FROM
Civil War
TO
Civil Rights
ALABAMA
1860–1960

D1120814

FROM

Civil War

TO

Civil Rights

ALABAMA

1860–1960

An Anthology
from *The Alabama Review*

COMPILED BY
Sarah Woolfolk Wiggins

THE UNIVERSITY OF ALABAMA PRESS
TUSCALOOSA AND LONDON

Copyright © 1987 by
The University of Alabama Press
Tuscaloosa, Alabama 35487
All rights reserved
Manufactured in the United States of America

Library of Congress Cataloging-in-Publication Data

Wiggins, Sarah Woolfolk, 1934–
 From Civil War to civil rights—Alabama, 1860–1960.

 Includes index.
 1. Alabama—History—1819–1950. 2. Alabama—
History—1951–   . I. Alabama review (University,
Ala.) II. Title.
F326.5.W54 1987   976.1′06   86-25068
ISBN 0-8173-0341-3

British Library Cataloguing-in-Publication Data
is available.

TO THE MEMORY OF
Milo Barrett Howard, Jr.

Contents

Progressive Era

The Twenties

The Great Depression

World War II and Beyond

Preface

The Alabama Review is the journal of the Alabama Historical Association. In 1987 the Association will complete forty years of publication of the *Review* with the cooperation of The University of Alabama Press in a successful effort between academics and the public. The journal has enjoyed remarkable continuity over these years in having only three editors: W. S. Hoole of The University of Alabama, January 1948 through October 1967; Malcolm C. McMillan of Auburn University, January 1968 through July 1976; and Sarah W. Wiggins of The University of Alabama, October 1976 to the present. The essays in this collection reflect the work of all three editors. Variations in editorial style have occurred in these years, and the articles are reprinted here *verbatim* as they were originally published.

The compiler of this collection wishes to acknowledge the assistance of many people. The Alabama Historical Association has encouraged this project. The staff of The University of Alabama Press has provided unfailing support, Malcolm M. MacDonald, director; Mike Burton, production manager. During the ten years with this journal the present editor has been blessed with extraordinary assistance in the mechanics of editing the *Review*: unselfish and skillful secretaries in Debbie Davis, Pam Franklin, Conita Fader; resourceful graduate assistants in Connie Kovac Radovanovic, Teresa Ceravolo, Michael Daniel, Guy Swanson.

Many issues of *The Alabama Review* are no longer available, and the intent of this publication is twofold: to make available again some of the outstanding scholarship in past issues of the *Review* and to provide an overview of an important period of Alabama's history.

SARAH WOOLFOLK WIGGINS

FROM
Civil War
TO
Civil Rights
ALABAMA
1860–1960

Introduction

This collection of essays from *The Alabama Review* spans the history of Alabama from 1860 to 1957, from the beginning of one revolution to the opening of another, the Civil War to the civil rights movement. To understand Alabama history one must appreciate the impact of the failure of secession on the state in the subsequent half century as well as the causes for the success of the civil rights movement in the state in the mid-twentieth century. The prophet of the first revolution was William Lowndes Yancey and the prophet of the second was Martin Luther King, Jr., two Alabamians who set in motion forces that shaped American history beyond the borders of their adopted state. In the years between their two lives, Alabama changed dramatically.

Yet, historians of Alabama have been timid in recounting this story for an adult audience in a sweeping history of our state; they have instead focused on one period or one subject. Frequently, prior to publishing a monograph, writers have explored their ideas in essay form, often published in *The Alabama Review*. Because there is no comprehensive state history many teachers have followed the same course as has been done here: to select essays from the *Review* to parallel classroom discussions. This solution at least samples the scholarship of writers of Alabama history and collectively provides a skeleton of the state's history. In reading issues of the *Review* one quickly perceives patterns in the essays and the scholarship they represent. Not many articles study Alabama before 1860 and even fewer for the years after the late 1950s. The dearth of appropriate articles about these periods has, therefore, established the time frame of this collection, 1860–1960.

The first group of articles centers around that watershed of the nineteenth century, the Civil War and Reconstruction era. Although Alabama's William Lowndes Yancey was the spokesman of the secession movement, the cause met far from unanimous support in Alabama. Yet, the state threw itself into the Confederate effort, enjoying momentary agricultural and industrial growth until the war cannibalized Alabama's resources along with those of the rest of the South. Physically lucky during the war when compared with the conditions of her neighbors, Alabama escaped with only cavalry raids through the state. But the war ended slavery, destroying a social structure as well as a labor system and leaving nothing in the place of either. Further changes, especially in political institutions, followed in the decade of Reconstruction. This most heatedly debated period in the state's history cannot be discussed with emotional detachment even after the passage of a century, as a session with students in a classroom or with adults on the street quickly attests. The Alabama public then and now has been preoccupied with villifying the Republican party for disasters that were basically the readjustments of a people defeated in a war, adjustments that represented unwanted, unpleasant, wrenching social, economic, and political changes.

By the 1880s Alabamians groped to improve their economic and political plight, too often looking backward at antebellum prosperity and methods. Greenbackers proposed to influence Congress, while Grangers proposed to influence the state legislature; eventually, both gave way to the Farmers' Alliance and to the Populists but with few positive long-range achievements. In frustration Alabamians lashed out at any convenient scapegoat, little realizing that larger forces beyond their control dictated their poverty. From the Civil War to the turn of the century politics in Alabama was the politics of pressure and intimidation of white as well as black poor who had not yet found any sense of the political power of their numbers. The 1900 U.S. Senate race that closed the decade of the 1890s was the ultimate in pressure politics. It provoked the passage of the famed succession law to prevent future governors from attempting to pressure the legislature to elect them to the U.S. Senate, circumstances very different from those when the succession law became an issue in the 1960s.

With the turn of the century subtle changes occurred in Alabamians. The agrarian-oriented generation who had survived the Civil War was dying off, and its successor was more influenced by industry-oriented matters. National progressive currents swept Alabama into movements for regulation of railroads, child labor reform, welfare capitalism, women's suffrage; religion was forced to adjust to urban growth. Progressives had a distinct sense that they could improve their world, that they could take on outside forces larger than themselves and win.

Industrial fever spread to the Tennessee Valley in the 1920s, while the Ku Klux Klan grew to be the most powerful social and political force in the state. The Klan influenced Alabama politics on every level in races for local, state, and national offices. The blessing or curse of this group made or broke the careers of powerful politicians in that decade.

After 1929 Alabama sank again beneath the weight of the forces of an outside world. The Great Depression spared no occupations in Alabama, and those who had seen economic hope in industry and mining in the state were as reduced to poverty as were those who had remained loyal to agriculture. Yet, through the despair there was a spirit that all was not hopeless.

World War II saw the revival of a sense that Alabamians could shape their world. Heretofore, Alabama governors had typified Alabama politicians generally: they all looked alike, and their administrations were like their faces, hardly distinguishable one from another. Now a new breed of politician appeared—plain, earthy, colorful, and successful. The political debut of "Big Jim" Folsom represented nothing so much as the emergence of the poor determined to act in their own behalf. The same sense that Alabama poor were no longer content to react to circumstances was broadcast around the world in the Montgomery bus boycott. If the Civil War had made revolutionary changes in the South in the nineteenth century, the civil rights movement had an equally revolutionary effect in the twentieth century. With unassuming beginnings the boycott was the first thunder of a social and political storm that would remake Alabama. Martin Luther King, Jr., an unknown black preacher, became the spokesman for the black poor in Montgomery. Within months his name was synonymous with the civil rights movement across the country. The movement fed upon the belief of the poor that they could make a difference, and a tidal wave of change was set loose.

The task of writing the history of these movements and events is an awesome one, so much so that historians have backed away. We need a history of our state that includes interpretations as well as facts, places events in their context, and weaves meaning from a series of episodes. A fresh history of our state must be based on original research rather than on a mere writing of filler between paraphrases of articles such as these by a variety of authors.

The essays in this collection also reflect a much larger problem in Alabama scholarship. Dramatizing the need for more than a history of our state, the collection pointedly demonstrates how numerous are the topics in each time frame that should be studied to fill the information gaps that stand between these selections.

In the end this collection is an introduction to a fascinating story that is waiting to be told and a reminder of how urgently that history is needed.

Civil War and Reconstruction

RALPH B. DRAUGHON, JR.

The Young Manhood of William L. Yancey

One of the most colorful politicians of ante-bellum Alabama was William Lowndes Yancey, the "Orator of Secession," who led the Southern walkout from the Democrat National Convention in 1860 and the withdrawal from the Union in the following year.[1] Indeed, one prominent American historian, Dwight Lowell Dumond, has made the statement that "Without Yancey's brilliant oratory and indefatigable labors there would have been no secession, no Southern Confederacy."[2] Whether Dumond's statement is exaggerated or not, Yancey has been noticed in the history books for his fire-eating speeches and for his participation in the heated events which preceded disunion. But of the man himself very little is known.

William Yancey's father was Benjamin Cudworth Yancey, a South Carolina politician whose bright career was cut short by death in 1817.[3] Benjamin's widow, Caroline Yancey, then took William, who was three years old, and William's infant brother from South Carolina to Georgia, where the little family made its home at the Shoals of Ogeechee, Mrs. Yancey's childhood home.

There at the Shoals lived Mrs. Yancey's mother, Catherine Bird, a former Virginian, renowned for her beauty and her beautiful daughters. William's grandmother, his mother, and his aunts, the Bird sisters, were such belles that an admirer dubbed their home "The

[1] This paper was read at the annual meeting of the Alabama Historical Association, Florence, Apr. 23, 1965. It was published in *The Alabama Review*, XIX (Jan., 1966).
[2] *Antislavery Origins of the Civil War in the United States* (Ann Arbor, 1939), 99.
[3] Charleston *City Gazette and Commercial Advertiser*, Oct. 21, 1817.

Aviary," since so many pretty Birds lived there.[4] Unfortunately, however, these ladies were noted not only for their good looks, but also for their bad dispositions, and William's mother and grandmother occasionally had truly remarkable temper tantrums.[5] A glance at his childhood home reveals that William came by his own temper quite naturally.[6]

When William was old enough to begin schooling, his mother gave him his first instruction. She trained him to be an orator, for his father had been a fine speaker and had been eulogized as a fountain of "the living waters of eloquence."[7] While her little boy declaimed some of the florid rhetoric which was so favored in the Nineteenth Century, Mrs. Yancey would knit but would interrupt him frequently to make corrections. Rather prophetically, young William's favorite recitation was a piece called, "On Jordan's stormy banks, I stand"[8]— a good choice for a boy who would one day lead his people in a stormy exodus from the Union.

Caroline Yancey sent her son for his first formal instruction to a nearby school taught by Presbyterian ministers, Mount Zion Academy, where William came under the supervision of that school's remarkable founder and headmaster, Nathan Sidney Smith Beman. A Northerner who had come to Georgia in 1812, Beman was a superior academician who exacted a stern discipline, neither sparing the rod nor spoiling the child.[9] He was a preacher of emotional and intellectual eloquence, but because he was also a man who sometimes interrupted his piety with displays of personal arrogance,[10] it is easy to speculate that he was not greatly loved by his students.

A widower with several grown children, Beman became charmed by Mrs. Yancey soon after her son came to Mount Zion and in 1821, when

---

[4] Benjamin F. Perry, *Reminiscences of Public Men with Speeches and Addresses* (Greenville, 1889), 54.

[5] William's grandmother and grandfather Bird had such severe quarrels that even their children took sides in the arguments (Louisa [Mrs. Robert] Cunningham to Benjamin Cudworth Yancey, Jr., Feb. 25, 1846, and another undated letter from the same correspondent). These and other manuscripts hereinafter cited are in the Benjamin Cudworth Yancey, Jr. Papers (Southern Historical Collection, University of North Carolina, Chapel Hill), unless otherwise indicated.

[6] His father had also been noted for a bad temper (John W. DuBose, *The Life and Times of William Lowndes Yancey* [New York, 1942], I, 30).

[7] Charleston *Courier*, Nov. 1, 1817.

[8] DuBose, I, 32.

[9] *Georgia, a Guide to Its Towns and Countryside* (Athens, 1946), 494–495.

[10] *Dictionary of American Biography* (New York, 1928–1940), II, 171–172.

William was seven years old, she and the schoolmaster were married.[11] Benjamin Yancey had left his widow some property[12] which, according to his will, should have passed to a trustee for the Yancey children in the event that Mrs. Yancey remarried.[13] Nevertheless, in spite of the will, Nathan Beman somehow came into control of the inheritance, and Yancey kinsmen later accused him of squandering the estate on himself and his own children.[14]

The year he married Mrs. Yancey, Beman asked to leave the Georgia Presbytery.[15] The preacher wanted to return to the North, and as he began to search for a new position in that region he took a step he was later to regret. On April 11, 1822 he sold to a man from Savannah for the sum of $700, three slaves—a Negro woman, her four-year-old son, and her infant daughter, whose name was Caroline.[16] Beman himself had been a slaveholder before his marriage to Mrs. Yancey, and there is considerable doubt about whether he sold his own slaves or those which came to him as a part of the Yancey estate.[17] No matter who owned the Negroes, however, the sale of them became extremely embarrassing to Beman when he became a prominent New York minister in pronounced opposition to slavery. The kinsmen and friends of William Yancey later pointed to the sale as evidence of

[11] "Early Marriages in Hancock County, Georgia," *Southern Historical Research Magazine*, II, 139 (Apr., 1937).

[12] She received a large sum for her husband's legal services in a South Carolina land claim case, and she also owned several slaves (John Belton O'Neall, *Biographical Sketches of the Bench and Bar of South Carolina* [Charleston, 1859], II, 324; United States *Census* (4th) 1820, Hancock County, Ga., 101 [original MSS returns, Library of Congress]).

[13] B. C. Yancey, Sr., "Last Will and Testament."

[14] ". . . this man [Beman] has spent many dollars of your Father's estate—& his [Yancey's] children—have been thrown on others . . ." (William Bird to B. C. Yancey, Jr., Oct., 1837). See also Caroline Beman to B. C. Yancey, Jr., Sept., 1837; Louisa Cunningham to B. C. Yancey, Jr., Feb. 25, 1846.

[15] James Stacy, *A History of the Presbyterian Church in Georgia* (Atlanta, 1912), 185–186, 331, 340.

[16] "True Copy, certified June 22, 1837, of State of Georgia, Hancock County, Bill of Sale, registered June 15, 1822."

[17] Before her marriage to Beman, Caroline had owned a Negro couple and a little Negro girl. Before marrying Caroline, Beman had also owned a Negro couple, a Negro girl and two Negro boys (U.S. *Census*, 1820, Hancock County, Ga., 101–102 [original MSS returns]). If the census is accurate, Caroline probably could not have owned a four-year-old boy in 1822, and the Negroes Beman sold were more likely to have come from his own and not his wife's estate. But what became of Caroline's Negroes? Though there is only one copy of a bill of sale in the Yancey Papers, one correspondent spoke of having certified copies of Beman's bills of sale—indicating that Beman made several slave sales and probably sold his wife's Negroes as well as his own (A. L. Alexander to B. C. Yancey, Jr., June 19, 1837).

Beman's false piety and charged that Beman was a hypocrite who preached against slavery after selling slaves himself.[18] And if the slaves were part of the Yancey property, then the Yanceys could charge that Beman had not only sold slaves, he had also pocketed the money.

Beman accepted a pastorate at the First Presbyterian Church in Troy, New York and brought his wife and stepchildren North in June, 1823.[19] William Yancey was almost nine years old when he left his Georgia home. The change was great from the mild winters of Georgia to the months of ice and snow in Troy, and far different from the Shoals of Ogeechee was life in the bustling young city by the Hudson River. Yancey probably encountered many problems of adjustment when he went to live in the Northern industrial town where people moved at a faster pace and spoke with a different accent. Moreover, he had to deal with the problems any boy has to face when he is identified as a preacher's son. The members of Beman's church were strict religionists. Indeed, the congregation had been disrupted when the previous minister offended conservative church members by installing heating and allowing music in the church.[20]

In later years William Yancey never said much about his New York boyhood, but his life in Troy appears to have been unstable and unhappy. Life in the Beman household was made up of increasingly angry and more acrimonious clashes between Caroline and Nathan Beman, while in strange contrast the household also glowed in the light of religious evangelism.

Like her mother, Caroline Yancey Beman had a violent temper and in Troy her rages became almost uncontrollable.[21] The hired girls at her home particularly upset her. She would scream in rage at them, threatening to knock them down or toss them into the street. When her husband tried to interfere, Caroline Beman would start a furious argument with him. William Yancey's mother had two children by her second marriage. In a fit of irritation she would slap the children or hit them on their heads with the heel of a shoe. If Beman objected, she would turn her fury on him. Beman in his own way was as pugnacious as his wife, but where Caroline was emotional and hot-tempered the preacher was cold, arrogant, and sarcastic. He piously refused to take

[18] Frances Bird to B. C. Yancey, Jr., June 27, 1837.
[19] Arthur James Weise, *History of the City of Troy* (Troy, 1876), 127–128.
[20] *Ibid.*, 64–65.
[21] Robert Cunningham to B. C. Yancey, Jr., July 9, 1837.

any part of the blame for the domestic difficulties, taunting his wife for being either deranged or immoral. In 1826 Beman threatened to take legal action to rid himself of his wife, but the argument ended when the preacher forced Caroline into admitting that she was a venomous and sinful woman. When Mrs. Beman in abject penitence confessed before the elders of Beman's church the wrongs she had done her husband, Beman and the elders allowed her to remain with the preacher and be admitted to the church.[22]

Young William Yancey was shaken by the vituperative disputes between his mother and stepfather and he was also intensely affected by the pervading atmosphere of religious fervor in the Beman household. In 1825 Beman held one of the greatest revivals in the history of Troy, and though the city was small, hundreds of people came to seek repentence for their sins and to join the church.[23] In the fall and winter of 1826–1827 Beman held another great revival with Charles Grandison Finney assisting in the preaching. Beman and Finney were developing the doctrines of the New School of Presbyterianism which liberalized the Calvinism of predestination and damnation and offered to mankind the hope of atonement and salvation.[24] Though Beman's doctrines disrupted the conservative Calvinists in his congregation, he stubbornly persisted in his evangelical labors. By 1830, when Yancey was about to enter college, the New School preaching had spread throughout the country and the American people were caught up in the greatest of the modern religious awakenings, the Great Revival of 1830.[25]

The Beman household was of course hotly involved in the fervor. William Yancey's life now became an unhappy mixture of family feud and religious crusade. Growing up in the emotionally charged atmosphere, he developed a temper that perhaps more than equalled his mother's, but he also acquired a great deal of his stepfather's crusading zeal. Unfortunately, the mixture of temper and crusading zeal in Yancey was as volatile as the mixture of bitter argument and religious evangelism in his boyhood environment.

[22] Beman to Caroline Beman, Feb. 15, 1836, Apr. 3, 1837. In these letters Beman wrote a long account of the quarrels.
[23] Weise, 224.
[24] N. S. S. Beman, *Christ, the Only Sacrifice; or the Atonement in its Relation to God and Man* (New York, 1844).
[25] Weise, 156–157; Gilbert H. Barnes, *The Antislavery Impulse, 1830–1844* (New York, 1933), 3–16.

There is no evidence that during his childhood Yancey took his mother's side in the fights between the Beman couple, but his later animosity towards Beman indicates a long-standing resentment of the treatment afforded Caroline Beman by the preacher.[26] Yancey loved his mother, in spite of her fierce temper, and he remained devoted to her all his life.[27] Had the relationship of Beman and his stepson been happier, Yancey might have followed Beman to become a preacher, or perhaps even an Abolitionist. Instead, Yancey became a wild, hot-tempered rebel, the fire-eater of secession.

Nevertheless, Yancey was not all temper. He was a curious mixture, and the other part of the mixture, the crusading zeal which Nathan Beman had inspired, was still below the surface. Later in Yancey's career his fervor for crusading reappeared, causing him to resemble his stepfather in many ways. But in marked contrast with Beman, Yancey's crusading fervor was always mixed with a hot temper, producing results unlike any that Nathan Beman intended.[28]

Beman saw to it that William Yancey had the opportunity for an excellent education. The preacher sent his stepsons to good schools, some of them presided over by friends of Beman in the Presbyterian ministry. Yancey attended the academies of Troy, Bennington, Chitteningo, and Lenox, and in 1830, at the age of sixteen, he entered Williams College.[29] The educational opportunities afforded William Yancey and his brother Benjamin tend to belie the charge that Beman misappropriated funds meant for his stepchildren's support and education. Nevertheless, Robert Cunningham, uncle of William Yancey, contributed most of the money to send his Yancey nephews to school. Cunningham was generous in supplying funds and Mrs. Cunningham, Caroline Beman's sister, was equally generous in supplying advice to the Yancey boys. To William's younger brother, Louisa Cunningham wrote on July 20, 1833, "Yes let your mothers [sic] trouble be an incentive to you—comfort her heart yet—succeed in business, and place her beyond the control of a tyrant. . . ."

William Yancey was in need of his aunt's counsel when he entered

---

[26] Yancey to B. C. Yancey, Jr., June 25, 1837.

[27] DuBose, I, 32.

[28] For further speculation on this theme see Ralph B. Draughon, Jr., "The Political Transition of William Lowndes Yancey, 1814–1848," unpublished master's thesis (University of North Carolina, 1963).

[29] DuBose, I, 32; *General Catalogue of the Non-Graduates of Williams College* (Williamstown, 1910), 15.

college. He was an unruly student and a member of a rowdy group.[30]
Several years after leaving college he reminisced:

> . . . I feel somewhat as I did of yore, when a
> wild student, I
>   'Threw by Euclid,
>   Closed the book lid
>   And turn'd the key, in the door lock,'
> And was ready to cut rare, fantastick [monkey]
> shines, which I would not that a dignified world
> should look upon.[31]

During Yancey's college days Beman occasionally visited the vicinity
of the college on preaching missions,[32] and on these visits Beman
probably preached as earnestly to his stepson as he did to the local
congregations.

During his years at Williams College, Yancey helped to edit a student
literary journal, joined an oratorical society, and had an opportunity
to study under a noted teacher of rhetoric, Mark Hopkins.[33] Nevertheless, Yancey's collegiate education lasted only three years, for he
withdrew from Williams College in 1833. When he became a Southern
leader, Northern newspapers charged that he had been kicked out of
college for tossing a pickle barrel through the window of a Methodist
meeting house.[34] This story is believable, but unsubstantiated. More
probably, he withdrew for financial reasons. His uncle was having difficulty educating his own children along with the Yancey boys.[35] Furthermore, in 1832 and 1833 Caroline and Nathan Beman engaged in
disputes which almost ended in their separation.[36] Mrs. Beman's troubles probably made William anxious to begin earning an independent
living.

After leaving college Yancey returned to the South, and he and
Nathan Beman went their separate ways. Beman went on to become
one of the most vehement opponents of slavery, and Yancey one of
its most adamant defenders.

---

[30] Yancey to N. T. Rosseter, Apr., 1837; Frederick Rudolph, *Mark Hopkins and the Log*
. . . (New Haven, 1956), 121, 121n.
[31] Yancey to B. C. Yancey, Jr., Dec. 25, 1838.
[32] *Williams College Adelphi,* Feb. 15, 1832.
[33] Rudolph, 28, 75; DuBose, I, 33.
[34] Boston *Atlas,* Jan. 20, 1845, quoting the Troy *Whig.*
[35] Louisa Cunningham to B. C. Yancey, Jr., July 20, Aug. 6, 1833.
[36] Beman to Caroline Beman, Apr. 3, 1837.

If the troubles between Beman and his wife did not begin with slavery, it became inextricably entangled in their arguments. Nathan Beman's opposition to slavery increased year after year during William's youth. In 1827 Beman held a religious service, which both races attended, to celebrate the final extinction of slavery in the State of New York. During Yancey's college years his stepfather helped to start a school for Negroes in the basement of a church.[37] In 1835, after Yancey had returned South, Beman took an uncompromisingly strong stand against slavery at a Pittsburgh meeting of the Presbyterian General Assembly. In fact, Beman's anti-slavery attack was one of the opening wedges which helped to split apart the Presbyterian Church.[38]

Furthermore, when Beman returned from the Presbyterian meeting, the difficulties between himself and his wife soon erupted in full fury. Beman accused her of slandering him, mistreating hired girls, and begrudging food to Henry Beman, a son by the preacher's first marriage who was dying of tuberculosis.[39] Beman threatened divorce, but the couple agreed instead that Mrs. Beman should sojourn in the South for a year and a half.[40] By this arrangement the preacher made certain that his wife would not interfere in his anti-slavery activities which he increased after her departure.[41]

During Mrs. Beman's visit to the South the couple engaged in a venomous correspondence. Caroline sent her husband a pro-slavery letter, and he sent back a stinging reply: "What you say on *abolition & slavery* is an *old* story, and has not at all altered my views. The attempt . . . to reconcile the abominations of slavery with the pure system of Jesus Christ is a complete failure, though it has made so deep an impression on your mind."[42] Caroline demanded more money

---

[37] Weise, 113–114, 172.

[38] For a Southern reaction to Beman's Pittsburgh stand, see John Witherspoon to Lyman Beecher, in Lyman Beecher, *Autobiography* . . . , ed. by Barbara M. Cross (Cambridge, 1961), II, 322.

[39] ". . . since he [Beman] returned from Pittsburgh in June he has not spoken a social [*sic*] word to me, why I cannot tell" (Caroline Beman to B. C. Yancey, Jr., Sept. 20, 1835).

[40] Beman to Caroline Beman, March 15, 1836 ("True & full copy BCY"). Some of the letters from Beman in the Yancey Papers are exact copies by Ben Yancey of the originals which William Yancey kept for his mother.

[41] The animosity Beman created in Troy has been blamed for the mobbing of a visiting Abolitionist in 1836 (Barnes, 85).

[42] Beman to Caroline Beman, Dec. 21, 1835.

from her husband and Beman intercepted his wife's letters to and
from their children. The preacher forbade Caroline to shorten her
Southern visit, to visit their daughter in boarding school, or to
correspond with friends in Troy.[43] Without telling his wife, he also
began making plans to attend the World Anti-Slavery Conference in
London.

When Beman returned from the conference, he wrote Theodore
Dwight Weld, the great Abolitionist leader, that he was thinking of
engaging permanently in "the cause of the oppressed," adding:
"There are some things in my *personal* situation which you can *guess*
which render it peculiarly necessary for me to see you."[44] The delicate
personal matter obviously referred to Caroline Beman, who was definitely an encumbrance to her anti-slavery husband. Caroline was to
end her Southern visit in the spring of 1837, but Beman had already
written her, April 3, "You can't return to the North. Should you
be rash enough to do it, you will not *find* me; & the children will be
beyond your reach. You can't force matters after all that has past."
Despite her husband's warning, Mrs. Beman returned, but Beman
refused to take her back. When she sneaked two trunks out of her
former house, Beman had the Troy City Council order them returned, and the couple engaged in bitter squabbling over their mutual possessions, which Beman himself divided.[45] After the division,
the preacher provided a small allowance for Caroline and sent her
packing. He could now devote his full time to "the cause of the
oppressed."

William Yancey was actively interested in the troubles of the Beman
couple and fully sympathetic to his mother's point of view. When the
Bemans began their last quarrel, Mrs. Beman reported to William's
younger brother, September 20, 1835, that "William wrote to your
Father [Beman] so dreadful a letter that I had to burn it and not
let your Father see it." If Mrs. Beman burned the letter, it must
have been truly dreadful. Furthermore, she saved the angry letters

---

[43] Beman to Caroline Beman, Fall and Dec. 21, 1835; Feb. 15, 19, March 15, 30, Aug. 15,
1836.
[44] May 10, 1837 (in *Letters of Theodore Dwight Weld, Angelina Grimke Weld, and Sarah
Grimke, 1822–1824,* ed. by Gilbert H. Barnes and Dwight L. Dumond [New York, 1934],
I, 383).
[45] Caroline Beman to B. C. Yancey, Jr., Aug. 13, Sept., Oct. 9, 1837; Jan. 15, Feb. 14,
23, Apr. 14, 1838.

the preacher wrote her and she sent them to William Yancey. She also wrote William, charging that the preacher had beaten her shamefully, though she denied the charge in her next letter.[46]

Nathan Beman's Yancey stepsons were infuriated at the way the preacher had treated their mother, and they were particularly galled at Beman's anti-slavery activities. The Yancey brothers sent Beman an insulting pro-slavery pamphlet, and they were careful to obtain a copy of the bill of sale by which Beman had sold three Negroes.[47] That a seller of slaves should now be preaching against slavery was particularly infuriating to the Yanceys and their kin. The Yancey brothers planned to prepare and publish a pamphlet attacking the preacher.[48]

Unfortunately, slavery became a point of debate in the conflict between Caroline and Nathan Beman. Had the couple confined their quarrel to personalities, the effect on Beman's stepchildren might have been less damaging. But the Bemans changed the ground of their debate from personalities to an issue on which every adult had to take a stand. Furthermore, the family's general sentiments on slavery intensified the Bemans' personal quarrel, and the Bemans' personal quarrel intensified the family's general sentiments on slavery. A general dislike for all Abolitionists added to Yancey's personal dislike for Beman, and a personal dislike for Beman added to Yancey's general resentment of all Abolitionists. The family quarrel and the conflict over slavery were mutually divisive, and conflict in one area encouraged conflict in the other.

To William Yancey, Beman personified the Abolitionist: a hypocrite who preached against slavery after selling slaves himself, who probably misused his stepchildren's inheritance, who abused and rejected his wife, denied her access to her own children, and refused to provide adequately for her support. And most irritating of all was the preacher's great self-righteousness. The South reacted strongly to the Abolitionist attack, but William Yancey reacted a great deal more strongly than most Southerners because he was spurred by his intense resentment of his stepfather.

[46] Beman to Caroline Beman, April 3, 1837.
[47] Beman to Caroline Beman, Dec. 21, 1835; Tuttle H. Audas to B. C. Yancey, Jr., June 22, 1837.
[48] "Would it not be advisable to publish it [the pamphlet], in one of the Troy papers, & pay for it, if required, as an advertisement? By that means, it would be more extensively read, than otherwise" (Yancey to B. C. Yancey, Jr., June 25, 1837).

Like the Beman household the Union was becoming a house divided. While Nathan Beman was putting on the whole armor of righteousness to attack slavery and the South, William Lowndes Yancey girded himself to wage a lone crusade against Abolitionism and the North. The fury of this family quarrel was one small sign that there was a terrible civil war in the making.

WILLIAM N. STILL

Selma and the Confederate States Navy

On February 21, 1861 the Provisional Congress of the Confederate States of America, meeting at Montgomery, Alabama, passed an act to create a navy and, shortly afterwards, Jefferson Davis appointed Stephen R. Mallory as secretary of the navy.[1] Mallory was immediately confronted with the lack of shipbuilding facilities in the South. There were no warships, of course, and only two shipyards, Norfolk and Pensacola. However, within three years Mallory had at his disposal at least eighteen shipyards, plus other naval facilities, in various parts of the Confederacy. Among these, two were established at Selma, a foundry for the manufacture of naval ordnance and a shipyard.

Selma, Alabama, an inland city 200 miles from the Gulf of Mexico, was chosen as the site for naval facilities for several reasons. In the first place, the Confederate States Navy had suffered a number of setbacks during the spring and summer of 1862, including the fall of New Orleans and Norfolk. As a result of these disasters, a number of interior points, including Atlanta and Columbus (Georgia), Richmond, Charlotte, and Selma, were selected as sites for naval establishments.[2] A second reason was the availability of facilities for manufacturing in Selma. These advantages were early recognized, as the following letter, written in January, 1862, suggests:

---

[1] This paper was read at the annual meeting of the Alabama Historical Association, Selma, April 22, 1960. It was published in *The Alabama Review*, XV (Jan., 1962).

[2] James D. Bulloch, *The Secret Service of the Confederate States in Europe* (London, 1883), II, 209–210; Arthur H. Noll, *Doctor Quintard, Chaplain, C.S.A.* (Sewanee, 1905), 130.

[Selma] is now connected by railroad and river with the great arteries of travel from South to North, and . . . is also most fortunately situated with regard to the means of manufacturing in iron. The coal beds of Bibb and Shelby [counties] are only fifty-four miles distant and are immediately upon the Alabama and Tennessee River Railroad . . . while iron ore . . . can be had by the same railroad from the iron mines . . . distant about sixty miles. . . .[3]

The writers could have added that Selma fortunately possessed a number of mechanics. But the last, and by no means the least, of the reasons for the selection of Selma was the persevering interest of Colin J. McRae, one of Alabama's representatives in the Provisional Congress. McRae, a native of North Carolina, had been a successful cotton commission merchant in Mobile before the war.[4] During the course of the war he was in turn a member of Congress, an agent for the Niter and Mining Bureau in Alabama, and the financial agent for the Confederate government in Europe. As a member of the Naval Affairs Committee in the Congress, McRae was instrumental in initiating defensive measures in Alabama, particularly concerning naval affairs.

The forerunner of the naval ordnance works in Selma was the Alabama Manufacturing Company, established in the early 1850's by a group of Selma businessmen.[5] In January, 1862 McRae was approached by a representative of this company concerning the possibility of selling or leasing the property to the government for a proposed foundry.[6] Secretary Mallory and Secretary of War Judah P. Benjamin rejected this offer and even a letter to President Davis failed to secure a favorable response.[7] McRae then turned to private sources for the necessary funds. Evidently, he was successful, for a group of

---

[3] *The War of the Rebellion: A Compilation of the Official Records of the Union and Confederate Armies* (Washington, 1880–1902), 4, I, 107–108 (hereinafter *ORA*).

[4] Thomas M. Owen, *History of Alabama and Dictionary of Alabama Biography* (Chicago, 1921), IV, 1139–1140.

[5] The earlier organizers included J. P. Perham, R. N. Philpot, F. X. Becton, Frederick Vogelin, Dr. I. Morgan, and William Icles. See John Hardy, *Selma: Her Institutions and Her Men* (Selma, 1879), 114.

[6] I. W. Lapsley to McRae (in McRae Letterbook, Alabama State Department of Archives and History, Montgomery).

[7] Feb. 24, 1862 (McRae Letterbook).

businessmen from Selma and Mobile, including McRae himself, purchased the foundry.[8]

With the transfer of ownership completed, McRae, who apparently assumed the responsibility of developing the newly acquired foundry, set about obtaining contracts from the government. This presented no problems and by the end of March, 1862 agreements had been reached with Colonel Josiah Gorgas, chief of the Confederate Ordnance Bureau, and Commander George Minor, in charge of the Office of Ordnance and Hydrography, to manufacture heavy ordnance and iron plates for gunboats. The contracts stipulated that the first cannon should be cast by September 1, and the plates by the following December.[9]

Having successfully obtained financial support and the all important contracts, McRae next concentrated on completing the foundry. He travelled extensively during the early months of 1862 for the purpose of purchasing machinery, tools, and supplies, and hiring workmen. In April he was in New Orleans. From there he returned to Selma in order to acquire more land and contract for the construction of new buildings. In Atlanta he examined the Atlanta Rolling Mill, and by the end of June he was in Richmond conferring with Confederate officials. While at Richmond McRae was appointed iron agent for Alabama, a position that afforded him many advantages.

During the summer of 1862 McRae first came into contact with a problem that would plague not only the Selma foundry, but all governmental establishments throughout the war. In August his superintendent was sent to various parts of the Confederacy to hire mechanics. Some were obtained, but not enough.[10] The scarcity of qualified workmen resulted in the first of many delays experienced by McRae in completing the foundry. He telegraphed Secretary Mallory, July 2, that it would be at least the middle of October before the foundry could begin operations. During September he complained about the failure to obtain the necessary labor, but added: "Notwithstanding these difficulties we shall be ready to commence cast-

---

[8] McRae to a friend, Nov. 10, 1862 (McRae Letterbook).

[9] McRae to Minor, Apr. 7, and Minor to McRae, March 25, 1862 (in McRae Papers, Alabama State Department of Archives and History, Montgomery).

[10] *Official Records of the Union and Confederate Navies in the War of the Rebellion* (Washington, 1894–1902), 2, II, 230–232 (hereinafter *ORN*).

ing cannon by the first of November and to roll iron by first of December."[11]

This optimism was premature, for the inevitable delays continued. November found McRae writing to the other shareholders requesting additional funds. He suggested that, if sufficient capital were furnished "by the first of January, 1863 we shall have the foundry . . . completed."[12] Unfortunately, McRae never saw the foundry completed while he was in charge. Shortly after the beginning of the new year, he received a communication from Richmond requesting him to accept an important financial mission to Europe for the Confederacy. Before agreeing to accept this assignment, McRae made it a "condition of his acceptance" to be relieved of the Selma foundry, "without pecuniary loss to himself."[13] Negotiations were opened with the War Department and the Navy Department, and by the middle of February both agreed to purchase and to operate the foundry jointly.[14] The transactions were completed by the first of March. Soon McRae was en route to Europe to begin the last of his services to the Confederacy.

On February 20, 1863 Colonel George W. Rains of the Confederate Army was ordered to assume command of the Selma Foundry Works "in behalf of the Army and Navy."[15] The choice was unfortunate, for Rains had frequently deplored the location of a large ordnance establishment at Selma.[16] Apparently, as commanding officer his views did not change. In a letter written from Selma, March 15, he expressed "regret that the Army [had] assisted in the purchase of the Foundry Works. . . ." Rains began advocating that the Navy Department be given complete responsibility for the works. He suggested that they were "well situated for that branch of the service having a Rail Road already graded immediately connecting . . . [Selma with the] Pensacola Navy Yard. . . ."[17] Rain's criticisms were effec-

---

[11] McRae to Minor, Sept. 8, 1862 (McRae Letterbook).

[12] McRae to Franklin Buchanan, Dec. 20, 1862 (McRae Letterbook).

[13] Josiah Gorgas, "Confederate Ordnance Department," *Southern Historical Society Papers*, XII, 83 (Jan.–Feb., 1884); see also Frank E. Vandiver, *Ploughshares into Swords* (Austin, 1952), 169.

[14] Gov. William Gill Shorter to McRae, Feb. 12, 1863 (McRae Papers).

[15] *ORN*, 1, XIX, 841.

[16] Vandiver, 159.

[17] *Ibid.*, 170.

tive, for on June 1, 1863 the Navy Department assumed complete control of the Works.[18]

Commander Catesby ap R. Jones of Virginia was the naval officer ordered to command the Selma Foundry Works. Jones was well qualified for the assignment. He was an expert in naval ordnance and gunnery and was highly respected by both Confederate and Union naval officers. Admiral David Porter, the second admiral of the United States Navy, remarked after the war that he only regretted the loss of two men—Jones and John Mercer Brooke, the developer of the Brooke gun.[19] Before assuming command of the Selma Naval Works, as the foundry was now designated, Jones had been the executive officer on board the Confederate ironclad, *Virginia,* and from there had gone to Columbus, Georgia to command the C.S.S. *Chattahoochee.*[20]

The condition of the foundry when Jones arrived at Selma was most discouraging. Not one gun or iron plate had been cast or rolled, although the works had been under construction for nearly sixteen months. Even more discouraging was the fact that much of the work already completed was not satisfactory. The gun pit was located in an area where water was constantly seeping in. The crane for lifting heavy objects had to be rebuilt, and many other minor alterations made.[21]

Although an expert in naval ordnance, Jones was not a foundryman. He needed someone who had had experience in casting cannon and other foundry work. Fortunately, he secured the services of George Peacock, an experienced English foundryman, who had been superintendent of an iron works that had been moved from Natchez, Mississippi to Columbiana, Alabama earlier in the war.[22]

Under the supervision of Jones and Peacock, rapid progress was made toward completing the works. By the end of July the foundry was ready to cast its first gun—a 7-inch Brooke rifle. This gun, as well as those that immediately followed, were experimental and used for test-

---

[18] Catesby ap R. Jones to John K. Mitchell, June 1, 1863 (in Jones Letterbook, Naval Records, Group 45, National Archives).

[19] See George M. Brooke, Jr., "John Mercer Brooke" (unpublished Ph.D. dissertation, University of North Carolina, Chapel Hill, 1955), II, 749.

[20] *Register of Officers of the Confederate States Navy, 1861–65* (Washington, 1931).

[21] *ORN,* 2, II, 548–549.

[22] Walter M. Jackson, *The Story of Selma* (Birmingham, 1954), 232; Ethel Armes, *The Story of Coal and Iron in Alabama* (Birmingham, 1910), 142–143. Peacock's appointment as superintendent was made possible by a special act of Congress.

ing purposes. It was not until January, 1864 that the first gun was shipped for combat use. From then until the end of the war over a hundred large naval guns were cast, and more than half of these were shipped to various parts of the Confederacy.[23]

The Brooke rifle, the principal type of gun manufactured at Selma, was probably the most powerful muzzle-loading rifled gun used during the Civil War. They were made of wrought iron or semi-steel, and for added strength hooped at the breech with bands of iron or steel. Some were singlebanded, but most of them were double-banded from the breech to the trunnion. Generally, two models were manufactured at Selma, the 6.4-inch, weighing over 10,000 pounds, and the 7-inch, weighing over 14,000 pounds. A few 8-inch, 10-inch, and 11-inch Brooke smoothbores were produced toward the end of the war, but most of these were used for harbor defense.

On December 24, 1863 Jones reported to Admiral Franklin Buchanan, in charge of the Mobile naval defenses, that he would be able to ship two 7-inch Brooke rifles to Mobile within a few weeks, in spite of the fact that a serious accident had occurred at the foundry. An explosion in one of the gun pits resulted in the burning of several buildings. Fortunately, damage to the foundry was negligible, with only two of the gun molds destroyed, although Jones later complained about losing his hat, coat, and pants.[24]

By the end of January, 1864, with the exception of the rolling mill, the works were nearly completed—a large number of brick buildings, including offices, gun foundry, machine shop, molding shop, melting furnaces, pattern shop, puddling furnace, and a blacksmith shop.[25] The gun lathes, molds, and other machinery necessary to cast cannon had come from various places. McRae had purchased most of it in New Orleans; some had been shipped from Pensacola, and probably the remainder had been brought in through the blockade.[26] Of course, replacement parts were not to be had. They were usually manufactured at the foundry.[27]

Under normal conditions about one gun was cast a week at the

[23] Walter W. Stephen, "The Brooke Guns from Selma," *Alabama Historical Quarterly*, XX, 464 (Fall, 1958).

[24] *ORN*, 1, XX, 858–859.

[25] Armes, 140–141.

[26] Walter Fleming, *Civil War and Reconstruction in Alabama* (New York, 1905), 151.

[27] *ORN*, 1, XXI, 858–859.

foundry, each gun requiring six weeks for completion. Jones had hoped
to cast one a day, but this was never achieved because of the insur-
mountable problems that were encountered, particularly the shortage
of iron ore, coal, and other materials, as well as the dearth of qualified
workmen.

On March 21, 1864 Jones wrote Major William R. Hunt, in charge of
the Niter and Mining Bureau in Alabama that "Our capacity to
furnish the guns is . . . limited [by the] supply of iron, none having
been received this month. . . ."[28] This problem was acute, not only
for the Selma foundry, but for the Confederacy as a whole. There was
never enough iron to go around. Railroads, ordnance works, shipyards,
and other industries were always handicapped. In Alabama the supply
of iron was exploited to the limit. At the beginning of the war there
were only four furnaces in the state, but by the end of the war the
number had increased to seventeen.[29] Three of these supplied iron to
the Confederate Navy, the Bibb Iron Works, directly under the
navy's supervision, and the Shelby Iron Works and Cane Creek Iron
Works, both by contract. The iron ore mined by the Bibb works was
suitable for the manufacture of ordnance, while ore from the other
companies was used in fabricating gunboat plates, shells, and machinery
parts.[30]

The problem of an inadequate supply of iron was never solved during
the war; and even if a sufficient quantity had been available, the
scarcity of trained labor would have limited ordnance production.
Agriculture, transportation, and industry were constantly struggling
with the military authorities for control of the rapidly decreasing
labor supply. Probably, there was a sufficient number of skilled mechanics in the South at the beginning of the war but, unfortunately,
these were not excluded from the general shift to the army. The
complexities of the problem were increased by the introduction of
military conscription shortly after the Battle of Shiloh. This completed the sweep of industrial manpower into the army. The government attempted to alleviate the problem by detailing mechanics

[28] *Ibid.,* 1, XXI, 882.
[29] Joseph H. Woodward, *Alabama Blast Furnaces* (Woodward, 1940), 21–23.
[30] Bassett to Jones, July 15, and McRae to Jones, Oct. 24, 1862 (in Shelby Iron
Company Papers, University of Alabama Library, University). This collection includes
a number of outgoing letters concerning iron for the Navy Department of which the
two cited are representative.

serving in the army to various industrial establishments, but for many reasons this proved unsatisfactory.

Before the war Selma possessed a relatively large number of mechanics employed in the various manufacturing establishments located in the city. As in other communities, most of these either volunteered or were drafted during the course of the war. Consequently, the Selma Naval Works was handicapped from the beginning as a result of the labor problem. On September 8, 1862 McRae wrote Lieutenant George Minor that:

> When I made the contract with the Secretaries of War and Navy it was understood between you, Colonel Gorgas & myself that the Departments were to give me all the aid they could in procuring both materials and mechanics. Though I have applied for the detail of a good many mechanics from the army I have never succeeded in getting but one and now a cancellation of his detachment by the army [has deprived me of his services]. . . .[31]

This appeal went unheeded (as did others written to various governmental officials),[32] not from the lack of any desire to furnish the needed mechanics, but simply because there was never enough manpower to go around.

Catesby Jones, as an officer in the Confederate Navy, could fare little better in procuring mechanics. His frequent letters to the Navy Department requesting details from the army produced negative results. Frequently, he enclosed long lists of mechanics and the army units to which they had been assigned. These lists were usually forwarded to the Secretary of War, who subsequently suggested that officers in charge of naval facilities send their request for details of workmen directly to the area commander. This inevitably proved unsatisfactory because the unit commanders were, of course, also faced with the manpower shortage, and were reluctant to part with their men. Eventually, Mallory went directly to the President stating that, "with a proper number of mechanics [Selma] . . . could manufacture one

---

[31] (McRae Letterbook).
[32] See, for examples, McRae to Gorgas, Oct. 24, to Admiral Buchanan, Nov. 27, 1862, and to Forney, Sept. 8, 1863 (McRae Letterbook).

[gun] every day. . . ."[33] Davis could only refer the matter back to the Secretary of War.

Probably the worst aspect of the labor problem was the bitter rivalry that developed over the procurement and retaining of skilled workmen.[34] This competition involved rivalries between the military authorities and private industry, between the army and the navy, and even intra-service rivalries among various facilities. As early as September, 1862 McRae wrote to the Navy Department, assuring Commander Ebenezer Farrand, in charge of the shipyard at Selma, of luring foundry mechanics to the shipyard by offering higher wages. He added, "so far from securing assistance from the Department in completing my works, its officers are embarrassing me. . . ." Even after the navy assumed control, competition between the ordnance works and the shipyard continued.[35]

This tug-of-war over labor was even more serious between the two branches of the service, particularly in cities where there were located both army and navy establishments. The commanding officer of the army arsenal at Selma wrote to the Secretary of War complaining of the competition between that establishment and the naval facilities of the city. Similar complaints from other army installations resulted in a recommendation by the Secretary that, "consultations be-tween the officers of the respective Departments commanding estab-lishments at the same posts. . . ."[36] would perhaps alleviate the situ-ation. This suggestion was never put into practice, however, and the dissention over labor continued to the end.

The exact number of workmen employed by the Selma Naval Works varied during the war. By 1865 over four hundred were on the payrolls, of whom at least three hundred were Negroes.[37] Negro slaves were usually hired by the year from local planters, and were employed prin-cipally in cutting wood for charcoal, and other tasks requiring unskilled labor.[38]

[33] July 1, 1864, *ORN,* 4, III, 520–521; see also Mallory to Davis, Jan. 5, 1865 (in Jefferson Davis Papers, Duke University Library, Durham, N.C.).
[34] McRae to Minor, Sept. 30, 1862 (McRae Letterbook).
[35] Jones to Farrand, June 10, 1863 (Jones Letterbook).
[36] Seddon to Mallory, Oct. 21, 1863 (National Archives, War Department Records, Record Group 109, Washington, D.C.).
[37] Brooke to Mallory, Feb. 1, 1865 (in Office of Hydrography Letterbook, War Depart-ment Records, National Archives); Bell Wiley, *Southern Negroes, 1861–1865* (New Haven, 1938), 112–113.
[38] Jones to Brooke, Feb. 24, 1864 (Jones Letterbook).

Despite the utilization of Negro labor, the shortage of workmen reached a critical stage by early 1864. "Can't start the gun pit while short-handed," wrote the officer in charge, "work every night in the foundry except Sunday. . . . Twenty five negroes working over-time in foundry tonight. Reckon they'll all be dead by the time you return."[39] In the summer of 1864 production had to be suspended. Jones became so discouraged that he seriously considered resigning his commission.[40]

In all, nearly two hundred guns were cast by the Selma foundry, including a number of mortars and field guns for the army.[41] The last gun was cast on December 19, 1864—three months before Selma was captured by the enemy. Toward the last the foundry was also manu-facturing projectiles for the Brooke guns at the rate of about twenty a day. A majority of the guns and projectiles were destined for the various naval vessels under construction in the Confederacy, includ-ing those that were built at Selma.

Selma was not only the site of a large naval ordnance establishment, but also of a shipyard of considerable importance. Several ironclads were constructed there, including the C.S.S. *Tennessee,* Admiral Bu-chanan's flagship at the Battle of Mobile Bay.[42] Colin J. McRae, who was largely responsible for the naval ordnance works at Selma, was also partially responsible for the shipyard. A few days after Congress appro-priated $1,200,000 for the defense of Mobile Bay, McRae wrote Sec-retary Mallory, recommending that, "our first class Iron Clad Rams . . . for the defense of the Bay . . ." be built at Selma.[43] A week later he wrote the Secretary again to introduce Henry D. Bassett, a Mobile shipbuilder, who constructed one of the first Confederate vessels along the Gulf Coast.[44] Bassett reached Richmond at a very oppor-tune time. As a result of the successes of the *Virginia* in the Hampton Roads affair, the Navy Department was in the process of contracting with private firms and individuals in various parts of the Confederacy for the construction of ironclad vessels. On May 1 Bassett signed a

[39] Van Zandt to Jones, May 24, 1864 (Jones Letterbook).
[40] Mallory to Jones, Sept. 10, 1864 (in Jones Family Papers, Library of Congress).
[41] Taken from notes provided by the late Walter W. Stephen of Oxford, Ala.
[42] Apparently, Selma had not been a shipbuilding center before the war. J. H. Scruggs, Jr., *Alabama Steamboats, 1819–1869* (Birmingham, 1953) does not include one steamboat constructed at Selma.
[43] Apr. 8, 1862 (McRae Papers).
[44] Apr. 15, 1862 (McRae Letterbook).

contract to build two floating batteries for $100,000 each. The first of these, the *Tuscaloosa*, was to be completed by July 1, 1862, and the second, the *Huntsville*, thirty days later.[45] The third was the *Tennessee*, and the fourth was damaged on launching and subsequently sold by the Navy Department.[46] Besides these ironclads, the only other vessels built at Selma during the war were several coal barges.[47]

Immediately after returning to Alabama, Bassett began preparations to construct the *Tennessee* and the *Huntsville*. A site for the yard was selected above the city, several buildings of rough timber were erected, and mechanics and carpenters were hired. The timber and iron were contracted for locally, the iron to be supplied by the Shelby Iron Company at Columbiana, Alabama.[48]

At the end of the stipulated period for the completion of the hull of the first vessel, Bassett had to report that the ironclad was only three-fifths completed.[49] When this report reached the Navy Department, Joseph Pierce, a naval constructor, was dispatched to investigate the delay. Pierce reported in August that the delay resulted from the non-arrival of the engines and iron plating.[50]

At the Navy Department the delays at Selma were noted along with similar reports from other shipyards. This serious situation provoked a decision to place naval officers either in direct command or in a supervisory position at the shipyards under contract with the government. On September 2, 1862 Commander Ebenezer Farrand, in command of the naval defenses at Drewry's Bluff on the James River, received orders to proceed to Selma and assume command of

---

[45] Contract of Henry D. Bassett with Navy Department, May 1, 1862, in *Report of Evidence Taken Before a Joint Committee of Both Houses of the Confederate Congress to Investigate the Affairs of the Navy Department* (Richmond, 1863), 455–456.

[46] Several authorities have mentioned the fact that other Confederate vessels, including the *Gaines, Morgan,* and *Nashville,* were constructed at Selma. The evidence clearly indicates that this is not true. The *Gaines* and *Morgan* were built at Mobile by Bassett and Hope, while the *Nashville* was constructed at Montgomery.

[47] Voucher of paymaster (in T. H. Ware Papers, United States National Park and Museum, Fredericksburg, Va.).

[48] Bassett to Jones, June 10, McRae to Jones, June 2, 1862 (Shelby Iron Company Papers). Shelby contracted for the delivery of 3,000 pounds of rolled iron for ship plates as early as April 13, 1863. See Frank Vandiver, "The Shelby Iron Company in the Civil War . . . ," *Alabama Review*, I, 114 (Apr., 1948).

[49] V. M. Randolph to I. W. Bennett, July 7, 1862 (Jones Papers); see also Ware to Bassett (Ware Papers).

[50] Pierce to V. M. Randolph, Aug. 6, 1862 (Ware Papers). McRae had earlier reported the same thing to Mallory, July 13, 1862 (*ORN*, 2, II, 217–218).

all naval construction there.[51] He had orders also to initiate and supervise construction of a large ironclad ram. Farrand arrived at Selma a few days after receiving these orders, and officially took charge with Lieutenant Julius A. Pratt as his executive officer.[52] By the end of September Farrand reported confidently to Admiral Buchanan that the first of the vessels would be ready in about six weeks.[53]

Two weeks later Farrand's optimism had toned down considerably. On October 15 he wrote Buchanan:

> I cannot write with the least encouragement with regard to the completion of the floating batteries here. They are at almost a dead stand still waiting for iron plating and machinery . . . not a particle of machinery for either, and only the boiler for one has been received.[54]

The delays again emphasized the inadequate resources and facilities in the South. At the beginning of the war there were only two rolling mills in the section capable of manufacturing suitable plate for ironclad vessels. Furthermore, before the war only seven steam warships had been built in the states forming the Confederacy, and only two of these had their machinery contracted for in these states.[55]

The engines for the Selma ironclads were to be supplied by the Columbus Iron Works.[56] These works in the fall of 1862 had orders to supply the machinery, including the engines and boilers, for war vessels under construction at Selma, on the Tombigbee River, at Columbus and Savannah, Georgia, at Charleston, South Carolina, and at Wilmington, North Carolina. With only limited facilities available, the Columbus foundry was never able to fill all of the orders, although a number of Confederate vessels did receive their machinery from it. Most of the iron used at Columbus came from the vicinity of Selma. In October, 1862 McRae wrote to the Shelby Iron Company to forward twenty-five tons of pig iron to Columbus.[57] Two-thirds of this order

---

[51] Mallory to Farrand, Sept. 2, 1862 (Jones Papers); for Farrand's career see the Attalla (Ala.) *Advertiser*, Aug. 24, 1933.

[52] Selma *Morning Dispatch*, Nov. 12, 1862.

[53] Buchanan to Mallory, Sept. 26, 1862 (Franklin Buchanan Letterbook, Southern Collection, University of North Carolina Library, Chapel Hill).

[54] Quoted in a letter from Buchanan to Mallory, Oct. 15, 1862 (Buchanan Letterbook).

[55] J. Thomas Scharf, *A History of the Confederate States Navy* (New York, 1887), 46.

[56] With the exception of the Tredegar Iron Works, Richmond, Virginia, the Columbus works was the only establishment in the Confederacy capable of building ship machinery.

[57] McRae to Jones, Oct. 23, 1862 (Shelby Iron Company Papers).

was held up at Selma because of inadequate transportation facilities. On October 31 McRae sent an urgent message to the army quartermaster at Selma to ship iron immediately, as "this iron . . . is required to complete the Engines and Machinery for the floating batteries at this place. . . ."[58] By January, 1863 the machinery for the *Tuscaloosa* had arrived and been installed; the *Huntsville's* engines and boilers failed to arrive before the vessel was taken down to Mobile for completion. The machinery originally designated for the *Tennessee* was never received. Eventually, old steam engines were taken off a Yazoo River boat, transported to Selma and installed on the ironclad ram.

The inadequate supply of iron also retarded the armoring of the vessels. When Selma was selected as a suitable site for a navy yard, one of its supposed advantages was the availability of iron for plate. McRae was under contract with the navy to erect a rolling mill along with the foundry, while the Shelby Iron Company was rapidly converting its facilities in order to roll plate. The Scofield and Markham Rolling Mill in Atlanta, Georgia was also producing gunboat plates for the navy. By the fall of 1862 this reassuring situation had changed considerably. McRae had encountered obstacles which made completion of the rolling mill at Selma uncertain. Some progress was made before the works were turned over to the navy, although the shortage of workmen prevented its completion. Catesby Jones found it impossible to complete the mill for the same reason. In February, 1864 the partially-completed rolling mill was leased to the Shelby Iron Company, provided it complete the mill and turn over to the navy a designated amount of iron plates for gunboats each month.[59] This transfer of responsibility had little effect; in October, Jones wrote: "They are not yet ready to roll . . . plate for gunboats, although they were to have commenced operation five months ago."[60] The mill, still inoperative, was destroyed along with the other naval facilities in Selma in 1865.

Even though the rolling mill at Selma was useless throughout the war, there were still the Atlanta and Shelby works to provide the navy with plate. A sufficient quantity arrived in December, 1862 and in January, 1863, from the Scofield and Markham works, to armor the *Tuscaloosa*. The *Huntsville* received her armor in the following spring

---

[58] McRae to Captain Harris, Oct. 31, 1862 (McRae Letterbook).
[59] Jones to Mallory, Feb. 6, 1864 (Jones Papers); Jones to Ware (Ware Papers); *ORN*, I, XXI, 876.
[60] Jones to Mallory, Oct. 11, 1864 (Jones Papers).

and summer, with both the Atlanta and Shelby works supplying the plates. Apparently, the *Tennessee* was also covered by plates from both companies.

On February 7, 1863 Farrand announced by telegram to Governor Shorter of Alabama the successful launching of the *Tuscaloosa* and the *Huntsville,* "amid enthusiastic cheering."[61] The *Huntsville* had not received her machinery and armor at the time, but was launched anyway to take advantage of the prevailing high water. Buchanan wrote a few days later to send the *Huntsville* down the river by tow if necessary, because of the "danger of the river falling so much that she cannot cross the shoals. . . ."[62] Both vessels were then taken to Mobile, the *Tuscaloosa* under her own power, and the *Huntsville* by tow. At Mobile the final stages of completing the vessels were carried out and they were then turned over to the navy. Similar in appearance to the *Virginia,* although smaller, the ironclads became units of the Mobile squadron and continued to operate until Mobile was evacuated in the spring of 1865. They were then scuttled to prevent capture.

Upon completion of the two Bassett ironclads, attention was then focused on the *Tennessee,* a much larger ironclad ram. Construction was started in October, 1862. Officers in Farrand's command were sent to various cities to hire mechanics and carpenters, while at the same time labor crews were ordered to fell the necessary timber. Late in October the keel was laid and construction was well underway. The work moved along rapidly, and by the end of February, 1863 the vessel was nearing completion. Because of the size of the *Tennessee* and the danger that the river might fall before launching, it was decided to tow her to Mobile and there install the machinery and iron plates. Buchanan ordered Lieutenant James D. Johnston to charter two steamboats for the towing. Johnston later wrote this description of the launching:

> About midday there was heard the sound of a gun, and immediately after-wards the *Tennessee* was shot into the swift current like an arrow, and the water had risen to such a height that she struck in her course the corner of a brick warehouse, situated on an adjoining bluff and demolished it. This was her first and only experience as a ram.[63]

[61] Governors Papers (in Alabama State Department of Archives and History, Montgomery).

[62] Buchanan to Farrand, Feb. 12, 1863 (Buchanan Letterbook).

[63] Quoted in Charles L. Lewis, *Admiral Franklin Buchanan* (Baltimore, 1929), 208.

The *Tennessee* was then taken to Mobile for completion. Her subsequent history is well known, for, as Admiral Buchanan's flagship, she fought valiantly in the Battle of Mobile Bay.

In the same month that the *Tennessee* was towed to Mobile, the fourth ironclad was laid down at Selma. This was to be a large side-wheel steamer, similar to the *Nashville,* then under construction at Montgomery. On March 28, 1863 John T. Shirley, the constructor of the *Arkansas,* and D. D. DeHaven of Missouri, signed a contract for the proposed ironclad steamer. They agreed to complete and turn the vessel over to the Confederate Navy at Mobile by December 14, 1863. In July a naval constructor was ordered to Selma to super-intend construction. By the middle of May the contractors were able to report that the "keel, stern, and sternpost . . . keelsons . . . and about 45 of the midship frames . . . were completed."[64] After this date very little is known about the construction of the vessel except that she was seriously damaged at her launching in April, 1864. Shortly afterwards the navy sold her.[65] With this unfortunate incident, naval construction at Selma came to an end.

During the winter of 1864–1865 General J. H. Wilson of the Union army, gathered a force of 13,500 men in northwestern Alabama for the purpose of making a raid through central Alabama. His objective was the destruction of Confederate stores, factories, mines, and ironworks in that section, including the naval establishments at Selma.[66] The raid began on March 22, and three days later Commander Jones received orders from Secretary Mallory to transfer his machinery to Columbus as soon as possible. Ten days previous to this Jones had written to General Robert Taylor, commanding Confederate defenses in Alabama, inquiring the course to be followed with the heavy machinery. He added rather discouragingly, "under favorable circum-stances it would require weeks to remove it. . . ."[67] But weeks were not available, for by April 1 the advance units of Wilson's forces were within a few miles of Selma. The night of the first was occupied by the workmen at the naval works in destroying as much of the machinery as possible. Tools and machines that were portable were taken by hand trucks to the river and dumped in. Many of the incompleted cannon at the

---

[64] Shirley and DeHaven to Ware, May 17, 1863 (Ware Papers).
[65] *ORN,* 2, II, 638; see also McCockle to Jones, Apr. 14, 1864 (Jones Papers).
[66] Fleming, 71.
[67] *ORN,* 1, XXII, 271.

foundry were also rolled into the river.[68] April 2 was a cheerless day for the Confederacy. Selma had the unwanted honor of falling to the enemy on the same day that Richmond was evacuated. After a brief but gallant fight the small force of Confederates defending the city was compelled to retreat. Shortly afterwards the Federal troops under General Wilson took possession of the city.[69]

The achievements of the Confederate Navy at Selma were considerable. The naval foundry produced nearly two hundred guns, second only to the famous Tredegar Iron Works at Richmond, while the shipyard constructed three ironclads, each of which played an important role in the defense of Mobile. In conclusion, one must emphasize that the problems faced by the Confederate Navy at Selma were typical of the many frustrating obstacles encountered elsewhere.[70]

---

[68] Jackson, 214–215.
[69] ORA, I, XLIX (2), 217.
[70] This paper was written before the publication of Charles S. Davis, *Colin J. McRae: Confederate Financial Agent*, Confederate Centennial Studies, No. 17 (Tuscaloosa, 1961).

PETER A. BRANNON

The Cahawba Military Prison, 1863–1865

Both Confederate and Federal military records indicate that there was considerable agitation in the spring and summer of 1864 for the establishment of a supplementary prison to accommodate the ever-increasing number of Federal prisoners being sent to Andersonville, Sumter County, Georgia.[1] That there was already one, and there had been one for more than a year, seems not to have occurred to the authorities. On July 11, 1864, General J. E. Johnston, then near Atlanta, wired General Braxton Bragg that he strongly recommended the distribution of United States prisoners "now at Andersonville, immediately."[2] And four days later Bragg wired General Samuel Cooper, Confederate States Adjutant and Inspector General, that he had ordered a "new depot" at Cahawba and not to send, for the present, any more prisoners "this side of South Carolina."[3]

Contrary to these official references, there were "Yankee" prisoners at Cahawba long prior to April 20, 1864, for Adjutant General Cooper on that date ordered General Leonidas Polk, whose headquarters were then at Demopolis, to send promptly the prisoners then at Cahawba "and all others that may be captured" to Andersonville. He further directed the "present guard" (at Cahawba) to go with the prisoners and remain with them at Andersonville.[4] Lieuten-

---

[1] This paper was read as the presidential address before the Alabama Historical Association, Cahawba, Dallas County, April 8, 1950. It was published in *The Alabama Review,* III (July, 1950).

[2] *The War of the Rebellion: A Compilation of the Official Records of the Union and Confederate Armies* (Washington, 1880–1901), 2nd Ser., VII, 458. Hereinafter cited as *Official Records.*

[3] *Ibid.,* 2nd Ser., VII, 467.

[4] *Ibid.,* 2nd Ser., VII, 76.

ant Colonel Henry C. Davis, commanding the post at Cahawba, on May 3 reported that all Federal prisoners, "except the sick, had been sent to Andersonville, including all Fort Pillow prisoners sent here."[5]

Orders were issued at Camp Sumter (the official Confederate name of the Andersonville, Georgia, Federal Soldier Prison) on June 27, 1864, for Captain C. E. Dyke, Florida Lieutenant of Artillery, to "proceed at once to Cahawba, and afterward to Union Springs in the same state, and examine thoroughly into the merits of the places for the establishment of a military prison." Dyke made an intelligent survey of the facilities at Union Springs and, while doing so, discovered the many advantages of Silver Run, on the Mobile and Girard Railroad, as a site for a prison.[6]

Accordingly, on July 7 General John H. Winder, from Camp Sumter reported to Adjutant General Cooper that Silver Run (the present town of Seale, Russell County) was the most suitable place to "establish a depot for prisoners of war," and asked whether he should proceed to establish it. He further said neither Cahawba nor Union Springs was suitable.[7] President Mitchell of the Mobile and Girard, on July 8, 1864, importuned the Secretary of War at Richmond not to locate the prison on his road,[8] but on July 13 Winder urged Cooper for authority to impress labor and teams to establish the prison at Silver Run.[9]

Six weeks later, on August 25, President Jefferson Davis wired Governor Thomas H. Watts of Alabama, who apparently was favorable to Silver Run, that the region around that place was too much drained of supplies for the Army and liable to raids. On the same day, John A. Seddon, Confederate Secretary of War, directed General Winder "to hasten to the utmost the preparation of the other prisons," and thus, by the order of the Commander-in-Chief, Jefferson Davis, the President of the Confederate States of America, Cahawba at the junction of the Alabama and Cahawba rivers, former site of the state capitol and then county seat of Dallas County, was

---

[5] *Ibid.*, 2nd Ser., VII, 110.
[6] *Ibid.*, 2nd Ser., VII, 441–444.
[7] *Ibid.*, 2nd Ser., VII, 446–469.
[8] *Ibid.*, 2nd Ser., VII, 448.
[9] *Ibid.*, 2nd Ser., VII, 463.

chosen as the site of the Cahawba Federal Prison, as the institution is officially called in all the records.[10]

Dr. Jesse Hawes of the 9th Illinois Cavalry, U.S.A., who twenty-three years after the war published *Cahawba, A Story of Captive Boys in Blue,* an on-the-spot account of his prison life there, says that there were Federal prisoners at Cahawba as early as the fall of 1863 and that "the idea of locating the great prison of the South at Cahawba, Ala., instead of Andersonville, Ga., had been advocated by a few Confederate leaders . . ."[11] Some claim that General Bragg—who, it will be recalled, had ordered a "new depot at Cahawba" on July 15, 1864—was President Davis' mouthpiece even that early. Captain H. A. M. Henderson who was appointed from retirement on August 14, 1863, as C.S.A. Assistant Commissioner of Exchange of Prisoners, while on duty at Demopolis on August 31 had recommended that a camp for Federal prisoners be located at Cahawba.[12]

Dr. R. H. Whitfield, on March 31, 1864 (the date is more than ninety days earlier than that on which Cahawba was officially selected as a prison site) reported to Medical Director P. B. Scott that there were 660 men then confined in an area of 15,000 sq. ft., that 1600 sq. ft. of this was open (to the heavens, no roof), and that there was no floor, except the natural earth, even under the leaky roof which was attached at but three sides. Since the report details conditions of the "past five months," it indicates that the site was a concentration camp as early as October, 1863.[13]

On April 2, 1864, the Selma *Morning Reporter* contained the following letter which is significant not merely because it gives a captured soldier's reaction to his imprisonment at Cahawba but also because it proves that out-going mail was censored:

> Cahawba, March 31, 1864
> *Mr. Editor:* Before sending Federal prisoners' letters North, by flag of truce, the duty devolves upon me of reading and approving what they write. From their correspondence I take from one letter the following extract:

[10] *Ibid.*, 2nd Ser., VII, 678.

[11] (New York, 1888), p. 12. Hawes calls the prison "Castle Morgan" (for General John H. Morgan) and the writer has many times heard it so described by ex-Confederate soldiers, but the name is not used in the official records.

[12] Service statement for Captain Henderson furnished by U.S. Adjutant General to Alabama Department Archives and History, Oct. 12, 1949, shows that he entered the Confederate service February 18, 1862, from Walker County and resigned September 18, 1862, on account of disability.

[13] *Official Records,* 2nd Ser., VI, 1124.

'*Dear Father:* You cannot imagine how many homes we have destroyed (and some of them those of poor widows) in this last raid. When I was captured I ran through the picket lines, and was not hurt by the fire opened upon me. My horse was shot by a citizen as I passed his burnt dwelling. When my horse plunged forward and fell, I was slightly hurt. After I arose, three citizens stood by me, with as many shot guns leveled at my head. They said I was the first Yankee that had fallen in their hands since their houses were burned and their families turned out to the mercy of the pitiless elements, and that they would make me suffer. Such had been the brutality of many of my comrades, that I could not ask for quarter. There was the wife of one of them, and three shivering hungry little children; their clothing and food had been burned or stolen by our cavalry, but they spared my life, the soldiers took charge of me, and I was well treated. I was sorry to be captured a few months before my term of enlistment expired. Since my capture I have seen more of the South and its slaves than I ever expected to see. Let no man ever, hereafter, speak to me about fighting to free negroes. The people of the South are humane, and the negroes well satisfied, until our army threw the firebrand of discontent into their midst. I took the oath, in good faith, to serve the United States three years. My time will soon be out, and I shall not re-enlist. I do not know whether I shall have a chance to see home or not when the election comes off this fall, but dear father, do all that you can to put the Democratic party in power. I think if this can be effected, the inhuman war will speedily end.'

The above extract is similar in spirit to many other views which come under my notice.

Respectfully,

H. A. M. HENDERSON.

Another story published in the same paper a few weeks later refers to the prison as a "receiving depot for the department of Alabama, Mississippi and East Louisiana," and reports the shipment of 1,500 prisoners from there to Andersonville.[14]

A Federal report of September 30, 1864, made by Major General C. C. Washburn at headquarters of the District of Tennessee, to Colonel William Hoffman, Commissary General of Prisoners at Washington, states that there were 350 prisoners belonging to the 16th Army Corps, U.S.A., then confined at Cahawba. An Agent of Exchange for the Confederate Government proposed to exchange these prisoners, man for man, the prisoners to be exchanged to belong to the Department of Alabama, Mississippi and East Louisiana. But General Washburn had no prisoners to offer and requested that some be sent from northern prisons. A significant feature of his report is

---

[14] May 16, 1864.

that there were no colored enlisted men then at Cahawba, but that there was one major of a colored artillery outfit who, he said, was badly treated. The Confederate authorities proposed to exchange him with the rest. Washburn also reported thirty or forty civilians, most of whom were U.S. Government employees, then in the Cahawba stockade. Hawes also mentions the imprisonment of these civilians.[15]

Assistant Adjutant and Inspector General D. T. Chandler, C.S.A., on October 16, 1864, recorded the only official "Diagram" and description of the reconverted "cotton shed" around which had been erected a stockade, though Hawes in his book brings out details not mentioned in the reports.[16]

From the Chandler report we learn that the prison was established to accommodate 500 prisoners. In October, 1864, there were 2,151 confined there. One-half the building, which had formerly been a bricked-around shed, was without a roof. Around this had been erected a stockade mainly of two-inch-thick plank, set three feet in the ground, and twelve feet high. There were 500 bunks under the wall roof, but no means of heating the structure. Open wood fires which were allowed in the enclosed area made the smoke nuisance intolerable. Each prisoner was required to do his own cooking. Confederate reports admit poor food, insufficient clothing to keep men warm, and a poor system of water supply. There was quite a sufficient quantity of water provided for the anticipated 500, for one of the many artesian wells of the town was diverted through the stockade, but this water flowed through part of the town in an open ditch where animals drank from it, clothes were washed in it, and it was otherwise polluted. Sanitary facilities were inadequate for the planned number and were terrible at the height of population. The inspector was very critical of the Commissary of Subsistance for furnishing no rice, peas, or beans to accompany the standard issue of raw meat and meal. There were a number of cases of scurvy. The ten Federal officers of the prison population lived in town in government-furnished quarters and while they were confined, on parole to the town limits, they expressed themselves as perfectly satisfied. Colonel Chandler recommended that, if the prison was to be made a permanent one, a site one mile out of town (on the plantation of a Mr. Matthews) should be used.

[15] *Official Records,* 2nd Ser., VII, 895–896; Hawes, *op. cit.,* pp. 223–225.
[16] *Ibid.,* pp. 12–21, 125 ff.; *WOR,* 2nd Ser., VII, 998–1001. Hawes, *op. cit.,* pp. xx, 128, contains a sketch of the prison "drawn from memory" and the diagram, a copy of which accompanies this article.

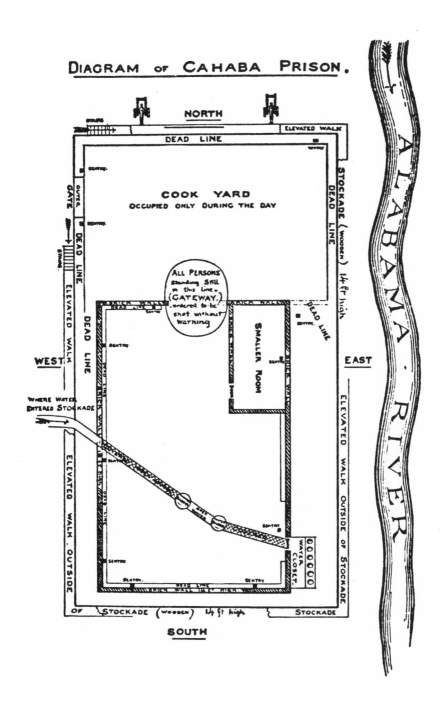

DIAGRAM OF CAHABA PRISON.

This was not endorsed by the authorities, however, and during the same month General Cooper ordered the surplus prisoners at Cahawba to be transferred to Millen, Georgia.

Captain Henderson, C.S.A., and Major General Washburn, U.S.A., entered into an agreement on November 15, 1864, whereby the Federal Army, District of West Tennessee, agreed to send Captain John Whytock of the latter's staff to distribute supplies and food to the prisoners. Henderson, who in addition to other duties then commanded the Cahawba Prison, signed the request of the Federal authorities subject to the approval of Major General D. H. Maury, commanding the District of the Gulf. Washburn proposed to send 2,000 coats, 2,000 pairs of pants, 2,000 pairs of drawers, 4,000 pairs of socks, 2,000 pairs of shoes, 2,000 hats, 1,500 blankets, 100 cooking pans, 5 reams of paper and 2,000 envelopes and sufficient medicine to supply the post, provided that his staff officer be allowed to make the distribution. Henderson requested of the Confederate authorities that Whytock be passed through the lines and suggested that he be allowed to entertain him at his own home in Cahawba while he discharged the distribution. Lieutenant Colonel S. Jones, Commander of the Post of Cahawba, requested permission for Captain Whytock to come from Memphis to Cahawba, but Maury at Mobile disapproved the request and Henderson so advised Washburn on December 8.[17] Maury was willing, however, in February, 1865, to allow General G. Granger, of the U.S. garrison at Fort Gaines, Alabama, to send clothing, under the flag of truce, to the prisoners.[18]

Hawes claims horrible conditions existed during the winter of 1864–1865 and in addition, the Cahawba River flooded and caused more suffering.[19] Prison restrictions were eased on account of the flood, however, and on January 20, 1865, the prisoners mutinied and captured the guards. The soldiers attached to the Post in the town put down the rebellion. The leader in the effort to escape was a man shown on the records as a civilian, George Schellar, but who was in reality, Captain Hiram S. Hanchett of Company M, 16th Illinois Cavalry, who was inside the Confederate lines as a spy.[20] Captain Hanchett was tried by Court Martial and sentenced to be confined in the county jail. An investigation made six months after the war by Federal officer W.

[17] *Official Records,* 2nd Ser., 1176–1177, 1205.
[18] *Ibid.,* 2nd Ser., VIII, 316.
[19] *Op. cit.,* pp. 444–446.
[20] *Official Records,* 2nd Ser., VIII, 117–121.

Boggs, commanding Company K, 47th Illinois Infantry, U.S.A., indicates that Hanchett was ordered released from jail to be sent to Demopolis for exchange as a prisoner of war, about the date of Wilson's Raid into Selma. This action was by the Cahawba Town Council. The Federal report indicates that he never reached Selma—in fact, he never lived to get two miles from Cahawba.[21]

Cahawba Prison was located on the river bank at the east end of Capitol Avenue, across Vine street, and was locally known as Babcock's Warehouse. Strange it is that Mrs. Anna M. Gayle Fry, who some years later wrote a vivid picture of life at Cahawba, makes only a casual mention of the incident of the location of the prison in the town. She gives the population of the prison as 3,000.[22]

Statistics show that the wall or stockade fence fronting Vine Street, was 258 ft. north and south. The back wall on the Alabama River bank was 212 ft. long and there was a 35 ft. offset at the main entrance in the left rear. Water was conducted into the prison through wooden pipes (really covered troughs) under the wall to a pit made of several barrels in the center of the enclosure, where free use for any and all purposes was permitted. A small, inadequate "sink" (latrine) was located at the back or river wall and water for its sanitation flowed from the central pool. The recreation yard, in which more than 2,000 prisoners got what exercise they could, was 35 ft. x 46 ft. Prisoners also cooked in this area.

Although Captain H. A. M. Henderson, Company E, 28th Alabama Infantry Regiment, detailed as C.S.A. Assistant Commissioner of Exchange of Prisoners, was Commander of the Prison, the Post of Cahawba was actually under the command of Lieutenant Colonel S. Jones, 22nd Louisiana Regiment of Infantry. Post officers, Captain J. J. Wheadon, Assistant Commissary of Subsistence, and Lieutenant V. Renaud, Quartermaster, were charged with furnishing the prison with supplies. The Prison Surgeon was R. H. Whitfield, of Demopolis. L. E. Profilet was Surgeon of the Guard. The hospital was totally inadequate. Dr. Whitfield significantly reported that "the two quartermasters at this Post, with only this prison and one small hospital to supply, have failed to be equal to the task of having this prison supplied with good and sufficient wood, water and bunks, and

---

[21] *Ibid.*, 2nd Ser., VIII, 794–795; Hawes, *op. cit.*, pp. 432 ff. This case was finally disposed of by a report of W. Winthrop, Brvt. Col. and Judge Advocate, Bureau Military Justice, August 8, 1866 (*ibid.*, 2nd Ser., VIII, 951).

[22] *Memories of Old Cahaba* (Nashville and Dallas, 1908), pp. 18, 68.

putting it in a condition in which it would be moderately comfortable, clean and healthy." The prison authorities had *one* wheelbarrow, and only that, with which to remove filth, garbage, rubbish and accumulations.[23] The Prison Guard was made of 161 effective men (October 16, 1864), and there was a special detail of eighteen men and two small pieces of field artillery. Colonel Chandler observed that the feeble garrison could easily be overpowered by the prisoners[24] and, it will be recalled, this actually happened in 1865.

The Post Commissary, who was the Tax-in-kind Collector for four adjacent counties, admitted that vinegar and rice, which were quite plentiful, could have been issued to the prisoners, but nobody ordered them. (There was much suffering from scurvy and dysentery.) The Richmond authorities ordered the deficiency of administration corrected, but during the lasts months of the war Captain Henderson was frequently absent, concerned with the exchange of prisoners, and nothing was done about it. Hawes found much fault and his complaints were in most cases justifiable.[25]

The large number of prisoners falling into the hands of the Confederate Army in the summer and fall of 1864 proved too great for the very inefficient personnel of the Post of Cahawba. Federal accounts find no fault with Captain Henderson and Dr. Whitfield, but they are very critical of Colonel Jones and his staff. Obviously, these Federal opinions are based somewhat on the reports of a few escaped prisoners, but Dr. Whitfield's official reports to his superiors show that there was much incompetency. At any rate, the authorities transferred the prisoners from Cahawba as promptly as was possible in the early weeks of 1865, and, when Wilson's army reached Selma on April 1, there were only a few sick men left. Most of the exchanges from Cahawba were released at Demopolis and by the end of April, 1865, the Cahawba Federal Prison was a closed episode in Confederate history.[26]

---

[23] *Official Records,* 2nd Ser., VI, 1124.

[24] *Ibid.,* 2nd Ser., VII, 998–1001.

[25] *Op. cit., passim.*

[26] That time ameliorates many of the passions of war is evidenced by the following experience of the writer who was a guest of the Cleveland, Ohio, Rotary Club on May 30 (Decoration Day) several years ago. Other guests were twenty-seven Union veterans, all but one of whom had been prisoners at Andersonville and the one at Cahawba. They all told of the horrors of prison life, but there was no bitterness, resentment or criticism, and their statements as to their treatment were, in every case, charitably expressed. When asked after the meeting by the Secretary how he enjoyed listening to Union veterans recall their war experiences, the writer reminded him that even though they had been in southern prisons, they seemed not resentful of the treatment they had received. The Secretary agreed that he had noted the same thing.

JAMES F. COOK

The 1863 Raid of Abel D. Streight:

Why It Failed

In the vast, ever-expanding literature of the Civil War, probably no aspect of the conflict has received more attention than the exploits of the cavalry. The raids of such colorful figures as J. E. B. Stuart, John Hunt Morgan, Earl Van Dorn, Philip Sheridan, and Nathan Bedford Forrest are well known even to beginning students. The life of Forrest has been recorded by no less than six biographers.[1] All of them portray the character and generalship of the dour, barely-literate Tennessean in highly complimentary terms, giving him such sobriquets as "the South's greatest cavalryman" and "the wizard of the saddle."

One of Forrest's most amazing achievements was his victory over the mule brigade of Abel Streight in the spring of 1863. In forcing Streight to surrender to a force only one-third as large as his, Forrest saved the city of Rome, Georgia from destruction and earned the everlasting gratitude of the Romans. He became the hero of the day, and Georgians, as they rejoiced, considered changing the name of Union County to Forrest County.[2] All of Forrest's biographers narrate this episode in considerable detail, yet none of them really analyze the raid in a critical and objective manner. Hence, this paper will attempt to do what they have neglected to do.

This essay was published in *The Alabama Review*, XXII (October 1969).
[1] Robert Selph Henry, *"First With the Most" Forrest* (Indianapolis, 1944); Thomas Jordan and J. P. Pryor, *The Campaigns of Lieut.-Gen. N. B. Forrest, and of Forrest's Cavalry* (New Orleans, 1868); Andrew Lytle, *Bedford Forrest And His Critter Company* (rev. ed.; New York, 1960); J. Harvey Mathes, *General Forrest* (New York, 1902); Eric William Sheppard, *Bedford Forrest, the Confederacy's Greatest Cavalryman* (New York, 1930); and John Allan Wyeth, *That Devil Forrest: Life of Nathan Bedford Forrest* (2nd ed.; New York, 1959).
[2] *Southern Confederacy* (Atlanta, Ga.), May 5, 1863; *Southern Recorder* (Milledgeville, Ga.), May 12, 1863.

In the first week of 1863 after the indecisive battle of Stone's River, the Union Army of the Cumberland commanded by General William S. Rosecrans and the Confederate Army of Tennessee commanded by General Braxton Bragg settled down for an extended period of relative inactivity. The two armies faced each other across Middle Tennessee virtually in a stalemate, the Federals occupying Murfreesboro, Franklin, and Nashville, and the Confederates located along the Duck River with headquarters at Tullahoma. The two antagonists made no large-scale movements until June and fought no major battle until Chickamauga in September. Only cavalry raids broke the monotony of camp life, and heretofore the Southern raiders had proved superior. Thus when Colonel Abel Streight of the 51st Indiana Infantry in late March suggested a daring cavalry raid behind the Confederate lines, the plan was accepted by Rosecrans and eagerly received by his chief of staff, General James A. Garfield (later to become President of the United States).[3]

The plan, when finally approved, called for Streight to lead a brigade of 2,000 men mounted on mules on a circuitous route to western Georgia to cut the Western and Atlantic Railroad. This railroad, which supplied Bragg's army, was the chief objective of the raid, but Streight also was instructed to "destroy all depots of supplies of the rebel army, and manufactories of guns, ammunition, equipments, and clothing for their use."[4] The expedition was to leave Nashville on steamers and go down the Cumberland River to Palmyra. From there it would march to Fort Henry on the Tennessee River, gathering additional mounts as it traveled. The raiders then would go by transport with gunboat escort down the Tennessee River to Eastport, Mississippi, where they would rendezvous with General Grenville Dodge's army. From Eastport they would march with Dodge to menace Tuscumbia, Alabama, but Streight's brigade would not participate in the attack unless the safety of Dodge's army required it. While Dodge kept the Confederates occupied, Streight was to slip away to Russellville or Moulton and proceed across northern Alabama to his destination in Georgia.[5]

---

[3] Theodore Clarke Smith, *The Life and Letters of James Abram Garfield* (New Haven, 1925), I, 289.
[4] U.S. War Department, *The War of the Rebellion: A Compilation of the Official Records of the Union and Confederate Armies* (hereinafter referred to as *O.R.*), ser. I. XXIII, pt. 1 (Washington, 1889), 282. All citations in this paper are series I.
[5] *Ibid.*

Was Streight's plan sound? Were the desired gains worth the possible loss of men and equipment? Without question the destruction of the Western and Atlantic Railroad would have been a severe blow to the Confederacy, which was hampered throughout the war by inadequate rail facilities. It would have impeded the flow of ammunition and supplies to Bragg, and would have deprived the Confederates of the advantages of their interior lines of communication.[6] The strategic importance of this railroad was recognized by both sides. In 1862 the Federals tried to destroy it with the Andrews raid; in 1864, when Sherman drove the Confederates from Chattanooga to Atlanta, Johnston never strayed far from the railroad as he retreated. In addition to this primary objective, there was also the strong possibility that the raid would destroy other valuable Confederate property. As it turned out, the one tangible accomplishment of the raid was the partial destruction of the Round Mountain Iron Works in Cherokee County, Alabama.[7] The chances of the raiders returning safely after accomplishing their mission were slim indeed, but their loss was a risk worth taking.

The success of this plan depended on the element of surprise, which could be achieved by secrecy of preparation, a convincing diversionary attack by Dodge, and rapid execution by Streight. The Union officers maintained the utmost secrecy and did not divulge the objective of the expedition to the raiders until the morning of April 23, when they were leaving Eastport for the attack on Tuscumbia.[8] The Confederates observed both Dodge's movements from Corinth and the transports descending the Tennessee, but they had no understanding of the true nature of the plan until Confederate scouts noticed a band of cavalry heading for Moulton on April 28. Even then the Confederates were not sure whether the cavalry movement was an independent raid or a flanking movement.[9] Superficially it appears that two of the ingredients for success were supplied, and obviously since Streight was captured before reaching Georgia, his execution was not rapid enough. But was Streight's failure a result of his negligence or incompetence, or were other factors responsible?

[6] Lytle, *Bedford Forrest*, 150; *O.R.*, XXIII, pt. 1, 281.
[7] *Southern Banner* (Athens, Ga.), May 13, 1863; Henry, *"First With the Most,"* 152.
[8] William Barton McCash, "Colonel Abel D. Streight's Raid, His Capture, and Imprisonment" (master's thesis, University of Georgia, 1959), 87, 92.
[9] Lytle, *Bedford Forrest*, 155.

Since Streight had suggested the raid he was placed in command of it, despite the fact that he was an officer in the infantry. In choosing the men he would lead, Streight selected four regiments of infantry and only two companies of cavalry. Streight did not command a cavalry brigade, but rather a brigade of mounted infantry. The selection of men was a mistake, for experienced cavalrymen could have borne the rigors of protracted riding better than the most trusted infantrymen unaccustomed to the saddle. One infantry sergeant recorded in his journal before the expedition even reached Tuscumbia that there was "considerable soreness" because the men were unaccustomed to the saddle.[10] In his report Streight acknowledged that his men, "unaccustomed as they were to riding" were "illy prepared for the trying ordeal through which they were to pass."[11]

The expedition was also hampered considerably by the decision to use mules instead of horses. Mules were selected because the terrain was rugged and the roads were in a wretched condition. It was believed that mules would be surer of foot in the mountainous country and that they could withstand greater hardships on less forage than horses.[12] This line of reasoning was questionable, to say the least, and it failed to take into consideration the fact that mules are both noisier and slower than horses. Furthermore, it appears that Forrest's horses got over the treacherous terrain as well as the mules and with at least equal endurance.

Even the use of good mules would have been a handicap to Streight, but the ones he received were sickly, unbroken, and in insufficient quantity. This deplorable situation resulted from Rosecrans' obsession that his cavalry was grossly inferior to Bragg's. Rosecrans contended that if he had 10,000 more mounted men he could have "all the stock and forage that the rebels have taken under our noses"; with 20,000 he could cut off the enemy's subsistence from Middle Tennessee.[13] The quartermaster, General M. C. Meigs, was unimpressed by Rosecrans' arguments and pointed out that he already had more horses than he could take care of.[14] Rosecrans pleaded so

[10] Frank Moore, ed., *The Rebellion Record: A Diary of American Events* (New York, 1864), supplement I, doc. 57, 340.
[11] *O.R.*, XXIII, pt. 1, 288.
[12] Wyeth, *That Devil Forrest*, 166.
[13] *O.R.*, XXIII, pt. 2, 289.
[14] *Ibid.*, 301.

often and so vehemently to the authorities in Washington that General in Chief Henry W. Halleck finally had to reprimand him on April 28, 1863. Halleck informed Rosecrans that "you now have a larger number of animals in proportion to your forces than any other general in the field."[15] On March 23, 1863 Rosecrans had 23,859 mules and 19,164 horses on hand, which indicates that his fears were exaggerated.[16] Yet, Rosecrans remained convinced of his cavalry inferiority and this belief made him unwilling to spare the necessary mounts for Streight's raid.

Only 800 mules were issued, because "the grand object of the expedition was to cripple the enemy as much as possible; and one very effectual way of doing this was to seize the animals whose labor furnished subsistence for the rebel armies."[17] This explanation, given by Streight's aide-de-camp, is unconvincing. When the outcome of the expedition was dependent upon speed of execution, such parsimony with over 40,000 animals on hand was foolish. Thus the commanding general, in trying to save a thousand mounts, burdened his men with such a severe handicap that he almost assured the loss of 800 mules and the whole brigade.

It should be pointed out that Rosecrans did make positive contributions to the expedition. He accepted the plan, permitted Streight to select the men he would lead, acquired the necessary transports and gunboats, and got assistance from General Dodge of General Stephen A. Hurlburt's army. Since Streight arrived at Eastport three days later than planned, as a result of difficulty in getting transports and unfavorable conditions for navigation, Dodge and Hurlburt attributed his defeat primarily to the delay.[18] Their arguments, however, appear to be merely efforts to exonerate themselves and place the onus of defeat on Streight and Rosecrans. Assembling at the desired spot Dodge's army of 7,500 men, Streight's brigade of 2,000 men, 1,200 cantankerous mules, and 130,000 rations without mishap indicates that the planning and coordination was adequate. To Rosecrans and Garfield, who frequently labored over the details until 4 A.M., must go the credit for this accomplishment.[19]

In Streight's official report he states that if Dodge had detained

[15] *Ibid.*, 284–85.
[16] *Ibid.*, 281.
[17] A. C. Roach, *The Prisoner of War and How Treated* (Indianapolis, 1865), 15–16.
[18] *O.R.*, XXIII, pt. 1, 243, 248–49.
[19] Smith, *Letters of Garfield*, I, 289–90.

Forrest one more day, the raid would have succeeded in spite of the poor mounts.[20] In view of the fact that Streight was captured only twenty miles from Rome, not by strategy or superior numbers but rather because his men were completely exhausted, another day probably would have been decisive. Why wasn't that day provided?

Grenville Dodge, commanding 7,500 troops, was opposed by the combined forces of Colonel P. D. Roddey and Forrest, which did not exceed 2,800 altogether.[21] The army under Dodge was capable of driving the Confederates across the Tennessee River toward their base at Tullahoma. It took Tuscumbia on the 24th "without severe fighting," drove the Confederates back steadily, and created "great alarm among the rebels."[22] Dodge continued to advance, and by the 27th he had driven the Confederates across Town Creek. The next day he crossed Town Creek but soon he abandoned the attack and retreated from the area, laying waste the Tennessee Valley as he went.

Despite this failure to exploit an opportunity to drive farther up the Tennessee Valley, Dodge and Hurlburt considered the mission a crowning success.[23] The statistics in Dodge's report are impressive indeed: six successful engagements, capture of Tuscumbia and Florence, destruction of 1,500,000 bushels of corn, 500,000 pounds of bacon, 60 flatboats, and the railroad from Tuscumbia to Decatur.[24] Laying waste the productive Tennessee Valley was a notable accomplishment, but was that Dodge's primary mission? Evidently Dodge understood his mission, for he recorded that "the intention and plan of the movement was to cover a raid by Colonel Streight, of Major-General Rosecrans' command, into Georgia, to break up the Atlanta and Chattanooga Railroad."[25]

The reason Dodge failed to continue his attack against Forrest seems to lie in the fact that Dodge was in Hurlburt's army and Streight was under Rosecrans' command. At the same time Streight was trying to cross Alabama, another Union cavalry raid was enjoying greater success crossing the Mississippi. Mounted on "the best horses avail-

---

[20] O.R., XXIII, pt. 1, 293.
[21] Ibid., p. 245; McCash, "Streight's Raid," 108; Jordan and Pryor, Campaigns of Forrest, 250–51.
[22] O.R., XXIV, pt. 3, 236.
[23] Ibid., XXIII, pt. 1, 243, 248.
[24] Ibid., 246–49.
[25] Ibid., 246.

able—captured Mississippi blood stock"—Colonel B. H. Grierson of Hurlburt's army led 1,700 men from La Grange, Tennessee to Baton Rouge on a highly successful mission.[26] In *Grierson's Raid,* D. Alexander Brown indicates that General Grant viewed Streight's raid, Dodge's movement, Grierson's raid, and two infantry movements as "five long-planned and well-synchronized" diversions which he hoped would "distract the Confederates' attention from activities around Vicksburg."[27] Although there is no evidence to indicate that either Rosecrans or Streight agreed with or was aware of such strategy, it is likely that Hurlburt and Dodge viewed Streight's raid as a diversion. Hurlburt agreed to let Dodge serve as a cover for Streight because it was convenient. Such a move would not interfere with Grierson's raid—indeed it would complement it by keeping Confederate pursuers occupied in Alabama chasing Streight.[28]

Having noted obstacles placed in the way of victory by Dodge and Rosecrans, let us now look at the fox and the hound and evaluate the part each played in determining the outcome on May 3. Colonel Abel D. Streight, a publisher from Indiana, was neither a brilliant soldier nor a great one. He was a brave man and a competent leader in search of glory. Forrest praised him as a "most excellent officer."[29] The adjectives "able," "wily," "skillful," "courageous" and "stalwart" have been used to describe him.[30] Yet, he surrendered his brigade to an adversary with less than half as many men. Could Streight have avoided this ignominious surrender by taking different action?

Wyeth suggests that Streight's biggest mistake was in marching all night on May 2. This forced march by exhausted men gained only a few miles, which Forrest covered the next morning in four hours. Thus, when Forrest demanded Streight's surrender, the rebels were rested and the Yankees could not stay awake.[31] Judging from the outcome the next day, it appears that Streight's decision was a grievous mistake. No doubt Streight did it because Forrest had consistently kept a small vanguard harassing Streight's rearguard,

---

[26] D. Alexander Brown, *Grierson's Raid* (Urbana, 1954), 38.

[27] *Ibid.,* 37–38.

[28] *O.R.,* XXIV, pt. 1, 520.

[29] *Southern Recorder* (Milledgeville, Ga.), May 19, 1863.

[30] Henry, *"First With the Most,"* 149; Lytle, *Bedford Forrest,* 157; Mathes, *General Forrest,* 109.

[31] Wyeth, *That Devil Forrest,* 197–98.

"shooting at anything blue." When it is remembered that skirmishing probably would have continued all night with Streight not knowing when Forrest's whole command might attack, Streight's decision to march rather than sleep does not appear unwise. In this situation the hound clearly has the advantage on the fox.

All of the advantages were not with Forrest, however, for a rapidly-pursuing force is an easy target for an ambush. On several occasions Streight left detachments in ambush which, on the whole, were well-planned and effectively carried out. On one engagement Streight captured two pieces of Forrest's artillery, and this loss left the Confederate leader furious with rage. The skillful use of the ambush and the example Streight set with his stamina and perseverance were the most obvious qualities of leadership he displayed.

Streight's major weakness as a commander was his inattention to details. On three occasions this defect proved costly. The first lapse was when the 800 mules were delivered at Nashville. Streight, tending to other details, had left in charge a subordinate, who accepted the animals. Streight, in fact, did not examine the mules until they disembarked at Palmyra. There he discovered that the mules were "poor, wild, and unbroken colts," many afflicted with the "horse distemper," and forty or fifty "too near dead to travel."[32]

The second mistake resulting from inattention occurred at Eastport. As soon as the transports anchored, Streight quickly rode twelve miles to consult with Dodge while the mules and supplies were being unloaded. During his absence a stampede occurred, which resulted in the loss of 400 of the best animals. Only 200 of them were recovered and much valuable time was lost in the process. Perhaps Streight should have left better instructions for the disembarkation, or commanded more men to do the job. It is also possible that Streight is without blame in this instance, for much controversy surrounds the cause of the stampede. Mathes and Henry do not explain the cause of the stampede, but Lytle and Wyeth attribute it to Roddey's men, who were attracted by the honking of the mules, a sound that carried for miles.[33] Dodge thought the carelessness of one of Streight's officers was the cause.[34]

[32] *O.R.,* XXIII, pt. 1, 286.
[33] Mathes, *General Forrest,* 111; Henry, *"First With the Most,"* 142; Lytle, *Bedford Forrest,* 152; Wyeth, *That Devil Forrest,* 168–69.
[34] *O.R.,* XXIII, pt. 1, 247.

A more serious example of Streight's negligence was in crossing Big Wills Creek on the night of May 1. During this crossing a quantity of the powder in canvas packs strapped to the backs of the mules got wet and was rendered useless.[35] Streight, being farther up the column, did not learn of the loss until the last mule had emerged from the creek. Ironically, Streight's antagonist was very attentive to details, particularly careful to protect his ammunition when crossing streams.[36]

In addition to inattentiveness to details, Streight was also remiss in not learning the size of Forrest's forces opposing him. Streight recorded that he was opposed by a force three times as large as his own when he surrendered, yet nearly the reverse was true. With approximately 1,700 mounted men left when he surrendered, it seems that Streight easily could have deployed half a dozen men at strategic spots to observe the approaching Confederates and ascertain their actual strength. By repeating this process several times Streight might have lost a few scouts, but that would not have jeopardized the success of the mission, and he would have gained valuable information. Had he possessed such knowledge it is quite likely that he would have made at least one pitched battle, and his chances of victory over Forrest would have been good indeed. Streight's failure to use his cavalry for this essential purpose probably resulted from his inexperience with cavalry.

The biographers of Forrest have heaped praise on their subject in gargantuan quantities. They do not state, but in general they do imply, that the outcome of the raid was determined on April 23 when Forrest received orders from Bragg to aid Roddey. A closer scrutiny of the evidence, however, reveals that in this particular instance Forrest is not altogether deserving of their accolades, for the outcome of the raid was by no means settled until May 3.

When Forrest received his orders at Spring Hill, he immediately dispatched 600 men of the Eleventh Tennessee to join Roddey near Tuscumbia. The next morning Forrest led the remainder of his brigade, the Fourth, Ninth, and Tenth Tennessee regiments and Morton's battery, in the direction of Courtland, Alabama. Just before crossing the Tennessee River he directed the Eighth Tennessee to

---

[35] *Ibid.*, 290.
[36] McCash, "Streight's Raid," 171.

Florence on the northern bank of the river, while the main body of troops continued to Courtland. Forrest's assistance was sorely needed, for Roddey's outnumbered brigade had been pushed east of Town Creek on April 27.

April 28, 1863 was the most eventful day of the raid. On that day a pitched battle took place with Dodge's superior numbers and artillery forcing Forrest and Roddey to retreat toward Courtland. That evening Dodge halted his advance only three miles from Courtland and then began his retreat and destruction of the Tennessee Valley. The night before, Dodge had informed Streight at Mount Hope that he had driven away the enemy and that Streight should push on. Streight did push on, thinking he was unopposed, for Dodge had promised that he would advance to Courtland and pursue the enemy if he should turn toward Moulton.[37] On the evening of the 28th, when the fighting had ceased, James Moon, a citizen of Tuscumbia, informed Forrest that approximately 2,000 mounted Union troops had passed through Mount Hope in the direction of Moulton.[38] The complexion of the raid had now changed considerably, for the diversionary force was withdrawing and Streight's movement was no longer a secret.

Most writers on the subject have erroneously concluded that on the night of April 28 Forrest realized the objective of Streight's movement. Mathes says: "He saw through it all in an instant, and formed his plans accordingly"; Jordan and Pryor relate that "he completed his preparations for the emergency of a prolonged pursuit as if he had fully divined the purposes of the enemy"; and Wyeth states that "his quick perception took in the situation at a glance."[39] Lytle and McCash, however, recognize that Forrest harbored doubts about Streight's objective until later.[40]

If Forrest was absolutely convinced that Streight was heading for Rome, it is difficult to understand why on the 28th he ordered Roddey to place his own regiment, the Eleventh Tennessee, and Julian's battalion between Dodge and Streight.[41] Equally baffling is his order

[37] O.R., XXIII, pt. 1, 287; Wyeth, *That Devil Forrest,* 172.
[38] Wyeth, *That Devil Forrest,* 171; Jordan and Pryor, *Campaigns of Forrest,* 253, who spell his name Mhoon.
[39] Mathes, *General Forrest,* 113; Jordan and Pryor, *Campaigns of Forrest,* 255; Wyeth, *That Devil Forrest,* 172–73.
[40] Lytle, *Bedford Forrest,* 155; McCash, "Streight's Raid," 117.
[41] Jordan and Pryor, *Campaigns of Forrest,* 255.

given the morning of the 29th splitting his forces by sending Biffle's regiment and the Fourth Tennessee to a point some miles northeast of Day's Gap.[42] These are not the actions of a general who "had fully divined the purpose of the enemy." And one can also wonder why he did not communicate with Rome immediately so that the city could be protected.

At one A.M. April 29, Forrest set out from Courtland with no more than 1,200 men in pursuit of Streight with approximately 1,500 men sixteen miles away.[43] The disparity in numbers does not clearly reveal the capabilities of the two forces. Streight commanded infantrymen mounted on poor quality mules while Forrest commanded veteran cavalrymen mounted on the best horses Forrest could acquire. Both forces already were tired—one having ridden from Eastport, Mississippi in four days, and the other having ridden from Spring Hill, Tennessee and fought a battle in four days.

Forrest caught up with Streight on the morning of April 30 and pressed hard on him with frequent skirmishing until the surrender. The continual harassment certainly delayed Streight, cost him some men, including Colonel Gilbert Hathaway, his most trusted officer, and denied him rest. At the same time, Forrest received a number of casualties, including his brother William, lost two of his guns, and got little rest. Without question Forrest displayed his usual boldness, speed of movement, and perseverance, but it is a mistake to conclude that his tactics were solely responsible for his victory. In addition to Forrest's skill, it took some fortunate circumstances for him to capture Streight before the railroad could be cut.

Emma Sansom proved to be a decisive factor, and Forrest certainly could not have anticipated her aid. After crossing Black Creek on May 2, Streight burned the bridge before Forrest could get over it. The stream was too deep and rapid to ford, and the nearest bridge was two miles away and unsafe. From a farmhouse nearby came sixteen-

---

[42] Broomfield L. Ridley, *Battles and Sketches of the Army of Tennessee* (Mexico, Mo., 1906), 172.

[43] It is extremely difficult to determine the exact number of Confederate or Federal troops used in this raid. Mathes (*General Forrest*, 114) says Forrest had 1,200 troops at this time. Streight said his command numbered 1,500 after leaving the physically unfit with Dodge (*O.R.,* XXIII, pt. 1, 287). The most recent and most thorough student of the raid believes that from the afternoon of April 30 until May 3, Forrest, with approximately 900 troops, faced Streight, who commanded approximately 1,650 men (McCash, "Streight's Raid," 153).

year-old Emma Sansom, who promptly directed Forrest to a ford only a few hundred yards away that the cows had occasionally used in low water. Forrest was so grateful for her assistance in solving his perplexing problem that he left her a note of thanks and took a lock of her hair.[44]

When it appeared to Forrest at Gadsden that there was a possibility that Streight might reach Rome, he dispatched a courier to warn the city to arm itself. Meanwhile Streight, eight miles east of Gadsden, sent Captain Milton Russell with 200 men to seize the bridge across the Oostanaula River at Rome. Before either the courier or Russell could carry out their missions, however, help came to Forrest from another unexpected source. Late in the afternoon of May 2, John Wisdom, a rural mail carrier, noticed his ferry boat was missing. He quickly learned that Russell had used it and was heading for Rome. Wisdom then immediately set out for Rome in his buggy via a different route. Being completely ignorant of Forrest's pursuit of the raiders, Wisdom traveled with all possible haste. By changing horses five times, he arrived at Rome at 2:30 A.M. and woke the town. Forrest's courier and Russell arrived in the morning, only to find that the citizens of Rome had control of the main bridge and that reinforcements from Dalton, Atlanta, and Kingston were on the way. Streight actually surrendered before he learned that Russell was too late. Hence the failure of his mission had no effect on the surrender. But it illustrates that Rome was saved from the deprivations of Russell's 200, not by any action on the part of Forrest, but by Wisdom's ride.[45]

These were the two most fortunate unforseen circumstances that aided Forrest, but there were others. Streight's wet ammunition and the stampede at Eastport were the result of human error, but also unforseen and highly advantageous to Forrest. Streight, on the other hand, was beset by misfortune from the beginning. The poor quality of his mules, the delay of the transports, Dodge's lack of vigor,

---

[44] A facsimile of Forrest's note is in Sheppard, *Bedford Forrest*, 111; and it is quoted in Henry, *"First With the Most,"* 151. For Emma Sansom's own account of her role see Wyeth (*That Devil Forrest*, 188–90), whose book is dedicated to her. The state of Alabama rewarded Emma with a grant of 640 acres of land (see Jordan and Pryor, *Campaigns of Forrest*, 269). For a contradictory view of the Emma Sansom episode see Roach, *Prisoner of War*, 30–33.

[45] *Southern Banner* (Athens, Ga.), May 13, 1863; George Magruder Battey, Jr., *A History of Rome and Floyd County* (Atlanta, 1922), 172–73.

terrible weather at the start of the chase, and the faulty guides at the end made Streight's task more difficult.

The first biographers of Forrest, Jordan and Pryor (1868), relate the story of Streight's surrender to Forrest, and subsequent biographers generally have followed their version. Taking for his example the cool and crafty Ulysses rather than the wrathful Achilles, Forrest sent Captain Henry Pointer forward with a flag of truce to demand the immediate surrender of the Federal force "in order to stop the further and useless effusion of blood." In a brief parley Streight demanded to see the Confederate troops, but Forrest declined. As they talked, Forrest's artillery was kept moving in a circle some 300 yards distant to deceive the Federal commander as to the Confederates' real strength. The ruse worked, and when all of Streight's regimental commanders advised surrender, he reluctantly agreed, yielding 1,466 officers and men.[46]

The true facts regarding the surrender may never be known, for legend has clouded the issue. General Dabney Maury recorded Forrest's rather fanciful account of the proceedings. In it Streight is supposed to have said: "Name of God! How many guns have you got? There's fifteen I've counted already!" To which Forrest replied: "I reckon that's all that has kept up." After Streight surrendered and learned that he was opposed by barely 400, he demanded his arms back to fight it out. Forrest just laughed at him, patted him on the shoulder, and said, "Ah, Colonel, all is fair in love and war, you know."[47]

Although it is generally assumed that Forrest's bluff was primarily responsible for Streight's surrender, the evidence reveals the improbability of such a conclusion. "It had," as McCash correctly points out, "at best, an indirect influence."[48] Sheer exhaustion and useless ammunition were more decisive factors.

Thus a daring cavalry raid, suggested and led by a brave infantry

---

[46] Jordan and Pryor, *Campaigns of Forrest*, 273–75. They probably arrived at that total from the newspaper accounts, and most writers agree that approximately 1,500 men plus Russell's 200 were surrendered to Forrest, who had from 410 to 700 troops. See *Southern Recorder* (Milledgeville, Ga.), May 19, 1863; Battey, *History of Rome*, 162; Henry, *"First With the Most,"* 155–57; and Sheppard, *Bedford Forrest*, 116. McCash, however, places Streight's total, including Russell's 200, at 1,305. See McCash, "Streight's Raid," 401–02.

[47] Dabney Herndon Maury, *Recollections of a Virginia in the Mexican, Indian, and Civil Wars* (New York, 1894), 209.

[48] McCash, "Streight's Raid," 230.

officer, was beset by misfortune and resulted in utter failure. Streight's inattention to detail was costly, but the errors of Rosecrans and Dodge proved fatal. The victor, Nathan Bedford Forrest, called "the South's greatest cavalryman," probably deserves that so-briquet for his exploits at Brice's crossroads, Thompsons's station, Murfreesboro, and dozens of other engagements. But the skill that this gallant and effective cavalryman displayed in the pursuit and capture of Abel Streight has been exaggerated. The leadership of Forrest, the only man in the war who rose from the rank of private to lieutenant general,[49] was bold and persistent, but that was not enough. He was lucky too.

[49] Henry, *"First With the Most,"* 13.

SARAH VAN V. WOOLFOLK

Five Men Called Scalawags

Among the most bitterly denounced figures of Reconstruction are the white Southerners who supported or participated in the Republican administration of Reconstruction in the South from 1865 to 1877.[1] They were called in derision "Scalawags" and have lived ever since in popular misconception as stereotypes. Traditionally, they are thought to have been from the small farmer class, Unionists with little education and no political experience. Once within the Republican fold they are supposed to have been outmaneuvered at every turn by Carpetbaggers and Negroes in the scramble for offices. Increasingly disillusioned at being ignored at the division of spoils, they are said to have fled back to the Democratic party when Negro equality, as provided under the Civil Rights Bill, seemed imminent. There, safe under the banner of White Supremacy, they are thought to have cooperated with the Democrats in the overthrow of the Republicans.

History books have familiarized the public with this portrait. For example, one 1956 text characterizes these men as "poor whites whose voice had been rarely heard . . . during antebellum days."[2] The same misconceptions have been applied to Alabamians who became Republicans.[3] But a study of one group of highly articulate Alabama Scalawags who eventually emerged as Republican leaders will serve to

---

[1] This paper was read at the annual meeting of the Alabama Historical Association, Birmingham, April 26, 1963. It was published in *The Alabama Review*, XVII (Jan., 1964).

[2] John Hicks, *Short History of American Democracy* (Boston, 1956), 394.

[3] Walter L. Fleming, *Civil War and Reconstruction in Alabama* (New York, 1905), 404–405, 765, and *Sequel to Appomattox* (New Haven, 1919), 222; L. D. Miller, *History of Alabama* (Birmingham, 1901), 252.

question the accuracy of the stereotype. Samuel F. Rice, Alexander H. White, Lewis E. Parsons, David P. Lewis, and Alexander McKinstry joined the Republican party in the months after the Republican victory in 1868. None of them fits the popular conception of the Scalawag, the man of small farmer background, little education, no political experience, and rabid Unionist sympathies.

Unlike representatives of the small farmer class, the five men studied or read law and practiced in Alabama. Samuel Rice graduated from South Carolina College and owned and edited a Talladega newspaper in addition to practicing law.[4] Alexander White, the son of a justice of the Supreme Court of Alabama, attended the University of Tennessee.[5] Lewis Parsons, the grandson of Jonathan Edwards, was educated in public schools of New York, read law there and in Pennsylvania, and settled in Talladega in 1840.[6] In 1860 Rice, White and Parsons owned considerable real property in several Alabama counties, and all lost large fortunes by the emancipation of their slaves.[7] David P. Lewis studied law in Huntsville and maintained a successful practice in Lawrence County, and Alexander McKinstry, who was orphaned at an early age, lived with relatives in Mobile, where he found mercantile employment and later read and practiced law.[8]

Prior to their affiliation with the Republican party, these men had had active public careers, including service in Congress and in the Alabama General Assembly, as provisional governor and judges. As a Democrat in 1840 and 1841 Samuel F. Rice represented Talladega County in the state legislature. In 1845, 1847, and 1851 he was defeated for Congress, the last time by Alexander White. Rice moved to Montgomery in 1852 and two years later was elected to the Alabama Supreme Court, where he served five years until 1859. During the last three he was chief justice. After serving in the House in 1859 as a

---

[4]Thomas M. Owen, *History of Alabama and Dictionary of Alabama Biography* (Chicago, 1921), IV, 1435; W. Brewer, *Alabama: Her History, Resources, War Record, and Public Men from 1540 to 1872* (Montgomery, 1872), 470–471; Montgomery *Weekly Alabama State Journal*, Oct. 7, 1870.

[5]*Biographical Directory of the American Congress, 1774–1949* (Washington, 1950), 1999.

[6]Brewer, 542.

[7]U.S. *Census* (8th), "Population and Slave Schedules," Dallas, Montgomery, Talladega counties, Ala. (original MSS returns, Library of Congress, Washington, microfilm copies in Alabama State Department of Archives and History, Montgomery).

[8]Owen, IV, 1043; Brewer, 423.

representative from Montgomery, he represented Autauga and Montgomery counties from 1861 to 1865 in the Senate.[9]

Alexander White was elected to Congress in 1851 as a Union Whig and to the Alabama Constitutional Convention of 1865.[10] White's law partner, Lewis E. Parsons, actively participated in the organization of the Know-Nothing party in Alabama in 1855 and 1856 and represented Talladega County in the state legislature from 1859 to 1865, when President Johnson appointed him provisional governor of Alabama. In December, 1865 the General Assembly chose him as national senator for a six-year term, but Congress refused him a seat. In 1868 he led the Alabama delegation to the Democratic convention and subsequently campaigned actively for Seymour. In ante-bellum Alabama, Yancey termed Parsons the ablest and most resourceful of the Union debaters that he had ever encountered.[11]

David P. Lewis' first political experience came in 1861, when he represented Lawrence County in the Alabama Secession Convention. Subsequently, he served as a member of the Provisional Confederate Congress, as the judge of an Alabama circuit court, and as a member of the delegation to the 1868 Democratic National Convention.[12]

Alexander McKinstry had a varied career. After serving as alderman of Mobile, commissioner of revenue of Mobile County, commissioner of county roads, and judge of the City of Mobile from 1850 to 1860, he held membership in the state legislature from 1865 to 1870.[13]

By virtue of their legal training and experience and their public careers in Alabama politics, all of these men were certainly not novices to the intricacies of politics and government. Their careers had given

[9] Owen, IV, 1435; Brewer, 470–471; *Weekly Alabama State Journal,* July 17, 1869, Oct. 7, 1870; Huntsville (Ala.) *Advocate,* Dec. 22, 1868.

[10] *Biographical Directory,* 1999.

[11] J. Morgan to Parsons, Aug. 28, 1863, M. T. Baldwin to Parsons, March 10, 1865, Mrs. E. A. Hunter to Parsons, Dec. 28, 1865 (in Lewis E. Parsons Papers, Alabama State Department of Archives and History); Brewer, 542; Lewy Dorman, *Party Politics in Alabama from 1850 through 1860* (Wetumpka, 1935), 123; Malcolm C. McMillan, *Constitutional Development in Alabama* (Chapel Hill, 1955), 153; Birmingham (Ala.) *Ledger,* Jan. 14, 1917; Montgomery *Daily Alabama State Journal,* Oct. 1, 1872.

[12] Owen, IV, 1043; Miller, 260–261.

[13] Brewer, 423–424; John W. DuBose, *Alabama's Tragic Decade . . .* (Birmingham, 1940), 274.

them experience in administrative, legislative, and judicial affairs in Alabama.

On the issues of secession and opposition to the Confederacy, the five men held widely differing positions. Rice was a supporter of Breckinridge in 1860, a Secessionist, and a member of the Alabama Senate, 1861–1865.[14] Alexander White, no firebrand like Rice, favored Bell and Everett, yet served in Hardee's infantry.[15] McKinstry opposed secession but, like White, served in the Confederate Army.[16] Lewis Parsons' actions in 1860 exemplified his adaptability in meeting political emergencies, a trait which would prove useful in his career as a Republican. After the Democratic National Convention of 1860 had been broken up by the slave states, he believed Yancey might still be held back in Alabama. Parsons left T. H. Watts of Montgomery and C. C. Langdon of Mobile to hold the Alabama Whigs in line for Bell and Everett, while he joined the Douglas Democrats in a vain effort to outflank the Yancey movement. During the war he continued his law practice in Talladega, serving in the state legislature from 1863 to 1865.[17] The only one of the five to fit the stereotype was David P. Lewis. He voted against secession in the 1861 convention and left Alabama in early 1864 for the duration of the war.[18] All Alabama Scalawags, then, were not examples of the ardent Unionists who refused to support the Confederacy and who suffered Confederate persecutions or fled the state.

Motivations of these men for joining the Republican party present intriguing problems. Three of them, Rice, White, and Parsons, made public statements regarding their defections from the Democratic party, statements which present interesting rationalizations of their motives, if nothing more. The other two, Lewis and McKinstry, did not publicly make known their reasons for becoming Republicans. Samuel F. Rice wrote several lengthy explanations of his motives. His opposition to the Republicans and his support of the Democrats in 1868 had been the means to accomplish the "salvation of free government, . . . the revival of industry and prosperity, the light-

[14] *Ibid.*, 275; William Garrett, *Reminiscences of Public Men in Alabama for Thirty Years* (Atlanta, 1872), 195.
[15] *Biographical Directory*, 1999; Garrett, 563.
[16] Brewer, 424; DuBose, 274.
[17] Brewer, 542; Dorman, 123.
[18] Owen, IV, 1043; Miller, 260–261.

ening of debt and taxes, and the perpetuation of the right of self-government." Rice believed that the defeat of the Democratic party ended the possibility of their achieving these goals for at least four years to come. "What," he asked, "is my duty in the meantime?" He desired to engage in neither "sullen inaction" nor war upon uncontrollable facts, however distasteful they might be. Such matters as the national and state administrations and Negro suffrage were conditions which could not be removed until given a fair trial and allowed to condemn themselves by their own works. In general, Rice felt that mere partisanship should cease to control the consciences and conduct of men concerned about good government.[19] In 1871 Rice reflected on his affiliation with the Republican party as a step which caused him considerable social ostracism. In 1868 he had considered his action as equivalent to "resignation for all time of anything in the way of political promotion."[20] However, as a Scalawag he did receive much in the way of political promotion.

Alexander White stated that reason alone guided him to join the Republicans. To him the Democratic party represented a by-gone age and a theory exploded at the cannon's mouth, while the Republicans had received new vigor and life as a result of the war. White realistically noted that it was useless to point out Alabama's vast undeveloped resources to Northern capitalists and then denounce them as adventurers and Carpetbaggers.[21] Likewise, he believed that the South's wants, such as railroads, internal improvements, and the removal of disabilities, could not be obtained by sending Democrats to a Congress which was two-thirds Republican.[22]

In 1871, while testifying before a congressional committee, Lewis Parsons acknowledged his support of the Democratic party in 1868 and spoke of his motives for his subsequent defection to the Republicans. After the 1868 election he felt that "having voted against the republican party as long as it was worth while," it was expedient "to make terms with them," work with them, and "acquire their confidence."[23] Thus, in their published statements explaining

---

[19] *Wilcox News and Pacificator* (Camden, Ala.), Dec. 15, 1868.
[20] U.S. 42 Cong., 2 Sess., *Senate Report* No. 22 (8), "Condition of Affairs in the Southern States," 95 (June 9, 1871).
[21] *Daily Alabama State Journal,* Nov. 25, 1865.
[22] *Ibid.,* Aug. 14, 1869.
[23] "Condition of Affairs in the Southern States," 95 (June 9, 1871).

their motives, these three men exhibited realistic and perceptive approaches to their own positions and to the needs of Alabama. Perhaps they were opportunists, but they were also political realists.

Not only the backgrounds of these men but also their roles in Reconstruction deserve reconsideration. In 1870 an opportunity came for them to extend their influence among Republicans. Party dissension flared openly as Scalawag Governor W. H. Smith accused Alabama's Carpetbagger Senator George E. Spencer of neglecting Alabama's interests for his own private ends. Meanwhile, Spencer was plotting against Smith as Spencer schemed to use the 1870 election as a preliminary for that of 1872. His colleague faced re-election in 1870; if he were defeated by a Democrat, Spencer would be the sole dispenser of Federal patronage in Alabama. Thus, Spencer intrigued to weaken Smith in order to elect a Democratic governor and legislature, which in turn would elect a Democrat to the Senate. Smith denounced Spencer further, and Judge Rice hurried to Smith's support questioning the motives of some Republicans who had come to Alabama since 1865.[24]

Reports appearing in Democratic newspapers suggested that there might be more to the warfare of Scalawags versus Carpetbaggers than a "sudden outbreak of bad temper." A Selma paper boldly stated that the conflict had been in the making for a long time and accused Smith and Rice of desiring an accession of conservative white men to their party to give the appearance of respectability and to secure leadership and power for themselves.[25]

Republicans made peace at the state convention and renominated Smith, but open bickering in the canvass resulted in a Democratic victory in 1870 and in Spencer's control of Federal patronage. The 1870 convention and election symbolize the battle between the two cliques for power.[26] The nomination of Smith and a dominantly native

[24] DuBose, 289; Selma (Ala.) *Weekly Times,* Oct. 29, 1870; Selma *Southern Argus,* Oct. 7, 1870; *Weekly Alabama State Journal,* June 24, 1870.

[25] *Southern Argus,* July 18, 1870.

[26] Thomas H. Peters and Alex White to Gov. William H. Smith, July 6, 1870 in Demopolis (Ala.) *Southern Republican,* July 20, 1870; Montgomery *Weekly Mail,* Sept. 7, 1870; Selma *Times,* Sept. 29, 1870; W. B. H. Howard to Robert McKee, Oct. 17, 1870 (in Robert McKee Papers, Alabama State Department of Archives and History); W. M. Byrd to John W. A. Sanford, Nov. 9, 1870 (in John W. A. Sanford Papers, Alabama State Department of Archives and History); W. H. Smith to W. B. Figures, Oct. 13, 1870, in *Southern Argus,* Oct. 28, 1870.

ticket suggested an apparent Scalawag victory; however, the defeat of the party in the election reflected a Carpetbagger victory in this fight for control of the party.

The next major confrontation of factions came at the 1872 Republican convention which drew another dominantly native white ticket, headed by David P. Lewis for governor, Alexander McKinstry for lieutenant governor, and Alexander White for congressman-at-large.[27] These nominations indicated that either the Scalawags were in full control or that Spencer acquiesced to their demands by backing this ticket, for he worked for their election and for their support for his re-election by the General Assembly.

Although the Republicans definitely controlled the executive by the 1872 election, many seats in the General Assembly were disputed, and the Republicans could do little, if they failed to control the legislature. Parsons is credited with concocting the scheme used by Spencer to secure a favorable assembly, and if no other example existed to undermine the Scalawag stereotype of men little experienced in practical politics, Parsons' maneuvers in 1872 would suffice to illustrate the dangers of historical oversimplification. Parsons advised the Radicals not to meet with the Democrats but to organize separately in the Federal court house, making two legislatures. Federal troops would be requested, and the Radical minority possibly could be converted into a majority. Both parties claimed a working majority, and rival legislatures met for four months in Montgomery. Eventually, the two rivals formed a fusion legislature which the Republicans controlled and which returned Spencer to the Senate. The Speaker of the House of Representatives in both the Court House Legislature and the Fusion General Assembly was Parsons.[28]

In 1874 Democrats accurately perceived the importance of an attempt to divorce the Republican party from the support of the white voters of North Alabama. The Civil Rights Bill made an opportune issue for the Democrats who proceeded to draw the color line in Alabama politics. In the face of new Democratic unity Republi-

---

[27] Mobile *Republican*, Aug. 17, 1872.
[28] Fleming, *Civil War and Reconstruction in Alabama*, 755; *Report of the Joint Committee of the General Assembly of Alabama in Regard to Alleged Election of George E. Spencer as United States Senator*... (Montgomery, 1875), 44; Sarah Van V. Woolfolk, "Republican Leadership in Alabama, 1865–1874" (unpublished Master's thesis, Louisiana State University, Baton Rouge, 1958), 33–37, 129–130.

cans again were divided. Party leaders such as Rice, White, and Parsons, who by 1874 was chairman of the Republican National Platform Committee, favored a moderate course on mixed schools and civil rights as well as a moderate, white-dominated party. But they found party control slipping from their grasp. Negroes grew outraged with the Scalawags, despite the fact that White had voted for the Civil Rights Bill in Congress. The result was a Democratic victory in the state executive and legislature, though two Republicans were returned to Congress.[29]

After 1874 the Republican party declined in Alabama, though these Scalawags continued to influence its course. In 1875 Alex White, chairman of the Republican State Executive Committee, and Parsons and Rice spoke out in opposition to the nomination of delegates for the Alabama Constitutional Convention.[30] Once the Constitution was revised, Parsons and White favored the revision, and Rice opposed it.[31]

Dissension in 1876 and the nomination of a weak state ticket sounded the death knell for Republicans as an influential party in Alabama. Scalawag defectors of 1868–1870 took various courses. Lewis returned to the Democratic party after the 1876 election, Rice ran for office as an independent in 1882, and McKinstry died in Mobile in 1879. White, defeated for re-election to Congress in 1874, left Alabama to resume his law practice, this time in Dallas, Texas. Contemporary accounts contain no reference to a change in Parsons' political affiliations after 1876, and he is considered to have remained a Republican for an indefinite period.[32] None of these men left the Republicans over the civil rights issue to aid the Democrats; instead, they remained Republicans until it was obvious that the Republican party had lost its hold on Alabama politics. Then they took their separate ways.

[29] Horace M. Bond, *Negro Education in Alabama* (Washington, 1939), 68; *Southern Argus,* Aug. 15, 1873, Oct. 9, 1874; Allen J. Going, *Bourbon Democracy in Alabama, 1874–1890* (University, Ala., 1951), 10–11.

[30] Willis Brewer to Robert McKee, Feb. 13, 1875, Walter L. Bragg to Robert McKee, May 29, 1875 (McKee Papers); McMillan, 175, 178; *Southern Argus,* July 2, 1875; Carrollton *West Alabamian,* June 30, 1875.

[31] W. L. Bragg to W. R. Dawson, Oct. 4, 1875 (McKee Papers); McMillan, 211.

[32] *Southern Argus,* May 25, June 1, 8, 15, 1876; *Biographical Directory,* 1999; Going, 51; Montgomery *Daily Advertiser,* Aug. 31, 1876; biographical sheet (in McKinstry File, Alabama State Department of Archives and History).

This brief review of the careers of five of the Democrats defecting after the 1868 presidential election who became Republican leaders illuminates variations in characteristics of background and experience of the Scalawag leaders when compared with the traditional view. None of these men represented the Alabama poor white farmer; all were men of some education and background. All possessed a knowledge of law and served in some political or judicial position prior to Radical Reconstruction in Alabama. Their experiences included service as congressmen, provisional governor, state legislators, and judges, ranging from the chief justice of the Alabama Supreme Court to city judges. They were not novices to the world of politics and government. On secession and the support of the Confederacy, they held varying positions.

The view of the role of the Scalawag in Alabama Reconstruction as one of little importance likewise needs revision. These five Democratic defectors alone garnered positions as governor, lieutenant governor, congressmen, state legislators, chairman of Republican State Executive Committee, chairman of the Republican Platform Committee, and speaker of the Alabama House of Representatives. They played a critical role in the dissension in the Republican party between 1870 and 1876, a dissension which was worsened, though not originated, by the Scalawags' efforts to gain predominance in the party. Obviously, the group had a far larger share in directing Reconstruction than is usually admitted.

Why these men became Republicans remains a question. Doubtless, they did not bare their complete motives to public scrutiny in letters to newspaper editors nor could they have been unaware of opportunities for personal aggrandizement as Republicans. Yet, with what evidence remains, some general evaluations of their motives may be made: they recognized the futility of further opposition to Radical Republican rule; they realized that their political alignment meant their personal success or failure in the immediate future; and they determined to join the Republican party and battle for control of it. These men exemplify clear-sighted political realism in assessing the political situation for what it was in Alabama, not as they might have wished it to be. Their actions certainly suggest at least tentative agreement with Lewis Parsons, when he said that "having voted against the republican party as long as it was worth while," it was expedient "to make terms with them," work with them, and "acquire their confidence." He might well have added, "and take over their party." A comment applied to a Carpetbagger in this period may be well applied to these men also; they played their "politics as a gambler shuffles his cards—to suit the occasion."[33]

[33] Robert H. Smith to Judiciary Committee of House of Representatives, July 20, 1870 (in Henry Churchill Semple Papers, Alabama State Department of Archives and History).

SARAH VAN WOOLFOLK

Carpetbaggers in Alabama:
Tradition Versus Truth

Over-simplified explanations of Carpetbaggers abound within the complex story of Reconstruction. These analyses ignore the multifarious individual differences among the immigrants and reduce their influence to a simple stereotype. Such a monistic picture has been drawn for Northerners who moved to Alabama during the post–Civil War years. As one historian has phrased it, "The Carpetbaggers, like the Carthaginians, had their history written by their enemy, with few exceptions."[1]

Throughout Reconstruction, according to traditional accounts, three groups composed the Republican party in Alabama—grasping, scoundrel Carpetbaggers; shiftless, poor-white Scalawags; and ignorant, beguiled Negroes. In this stereotype Carpetbaggers, who controlled Reconstruction through the establishment of the Republican party based on black votes, occasionally awarded insignificant offices to Scalawags, while reserving the juicier plums for themselves. An analysis of Carpetbaggers illuminates traditional and novel characteristics of these Republican leaders, all of whom do not conform to the accepted stereotype.

Carpetbaggers were Northerners who came South for political, ideological, or avaricious motives and who utilized politics to advance their respective causes. Northerners who entered community economic life and abstained from political activities never drew the opprobrium of the natives. Early in Reconstruction all types appeared

---

This essay was published in *The Alabama Review*, XV (Apr., 1962).
[1] Robert S. Henry, *The Story of Reconstruction* (New York, 1938), 597.

in Alabama. The meeting for the formal organization of the Republican party in Alabama in 1867 presented Carpetbaggers resembling Northern Republicans, and equally as diverse. The conduct of these Carpetbagger Republicans in Alabama illuminates the inducements which lured them southward.

Willard Warner and General Wager Swayne combined ideological and political motives, when they immigrated to Alabama from Ohio. They desired to institute an important social change in the state by altering the current position of the Negro freedmen and to superimpose on Alabama the civilization, thoughts, and identity of the North. Thus, these men represented a far more potent danger to the Southern social framework than men primarily interested in quickly acquiring wealth and returning home. In January, 1868 Warner moved to Prattville, Alabama, where he engaged in cotton planting. After holding several local and state offices, he was elected a United States senator in July, 1868. Warner's respectability and moderation in actions and utterances so infuriated his Alabama colleague in the Senate that he denounced Warner for his "lukewarmness."[2] Swayne's policies as assistant commissioner of the Bureau of Refugees, Freedmen, and Abandoned Lands in Alabama elicited praise from his inspectors as "discreet, liberal, and enlightened."[3] The favorable public opinion created among the whites toward the bureau further testified to his sagacity as an administrator. Contrary to the tradition that there were no temperate Carpetbaggers, General Swayne, as head of the Freedmen's Bureau, and Senator Warner exercised moderating influences on the Republican party during its early years in Alabama.

Others came unaffectedly as plunderers. Post-war Alabama presented a fertile field for Richard Busteed of New York and Andrew J. Applegate of Ohio. Busteed, a Douglas Democrat in 1860, reported for duty as Republican district judge of Alabama shortly after the arrival of Federal troops and inaugurated a flood of trials which resulted in few convictions but in a ripe harvest of costs.[4] With an army behind him he proceeded to mete out a justice favorable to Busteed primarily and to the United States incidentally. To ensure the court's func-

[2] Walter L. Fleming, *Civil War and Reconstruction in Alabama* (New York, 1905), 739; John W. DuBose, *Alabama's Tragic Decade* . . . (Birmingham, 1940), 100, 342.

[3] New York *Times,* Aug. 10, 1866.

[4] William H. Brantley, *Chief Justice Stone of Alabama* (Birmingham, 1943), 228.

tioning without interference from any former Rebels, Busteed brought his own assistants: Lawrence Worral, who would complete all legal papers; Rufus F. Andrews, who would be the Judge's law partner; and Jacob Wilson, his valet, who would receive the duties and title of deputy marshal. On his arrival in Alabama Busteed soon acquainted himself with John Hardy, former marshal of the United States District Court, a man in a position to know all Alabamians rich enough to stand a Busteed trial. Busteed added Hardy to his trio and "drove right royally his four in hand. Andrews beat up business; Busteed judged the case as per purse; Worral made out the papers; Wilson bullied the small debtor; and Hardy sold out the big. Then they portioned out the spoil."[5] For instance, according to one witness, the cost of a suit in Judge Busteed's court to foreclose two mortgages on the Alabama Central Railroad, paid by New York creditors, amounted to $120,000.[6]

Others were equally avaricious but momentarily less successful than Busteed. Andrew J. Applegate, Republican lieutenant governor in 1868, called the state Senate to order on February 17, 1868 in the office of the Republican Montgomery *Daily State Sentinel,* rather than wait for Congress to act on the bill to admit Alabama to the Union. Applegate feared time. More important, he was afraid some loot might escape the Republicans.[7]

While these grasping outsiders enriched themselves at Southern expense, others busied themselves with organizing an electorate to continue them in positions of power and profit. Traditionally, the Carpetbagger controlled Reconstruction through the establishment of a Republican party based on black votes. Early in Reconstruction this was true in some measure for Alabama. After the war secret associations were begun among Negroes under the direction of several Freedmen's Bureau agents. Among the arch organizers was Pennsylvanian John C. Keffer, active in the formation at Montgomery of the "Lincoln League," composed only of Negroes. While Negro suffrage was assured, the league directed its energies in full force to the organization of prospective Negro voters. Unquestionably, the league served as the effective propaganda organ of the Republican

---

[5] Montgomery *Weekly Advertiser,* Aug. 5, 1868.
[6] Eyre Damer, *When the Ku Klux Rode* (New York, 1912), 69.
[7] Fleming, 546.

party, financed by industrialists and financiers who composed the
Union League in the North. After 1868 the organization declined
primarily because its sponsors considered their work completed when
Republican control was assured in Alabama.[8]

Not wholly trusting the electorate to return them to office, many
unscrupulous politicians plotted elaborately for their own re-election,
even against Scalawag members of their own party. Former Brigadier
General George E. Spencer, Warner's colleague in the United States
Senate until Warner's defeat in 1870, devised a scheme to manipulate
the 1870 election as a preliminary for that of 1872, when he faced re-
election himself. If a Democrat could displace Warner, Spencer, an
intimate of President Grant, would become the sole dispenser of
Federal patronage in Alabama. With Warner gone Spencer could utilize the officials for whom he had secured appointments and the money
they held to put the Democrats out of competition and simultaneously carry Alabama for Grant. Spencer intrigued to weaken Scalawag
Governor William H. Smith, candidate for re-election in 1870, in order
to elect a Democratic governor and a Democratic legislature which
would speed Warner's disappearance from Congress.[9]

Spencer astonished Alabamians by pronouncing that the Republicans held the state by a slender thread because every day defections
depleted the party which was "hampered by weak-kneed officials."[10]
Further, Spencer charged that Governor Smith had been "crim-
inally derelict and flagrantly wanting in the most commonest essentials
of his office."[11] Spencer successfully disposed of his Republican colleague in the Senate and eliminated any competition for White House
patronage.[12]

Carpetbaggers often used blatant fraud to maintain possession of
their offices. Foremost among these men was Senator Spencer, who

[8] DuBose, 86; Fleming, 554–559; Arthur Williams, "The Participation of Negroes
in the Government of Alabama" (Master's thesis, Atlanta University, Atlanta, Ga.,
1946), 10; Walter L. Fleming, "The Formation of the Union League in Alabama,"
Gulf States Historical Magazine, II, 84 (Sept., 1903); Horace M. Bond, "Social and
Economic Forces in Alabama Reconstruction," *Journal of Negro History*, XXIII, 327, 329–
330 (July, 1938).
[9] DuBose, 289; Selma *Weekly Times*, Oct. 29, 1870; Selma *Southern Argus*, Oct. 7, 1870;
see also Wm. Stanley Hoole, *Alabama Tories . . .* , Confederate Centennial Studies, No.
16 (Tuscaloosa, 1960), 138–141.
[10] Montgomery *Weekly Alabama State Journal*, Aug. 5, 1870.
[11] Huntsville *Advocate*, July 2, 1870.
[12] Montgomery *Weekly Mail*, Nov. 16, 1870.

schemed in the 1872 election to obtain a General Assembly which would return him to office. Accordingly, he dispatched an emissary to another Republican to ask the latter to run as an independent candidate to defeat Lewis E. Parsons of Talladega and to offer to defray the campaign expenses. "Go to Talladega," instructed Spencer, "and block that game; I must not, however, be known in the matter."[13]

Spencer dispatched two other agents to Dallas County to aid the opposition to Alexander White, a Scalawag candidate for the legislature who supported Parsons. "Can't you manage to get White off the legislature track in Dallas" Spencer asked Robert Barber on October 16, 1872. "Parsons has a deep laid scheme to elect himself, and has now gone to New York to try and raise money to be used in the legislature." See Beach and Coon, two Carpetbaggers, he advised, and "urge them to see that White is taken down."[14] The best Spencer's henchmen could manage was unimaginatively to leave White's name off almost one-half the tickets. Unfortunately for Spencer, White discovered the fraud in time to have his name printed in the blanks.[15]

In 1875 Jerome J. Hinds of Decatur, a particular friend of Spencer and perhaps a business partner, was indicted for fraud in the Post Office Department. His specialty was mail contracts, "to which he was generously helped by his patron and his own wit," and from which he reaped a "prolific harvest."[16] Hinds, however, was acquitted of these charges.[17]

Tradition accuses Carpetbaggers of implementing fraud with bribery for political ends. This accusation proves accurate in at least one instance in Alabama. One of Spencer's agents admitted near the end of Reconstruction that the Senator "furnished me money at any time and place I wanted it," in his campaign for re-election. Spencer rewarded many of the persons who most actively aided him by assisting them to secure Federal offices. These promises he made before and while the services were being rendered. For one of his assistants Spencer

[13] *Report of the Joint Committee of the General Assembly of Alabama in Regard to Alleged Election of George E. Spencer as United States Senator* . . . (Montgomery, 1875), 19, 20 (hereinafter *Report on Spencer Election*).
[14] *Ibid.*, lxiii.
[15] *Ibid.*, lxiv–lxv, 19.
[16] Selma *Southern Argus*, Apr. 9, 1875; Mobile *Daily Register*, Apr. 13, 1875.
[17] Selma *Southern Argus*, July 2, 1875; see Hoole, 140.

obtained the position of inspector of customs at the Port of Mobile. By his own admission this inspector was not there during his term of office, except when he was sworn in.[18]

Undoubtedly, Republicans used questionable methods in the 1874 campaign. Ostensively for flood relief, they distributed 200,000 pounds of army bacon in communities nowhere near a stream—areas which "had not been under water since the days of Noah's Ark."[19] Before distributing the bacon in Monroe County, Republicans circulated the story that recipients of bacon must vote the straight Republican ticket. If they afterwards refused or neglected to vote, they would forfeit their rights in law. In Dallas County an ingenious Republican politician required the Negroes who applied for bacon to make an affidavit that they had been overflowed and for witnessing these papers charged each man about twenty-five cents. Each applicant received about two pounds of bacon. He could have bought nearly three pounds also for twenty-five cents.[20]

Republicans divided early over the need for Federal troops in Alabama. Governor Smith explained in 1869 that the constitutional provision for the organization of the state militia had not been put into operation because there had been no resistance to civil authority.[21] However, Carpetbaggers disagreed, because they keenly felt the contrast between their report and Smith's report to Washington concerning the turmoil in the state. Many systematically misrepresented the condition of Alabama as to peace and order to retain Federal troops.[22]

One United States deputy marshal indirectly notified Spencer that, if troops could be sent into certain counties in Alabama, "enough voters would be run out of them, through fear of arrest, to secure the election of Republican representatives for these counties" to the legislature in 1872.[23]

---

[18] Report on Spencer Election, 21, 26–29, clxxix, clxxxi.
[19] Hilary A. Herbert (ed.), Why the Solid South? . . . (Baltimore, 1890), 61–62; Joseph F. Johnston, Frederick G. Bromberg vs. Jeremiah Haralson, Contest for Seat in 44th Congress from First Congressional District of Alabama (n.p., n.d.), 2–4.
[20] New York Herald, June 12, 1875.
[21] Message of William H. Smith, Governor of Alabama, to the General Assembly, November 15, 1869 (Montgomery, 1870), 5–13.
[22] Charles Nordhoff, The Cotton States in the Spring and Summer of 1875 (New York, 1876), 90.
[23] Report on Spencer Election, 20, 50.

Riots occurring during the 1870 campaign and election collaborated Spencer's reports to President Grant of the unsettled conditions in Alabama caused by the ghostly visitations of the Ku Klux Klan. James S. Perrin, a deputy marshal indebted to Spencer for his appointment, provided proof for Spencer's insistence that the preservation of order in Alabama necessitated the presence of troops. On one occasion Perrin rode ahead out of the sight of a company of troops, shot a hole in his own hat, and waited for the troops to catch up. Then, shouting that he had been set upon by members of the Ku Klux Klan in ambush, Perrin deployed the company as skirmishers against the imaginary enemies. Several Northern papers reported this incident as a "southern outrage," and the government in Washington felt satisfied that such events necessitated the continued presence of troops in Alabama.[24] Again, in 1874, Republicans circulated stories of violence to ensure the maintenance of troops in the state for the November election.[25] In these instances Alabama Carpetbaggers complement tradition; however, contradictions equal stereotypes in the characteristics of the actions of Carpetbaggers as a group.

Carpetbaggers did not maintain themselves in power throughout the whole of Reconstruction primarily on a base of Negro votes. After 1868 and the decline of the Union League the importance of the Negro electorate diminished. Republicans successfully favored white supremacy in white counties while seeking Negro votes in the Black Belt.[26] The nomination of two Negroes on the 1870 Republican ticket signalized that the Negroes were not as willing as they had been earlier to serve as a tool for Carpetbaggers and Scalawags without receiving compensation for their votes.[27] The white Radicals were now determined, regardless of what happened to the rest of the ticket, to defeat these Negroes, thinking that their fate would deter other Negroes from later also demanding offices.[28] However, the entire ticket failed.

Carpetbaggers entertained no scruples against profitable alliances with Democrats. In the 1870 gubernatorial campaign rumors spread that Senator Spencer, the bitter rival of Governor Smith, secretly

[24] *Ibid.*, xliii.
[25] Carrollton *West Alabamian,* Sept. 9, 30, 1874.
[26] Selma *Weekly Times and Messenger,* Sept. 22, 30, 1870.
[27] Selma *Weekly Times,* Sept. 7, 1870; Selma *Southern Argus,* Sept. 9, 1870.
[28] Selma *Weekly Times,* Oct. 29, 1870.

backed the Democratic candidate in some North Alabama white counties in an attempt to defeat Smith in his campaign for re-election.[29]
Judge Busteed's political affiliations in 1871 were equally uncertain. He
was rumored to have declared himself a good Democrat in Montgomery, and later that spring he was seen in Washington with Democratic
Governor Lindsay.[30] In the summer of 1871 Busteed appeared in New
York arm in arm with Senator Spencer and, again, with Governor
Lindsay. When Lindsay was questioned about this and admonished
that it ill became a man of his standing to be associated with these
men, Lindsay replied: " 'Mr. . . . , you do not know Busteed as well
as I do; he is a good fellow,' and if we mistake not, 'twas said, 'He is
a G——d d——d good fellow.' "[31] Despite this contact with the Democratic administration through Governor Lindsay, Busteed warmly
supported Republican candidates in the campaign of 1872. On his resignation from office in 1874 to avoid impeachment complete meta-
morphosis occurred when he arrived in New York City an eager Democrat.[32] Men like Spencer and Busteed used their "politics as a
gambler shuffles his cards—to suit the occasion."[33]

Scalawags and Carpetbaggers could not always live harmoniously
together within the Republican party. Senator Spencer's action in the
1870 campaign exemplified this. While Spencer concerned himself primarily with his own political welfare, more conscientious Republicans
criticized him for his part in the introduction of "internecine
warfare in the Republican party of this State."[34] However, Republicans
did not always divide along strictly Carpetbagger-Scalawag lines. In
the presidential campaign of 1872 many prominent Scalawags joined
former Senator Warner in supporting Greeley and the Cincinnati
Platform while others, such as former Governor Smith, joined Spencer to back Grant and the regular Republicans.[35] Thus, the methods

[29] Allen J. Going, *Bourbon Democracy in Alabama, 1874–1890* (University, Ala., 1951), 4;
DuBose, 342.
[30] Montgomery *Weekly Alabama State Journal*, Apr. 7, 1871.
[31] Selma *Southern Argus*, Jan. 26, 1872.
[32] Going, 11.
[33] Robert H. Smith to Judiciary Committee of the House of Representatives, July
20, 1870 (in Henry Churchill Semple Papers, Alabama State Department of Archives
and History, Montgomery).
[34] Mobile *Republican*, Apr. 27, 1872.
[35] Montgomery *Daily Alabama State Journal*, July 21, 23, Aug. 12, Sept. 6, 11, 13, 19, Oct.
1, 26, 31, 1872; Lauderdale *Times*, Oct. 29, 1872; Eufaula *Daily Times*, Oct. 4, 1872; Montgomery *Daily Advertiser*, Aug. 20, 1872.

by which Carpetbaggers as Republicans maintained themselves in power varied widely and demonstrated the marked adaptability of these men to meet novel political needs.

Carpetbaggers are universally accepted as having courted the Negroes and championed their right to vote. However, at least one Carpetbagger in Alabama early in Reconstruction viewed Negro suffrage with disfavor. Judge Busteed, who owned a plantation in Lowndes County, urged Negroes to keep aloof from politics for the present, attend to their labor, and leave the voting to the whites. They were, according to the Judge, not prepared to vote intelligently and therefore should not vote at all.[36]

One analyst of Alabama Reconstruction wisely observed that "certain facts add piquancy to the general notion that Reconstruction in Alabama was a tightly drawn struggle between virtue, as represented by the Democrats, and vice, as represented by the Republicans."[37] And among the Republicans, probably those most damned have been the Carpetbaggers. One traveller through Alabama in 1875 surmised that the state suffered far less from Carpetbaggers than any of the other Southern states which he had seen, Arkansas, Louisiana, or Mississippi. Rather, it was the "native Alabamian under the tuition of the United States Senator" who showed himself "very capable of misrule and particularly of the most unscrupulous political trickery." Also, wherever "conspicuous financial jobbery took place, Democrats oftener than not, have been parties in interest."[38]

Northerners who eschewed political activities were readily accepted in Alabama. Willard Warner wrote John Sherman in April, 1866 that his partner who remained alone on an Alabama plantation all winter had met with only the "kindest treatment and the heartiest encouragement from all our neighbors. I have yet to hear (and I inquired of the Bureau in Montgomery) of the first instance in this state of injury of Northern men. A Northern man, who is not a natural fool, or a foolish fanatic, may live pleasantly anywhere in Alabama without abating one jot of his self-respect or independence."[39] After

---

[36] Selma *Weekly Messenger*, March 29, 1867.
[37] Bond, 333.
[38] Nordhoff, 89.
[39] Quoted in E. Merton Coulter, *The South During Reconstruction, 1865–1877* (Baton Rouge, 1947), 209.

his failure to be re-elected to the Senate in 1870, Warner retired from politics and continued to live in Alabama after the Democrats' permanent return to power in 1874. Perhaps, actions of such men as Warner are the best barometers for the motives of Carpetbaggers. Those who remained beyond the end of Reconstruction and entered the economic life of the community may justly be evaluated as having come South for motives other than those of a quick profit. Yet, the ideologist, rather than the rogue, constituted the greater threat to the Southern social structure.

Without the Carpetbaggers there probably would have been no Republican party in Alabama. One Democratic newspaper accused the Scalawag of taking his "seat at the table" only "when the feast was spread to his liking." Northern control over Alabama Reconstruction has, however, been vastly overestimated. None of the Republican candidates for governor between 1865 and 1877 was a Carpetbagger, and only nine of the thirty-eight Congressmen were Northerners. Among the seven justices of the Alabama Supreme Court none was a Carpetbagger.[40] If Northerners directed so small a part of Reconstruction, they exercised a much less potent influence on the Republican party in Alabama than is usually admitted. Correspondingly, they deserve less criticism for misdeeds of the period than they have heretofore received. Carpetbaggers, like the Carthaginians, have suffered from the hands of their chroniclers.

[40] Selma *Southern Argus,* Sept. 7, 1877; Fleming, *Civil War Reconstruction in Alabama,* 750, 755, 795, 796; *Biographical Directory of the American Congress, 1774–1949* (Washington, 1950), 290, 299, 308, 327, 338; Montgomery *Daily State Sentinel,* Dec. 3, 7, 1867; Montgomery *Daily Alabama State Journal,* Sept. 25, 1873.

FRANK E. VANDIVER

Josiah Gorgas and the Brierfield Iron Works

As Brigadier General Josiah Gorgas made his way south from Virginia at the close of the Civil War, he realized it would not be easy to readjust himself to the comparative inactivity of private life.[1] A large portion of his personal fortune had been invested in Confederate securities, and, since these were now valueless, he had very little money with which to begin the process of starting over. While serving as Chief of Ordnance of the Confederate Army he had been unable, perhaps unwilling, to decide what course he would follow if the South were defeated. But after April 2, 1865, and the abandonment of Richmond, he had been forced to face the issue. For a man of forty-six he saw a bleak future.

His wife, Amelia Gayle Gorgas, daughter of a former Governor of Alabama, and their six children had been trapped in the tottering capital of the Confederacy, but Gorgas had escaped with Thomas L. Bayne, his brother-in-law and fellow officer, and made his way to Danville, Virginia. Here, along with Jefferson Davis and some of the members of his Cabinet, the two men awaited news of General Lee, who, they knew, was trying to join forces with General Joseph E. Johnston in North Carolina. When, on April 10 the news came that Lee had surrendered the Army of Northern Virginia, Gorgas and his companion began their long and hazardous trek to Alabama. Equipped with a wagon and some Confederate money, they made their

This essay was published in *The Alabama Review*, III (January, 1950).
[1] This paper has resulted from research made possible by a grant-in-aid from the Rockefeller Foundation.

way toward Charlotte, which they reached shortly before it fell to the advancing Federals. Gorgas's point of destination was Greensboro, Alabama, and that of Bayne was Selma, some fifty miles nearer.

Long before the two reached Montgomery, May 26, the ravaged, chaotic condition of Alabama had become obvious. There was extremely little food in the country, and only in cities where the Freedmen's Bureau and Federal troops were located did the people appear to eat with any regularity. Gorgas was worried about the possibility of being arrested, but an old friend of his from pre-war service in the U.S. Army, General A. J. Smith, told him in Montgomery that there were no orders to arrest Confederate officers. Unmolested, Gorgas and Bayne continued their journey by river steamer to Selma. Bayne disembarked at that place and Gorgas continued on alone, finally reaching his destination on May 29, 1865.[2]

For some time after Gorgas arrived in Greensboro he could not fully grasp the disaster that had befallen the Confederate States. While he allowed himself time to readjust gradually to the new conditions existing, making no serious efforts to explore the possibilities of obtaining a job, he observed the pathetic conditions about him. Alabama, as well as most of the other former Confederate States, had sustained almost incredible material losses and the standard of living had sagged alarmingly. Everywhere was first-hand evidence of the economic paralysis of his adopted state. Property losses were estimated to have amounted to $500,000,000, including the value of the slaves. Widespread confiscation of livestock by both contending armies had reduced the number of animals far below that of the prosperous pre-war days. The total value of farm property, which in 1860 had amounted to over $250,000,000, was now estimated at only $97,716,055. Damage had proved so thorough in the farming areas of the state that by the turn of the century agricultural standards had not yet re-attained the level of 1860. All banking capital, of course, was worth nothing, and assets of the state had greatly depreciated.[3] The transportation network of the state was bankrupt. Alabama had

---

[2] Diary of Josiah Gorgas (May 29, 1865). Hereinafter cited as Diary. This manuscript and others cited (unless otherwise stated) are in possession of General Gorgas's daughters, Gorgas Home, University of Alabama. The writer is deeply grateful to Mrs. George Palfrey and Miss Maria Bayne Gorgas, daughters of the General, for their unfailing cooperation and assistance.

[3] Walter L. Fleming, *Civil War and Reconstruction in Alabama* (New York, 1905), p. 254.

boasted some 800 miles of track in 1860, and during the war little or no additions were made. The continual use of rolling stock in the face of governmental inability or refusal to repair it had brought ruin to the roads. At the close of the fighting the Tennessee & Alabama Railroad had no more than three serviceable cars. Rails were unsafe, locomotives out of order and depots, bridges and trestles destroyed. The Mobile & Ohio had lost $5,228,562.23 in Confederate currency; 37 miles of track were worn out, 21 miles had been burned, and 184 miles were devoid of bridges, trestles and stations. In addition, the Federal Army had destroyed shops and other repairing facilities. The Alabama & Tennessee Rivers Railroad alone had lost at least a million dollars in Confederate money, "its shops, tools, and machinery at Selma, 6 bridges, its trestle, some track and many depots, its locomotives and cars."[4]

Perhaps the general apathy of the people of the South immediately following the Civil War may be partially attributed to this economic stagnation in the wake of widespread destruction. But to a man in Gorgas's position lethargy was an ill-afforded luxury. His family had by now moved to Maryland and they looked to him for money. Good fortune he had in obtaining a small sum from cotton rescued from the war, and some funds came to him as a result of a blockade running enterprise, but his stock of capital was quite limited. He needed a means of permanent support, and he needed it quickly.

There were some possibilities: the Red Mountain Iron Company, not far from Elyton, Alabama (now Birmingham), appeared to offer an opportunity in a business with which he was moderately familiar. Then, too, several railroad companies, in need of an executive officer, also were to be considered.[5] Gorgas wrote to Robert Jemison, Jr., a former Confederate senator and would-be industrialist, concerning the possibility of resuming work on the North East & South West Railroad (which might serve Elyton), confiding in Jemison that he thought seriously of "applying myself to the development of the mineral resources of the region of country which that road will penetrate. . . . One can hardly go wrong in that region so fertile in the elements of future wealth. The mining interest and the Rail Road interest must go hand in hand—that latter must lead the former &

[4] *Ibid.*, pp. 259–60.
[5] Diary, June 12, 16, 19, 1865.

must then be sustained by it—"[6] Jemison seemed a likely person to write to about this problem, since he belonged to that class of men whom Gorgas recognized as anxious to forget the war as soon as possible and return to their former business pursuits.[7] But in this case Jemison could offer the ex-General nothing.

Gorgas did not by any means abandon hope. On July 1, 1865, he wrote in his journal: "I am now at the age of 47, beginning life anew so far as my provision for my family is concerned. If the country were in a prosperous or even settled condition, it would be easy enough to earn one's bread and something more, but prospects are gloomy enough and it may be some time before I get at settled work."[8]

The necessity of earning a decent living had evidently caused a significant change in Gorgas's personal attitude toward Andrew Johnson's Proclamation of Amnesty. Bitter at the thought of taking an amnesty oath when he first heard about them, Gorgas had so modified his views by August, 1865, that he wrote his wife on the twenty-first: "I have not yet taken the oath of amnesty, tho' I am entirely ready to do so, whenever I get a good chance." True, he sought reasons why it would be unnecessary for him to take the oath: "I dont want to vote and have no property which is confiscable . . . no object in being in a hurry"—but this admission was a large concession to existing conditions.[9] He had decided to make the best of a bad situation.

By August, 1865, another idea had crystallized in his mind. Although he heard that he could have obtained the superintendency of the Selma & Meridian Railroad, and although he really thought that this would be a better job, he had made up his mind to try the iron business. The rationalization he used in arriving at this decision had the advantage of being the truth. He told Amelia, his wife, that all of his training fitted him much more adequately for that sort of work than for the management of a railroad. It was also a "business which I have more *heart* for than any other I have tho't of." There was one drawback: Amelia hated just the sort of isolated existence which the

---

[6] Letter, Gorgas to Robert Jemison, Jr., Greensboro, Ala., n.d. (in Robert Jemison Collection, University of Alabama Library).

[7] See letter, Gorgas to Amelia Gorgas, [Greensboro, Ala.], July 1, 1865.

[8] Diary, July 1, 1865.

[9] Letter, Gorgas to Amelia Gorgas, Greensboro, Ala., August 21, 1865. Gorgas took the oath of amnesty on August 22 (see Diary, entry of that day).

administration of an iron factory would necessitate. But Gorgas had decided, and he maintained that the thing to do was to make the best of the isolation.[10]

Now that the problem of what he would do had been practically settled, the remaining questions were where to find suitable iron works and the money necessary to buy the plant. He believed that he could obtain the presidency of the Shelby Iron Company, near Columbiana, Alabama, without too much trouble. These works were well known to him, since they had supplied much vital iron to the Confederate Ordnance Bureau during the war, and this enterprise seemed to be ideally suited to him.[11] Though bitterly lonely and longing to go to Cambridge, Maryland, to see his family, he persevered in trying to find a permanent home for them in Alabama. Throughout the month of September and early October, 1865, therefore, he tried to work out an arrangement with Shelby which would give him gainful employment. But the Company, badly in need of money, could offer little encouragement.[12]

After trying for several weeks to locate some fairly promising sites for an iron establishment, Gorgas's attention was called to the furnace and plant at Brierfield, near Ashby, Alabama. This Company had been established in 1860 under the management of Caswell C. Huckabee and Jonathan N. Smith, who had sold out to the Confederate government during the war. Consequently the plant now belonged to the Federal government as the successor to the defunct Confederacy. It would require government permission to buy the Company, and Gorgas felt he would have to go to Washington to secure this permission. Here, too, he was probably rationalizing, since he was on personally friendly terms with General Wager Swayne, Assistant Commissioner of the Freedmen's Bureau in Alabama, who easily could have obtained the property for him. But a trip to Washington for the ostensible purpose of purchasing land would also offer an opportunity to see the family in Maryland. His departure for the North hinged on the uncertainty of obtaining special authority to make such a trip.

A request for aid from his brother-in-law, Thomas L. Bayne, who

---

[10] Letter, Gorgas to Amelia Gorgas, Greensboro, Ala., August 21, 1865.

[11] *Ibid.*, September 11–12, 1865. See also Frank E. Vandiver, "The Shelby Iron Company in the Civil War: A Study of a Confederate Industry," *Alabama Review*, I (January, April, July, 1948).

[12] Diary, October 14, 1865.

now lived in New Orleans, brought prompt response in the form of approval by General Philip Sheridan.[13] Consequently, armed with official permission, he started for Maryland on October 26 or 27 and arrived there on November 2, 1865.[14]

On November 11, after spending about a week with his family on Chesapeake Bay, Gorgas went to Washington to inquire at the Treasury Department about the possibility of purchasing the Brierfield plant. He hoped to form a company to help him finance it, and was anxious to have something definite to tell prospective stockholders. After a delay of several weeks, he obtained a letter from General O. O. Howard to General Swayne, authorizing the sale of the property, if it was not needed for the Freedmen's Bureau.[15] Elated, Gorgas returned to Alabama and set about finding money. His efforts were successful. Francis Lyon, a former Confederate congressman and close personal friend of Gorgas, brought several others into the project with him, and soon the Company boasted some eleven stockholders, commanding a combined capital of $95,000, with $5,000 in reserve.[16] General Swayne consented to the disposal of the property as authorized by General Howard, and the "Canebrake Company" purchased the plant at auction in January, 1866, for $45,000.[17]

The iron Works, as they had existed during the war, had not been operated on an imposing scale, nor was the physical plant large or especially well developed. But the Federal army, during the great cavalry raids directed against Alabama's iron regions, had not spared Brierfield, and the damage was considerable. Gorgas observed, however, that a good train connected the mills and the furnaces and that two serviceable stacks, with one arranged for hot blast, were

---

[13]Letters, Gorgas to Amelia Gorgas, Greensboro, Ala., August 14, September 29, 1865. Sheridan's approval was further strengthened during a trip to New Orleans in late September, when Gorgas and Bayne both visited General E. R. S. Canby, Federal department commander. He told Gorgas, whom he had known when they were both still in the "old army," that he did not foresee any trouble arising over Gorgas' trip to Maryland. By the middle of October Gorgas had abandoned hope of obtaining title to the Brierfield property without a trip to Washington.

[14]Diary, October 15, 21, November 4, 1865. The equivocation about the date of departure is Gorgas' own.

[15]*Ibid.*, December 17, 1865.

[16]*Ibid.*, January 20, 1866.

[17]Ethel M. Armes, *The Story of Coal and Iron in Alabama* (Birmingham, Alabama, 1910), p. 204. The Alabama legislature incorporated the company on January 28, 1867 (see "An Act To incorporate the Brierfield Iron Works Company of the county of Bibb," in *Acts of the Session of 1866–7 of the General Asembly of Alabama . . .*, Montgomery, 1867, pp. 229–230).

there, in addition to 4,000 acres of land.[18] The iron ore was scattered, but sufficient, and he had no real doubt about the future success of his enterprise. Gorgas, who was to act as manager of the Works for the Company, planned to utilize $30,000 of the remaining capital of the stockholders to repair the plant and put in new machinery. This would leave $25,000 with which to begin operations. The Company had no fears about being able to increase the number of stockholders, and looked forward to larger capitalization.[19]

The outstanding objection to Brierfield, as far as the Gorgases were concerned, was the primitive surroundings and the isolation. Although Amelia and the children had been exposed to living of this kind when Gorgas was in the United States Ordnance Department, they had grown to dislike it intensely. Gorgas did not wish to impose it upon his family, but there was nothing else he could do. As it turned out, the family discovered certain compensations, when they began to consider Brierfield carefully. Many of Gorgas's Confederate cronies were living fairly close at hand, and General William J. Hardee, whose plantation was within a day's trip, was a frequent visitor to the Works.[20] Then, too, the people who lived in the vicinity established a neighborliness which it would have been impossible to achieve in a city. "Storms," as some parties were called, were organized and eagerly attended. Society, while lacking much in fashion, lacked little in energy and enthusiasm. The Gorgases were somewhat better off than others might have been in similar circumstances, since there were many family connections and old friends throughout Alabama.

Gorgas had made plans to receive his family in January, 1866, but delays in arranging a place for them to stay had made it impractical to have them come down from Maryland until April. By then he had succeeded in having a house made ready for their occupancy and had made some arrangements for civilized living. Amelia and the children reached Brierfield on April 12, and moved into the home that all of them hoped might be permanent.

The house itself was not pretentious, since pretention had given way to necessity in the South of that era. It needed paint and was situated distressingly close to the railroad, but it had several advantages. It had been built atop a small rise in the hilly ground near the

---

[18] Diary, October 15, 1865.
[19] *Ibid.*, January 20, 1866.
[20] *Ibid.*, July 12, 1865; Gorgas to Amelia Gorgas, Greensboro, Ala., August 21, 1865.

rolling mill and on one side the lawn sloped gently down toward a small creek that gave Gorgas's garden added lushness. The house had been located high enough to catch whatever breeze might blow during the hot summer days, and the general effect was that of easygoing comfort.[21]

Gorgas had effected a workable compromise with his family, and had gained their acquiescence to the country life by promising that during the winter months the family might visit New Orleans. Amelia could take comfort, too, from the guests that frequented her house, including such notables as Generals William J. Hardee and Joseph E. Johnston.[22] Railroad connection with Selma provided mail service for the family and brought them newspapers which prevented their complete stagnation.[23] Food came by the same medium. On the whole, Brierfield was a fairly pleasant place to live.

As the days went by, Gorgas's outlook became progessively darker, not because of the living conditions, but because of the troubles he continually encountered in getting and keeping the Works in operation. His own bitterness and growing disillusionment added to the problems of the family. His depression, partly a carry-over from the last hectic months of the War, was heightened by the election of Alabama's Reconstruction Convention. "What an end to our great hopes!" he wrote in his diary. "Is it possible that we were wrong? Is it possible after all that one set of men can force their opinions on another set? It seems so, and that self government is a mockery before the Almighty. . . . Let us bow in submission and learn to curb our bitter thoughts."[24] Since the failure of the Confederacy, he confessed, his life had been "bitter and barren."[25] As a matter of fact, his despondency grew so marked that the material needs of his family on several occasions were the only things that carried him

---

[21] This description is partly based on observation of the site of the Gorgas house.

[22] Letter, Johnston to Gorgas, Selma, Ala., January 19, 1867; Diary, January 7, 1867. It is interesting to note that among the cherished relics of the Gorgas family is a bed 7½ feet long, affectionately called "the Hardee bed," which Gorgas had built especially to accommodate the long frame of his friend.

[23] Letter, Gorgas to Col. J. L. White, Brierfield, Ala., January 23, 1867 (in Letter Book, 61, Brierfield Iron Works Collection, University of Alabama Library).

[24] Diary, August 3, 1865.

[25] Ibid., July 1, 1866.

through, though a continuing interest in current events helped considerably.[26]

There appeared in his depression an essentially new facet, one that seemed so unlike him as to indicate the possible existence of illness. He became frightened at the thought of the responsibility that management of the Company entailed and confessed that "I am in constant terror lest our funds may fail before I can get any returns from them. The load of responsibility is even greater than that of Chief of Ordnance in the Confederacy."[27] He could not throw off the dread of failure at Brierfield, and this possibility preyed constantly on his mind.[28] His anxiety grew so acute that he recognized its abnormality, and sought to attribute it to dyspepsia or to some other organic ill.[29] The lowest point in his outlook came in January, 1867, when he wrote in his journal: "For no imaginable recompense would I live this life over again. I can now see how these poor doomed, destroyed wretches whose life destruction we daily see chronicled, are forced to their doom. Nothing is so terrible as despair."[30] By April, 1867, something of his old determination had returned, however, and although reasonably convinced that the Works would fail, he vowed his intention to "persevere to the last."[31] Certainty of failure came fully upon him in June and made the Fourth of July hardly a day for celebration. The political sham of the Carpetbag régime, although not actually in full swing as yet, doubtless contributed to his feeling of disgust and he had almost reached the point of being ready again to take up arms against the Union had it all not seemed so futile. In September, after alternate hope and gloom, Gorgas received the news that President Johnson's latest Amnesty Proclamation included everyone except Jefferson Davis and members of the Confederate Cabinet, governors of states and officers above the rank of brigadier general. This news meant little to him, and he did not look with pleasure upon the necessity of taking the oath of

---

[26] *Ibid.*, August 6, 21, September 16, 1866.
[27] *Ibid.*, September 16, 1866.
[28] See *ibid.*, September 30, 1866, for typical entry.
[29] *Ibid.*, October 15, 1866.
[30] *Ibid.*, January 7, 1867.
[31] *Ibid.*, April 3, 1867.

allegiance.[32] Christmas of 1867 did not pass happily at the Gorgas home, and Amelia observed that "our misfortunes seem to come towards Christmas . . . it is never a season of rejoicing with us." The children, fortunately, were more than content with the little gifts that could be given them, and seemed oblivious to the fact that their father was so downcast that he took a long, lonesome walk by himself.[33]

In January, 1866, when Gorgas had begun his work at the Brierfield Iron Works, he had planned to build the firm up along the same lines he had used in building up the Confederate Ordnance Bureau. First, he wanted able men as his subordinates, and it was natural that he should seek the services of those who had served him well during the war. As his first assistant he employed W. H. McMain, who had been in charge of the Dalton Ordnance Depot, and later, as chemist, his friend, John William Mallet, who was also a stockholder. Mallet had been Superintendent of Confederate Ordnance Laboratories.[34]

From the outset Gorgas realized that the task of getting the plant into operation was not to be as easy as he had hoped. Expenses were overwhelming—over $200 per day for labor alone—and the purchases of material, machinery and food continued heavy. He estimated that it required fully $10,000 per month to cover the plant's outlay. The only salvation that he could imagine in July, 1866, was to get the furnace in blast by August,[35] and at best this was an uncertain prospect. The labor supply was an indeterminate factor. Negroes proved particularly unreliable, and those who did work well were not entirely satisfactory, chiefly because of the activities of the Ku Klux Klan, which on at least two occasions, frightened them away from their work.[36] In addition, the Freedmen's Bureau did not function with efficiency in that section of Alabama and this left Brierfield at times in possession of "workers" who would not work.[37] As early as March,

---

[32] *Ibid.*, September 15, 1867.

[33] *Ibid.*, December 14, 25, 1867.

[34] *Ibid.*, May 3, July 1, 1866.

[35] *Ibid.*, July 1, 1866.

[36] Gorgas to Francis S. Lyon, February 22, 1867, Letter Book, 104.

[37] Gorgas to Lt. George Shakley, April 1, 1867, *ibid.*, 152. In this letter to an officer of the Freedmen's Bureau, Gorgas wrote, "An aged Freedman named *Brutus* is here in a very destitute & helpless condition. He was brought here from Georgia during the war & can look to no one here for care in his old age. This company has supplied him with food & shelter for a year past for which he has been unable to render much return. It is a case you will find calling for immediate relief & I beg your *earliest* attention to it."

1867, the lack of money had forced Gorgas to refuse to hire additional labor. Even his skilled workers could not be increased, nor could those he already had be relied upon to any great extent.[38] All things considered, the labor supply was almost a liability.

Another major problem in the initial operation of the plant was the purchase of needed equipment. One example will suffice to show the sort of trouble encountered in securing machinery for the rolling mill. On September 11, 1866, Gorgas ordered some small rolls from a manufacturer in Pittsburg, Pennsylvania. They failed to arrive for several weeks and Gorgas wrote several letters to the factory between November 16, 1866, and February 8, 1867. Finally, he learned that shipment had been delayed by ice and that the rolls would ultimately arrive. But in the interim he had been forced to put off prospective orders for rolled iron and for hoops and iron ties, much to the detriment of the Company's trade.[39]

Underlying all the other problems of the management of the Works was that of money, just as it had been with Gorgas in the management of the Confederate Ordnance Bureau. Banks in the South had been wiped out because of the worthlessness of Confederate currency, and by 1867 they had not been able to recuperate. Of course, Gorgas had begun his work with the confident hope that the Company would make money. But in this he was sorely mistaken—by later 1866 he had to scrimp even to secure cash to buy corn. He requested some of the Company creditors to extend their loans or bills, and urged upon the stockholders the necessity of a loan of $25,000.[40] As president of the Company, a position the stockholders voted upon him in February, 1867, Gorgas had more authority to make financial arrangements than before. He left no stone unturned.

Among the attempts he made were liens against future production of the Works, sightdrafts, and sales of the Company's foodstocks. As credit became tighter (it finally became impossible to deal in credit at Selma), Gorgas grew almost desperate. "We are heavily in debt and with the present condition of our country—the South—it is

---

[38] Gorgas to William T. Quimby, March 3, 1867, *ibid.*, 121; Gorgas to Fowler, Hessee & Co. (Mobile), June 18, 1867, *ibid.*, 268.
[39] Gorgas to Messrs. A. Garrison & Co. (Pittsburgh, Pa.), November 16, 30, December 5, 1866, February 7, 1867, *ibid.*, 3, 12, 22, 84.
[40] Gorgas to Col. J. L. White, December 16, 26, 1866, *ibid.*, 27–28, 36; Gorgas to Dr. J. W. Watkins, January 1, 1867, *ibid.*, 39; Gorgas to D. F. Prout, January 23, 1867, *ibid.*, 62–63.

impossible to sell stock or to borrow money," he wrote Colonel J. L. White. In view of these conditions he feared that Brierfield might be forced to sacrifice its property. "We could make money and work ourselves out of debt could we but find a market for our products at any rate which we had a right to calculate on."[41]

As the financial condition grew worse, Gorgas resorted to frantic measures to keep it going. On June 20, 1867, he mortgaged the Iron Works to his wife for the sum of $5,224.74, and on October 1, he borrowed from her the amount of $1,354.[42] Decreasing returns from sales of its products and the stringency of the currency forced the Company into a practice of barter, not unlike that practiced in war days, which it should have avoided if at all possible. The large quantities of food needed at the Works cost more than the receipts would cover, and Gorgas sought to exchange iron for food. He tried the same scheme to obtain coke and other supplies.[43]

The sale of iron, which should have been the source of greatest revenue, did not pay anything like the expected profits. The reasons were several. Cost of production of foundry pig iron ran more than $32 per short ton. The Company made other, "fancier," types of iron and sold its best charcoal iron for $60 to $70 per short ton. New York offered a better, more lucrative market than the South, but Gorgas recognized several drawbacks to making New York profitable as an outlet. These included charges for drayage, breakage and weighing, plus the cost of transfer from railroad to steamboat at Selma, Alabama.[44] On the other hand, prices for iron in nearby markets, such as Mobile, scarcely paid the cost of production. A firm in Mobile sold some Brierfield iron for $43 per ton. Better prices could have been obtained, except for competition from Selma, where an individual offered "number one" iron for $35 and "number two" for $34 per ton. In view of this, Gorgas thought it might be well to raise

[41] See Gorgas to White, May 16, 1867, *ibid.*, 202; Gorgas to Guyol, Gayle & Co. (New Orleans), June 11, 1867, *ibid.*, 251; Gorgas to Col. James Crawford, June 17, 1867, *ibid.*, 264; Diary, June 30, 1867.

[42] See mortgage, June 20, 1867, and note, signed by Gorgas as president of the Brierfield Works, October 1, 1867 (in Gorgas Home).

[43] Gorgas to J. E. Prestridge, November 15, 1866, Letter Book, 1; Gorgas to L. F. Mellen, February 7, 1867, *ibid.*, 83–84; Gorgas to Messrs. G. & C. Place, February 12, 1867, *ibid.*, 88; Gorgas to Harville Steren, Superintendent, Central Mining and Manufacturing Company of Alabama (Montevallo), February 18, 1867, *ibid.*, 95.

[44] Gorgas to Messrs. J. C. Graham & Co. (Selma), December 3, 1866, *ibid.*, 15; Gorgas to Z. C. Deas, December 4, 1866, April 13, 1867, *ibid.*, 21, 156–157.

the price of his product in the local market. The low prices brought by all types of iron in the South had pushed Brierfield's down so low that the Company was probably taking a loss in much of its production. In one letter, dated May 9, 1867, Gorgas stated that he would deliver pig iron "on the cars" at Brierfield for $32 per short ton, while in another letter, dated June 15, he said that production costs were more than $32.50 per ton[45]

Another factor in the decreasing returns on production was an error in management, almost as costly as operating expenses. In the frenzy attending the efforts to sell iron, the Company made a tactical blunder in permitting too many concerns to market its products, both in the North and South. This mistake was made worse because of the practice of carrying the price according to the wishes of the agencies. By April, 1867, Gorgas, in a letter to General Zachariah Deas, his New York agent, admitted this error and confessed that "it is undoubtedly unfortunate that all of our iron was not placed with you or some other one party but as we had to sell *here* we could not control it."[46]

The ultimate result of this policy, of course, was that the company, through its selling agents, competed with itself for a market, in addition to competing with the other iron manufacturers. As each of the many official outlets for Brierfield iron put their stock on the market, the prices came down in proportion, and some of the northern agents advised Gorgas "how much our iron suffered by being forced on the market thro' various hands."[47] This practice created a "bull market" condition, which the Company could ill afford, and badly affected future production.

Most of the raw materials for iron production were secured from the near vicinity of Brierfield. Coal and coke came from the Cahaba Coal

---

[45] Gorgas to J. M. Parkman, April 1, 1867, *ibid.*, 171–172; W. H. McMain to Messrs. Gilkerson & Sloss (St. Louis), May 9, 1867, *ibid.*, 189; Gorgas to Deas, June 15, 1867, *ibid.*, 261–262. On February 1, 1867, Gorgas had quoted the price of $35 per short ton in Selma, and added that "these prices are much too low & must soon go up we think" (Gorgas to B. H. Micou, February 21, 1867, *ibid.*, 103–104).

[46] Gorgas to Deas, April 13, 1867, *ibid.*, 156–157; Gorgas to J. C. Graham & Co., December 3, 1866, *ibid.*, 15; Gorgas to N. M. Robinson, January 15, 1867, *ibid.*, 50; Gorgas to Messrs. Ware & Davis (Montgomery), February 12, 1867, *ibid.*, 88; Gorgas to D. F. Prout, April 9, 1867, *ibid.*, 160; Gorgas to J. M. Parkman, April 16, 1867, *ibid.*, 171–172; W. H. McMain to Messrs. Gilkerson & Sloss, May 9, 1867, *ibid.*, 189; Gorgas to Charles M. Williams, May 31, 1867, *ibid.*, 230–231.

[47] Gorgas to Deas, June 15, 1867, *ibid.*, 261–262.

Mines, with offices in Selma, and most of the ore came from Brierfield's own fields.[48] But the transportation of the raw materials posed a problem intimately connected with the reasons for the failure of the Brierfield Iron Company.

If money was the prime factor in keeping the plant running, Gorgas discovered that troubles over railroad transportation formed the greatest reasons for the gradual collapse of the company's venture. High freight rates on the Alabama & Tennessee Rivers Railroad made the shipping of iron to Selma ruinously expensive, since the price stood at $3.25 per short ton in November, 1866, and was raised to $3.92 by January, 1867.[49] Gorgas complained strenuously about these rates to officials of the road, but got only unsatisfactory responses. He carried his campaign to his friend, General William J. Hardee, president of the Selma & Mobile: "The rates over your road are sufficiently moderate & if we can get the same rates over this road, we may be able to compete in the market of St. Louis, as our iron is of such a nature as to command an advanced price. . . . Perhaps you can assist me in this matter."[50]

These gestures resulted only in higher rates. While, in 1866, the freight charge per mile had amounted to 6½¢, the rate climbed steadily, until, in June, 1867, Gorgas had to pay 12¢ per ton per mile for wrought iron to Selma. By that time he had become convinced that the railroad did not want to aid the Works—"I fear it is not the design of this company to accommodate us"—and he did not like the necessity of having to beg for a reduction to 6½¢ again. But without a return to something like that rate, "it seems impossible to struggle on against such very high freight."[51]

The railroad proved uncooperative in many ways other than high costs. The Iron Works depended on the line for the importation of coal and coke from the Cahaba company, and if the service did not remain efficient, the daily production of iron would suffer accordingly.

---

[48] Gorgas to L. F. Mellen, January 4, 1867, *ibid.*, 41; Gorgas to Col. R. M. Moore, January 18, 1867, *ibid.*, 53–54; Gorgas to Moore, February 19, April 12, 1867, *ibid.*, 99, 166–167.

[49] Gorgas to Gen. W. J. Hardee, November 23, 1866, *ibid.*, 6; Gorgas to E. G. Barney, Superintendent, Alabama & Tennessee Rivers Railroad, November 23, 1866, *ibid.*, 7–8; Gorgas to Messrs. A. J. Moses & Co. (Mobile), January 5, 1867, *ibid.*, 43.

[50] Gorgas to Hardee, November 23, 1866, *ibid.*, 6.

[51] Gorgas to E. G. Barney, November 23, 1866, *ibid.*, 7–8; Gorgas to White, June 25, 1867, *ibid.*, 242; Gorgas to Barney, June 25, 1867, *ibid.*, 280–281.

The railroad apparently made no consistent effort to see that freight trains stopped to pick up cars loaded with iron at Brierfield. This resulted in several cars waiting several days for movement to Selma. Then, too, the road made no great effort to move coal from the Cahaba and Montevallo mines to Brierfield in adequate quantity and on time. This resulted in the partial suspension of activity in April, 1867.[52]

In other ways the railroad managed to hamper Gorgas's operations with almost as much effect as deliberate failure to accept freight. Maintenance of track and switch connections, a vital function of the road, was never looked after adequately, and damaged side tracks in the Brierfield yards frequently held up shipments. The poor condition of the switch, connecting these yards with the main line of Alabama & Tennessee Rivers track, had the same effect. In addition, the railroad overlooked numerous little courtesies which would have improved the working chances of the Iron Works. No freight agent was designated for Brierfield and consequently no one could sign for freight. Brierfield was not made an approved stopping point, but was kept on the list of flag stations. Mail, addressed to the plant, was frequently put off the trains at Ashby Station, some distance from the Works. While these little irritations were not disastrous in themselves, they were the added straws that finally broke the back of the Company.[53]

There were other adverse factors hampering Gorgas's endeavors. He complained in March, 1867, to tax collector William Berney, that it seemed wrong that the Company should be taxed for castings "made for our own works & used in putting up the machinery for making the products covered by our license. I cannot think this correct. . . . We are taxed for example for castings used in building our blast furnace the products of which *namely;* pig iron are exempt from taxation."[54]

It would be unfair, however, to give the impression that Gorgas

---

[52] Gorgas to Cahaba (Alabama) Coal Company, June 9, 1867, *ibid.,* 48; Gorgas to M. Stanton, January 8, 9, April 10, 1867, *ibid.,* 45, 46, 165; Gorgas to Mellen, January 7, 1867, *ibid.,* 43; Gorgas to C. B. Barnes, April 9, 1867, *ibid.,* 164; W. H. McMain to C. B. Andrews, May 4, 1867, *ibid.,* 187.

[53] Gorgas to Stanton, January 5, March 12, April 1, 1867, *ibid.,* 41–42, 135, 150–151; Gorgas to C. B. Andrews, April 12, 1867, *ibid.,* 151; Gorgas to E. G. Barney, June 25, 1867, *ibid.,* 280–281.

[54] Gorgas to Collector William Berney (Selma), March 15, 1867, *ibid.,* 139.

and his assistants failed to make any progress whatever in the face of these obstacles. On the contrary, they did very well with the Brierfield project for a time, and were particularly successful in perfecting the physical condition of the Works to produce iron. An officer of the United States Army Engineer Corps, in writing about the condition of these works in 1868, described them as follows:

> All of the structures are of the most substantial kind. First, within one hundred yards of the railroad is the large rolling mill; within this there are three engines at work, one driving the 'muck train,' and intended also to drive the 'nail plate train,' a second which makes bar iron, and a third which pumps water, cuts off iron, and a machine for making buckles for cotton ties. Here are eight puddling furnaces, two heating furnaces, and four boilers supplying steam to the engines. The boilers are placed by the heating furnace, and the steam is made by the waste heat from those furnaces. The machinery all appears to work well, is placed on stone foundation, and is well disposed for work. The puddling furnaces will convert sixteen gross tons of pig iron into muck bar in twenty-four hours, and these are daily converted into twenty thousand pounds of bar iron, and one hundred kegs of cut nails—the machinery for which is all on the spot, though not yet put up.

The engineer then described the cupola crane, machine shop, pattern shop, small brass factory, blacksmith shop, school and the building intended for the nailery, all of which he considered to be of the first order. He described the hot blast furnace and the ore beds feeding the Works in complimentary terms and thought that the plant showed great promise—and this was as late as 1868.[55]

In spite of the progress made, however, the passage of time pointed clearly to the fact that Brierfield would probably fail. The periodic stoppage of work at the furnaces for a variety of reasons was as clear an indication of this eventuality as could be desired.[56] Gorgas managed, somehow, to keep the plant in sporadic operation throughout 1867, but by June, 1868, he had become so convinced that it would be fruitless to hang on at Brierfield that he began to think of other employment. His idea about the futility of staying was shared by

---

[55] Quoted in Armes *op. cit.*, pp. 204–207.
[56] These factors included bad weather, needed repairs, lack of an adequate market, and breakdowns. See for example, Gorgas to J. C. Graham & Co., March 1, May 31, 1867, Letter Book, 142, 229–230; Gorgas to Messrs. Prestridge & Knox (Selma), April 10, 1867, *ibid.*, 166; Gorgas to Guyol, Gayle & Co., May 28, 1867, *ibid.*, 225.

Colonel Mallet, who himself quit the Works on August 31, 1868, and went to the University of Virginia to teach.[57]

By mid-July, 1868, Gorgas heard about a movement afoot to get him appointed to the University of the South at Sewanee, Tennessee. This institution needed a headmaster for its Junior Department, and seemed to offer a fine opportunity to indulge the propensities for teaching which Gorgas had always felt. After several trips to Sewanee, he secured the position and made definite plans to move there as soon as possible.

Since his appointment was not to become effective until 1869,[58] he had time to arrange for the transfer of Brierfield to other hands. He did not succeed for a year, however, when he finally leased the Works to Captain Thomas S. Alvis, who had been familiar with them during the war.[59] Meanwhile, he had been forced to dismantle the furnace and install a new hearth. By July, 1869, the supply of ore had run out entirely, putting the final touch to Gorgas's ill-fated administration of the Brierfield Iron Works Company.

He moved to Sewanee July 1, 1868, to accept his new position,[60] a place he was destined to hold for eight years. Behind him he left a reminder of dual tragedy: the economic prostration of the South in the late 1860's and that of his own personal failure as a businessman.

---

[57] Diary, August 31, 1868.

[58] *Ibid.*, June 7, July 10, August 9, September 23, 1868.

[59] Articles of Agreement, signed by Gorgas and Thomas S. Alvis, August 2, 1869 (mss. in Fitch Papers, University of Alabama Library). Gorgas attained the position of Vice-Chancellor of the University of the South before his resignation.

[60] Diary, November 5, 1868.

JONATHAN M. WIENER

Female Planters and Planters' Wives in Civil War and Reconstruction:
Alabama, 1850–1870

Studies based on literary sources suggest that the Civil War brought about a transformation in the position of white plantation women in the South. During the war many women operated plantations while planter-husbands fought on the battlefields; war deaths created a "generation of women without men," it has been argued, and defeat of the planter regime undermined the patriarchal ideology that had defined the role of the "lady" in plantation society. As a result, a "significant social change" occurred: women became planters on their own account after the war.[1]

Evidence from the manuscript census does not support this view. On the contrary, it suggests that in many respects the continuities of antebellum patterns were more important than the changes. No increase in the proportion of female planters followed war and Reconstruction; in spite of wartime deaths, females were less likely than males to persist as planters through the war decade. The manuscript census also reveals much about how the war affected the composition of planter families. While there is little evidence of a "generation of women without men" among the elite, certain generalizations may be drawn. More young women were in households headed

This essay was published in The Alabama Review, XXX (April 1977).
[1] Anne Firor Scott, The Southern Lady: From Pedestal to Politics, 1830–1930 (Chicago, 1970), 81, 96, 106–07. Scott's argument has been noted recently in George B. Tindall, "Beyond the Mainstream: The Ethnic Southerners," Journal of Southern History, XL (February 1974), 15, and W. R. Krauss, "Political Implications of Gender Roles: A Review of the Literature," American Political Science Review, LXVIII (December 1974), 1706. See also Susan E. Bloomberg et al., "A Census Probe into 19th Century Family History: Southern Michigan, 1850–1880," Journal of Social History, V (January 1971), 26–45.

by older men, and there is a missing generation of children in planter families after the war. These conditions reflect the extent of wartime deprivation.

The manuscript schedules of the U.S. census of population are an invaluable source, both for identifying the South's planter elite and for studying its sexual composition and transformation through the Civil War decade. In 1850, 1860, and 1870, the census asked each individual for the "value of real estate" he or she owned.[2] The responses can be used to identify the wealthiest landholders in each census year by sex and to study persistence and change in the composition of this planter elite, in order to compare antebellum patterns with the developments that accompanied war and Reconstruction.

Five adjacent Alabama counties were selected as the focus for this study. The five made up the western half of the Alabama Black Belt; in 1860 they had a population of 114,000, of which 74 percent were slaves.[3] Landholding was extremely unequal in the region. In the Black Belts of Alabama and central Mississippi in 1860 the top 5 percent of landowners held 24 percent of the improved acreage, 26 percent of the slaves, 26 percent of the cotton output, and 30 percent of the farm value.[4] Politically, the five counties were a bedrock of planter support; their vote in favor of secession in December 1860 was overwhelming, as was their opposition to Republican, Greenback, and Populist candidates for state office in the last quarter of the century.[5]

This study analyzes the 236 planters with the greatest wealth in real estate in each of the three censuses. The number 236 provided the most straightforward wealth cutoffs: the group included all planters with at least $10,000 in real estate in 1850, $32,000 in 1860, and $10,000 in 1870. These 236, who will be referred to hereinafter as the

[2] For the instructions to census enumerators, see Carroll D. Wright and William C. Hunt, *The History and Growth of the U.S. Census*, Senate Doc. No. 194, 56th Cong., 1st Sess. (Washington, 1900), 152.

[3] The five are Greene, Hale, Marengo, Perry, and Sumter. Hale was created in 1866 out of parts of Greene, Marengo, Perry, and Tuscaloosa.

[4] Gavin Wright, "'Economic Democracy' and the Concentration of Agricultural Wealth in the Cotton South, 1850–1860," *Agricultural History*, XLIV (January 1970), 63–93.

[5] William L. Barney, *The Secessionist Impulse: Alabama and Mississippi in 1860* (Princeton, 1974), 317–18; Allen Johnston Going, *Bourbon Democracy in Alabama, 1874–1890* (University, Ala., 1951), 220–31; William Warren Rogers, *The One-Gallused Rebellion: Agrarianism in Alabama, 1865–1896:* (Baton Rouge, 1970), 223, 284, 315.

"planter elite," constituted approximately the top 8 percent of the landholders in the western Alabama Black Belt and 3 percent of white adult males. Their mean real estate holding in 1860 was roughly 1,600 acres; the smallest holding was around 800 acres, and the largest close to 9,000 acres.[6]

Evidence from the Alabama Black Belt indicates no increase in the proportion of females in the planter elite between 1860 and 1870, the decade of war and Reconstruction. Ten percent of the planter elite was female in 1870, the same proportion as in 1860. Planter war deaths did not increase the proportion of women operating plantations in 1870; a generation of Southern women without men after 1865 may have existed, but elite plantation women do not seem to have been part of it.[7]

The women who were planters in 1870 appear to have been the elderly widows of elderly men who died of natural causes, rather than young widows of young male war victims, since female planters in 1870 were considerably older than male planters as a group (see Table I). Though evidence is not conclusive, it suggests that the females who became planters tended to do so relatively late in life as a result of inheriting the plantations of their elderly husbands.

Of course, females had held plantations in their own names before the war. As Anne Firor Scott points out, some Southern women had been planters in their own right since the earliest settlement of the South.[8] In the Black Belt of western Alabama, however, no females were among the planter elite in 1850; not until 1860 did females appear in the census lists as elite property owners. This relatively late appearance of women as property owners may have been a consequence of the recent settlement of western Alabama in 1850; that the frontier was settled by men, single or married, rather than by single women might account for the absence of women from the 1850 planter elite.

From this perspective, females became planters in their own right primarily through inheritance—as the widows of male property owners or as daughters of planters without male heirs. Scott discusses a widow

[6] The figure of $40 an acre for good plantation land in the Alabama Black Belt is suggested by Lewis C. Gray, *History of Agriculture in the Southern United States to 1860* (2 vols., Washington, 1933), II, 642–44.

[7] See also Jonathan M. Wiener, "Planter Persistence and Social Change: Alabama, 1850–1870," *Journal of Interdisciplinary History*, VII (Autumn 1976), 235–60.

[8] Scott, *Southern Lady*, 34.

Table I
Female and Male Planters in 1870

	Planters	
	Male	Female
Real Estate		
Top ⅓	35%	17%
Middle ⅓	34	26
Bottom ⅓	31	57
Number of sons:		
None	75	65
At least 1	25	35
Four or more	2	4
Age:		
Youngest ⅓	32	26
Middle ⅓	31	30
Oldest ⅓	29	44
Birthplace:		
South	92	91
Non-South	8	9
Persist from 1860	43%	30%
Do not persist	57	70
Number	213	23

who ran an antebellum plantation "from the time her husband died until her son was old enough to assume responsibility."[9] This pattern may well have been typical: females were landowners in their own right primarily as widows without adult sons. Scott cites one case of a daughter inheriting a plantation from her planter-father and another of a daughter following in the footsteps of her planter-mother. Single men regarded such unmarried female landowners as highly desirable spouses, and, given the stigma attached to spinsterhood, it is extremely unlikely that daughters who inherited plantations remained single for very long.[10]

The persistence rate of female planters during the war decade was

[9] *Ibid.*
[10] *Ibid.*, 23–25.

considerably lower than that for males. Thirty percent of the female planters of 1860 were still members of the elite in 1870, in comparison to 43 percent of the males.[11] Such a percentage would be the expected finding if women became planters relatively late in life and only until their sons were old enough to become planters themselves. Many sons would be able to take over the plantation between the beginning and end of a decade; elderly female planters would be more likely to die during the decade than the younger male planter group. Any female heirs would be likely to marry and change their names during the decade. Thus the lower persistence rate of females appears to have been a consequence of the circumstances under which females became planters. Female planters in 1870 were also considerably less wealthy than males. The biggest plantations were almost exclusively operated by males rather than females; women were in the elite, but they tended to be at the bottom rather than the top in 1870.

Scott makes a telling point when she observes that, after the war, the census enumeration of occupations did not indicate the full extent to which women were effectively operating plantations by themselves; she points out that, in many planter families with male household heads, the wives were left in charge of the plantation because husbands were engaged in politics, law, or medicine.[12] While the census did not indicate whether wives were in fact operating plantations listed as the property of their husbands, the occupations of household heads were recorded, and some big landowners gave occupations other than "planter." The elite of Marengo County (one of five Black Belt counties) was studied in greater detail than that of the other four counties, and the number of such "non-planter" occupations among elite landowners in 1870 was found to have increased considerably over 1860. Twenty-one percent of the 1870 planters listed an occupation other than, or in addition to, "planter," in comparison to only 4 percent of the 1860 elite. If Scott is correct in arguing that wives often operated the plantations of landowning males who had other occupations, the number of females effectively operating plantations after the war may have increased.

Some idea of how the war affected female planters can be gained by

---

[11] To compare these persistence rates to the national pattern, see Stephan Thernstrom, *The Other Bostonians: Poverty and Progress in the American Metropolis, 1880–1970* (Cambridge, 1973), "The Boston Case and the National Pattern," 220–61.

[12] Scott, *Southern Lady,* 108.

comparing the female planters of 1870 with their counterparts of 1860. The postwar female planters were considerably poorer (see Table II). Before the war there was little difference in the landholdings of male and female planters; after the war females were considerably less wealthy. Apparently, the decade of war and Reconstruction had a more dele-terious effect on female planters than on males, but without more detailed evidence it would be incorrect to conclude that female planters were less able to "cope" with war and Reconstruction than males. The postwar female planters were considerably older than their antebellum counterparts. If females became planters primarily as heirs of husbands or fathers, perhaps postwar females tended to be widows while the antebellum females were more likely to be daughters who had inherited land.

The postwar female planters had families with fewer sons than their antebellum counterparts, perhaps as a consequence of a lower wartime birth rate, a higher wartime infant mortality rate, and also the

Table II
Female Planters, 1860 and 1870

	Female Planters	
	1860	1870
Real Estate		
Top ⅓	35%	17%
Middle ⅓	35	26
Bottom ⅓	30	57
Number of sons:		
None	50	69
At least 1	50	35
Four or more	15	4
Age:		
Youngest ⅓	50	26
Middle ⅓	30	30
Oldest ⅓	20	44
Birthplace:		
South	90	91
Non-South	10	9
Number	20	23

greater age of the postwar female planters in comparison to the age of the female planters of 1860.[13] The census did not list any planter families in which both mother and son were elite landholders (though there were a few in which father and son were elite landholders). Probably older female planters had inherited the land from their husbands because they had no sons.

In a society in which social life was an intensely local and kinship-based experience, women born outside the region found themselves in a difficult situation, at least at first. As Scott describes life for plantation wives, "the domestic circle was the world," and "visiting was the essence of life." The extended family was usually the basic social unit; the health of relatives was a constant subject of concern, and the courtship and marriage of members of the extended family were social events that received the greatest attention.[14] Women from outside the region were not part of this lifetime web of family ties; more likely than not they had no neighboring blood relatives of their own who could be visited, cared for when sick, or greeted in church. However, since the census listed only the state of birth, rather than the year of migration to the South, it is not possible to determine when non-Southern women came to the region—whether they did so just before marriage, or long before, as children, perhaps with their entire families. Nor is it possible to ascertain whether siblings, parents, or other relatives also migrated into the South. This discussion, then, is in part necessarily speculative.

Women born outside the South made up a small proportion of planter wives, and the proportion did not change over the decade of war and Reconstruction. Six percent of planter wives had been born outside the South, in both the 1860 and 1870 elite groups. Some of these non-Southern women had husbands who also had been born outside the South. In the antebellum period 20 percent of non-Southern planter wives had non-Southern-born planter husbands (see Table III). These were couples in which both members had migrated to the South rather than being native to the region—although the

[13] Daughters of planters were not coded for this persistence study because marriage makes it impossible to trace them from one census list to the next. See Jonathan M. Wiener, "Planter-Merchant Conflict in Reconstruction Alabama," *Past and Present*, No. 68 (August 1975), 73–94.

[14] Scott, *Southern Lady*, 42–43. The family "was the core of Southern society; within its bounds everything worth while took place." Francis Butler Simkins, *A History of the South* (3rd ed., New York, 1963), 388.

Table III
Planters' Wives: Husbands' Birthplace and Age

	1850	1860	1870
Southern-born wives:			
Southern-born husband	95%	97%	96%
Non-Southern-born husband	5	3	4
Non-Southern-born wives:			
Southern-born husbands	82%	78%	50%
Non-Southern-born husbands	18	22	50
Age difference from husband:			
Wife older	3%	3%	3%
Same ± 1	18	5	5
Wife 2–5 yrs. younger	24	43	29
" 6–10 " "	37	16	24
" 11–20 " "	16	30	26
" 21+ " "	3	3	13
Husband's age minus wife's age:			
Mean difference	12.0	8.2	8.6 yrs.
Median	7	6	6

census does not indicate whether this migration took place when they were children or adults. The great majority of wives born outside the region—80 percent—had married planters born within the South.

The decade of war may have brought dramatic change to this antebellum pattern of non-Southern-born women marrying Southern-born planter men. Fully half of the non-Southern-born wives in 1870 were married to husbands who had also been born outside the South. This fact suggests that the pattern of marital choice may have changed over the war decade: before the war, more than three out of four non-Southern wives were married to Southern-born planters; after the war, only 50 percent were. But it is not clear that these marriages actually took place after the war, or that these were cases of carpetbag couples. The non-Southern-born planter couples of 1870 might very well have come to the South and married before the war, and simply not have moved to the Alabama Black Belt until the sixties; or they may have been Alabama Black Belt residents in 1860 but not yet members of the planter elite. And the actual number of such couples in 1870 is not large enough to permit solid general-izations.[15]

The census also makes it possible to ascertain how many Southern-born women had planter husbands who had been born outside the South. Very few such cases existed, and the war did not change the proportion. Three percent of Southern-born wives had non-Southern-born planter husbands in 1860, as compared with 6 percent in 1870. When Northern men came South to become plantation owners, they seldom took Southern-born women as their wives.

One might hypothesize that, if young men died in the war, women who got married after the war would marry older men more often than before. Actually, there was little difference between the 1860 and 1870 patterns of age differences of husbands and wives, further corrobora-tion of the view that the postwar planters had remained unscathed by the war in many aspects of their lives. The differences between 1850 and 1860 were greater than those between 1860 and 1870.

Wives tended to be younger than husbands by several years in both antebellum and postwar periods. The median wife was six years younger than her husband in 1860, as well as 1870, while the mean age of wives was 8.2 years less than husbands in 1860 and 8.6 years less in 1870. Only 5 percent of couples were within one year of each other's age in both 1860 and 1870, and only 3 percent of the wives were more than one year older than their husbands. Virtually none of the wives were considerably older; the Southern elite was not a society in which young men married older women. On the other hand, many wives were con-siderably younger than their husbands; this pattern was shared by the elite of contemporary Victorian England.[16] A third of all wives were more than ten years younger than their husbands, both in 1860 and 1870. Thus the pattern of age differences between spouses is another area that was changed little over the decade of war and Recon-struction.

The war seems to have brought about an increase either in the number of young women married to older men, or in the number of unmarried young women living at home with their widower fathers. If indeed the war had reduced the number of marriageable men in the

---

[15] On landholding by carpetbaggers, see Wiener, "Planter Persistence and Social Change."

[16] J. A. and Olive Banks, *Feminism and Family Planning in Victorian England* (New York, 1964).

planter elite, then the effect of the war on planter women was to create not a "generation of women without men," but rather an increase in the proportion of women living with elderly men. Since the census did not indicate the relationship of household members to each other, these men could have been either husbands or fathers. Thirteen percent of females in planter elite families in 1870 lived in households in which the male household head was at least twenty years older than the oldest female; this increase was 10 percent over the 1860 figure.

The Civil War, like most major wars, left a permanent mark on the composition of planter families, particularly in the number and ages of children. Planter families in 1870 had few sons aged five through seven, sons born in the depth of war who survived it. The sons in planter families in 1870 were primarily eight years old or older, or else infants, one and two years old. And, to the extent that the number of surviving sons measures the wartime deprivations experienced even by the South's planter elite, it reveals two noteworthy facts: little deprivation existed in the first two years of the war, and the deprivation during the two years after the war appears to have been considerable.

The census gave the ages of all members of the planter households in 1870, and a study of the ages of sons reveals that in 1870 few planters had sons between the ages of two and seven, sons born between 1861 and 1867 who had survived until 1870. The relative absence of this birth cohort from planter families is a consequence of a low birth rate in those years, and a high rate of infant and childhood mortality. However, the census gives no way of determining the relative importance of each factor. Before the war between seven and eight sons were born per year who survived until 1870 in the 236 planter families. In 1870 nine planter families had ten-year-old sons, who had been born on the eve of secession (January 1861); eight families had sons born in the first year of the war, who had been conceived in peacetime but born after the war reduced the number of doctors and the amount of food and medicine available. The same number of surviving sons was born in 1862 as in 1861, indicating that the second year of the war did not bring noticeable change in the number of planter sons who survived birth and infancy.

The change came in 1863. Only two out of 236 planter families had sons born in 1863 who survived until 1870. The census gives no way of measuring the relative importance of fewer conceptions, fewer live births, and more cases of infant mortality. The same small number of sons was born in 1864 and 1865 who survived until 1870 in planter families—three in 1864, and two in 1865, the final year of the war, when hunger was pervasive and starvation a threat to many poorer Southern families.[17] It is remarkable that the number of sons surviving from 1865 births was as high as the preceding two years, given the greater deprivation they and their mothers experienced in the year of their birth.

One might think that the end of the war, the return of men to their wives, doctors to their communities, and laborers to the task of raising food crops, would have brought a return of the birth pattern to its antebellum levels, but the birth rate does not seem to have increased for two more years. Six families in 1870 had sons born in 1866, and five had sons born in 1867. While more surviving sons were born in the two years after the war's end than in its final three years, still significantly fewer sons survived from 1866 and 1867 than from 1861 and 1862. If the number of surviving sons is a measure of deprivation, such deprivation was greater in the two years after the war than in the first two years of the war itself.

If deprivation reduced the number of surviving sons, that deprivation came to an end in 1868, when eleven sons were born who survived until 1870. The following year, 1869, twelve sons were born who survived at least until the census taker arrived the next year. Some qualifications of this argument are necessary. First, the number of surviving sons in 1870 is not a birth rate, although it is undoubtedly related to the birth rate. Secondly, census enumerators did not record ages very precisely. This list of children's ages depended on the month the census enumerator visited planter homes in 1870 and on the way planters calculated and reported their children's ages. The census gave ages in years, but not months. If the census taker arrived on schedule in June of 1870, children born between May 1868 and June 1869 could have been recorded as being one year old. The dates in the above discussion could be off as much as a year, but no other way seems obvious to calculate birth years. The deprivation that resulted in a

---

[17] Paul W. Gates, *Agriculture and the Civil War* (New York, 1965), ch. 5. On the effect of wartime deprivation on fertility and childbirth in World War I, see Peter Loewenberg, "The Psychohistorical Origins of the Nazi Youth Cohort," *American Historical Review*, LXXVI (December 1971), especially 1473–80.

smaller number of surviving sons might have set in several months before the close of 1862 and stopped several months before the end of 1867.

In conclusion, evidence from the manuscript census for 1850, 1860, and 1870 indicates that, while the Civil War had a profound effect on the composition of planter families, it did not transform the social position of female planters and planters' wives to the extent that literary sources suggest. The image of white plantation women may have undergone a significant change in the wake of the war, but this change does not seem to have been accompanied by a corresponding change in the social position of planter women, at least to the extent that such developments are revealed in the manuscript census. This gap between the changing ideological representation of elite Southern women and the social reality of persistent antebellum patterns deserves further study.

Bourbonism
and Populism

GRADY McWHINEY

The Revolution in Nineteenth-Century Alabama Agriculture

How the Civil War and Reconstruction shaped Alabama history has been told often and in considerable detail—especially how whites and blacks suffered through invasion, emancipation, military occupation, Republican government, and a host of other developments—but too little has been written about the monumental change in the way most Alabamians lived during this period. Alabama was an agricultural society both before and after the war with ninety-five percent of its citizens living in rural areas. What changed so sharply between 1860 and 1870 was the nature of that agrarian society. "Whilst houses, fences, and everything have gone and are going to ruin and decay," noted a contemporary observer, "the poor farmer can only get advances to make cotton. [There are] no fences, no hogs, no cattle, no agriculture, no nothing. Bald, barren, uncultivated, and washed spots are seen everywhere. . . . The products of the soil of Alabama do not sustain and support the population of the State. . . . Not one [man] in a hundred makes a crop now without mortgaging for his year's support and supplies. Farm after farm, acre after acre, is eaten up in this way, until now it is hard to ascertain to whom the lands in Alabama really belong." What a contrast from the antebellum period. "Once [Alabama was] the wonder of the agricultural world," recalled this same observer, but "now [she is] groveling in the dust, and her children selling their birthright for bread."[1]

This article is an expansion of a paper read at the meeting of the Alabama Historical Association in Montgomery, April 30, 1976. It was published in *The Alabama Review,* XXXI (January 1978).

[1] Donald B. Dodd and Wynelle S. Dodd, *Historical Statistics of the South, 1790–1970* (University, Ala., 1973), 2–3; John T. Milner, quoted in Ethel M. Armes, *The Story of Coal and Iron in Alabama* (Birmingham, 1910), 269–70.

Alabama had changed from what before the war was a relatively self-sufficient society that fed itself and where perhaps seventy percent of the white farmers owned land[2] to what after the war was a colonial economy that was not allowed to feed itself and where scarcely half of the farmers owned any land. The acreage farmed by Alabamians after the war was nearly the same as before, but vital differences existed in farm size and land tenure and in what was produced and how. There were 80,736 more farms in Alabama in 1880 than in 1860, and during this period the average size and value of a farm declined from 347 acres worth $3,189 to 139 acres worth $581. Not only were tenants farming smaller plots than before the war, but by the end of Reconstruction, Alabama farm owners and tenants alike were trapped into devoting more and more of their acreage and efforts to a crop they could not eat and had to sell for whatever price outsiders set. By 1880 concentration on cotton in Alabama produced 699,654 bales—twelve percent of the nation's production as compared with eighteen percent (989,955 bales) produced by Alabamians in 1860,[3] but the state could no longer feed its citizens, and a distinctive way of life was being systematically destroyed by the forced concentration on cotton growing.

What made the lifestyle of antebellum Alabamians—indeed, of all Southerners—so distinctive was their attitude toward leisure. The Puritan work ethic that dominated most Northerners was not at all pervasive in the Old South.[4] To be lazy—which good Yankees regarded as reprehensible and defined as being indolent, shiftless, slothful, and worthless—was viewed differently by Southerners. To them lazy meant being free from work, having spare time to do as they pleased, being at liberty, and enjoying their leisure. When, unlike a conscientious Northerner, a Southerner said that he was being lazy, he was not reproaching himself but merely describing his state of comfort. He suffered no guilt when he spent time pleasantly—hunting, fishing, dancing, or just talking.

Two dominant institutions—black slavery and the open range system of grazing livestock—made it possible for most white Southerners to practice their preference for leisure. At the middle of the nineteenth century only eight million of the nation's twenty-three

[2] Frank L. Owsley, *Plain Folk of the Old South* (Baton Rouge, 1949), 9.
[3] Dodd and Dodd, *Historical Statistics of the South*, 2–5.
[4] For an excellent example see James R. McGovern, *Yankee Family* (New Orleans, 1975), 79, 82–84.

million inhabitants lived in the 900,000 square miles of mostly un-
cleared forest that constituted the Old South, but three million of
these Southerners were blacks and ninety percent of those were slaves.
The South produced nearly all of the nation's cotton, rice, and sugar
cane, three-fourths of its tobacco, and more than half of its corn.
Much of this production was done with slave labor. Yet only a fourth
of the Southern whites owned, or were members of families who owned,
slaves. In Alabama the percentage was slightly higher—about a third
of the families owned slaves, but half of these owned fewer than five
each. Only 1,687 Alabamians owned more than fifty slaves.[5]

The labor of slaves, which allowed some whites to enjoy opulance
and leisure, also tended to discredit the value of work. A major and
often overlooked reason why Southerners—even nonslaveowners—con-
doned slavery was their commitment to leisure; they frequently said
disdainfully that only slaves and Yankees worked. "No Southern
man," claimed John C. Calhoun, "not even the poorest or the
lowest, will, under any circumstances, . . . perform menial labor. . . . He
has too much pride for that." Though Calhoun's words were not
absolutely true, the Southerner's attitude toward work differed from
the Northerner's. "If I could get such hired men as you can in New
York," a Southerner told a Yankee, "I'd never have another
nigger on my place; but the white men here who will labor, are not a
bit better than negroes. You have got to stand right over them
all the time, . . . and then, if I should ask, now, one of my white men
to go and take care of your horse, he'd be very apt to tell me to do
it myself, or, if he obeyed, he would take pains to do so in some way
that would make me sorry I asked him; then if I should scold him, he
would ask me if I thought he was a nigger, and refuse to work for me
any more."[6]

Many Southerners managed to avoid excessive or menial labor by
depending upon animals for their livelihood. Though the Old South
produced most of the nation's staple crops, a significant portion of

----

[5] Dodd and Dodd, *Historical Statistics of the South*, 2–61; Bureau of the Census, *The
Statistical History of the United States* (Washington, 1957), 4–11; Emory Q. Hawk, *Economic
History of the South* (New York, 1934), 222; Albert B. Moore, *History of Alabama* (University,
Ala., 1934), 354.
[6] Calhoun quoted in E. Merton Coulter, "The Movement for Agricultural Reorganization in the Cotton South during the Civil War," *Agricultural History*, I (January
1927), 11; Frederick Law Olmsted, *A Journey in the Back Country* (new ed., New York, 1970),
228.

which was grown on plantations with slave labor, neither slavery nor plantations were as widespread or as distinctively Southern as the raising of livestock, especially hogs and cattle. In 1860 hogs and other Southern livestock were worth half a billion dollars—more than twice the value of that year's cotton crop; indeed, Southern animals probably were worth much more because there was every reason for owners to undercount the actual number of livestock they reported to tax collectors and census takers. Not all of the Old South's animals were sold each year, of course, but for twenty years between 1830 and 1850 one small area of the South extending from western Alabama through southern Mississippi into eastern Louisiana had raised "one million head of cattle yearly" and sold them for "from $10 to $12 per head." Two-thirds of the nation's hogs were grown in the Old South. Just before the Civil War the hogs and other livestock slaughtered in the South were worth some $106 million; this was $237,000 more than all the livestock slaughtered in the North.[7]

Practically all Southerners kept livestock for their own use, including some townspeople, and a surprisingly large number of people whom historians have regarded only as plant growers derived as much or more of their livelihood from the animals they raised as from their crops. Those who raised substantial numbers of livestock included at least three groups, each with countless gradations both in the extent of their specialization and the volume of their business: planters, who frequently tried to produce their own meat supply; yeoman farmers, who almost universally kept some hogs and often raised sizable herds; and drovers, whose main or sole occupation was herding, and who, when they raised crops at all, did so mainly for fattening their stock or for distilling into whiskey. In many areas of the Old South people by tradition and choice raised cattle and hogs as their principal

[7] *Agriculture of the United States in 1860 . . . Compiled from . . . the Eighth Census . . .* (Washington, 1864), 184–87; *Report of the Commissioner of Patents, for the year 1850:* Part II, *Agriculture* (Washington, 1851), 260; cited hereinafter as *Patent Office Report, 1850.* The average price for middling upland cotton between 1856 and 1860 was 11.5 cents on the New York market and 6.7 cents on the Liverpool market. The weighted average price in 1860 on the New Orleans market was 11.1 cents per pound. M. B. Hammond, *The Cotton Industry: An Essay in American Economic History* (New York, 1897), Appendix I; Lewis C. Gray, *History of Agriculture in the Southern United States to 1860* (2 vols., Washington, 1933), II, 1027. For this study an average price of ten cents per pound was used. It should be noted that cotton prices fluctuated "as much as 5 cents per pound—and more—throughout the season in every market. . . ." Harold D. Woodman, *King Cotton & His Retainers: Financing & Marketing the Cotton Crop of the South, 1800–1925* (Lexington, 1968), 19–20.

occupation.[8] "The people [in much of Alabama and Mississippi] are for the most part pastoral," noted a traveler in the 1840s, "their herds furnishing their chief revenue." Another observer recalled that "most of the people [of northern Florida and southern Georgia] lived by raising stock." And a visitor to east Tennessee reported: "The principal revenue of the people . . . is derived from the business of raising cattle."[9]

Customs, laws, and the physical environment combined to make the raising of livestock a leisurely activity in the Old South. Throughout the antebellum period conditions in Alabama and other Southern states, including a mild climate and abundant forage, encouraged a special type of herding—the open range system, which allowed animals to roam freely and to graze upon any unfenced land, whether or not it belonged to the owner of the animals. From early times until after the Civil War the laws were written to favor open range herding. *The Code of Alabama* permitted "cattle, hogs, sheep, or goats" to run "at large" with only the restriction that these animals "must have an ear mark or brand." All marks and brands were registered and kept in a book at the county courthouse, and the altering of a brand was a serious offense. No slave or Indian was allowed to mark or brand an animal unless some white person was present. Once branded or marked, animals could wander the countryside. The law required that they be fenced *out,* not in, and that all "enclosures and fences . . . be at least five feet high, . . . and so close as to prevent stock of any kind from getting through." The owner was not liable if his animal damaged crops that were unprotected by a lawful fence. If, instead of a lawful fence, a property owner resorted to "stakes, pits, poison, or any thing" that might "injure, or kill, any animal or stock" that person could be fined "fifty dollars for every such act" and compelled to pay the animal's owner "five times the amount of the injury done." Moreover, "any stakes, pits, or poison" discovered were considered by law as "presumptive evidence that the same were set by the person in charge of such land." The law allowed

---

[8] For a more detailed treatment of this topic see Forrest McDonald and Grady McWhiney, "The Antebellum Southern Herdsman: A Reinterpretation," *Journal of Southern History,* XLI (May 1975), 147–66.

[9] John F. H. Claiborne, "A Trip Through the Piney Woods," Mississippi Historical Society, *Publications,* IX (1906), 514–38 (quotation on page 515); Simon P. Richardson, *The Lights and Shadows of Itinerant Life: An Autobiography* (Nashville, 1900), 26–27; Charles Lanman, *Letters from the Allegheny Mountains* (New York, 1849), 153.

unidentified stray animals found on one's property to be retained under certain circumstances, but any person who took up an estray had to testify under oath before a county court that he had not "defaced or altered" the animal's brand or mark. Furthermore, it was strictly illegal to take up as estrays any beef "cattle, . . . sheep, or hogs" between April 1 and November 1.[10]

The open range method of grazing required little expenditure of either labor or money. Animals were simply turned out to run wild and root for themselves on just anybody's land. As one Alabamian recalled, "Cattle and hogs became wild and . . . were driven up only once a year. . . ."[11] Another man remembered that animals were rarely seen until they were hunted up in the late fall. "Usually," he noted, "when we found them they were in good condition and fat." The rounded-up cows and hogs were often sold to a local buyer who, when he had purchased a large herd, would drive them to some market town.[12] "As a general thing," said one man, "we did not buy pork, except now and then a little fat bulk pork, but every year droves of hogs would be driven through the country from Tennessee and North Alabama, and the farmers who were newcomers or did not raise enough meat for home consumption would select their supply and buy the hogs on foot from these droves."[13] Newspaper advertisements indicate a brisk trade in pork. For example, in 1859 in Greene County, A. Jarvis of Eutaw offered "8,000 pounds Bacon, Sides, Hams and Shoulders" as well as "20 barrells Mess Pork, on hand and for sale"; A. S. Gilbert sought buyers for "Fresh Lard, and country cured Hams"; and H. B. Dugger, proprietor of the Greensboro Hotel, announced that "Drovers will find it to their interest to give him a call."[14]

---

[10] *Statutes of the Mississippi Territory* . . . (Natchez, 1816), 214–15, 392–96, 424–26; *Acts of Alabama* . . . (Cahawba, 1820), 27, 78; *Acts of Alabama* . . . (Cahawba, 1824), 53; *Acts of Alabama* . . . (Cahawba, 1826), 14–15; *Acts of Alabama* . . . (Tuscaloosa, 1829), 32; *The Code of Alabama* . . . (Montgomery, 1852), 245–51.

[11] Fred S. Watson, *Coffee Grounds: A History of Coffee County, Alabama, 1841–1970* (Anniston, 1970), 29.

[12] Eddie B. Rozelle, *Recollections: My Folks and Fields, 1900,* ed. by Lenore Bishop (Talladega, 1960), 66–67.

[13] R. C. Beckett, "Antebellum Times in Monroe County," Mississippi Historical Society, *Publications,* XI (1910), 92. (The author is indebted to Dr. Jerry C. Oldshue for this reference.)

[14] Eutaw *Alabama Whig,* October 13, 20, June 30, 1859. (The author is grateful to Dr. Warner O. Moore for these items.)

Prices varied. In the early 1840s cows in Sumter County were worth ten to twenty dollars each; pork sold for four or five cents a pound; bacon for ten cents cash or twelve and a half cents on credit. In comparison, cotton was five to eight cents a pound, and corn brought from fifty cents to a dollar a bushel.[15] In 1846 James Mallory of Talladega County raised 5,000 pounds of pork that was worth eight cents a pound and twenty-four bales of cotton that he sold for nine cents a pound—a total of $400 worth of pork and $1,080 worth of cotton. Hogs and cotton appear to have been his main products. Four years later, when he butchered some 4,500 pounds of pork and made $2,600 on the thirty-six bales of cotton he sold at the high price of twelve cents a pound, Mallory wrote in his diary: "pork scarce and six dollars per hundred. Cotton seems to rule the price of everything, lands, negroes and stock are all advancing in price."[16]

In most areas of Alabama natural vegetation was so abundant that animals could subsist on it all year. "The oak forest throughout the greater part of . . . [Morgan] county furnished considerable mast for hogs," observed a local historian. "Cattle in the southern part of the county were driven, in the fall, to the Tennessee river bottoms to winter in the corn fields and canebrakes. Wild grasses furnished . . . hay for livestock." One writer noted that since "the earliest settlement" of Conecuh County extensive parts "have been held in high esteem as pasturage lands." Another authority stated that Limestone County's natural vegetation provided "a fine range for stock." Indeed, the ease with which livestock subsisted on the open range in Alabama is described by numerous local historians. Coffee County has been called "ideal cattle" country where animals "were not only raised for home use, but were one of the farmers' largest sources of income." The historian of Pike County concluded that a "large proportion of those who came first . . . were herders of cattle, sheep and hogs." In Walker County, where "cattle, hogs and sheep roamed the hillsides," the population consisted "largely of independent farmers, stock raisers and small

[15] George H. Sheldon to John Benson, December 16, 1841, November 4, 1842, George H. Sheldon Papers, University of Alabama, Tuscaloosa.

[16] James Mallory Journal, December 31, 1846, January 7, 1847, December 23, 31, 1850, January 2, 12, 1851, James Mallory Diary, 1843–1877, 2 vols., Southern Historical Collection, University of North Carolina, Chapel Hill (original owned by Edgar A. Stewart, Selma, microfilm copy at University of Alabama, Tuscaloosa).

business men." One of the leading citizens of Butler County "spent the earlier days of his life driving cattle."[17]

The raising of livestock was so widespread in antebellum Alabama that it could almost be described as a universal activity, yet some Alabamians practiced it differently from others and to a lesser extent. Elbert A. Holt of Montgomery County grew oats for his animals. "We cut some for summer feeding of horses, and the rest is fed off the land by the cattle and hogs," he explained in 1850. Holt also fattened his hogs on boiled corn. He claimed that it was impossible to "raise stock on grass" in his area because "cotton at 10 to 12½ cents per pound is much more profitable. All our planters who consult their best interests will attend to their dairies, neat cattle, sheep, hogs, and horses, for their own use, not for profit, but for saving," concluded Holt.[18]

James Mallory of Talladega County sometimes fattened his hogs on sweet potatoes or peas before butchering them. "Our hogs are not so large or fat as usual," he recorded on December 14, 1849. "They lacked the pea crop." He agreed with Holt that when cotton prices went up people tended to neglect everything else. In 1851, when cotton rose to twelve cents a pound, Mallory wrote: "fear that it will make many go in debt and be ultimately injured in it."[19]

In Barbour County herdsmen never fed boiled corn to livestock, insisted J. H. Dent, but they turned their animals into fields of rye and peas during the winter. Dent also noted how high cotton prices influenced farmers. "Cotton is now bearing a high price," he wrote

---

[17] John Knox, *A History of Morgan County, Alabama* (Decatur, 1967), 15; Benjamin Franklin Riley, *History of Conecuh County, Alabama* (Columbus, Ga., 1881), 215, 216–17; Captain R. A. McClellan, *Early History of Limestone County* (Athens, 1881), 9; Watson, *Coffee Grounds,* 18, 23, 90–91; Margaret Pace Farmer, *One-Hundred and Fifty Years in Pike County, Alabama, 1821–1971* (Anniston, 1973), 76; John Martin Dombhart, *History of Walker County, Its Towns and People* (Thornton, Ark., 1937), 35, 42; John Buckner Little, *History of Butler County, Alabama, 1815–1885* (Cincinnati, 1885), 108. See also James F. Clanahan, *The History of Pickens County, Alabama, 1540–1920* (Carrollton, 1964), 17; Margaret Jean Jones, *Combing Cullman County* (Cullman, 1972), 19, 179; Anne Kendrick Walker, *Backtracking in Barbour County* (Richmond, Va., 1941), 105–06; Rozelle, *Recollections,* 13; Mitchell B. Garrett, *Horse and Buggy Days on Hatchet Creek* (University, Ala., 1957), 3–4, 56–57; Fred S. Watson, *Forgotten Trails: A History of Dale County, Alabama, 1824–1966* (Birmingham, 1968), 80; John Simpson Graham, *History of Clarke County* (Birmingham, 1923), 145; Fred S. Watson, *Hub of the Wiregrass: A History of Houston County, Alabama, 1903–1972* (Anniston, 1972), 119; Nelson F. Smith, *History of Pickens County, Alabama, 1817–1856* (Carrollton, 1856), 188–89.

[18] Elbert A. Holt to Thomas Ewbank, December 10, 1850, *Patent Office Report, 1850,* 301–02.

[19] Mallory Journal, October 21, 22, 1846, December 14, 1849, January 12, 1851.

in 1850, "and the whole energies of the planters are bent on making all they can. The result will be, that they will find themselves dependent upon others for every thing they need, having neglected their provision crops, stock &c. for cotton."[20]

Whatever herdsmen added to the diet of their stock—corn, rye, oats, potatoes, or peas—was merely a supplement to what the animals obtained for themselves on the open range. J. H. Dent pointed out that the cost of raising beef cattle was "merely nominal; for, in summer, they are sustained by the range, and, in winter, the run of the fields with shucks is found sufficient." A three-year-old cow was worth from seven to nine dollars. "Beef is used only in the summer months, where fattened by the range," reported Dent. "Fall beeves, killed and cured for winter use, are generally fattened in the peafields." Another Barbour County man, who considered fifteen cows sufficient to supply fifty or sixty people with meat, noted that "we must in a great degree depend on the range for . . . green food or grazing." James Mallory turned his hogs out after marking them in January or February and did not round them up again until late October or November. "The native or common stock," wrote Dent, "we find to answer our purposes best, owing to its hardy habits, and being the most thrifty range-hog."[21]

A major problem that hog raisers shared was that meat might spoil before it could be preserved in Alabama's mild climate. "[M]any are killing hogs," noted James Mallory on December 13, 1848. "It is too warm to be safe, all who killed the past week have lost a portion [of their pork]." Five days later he complained: "Warm yet, many persons have killed their pork hogs and much of it is spoiled by the hot weather." Mallory waited until early January to kill his hogs, but even then he reported: "Turning warm, fear it will damage pork." J. H. Dent insisted that the Alabama climate "is so variable and uncertain, that it is a hard matter to save what pork is raised in the country. The drove-pork purchased is often much injured in saving, and the risk is so great, that the planters feel safer in purchasing their bacon from New Orleans, than in raising and curing. In putting up our meat, the worst enemy we have to contend with is the skipper-fly,

[20] Jno. H. Dent to Thomas Ewbank, November 9, 1850, *Patent Office Report, 1850*, 284–88.

[21] *Ibid.*; Walker, *Backtracking in Barbour County*, 105; Mallory Journal, December 5, 1843, January 20, February 6, October 21, 1846, December 13, 1848.

which produces a bug that in summer destroys it [pork]. Many preventatives against this enemy have been resorted to, but none, so far as I have heard, has proved entirely successful." John M. Swoope of Lawrence County echoed Dent's contention that pork was difficult to preserve. "The climate is changeable," he wrote, "and it requires strict attention to save meat that will be palatable."[22]

Despite the problem of meat preservation, pork was a mainstay of the Alabama diet, and during the three decades before the Civil War vast herds of hogs and cattle roamed the open range throughout the state. The 1840 census, which doubtless understated the number of livestock, reported that there were 77,000 more beef cattle and 800,000 more hogs than people in Alabama. Though people outnumbered cows by 300,000 in 1850 and by a half a million in 1860, hogs maintained their numerical supremacy—there were 1,100,000 more hogs than people in the state in 1850; 780,000 more in 1860.[23]

The open range system of livestock grazing and the leisurely lifestyle that it promoted were not mere creations of the Southern physical environment. The South's mild climate may have contributed to the Southerner's laziness, as is often claimed, but a leisurely way of life was an established part of a culture brought to the South by settlers whose ancestors had acted remarkably like antebellum Southerners as early as 600 B.C. It is a commonly accepted myth that the people who settled south of the Ohio River were of Anglo-Saxon descent; actually, most of them were of Celtic heritage—quite a different culture from the one that shaped Yankee values.

The ancient Celts, who created the first civilization north of the Alps and who dominated Europe from the Black Sea to the Atlantic and from the North Sea to the Mediterranean in the eight centuries before Christ, successfully resisted being Hellenized or Romanized. To protect their culture, they retreated ever westward to new lands where they could retain their old ways. During the Middle Ages, when Britain was successfully dominated by Anglo-Saxons (a Germanic people, lin-

[22] Mallory Journal, December 13, 18, 1848, January 2, 10, 14, 1849; Dent to Thomas Ewbank, November 9, 1850, *Patent Office Report, 1850,* 284–88; Swoope to Thomas Ewbank, December 4, 1850, *ibid.,* 194–96.
[23] *Compendium of the . . . Inhabitants and Statistics of the United States . . . Returns of the Sixth Census* (Washington, 1841), 54, 215; *The Seventh Census of the United States: 1850* (Washington, 1853), ciii, 429–31; *Population of the United States in 1860; Compiled from the Original Returns of the Eighth Census* (Washington, 1864), 8; *Agriculture of the United States in 1860; Compiled from the Original Returns of the Eighth Census* (Washington, 1864), 2–3.

guistically and culturally significantly different from the Celts) and then by Normans, the Celts were pushed into the extreme western and northern upland parts of the British Isles, where they experienced some infusion of Viking blood and culture and hardened into five distinct but still culturally related groups—the Cornish, the Welsh, the Highland Scots, the Lowland Scots, and the Irish. A sixth group, the Ulster Scots or Scotch-Irish, developed still later. During the seventeenth century many of these Celtic people, together with west-of-England folk with whom they had interacted, fled the Puritan Commonwealth. They settled in the colony of Virginia after being on the losing side in a war against the purely English, or Germanic, part of Britain, the same part that peopled New England. In the eighteenth century, subjected to powerful pressures for amalgamation at home, additional Scotch-Irish came to America, either to North Carolina or to Philadelphia, whence they moved westward along the Ohio Valley or southwestward through Virginia into Tennessee and the Carolina and Georgia piedmont. In the nineteenth century they moved farther south and west to settle Alabama, Mississippi, northern Louisiana, Arkansas, and Texas. Throughout this 2,000-year migration, these Celtic people proved remarkably resistant to change.[24]

Not all herdsmen were Celts and not all Celts were herdsmen, but the description of Celtic customs and values—made by such ancients as Diodorus, Strabo, and Julius Caesar; by the fourth-century sage of Cú Chulainn; and by eighteenth-century travelers in the British Isles—are remarkably similar to those customs and values attributed to Southerners by nineteenth-century observers. The ancient Celts were a pastoral people who grazed their large herds of hogs and cattle on the open range. "They have large quantities . . . of meat, especially fresh and salt pork," noted Strabo. "Their pigs are allowed to run wild, and are noted for their height, and pugnacity and swiftness." The pig was their favorite animal; they hunted and ate him with equal delight and amused themselves while he multiplied. The ancient Celts, like their descendents in the Old South, enjoyed

---

[24] McDonald and McWhiney, "Antebellum Southern Herdsman," 156–61; Forrest McDonald, "Ethnicity in the History of Alabama: A Neglected Dimension" (unpublished paper read at the Alabama Historical Association Meeting, April 30, 1977). The best works on the ancient Celts are: Anne Ross, *Everyday Life of the Pagan Celts* (London and New York, 1970); T. G. E. Powell, *The Celts* (New York and Washington, 1958); and Gerhard Herm, *The Celts: The People Who Came out of the Darkness* (New York, 1977).

feasts and heavy drinking, instrumental and vocal music, hunting
and fishing, horse racing, and oratory. They favored the oral to the
written word. Their society was aristocratic, and they practiced slavery. Though they highly regarded the truth and honor, Diodorus
claimed that they "frequently exaggerate, with the aim of extolling
themselves. . . . They are boasters and threateners, and given
to bombastic self-dramatisation, and yet they are quick of mind and
with good natural ability for learning." They estimated a wrong according to the damage suffered and the social rank of the person
injured. Later described as "indolent to a high degree, unless
roused to war, or to any animating amusement," they were full of
"pride, and consequently are impatient of affronts, and revengeful
of injuries. They are decent in their general behaviour; inclined to
superstition, yet attentive to the duties of religion." Sustained by
their faith in the immortality of the soul, Celts considered combat
noble and were brave to the point of foolhardiness. Their ideal was
the heroic warrior aristocrat. "It is a wonderful thing, if I am but
one day and one night in the world," said Cú Chulainn, "provided
that my fame and my deeds live after me." Because of their pride and
short tempers, Celts often fought duels over fancied insults; one
might fall out with a friend at dinner, challenge and kill him. Strabo
considered the Celts "all naturally fine fighting-men," but
"better as cavalry than infantry." As soldiers they were too individualistic and undisciplined. They could terrify an opponent with
their bold charges accompanied by fearsome yells, but like most
unstable and impulsive people they lacked tenacity.[25]

---

[25] Ross, *Everyday Life of the Pagan Celts,* 99, 100, 108–09, 114, 97, 98, 102, 104, 105, 107,
35, 36, 124–25, 110–13, 115, 132–33, 74, 77, 55, 56, 65, 46; Thomas Pennant, *Tour of Scotland*
(1759), quoted in Maurice Lindsay, ed., *Scotland: An Anthology* (New York, 1974), 280–81.
Confederate soldiers, like their Celtic ancestors, tended to be brave, impulsive, and
often undisciplined. They liked to attack but were bored by the routine of war. General
Winfield Scott, himself a Virginian, believed that Southerners were too undisciplined
to fight a defensive war. They "will not take care of things, or husband [their] . . .
resources," he insisted. "If it could all be done by one wild desperate dash [then
Southerners] . . . would do it, but [they cannot] . . . stand the long . . . months between
the acts, the waiting!" Mary B. Chesnut, *A Diary from Dixie,* ed. by Ben Ames Williams
(Boston, 1961), 245. In describing what he called "the greater impetuosity of the Southern temperament," Thomas Livermore pointed out that "Southern leaders were, at
least up to 1864, bolder in taking risks than their opponents, but also that
they pushed their forces under fire very nearly to the limit of endurance." Livermore,
Numbers and Losses in the Civil War in America: 1861–65 (Bloomington, 1957), 71. David
Herbert Donald stated that the "Southerner made an admirable fighting man but a
poor soldier." Donald, "The Confederate as a Fighting Man," *Journal of Southern
History,* XXV (May 1959), 178–93.

The settlers of Alabama and the Old South, like their Celtic ancestors, imposed their customs upon their environment. The frontier experience did not do to them what Frederick Jackson Turner said it should have—strip away their cultural baggage and homogenize them into unique Americans.[26] Instead, they maintained to a remarkable degree the values and old ways that their people had followed for centuries. Their adherence to ancient customs is confirmed by a comparison of the agricultural practices of Northern and Southern farmers, who differed significantly in their tastes, work habits, and use of land. Pork, which by tradition was the mainstay of the Southern diet, was not so popular with Yankees. In Alabama in 1860 there were twenty-three times as many hogs in proportion to the population as there were in Maine; thirty-six times as many as in Massachusetts. Yankees preferred mutton and beef to pork. Diners at Boston's Revere House consumed each week seven times as much beef and five times as much mutton as pork. Between 1854 and 1860 a million more sheep than swine were brought into the New York livestock market, and most of the hogs slaughtered and packed there were "sent to other places for consumption." There was nothing in the South comparable to the movable sheep fence that was changed every day in New England "so that each commoner's cropland eventually had the benefit of a night's manuring." Northern farms generally were smaller and more intensely cultivated than those in the South. In 1850 Southern farms averaged 384 acres each—289 acres each in Alabama—compared to the national average of 203 acres, but Southerners rarely planted crops on more than a third of their land—herds of hogs and cattle usually roved the remainder. Only fifty-two million of the South's 171 million farm acres were under cultivation in 1850; improved farm acres varied from forty percent in Virginia to thirty-seven percent in Alabama to ten percent in Texas. Nowhere in the North was so much land left unplanted; even in frontier Illinois, sixty-three percent of the land was in crops. From New England through New York, Michigan, and Wisconsin farmers usually produced their own food as well as a variety of such saleable items as grains, hay, wool, maple sugar, fruit, dairy products, eggs, potatoes, and meat. This mixed farming, which seemed to suit the Yankee character, was hard work; it required the year-round efforts of the whole family and left them little free time

---

[26] Turner, "The Significance of the Frontier in American History," American Historical Association, *Annual Report* (1893), 199–227.

from their labors. Their animals had to be sheltered, fed, and cared for during the cold winter months.[27]

By contrast, the Southern system of raising livestock on the open range was simple and easy. Aside from marking or branding their animals, Southerners had little more to do than round them up in the fall and either sell them to a local buyer or drive them to market—the driving of large herds over long distances to market prevailed in the Old South just as it had among the Celtic peoples for centuries.[28] One could even raise livestock without owning land. An analysis of Covington County, Alabama, reveals that of the 497 heads of household listed in the 1850 census, forty-two percent were landowners and fifty-eight percent were tenants. None of the tenants owned land, of course, and only six percent of them owned any slaves, compared to twenty-nine percent of the landowners. But fully ninety-five percent of the tenants and ninety-six percent of the landowners owned animals. As might be expected, a higher percentage of landowners than tenants possessed livestock worth more than $500—twenty-four percent to five percent—but there was little difference between the percentage of landowners and tenants who owned animals worth between $100 and $500—fifty-eight percent compared to sixty percent. The census material also shows that sixty percent of the landowners and forty-six percent of the tenants slaughtered livestock valued at $50 or more in 1850. These figures show that in one year alone more than half of Covington County's heads of household butchered or sold more than six cows each. Covington was predominately cattle country; in 1850 it produced some 3,292 more cows and 10,253 more hogs than were needed to feed its population.[29] Many of these animals were raised by people who owned no land. One such tenant possessed 160 beef cattle and 250 swine valued at $2,104; another held 200 cows

[27] Paul W. Gates, *The Farmer's Age: Agriculture, 1815–1860* (New York, 1960), 146, 214–17, 247–48; Dodd and Dodd, *Historical Statistics of the South*, 2–61; Howard S. Russell, *A Long, Deep Furrow: Three Centuries of Farming in New England* (Hanover, N.H., 1976), 25–27, 152–53, 155, 325–414, 497.

[28] McDonald and McWhiney, "Antebellum Southern Herdsman," 159–62.

[29] One authority has estimated that each person living in the Deep South during the nineteenth century consumed approximately 150 pounds of pork and 50 pounds of beef per year, and that these amounts convert into an individual yearly consumption of about 2.2 hogs and one-sixth of a cow. Sam B. Hilliard, *Hog Meat and Hoecake: Food Supply in the Old South, 1840–1860* (Carbondale, Ill., 1972), 124–30.

and 70 hogs worth $1,390; still another owned 15 cows and 300 hogs valued at $808.[30]

Most antebellum Alabamians and Southerners differed from most Northerners in ways other than their work habits, land use, and ancestors. Few Southerners believed as wholeheartedly in the perfectability of man and in material and social progress as did good Yankees, who were confident that they had not only the wisdom to recognize the world's problems but also the ability to solve them. In contrast to the Yankee ideals of hard work, thrift, and a desire to improve oneself and indeed the whole world, Southerners usually exerted less effort to make money or to acquire material things. An Alabamian told a traveler that he and his neighbors "try to enjoy what they've got, while they ken. . . . Now, I never calculate to save any thing; I tell my wife . . . I mean to enjoy what I earn as fast as it comes."[31] Southerners also doubted generally that much could, or should, be done to improve things in this world. They looked more to the next world, where they believed life would be all leisure and comfort, and which could be reached simply by belief and baptism. Contemporaries claimed that Southerners were neither introspective nor much concerned with social betterment. Many, it is true, were outright romantic reactionaries, but they—more than most Northerners—were willing to tolerate the irregularities in man and nature. As one Alabamian said, when pressed by a Yankee for an explanation of why the state capital had been moved from Tuscaloosa to Montgomery, "The fact is, sir, the people here are not like you northern people; they don't reason out every thing so."[32]

The way of life of most Alabamians, especially those who gained much of their livelihood from livestock that roamed the open range, changed significantly after 1861. Put simply: the Civil War and Reconstruction were devastating to Alabama's animal growers. Between 1860 and 1870 the value of livestock fell from $43,000,000 to

---

[30] This information was computed from the published census returns and from notes taken by Professor Frank L. Owsley and his students. These notes are on deposit at The University of Alabama. Much of the statistical work for this paper was done by Michael J. Daniel and Boyd Childress, and the author is grateful to them for their assistance.

[31] Olmsted, *Journey in the Back Country*, 211.

[32] *Ibid.*, 206.

$26,000,000; the value of animals slaughtered from $10,000,000 to $4,000,000. What is important is that Alabama shifted from a society that in 1840 could feed itself and produce a surplus of 100,000 hogs to a society that in 1880 fell a million and a half hogs short of the number needed to feed its citizens.[33]

At first it appeared that herdsmen would profit from the Civil War because meat was in great demand and high in price, and plenty seemed available in 1861. A man from Flat Woods, Alabama, informed a friend in Marengo County that a herdsman had promised to supply an additional thousand pounds of pork and "perhaps he can let you have 2,500 lbs. He gives us the choice of hogs and we are to say when they are fat enough to kill. This is a fine bargain for we get fat or in other words, 'whole hog.' Several want the meat, but he says he will wait until he hears from you. You had better take all you can get from him for he has the largest hogs about."[34]

Animals were still available in 1863, though a Confederate army officer who had established a subsistence depot at Oxford, Alabama, complained that the prices asked for livestock and other items exceeded the amount he was authorized to pay. "I find . . . in the vicinity of Uniontown and Demopolis," he reported, "lots of bacon, some in the hands of speculators and some in the hands of wealthy planters, who, like the speculators, are holding it up for prices much above the maximum established by the Secretary of War. . . ." If this officer received authorization to impress meat for the army, he was confident that he could "secure many thousand pounds of bacon" from Alabama. "I have purchased above 60 head of good beef-cattle, and will be able to start a drove of from 80 to 100 to the army by the middle of the present week," he announced, "and I think I will be able to secure from 400 to 600 before the grass beef comes in, after which a great many may be bought."[35]

[33] *Compendium of the . . . Sixth Census,* 54, 214, 216, 218, 222, 224; *The Seventh Census,* 430–32; *Population . . . in 1860,* 8, 10–11; *Agriculture . . . in 1860,* 2–5; *Statistics of the Population of the United States . . . 1870* (Washington, 1872), 11–12; *Statistics of the Wealth and Industry of the United States . . . 1870* (Washington, 1883), 94–96; *Statistics of the Population of the United States at the Tenth Census . . . 1880* (Washington, 1883), 49, 380, 427; *Report on the Productions of Agriculture . . . 1880* (Washington, 1883), 104, 142, 178, 213, 252–53.

[34] William Watkins to Jonathan G. Allen, November 18, 1861, W. C. Allen Family Papers, University of Alabama, Tuscaloosa.

[35] Major W. W. Guy to Colonel B. S. Ewell, March 9, 1863, *The War of the Rebellion: A Compilation of the Official Records of the Union and Confederate Armies* (128 vols., Washington, 1880–1901), Series I, XXIII (pt. 2), 674–75 (hereinafter cited as *OR,* with all references to Series I).

By 1864 Alabamians, like most Southerners, were reluctant to exchange their livestock for Confederate money. "There are large quantities of cattle and hogs still to be collected [in Alabama and Mississippi]," reported a Confederate officer, "but we require military aid to secure them." Another officer in the area admitted: "I find it almost impossible to buy more hogs with Confederate money, and cannot promise any more except from tax in kind. But if you can procure me an order from the commanding general to impress hogs in the northern and bottom counties of my district as a military necessity—for the citizens will not sell for our money—I can get 3,000 to 4,000 hogs more from that portion of the State."[36]

As Yankee armies invaded the lower South, whole areas were stripped of animals. The Confederacy's Commissary General, Lucius B. Northrop, had promised to impress so ruthlessly that "there will be no portion of the Confederacy which is not thoroughly drained." By February 1864 General Joseph E. Johnston reported that much of northern Alabama and Georgia was devoid of meat—the area, in his words, was "an exhausted country." Advancing Union and retreating Confederate forces had stolen or impressed everything eatable. Even breeding stock had disappeared. Jeremiah Clemens of Huntsville, Alabama, claimed that he was robbed by Confederate General Joseph Wheeler's cavalrymen of "thirty-five mules, four horses, and every hog, sheep, and goat, with every hoof of cattle, besides corn, provisions, etc., to an unknown amount. . . ."[37]

What animals survived the war were in constant danger during Reconstruction. "We cannot raise a turkey, chicken, or a hog," announced James H. Clanton in 1871. "Planters of Montgomery [County], who before the war used to raise bacon at 5 cents a pound, have actually had to kill their shoats, and in some instances, every sow they had, in consequence of the stealing by the negroes; and we now have to pay 25 cents for bacon. We dare not turn stock out at all. One man, within a mile of Montgomery, had . . . five out of seven cows killed."[38]

---

[36] Major W. H. Dameron to Colonel Thomas M. Jack, January 6, 1864; Major Samuel Mellon to Major W. H. Dameron, January 1, 1864, *OR*, XXXII (pt. 2), 523.

[37] Colonel L. B. Northrop to Major W. H. Dameron, April 15, 1863; J. E. Johnston to Jefferson Davis, February 1, 1864, *OR*, XXXII (pt. 2), 525, 645; Jeremiah Clemens, *Tobias Wilson: A Tale of the Great Rebellion* (Philadelphia, 1865), 304.

[38] Walter L. Fleming, ed., *Documentary History of Reconstruction* (2 vols., Cleveland, 1906), II, 279.

Complaints against black thieves during Reconstruction were wide-spread in other Southern states as well. Freedmen simply foraged widely and stole and butchered the animals they found roaming the woods. The situation became so bad in Mississippi that the first Redeemer-dominated legislature passed "a bill which declared the theft of any property valued at more than ten dollars, or of any kind of cattle or swine, regardless of value, to be grand larceny, subjecting the thief to a term up to five years in the state penitentiary. This was the famous 'pig law,' which was largely responsible for an increase in the population of the state prison from 272 in 1874 to 1,072 at the end of 1877."[39]

No such law was passed in Alabama; indeed, the state's livestock raisers suffered during Reconstruction and beyond from a changing agricultural system and a series of legislative acts that circumscribed their operations and changed their lifestyle. The Confederacy's defeat left Alabama and the South defenseless; exploiters of all sorts came and found some Southerners ready to assist them. In the scramble for place and favors that followed the war some became rich and powerful, others became hopelessly trapped in tenancy, and Alabama became—like the rest of the South—a colonial economy in which Yan-kees and their local allies controlled nearly everything—land, railroads, banks, mercantile houses, mineral and timber resources. In this new order self-sufficiency was discouraged. As a visiting Northerner ex-plained after talking with a German provision merchant who came to the South just after the war:

> He has some interesting facts to tell about the way things are done in the cotton country and as I heard the same story not long since from the lips of a former cotton farmer I feel justified in relating it. . . . The gist of the matter is that the merchants and cotton farmers are so situated that the latter work hard the year around for a mere subsistence while the former . . . pocket all the surplus. The war left the cotton farmers throughout the South penniless. To keep going they had to borrow money. Interest was enormous and profits not large enough to cover it, so they must borrow again at an exorbitant rate. The result is that all through the South the cotton growers are bankrupt; their creditors being generally the mer-chants. However, if they could raise enough provisions to last them over the season without borrowing, the farmers would soon be independent. But there's the rub: They are not allowed to do it. Suppose a farmer having

[39] Vernon L. Wharton, *The Negro in Mississippi, 1865–1890* (Chapel Hill, 1947), 237.

50 acres determines instead of putting it all in cotton, to plant 10 acres in corn and wheat so as to be independent next season of the provision merchant. But meanwhile he must live, so he goes to the market and says, "I want you to sell me provisions enough to last me until cotton harvest. I have no ready money but I will give you a lien on my cotton crop which is the best kind of security." "Well," says the merchant, "What are you going to plant this year. All cotton I suppose?" "Not entirely," says the farmer, "I want a few acres in corn and wheat." "No," replies the merchant, "I cannot give you credit if you intend to raise your own provisions." So the poor farmer must raise cotton alone or nothing. When he finally agrees not to raise provisions the merchant says, "All right, here is $120 worth of provisions but as you cannot pay me for several months you must give me a lien of $200 on your crop"; and he gets it. So the farmer has sold his crop before it is planted for half its value in provisions and must go through the same process next season.[40]

The trains that took out the South's cotton and other raw materials brought in not just finished products but food as well. As one Alabamian expressed it, freight rates were so discriminatory that local producers were "debarred from selling our goods." Alabamians paid endlessly for the railroads, all of which were owned by outsiders concerned mainly with profits. In 1873 the railroad owners got a bill through the legislature that allowed them to charge up to fifty percent more for moving freight within Alabama than they charged "for the transportation of the same description of freight over the whole line." Discrimination between towns became common—for example, the rate on cotton shipped 180 miles from Montgomery to Mobile was seventy-four cents a bale, while the rate on that shipped 135 miles from Greenville to Mobile was $2.30 a bale. When a man in Opelika complained that because of freight rate discrimination "produce shipped from the West costs us nearly double what it does Montgomery," he was told that Opelika was lucky to be "within the circle" of a national railroad system.

In 1880 the Louisville and Nashville Railroad, which had leased the Montgomery to Selma line of the Western of Alabama, stopped the shipment of goods from New Orleans that previously had been distributed in Alabama. The L.&N. simply wanted to force all trade

---

[40] Charles H. Cooley to his mother, June 9, 1883, Charles H. Cooley Papers, Michigan Historical Collection, University of Michigan, Ann Arbor. See also Woodman, *King Cotton*, 295–359, and Margaret Pace Farmer, "Furnishing Merchants and Sharecroppers in Pike County, Alabama," *Alabama Review*, XXIII (April 1970), 143–51.

over its lines. This company, which discriminated in various ways against Cincinnati jobbers and those local merchants who traded with them rather than with their rivals in Louisville, often delayed freight from Cincinnati at Birmingham and then charged nearly as much to move it from there to Montgomery as the full rate from Louisville to Montgomery. Such arrogant disregard for public welfare caused a Barbour County man to denounce all railroads and sawmills; he wanted to draw "a line around his acres" and keep them both out. But they were too strong. By 1876 the merchants of Eufaula—where the streets were clogged with cotton and the "stores bulged with bacon and flour" shipped in from the North—were supplied by Yankees with nearly everything, including "unlimited credit." It was that way throughout Alabama. The merchants, in turn, encouraged the farmers who were dependent upon them for credit to plant only cotton and to buy everything else, including their meat and corn, at the store.

In this way Alabama's livestock industry, which the war and its aftermath nearly destroyed, was mortally injured by the rise of tenancy and sharecropping. Landowners, who quit keeping animals because so many of them were stolen, tended to discourage their croppers from raising anything eatable. It was simpler and more profitable for merchants and landowners to import barreled meat from the North and to sell it on credit at a smart mark-up to their customers and tenants. Any attention croppers gave to animal husbandry took time away from making the cotton crop they were expected to share with the landowners. One reason why cotton became so popular with postbellum landowners and merchants alike was because the tenants could not eat it.[41]

Instead, they ate mostly fat pork and processed cornmeal brought in from the North. Such a diet, though it featured the items Southerners had long favored, did not include much of the lean, range-hog pork, high in protein, or the unrefined corn that was eaten in the antebellum period; meals after the war consisted mainly of fat, pen-

---

[41] Allen J. Going, *Bourbon Democracy in Alabama, 1874–1890* (University, Ala., 1951), 92, 146; James F. Doster, *Alabama's First Railroad Commission, 1881–1885* (University, Ala., 1949), 57, 10–14, 27–28, 31; Walker, *Backtracking in Barbour County,* 329, 290–91. Merchants frequently acted as bankers. Tallapoosa County, for example, had no banks before 1887, but one of those organized soon after that date by Reuben Herzfeld started in the general store of Herzfeld and Frohsin. Voncyle Young Allen, "Banks and Bankers," *Tallapoosa County: A History* (Alexander City, 1976), 174.

fed pork, and milled corn from outside the South that were low in essential vitamins. This new, inadequate diet forced upon Southerners contributed directly to such diseases as pellagra. An authority on Southern eating habits observed that as:

> share cropping and tenancy became entrenched throughout the cotton belt, the plantation store came to be a landmark. In the store were ... goods sold or "furnished" to the tenants of which "side meat" was one of the more important items. Many persons today can recall seeing the "meat box" in the corner of these stores filled with large pieces (perhaps fifteen by thirty inches in size and four inches thick) of white salt meat. Many, too, can remember seeing warehouses in Memphis, Nashville, Atlanta, Montgomery, or Jackson filled with stacks of such white slabs. It is this writer's opinion that extreme dependence upon these white slabs of side meat by tenants in the South during the early twentieth century has influenced students of Southern history to assume that Southern pork during the antebellum period was similar.[42]

It was not. Some planters believed that slaves needed "fat bacon, pork, corn, and peas because such 'carbonaceous' foods generated heat" and supposedly blacks possessed "feeble heat generating powers."[43] But generally the lean, muscular rangehogs, that rarely weighed more than 150 pounds each, were a staple of the antebellum Southerner's diet. Pellagra was first recognized as a problem in the United States about the end of the nineteenth century. It was found to be far more prevalent in the South than in any other part of the country. A study of the eating habits of Alabamians in the 1890s revealed that they consumed large amounts of fat pork that was high in energy but deficient in protein. Had the "muscle meat" eaten by most antebellum Southerners been a part of the postbellum Alabama diet, it would have prevented pellagra, whereas the fat pork that had replaced it left the people vulnerable.[44]

Kenneth K. Kiple and Virginia H. Kiple, "Black Tongue and

---

[42] Hilliard, *Hog Meat and Hoecake*, 252.

[43] William D. Postell, *The Health of Slaves on Southern Plantations* (new ed., Glouchester, Mass., 1970), 85; Weymouth T. Jordan, "Plantation Medicine in the Old South," *Alabama Review*, III (April 1950), 101.

[44] Wilbur O. Atwater and Charles D. Woods, *Dietary Studies with Reference to the Food of the Negro in Alabama in 1895 and 1896* (Washington, 1897), 64–69; Joseph Goldberger, "Pellagra," *Essays on History of Nutrition and Dietetics*, comp. by Adelia M. Beeuwkes et al. (Chicago, 1967), 103–06. (The author is grateful to Dr. Vera J. Wall for both expert advice on nutrition and this reference on pellagra.)

Black Men: Pellagra and Slavery in the Antebellum South," *Journal of Southern History,* XLIII (August 1977), 441–48, argue that pellagra probably "existed in endemic form" among slaves whose diet mainly consisted of "fat pork" and corn, but these authors offer no explanation for the absence of pellagra among antebellum white Southerners and fail to note that before the Civil War most white and many black Southerners ate lean, range pork, which contained much more protein than the fat pork so often consumed by postbellum Southerners, white and black.

While the railroads brought in more and more of the fat pork that made Alabamians susceptible to pellagra, new fencing laws and disease further reduced the number of range hogs available. "Killed six hogs, lost most of our stock by cholera, the first time in 30 years that we failed to make meat for family use," wrote James Mallory in December 1875. A few weeks later he noted: "More meat spoiled through the South than ever known, the already high price will be increased."[45] Systematically, in county after county, the open-range herdsmen began to be squeezed out by law. Plant-growing landlords, supported by the railroad and lumber interests, managed to get a series of special bills enacted that prohibited the free ranging of livestock. These restrictions on the open range began as early as December 3, 1866, when the state legislature made it unlawful "for any stock of any description whatever, to run at large at any time between the fifteenth day of February, and the twenty-fifth day of December in any year, in a district of land in the county of Dallas. . . ."[46] Soon laws limited the areas in which animals could run free in various counties. In 1869 Lauderdale County planters were authorized to run a public fence across part of the county for "the protection of plantations and crops," and no animal was allowed "to run at large in the district of country lying between the Tennessee river and said public fence."[47]

By the 1880s the open range was closed in many parts of Alabama. Dozens of counties had restricted the free grazing of livestock. Power had passed from the herdsmen to the plant growers and their masters, and their intent was clear. They and their friends in the state legislature were determined, as the titles of some of their laws indicate, to "prohibit stock from running at large," "to reg-

[45] Mallory Journal, December 16, 1875, January 10, 1876.
[46] *Acts of . . . Alabama, 1866–67* (Montgomery, 1867), 46.
[47] *Acts of . . . Alabama, 1869–70* (Montgomery, 1870), 9–16.

ulate the enclosure of stock," "to prohibit the owner . . . from allowing any . . . animal to go at large off the premises of such owner," and to protect "lands and plantations from depredations by stock."[48]

To protect themselves, the plant growers and their allies destroyed an important economic and social activity and a way of life. The livestock industry would revive in Alabama and in the South after World War II, but the new animal growers were unlike the old either in motive or in method. The mid-twentieth-century herdsmen were capitalists—sometimes corporations or groups of investors looking for tax shelters—who owned or leased the land on which their animals grazed.[49] Alabama's twentieth-century livestock growers actually have less in common with the antebellum herdsmen than with the plant growers who helped to destroy the open-range herdsmen.

It is easy to dismiss the antebellum livestock grower as a historical dinosaur who perished because he could not adapt to a changing world. But to do so is to ignore both his central role in the Old South's economy and the significance of his uniquely Southern way of life. The open-range herdsman—the man who let his animals make his living— was an independent character, for his wealth was mobile and he had the use of even the great planter's land. He was less tied to the land and less dependent upon the weather than the plant farmers, and his product was always in demand. Unlike the men who devoted most of their energy to cultivating plants, the livestock raiser had abundant free time for such pursuits as hunting and fishing. His lifestyle promoted leisure rather than the compulsive pursuit of wealth. To the outsider, caught up in the race for profits, the Southern herdsman appeared to be both indolent and shiftless. Because he shunned hard and con-stant work, he was sometimes mistakenly described as a "poor white." To Yankee travelers who were imbued with the work ethic, the South-ern herdsman seemed despicably un-American.[50]

Indeed, he may have been un-American. How else can one explain a man who valued comfort more than wealth and who was not ambitious

---

[48]*Acts of . . . Alabama, 1870–71* (Montgomery, 1871), 94; *Acts of . . . Alabama, 1880–81* (Montgomery, 1881), 175, 260, 184, 189.

[49]Charles P. Roland, *The Improbable Era: The South since World War II* (Lexington, 1975), 20–23; W. M. Warren, "Livestock," *Atlas of Alabama,* ed. by Neal G. Lineback (University, Ala., 1973), 70–71.

[50]Olmsted, *A Journey in the Back Country,* 197–242.

enough to work and scheme to get ahead? In most ways the antebellum Southern herdsman simply did not act like other Americans. He sacrificed material goods for the time to do what he enjoyed doing. Leisure meant more to him than luxury. His unhurried pace was reflected in his manners, in his speech, and in the very way he walked. Courteous, modest, and even deferential, he could yet be deadly if provoked. Though far from class-conscious, at least in a Marxian sense, he was proud and possessed of strong ethnic and racial prejudices. Such a man, understandably, confused outside observers. Before the war they had often mistaken him for an unsuccessful planter because the forests hid his livestock and what he planted frequently was poorly tended, and the self-righteous considered it lamentable that after the war, when the herdsman was forced to become a cotton-growing tenant, he did not take to this labor like a good Yankee farmer. The antebellum Southern livestock grower and his ways stood against all those smug, progressive-industrial values that have captivated most Americans and most historians since the nineteenth century. That concept alone is reason enough for most historians to ignore and thus to deprecate the Southern herdsman. But there is a further reason: a trace of him and his values can still be seen in that elusive but quite real quality known as the Southern character.

WILLIAM WARREN ROGERS

The Alabama
State Grange

After the Civil War the widespread and crippling agricultural depression in the South prompted the United States Department of Agriculture to send agents into the devastated region for the purpose of gathering statistical information. One of these agents was Oliver H. Kelley, a clerk in the department, who was determined that the *"people* North and South must know each other as members of the same great family, and all sectionalism be abolished."[1] Impressed with the general demoralization, Kelley conceived the plan of an organization for social and educational purposes which would benefit the farmers. As a Mason he thought of an order with a similar ritual of secrecy and fraternity.[2] After his tour, which included Alabama,[3] Kelley returned to Washington and on December 4, 1867 he and six other government employees organized the National Grange of the Patrons of Husbandry. One writer commented, "There was none to dispute the title, and they enjoyed it alone for the next five years."[4]

Despite these slow beginnings the Grange, as the movement was

This essay was published in *The Alabama Review*, VIII (April, 1955).
[1] Oliver H. Kelley, *Origin and Progress of the Order of the Patrons of Husbandry in the United States; A History from 1866 to 1873* (Philadelphia, 1875), p. 14. See also Solon J. Buck's *The Agrarian Crusade: A Chronicle of the Farmer in Politics* (New Haven, 1920), pp. 1–10, and *The Granger Movement: A Study of Agricultural Organization and Its Political, Economic and Social Manifestations 1870–1880* (Cambridge, 1913), pp. 40–52.
[2] Charles W. Pierson, "The Rise of the Granger Movement," *Popular Science Monthly*, XXXI, 199–208 (December, 1887).
[3] Kelley, *op. cit.*, p. 14. At Mobile Kelley received a letter from his niece, Mrs. C. A. Hall, who later gave him the idea of admitting women into the Grange.
[4] Pierson, *op. cit.*, XXXI, 200 (December, 1887).

popularly called, caught the interest of the Middle West and grew rapidly. By the early 1870's the order had expanded into the Southern states. Agents or deputies were sent out by the National Grange to organize state and local granges. The destruction of the war, poor agricultural prices, and an uncertain labor system prompted many farmers of the South to join, especially those of Alabama ready for any organization that offered relief.

The first beginnings in Alabama came in 1872, when a deputy from Mississippi organized eight subordinate granges in Pickens and Sanford counties.[5] Chief credit for the permanent and soon flourishing establishment of the Alabama State Grange belongs to Evander McIver Law, better known by his initials "E. M." Scion of a distinguished South Carolina family, Law was graduated from the South Carolina Military Academy in 1856, taught school in his native state, and in 1860 moved to Tuskegee, Alabama, where he established and became principal of the Tuskegee Military High School. At the outbreak of the war, Law was commissioned a captain in the Confederate Army. He rose to the rank of major general, achieving a brilliant combat record. He returned to South Carolina after the conflict and, like many of his contemporaries, engaged in planting and railroad ventures. However, in 1872 he again moved to Alabama and began farming.[6] Because of his prestige and success as a planter he received a commission from the National Grange as deputy for Alabama and on May 17, 1873 he organized Tuskegee Grange No. 9. After this, the number of granges leaped so phenomenally that, when the Alabama State Grange was formed, there already existed 320 subordinate granges, representing fifty out of the state's sixty-five counties.[7]

---

[5] *Journal of Proceedings of the Third Annual Session of the Alabama State Grange, Patrons of Husbandry* . . . [1875] (Montgomery, 1876), p. 9. Hereinafter cited as *Annual Session*, with appropriate date. John B. Clarke, *Populism in Alabama* (Auburn, 1927), p. 54, credits the first official Grange as being established at Yorkville, July 15, 1872. Kelley states (*op. cit.*, p. 320) that the first inquiry received about the Grange from Alabama came from one J. H. Barger of Eutaw in 1871.

[6] Law served as secretary of the Alabama State Grange from 1873 to 1876. His later career included the establishment and operation of the South Florida Military Institute at Bartow (Thomas M. Owen, *History of Alabama and Dictionary of Alabama Biography*, IV, 1014–1015, Chicago, 1921). By 1875 Law had personally organized 78 subordinate granges (Kelley, *op. cit.*, p. 431). See also *Rural Alabamian* (Mobile), II, 330 (July, 1873).

[7] *Third Annual Session*, 1875, p. 9.

Concerted action became the driving mania for Alabama farmers. Dedicated to the notion that "agricultural interests demand an organization of some kind"[8] the grangers preached the "imperative duty of every farmer . . . to attach himself to this organization."[9] Farmers responded with great zeal. With National Master Adams present, 129 delegates met at Montgomery November 27, 1873 and organized the Alabama State Grange.[10] From this beginning the order continued to grow, reaching its probable peak in 1877, at which time it boasted of 678 granges and 17,440 members.[11]

The organizing convention selected William H. Chambers of Oswichee, Russell County, as master. The decision proved wise, for Chambers was well equipped to lend dignity as well as enthusiasm to the movement. Born in Georgia and able to trace his progenitors back to a leading English family, Chambers had led his class at Emory University and in 1847 had earned a law degree from Harvard. He had moved to Eufaula, Alabama in 1854 and become a successful attorney in partnership with John Gill Shorter, Alabama's Civil War governor. His career had also included membership in the state legislature, editorship of the *Southern Cultivator* and service in the Confederate Army. After the war he had retired to his plantation at Oswichee and been elected state senator.[12] Chambers may safely be classified as an intellectual conservative. Indeed, the leaders of the Alabama State Grange may uniformly be categorized as large land-owners, usually connected with politics and imbued with a basically conservative philosophy. Although it has been said that the Grange in the South was in the main made up of small white farmers rather than large planters,[13] this does not appear to have been the case in Alabama.

---

[8] *Alabama Farm Journal* (Auburn), I, 5 (February, 1878).

[9] *Rural Alabamian*, II, 469 (October, 1873).

[10] *First Annual Session*, 1873, p. 6.

[11] These figures placed Alabama ahead of Florida, North Carolina, South Carolina, Louisiana, Maryland, Virginia and West Virginia, with more granges but fewer members than Mississippi and Arkansas. In the South only Texas, Tennessee, Georgia and Kentucky surpassed the Alabama Grange in size. See *Southern Plantation* (Montgomery), II, 173 (January 18, 1877).

[12] Owen, *op. cit.*, III, 310–311; Birmingham *News*, October 7, 1932. Chambers spent his last years as a professor of literature and agriculture at the Alabama Agricultural and Mechanical College, Auburn. He died in 1881.

[13] Theodore Saloutos, "The Grange in the South, 1870–1877," *Journal of Southern History*, XIX, 475 (November, 1953).

While many small farmers did flock to join the organization, the leadership was furnished by the men of wealth and property.[14]

Founded to aid farmers, the Grange took the undeviating position that politics offered no solution. One member wrote, "We are not interested in the Democratic party, not the Republican party, its nominees or its isms," because the grangers had "abrogated . . . allegiance to party."[15] Even in 1890, when the Grange had declined almost into oblivion, Master Hiram Hawkins admonished the annual convention to "stand as the strong and impregnable bulwark against the communistic, the socialistic and agrarian heresies" then rampant.[16] This noble creed was extremely difficult to uphold, especially when the patrons attempted to "exert a benign influence on government and legislation."[17] The Grange did wield a political influence, although it was in no sense politically inspired or controlled. This may be seen in the refusal of the *Southern Plantation,* official organ of the Grange, to print political matters.[18] In state and local meetings politics was rarely an issue. Only in the later years did the order openly endorse free coinage of silver, radical tariff reduction and war on the monied interests.[19] Thus "the true design of the Order . . . [was] to reform and elevate . . . agriculture, by making it independent and profitable, and its followers intelligent and prosperous."[20]

Vast in scope, the program advocated by the Alabama State Grange included social and educational benefits and a panacea for the farmers' economic plight in the form of co-operative ventures in buying and selling. A third aspect, though not expressed, was that of political reform; that is, the subtle exercise of a non-partisan franchise

---

[14] Hiram Hawkins, long master of the Alabama State Grange, owned 1,500 acres in Barbour County, served in the state legislature and was twice a candidate for commissioner of agriculture (Montgomery *Advertiser,* July 29, 1913; *Memorial Record of Alabama,* I, 430–439, Madison, Wis., 1893). Other prominent members included I. F. Culver and E. C. Betts, both of whom later served as commissioner of agriculture. See Birmingham *News,* October 10, 1936, and *Report of the Commissioner of Agriculture of the State of Alabama from September 1, 1883, to September 1, 1886* (Montgomery, 1886), pp. 6–7. The Grange did not restrict its membership to farmers. Lawyers, merchants and doctors frequently held important positions in the order. Other examples are legion, all illustrating that the Alabama State Grange was anything but a small farmer movement.

[15] *Southern Plantation,* I, 370 (June 24, 1875).

[16] *Eighteenth Annual Session,* 1890, pp. 12–13.

[17] *Third Annual Session,* 1875, pp. 12–13.

[18] *Southern Plantation,* I, 360 (June 17, 1875).

[19] *Eighteenth Annual Session,* 1890, pp. 48–50.

[20] *Second Annual Session,* 1874, p. 11.

which would elect "more farmers, and fewer lawyers, merchants and railroad men to make the laws."[21]

Grange meetings served as educational and social gatherings also. Because of the nature of his work, the farmer lived in virtual isolation. Regular meetings of the order offered him a chance to mingle with his neighbors. As enthusiastic participants the women often took an active part in the Grange, which was a "real source of social enjoyment to its lady members."[22] At the meetings songs from the books issued by the National Grange were sung, programs offered, and Grange sponsored picnics were legion.[23] This festive air led to the charge that the Grange as an "intellectual gymnasium . . . is almost ignored."[24]

However, each Grange had supporters who read papers on agriculture, and the members themselves exchanged information on planting, harvesting and other aspects of farming. Lecturers, paid by the Alabama State Grange, held regular speaking engagements in the various counties. Their central themes were usually crop diversification and the wage system of labor. Though cotton "used to be called King—he seems now to have risen to the proportions of a heathen deity, and our people sacrifice upon his altar everything that is desirable in life,"[25] stated the *Southern Plantation*. To offset this, *"farming must take the place of planting,"* and farmers must raise their "own stock, . . . devote more land to grain, grasses and pasturage, and give more attention to the improvement of the soil," declared the *Farm Journal*.[26] In labor the wage system was strongly urged as being infinitely superior to the renting and share-cropping systems. To further this program the Grange favored immigration by small farmers from the Northwest and from Europe, "the stream of which has heretofore been to the bleak and ice-bound regions of this country."[27] Such an ambitious program failed to offer any pragmatic remedy for the burden of debt which had resulted from the dedicated system of planting

---

[21] *Rural Alabamian*, I, 525 (October, 1872).
[22] *Wilcox Vindicator* (Camden), December 8, 1875; *Third Annual Session*, 1875, p. 13. In the Grange the offices of Ceres, Flora and Pomona were held by women.
[23] *Southern Plantation*, I, 33 (January 28, 1875).
[24] *Third Annual Session*, 1875, p. 15.
[25] I, 50 (February 3, 1875).
[26] I, 2 (February, 1878).
[27] *Second Annual Session*, 1875, p. 17; *Southern Plantation*, III, 141 (January 4, 1877).

cotton for the sole cash crop. Paying money wages, while admirable, was impossible because of the contracted currency system and the low agricultural prices which dipped lower as surpluses piled up. In this depressed agricultural situation the farmers simply did not have the ready cash to engage in the payment of money wages. Nor could immigrants be induced to come to Alabama in any appreciable number to compete with "African bone and muscle."[28] As a consequence, despite all that the Grange could do, the share-cropping and renting systems became more firmly entrenched and the poor-whites and Negroes remained as laborers, while "King Cotton" retained his sovereignty.

As a part of the educational program several grammar schools were organized and conducted by the granges. One of these was at Trinity, Morgan County, and another at Mount Willing, Lowndes County. These schools had regular teachers and were supplied with books. The rooms were usually attached to Grange meeting halls. Stressing the application of scientific agriculture, the schools also instilled the "noble principles and purposes of the Grange."[29] On a higher level the organization heartily endorsed and supported the Alabama Agricultural and Mechanical College at Auburn.[30]

As a more informal educational program, the larger granges had libraries or reading rooms and encouraged farmers to subscribe to newspapers and magazines.[31] There were three organs for the Grange in Alabama: the *Southern Plantation,* the *Alabama Farm Journal,* and the *Alliance Journal* (Montgomery). The last-named was published in the early 1890's and seems to have promoted the Grange chiefly out of spite, when its editor disagreed with the policies of the Farmers Alliance.[32] Only the *Southern Plantation,* published from 1874 to 1877 and succeeded by the *Farm Journal* which ran until 1880, were of significance. Both journals carried farm advertisements, letters, articles copied from other periodicals, feature stories, news of the state and subordinate granges, and departments for poultry and livestock, but

---

[28] *Second Annual Session,* 1874, p. 17. Despite the propaganda campaigns to get immigrants, Alabama's native born population in 1890 was 99.02 per cent. In 1850 it had been 99.03 per cent. See *U.S. Census* (11th), 1890, Pt. I (Washington, 1894), p. lxxxiii.

[29] *Southern Cultivator,* XLVI, 569 (December, 1888), *Third Annual Session,* 1875, p. 14.

[30] *Ibid.,* pp. 20–21.

[31] Saloutos, *op. cit.,* XIX, 487 (November, 1953).

[32] *Nineteenth Annual Session,* 1891, p. 48; *Alliance Journal,* I, 23 (April, 1890). Another Alliance paper, the *Alliance Herald* (Montgomery), printed some Grange news in the later period, as did the *Rural Alabamian* in the early 1870's.

little or no politics. By circulating the latest agricultural knowledge and methods, they performed a valuable service for the farmers. One historian has written that, if the movement had created nothing else than the desire to read, it would have been worthwhile.[33] Certainly, the educational program gave a medium of expression to many farmers who otherwise would have never had an opportunity to develop their talents.[34]

The Grange-sponsored Alabama State Fair was an event combining social and educational features. In 1875 it was held at Selma. Chambers was probably correct in his claim that to "Alabama belongs the credit of having held the first State Fair under the auspices of the Grange."[35] Although well attended, the fairs were not financially successful. They reflected a certain vitality of the order and interest in promoting agriculture, but the educational and social aspects of the Grange remained its most significant and most successful achievements.

Blaming the economic situation on the middlemen, commission merchants and retailers, the Grange sought alleviation by going into business for itself. The fact that the credit system was the "prolific source of . . . financial troubles" suggested the inexorable logic of abolishing credit and establishing co-operative stores [36] which were to be run by and in the interests of the farmers. The resulting war on the middlemen attracted many farmers to the Grange.[37] Ignoring almost entirely the factors of over-production, poor transportation and extremely limited state and national farm legislation, the farmer was inclined to hold the commission merchant responsible for his impoverished condition. He considered the merchant a non-producer, waxing rich on the farmer's labor, taking each year the major portion

[33] Buck, *Agrarian Crusade*, p. 76.
[34] James S. Ferguson, "The Grange and Farmer Education in Mississippi," *Journal of Southern History*, VIII, 76 (November, 1942).
[35] *Third Annual Session*, 1875, p. 18. At the 1875 fair there were departments of Field Crops; Horticulture; Horses, Mules and Jacks; Cattle, Sheep and Swine; Poultry; Home Industry; Fine Arts; Manufactures; Machinery; Tools and Implements, and Miscellaneous. Premiums were awarded for every conceivable article from sponge cakes to Shepherd dogs (*Southern Plantation*, I, 129, 142, March 11, 1875). See also *Alabama State Grange Fair, Selma, Alabama* [1875] . . . *Program and Schedule of Premiums* . . . (Selma, 1875), pp. 1–56. State fairs had been held before the Civil War (See Weymouth T. Jordan, "Agricultural Societies in Ante-Bellum Alabama," *Alabama Review*, IV, 241–253, October, 1951; Allen J. Going, *Bourbon Democracy in Alabama 1874–1890*, (University, Ala., 1951), p. 105, and *American Cotton Planter and Soil of the South*, XI, 50–56 (January, 1860).
[36] *Fourteenth Annual Session*, 1886, p. 37.
[37] Charles W. Pierson, "The Outcome of the Granger Movement," *Popular Science Monthly*, XXXII, 368–373 (January, 1888).

of his crop. While this animosity was not completely warranted, there was perhaps some justification for the complaints.[38] Moreover, the chief opposition to the Grange came from the commission merchants.[39]

The first attempts at co-operation on a national scale failed because of the diversity of interests within the Grange.[40] After this, the various experiments were carried out on a state and local level. Alabama patrons took a dim view of large-scale business activities. No regular selling or purchasing agent was appointed, and the Grange thus escaped losses through mismanagement that occurred in other states.[41] State Master Chambers doubted the wisdom of turning farmers into storekeepers and believed the Grange would best serve agriculture "by sticking to our own business, and permitting the merchants to attend to theirs."[42] But in this instance his was a minority voice, and the patrons plunged into the co-operative venture with great expectations. To secure fair prices the plan involved the establishment of joint stock companies made up of grangers. Supplies were to be sold at low prices. The profits, if any, were to be divided at the end of the year. However, the stores were seldom able to operate for any extended period of time. Regular merchants, with superior capital and experience, consistently undersold the co-operatives and, as a result, most of the stores were forced to close. One such co-operative, Friendship No. 656, reported that it had forced its competition to lower prices, but admitted laconically that this was only done to run them out of business.[43]

Beginning in 1876 the Rochdale Plan was proposed by the National Grange. Borrowed from England, this plan entailed the sale of a limited amount of stock at a uniform price. The store was thus owned by a large number of stockholders with equal voice in management. At the end of the year a small dividend was paid and the profits were divided among the purchasers, according to the amount purchased.[44]

---

[38] Thomas D. Clark, "The Furnishing and Supply System in Southern Agriculture Since 1865," *Journal of Southern History*, XII, 32–36 (February, 1946).

[39] Buck, *Granger Movement*, p. 55.

[40] Pierson, *op. cit.*, XXXII, 372 (January, 1888).

[41] *Third Annual Session*, 1875, p. 16; Saloutos, *op. cit.*, XIX, 480 (November, 1953).

[42] *Fourth Annual Session*, 1876, p. 11. In *Rural Alabamian*, II, 543 (December, 1873). C. C. Langdon, agreeing with Chambers, wrote, "*Make no war upon middlemen.*"

[43] Others, such as Pintala Grange No. 175 and L. M. Edwards No. 316, reported temporary success with co-operative stores (*Fourth Annual Session*, 1876, pp. 28–32).

[44] Buck, *Agrarian Crusade*, pp. 67–68.

The Rochdale Plan worked well in Texas, but gained few adherents in Alabama, due chiefly to the spirited opposition of Master Chambers, who seems to have mistrusted its foreign origins.[45]

After the co-operative stores failed, the Grange was more successful in what became the contract order system of the 1880's. This plan relieved farmers from becoming merchants themselves by putting money into goods and supplies. Rather, a written contract, usually limited to one year, was entered into with merchants for supplies in quantity at reduced prices.[46] The chief difficulty was that the plan depended on cash payments which the patrons could not meet. The merchants thus disappointed them and were in turn disappointed by what seemed to be an indisposition on the part of the farmers to trade with them.[47] Finally, in 1889 the Alabama State Grange, under the leadership of Hiram Hawkins, made a series of contracts with wholesale houses and manufacturers by which the patrons, individually or collectively, could with a Grange seal or trade-card buy supplies at the lowest wholesale rates. Confidential circulars giving names and terms of the houses were furnished to the local granges.[48] Though highly imperfect, this system did result in savings for the farmers.[49]

As another part of the co-operative program various individual granges appointed purchasing agents to buy goods in bulk and thus secure a saving. This appears to have worked particularly well in the purchasing of fertilizers and in the rental of warehouses for storing cotton.[50]

The entire Grange effort, beginning with co-operative stores and culminating in the efforts at direct purchasing, was calculated to aid the farmers, of course. But its unremitting war against the middlemen usually failed. In the longer view business setbacks discouraged and disillusioned many farmers—the promised delivery from their woes never came. Mismanagement and even fraud often served to dampen the ardor of the stoutest patrons. Following these losses the order began to decline, and its failure in business must be held largely responsible.[51]

[45] *Fourth Annual Session*, 1876, pp. 37–38.
[46] *Sixteenth Annual Session*, 1888, p. 48.
[47] *Third Annual Session*, 1875, p. 16.
[48] *Seventeenth Annual Session*, 1889, pp. 10–11.
[49] Clark, *op. cit.*, p. 57.
[50] *Sixteenth Annual Session*, 1888, pp. 27–28; *Southern Cultivator*, XLVI, 414 (September, 1888); XLVI, 476 (October, 1888).
[51] Pierson, *op. cit.*, XXXII, 664 (January, 1888); Buck, *Agrarian Crusade*, pp. 62–63.

In politics the Grange exerted an influence in its early years, but this power was by no means designed to aid the agrarian class, which was a numerical majority, by destroying or warring on other economic groups. For example, in extant Grange publications there is little evidence to show that there was ever a concentrated attack on the railroads.[52] Yet the order was so strong that "Grange Legislature" was applied to the session of 1875–1876.[53] Patrons were often elected to the legislature and were important in getting bills passed that aided agriculture and conformed to the Grange policy of being non-partisan. The law making it a misdemeanor to deal in agricultural products between sunset and sunrise had Grange support and votes. Other acts receiving Grange endorsement were those regulating the weighing and sampling of cotton, providing for a geological survey, protecting farm products and animals, and the law appointing a commissioner of immigration.[54] Perhaps the most significant legislation was the establishment of the Department of Agriculture in 1883. Hiram Hawkins, a leading granger and chairman of the House Agricultural Committee, was instrumental in preparing the bill and getting its final approval.[55]

Not until the 1890's did the Grange become radically political, and then only on a national scale. Denunciations of the tariff, demonetization of silver and freight rates became a part of the Granger program.[56] Yet the Grange would not make a common cause with the Farmers Alliance, which had become a potent force in Alabama. Differing with the Alliance, the state Grange opposed any coalition with labor unions. It also looked askance at the political proclivities of the Alliance on both state and local levels. Fundamentally, the two were different in that the Alliance was a militant agrarian organization that soon sought economic redress by the exercise of the ballot, and the Grange, as Hawkins said, had for many years been recognized as a "great conservative . . . organization."[57]

[52] Allen J. Going, "The Establishment of the Alabama Railroad Commission," *Journal of Southern History,* XII, 367–368 (August, 1946); Saloutos, *op. cit.,* XIX, 482 (November, 1953).

[53] Albert B. Moore, *History of Alabama* (University, Ala., 1934), p. 572.

[54] See Alabama *Acts,* 1872–1873, 1874–1875, 1876–1877, 1878–1879 (Montgomery, 1873–1879), *passim,* and Going, *Bourbon Democracy,* pp. 92–108.

[55] Alabama *House Journal,* 1882–1883 (Montgomery, 1883), pp. 41, 667–669; Alabama *Acts,* 1882–1883 (Montgomery, 1883), pp. 190–197. *Southern Plantation,* III, 24 (November 9, 1876) had earlier urged establishment of such a department.

[56] *Nineteenth Annual Session,* 1891, pp. 49–50.

[57] *Eighteenth Annual Session,* 1890, pp. 13–14.

In general it may be assumed that the Grange was responsible for practical farm laws. It was able to get these acts through without being charged with the stigma of sponsoring class legislation. The fact that the Grange was so large and filled with diverse groups, including planters, small farmers and others entirely unconnected with agriculture, prevented it from having a united, concentrated program. Beneficial laws were passed, but they were political only in that they required the organic function of a political body. Many of the patrons were politicians, yet they did not use politics to promote the Grange. If anything, they used the order to promote their personal politics. A profession of love for agriculture and the soil was not far behind service in the Confederate Army for getting votes. Politically, the Grange never did and never pretended to represent the farmers, *en masse*.

After the peak years of the mid-seventies the Alabama State Grange began to decline. The order kept its organization until the 1890's but after 1880 it was no longer a potent force in the state. Its failure may be attributed to several causes. Foremost among these was the failure to bring economic relief to farmers by business ventures. The order fell into such disrepute that at one time there were only ten granges and barely enough delegates at the state convention to transact business.[58] Many of the granges had been carelessly and rapidly organized and were composed of members who misunderstood the purposes of the order.[59] Non-farmers in policy-making positions were hardly dedicated to improving the condition of the farmer. Objections were also raised to the secrecy of the meetings as violating the democratic tradition. Faced with these discordant factors, the Grange was unable to survive.

When its program failed, the farmers, disappointed and despondent, resigned from the order. The Grange refused to adopt a political tack and thus lost out to the more aggressive Farmers Alliance. As membership fell, the once-brimming Grange treasury dwindled also. In these years Grange publications were filled with gloomy discussions of inadequate finances. Grange fairs, reports, pamphlets, periodicals and other publications ceased. However, in 1887 the order underwent a slight revival that saw six granges reactivated and nine new ones formed. This raised the number to twenty-four and added 2,500 new

[58] *Seventeenth Annual Session*, 1889, p. 22.
[59] *Alabama Farm Journal*, III, 46–47 (May, 1880).

members. Heartened, a patron wrote, probably with more enthusiasm than confidence, that "the Grange is not dead—certanly [*sic*] not in Alabama."[60] Such a resurgence was only temporary, however, and in the last years there was only one chapter in North Alabama.[61] The last state-wide meetings were all held in South Alabama towns. In this section the organization remained fairly strong and was able to hold its own against the Alliance.

The Alabama State Grange rose spectacularly, declined sharply and, while not falling completely, gradually gave way to more radical organizations, such as the Farmers Alliance and the Agricultural Wheel. If the Grange failed in its declared purpose, its achievements were significant and far reaching. Educational and social action by an economic class, later brought to perfection in this country by the Alliance, was first practiced by the Grange. Even the business failures made the farmers cognizant, at least, of those aspects of farming other than production. Its co-operatives paved the way for the more ambitious ventures. On the national level the Grange helped allay sectional prejudices, and Alabama farmers learned that poverty was no respecter of sections or state lines. The Grange was the first large-scale agricultural organization Alabama had ever known. Its aims were noble, its accomplishments somewhat less, but still of profound significance. Not the least of these were the sponsoring of a high degree of self respect in farmers and a pride in agricultural pursuits. The predecessor of the later agrarian movements, the Grange was an ardent champion of progressive agriculture in Alabama.

---

[60] *Southern Cultivator,* XLVI, 414 (September, 1888).
[61] *Seventeenth Annual Session,* 1889, p. 46.

FRANCES ROBERTS

William Manning Lowe and the Greenback Party in Alabama

The Republican party ceased to be an important factor in Alabama politics after 1876.[1] Complete political victory of the Democratic-Conservative party in 1874 (it was not officially entitled simply the Democratic party until 1906), the adoption of a new constitution the year after, and the powerful "White Man's Movement" to restore white supremacy had combined to re-start the state on the road to political stability. As soon as the restoration got under way, many leaders began to assume an air of independence to which they had been unaccustomed since before the Civil War.[2] They began to fight for issues which they deemed right, even though they knew that in so doing they would be taken, perhaps permanently, out of the Democratic ranks.[3] Among these was William Manning Lowe of Madison County, a fearless Confederate veteran who became the champion of the masses struggling for financial relief from mortgage-ridden farms and low farm prices.

Up until 1878 Lowe had always been a staunch Democrat, but his chief political contribution to Alabama was as a leader of the Greenback party which rose to prominence in the eighth congressional district between 1878–1882. Indeed, the beginning of the party in Madison County can be traced to Lowe's open attack on convention rule in county politics in 1878, an outburst which resulted from his

---

[1] This paper was read at the annual meeting of the Alabama Historical Association, Alabama Polytechnic Institute, Auburn, April 7, 1951. It was published in *The Alabama Review,* V (April 1952).

[2] Albert B. Moore, *History of Alabama* (University, 1934), pp. 502–519, 578–582.

[3] Thomas J. Taylor, "History of Madison County [Alabama]," unpublished MS in possession of Douglas Taylor, Huntsville, Alabama.

failure to secure the Democratic nomination for Congress in 1876. At this meeting Lowe was supported by Jackson, Limestone, Madison counties, while Joshua Burnes Moore, a Franklin County legislator, had the support of the western counties of the district. After balloting for more than a hundred times, both contenders withdrew their names from nomination in an attempt to break the convention deadlock. At this point a "dark horse" candidate, W. W. Garth of Huntsville, was nominated along with Laurence R. Davis of Limestone and John D. Rather of Decatur. Although Lowe and Moore were again placed before the convention, Garth won the nomination. Lowe felt that Garth, in letting his name remain before the convention after Lowe had been renominated, had caused a split in Madison County vote, thus leading to his defeat.[4] Since nomination by the Democratic and Conservative party at that time meant victory in the general election in November, Garth represented the district in Congress, 1876–1878, and of course became a strong contender for re-election. Lowe, realizing that the Madison County Democratic and Conservative Executive Committee would most likely seek Garth's renomination, launched an attack on the convention method of nominating candidates, calling it undemocratic and machine-controlled. He also challenged Garth to meet him in a primary election in order to let the people of Madison County decide who should receive the county nomination for congressman.

Up until this time Lowe's record as a public servant and a Democrat had been without question. After the Civil War, in which he had served as lieutenant colonel on General James H. Clanton's staff, he had been elected solicitor of Madison County, a post which he held until ousted by Reconstruction measures in 1868. For the next two years he had served as county chairman of the Democratic and Conservative Executive Committee, and he had represented Madison County in the state legislature, 1870–1872. In 1875 he had been elected as a delegate to the Constitutional Convention where he worked to bring about restoration of sound government for Alabama.[5] Because of his power as a speaker with a keen sense of humor and straightforwardness in political argument, he was popular with the masses.[6] He also

[4] Huntsville *Advocate*, August 28, 1878; Huntsville *Democrat*, August 14, 1878.

[5] Thomas M. Owen, *History of Alabama and Dictionary of Alabama Biography* (Chicago, 1921), IV, 1075.

[6] William C. Oates, "Memorial ... Lowe," *Congressional Record*, XIV, pt. 3, 2057–2058 (February 3, 1883).

had the friendship and support of older independent thinkers of Madison,[7] and one of his best political friends had been his brother-in-law, Nicholas Davis, Jr., an old line Whig and often an independent in political matters. Both the Lowe and Davis families had long been prominent in political affairs of Madison and Limestone Counties.[8]

On the contrary, William Willis Garth, Lowe's leading opponent in Madison County, had been in public office only once, as a congressman in 1876–1878. The son of a wealthy financier and railroad builder, he had received his early education in a private school and his law degree from the University of Virginia, and, after serving as a volunteer in the Mexican War, he had practiced law in Decatur until 1855, at which time he had joined a law firm in Huntsville. In 1861 he had entered the Confederate Army and, as a lieutenant colonel, he had served on General James Longstreet's staff throughout the war. After Appomattox he had resumed his law practice in Huntsville, remaining in this capacity until he entered politics in 1876.[9]

Rumblings of political warfare could be heard when "Common Sense and Scriptures to Prove It," a stirring attack on the convention method of nominating candidates, appeared in the Huntsville *Democrat*, May 22, 1878 over Lowe's pseudonym, "Veteran." John Withers Clay, the *Democrat*'s editor for more than thirty years, having first failed to read the essay carefully before printing it, devoted four weekly issues to editorials explaining his stand favoring conventions. In his comments he stated the need for continuing strict control of nominations in order to avert a return to Radical rule and apologized for having printed the original article without an accompanying note of condemnation. And judging from the "Letters to the Editor," there was growing sentiment against convention nomination of candidates.[10] The rival Huntsville *Advocate*, edited by A. H. Brittin, an independent in politics, strongly endorsed Lowe's stand against conventions.[11] The Huntsville *Independent*, another Democratic paper, edited by Frank Coleman, favored the primary election as a substitute for the convention.[12]

Lowe's second attack came in the form of a personal letter to

---

[7] *Advocate*, September 25, October 30, 1878; *Democrat*, October 9, 1880.
[8] Owen, *op. cit.*, III, 463–486; IV, 1074–1075.
[9] *Ibid.*, III, 642–643.
[10] *Democrat*, May 22, 29, June 5, 12, 19, 1878.
[11] May 29, June 5, 12, 19, 26, 1878.
[12] June 6, 1878.

A. W. Brewer of Scottsboro and later published in leading papers of the state. In his "Scottsboro Letter," as it was called, he again attacked caucus politics, although most of his comments dealt with what he called the only important issue of the day—"Finance." In endorsing the Greenback party, he urged the speedy payment of the national debt in greenbacks, the repeal of the Resumption Act, abolition of the National Banking System, taxation of government bonds and securities, unlimited coinage of silver on equal terms with gold, and that all paper money as well as metal money of the United States be issued directly by the Federal government. All money issued, he declared, should by law be made absolute legal tender for all debts and dues both public and private and such money should be kept up to a minimum of at least $50 per capita.[13]

Until 1878 the national financial issue had not played an important part in Alabama county and state politics. Though strong in its advocacy of economy in expenditures and reduction of taxation, the state Democratic and Conservative party made no attempt to take a financial stand contrary to that of the National Democratic party. Early in the summer of 1878, Madison County's Democratic and Conservative Executive Committee had endorsed the state platform.[14] Some of its members, including Chairman Paul Jones, later avowed the cause of Greenbacks in July when a Greenback Club was formed at a political meeting at Kelly's Mill. Elsewhere in the district the Greenback movement had gained some momentum. Two legislators from Lawrence County were elected on a Greenback and Labor ticket in August and J. A. Steele of Colbert County was victorious as an independent candidate.[15]

On August 3 in a rally at Gurleysville, Lowe had challenged Garth to meet him in a primary in order to let the people decide who could receive Madison's thirty-two votes at the nominating convention. At this time he restated his stand on money matters and criticized Garth's action in Congress. Editor Clay had been present to defend Garth's position and J. B. Moore of Colbert County spoke in his own behalf for the congressional nomination. Instead of calling a primary election as Lowe had suggested, the county executive committee announced that a convention would be held in Huntsville on

[13] *Advocate* and *Democrat*, July 31, 1878; *Independent*, August 1, 1878.
[14] *Democrat* and *Advocate*, June 5, 1878.
[15] *Ibid.*, August 14, 1878.

August 9 for the purpose of electing delegates to the Decatur Convention.[16] On August 7 the delegates chosen from sixteen voting precincts of Madison county assembled at the court house to elect delegates to the Decatur Convention. According to the glowing report in the *Democrat,* the meeting was harmonious in every respect. Garth received the nomination without opposition and thirty-two delegates were instructed to vote for him at the district convention. The *Advocate,* on the other hand, contended that the harmonious meeting had been due to the absence of Lowe's supporters, and a liner in its editorial column warned Garth's supporters to "beware of the Ides of November."[17] At the Decatur Convention, August 16, things did not move so smoothly as they had earlier. Garth's forces met with stiff opposition from the western counties which were in favor of J. B. Moore, contender for the nomination two years earlier. On the thirty-second ballot, Rip Davis of Limestone County proposed that Moore and Garth meet in a district primary to let the people decide between them. This resolution was promptly voted down and on the next ballot Franklin County switched its full support to Garth, thus giving him a majority vote.[18]

The battle lines were now tightly drawn: one week after Garth's nomination Lowe announced his candidacy as an Independent in the congressional race. Even at this point, however, he did not break with the Democratic-Conservative party, but merely with its convention form of nomination. In an address to the people, published in all the papers of the district, he restated what he had already made clear in his "Scottsboro Letter."[19]

During September and October the battle, which spread itself over the entire district, was conducted in three distinct phases. In the first phase both candidates used basic principles in their arguments. Garth's forces contended that preservation of the Democratic and Conservative party was all important. They avowed the cause of

---

[16] *Ibid.,* August 7, 1878; *Democrat,* August 7, 1878.
[17] *Advocate* and *Democrat,* August 14, 1878.
[18] *Democrat,* August 21, 1878.
[19] *Advocate,* August 28, 1878; *Democrat,* August 28, October 9, 1878. In the meantime J. B. McClellan of Athens, an Independent who polled a small vote in the 1876 race against Garth, announced that he would again be a contender for the congressional post. According to the *Democrat,* McClellan's withdrawal from the race a few weeks later was due to a compromise between the two Independents. Editor Clay pointed out that a committee had met and decided in favor of Lowe after both candidates had submitted the question to them for a decision.

Greenbacks but said that money matters could be solved by their party's action. Lowe attacked Garth's "lukewarm" stand on finance and asserted that, in preserving the Democratic and Conservative party by means of a machine dedicated to "class" interests, real democracy had become only a myth.[20] After two or three weeks of canvassing on a high plane, both candidates moved into the second phase of the battle, that of debunking each other's political records. Lowe singled out Garth's affirmative vote on a bill to require a $3,000 property qualification for holding office in the District of Columbia in an attempt to prove that his vote had been for the classes instead of the masses.[21] Garth also found flaws in Lowe's legislative record which seemed to indicate discrimination against the Negro.[22] By the end of the sixth week the campaign was nearing its close and the "mud-slinging" phase began. Lowe accused Garth of not fighting in the recent war and being a bond-holding aristocrat who worked for the rich and of buying votes in some instances and frightening Negroes away from the polls in others. One story about Garth contended that he had sold a Confederate soldier a chicken and demanded that it be paid for in gold.[23] These accusations were promptly denied by Garth and his followers who retaliated by accusing Lowe of being a drunkard, a gambler, a debt dodger, and an egotist who had deserted party ranks because of ambition.[24]

By the time election day drew near some members of the press were beginning to admit that Lowe's Greenback following was growing. The Democrats and Conservatives showed some signs of anxiety too, because several state leaders, including Governor George Houston and Senator John Tyler Morgan, were brought into the district on the eve of the election to speak for Garth. When Lowe's printed ballots were circulated, they bore the heading, "People's Greenback Party" thus showing that he had agreed to run under that party's banner. The steady growth of the Greenback movement was also evidenced by the fact that a state convention was called in September to formulate a platform of principles and to perfect its organization. At this time J. N. Carpenter of Birmingham was chosen president of the group and A. H. Brittin secretary.

[20] *Ibid.* and *Advocate,* September 4, 11, 18, 25, 1878.
[21] *Ibid.,* October 2, 1878.
[22] *Democrat,* October 2, 1878.
[23] *Advocate,* October 9, 16, 23, 30, November 6, 1878.
[24] *Ibid.* and *Democrat,* October 9, 16, 23, 30, November 6, 1878.

When the votes were counted, it was found that Lowe had won by a majority of something over 1900. Jubilant over their victory, the Greenbackers gathered at the Huntsville courthouse the night following the election, formed a torchlight parade and led by a brass band marched to Lowe's home. From the colonade of his home Lowe spoke in a clear, forceful voice to a hushed, attentive audience, expressing his appreciation to all who had supported him. In reasserting his belief in the financial platform of the Greenback party, he stated that he would fight for the plain people's cause until victory was won. He pointed out that he had always been a Democrat and that in entering the race for Congress he had done so because of his sense of duty to his people. In concluding his remarks he declared, "Whosoever casteth out bondholding devils in the name of liberty, we hail him as friends and brother. We lock shield and shoulder with him now and in 1880 we will march forward with him to victory in the great and final contest between the money power and the people."[25]

As the smoke cleared from the political battlefield each party began to analyze Lowe's victory. Editor Clay of the *Democrat* claimed (November 6) that the Democratic defeat had been due to Radical efforts supported by money from Washington Republicans, to Communists who stirred up the poor against the rich, and to disappointed Independent office-seekers who used falsehood as a brazen front to "clamor for inflected, irredeemable greenback currency in place of gold and silver" and at the same time attempt to destroy the established party. On the same day Brittin of the *Advocate* asserted: "The rule of the caucus is broken. In all history of our beloved Alabama is not recorded such a victorious uprising of the hard working patriotic, independent voters of the state as we displayed in the Congressional election in this district, which has just closed. They have had the independence to defy the tyranny of caucus and party dictation. . . ." And in the *Independent* (November 7) Editor Frank Coleman, a Garth supporter, made only one editorial comment: "In the far future it may possibly be permitted unto us, as we dandle our grand-children on our knee, to tell them of a time when the Democrats practiced the convention system in North Alabama."

Encouraged by such a decided victory, the Greenbackers set out

[25]*Advocate* and *Democrat,* September 4-November 13, 1878. Lowe's majority of votes came from Madison, Lawrence, Limestone and Franklin counties. Morgan, Lauderdale and Colbert supported Garth.

to perfect their organization so that they might make good show-
ings in all local, state and national elections of 1880. The Democrats
and Conservatives, on the other hand, were determined to turn
defeat into victory in the coming election.

For the Greenbackers 1879 was a year of organization. When the
new party began to take shape, various groups had brought with them
their own ideas of local, state, and national reforms. Thus was the
party a "catch all" for discontented groups, and its original objectives were easily modified from time to time until the party's identity
was at last to become lost in a greater insurgency movement, the
Populist Revolt. Complete party organization in Madison County
was achieved at a Greenback rally held at Hickory Flat, August 30,
1879. J. P. Whitten of Madison was elected chairman of the county
committee and W. B. Jones of Huntsville secretary. Congressman
Lowe and Paul Jones, former chairman of the Democratic and Conservative Executive Committee, were the principal speakers. Lowe
spoke of his fight for the Greenback cause in Washington and reas-
serted his belief in the ultimate victory of the people in their struggle
against the money interests of Wall Street. At the conclusion of his
speech the crowd endorsed Lowe as their leader in Congress.[26]

To aid in perfecting the district organization of the Greenbackers, Lowe and Jones made a three months tour of the district.
According to William H. Moore, a special reporter who covered each
meeting for the *Advocate,* they were well received. Upon his return to
Huntsville in late November, Lowe stated that he had observed a
rapid growth of the Greenback party in the district and that he felt
sure of a party victory in 1880.[27]

Meanwhile, the Democrats had not been idle in this political "off
year." Besides sending out speakers to combat the spread of Green-
backism, they had aided in the reorganization of Alabama's election
laws. Early in 1879 the Democratic legislature had enacted a new law
that called for a ballot of white paper which could bear no marks,
figures, rulings, characters or embellishments, and on which the names
should be printed or written, together with the designated office for
which they were running. These ballots were to be folded by the voters
and handed to election officials who would place them in the ballot
boxes without being numbered. Advocates of the law said that it

[26] *Advocate,* September 2, 1879.
[27] *Ibid.,* September 2, 10, November 26, 1879.

would insure secret ballot and decrease political intimidation at the polls. Opponents of the measure concluded that it was a sure way of giving election officials power to govern election results.[28]

During the year the state Democratic Executive Committee issued several policy statements, urging its members to consolidate its forces, compromise its differences, and rally its full support in obtaining a Democratic victory in 1880.[29]

What had seemed to be a hard political fight in 1878 proved to be only a skirmish in comparison to the political struggle which took place in the Tennessee Valley in 1880. In every elective political office, Greenbackers and Independents opposed the Democratic and Conservative candidates and in many instances furnished stout opposition. Meanwhile, in the House of Representatives, Congressman Lowe and fourteen other Greenbackers continued their fight for financial aid to the laboring classes. Since the Resumption Act had become an accomplished fact about which they could do nothing, their attention was turned to the question of funding the national debt.[30] Although Lowe seemed to have tried hard to accomplish what he set out to do in Congress, he met with little success. Congressman Oates of Alabama said that Lowe came to Congress as a teacher, but had to return to the rank of a student in order to learn that national policies could not be changed rapidly.[31] As election time drew near Lowe returned to the state to aid the Greenback fight for political control of Alabama.[32]

In April, 1880, when A. H. Brittin's suggestion of organization was adopted by the State Executive Committee, the final step was taken to transform Greenback Clubs into political organizations. According to this method meetings were to be held in each of the eight congressional districts for the purpose of selecting delegates to the national convention in Chicago, June 9. The state committee was then to select two delegates at large. After the national convention a state convention was to be held to elect a new committee and to put out a state ticket. The district meetings were also instructed to select two delegates in each county to perfect their organizations.[33]

[28] *Ibid.*, February 5, 1879 and *Democrat,* February 5, 12, 1879.
[29] *Democrat,* March 10–June 24, 1879.
[30] *Ibid.*, April 21, 1880.
[31] Oates, *op. cit.,* XIV, pt. 3, 2057.
[32] *Advocate,* June 23, 1880.
[33] *Ibid.*, April 14, 1880.

In accordance with this plan, a district meeting was called in Decatur on May 10. A. H. Brittin and J. J. Woodall of Decatur were elected delegates to the national convention and the Huntsville *Advocate* was voted the official state organ of the Greenback Labor party. After the business session, J. H. Randall, who had been on a four months' speaking tour of the state, made his concluding speech in Alabama, in which he urged support of the national party's program. After the district meetings were held, J. N. Carpenter, state president, issued a call for a state convention in Montgomery on June 24. He urged all clubs, farmers clubs, and workingmen's groups to send delegates, and he especially invited people who were opposed to "ring rule" to call mass meetings and send delegates. A week before the convention a conference of Greenbackers was called in Huntsville and William Lowe, L. W. Day, W. H. Moore, Paul L. Jones and A. H. Brittin were among those chosen to represent Madison County.[34]

On June 24 the state convention met and discussed means for more effective state and national organizations as well as measures for the political and economic relief to a "caucus-ridden, tax-burdened people of the state." An attempt was made to give all discontented groups some consideration. The platform of the Green-back Labor party (which had been adopted in Chicago on June 12) was reaffirmed and its candidates were endorsed. The state adminis-tration was denounced for changing the election laws so as to open the door for fraud and perjury, and reforms in the educational and convict systems were urged. Demands were made that all property bear equally the burden of taxation, and ring rule, favoritism, and class legislation of the Democratic administration were condemned. Members of the Huntsville delegation were placed on all key commit-tees of the convention. Lowe served on the committee on perma-nent organization, while Brittin and Day worked with the committee on nominations. Day was also elected to succeed Brittin as secretary of the organization. On the state ticket James M. Pickins, of Law-rence County, was nominated for governor and Paul L. Jones, of Madison, became the party's choice for attorney general.[35]

During this time the Democrats had not been idle. The April

---

[34] *Ibid.*, May 10, 26, June 23, 1880.
[35] *Ibid.*, June 29, 1880. At this time the state and national platform of the Greenback Labor party were shifted from financial to social-economic reform.

municipal elections in Huntsville had sounded a serious note of warning. Zeb Davis had been re-elected mayor by only one vote and two Negroes had won places on the town council.[36] John Brandon, county chairman of the Democratic-Conservative party announced that a mass meeting (instead of a convention) would be held in order to nominate delegates to a state convention. Care was taken to assure members of the meeting that the delegates were chosen democratically.[37] Twenty-four delegates were sent to Montgomery on June 9 to help draw up a strong platform and to nominate a slate of state officers which would insure victory in the August elections. Governor Rufus W. Cobb was renominated to head the ticket which was backed up by a platform pledged to economy and efficiency of government and tax reduction. The party also advocated needed reforms similar to those voiced by the Greenbackers.

Since all Madison County officials were up for election, the executive committee announced that primary elections would be held in July to allow the people to decide who should represent them in the August elections. It warned, however, that all people voting in the primary would be expected to support the Democratic-Conservative platform in August.[38] Forty-two candidates announced for various positions and on July 9 a complete slate was chosen.[39]

To oppose this ticket the Greenbackers joined with the Republican faction in Madison County and brought out a compromise ticket which included two Negro candidates.[40] This fusion was probably brought about because the Republicans, instead of putting out a state ticket, had urged their forces to vote for Greenback candidates.[41] Rather than strengthening the Greenback forces in Madison County, however, the idea seemed to confuse issues and the people. Some of the Negroes of the Democratic-Conservative party voted

[36] *Democrat*, April 7, 1880.
[37] *Ibid.*, April 14, 1880.
[38] *Ibid.*, June 16, 23, 30, 1880.
[39] W. W. Richardson, probate judge; John W. Cooper, sheriff; Thomas J. Taylor, circuit court clerk; James H. Ware, tax collector; J. H. Landman, tax assessor; A. M. Wynn, county treasurer; E. C. Betts, John W. Grayson, B. C. Lanier, Jr., legislators.
[40] Others on the ticket were: Richard Medlin, sheriff; Henry Barnard, circuit clerk; Frank A. Hamer, tax assessor; Hugh L. Toney, tax collector; J. W. P. Kelley, treasurer; Hermon Humphrey, Richard C. Carter, Henry C. Binford, representatives.
[41] *Democrat*, July 21, 1880; *Advocate*, July 28, 1880; Walter L. Flemming, *Civil War and Reconstruction in Alabama* (New York, 1905), p. 798.

for Negroes on the Greenback ticket, while some white people who supported the Greenback ticket voted for the white candidates on the Democratic-Conservative ticket.[42]

In July James B. Weaver, Greenback nominee for president, made an extensive tour of Alabama, and Congressman Lowe and James Pickens also spoke in almost every county. But the efforts of the Greenback Labor party were all in vain. In Madison County, as well as all over the state, the Democrats and Conservatives won the major victories.[43]

Although there were three contenders for the Democratic-Conservative nomination for Congress at the Decatur Convention in August, 1880, General Joe Wheeler of Lawrence County was easily nominated because of his brilliant Civil War record and untiring efforts on behalf of the party. As a member of the Congressional Executive Committee of the district he had become well known as an able speaker and politician.[44] And as the battle lines formed for the next political struggle the Democrats felt that they had at least found a match for William Manning Lowe.

But a September 1, 1880, issue of the *Advocate* suddenly announced that Lowe would not be a candidate for re-election, adding that his withdrawal was due to the recent election law and to a Garfield ticket which was being circulated in the state.[45]

At a Greenback rally held at New Market, August 30, Lowe spoke on behalf of the Greenback cause. He reviewed his congressional attempt to relieve the financial distress of the country. He said that he had "introduced a bill to abolish National Banks which Speaker Randall referred to a hard money committee, and it there sleeps the sleep of the righteous." After speaking for more than an hour he introduced J. B. McClellan to the audience as an able Independent leader. McClellan's speech was well received, but in the discussion which followed he differed from the Greenbackers by stating that he would support the Hancock ticket in the presidential race. According to

[42]*Democrat,* July 21, 1880; *Advocate,* August 4, 1880; *Independent,* August 5, 1880. Judging from later events, the Greenback party during this campaign probably lost some of its original agrarian supporters and became dominated by Republicans under a new name.
[43]*Democrat,* July 14, August 14, 1880.
[44]*Ibid.,* August 25, 1880.
[45]*Ibid.,* August 25, 1880, had printed a rumor to this effect. J. B. McClellan, Independent candidate, stated that he had heard Lowe say he would not seek reelection.

Brittin, this stand did not set well with the Greenbackers who had worked hard for the Weaver ticket.

The actual happenings within the ranks of the Greenbackers were not recorded in any of the weekly papers, but Clay of the *Democrat* made a prediction. He said that Lowe was using McClellan as a "decoy duck" for his own benefit and added that, if McClellan could not get the votes, Lowe figured that McClellan would withdraw from the race. If the Republicans could be prevailed upon not to nominate a candidate, Clay concluded, Lowe would feel that his chances of election were good and would therefore become a candidate.[46] On September 21 Lowe in Florence announced his candidacy for re-election. The Democrats had anticipated this announcement and Leroy Pope Walker, veteran Democrat of forty years, was on hand to challenge Lowe. Walker said later that he had gone to Florence, confident that he knew all the answers, but after Lowe's speech he had not been quite sure of his own position.[47] Contrary to the Clay prediction, the Republicans brought out former Congressman C. C. Sheats of Decatur as their candidate. However, before the fight was over both McClellan and Sheats withdrew, leaving the field of battle to Lowe and Wheeler.[48] The six-weeks contest which followed Lowe's announcement proved to be hard and exciting, but it never degenerated to the "mud-slinging campaign" of 1878.

Both Wheeler and Lowe had good military and political records. Neither candidate was embarrassed by personal wealth. Both were generally liked by the masses. (By this time the Greenback organization had been perfected to such an extent that Lowe became vulnerable to the caucus attack which he had used against Garth in 1878). Lowe centered his attack on the Democratic and Conservative party and its inability to relieve the distress of the people. He accused its party leaders of being dominated by capitalists of the state and nation who were interested in making the rich richer and the poor poorer. Wheeler, on the other hand, attacked Lowe's congressional record in a gentlemanly fashion, accusing him of siding with Republicans in Congress. He further urged the people to stick to their party which had done so much for them in recent years. He contended that the

---

[46]*Advocate* and *Democrat,* September 1, 1880.
[47]*Democrat,* September 22, 1880; Oates, *op. cit.,* XIV, pt. 3, 2058.
[48]*Democrat,* November 3, 1880.

financial issue could be solved in due time by the Democrats. As the campaign drew to a close, Lowe and Wheeler both accused each other of issuing a secret circular letter to stir up trouble. And when election day came, the Democrats carried the district for Hancock, the Republicans showed up with considerable strength for Garfield, and Weaver received only a negligible vote; but a majority of the people cut across party lines and voted for Lowe.

It was now the Greenbackers turn to celebrate. A large crowd with the usual torchlights, placards and music assembled at the courthouse on election night to celebrate Lowe's victory. But Lowe's triumph proved to be short-lived. It was discovered that the Greenback ballot had had some extra printing on it which designated the districts of the Weaver electors. These ballots were thrown out, as were a number of votes cast by people who, it was claimed, had not been legally registered. After this purge Wheeler was declared to be elected by a majority of forty-three votes.[49]

Lowe's lawyers immediately served notice that the election would be contested and, accordingly, a preliminary hearing was called before Judge Henry C. Speake at which time Lowe and Wheeler were both present. After hearing a number of witnesses the session was adjourned and the case was continued until December. By March Lowe's forces had not been able to establish the necessary evidence to effect a victory, so Wheeler was admitted to Congress with an election certificate granted him by the Attorney General of Alabama.[50]

But the fight was still not over. Lowe and his friends worked for months to get enough evidence to unseat Wheeler. Finally, after nearly a year and a half the Congressional Committee on Elections presented a majority report to the House of Representatives in which it recommended that Lowe receive his seat in Congress.[51] This report, based on thousands of pages of evidence presented by both sides, contended that the election laws of Alabama did not give the election officials the right to reject ballots on the grounds that the district electors on the Greenback ticket were numbered as to district. These numbers, the report went on to state, could in no way affect the vote and therefore were unimportant. It contended fur-

[49] *Ibid.,* September 22, 29, October 6, November 17, 1880; *Advocate,* September 22, November 3, 17, 1880; *Independent,* November 18, 1880.

[50] *Democrat,* November 24, 1880, March ?, 1881; *Advocate,* December 1, 1880.

[51] "Contested Election—Lowe *vs.* Wheeler," *Congressional Record,* XIII, pt. 5, 4455–4505 (June 2, 1882).

ther that in three instances there had been sufficient evidence presented to prove that the contestee's party had been guilty of fraud
at election time. After reviewing the hazy registration laws of Alabama, the report concluded that the contestant had received
enough legal votes to give him a majority and should therefore be
admitted to Congress. The minority report, on the contrary, contended that all ballots rejected were properly rejected, that many
more should have been rejected, that many votes were cast for the
contestant by unregistered or otherwise disqualified voters, and that
fraud had been committed in some precincts in the interest of the
contestant.[52]

On the second day of debate in the House, Wheeler appeared in his
own behalf to declare that the election had been carried out in
accordance with the laws of Alabama. Lowe, who was also present and
suffering from a throat infection, asked that his defense speech be
printed in the *Congressional Record*. At the close of debate, June 2,
1882, the House voted 140 to 3 in favor of seating Lowe (140 members
did not vote).[53] He remained in Congress until July 1, at which time
he traveled to Colorado Springs in an attempt to regain his health
which had been impaired by a severe attack of bronchitis and
pneumonia.[54]

It was evident by this time that Lowe had broken completely with
the Democratic-Conservative party and had become an outright
Greenback who was willing to acknowledge the support of Independent
Republicans of his district. This fact was clearly brought out when he
addressed his remarks to Greenbackers, Independent Republicans and
true Democrats in a letter describing his victory in Washington.[55]

Meanwhile, in Madison County the Greenbackers (now called
"Greenblackers" by the Democrats) decided to bring out candidates
for the legislature. D. D. Shelby was nominated for the Senate and
W. P. Williams, a Negro, W. W. Haden, and John W. Cochran were
nominated for the House. James Sheffield, former legislator from
Marshall County, contended for the Governor's post while George
P. Lane, of Madison County, ran for attorney general. "Fair elections"

[52] Chester H. Rowell, *A Historical and Legal Digest of All the Contested Election Cases in House of Representatives of the United States from 1st to 56th Congress 1789–1901* (Washington, 1901), pp. 365–368.
[53] "Contested Election—Lowe *vs.* Wheeler," *op. cit.,* XIII, pt. 5, 4505.
[54] Oates, *op. cit.,* XIV, pt. 3, 2057; *Advocate,* October 18, 1882.
[55] *Ibid.,* June 7, 1882.

became the chief cry of the Greenbackers, although they retained all of their suggested social and economic reforms in their platform. In August, 1882 the Greenbackers won their first Madison County victory, when their entire slate was elected to the legislature. In fact, five counties in the district sent Greenbackers to the legislature. Sheffield carried Madison and Lawrence Counties, but made no showing in the state.[56]

At this point the Democrats became thoroughly alarmed. The *Democrat* warned that the basic issue of the day had grown to be White *vs.* Black Supremacy. He pointed out that in 1880 Hancock had received 13,007 votes in the district, Garfield 9,752 and Weaver only 2,828, thus showing that the Greenback following was primarily Republican, except in national elections when they refused to support the Greenback ticket. Quoting from the 1880 *Census,* he showed that the whites had a 9,000 majority of the 34,000 men in the district over twenty-one. This, he concluded, meant that in the next election the Democratic majority should be 9,000 to insure white supremacy.

All differences within the party seemed to have been erased before convention time, for Luke Pryor, former state senator and planter of Limestone County, was nominated in less than two hours at the Decatur Convention. Joe Wheeler, who had a strong following at the meeting, nominated Pryor for Congress and then spoke in his behalf. Warning the delegates of grave danger ahead, he urged the party to stick together on every issue. "Pryor Clubs" were organized throughout the district in an attempt to solidify the Democratic forces. At meetings held in all parts of the district Pryor was aided in his campaign by Governor-elect O'Neal of Florence, Leroy Pope Walker of Huntsville, Joe Wheeler of Lawrence County and Senator John Tyler Morgan of Selma.[57]

D. D. Shelby, Charles P. Lane and Lionel W. Day then began a counter-attack in favor of Lowe, who was still in Colorado Springs.[58] Early in September Lowe returned to Huntsville to take up his own fight, but his health prevented him from doing so. In October he was forced to abandon his speaking tour of the district and on October 12 he died.[59]

---

[56] *Ibid.,* July 19, August 16, 23, 1882.
[57] *Democrat,* August 16, 23, 30, September 27, 1882.
[58] *Advocate,* September 20, 1882.
[59] Oates, *op. cit.,* XIV, pt. 3, 2058; *Advocate,* October 18, 1882.

Realizing that the political fight must continue, the Greenbackers nominated D. D. Shelby, Huntsville attorney, who had recently been elected state senator on the Greenback ticket. Shelby, considered to be an Independent Republican rather than a true Greenbacker, carried Madison, Lawrence, and Colbert Counties, but made only a fair showing against Pryor in November. Thus the post of congressman from the eighth district passed from the control of the Greenbackers into the hands of the Democrats where it has since remained.[60]

To say, as the papers did at the time, that "the Independent movement in North Alabama died with its leader," would not be true in its broadest sense.[61] It is evident from a study of the 1880–1882 elections that the leadership of the Greenback party shifted from those who had been Democrats to those who were considered to be more Republican than Greenbacker. This shift seemed to have come with the fusion of the two groups in the 1880 election. After that time Lowe was one of the few original leaders who continued to be prominent in all the Greenback affairs. After Lowe's death many of his followers returned to the Democratic and Conservative party, probably because the insurgency movement had become a threat to white supremacy. Though they had been willing to vote for Lowe along with the Negroes who had avowed the Greenback cause, they were not willing to do so for other Greenback candidates, especially when Negroes once again began to seek public office.[62] The Greenback Labor party, unimportant in national affairs after 1884, continued to function as an organization in Alabama until 1890, but after 1882 its political influence was no longer that of an insurgency movement to right the grievances of discontented groups.[63] In the political history of this period Lowe and his Greenbackers may be placed with the idealists who helped to point the way for others to follow in gaining needed reforms for the people of Alabama.

[60] *Ibid.*, November 8, 1882.

[61] *Iron Age* (Birmingham), October 19, November 16, 1882; Montgomery *Advertiser*, March 4, 1883.

[62] Returns showed that Democrats won in city, county and state elections in 1884.

[63] Solon J. Buck, *The Agrarian Crusade; a Chronicle of the Farmer in Politics* (New Haven, 1919), p. 96; John B. Clark, *Populism in Alabama* (Auburn, 1927), pp. 27–28; Moore, *op. cit.*, p. 603. That the Republicans had taken over the Greenback party in Madison County is evidenced by the fact that in 1884 Lionel W. Day, Greenbacker, carried the county while the Republican ticket in the national election won a majority in the county.

WILLIAM WARREN ROGERS

The Farmers' Alliance
in Alabama

The Farmers' Alliance was the most important agricultural organization to appear in Alabama between the Civil War and 1900. Its close affiliation with the Populists and the attendant political battles of the 1890's against the regular Democrats have been carefully studied.[1] Less familiar are the extensive social, educational, and economic activities of the Alliance. The order originated in Texas as early as 1875 as a protective association of Lampasas County farmers against cattle and horse thieves.[2] After some early difficulties the Alliance reorganized and spread into the other Southern states.

Organizers sent into the various states usually were assigned to territory encompassing one or two congressional districts. Once the Alliance was established in Alabama it mushroomed into importance. The first Alliance in the state was formed by A. T. Jacobson, a Texas organizer, at Beech Grove, Madison County, in March, 1887. Other Alliances were soon organized in the neighboring North Alabama counties of Limestone, Jackson, and Marshall. The pattern of growth in Alabama followed a general north-to-south direction. Other organizers were sent into several counties by National Farmers' Alliance President Dr. C. W. Macune. Their work was effective and in

This essay was published in *The Alabama Review,* VIII (Apr., 1955).

[1] See John B. Clark, *Populism in Alabama* (Auburn, 1927); Allen J. Going, "Critical Months in Alabama Politics, 1895–1896," *Alabama Review,* V, 269–281 (Oct., 1952); Charles G. Summersell, "The Alabama Governor's Race in 1892," *ibid.,* VIII, 5–35 (Jan., 1955).

[2] Ralph A. Smith, " 'Macuneism,' or the Farmers of Texas in Business," *Journal of Southern History,* XIII, 220 (May, 1947); Roscoe C. Martin, *The People's Party in Texas* (Austin, 1933), 15–29.

the spring of 1887 a state organization was perfected. W. J. McKelvey was elected president and G. W. Jones, secretary.[3]

From the first the Alliance got a mixed reception. In 1887 a Texas organizer in Bibb and Shelby counties was criticized. A local paper believed that "The organization admits to membership farmers, farmer laborers, mechanics, doctors, ministers of the gospel, ladies and boys of sixteen."[4] Alliance organizers were trying to pocket the membership and initiation dues of the gullible farmers and were no more than "mountebank frauds and humbugs," charged a hostile observer.[5] Alliance advocates defended the respectability of their order and the Bibb County Alliance passed a resolution condemning its detractor.[6] This was perhaps the first in what was to prove a long line of condemnations, censures, and defamatory resolutions passed on the part of both the Alliance and its critics.

The composition of the Alliance helped shape its policies. Many farmers, who either owned only a small amount of land or were tenants, became enthusiastic members. In addition, many large farmers joined the order. In some instances affiliation with the Alliance was a group action. In Marshall County there were various farmers' clubs that passed *en masse* into the movement, and in Tuscaloosa County the Alliance leaders were the same men who had been active in the Alabama State Grange. One study has revealed that Elmore County Alliance members were more economically solvent than their Democratic counterparts.[7]

Ministers, especially rural Baptists, were interested in the Alliance. Samuel M. Adams of Bibb County was State Alliance president and also fulfilled his clerical duties as Baptist minister. The Reverend J. M. Loftin, a Bullock County minister, was an Alliance leader, and the same was true of John L. Stuart, a Covington County Baptist minister. The Reverend A. J. Hearn of Choctaw County, a Baptist,

---

[3] N. A. Dunning (ed.), *Farmer's Alliance History and Agricultural Digest* (Washington, 1891), 237.
[4] Centreville *Bibb Blade,* Apr. 7, 1887.
[5] Montgomery *Advertiser,* July 14, 1887.
[6] Centreville *Bibb Blade,* Aug. 4, 1887.
[7] Thomas Kermit Hearn, "The Populist Movement in Marshall County" (unpublished Master's thesis, University of Alabama, University, 1935), 24; Houston Cole, "Populism in Tusacloosa County" (unpublished Master's thesis, University of Alabama, 1927), 44; O. M. Bratton, "Elmore County Politics, 1890–1900" (unpublished Master's thesis, University of Alabama, 1938), *passim.*

proved an active Alliance worker.[8] Once the organization entered
politics, people without agricultural connections supported it, but
in general the response to the Alliance was confined to farmers, white
and black, with both large and small farmers joining in large numbers.

The first state organization proved impermanent. This necessitated the calling of a second state convention in August, 1887. The
strong Bibb County Alliance selected the red-haired and fiery-tem-
pered divine, S. M. Adams, as chairman of its delegation. The meeting
also recommended that the *Alliance News,* published at Calera, Shelby
County, be made the state organ for the Alliance. The paper became
the first official journal and the first of many Alliance and Populist
newspapers in Alabama. Adams told his fellow members that the moral
and educational influence of the Alliance was "the next thing to
the church of Christ."[9]

Over three thousand people attended the state meeting which
convened at Cave Spring in Madison County. Another state organization was formed. Adams was elected president and delegates were
selected to attend the national meeting at Shreveport, Louisiana
in October, 1887. These delegates were instructed to apply for admission into the national order, an application which was duly made and
granted.[10]

The Alliance continued to expand. An editor observed that the
existence of the Alliance was "in itself convincing proof that the
farmers of the country need both protection, and cooperation among
themselves to secure the benefits and privileges to which they are
entitled."[11] The organization's rapid growth made it difficult to get
enough organizers into the field to meet the demand. The Alliance
had indeed "arrived" when Senator John Tyler Morgan tendered
his regrets at being unable to attend a Shelby County Alliance barbecue in 1888. His letter of apology, praising the organization, was

[8] Joel Leontz Bates, "Politics In Bullock County, 1890 to 1900" (unpublished
Master's thesis, University of Alabama, 1942), 18; Gladys S. Love, "Politics in
Covington County, Alabama from 1890 to 1900" (unpublished Master's thesis, University of Alabama, 1941), 9.
[9] Centreville *Bibb Blade,* Aug., 4, 1887. For recent appraisals of the Alliance and
Populist press see Charles G. Summersell, "Kolb and the Populist Revolt as Viewed
by Newspapers," *Alabama Historical Quarterly,* XIX, 375–394 (Fall-Winter, 1957); William W.
Rogers, "Alabama's Reform Press: Militant Spokesman for Agrarian Revolt," *Agricultural History,* XXXIV, 62–70 (Apr., 1960).
[10] Huntsville *Daily Independent,* Aug. 4, 1887; Dunning, 237.
[11] Troy *Enquirer,* Aug. 13, 1887.

printed on the front page of the Montgomery *Advertiser*.[12] As Alliances were established across the state, enthusiasm for the program was strongly evident. The order was welcomed into Monroe County because "Necessity is the mother of invention and the Farmers' Alliance is her offspring which is ordained to be the Moses that is ultimately to lead our farmers out of the bondage of Debt, though the journey may be long and tedious."[13]

The Alliance was weakest in the Black Belt, the richest and most extensive agricultural section of Alabama. A considerable portion of the farming lands in the Black Belt was owned by merchants or professional men who lived in the cities and hired tenant farmers to operate their lands. The owners were not farmers and, seeing no benefit in the Alliance for themselves, were inclined to discourage rather than promote the organization. Another reason for the failure of the Alliance to make deeper inroads in the Black Belt was that almost all of the farming in the region was done by Negroes. Although Alliances were quickly organized for the Negroes, they never had equal status with those of the white citizens. There were many Alliance members in the Black Belt, but there was not present the spontaneous enthusiasm that existed in other sections. The reasons for this were racial and economic.[14]

The movement permeated every section of rural Alabama. Frequently, the county seats, which were no more than villages themselves, served only as meeting places for the county groups. The real strength of the order lay in the remote hamlets and communities with picturesque names, such as Midway, Perote, Inverness, Farriorville, Bug Hall, Aberfoil, Indian Creek, Chennunuggee, and Greenwood in Bullock County.[15] The Alliance was so well received that State Lecturer B. W. Groce of Talladega County was treated as a celebrity wherever he went.[16] An advocate said of the Alliance, "It has gone before the public with its principles clearly defined, its mission being to free the farmers from the oppression of debt, restore the country to cash basis, to bring prosperity to the farming interest and hap-

---

[12] July 15, 1888.

[13] Monroeville *Monroe Journal*, Jan. 4, 1889.

[14] See William W. Rogers, "The Negro Alliance in Alabama," *Journal of Negro History*, XLV, 38–44 (Jan. 1960).

[15] Union Springs *Herald*, March 20, 1889.

[16] Carrollton *West Alabamian*, July 24, 1889. Frequently, as in Pickens County, Groce and other lecturers had little to do other than commend the work already in progress.

piness to the farmers['] home[s]."[17] This belief in future relief from economic distress and in victory over the authors of their trouble contributed to the loyalty that the farmers had for their order.

A significant increase in the membership of the Alliance occurred in 1889. The Alabama State Alliance met at Auburn, site of the Agricultural and Mechanical College. This meeting was attended by national agricultural leaders and such state leaders as Commissioner of Agriculture Reuben F. Kolb. Among several matters considered was the proposed merger with the Agricultural Wheel, a national farm organization somewhat similar to the Alliance but more militantly inclined toward politics. Its chief strength in Alabama was in the Tennessee Valley, but even there it had been eclipsed in popularity by the Alliance. The numerical increase and power that this union promised offset any objections, and the Alliance voted to unite.[18]

The phenomenal growth of the order made an accurate estimate of its membership difficult to chronicle. By late 1889 the concensus of state newspapers was that the Alliance had between 120,000 and 125,000 members and 3,000 lodges.[19] This was perhaps the period of its greatest strength.

The Farmers' Alliance emphasized the importance of a social and educational program. This is attested by the barbecues and picnics that were usually held in conjunction with alliance meetings. The Mulberry Alliance at Ivey Creek Church, Autauga County, held enjoyable meetings because, as one satisfied member said, he had "plenty to eat as we always do at that place."[20] At Blackman's Grove in Calhoun County a barbecue in 1891 was attended by 1,000 persons.[21] Most of the food was prepared by the women who formed a considerable part of the Alliance membership. A member remarked "our heart honors and reveres woman alike for her goodness and wisdom, and we are delighted to meet her in our Alliance halls."[22] An ardent woman member of the Alliance vowed that she and others would stand by the order "until shouts of victory shall sound throughout the

[17] Newton *Messenger*, March 2, 1889. For a list of the declarations and purposes of the order see Eufaula *Weekly Times and News*, May 2, 1889.

[18] Opelika *Semi-Weekly Democrat*, Aug. 9, 1889. The merger was complete by October (see Marion *Standard*, Oct. 30, 1889; Moulton *Advertiser*, Oct. 31, 1889).

[19] Troy *Enquirer*, Aug. 17, 1889; Anniston *Evening Watchman*, Sept. 5, 1889; Greensboro *Alabama Beacon*, Sept. 10, 1889; Union Springs *Herald*, Sept. 11, 1889. The Grove Hill *Clarke County Democrat*, Oct. 3, 1889, asserted that the Alliance had 175,000 members.

[20] Prattville *Progress*, Aug. 1, 1890.

[21] Anniston *Weekly Times*, July 30, 1891.

[22] Troy *Enquirer*, Jan. 26, 1889.

farming world."[23] Gatherings of the order were lively and well attended. "Piney Woods," a Conecuh County member, wrote, "These Alliance meetings are schools that will educate the farmers in the arts, skill, science and experience, that will improve all farming methods with such other interests as are of vital importance."[24]

Alliance leaders supported the Agricultural and Mechanical College at Auburn and advocated a better secondary educational system. The Alliance administered a high school in Choctaw County in 1891.[25] As late as 1893 the Alliance Cooperative School at Echo, Dale County, had two male professors and a woman music teacher. The Echo school had 110 students and held sessions of seven months' duration.[26] The vitality of the order was demonstrated at the various state fairs and local exhibitions. Almost without exception a day was set aside to honor the Alliance. At the 1889 Southern Exposition at Montgomery an Alliance wedding was held with the trousseau of the bride and the suit of the groom being made of cotton bagging.[27]

Important as the educational and social activities of the Alliance were, its most significant work was in its ambitious program to bring economic relief to the farmers. There was speculation that the organization would declare war against all businessmen. One farmer denied this and explained, "The Alliance is not here to slay the merchants, but to co-operate with them, to publish glad tidings of peace to all men."[28] As a class beset by agricultural surpluses, low prices, and mortgage foreclosures, farmers subscribed wholeheartedly to "Beat II's" contention that "the farmer has as much right to make a profit on anything he sells as any other man—regardless of race, color, . . . or present condition of servitude."[29]

The Alliance did not undertake a sustained attack on the railroads and seemed satisfied that the freight rates of such lines as the Louisville & Nashville were not too discriminatory.[30] The severely depressed times made economic salvation for farmers difficult to achieve. When

---

[23] *Southern Farmer* (Athens, Ga.), IV, 205 (Apr., 1889).

[24] Evergreen *Star*, Sept. 4, 1890.

[25] Butler *Choctaw Advocate*, Sept. 2, 1891.

[26] Ozark *Banner*, Jan. 5, 1893.

[27] Brewton *Standard Gauge*, Nov. 11, 1889.

[28] Monroeville *Monroe Journal*, Feb. 1, 1889.

[29] Eufaula *Weekly Times and News*, Sept. 6, 1888.

[30] Grove Hill *Clarke County Democrat*, Nov. 27, 1890; Montgomery *Advertiser*, Oct. 29, 1889. For a full discussion of this point see James F. Doster, "Were Populists Against Railroad Corporations? The Case of Alabama," *Journal of Southern History*, XX, 395–399 (Aug., 1954), and *Railroads in Alabama Politics, 1875–1914* (Tuscaloosa, 1957), 43.

the Alliance attempted co-operative programs withholding cotton from the market until prices rose, the desperate need for cash, even at dictated terms of unfairness, often forced many farmers to sell. Faced with such problems, Alliance members determined to enter business for themselves. Occasionally, a lodge sought relief by resorting to a strict regimen of austerity. The Pike County China Grove Alliance resolved to "buy for clothing nothing but that which is essential for warmth and comfort and guard against everything which has a tendency to extravagance."[31]

So extensive were the Alliance's ventures that there was scarcely a county in the state unaffected by its business activities. A typical pattern was that of Bibb County where a co-operative association, complete with constitution and by-laws, was organized. A general manager and board of directors were selected to operate a co-operative trade and mercantile business. Money was to be raised by selling shares, and any profits were to be divided among the stockholders. Those who held no shares were to be entitled to half the net profits arising from their purchases.[32] Rather than go into business for themselves, some county Alliances designated particular merchants with whom to do business. This guaranteed the businessman a significant volume of business and was a strong inducement to "put his figures down to the limit of reason, to the live and let live policy."[33]

The most widely used and patronized Alliance business enterprise was the Alliance warehouse. This gave the Alliance an opportunity to deal in agricultural commodities, principally cotton, and to avoid the risks of operating mercantile businesses. By 1888 warehouses were flourishing at Opelika and Ozark. The next year St. Clair County had three cotton warehouses. Frequently, the threat of opening a warehouse was sufficient to secure a reduction in the price of cotton storage from established firms.[34] A sectional warehouse at Eufaula provided cheap storage facilities for Alabama and Georgia farmers.[35] The various establishments appear to have effected considerable savings for

[31] Union Springs *Bullock County Reporter,* Feb. 1, 1889.
[32] Centreville *Bibb Blade,* Oct. 27, 1887; Sept. 27, 1888.
[33] Brewton *Standard Gauge,* Jan. 17, 1889.
[34] See Opelika *Democrat,* July 26, 1888; Ozark *Southern Star,* Oct. 31, 1888; *Southern Cultivator* (Atlanta, Ga.), XLVII, 504 (Oct., 1889); Union Springs *Bullock County Reporter,* July 27, 1888.
[35] Eufaula *Weekly Times and News,* June 13, 20, Aug. 8, 1889. Frequently, as at Evergreen, the Alliance operated both a store and a warehouse (see Evergreen *Star,* March 20, 1890).

Alliance members and lasted longer than any of the order's business enterprises.[36]

The Clayton Fertilizer Company of Barbour County was sponsored by the Alliance.[37] At Centre, Cherokee County, the Alliance raised funds to put a cotton factory in operation.[38] More ambitious, the Bullock County Alliance made plans to build an oil mill and a cotton factory at Union Springs. At Selma an Alliance bank was capitalized at $100,000.[39] There was a strong movement for the State Alliance to set up a state bank, but this was not done. Everywhere, as in Geneva County, the attitude was that business "promises great things for the alliance. . . ."[40] In Butler County a manufacturing and commercial company, capitalized at $125,000, was organized.[41] The southwestern counties attempted to revive the old Grange policy of operating a boat on the Tombigbee River in an effort to secure better rates. Although put into effect, the operation did not last long.[42] A visitor at a Choctaw County Alliance store remarked, "I found [it] completely stocked with a full assortment of goods to supply the farmers' needs."[43]

The magic word Alliance had wide appeal and was soon associated with businesses that appropriated the name for its commercial value. There were Alliance hotels at Montgomery and Monroeville, while a Negro café called "The Alliance Restaurant" was opened at Union Springs.[44] Many warehouses took the name Alliance, whether or not owned or sponsored by the local lodge. The line was finally drawn when the Dale County Alliance passed resolutions condemning the Alliance Bar in Ozark.[45]

The Alliance also established the Alabama State Exchange. This

---

[36] See Ozark *Banner Advertiser,* May 9, 1895; Eufaula *Times and News,* June 13, 1895. At Dothan in Henry (now Houston) County opposition to an Alliance warehouse resulted in a gunfight in which two men were killed and another wounded (see Newton *Messenger,* Oct. 26, 1889).

[37] Clayton *Courier,* March 2, 1889.

[38] *Southern Cultivator,* XLVII, 26 (Jan., 1889).

[39] Union Springs *Herald,* Apr. 1, 1889.

[40] Geneva *Record,* May 15, 1889.

[41] Union Springs *Bullock County Reporter,* Oct. 18, 1889.

[42] Grove Hill *Clarke County Democrat,* Nov. 7, 1889; Feb. 20, 1890. The counties involved included Washington, Clarke, Choctaw, and Marengo.

[43] Butler *Choctaw Advocate,* May 6, 1891.

[44] Monroeville *Monroe Journal,* Nov. 1, 1889; Aug. 29, 1890. See also *Alliance Journal* (Montgomery), I, 23 (Dec., 1889).

[45] Ozark *Southern Star,* Feb. 5, 1890.

was the largest business enterprise ever attempted by any farm group in Alabama, and it proved to be an operation of considerable importance. In 1888 a slate of officers and board of directors was selected, and Dr. John S. Bird of Henry County was made president.[46] It was incorporated early in 1889, and had almost unlimited privileges to engage in business. The capital stock of $250,000 was to be divided into equal shares of $100 each. Subscriptions for shares of stock were to be made by primary Alliances, rather than by individuals, and each group was to be entitled to one trustee stockholder who was to represent his county in the Exchange. Meetings of the stockholders were to be held in conjunction with the State Alliance. A seven-man board of directors, elected by the stockholders from their number, made policy for the Exchange. This board of directors elected the Exchange president and other officers.[47]

Montgomery won out over other cities as the site for the Exchange and operations were begun in 1889. A branch was later opened at Birmingham.[48] The Exchange functioned as a purchasing agency through which the orders of the farmers were received and executed. No goods or material were stocked. Rather, the Exchange purchased almost entirely from Montgomery merchants. The Exchange also made plans to engage in manufacturing by establishing factories to produce cotton bagging, farm implements, plows, and cottonseed oil.[49] President Bird announced that the Exchange would, in its capacity as purchasing agent, advance the necessary funds to farmers in order to enable them to buy for cash, thus protecting them from "grasping monopolies, blood sucking trusts, heartless usurers and extortionists."[50]

The biggest transactions of the Exchange were in cotton. In October, 1889 General Manager George F. Gaither claimed that the organization averaged cash receipts of from $2,000 to $5,000 a day.[51] In 1889 it boasted that it had done a business of $100,000 and in 1890 $140,000.[52] Despite a general rise in fertilizer prices in 1890 over

---

[46] Union Springs *Bullock County Reporter,* Sept. 9, 1888.
[47] Alabama *Acts,* 1888–1889 (Montgomery, 1889), 287–289.
[48] Greensboro *Alabama Beacon,* May 28, 1889; Montgomery *Advertiser,* July 4, 1889; Eufaula *Times and News,* Aug. 14, 21, 1890.
[49] Troy *Enquirer,* Apr. 20, 1889.
[50] Eufaula *Weekly Times and News,* July 25, 1889.
[51] Montgomery *Advertiser,* Oct. 29, 1889.
[52] Carrollton *West Alabamian,* Aug. 12, 1891; Montgomery *Advertiser,* Aug. 8, 1891.

those of 1889, the Exchange made purchases for farmers at prices below those of 1889.[53] In 1889 the Exchange purchased a cotton factory near Florence in North Alabama. This was done during the campaign to break the jute-bagging monopoly. The factory was supposed to manufacture cotton bagging that could be used as a substitute for jute. New equipment had to be purchased and the bagging proved inferior to that obtainable from other sources. In 1890 the plant was closed and the machinery sold.[54]

The fortunes of the Exchange deteriorated rapidly and the agency ceased to be effective after 1891. There was some evidence of mismanagement, but the major reason for its failure was that it attempted too much. Many farmers never really understood how the Exchange functioned. Although supposedly limited to dealing with Alliances, the Exchange permitted individual farmers to make purchases and receive advances. This meant additional bookkeeping and gave a wide margin for error and mismanagement by people who were not well schooled in business operations.

By 1890 the economic program of the Alliance was faltering on all fronts. The members began to accept the idea that economic redress lay in politics rather than business. Alliance business ventures failed for the same basic reasons that the earlier Grange co-operatives of the 1870's had failed. When an Alliance store at Calera in Shelby County went bankrupt, a paper recorded, "Bad management at the outset is alleged as the cause of its unsuccessful career."[55] At least two co-operative stores, one at Heflin, Calhoun County, and another in Choctaw County, were burned by incendiaries.[56] Democratic papers used co-operative store failures to underscore their belief that business should be reserved for businessmen. In 1892 a Tuscaloosa Alliance store closed and an editor wrote, "It seems that people never learn from the school of experience, until it is too late to be of any use to them."[57]

Some Alliance businesses proved profitable, but the majority enjoyed only brief success. Price wars by other merchants, mismanagement,

---

[53] Prattville *Progress*, March 21, 1890, quoting Montgomery *Alliance Herald*.

[54] Monroeville *Monroe Journal*, Nov. 1, 1889; Grove Hill *Clarke County Democrat*, Sept. 18, 1890.

[55] Opelika *Semi-Weekly Democrat*, Aug. 2, 1889.

[56] Union Springs *Herald*, Nov. 11, 1891; Butler *Choctaw Alliance*, Jan. 21, 1896.

[57] Union Springs *Herald*, June 1, 1892.

and the continuing depression were all factors in their failure. Yet the co-operatives were evidence of the order's determination to help the farmers. The extent of its ventures indicated that many farmers mistrusted the regularly constituted channels of commerce. If the Alliance failed in most of its efforts, it was successful in its major war against the jute-bagging trust. By raising their prices in 1888, the jute manufacturers saddled debt-ridden farmers with additional expenses. In retaliation the State Alliance embarked on a campaign to substitute cotton bagging for jute. This was done and, by an organized boycott of jute, the Alliance forced the price down and achieved a major economic victory in 1890. Exchange General Manager Gaither announced that jute had dropped from thirteen cents to five cents.[58]

Unlike the Grange, Alliance business failures did not cause the order to decline rapidly. As the farmers abandoned their economic ventures, they became increasingly political. Rather than dispersing, they united more closely otherwise to achieve their goals. From 1887 to 1892 the Alliance was a non-political order. Even after it became an integral part of the Populist movement, it maintained its separate existence down to 1897. It is significant that it did not become political until its economic program failed.

There seems little doubt that the Farmers' Alliance gave the farmers a genuine feeling of brotherhood and made them proud of the historic role of the farmer. Their annual conventions and numerous county and local meetings were important social events. The order sponsored schools and fairs and concentrated on an economic program. It was a statewide movement that appealed to all farmers. A South Alabama editor accurately wrote that the Farmers' Alliance "was the child of discontent . . . nurtured on calamity, the chief ingredient of which was the farm mortgage."[59]

---

[58] Eufaula *Times and News,* July 17, 1890.
[59] Monroeville *Monroe Journal,* June 11, 1896.

JOSEPH A. FRY

Governor Johnston's Attempt to Unseat Senator Morgan, 1899–1900

In "one of the most exciting political contests ever waged in Alabama,"[1] Governor Joseph F. Johnston sought unsuccessfully to unseat U.S. Senator John Tyler Morgan. The bitter contest produced high personal drama. Nearing his seventy-sixth birthday and the end of his fourth Senate term, Morgan had established a national reputation as an expansionist and a staunch defender of Southern interests. Although age and declining health had begun to diminish a once-boundless store of energy, he was hardly ready to retire with his quest for a Nicaragua Canal still unrealized. Johnston, a former Morgan protégé, had been a key member of the party for a quarter century, had chaired the state Democratic Executive Committee in 1874, and in 1895–1896 had assembled a formidable freesilver coalition that defused Alabama Populism and elected him governor. By 1900 the fifty-seven-year-old governor aspired to Morgan's Senate seat. For these old friends to become enemies seemed almost fratricidal; it was an ugly "family row" within the Alabama Democracy.[2]

The struggle, however, embodied far more than two political ca-

This essay was published in *The Alabama Review*, XXXVIII (October 1985).

The author would like to thank the American Philosophical Society and the University of Nevada, Las Vegas, Research Council for aid in the researching of this article. He also expresses appreciation to Paul Burns, Brent Tarter, and the *Alabama Review*'s referee for their helpful readings of the manuscript.

[1] New York *Times*, November 24, 1899.
[2] Mobile *Register*, November 22, 1899.

reers. Control of the Democratic party and a constitutional convention to disfranchise blacks were also at stake. Morgan led the "Big Mule–Black Belt" coalition of north Alabama industrialists and Black Belt planters who dominated the party and favored a constitutional convention. Johnston, in turn, headed a reform faction that appealed to Populists and other disaffected groups and opposed a convention. Finally, numerous contemporary observers interpreted the battle as a test of Southern attitudes on U.S. expansion and William Jennings Bryan's 1900 presidential prospects.

As confrontation loomed, both men boasted impressive credentials. After service in the Confederate Army Governor Johnston had moved to Selma, where he practiced law and chaired the Dallas County and the state Democratic Executive Committees. Johnston's first tenure as state chairman had been a controversial one. In 1874 he both presided over the Democratic campaign that redeemed the state from Republican control and resigned under pressure. He had angered the party by offering to share the fees from a claims bill with Republican Congressman Charles Pelham of Talladega. Morgan defended Johnston but could not counteract the party's general dissatisfaction. Although the episode revealed a tendency to mix personal and public affairs that would subsequently prove disastrous to Johnston, this misfortune proved only temporary. By 1878 he had regained the state chairmanship. Six years later he demonstrated a keen eye for political and business opportunity by moving to Birmingham, then developing into Alabama's industrial center. Johnston led in this growth, first as president of the Alabama State Bank and later as head of the Jasper Land Company and the Sloss Iron and Steel Company.[3]

These lucrative business activities did not preclude continued political involvement. After loyally, if impatiently, accepting the party's decisions to nominate Thomas Goode Jones for governor in 1890 and 1892 and William C. Oates in 1894, he captured the prize in 1896. He had emphasized free silver, honest elections, support for public education, and the reincorporation of Populist and other party bolters. Morgan had been one of his most influential backers in

[3] Lorena Dale Parrott, "The Public Career of Joseph Forney Johnston" (M.A. thesis, University of Alabama, 1936), 1–5; Ethel Armes, *The Story of Coal and Iron in Alabama* (Birmingham, 1910), 341–42, 347–49; Montgomery *Advertiser,* November 19, 1899.

both of the latter campaigns, and the senator was convinced that
in extending his aid he had "never done a better work for Alabama."[4] Morgan's confidence seemed warranted. Much of Johnston's
first three years as governor featured the typically Bourbon policies
of economy in government, strict valuation of property and collection of taxes, and encouragement of Northern investors. But his
administration was also identified with Alabama's emerging Progressive movement. Johnston augmented mine inspections, regulated
insurance companies, resisted indiscriminate tax exemptions for corporations, and called for an extension of the railroad commission's
powers.[5]

While the governor's long public service, acute political instincts,
and colorful oratory made him a formidable opponent, he faced a
virtual institution in John Tyler Morgan. Termed by newspapers as
the "greatest democrat in the senate" and "one of the greatest men the south has produced since the war," Morgan, in the opinion
of one Alabama editor made Johnston seem "Liliputian" by comparison.[6] Morgan had begun his political career as a lieutenant of
William Lowndes Yancey in Alabama's secession movement, and he
had become a brigadier general in the Confederate Army. After the
Civil War he, too, had returned to Selma, resumed his law practice,
and emerged as a leading opponent of Republican Reconstruction.
First elected to the Senate in 1876, he had earned a reputation as a

[4] Parrott, "Joseph Forney Johnston," 7–38; Julian Carlton Braswell, "Senator
Joseph Forney Johnston: Brinksmanship and Progressivism" (M.A. thesis, Auburn
University, 1969), 9–19; John T. Morgan to Joseph F. Johnston, December 4, 1896,
Cocke-Johnston Papers, Alabama State Department of Archives and History, Montgomery. This collection of papers should be distinguished from the Joseph Forney
Johnston Papers that are also housed at the state archives. See also John T. Morgan
to Chappell Cory, November 17, 1896, Chappell Cory Papers, Alabama State Department of Archives and History, Montgomery. John T. Morgan, Joseph F. Johnston,
and Alabama State Department of Archives and History will be cited as JTM, JFJ,
and ASDAH, respectively.

[5] Sheldon Hackney, *Populism to Progressivism in Alabama* (Princeton, 1969), 138; Parrott,
"Joseph Forney Johnston," 45–64; David Alan Harris, "Racists and Reformers: A Study
of Progressivism in Alabama, 1896–1911" (Ph.D. thesis, University of North Carolina
at Chapel Hill, 1967), 59–109; Allen Woodrow Jones, "A History of the Direct Primary in
Alabama, 1840–1903" (Ph.D. dissertation, University of Alabama, 1964), 229–36. On the
mix of progress and tradition in Southern Progressivism, see Dewey W. Grantham,
Southern Progressivism: The Reconciliation of Progress and Tradition (Knoxville, 1983), 34, 47,
passim.

[6] Washington *Times* and Knoxville *Sentinel* quoted in unidentified clipping, n.d., John
Tyler Morgan Papers, Manuscript Division, Library of Congress, Washington, D.C.;
Tuscaloosa *Times* quoted in Mobile *Register*, November 24, 1899.

tireless, well-informed legislator, a knowledgeable constitutional lawyer, and a "long distance talker." Much of his talking had been
devoted to his pet project—the building of a Nicaragua Canal; but
he had also supported late-nineteenth-century economic and territorial expansion, favored free silver and a low tariff, and opposed all
potentially anti-Southern, domestic legislation.[7] By 1900 his forty
years of public service had already spanned several of the most tumultuous periods in Alabama history, and he had been an important
actor in each.

Johnston had been mentioned for the Senate as early as 1895, and
by September 1898 he contemplated the race. Although he regretted
to conflict with Morgan, friends assured him that he would "best
the field," because Morgan had given "too little attention" to
Alabama and had "lost contact with the present leaders." The
governor's ambition became increasingly evident in early 1899. Supporters warned Morgan of Johnston's "strenuous scheming, and
unscrupulous efforts"; Johnston was using his position as governor
for political gain and "to arrange for his friends to be elected to
the General Assembly." One Democrat friendly with both Morgan and
Johnston recounted two conversations with the governor. When
approached on the question of his candidacy for the U.S. Senate,
Johnston "*shied*." In response to a subsequent query regarding the
Senate Johnston again "turned the subject," convincing his
interrogator that he would make the race.[8]

This nascent rivalry became entangled with the movement for a
constitutional convention to disfranchise Alabama blacks. Johnston
had endorsed constitutional revision in 1892 and 1897 and had signed
the 1898 bill providing for the convention; but he reconsidered as
he eyed Morgan's Senate seat. In his successful campaigns the governor
had appealed effectively to Populists, to former followers of Reuben
F. Kolb who had recently challenged the conservative Democratic
establishment, and to north Alabama whites generally. Such support

[7] For JTM's career see August Carl Radke, "John Tyler Morgan, An Expansionist
Senator, 1877–1907" (Ph.D. dissertation, University of Washington, 1953), and James
Marvin Anders, "Senatorial Career of John Tyler Morgan" (Ph.D. dissertation,
George Peabody College for Teachers, 1956).

[8] JFJ to Billie, September 5, 1898, Joseph Forney Johnston Papers, ASDAH; Parrott, "Joseph Forney Johnston," 86; Thomas Carruth to JTM, February 24,
1899, R. T. Ervin to JTM, April 10, 1899, Sam'l Will John to JTM, April 20, 1899,
Morgan Papers.

was essential in any contest against Morgan. When these groups worried that suffrage restriction would eliminate both the blacks and less-affluent whites, Johnston declared for a specific constitutional amendment rather than a convention.[9]

Subsequent events solidified Johnston's resolve. Numerous anti-Johnston gold Democrats were selected as convention delegates, and opposition to the convention rose in north Alabama. Meeting in late March, the Democratic state convention narrowly voted to make the constitutional convention a "party issue," despite the opposition of Johnston's backers. With his political enemies pushing for the convention and his allies protesting against it, Johnston acted boldly. After polling the legislators and determining that a majority would vote to repeal the convention bill, he called a special legislative session for May 3, 1900.[10]

An overwhelmingly adverse press reaction accurately reflected the position of the majority of Alabama's Democratic leadership,[11] and no Democrat was more outraged than John Tyler Morgan. The old senator's opposition to black suffrage was longstanding and unqualified.[12] When the state Democratic Executive Committee met in Montgomery in April to censure Johnston, Morgan sent an unequivocal telegram: "The democrats can only march straight to the front. To recede or to hesitate invites disaster to the white voters." The legislature, Morgan continued, had "exhausted its powers" with the enabling bill; its action was "irrevocable," and the process had passed to the people who could vote for or against a convention. The executive committee greeted his message with "deafening applause."[13]

Morgan elaborated his position in a public letter, stating that the

[9] Birmingham *Age-Herald*, January 24, 1893; Malcom Cook McMillan, *Constitutional Development in Alabama, 1798–1901: A Study in Politics, the Negro, and Sectionalism* (Chapel Hill, 1955), 250–55; Harris, "Racists and Reformers," 123–32.

[10] McMillan, *Constitutional Development in Alabama*, 255–56; Hackney, *Populism to Progressivism*, 165–67; JFJ to The People, October 7, 1899, in Montgomery *Journal*, October 7, 1899.

[11] See for example Birmingham *Age-Herald*, February 22, April 12, 1899; Montgomery *Advertiser*, March 11, 1899; Mobile *Register*, April 18, 22, 1899.

[12] See for example, JTM, "Address Delivered by Gen. Jno. T. Morgan, Before the Erosophic and Philomathic Societies, of the University of Alabama, July 6th, 1875" (n.p., n.d.), 14–15; JTM, "Shall Negro Majorities Rule?" *Forum*, VI (February 1889); JTM, "Remarks on Negro Suffrage Submitted to the Members of the Constitutional Convention of Alabama" (Washington, D.C., 1901).

[13] McMillan, *Constitutional Development in Alabama*, 256; New York *Times*, April 23, 1899; Birmingham *Age-Herald*, April 22, 1899.

governor had no role in the process of amending the constitution. The legislature approved an enabling bill, the people voted for a convention, and the convention delegates revised the document. Once each group acted, "the jurisdiction of the next" became a "constitutional right" that could not be changed. Therefore, the legislature had no authority to repeal its previous action. Morgan argued that Alabama could and should disfranchise blacks, and he suggested a $2 poll tax and rigorous screening by local registrars as the appropriate mechanisms. As long as black suffrage continued, there would be "friction, discord, and fraud." Clearly referring to Johnston, Morgan regretted that "party jealousies, more personal than patriotic," blocked disfranchisement.[14]

At the urging of the chairman of the state Democratic Executive Committee Morgan also traveled to Montgomery on May 2 for a mass meeting opposing repeal of the convention bill. He joined his colleague in the U.S. Senate, Edmund W. Pettus, and former governors Thomas Goode Jones and William C. Oates on the stage at the Montgomery Theater. In an hour-long speech he repeated his brief against further gubernatorial or legislative action, emphasized the need for white unity and supremacy, and pointedly criticized Johnston. Asserting that Alabamians were refighting the battle of 1874, he condemned the black man's political participation and asked why some modern governors seemed to "need him." After suggesting that Johnston's political ambition exceeded his ability, he stressed that race, not monetary policy, was the critical consideration. Morgan concluded by reading Johnston out of the party: anyone who had defied the party's convention and executive committee was "no democrat."[15]

Governor Johnston's rebuttal was equally sharp revealing that more than the constitutional convention was at stake. Addressing the special session he denied that the executive committee could dictate to the governor and legislature, and he berated the committee for seeking to "shackle" voters. Given their refusal to trust white Democrats to vote intelligently, did it not "ill-become" committee members to advocate disfranchising blacks? Since white supremacy was "complete and all pervading," he found

[14] JTM to Sam Will John, April 23, 1899, in Birmingham *Age-Herald*, May 2, 1899.
[15] Robert J. Lowe to JTM, April 24, 1899, and Francis L. Pettus to JTM, April 26, 1899, Morgan Papers; Montgomery *Advertiser*, May 3, 1899; Birmingham *Age-Herald*, May 3, 1899.

no reason for haste. Turning to the mass meeting, he flayed the attempt to coerce the legislators and denounced Morgan's and Pettus's "gratuitous" advice.[16]

Morgan's oratory proved unavailing. Johnston had the votes, and the General Assembly repealed the convention bill. As the sparring continued into early fall, the governor concentrated on deflecting charges that he had endangered white supremacy. In a July letter to the New York *Independent* he not only reiterated his anti-convention arguments but also endorsed a suffrage change since continued black voting provided opportunities for disruptive "agitators."[17]

Johnston backers also seized upon an interview in the Washington *Post,* in which Morgan suggested that Bryan might not be the most available Democratic presidential candidate for 1900. The senator declared his support for free silver but bemoaned the futility of party division on the money question. Without sufficient pro-silver votes in Congress nothing could secure free coinage. Morgan's solution was to nominate a man in whom all Democrats had confidence and who would agree to sign a silver bill if Congress approved. Morgan would "then go about the business of electing free silver men to congress."[18]

Both his friends and enemies immediately pronounced the interview a "great mistake."[19] Johnston had made an unsuccessful overture for Bryan's support the previous April, and he followed Morgan's comments with a strong endorsement of the Nebraskan. The pro-Johnston Montgomery *Journal* charged that the senator had abandoned Bryan and the Democrats' 1896 Chicago platform and deserted to the "Eastern democrats." Even the friendly Birmingham *Age-Herald* scolded Morgan and predicted that his strategy would divide the party in the South. Realizing his blunder, Morgan hastily explained his position. After reaffirming his support of the Chicago platform and praising Bryan's 1896 campaign, he repeated his doubts about Bryan's chances for election.[20]

[16] *Journal of House of Representatives of the State of Alabama, Extra Session of 1899* (Jacksonville, 1899), 9–20; Montgomery *Advertiser,* May 3, 1899.

[17] JFJ, "Negro Suffrage in Alabama," New York *Independent,* LI (1899), 1535–37.

[18] Washington *Post,* July 11, 1899.

[19] Albert Elmore to John W. A. Sanford, July 17, 1899, John W. A. Sanford Papers, ASDAH; W. J. Wood to JFJ, July 16, 1899, Governor Joseph F. Johnston Papers, ASDAH.

[20] W. J. Bryan to JFJ, April 22, 1899, Cocke-Johnston Papers; Montgomery *Advertiser,* July 19, 21, 1899; Montgomery *Journal,* July 13, 15, 17, 1899; Birmingham *Age-Herald,* July 13, 15, 1899; New York *Times,* July 22, 1899.

Recognizing that the senator was in an "awkward position," the Montgomery *Journal* elaborated the anti-Morgan case. The *Journal* complained of Morgan's long absences from Alabama, decried his support of imperialism, and belittled his legislative accomplishments and his failure to secure a Nicaragua Canal. The governor's "Evening Echo" concluded its pre-campaign blitz by dismissing Morgan as a "feeble old man" surrounded by a "coterie of amateur politicians" and advising him to return to Washington.[21]

Johnston's activities extended beyond newspaper sniping. He maintained an extensive political correspondence and on September 29 distributed a circular letter designed to gauge preferences for governor, senator, and president. While he did not mention Morgan specifically, his declaration for "Bryan and the Chicago platform, and against Imperialism" obviously struck at the senator. To accentuate his opposition to Morgan's expansionism, the governor accepted an invitation to become an honorary vice-president of the American Anti-Imperialist League.[22]

Johnston became even more caustic in an early October letter to the *Journal*. Stopping just short of officially declaring his candidacy, he opened with a summary of his accomplishments as governor. By reforming the assessment and collection of state taxes and instituting an economical regime, he had retired a general fund debt of more than $568,000. He boasted of firing corrupt and negligent officials, increasing allocations for education by $350,000, and saving more than $155,000 in the convict lease system. These reforms, Johnston proclaimed, had prompted attacks by disappointed spoilsmen and newspapers "unable to dictate" appointments.[23]

Within the context of another explanation of his calling of the special legislative session, the governor noted that "supposedly wise and venerable men" had argued that the legislature could not repeal the convention bill. Where, Johnston taunted, was the "senior senator" who had promised to fight for the new constitution? Apparently, he and Senator Pettus could "discuss constitutions for Cuba and Hawaii and the Philippines but not for Alabama."

[21] Montgomery *Journal*, July 17, September 8, 25, October 9, 31, 1899; see also John W. DuBose to JFJ, November 13, 15, 1899, Governor Johnston Papers.

[22] Montgomery *Advertiser*, October 1, 1899; Edward Atkinson to JFJ, October 10, 1899, and W. J. Mize to JFJ, October 27, 1899, Governor Johnston Papers.

[23] Montgomery *Journal*, October 7, 1899.

Unable to ignore the popularity of Morgan's Nicaragua Canal project, Johnston endorsed the concept but contended that the senator had done little more than talk during the previous twenty years: "We want a canal full of water, not wind."[24]

Johnston's barbs hit their mark. Morgan complained privately that his opponent had treated him with "unwarranted severity and injustice," and he arraigned Johnston's transparently concealed candidacy as "political bushwacking." Troubled by the "rumors" that Johnston was resorting to "secret practices" to capture his Senate seat, Morgan felt compelled to announce his candidacy for the "first time." He stubbornly maintained, however, that he had "never asked any man, directly or indirectly" for his vote and that he would keep that record intact.[25]

Morgan made this official announcement on August 31, 1899, at Maplesville in Chilton County. Before nearly two thousand admirers the aging legislator declared for Bryan, the Chicago platform, and free silver; explained his prolonged absences from Alabama with the assertion that he worked very hard in Washington; and defended the acquisition of the Philippines. Elaborating on expansionism, Morgan underscored the South's special interest in the acquisition of Hawaii, Cuba, and Puerto Rico. Together with the western territories soon to be made states, these regions would help redress the South's minority positions in the U.S. Senate. More immediately, Manila would replace Liverpool as the entrepot for Alabama cotton en route to Asia. With the construction of the Nicaragua Canal these markets would provide the beginnings of "commercial independence for the cotton growers."[26]

As Morgan and Johnston traded insults, critical maneuvering was under way within the Democratic party. Hoping to bypass the local courthouse cliques, Johnston and his followers had favored a direct primary to choose nominees. When this effort failed, they shifted their attention to procedures for nominating Democratic legislative candidates. Assured of victory in the perfunctory general elections,

[24] *Ibid.*

[25] JTM to [W. H. Denson], October 29, 1899, and JTM to John W. A. Sanford, September 2, 1899, Morgan Papers.

[26] Birmingham *Age-Herald*, September 1, 1899; Washington *Post*, September 1, 1899; see also JTM to Clarke Howell, July 21, 1899, Morgan Papers; JTM to Virginia Clopton, March 31, 1895, Clement C. Clay Papers, Duke University, Durham, N.C.

these nominees would designate Alabama's U.S. senator. By the late 1890s most counties had adopted primaries to choose these candidates, virtually all of whom ran as Morgan or Johnston men. Johnston sought to continue to allow counties to schedule their primaries and conventions, a practice that stretched elections from December 1899 through April 1900. This procedure would have harmed Morgan, who was less physically able to visit all the counties and had responsibilities in Washington. Therefore, it was significant when the state Democratic Executive Committee directed that all county primaries or beat meetings be held on April 14, 1900, and all county conventions on April 21.[27]

Although Johnston resented the "April 'Derby,'" he remained confident. On November 12 he assured supporters that the statewide outlook was "all that I could ask."[28] As Johnston penned this letter, he received a sharp telegram from Morgan, demanding to know if the governor were a candidate and challenging him to a debate. When Johnston agreed, the stage was set for a dramatic confrontation.[29]

Nearly a thousand people jammed into the Athens courthouse square on November 17. Each man spoke for an hour and a half. The governor denied "personal" differences with his old "friend" and asserted that he would never have become a candidate had Morgan retained his "allegiance" to Bryan and free silver. He read from the Washington *Post* interview and charged Morgan with hugging Bryan with one hand while stabbing him with the other. Reiterating his position on constitutional revision, he argued that the Fifteenth Amendment precluded Morgan's call for black disfranchisement. Johnston closed by criticizing U.S. imperialism and asking if Alabamians desired more "dark-skinned people in this country."[30]

Morgan's caustic rejoinder demonstrated how personal he considered the struggle. Recalling his previous support for Johnston, he deemed

[27] Jones, "Direct Primary in Alabama," 172, 238–41; Harris, "Racists and Reformers," 139–41; Birmingham *Age-Herald*, October 11, 1899; Montgomery *Advertiser*, June 7, 1899.
[28] JFJ to M. Walker, November 6, 1899, and JFJ to J. C. McClellan and Ryan Walker, November 12, 1899, Johnston Papers.
[29] JTM to JFJ, November 12, 1899, Governor Johnston Papers; JFJ to JTM, November 13, 1899, Morgan Papers.
[30] Birmingham *Age-Herald*, November 19, 1899; Montgomery *Advertiser*, November 19, 1899.

the governor's delay in announcing his candidacy especially offensive. Rather than running openly, Johnston had clandestinely laid "pipes and underground wires" and fired "smokeless powder." Morgan again explained the Washington *Post* interview and accused Johnston of swinging upon Bryan's "coat tail." How, he asked, could a "converted bank president" be considered a better silver man than he? After defending expansionism, he focused on Johnston's handling of the constitution and race issues. Morgan bluntly asserted that he would inform blacks, "I am in favor of taking away from you the right of suffrage." He then solicited Johnston's position. When the governor replied that he favored "white supremacy," Morgan charged him with evading the question. Warming to his task, he compared Johnston's reversal on the constitutional convention to a "cannibal" eating his "own offspring," and he condemned the governor for forming a black regiment to fight in the Spanish-American War.[31]

In closing his remarks Johnston invited Morgan to continue their debates over the entire state. The old senator promptly agreed, but several observers questioned whether he could withstand the rigors of touring rural Alabama.[32] While it is unclear that Johnston intended to exploit Morgan's poor health, the governor did judge that he was "cleaning up" in the debates.[33]

The fears for Morgan's health seemed justified when he was sick much of the night before the second debate on November 20. Morgan set the tone for another bitter exchange by refusing to shake hands with Johnston. Both men repeated their previous positions, and Morgan focused on the race issue. He accused Johnston of "stumbling" on disfranchisement and asked how Johnston would be able to defend constitutional revision in Louisiana and Mississippi.[34]

The third and final debate followed the next day. The high point of this exchange came when Johnston began his usual reading of Morgan's Washington *Post* interview. The older man jumped to his

---

[31] *Ibid.*

[32] Mobile *Register,* November 22, 1899; Montgomery *Advertiser,* November 19, 21, 1899; Jno. O. Turner to JFJ, November 20, 1899, Governor Johnston Papers.

[33] JFJ comment on the verso of J. R. Cowan to JFJ, November 17, 1899, Governor Johnston Papers.

[34] Birmingham *Age-Herald,* November 21, 1899; Montgomery *Advertiser,* November 22, 1899.

feet, stalked across the platform, shook his finger at the governor, and crossly stated that he had already explained his comments on Bryan and silver: "I say to you now, that if you do it again, Governor or no Governor, I will hold you to account." With Johnston supporters shouting for him to sit down and Morgan responding that he was "not afraid," several minutes passed before order was restored. Less inflammatory, but ultimately much more significant, was Morgan's almost passing reference to "rumors" of misconduct surrounding the sale of university coal lands. The debates ended when Vice-President Garret A. Hobart's death called Morgan back to Washington.[35]

Undoubtedly relieved to escape the grueling prospect of a statewide trek, Morgan spent the remainder of the campaign in Washington pushing for the Nicaragua Canal. He adopted the convenient position that he would rather lose than sacrifice his public duties. Significantly, the veteran senator found that these responsibilities included the printing and circulating of at least five of his Senate speeches. In what were essentially 30,000 pieces of campaign literature, Morgan reaffirmed his support for silver, attacked national banks and bonded indebtedness, defended black disfranchisement and territorial expansion, and identified Johnston with allegedly predatory corporations.[36]

Morgan's absence did not diminish the campaign's intensity. As the senator assumed a statesman-like posture in Washington, anti-Johnston papers harshly attacked the governor. These journals charged that Johnston had failed to investigate dishonest state officials in Mobile and had mismanaged the Montevallo School's lands.[37] Johnston denied both accusations; and while neither proved more than an irritant, they set the stage for revelations concerning University of Alabama lands.

That story broke on November 16, 1899. Two months earlier The University of Alabama Board of Trustees had decided to sell 3,480

[35] Birmingham *Age-Herald,* November 22, 1899; Montgomery *Journal,* November 23, 1899; Mobile *Register,* November 23, 1899.

[36] Birmingham *Age-Herald,* November 29, 1899; *Congressional Record,* 56th Cong., 1st sess., Vol. XXXIII, Pt. 1, 565–69, 671–75, 983–86, Pt. 2, 1816–17, Pt. 4, 3359–65. Copies of these speeches with notations indicating the number printed are located in the main collection of the Library of Congress.

[37] Selma *Times,* quoted in Birmingham *Age-Herald,* November 16, 1899; Montgomery *Advertiser,* November 11, 14, 15, 1899; Mobile *Register,* October 7, 1899.

acres of university-owned coal lands to the Sloss-Sheffield Iron and Steel Company at $12.50 per acre. Ironically, these lands were part of a 46,080-acre grant that Senator Morgan had been instrumental in securing from the U.S. government in 1884. Revenues from these lands were to have been used to restore university buildings and equipment destroyed during the Civil War. Although nearly 13,000 acres had been sold by 1891, the trustees had adopted a policy of leasing in the mid-1890s. The decision to resume land sales had come at Johnston's behest. He personally had called the special meeting, rather than following the stipulated procedure requiring a written request from four board members; he had not informed the board that land sales would be the principal item of business; he had previously exceeded his authority by extending purchase options to Sloss-Sheffield; and he had convinced a majority of the board of the sale's advisability.[38]

Both Dr. Eugene Allen Smith, the state geologist, and J. H. Fitts, university treasurer, denounced the terms of the sale. Had the property been leased like a comparable tract in Bibb County, Smith declared with considerable exaggeration, it would have yielded $500,000 rather than $50,000. Fitts further revealed that Johnston had rejected coal and iron magnate Henry F. DeBardeleben's application for a lease. If proved, these charges would have impugned the governor's judgment. A second round of more damning revelations threatened to undermine his integrity by disclosing that Johnston and his business associate, Edmund W. Rucker, had been instrumental in the formation of the New Jersey–based Sloss-Sheffield corporation. Johnston and Rucker not only had sold their stock in the American Coal and Coke Company to Sloss-Sheffield but also had sold American Coal and Coke lands to the New Jersey company at $49 per acre.[39]

The disparity in the price of the university and American Coal lands and the procedural irregularities of the sale attracted the attention of the university's alumni association, which called for an investigation. A special committee reported on December 19, citing the governor's violation of the rules for summoning the September

[38] Birmingham *Age-Herald*, November 16–December 22, 1899; Montgomery *Advertiser*, November 17–December 24, 1899; James B. Sellers, *History of the University of Alabama* (University, Ala., 1953), Vol. I, 345–54.

[39] *Ibid.*

trustees meeting and the allegedly poor agreement with Sloss-Sheffield. The committee charged that Johnston was both "greatly
misinformed" and "recklessly disregardful" of the law, characterized
the sale as "illegal, injudicious, and unwise," and called on the
trustees to nullify the contract. The alumni also noted the "remarkable simultaneousness" in Johnston's sale of the university and
American Coal and Coke lands. The following day, the trustees essentially adopted the alumni report, declared the contract illegal, and
agreed to institute the legal proceedings necessary to void the sale.[40]

Johnston and his supporters attributed the flap to partisan politics. Johnston defended the $12.50 sale price by asserting that he
had sold lands in the same vicinity for only $10 per acre; moreover,
the university's lands were widely scattered and unsuitable for leasing.
In contrast to the "raw" university lands the American Coal and
Coke properties had been developed sufficiently to command $49. He
denied that he owned any stock in Sloss-Sheffield or that he profited
personally from the university land deal. When the alumni committee
wrote him posing a series of questions, he charged that they were
"tools" in the political struggle and curtly rejected their request to
interrogate the governor.[41]

Although there was no concrete proof of Johnston's personal involvement in Sloss-Sheffield, his explanations left crucial questions
unanswered. After all, he had once been president of the Sloss Iron
and Steel Company, which provided the basis for this new corporation. The Mobile *Register* pointedly asked if the sale of American Coal
and Coke lands (from which the governor clearly profited) had been
contingent on the university's agreement with Sloss-Sheffield. Why
had the governor clearly extended unauthorized options? Why had
he disregarded established procedures in calling the trustees meeting?
Why had he acted in such haste in September? Why had the transaction
been kept secret until discovered by the press? The *Register* also
perceptively observed that the controversy over the land sale had
halted much of Johnston's early campaign momentum and left the
governor on the "defensive."[42]

Morgan confided his impressions of the controversy to former

----

[40] Birmingham *Age-Herald*, November 29, December 20, 21, 1899.

[41] *Ibid.*, December 14, 20, 21, 1899; Montgomery *Journal*, December 19, 21, 1899.

[42] Mobile *Register*, November 28, December 2, 1899, January 11, 1900; Armes, *Coal and Iron in Alabama*, 347–49, 451–53.

Governor Thomas Goode Jones in early December. He complained of Johnston's "overmastering greed for power and money" and his "willful abuse" of statutes, but Morgan worried more about the danger to the Democratic party. To impair the "organization, or the morale" of the body that safeguarded the state ranked with "patricide."[43] Two weeks later Morgan criticized Johnston in a Senate speech, citing Sloss-Sheffield as an example of the "rapid and dangerous" growth of corporations and their "usurpation of powers." By incorporating in New Jersey, the company had escaped legal and financial obligations in Alabama. It was, he concluded with a flourish: "a monster monopoly, that had to leave Alabama to find a home and shelter in New Jersey, and a large corporation in which the governor of Alabama has or had, a large amount of stock, . . ." Incensed, Johnston demanded that Morgan "retract" the charge or locate reputable witnesses to sustain it.[44]

The senator's response provoked a sizzling exchange of letters. After defending his statement, he asserted that Johnston had participated in the formation of Sloss-Sheffield, had helped to establish a "cover for a combination" that was "unlawful in Alabama." He had also acted illegally by calling the special legislative session, by unilaterally extending options on university lands, and by appointing two men (rather than one) to select public lands for Tuskegee Institute and the Montevallo School.[45]

In a patronizing rebuttal Johnston pledged to remember the "respectful consideration" due Morgan's "age, feebleness and irritability." He denied owning any stock in Sloss-Sheffield and saw no crime in having sold his American Coal lands to the corporation. Nor did he see any wrongdoing in helping form a company that promised to bring $2 million into the state. Responding to charges of subserviance to big business, he criticized Morgan's "republican" votes on antitrust bills and inquired if the Maritime Canal Company were not "something of a trust or monopoly." Johnston closed by

[43] JTM to Governor [Thomas G. Jones], December 2, 1899, Robert McKee Papers, ASDAH.

[44] *Congressional Record*, 56th Cong., 1st sess., Vol. XXXIII, Pt. 1, 568–69; JFJ to JTM, December 20, 1899, "Correspondence Between Governor Joseph F. Johnston . . . and Senator John T. Morgan . . ." (n.p., n.d.), Morgan Papers, hereafter cited as Johnston-Morgan Correspondence.

[45] Birmingham *Age-Herald*, December 27, 1899; JTM to JFJ, December 25, 1899, Johnston-Morgan Correspondence.

asking why Morgan had waited so long to denounce his allegedly "wicked and unconstitutional and lawless" acts. Answering his own questions, he declared that his real "offense" had been to run for the Senate.[46]

Morgan concluded the exchange in January in a thirty-five-page letter berating the governor for joining the "speculators" rather than protecting Alabama from increased "bondage" to the Northeast. He defended his support for the Maritime Canal Company and charged Johnston with trying to "discourage" the waterway that was critical to Alabama's development. Morgan then returned once again to the issue of race. He pronounced Johnston's position an "enigma" and criticized his organization of the black army regiment. Were Johnston to serve three years in the Senate and have his conduct stir as much "serious criticism" as had his governorship, Morgan was certain he would be the "most notorious man" ever elected from Alabama.[47]

While the debates and public exchange of letters provided the candidates' most dramatic personal confrontations, the campaign had a less visible, but no less important, organizational dimension. Long recognized as a skilled politician by his friends and a "political wire worker of much cunning" by his enemies,[48] Johnston used state patronage to consolidate his following. He had carefully recorded political favors in a " 'red' book," and as the struggle entered its final months, he sought to convert these favors into votes. In January he characteristically acknowledged that a prospective appointee was a competent Democrat but asked whether the man was his "friend."[49] Although Johnston augmented this appointment policy with a massive correspondence and a rigorous travel schedule, his organization suffered by comparison to Morgan's. Numerous Johnston followers bemoaned the lack of systematic activity in their counties. One Birmingham report was typical: "It is all one-sided, nobody at work for you." An Ashland backer found the governor's friends "almost idle." And a Gadsden supporter predicted defeat

[46] JFJ to JTM, January 4, 1900, Johnston-Morgan Correspondence. The Maritime Canal Company was the corporation JTM favored to build the Nicaragua Canal.

[47] Birmingham *Age-Herald*, January 18, 1900; JTM to JFJ, January 10, 1899, Johnston-Morgan Correspondence. JTM's thirty-five-page draft is in the Morgan Papers.

[48] J. T. Holtzclaw to Thomas G. Jones, January 27, 1891, Thomas Goode Jones Papers, ASDAH.

[49] JFJ to D. H. Riddle, January 1, 1900, in Montgomery *Advertiser*, March 21, 1900; JFJ to E. L. DeBardeleben, February 19, 1900, in Montgomery *Advertiser*, April 5, 1900.

unless every county was "thoroughly organized *at once*," because "you are trying to do too much [yourself] without organized assistance."[50]

The difficulty of incorporating political "outsiders" greatly complicated Johnston's organizational efforts. Johnston partisans allied themselves with Populists and ex-Populists throughout the state, and their backing was crucial to Johnston victories in some counties. Interestingly, Johnston received the aid of Philander Morgan, the senator's Populist brother. Philander urged the governor to consummate an "*open* alliance with the Bryan populists." Only by securing their "full cooperation" and granting them a "full share of the honors" could Johnston defeat the "anti-democratic democracy."[51]

Johnston organizers also counted variously on the aid of blacks, Republicans, and German immigrants. The probate judge of Choctaw County predicted significant black assistance, and blacks were reportedly "drilled" in Barbour. Two Sumter County Republicans assured Johnston of GOP support and sought advice on how best "to stir" their "boat" in his "direction." Still another Johnston backer thought the governor's anti-imperialism would attract Germans in New Decatur, Huntsville, Athens, Florence, and Tuscumbia.[52]

Unlike Johnston, Morgan played virtually no role in the campaign's organization. He had worried that his first formal announcement for the Senate had made him appear a "self seeker," and he personally avoided grass-roots political work. After the election he somewhat naively reiterated his claim that he had never "solicited the support of any man"—that he had sought the party's nomination "unbought" without "incurring obligations, of a personal nature, to anyone." Defeat was preferable "to any arrangement to secure the support of any man, or any journal, for a consideration."[53]

[50] E. W. Lucken [?] to JFJ, January 18, 1900, R. L. Windham to JFJ, January 29, 1900, Martin W. Whatley to JFJ, February 9, 1900, Wm. J. Boykin to JFJ, February 6, 1900, Governor Johnston Papers.

[51] James Crook to O. D. Street, November 21, 1899, Oliver Day Street Papers, University of Alabama Library, Tuscaloosa; T. A. Street to JFJ, November [1899], Geo. P. Jones to JFJ, December 15, 1899, Philander Morgan to JFJ, February 1, 9, 1900, Governor Johnston Papers.

[52] C. E. McCall to JFJ, February 14, 1900, B. A. Forrester to JFJ, February 12, 1900, J. T. J. James and A. C. Schiel to JFJ, February 9, 1900, Hugo Lehmann to JFJ, December 2, 1899, Governor Johnston Papers.

[53] JTM to Frank S. White, January 11, 1900, in unidentified clipping, n.d., and JTM to Max Hamburger, October 11, 1900, Morgan Papers.

Despite Morgan's lack of personal involvement, his organization was at once more easily erected and more elaborate than Johnston's. More than one-hundred Morgan partisans met at the Morris Hotel in Birmingham in late December 1899, and the Morgan Campaign Committee chose a chairman and a secretary, established headquarters in Birmingham, and made plans to organize "Morgan Clubs" throughout the state. The committee promised to compensate for what the senator lacked in the "wiles and arts of politics," and Morgan organizers energetically set about their task. Johnston men soon reported that their opponents were "straining every nerve" in Talladega County, "most active all through" Jefferson, "making a home to home canvass" in Washington County, and "attempting to bulldoze" anti-Morgan Democrats in Marion County.[54] While this concerted effort was significant, the Morgan Committee built upon existing Democratic organizations in most counties. A Franklin County observer wrote representatively: "The party machinery or rather the ring . . . so common in all the courthouse towns . . . are for Morgan." To construct an organization based on these "insiders" was an easier task than that which Johnston had undertaken.[55]

Morgan's wide appeal as a public figure was the final, critical ingredient for a superior organization. Support from local courthouse cliques was not surprising. As the representative of the conservative Big Mule–Black Belt coalition, he opposed the Johnston forces' threat to displace the established leadership. Johnston was attempting to build his own political machine, and the effort would continue if he were elected senator. Morgan also garnered the backing of Alabama's gold Democrats, leading Johnstonites to question his loyalty to free silver and one historian to term him a "lamb . . . dressed in a wolf's clothing." Given his thirty-year battle for free silver and his thorough dislike for the Northeastern wing of the party, these erstwhile opponents could hardly have counted him as an ally on the money question. Some Alabama newspapers had castigated him for

---

[54] Birmingham *Age-Herald,* December 30, 1899; unidentified clipping, n.d., Morgan Papers; C. C. Kimbrough to JFJ, January 24, 1900, E. W. Lucken [?] to JFJ, January 18, 1900, Martin W. Whatley to JFJ, February 9, 1900, S. E. Wilson to JFJ, January 22, 1900, Governor Johnston Papers.
[55] M. C. Gantt to JFJ, February 9, 1900, N. D. Denson to Chappell Cory, February 15, 1900, B. H. Sargent to JFJ, January 8, 1900, Governor Johnston Papers.

years on the currency issue and only changed their policy when he became the candidate least likely to disturb the existing party structure and thus the lesser of two evils. The gold forces saw Morgan's candidacy as an opportunity "to restore some of their men to power" in the legislature.[56] And even with this following of gold backers and the Bryan interview, Morgan's long pro-silver record enabled him to retain the loyalty of many silver Democrats.[57]

More importantly, over his long career he had generated loyalties that surpassed those Johnston could command. Civil War comrades and their families rallied to his support,[58] and many Morgan followers gratefully remembered his tireless efforts to help defeat the Republicans in 1874.[59] Others warmed to his advocacy of the Nicaragua Canal and judged him able "to do more for it than any other half dozen" senators.[60] For uncounted Alabamians, Morgan had been the state's most prominent person from the time they first became politically aware. One ally succinctly expressed this sentiment when he acknowledged that the organizational work of Morgan's friends was "needed, demanded and effective; but high over all and chief among all was *your own personality,* the esteem, the reverence, the deep seated affections enshrined in the hearts of the honest white people of Alabama for one who has served them so long, so faithfully and so well."[61]

Johnston's strategy had been to overcome such obstacles with a fast start in several "early bird" December primaries. Morgan's newspapers charged that these counties had meant to aid Johnston by "deliberately" disregarding the Democratic Executive Committee's April schedule. Even so, the governor secured specifically instructed legislators from only two counties; his candidates carried two other counties, only to be instructed later by conventions. Although the Montgomery *Journal* promptly pronounced that these "sweeping victories assured" Johnston's election, Morgan essen-

[56] Hackney, *Populism to Progressivism,* 170; Sam'l Will John to JTM, April 20, 1899, Morgan Papers; J. R. Cowan to JFJ, August 28, [1900], Cocke-Johnston Papers.
[57] John M. Wilson to JFJ, January 20, 1900, Governor Johnston Papers.
[58] D. S. Bethune to JTM, April 27, 1900, and W. H. McCain to JTM, April 28, 1900, Morgan Papers.
[59] George K. Miller to JTM, April 18, 1900, Morgan Papers.
[60] J. E. Brown to O. D. Street, January 3, 1900, Street Papers.
[61] John R. McCain to JTM, April 19, 1900, Morgan Papers.

tially matched his tally of instructed representatives by winning two potentially pro-Johnston, north Alabama counties.[62]

Therefore, neither man had established a clear advantage as he approached the crucial portion of the campaign in early 1900. Six additional counties were decided in January and February before the "April Derby" determining the remaining fifty-three. The superiority of Morgan's organization and appeal surfaced as he swept three counties in January and one in February. Johnston captured Winston's one representative but suffered a bitter reversal in Russell, where both sides had worked feverishly and predicted a hard struggle. One of the Morgan committee's "flying squadrons" of speakers had toured the county, and Johnston appointees had stumped for the governor. Cries of foul arose from both camps in the wake of the February vote, which gave Johnston a majority of sixty-one. Johnston supporters boasted that the governor had won over a "bold and open attempt at bribery, and the purchase of votes by the Morgan men." The senator's allies countered that the Johnston forces had distributed a $1,500 "corruption fund" from a small shed behind the Girard post office in Russell County and had imported 100 to 150 voters from Columbus, Georgia, and Phenix City. Citing these irregularities, the county executive committee threw out the votes from the Girard Beat and scheduled a second election for April 14.[63] Johnston's apparent victory had been nullified, and he came no closer to winning any of the remaining counties.

Morgan's campaign received added impetus when two secondary candidates, John D. Roquemore and William C. Oates, dropped out of the race. Although Roquemore was not expected to be a factor beyond Montgomery County, his stroke in early February and subsequent death cast anti-Johnston support to Morgan. A former congressman and governor, Oates was a staunchly conservative gold Democrat and a greater threat to attract potential Morgan voters. Oates had already won in Coffee and Geneva counties and might well

---

[62] Montgomery *Journal*, December 18, 1899; Montgomery *Advertiser*, September 21, 1899; Birmingham *Age-Herald*, February 20, 1900; Ed. M. Johnston to JFJ, December 12, 1899, and John P. Proctor to JFJ, December 18, 1899, Governor Johnston Papers.

[63] Robert J. Lowe to JTM, January 27, 1900, and A. D. Sayre to JTM, January 28, 1900, Morgan Papers; J. W. Knowles to JFJ, January 8, 1900, and F. W. Mosley to JFJ, February 16, 1900, Governor Johnston Papers; Birmingham *Age-Herald*, January 28, February 3–5, 20, 1900; Montgomery *Advertiser*, January 30, February 3, 4, 6, 23, 1900; Montgomery *Journal*, February 5–7, March 2, 1900; Russell *Register*, January 12, 26, February 2, 9, 23, 1900.

have carried another half-dozen southeastern, wiregrass counties or have badly divided the anti-Johnston vote generally. On March 21, 1900 he withdrew his candidacy and pledged his support to Morgan, declaring that the race had become a two-man affair and that he wished to avoid dividing the anti-Johnston forces. In fact, Morgan and Oates backers had carefully cooperated in several counties, and Oates's earlier withdrawal from Crenshaw clearly had aided Morgan. Acutely aware of the damage to the Johnston cause, the Montgomery *Journal* berated General Oates's "full retreat from the wiregrass" and proclaimed the "Oates-Morgan combination" the rankest specimen of "ward politics" ever witnessed in an Alabama Senate race.[64]

Such invective was typical of the mutual accusations of corruption and the increasingly caustic nature of the campaign. Johnston backers complained that *"money was thrown into"* Clark County *"the like of which has never been known before,"* that "deplorable" practices had occurred in DeKalb, and that there had been "all kinds of swindling" in the city of Hamilton. In the latter, the Morgan forces were charged with voting "pronounced Republicans" and "boys under age." Liquor flowed in other areas, and voting of unregistered, unborn, or deceased blacks was also alleged in the Black Belt.[65]

Morgan partisans replied in kind, claiming that Johnston had a "very fat pocket-book" and circulating the rumor that his followers were prepared to spend $20,000 to carry Montgomery County. From Selma a Morganite warned that "Some counties are held by appointments, some by non-examinations, and some by the 'cool cash.'" The senator concurred and accused Johnston of employing tactics in Jackson and Russell counties "never known, or heard of, in our former canvasses in Alabama." In a charge calculated to highlight Johnston's association with Northern capitalists the *Advertiser* cited Collis P. Huntington and the transcontinental railroads as major sources of the governor's campaign funds. Although the meager evidence amounted only to Huntington's passing through the state in 1899, Morgan told the Atlanta *Constitution* that the railroad mag-

[64] Montgomery *Journal,* January 22, 27, February 2, 19, March 22, 1900; Montgomery *Advertiser,* March 22, 1900; Washington *Post,* March 26, 1900; unidentified clipping, n.d., Morgan Papers.
[65] D. C. Case to JFJ, January 27, 1900, John M. Wilson to JFJ, January 28, 1900, W. A. Livingston to JFJ, February 12, 1900, Governor Johnston Papers; S. E. Wilson to JFJ, April 19, 1900, and Robert Cruse to JFJ, May 7, 1900, Cocke-Johnston Papers; Montgomery *Journal,* January 29, 1900.

nate and his anti-canal allies were "trying to prevent" his re-election.[66]

As this barrage of newspaper charges continued through the final weeks of the campaign, no slur seemed to be too trivial or to need substantiation. The *Journal* castigated Morgan for voting to confirm Frederick Douglass as a U.S. marshal in 1878, for opposing public education, for favoring unlimited Asian immigration, for attending the wedding of a black senator, and for arranging the appointment of a "saloon keeper" to senate clerkship. The *Age-Herald* replied with a series of front-page cartoons pilloring Johnston; and the *Advertiser* charged him with reducing Confederate pensions, appointing a black chaplain, calling a Negro "Mr.," and using foul language. These mutual recriminations led the New York *Times* to predict "serious trouble," and in at least one instance injuries were narrowly averted. As a Morgan campaigner spoke in Jackson County, he was harassed from the audience. The Morgan orator answered with a drinking glass that narrowly missed his tormentor's head, and the heckler tried unsuccessfully to shoot him.[67]

The campaign attracted national attention. The Washington *Star* editorialized that Morgan was a "man of national fame and truly national usefulness" and that his fate had not just "local, but national implications." Almost without exception, non-Alabama papers expressed surprise and dismay that the senator might be replaced. The New York *Times* termed the prospect a "calamity to the State and a misfortune for the country"; the Washington *Times* described the possibility as "amazing" and "incomprehensible"; the Washington *Star* was appalled that Alabama could consider turning "from this most famous and useful of all her living sons" to a "new and an untried man."[68]

The *Star*'s concern proved unwarranted. In April Morgan carried each of the remaining primaries, winning sixty-one of sixty-six counties.

[66] JTM to Dan Gordon, April 6, 1900, and C. W. Hooper to JTM, April 3, 1900, Morgan Papers; Montgomery *Advertiser*, January 19, 21, March 31, 1900; Mobile *Register*, March 30, April 1, 5, 1900.

[67] Montgomery *Journal*, February 8, March 17, April 2, 1900; Montgomery *Advertiser*, March 29, April 6, 1900; New York *Times*, November 24, 1899; Birmingham *Age-Herald*, December 17, 1899.

[68] New York *Times*, January 21, April 17, 1900; Washington *Star*, n.d., Florida *Times-Union and Citizen*, n.d., New York *Mail and Express*, n.d., Washington *Times*, n.d., New York *Commercial*, n.d., Morgan Papers.

Johnston accepted the verdict without a public murmur, while privately confiding that those "worthy of success" had to "accept reverses with equanimity." He would leave office with "clean hands and a clear conscience" and although his rejection of the "plunderers and privileged class" had led to "the fate of nearly every reformer," he was confident the people would eventually comprehend and reward his service. Even the *Age-Herald* concluded that his gubernatorial work warranted recognition, "that he deserved well of the people." His "mistake" had been to seek that recognition by challenging Morgan. In short, he had "attempted the impossible."[69]

In retrospect, the *Age-Herald*'s conclusion appears sound. Although slowed by age and impaired health, Morgan remained Alabama's most important public figure. He had established lasting loyalties and strong obligations. He had devoted less time to patronage, personal favors, and state matters than many Alabamians would have liked; but his war record, his struggle against Reconstruction, his tireless support for the Nicaragua Canal, and his vehement battles against Northern domination of the South's economy and politics commanded widespread respect and affection.

Furthermore, he benefited from specific developments in 1899–1900. Even though his backers incessantly denounced Johnston's political machine, Morgan's lieutenants constructed a superior campaign organization. Based on the traditional courthouse cliques, Morgan's personal following, and Alabama's gold Democrats, the senator's forces overwhelmed Johnston. Morgan also exploited the race issue. While many white Alabamians were ambivalent about a constitutional convention, most favored black disfranchisement, and Morgan was much closer than the governor to the dominant trend in Southern race relations. The senator unquestionably profited from portraying Johnston as threatening white solidarity and Democratic party integrity. Finally, Morgan received unexpected aid from the scandal surrounding the university coal lands. The "land deal" impugned Johnston's integrity, identified him with widely resented Northeastern capitalists, and left him on the defensive.[70] Following

[69] JFJ to O. D. Street, April 23, 1900, quoted in Braswell, "Senator Joseph Forney Johnston," 49, n. 80; Montgomery *Journal*, April 17, 1900; Birmingham *Age-Herald*, April 16, 1900.
[70] E. F. Fulton to JTM, April 24, 1900, Morgan Papers.

the initial press disclosures, he spent much of his time explaining his conduct. Although many allegations were exaggerated or groundless, the damage was extensive.

The significance of Morgan's victory was widely discussed. Both his personal followers and a broad spectrum of the press dubiously but sincerely touted the vote as a "triumph of statesmanship" over "bossism, demagoguery," and "machine politics."[71] One of the senator's most earnest backers also asserted that "the integrity of Democratic party organization" had been in the balance; and to the extent that he referred to preservation of the Big Mule–Black Belt coalition, the reference was correct.[72] Morgan's victory had repulsed the challenge of Johnston's reform group and his Populist allies and had paved the way for a constitutional convention.

The governor had warned that a Morgan victory would be viewed as an endorsement of a constitutional convention, and the chairman of the Morgan Campaign Committee interpreted the results in precisely that light.[73] Under Morgan's inspiration the Democratic state convention in 1900 made the constitutional convention part of the party platform, and Johnston's successor dutifully signed the enabling bill. Again as Johnstonites had feared, the Big Mule–Black Belt alliance dominated the ensuing convention and disfranchised both blacks and poor whites. Interestingly, Johnston's challenge to Morgan also prompted a constitutional restriction against an Alabama governor being selected for the U.S. Senate during his gubernatorial term or for one year thereafter. Anti-Johnston Democrats were determined that his possible reelection as governor in 1902 would not bring elevation to the Senate.[74]

Johnston and his backers had also proclaimed that Morgan's election would be interpreted as an Alabama endorsement of a "dangerous imperialistic policy," and the Louisville *Courier-Journal* led

[71] John T. Ashcraft to JTM, April 16, 1900, B. A. Rogers to JTM, April 16, 1900, Eli L. Shorter to JTM, April 17, 1900, William J. Sanford to JTM, May 3, 1900, John V. Smith to JTM, May 24, 1900, Lafayette *Sun*, n.d., Concord *Monitor*, n.d., Morgan Papers; Birmingham *Age-Herald*, April 15, 1900; Montgomery *Advertiser*, April 15, 1900.

[72] Sydney J. Bowie to JTM, April 17, 1900, Morgan Papers; Karl Louis Rodabaugh, "The Turbulent Nineties: The Agrarian Revolt and Alabama Politics, 1887–1901" (Ph.D. dissertation, University of North Carolina at Chapel Hill, 1981), 285–86.

[73] Montgomery *Advertiser*, April 11, 1900; Montgomery *Journal*, April 17, 1900; T. A. Street to JFJ, April 19, 1900, Cocke-Johnston Papers.

[74] Mobile *Register*, April 29, 1900; McMillan, *Constitutional Development in Alabama*, 265–322; Hackney, *Populism to Progressivism*, 173–229.

numerous papers in portraying the outcome as proof that "The South is an Expansionist."[75] To be sure, the major Alabama papers and many important state politicians applauded Morgan's calls for commercial expansion and a Nicaragua Canal. However, Morgan's imperialism—of general territorial as well as economic expansion—remained a minority position among Alabama and Southern Democrats. Significantly, the 1900 state Democratic platform endorsed canal construction and the "legitimate expansion of home and foreign trade" but did not mention the Philippines. The Chattanooga *News* was more perceptive in assessing the imperialism issue among Alabama voters, acknowledging that Morgan was the "jingo of jingoes" among Senate Democrats and that he favored "grabbing all the territory possible." Still, he remained the popular choice regardless of these views. Alabamians were not prepared "to turn him out in his old age for advocating principles that he has contended for all his life."[76]

Just as Morgan's victory fell short of a Southern endorsement of imperialism, his election failed to provide a definitive commentary on Bryan or free silver. The senator was a life-long silver man, and in response to Johnston's attacks he had competed with the governor in attempting to establish fidelity to Bryan and the Chicago platform. On the other hand, he had equivocated regarding Bryan's renomination and had garnered strong support from Alabama's gold Democrats. Given these mixed signals and the presence of other more important issues as well as Morgan's personality and influence, the senator's victory can hardly be seen as either a rejection or a ringing endorsement of the Nebraskan and his currency policy.

The election's ultimate significance lay in Morgan's personal triumph, ensuring that he would remain the dominant political per-

[75] Montgomery *Journal*, December 5, 1899, March 5, 1900; Louisville *Carrier-Journal*, April 17, 1900. For an extensive sampling of national press opinion, see Scrapbook #8, Box 31, Morgan Papers.

[76] Montgomery *Advertiser*, April 27, 1900; Birmingham *Age-Herald*, December 15, 1899; O. Lawrence Burnette, Jr., "John Tyler Morgan and Expansionist Sentiment in the New South," *Alabama Review*, XVIII (July 1965), 163–82; Tennant S. McWilliams, "Expansionism in Southern History: A Speculative Essay"(Paper delivered at the Society for Historians of American Foreign Relations Meeting, Washington, D.C., August 2–4, 1984), 6, and "The Lure of Empire: Southern Interest in the Caribbean, 1877–1900," *Mississippi Quarterly*, XXIX (Winter 1975–76), 43–63; Edwina C. Smith, "Southerners on Empire: Southern Senators and Imperialism, 1898–1899," *Mississippi Quarterly*, XXXI (Winter 1977–78), 89–107.

sonality in Alabama. Morgan initially seemed inclined to assuage the bitterness that had developed between him and the governor. In September 1900 Johnston traveled to Portsmouth, New Hampshire, to accept a bas-relief honoring the battleship U.S.S. *Alabama*. The governor's address drew favorable notices from Alabama's press, and Morgan publicly congratulated him on his "eloquent and impressive speech." Any hope for a truce faded the next year when Johnston led the opposition to the new constitution, declaring that he sought to protect poor whites against the "bosses." Although Morgan was unhappy with the document's "grandfather clause" and did not actively canvass for its adoption, he did declare that the constitution was "necessary" as a "measure of harmony, peace and safety," and he could hardly have been pleased with the charges of "bosses" abusing white suffrage opportunities.[77]

Morgan's displeasure became apparent when Johnston made these issues the central focus of his 1902 campaign for governor. Johnston again denounced the "bosses" who had written the constitution and prevented the 1900 Democratic convention from endorsing his second gubernatorial term. Morgan wrote a public letter castigating Johnston and endorsing his opponent, W. D. Jelks. Black suffrage, Morgan asserted, was the key issue, as it had been in 1900. He characterized Johnston's demand for vindication as a "deliberate defiance of the Democratic party," a "declaration of war against the new constitution," and a strategy to restore "the negro to the ballot." The senator concluded his tirade with the warning that Johnston sought the governorship only as a "stepping-stone to federal office." Alabama voters apparently agreed, and Jelks handily won the Democratic primary.[78]

Undeterred, Johnston resumed his dogged pursuit of a Senate seat in 1906. Although reportedly Johnston planned to challenge Morgan again, the confrontation was avoided by Alabama's bizarre "dead shoes" senatorial primary. With both Alabama's incumbent senators over eighty years old and unlikely to survive another term, the party

[77] Louisville *Courier-Journal*, April 17, 1900; JTM to JFJ, September 21, 1900, Cocke-Johnston Papers; Mobile *Register*, November 7, 1901; Parrott, "Joseph Forney Johnston," 83, 112–14; McMillan, *Constitutional Development in Alabama*, 293, 349; Hackney, *Populism to Progressivism*, 195–98, 227–29.

[78] Mobile *Register*, August 3, 1902; W. D. Jelks to JTM, June 20, 1902, Morgan Papers; Albert B. Moore, *History of Alabama* (University, Ala., 1934), 660–62; Parrott, "Joseph Forney Johnston," 115–17.

arranged a two-track primary; the first virtually assured reelection to the incumbents, and the second allowed Alabama voters to designate the two "senators-in-waiting" that they preferred the governor to appoint to Senate vacancies from Alabama. After waging a vigorous campaign on what Morgan dubbed the "pallbearers' ticket," Johnston finished second to John Hollis Bankhead, Sr. When Morgan died in June 1907 and Senator Pettus succumbed the following month, Bankhead filled the first seat and Johnston the second.[79] Johnston's vindication had come, and his rivalry with Morgan had ended. But it was both ironic and symbolic that even in this moment of triumph Johnston had gained his coveted Senate seat via a route that acknowledged Morgan's political dominance and that the prize was obtainable only upon the death of "Alabama's grand old man."

[79] Birmingham *Age-Herald,* December 17, 1905; Mobile *Register,* August 12, 1906; Allen W. Jones, "Political Reform and Party Factionalism in the Deep South: Alabama's 'Dead Shoes' Senatorial Primary of 1906," *Alabama Review,* XXIV (January 1973), *passim.*

Progressive Era

ALLEN W. JONES

Political Reforms of the Progressive Era

The progressive era was an epoch in United States history that began during the late 1890's and continued through the first two decades of the twentieth century.[1] This period of social, economic, and political reform is not confined to any single movement, organization, political party, social or economic class, or geographical section of the United States. The progressive crusade began in the states and rapidly developed into a national reform movement. For years historians ignored or neglected the progressive era in the Southern states, believing that the South was a backward, conservative, or even reactionary region controlled by white-supremacy demagogues and one-party political machines. Recent studies indicate, however, that the Southern states not only participated in the reforms associated with progressivism, but in some cases provided leadership for the rest of the nation.[2]

In Alabama, as in other Southern states, the progressive movement evolved from the agrarian radicalism and turbulent political

[1] This paper was read at the annual meeting of the Alabama Historical Association, Selma, Apr. 26, 1968. It was published in *The Alabama Review,* XXI (July, 1968). The author acknowledges the assistance of the Auburn University Grant-In-Aid Program for making a larger study of this whole era possible.

[2] See Arthur S. Link, "The Progressive Movement in the South, 1870–1914," *North Carolina Historical Review,* XXIII (April, 1946), 172–95; Dewey W. Grantham, Jr., *The Democratic South* (Athens, Ga., 1963); Arthur S. Link, "The South and the 'New Freedom': An Interpretation," *The American Scholar,* XX (Summer, 1951), 314–24; Anne F. Scott, "A Progressive Wind from the South, 1906–1913," *Journal of Southern History,* XXIX (February, 1963), 53–70; T. Harry Williams, *Romance and Realism in Southern Politics* (Baton Rouge, 1966), 44–64; Dewey W. Grantham, Jr., "The Progressive Era and the Reform Tradition," *Mid-America,* XLVI (October, 1964), 227–51.

era of the 1890's. The Populist and Jeffersonian Parties were formed in Alabama in 1892 in an effort to combat the conservative Democratic control of the state government. Agitation for political reforms that would ensure a "free ballot and a fair count" and a return of the government to the people poured fervently from agrarian leaders and Populist newspapers. Their demands included the Australian or secret ballot, the state-wide direct primary, the popular or direct election of President and Vice President of the United States, the direct election of United States Senators, and laws to regulate elections and primaries.[3]

The Populist challenge caused the Democratic Party to alter many of its political methods in order to perpetuate its power. It caused the Democratic state convention of 1892 to extend unusual powers and authority to the state executive committee, which had been subservient to the convention since the days of Reconstruction. After the turn of the century when the direct primary replaced the convention system for nominating party candidates, the convention gradually faded away and the executive committee became the directive arm of the party.[4]

The reorganization and reorientation of the Democratic Party in Alabama became obvious in 1896 when the national party nominated progressive-minded William J. Bryan and the state party elected a "half-way" Populist, Joseph F. Johnston, as governor. The four-year term of Governor Johnston served as a transitional period between Populism and Progressivism.[5] This period marked the return of Populists to the ranks of the Democratic Party and with them they "brought along . . . their ideological baggage, for which room had to be found."[6]

---

[3] Montgomery *Alliance-Herald*, Nov. 11, 1893; William W. Rogers, "Agrarianism in Alabama, 1865–1896" (unpublished Ph.D. dissertation, University of North Carolina, 1959), 371–99; Link, "The Progressive Movement in the South," 175–76; Allen W. Jones, "A History of the Direct Primary in Alabama, 1840–1903" (unpublished Ph.D. dissertation, University of Alabama, 1964), 194–237.

[4] Minutes of Democratic State Convention, June 8–10, 1892, in Alabama State Department of Archives and History, Montgomery (all "minutes" hereinafter cited are in same archives); Jones, "History of the Direct Primary in Alabama," 323–31.

[5] David A. Harris, "Racists and Reformers: A Study of Progressivism in Alabama, 1896–1911" (unpublished Ph.D. dissertation, University of North Carolina, 1967), 7–9; Lorena D. Parrott, "The Public Career of Joseph Forney Johnston" (unpublished Master's thesis, University of Alabama, 1936), 36–119.

[6] C. Vann Woodward, *Origins of the New South, 1877–1913* (Baton Rouge, 1951), 372.

While Populism in Alabama sprang from the rural regions and the agrarian class, Progressivism reflected the ideals and discontent of the middle class in the urban centers of the state. Its leadership came from businessmen, school teachers, editors, lawyers, and other professional groups.[7] To a large degree the aims and objectives of the Populists—greater popular control of government, popular education, and abandonment "of laissez-faire as a guide for economic and social action"—became the platform of the progressives. These reformers expressed a spirit of moderation in certain areas, but in some of their basic assumptions, such as race relations, they were extremely conservative.[8]

The major issues of the progressive movement in Alabama from 1896 to 1920 were primarily political, which seems to be typical of the other Southern states as well as the entire nation. An examination of some of the political reforms that occurred in Alabama will help substantiate the importance of the South in the Progressive movement.

One political reform basic to all others and designed to restore effective control of election machinery to the people was the direct primary for nominating candidates. In a one-party state like Alabama the nomination was tantamount to election and whoever controlled the county and state conventions controlled the nominations and the Democratic Party. Charges of "ring rule" and corruption in the 1870's and 1880's caused many county politicians to abandon the "time honored convention system" in favor of the direct primary.[9] The extensive use and successful operation of the primary system in municipal and county politics during the 1880's and 1890's led reformers to urge its use in nominating state officers in 1891 and 1893.[10] These early efforts for a state primary were blocked by Black Belt conservative Democrats who argued that the adoption of a

---

[7] *Ibid.*, 371–72; Link, "The Progressive Movement in the South," 179; Eric F. Goldman, *Rendezvous with Destiny, A History of Modern American Reform* (New York, 1953), 83; Grantham, *The Democratic South*, 51–55.

[8] Grantham, "The Progressive Era and the Reform Tradition," 228; Link, "The Progressive Movement in the South," 179; Harris, "Racists and Reformers: A Study of Progressivism in Alabama," 117, 122–24; Woodward, *Origins of the New South*, 373.

[9] Jones, "History of the Direct Primary in Alabama," 95–146.

[10] Union Springs *Herald*, May 27, 1891; Eufaula *Times and News,* June 4, 1891; Prattville *Progress*, May 19, June 9, 1893; Athens *Limestone Democrat*, May 20, 1893; Alexander City *Outlook*, Sept. 15, 1893; Boaz *Sand Mountain Signal*, Oct. 20, 1893.

state primary without any state regulation was "impracticable and would lead to interminable confusion and discord."[11]

With the election of Governor Joseph F. Johnston in 1896, the reform wing of the Democratic Party began a push for the passage of a primary election law. The Democratic state platform for 1896 called for such a law and Governor Johnston in his inaugural address asked the legislature to "enact laws under which the various political organizations in the State may hold primary elections and secure fair nominations."[12] When the legislature did not honor his request in 1897, he issued a stronger demand in his biennial message of 1898. Erle Pettus, a young progressive representative from Limestone County, accepted the governor's challenge and introduced a measure "to regulate primary elections of recognized political parties in Alabama." This bill became Alabama's first general primary election law on February 8, 1899.[13]

The new law was very incomplete and was only "a start towards legalized primaries."[14] The act merely surrounded primaries with the same legal safeguards that protected regular elections. It did not include any positive rules for the conduct of primaries; this was left to the political parties.[15] Because of the political situation in the state, the act made the primary election system optional for all political parties. With this law Alabama had made a start toward securing a state-wide primary election, but "the problem of the Negro voter," who was blamed for all of the fraud and corruption in elections, had not been solved.[16]

Politicians in Alabama were quick to see that the voice of the Negro could be eliminated from politics through the use of the white primary. In 1897, the Democratic state executive committee left the

[11] Birmingham *Age-Herald*, June 6, 1891.

[12] Minutes of the Democratic State Convention, Apr. 22–23, 1896; *Journal of the House of Representatives of the State of Alabama, 1896–1897* (Montgomery, 1897), 372. Hereafter cited as *House Journal*.

[13] *Biennial Message of Governor Joseph F. Johnston to the General Assembly of Alabama* (Birmingham, 1898), 16; *Acts of the General Assembly of the State of Alabama, 1898–1899* (Montgomery, 1899), 126–28 (hereafter cited as *Acts of Alabama*); *House Journal, 1898–1899*, 35.

[14] Birmingham *Age-Herald*, Dec. 17, 1898. The *Age-Herald* suggested adding an amendment to the law which would require the voters to register their party preferences. The editor made this recommendation because he expected Negro disfranchisement and the rise of a two party system in Alabama.

[15] *Acts of Alabama, 1898–1899*, 126–28.

[16] Harris, "Racists and Reformers: A Study of Progressivism in Alabama," 122; Malcolm C. McMillan, *Constitutional Development in Alabama: A Study in Politics, the Negro, and Sectionalism* (Chapel Hill, 1955), 250–53.

decision of Negro participation in the primaries to the county executive committees, but in 1900 the state committee decided that
"only white Democrats" could participate in the primaries, beat
meetings, and conventions.[17] Prior to 1901, the possible inclusion of
Negroes in Democratic primaries seems to have been the reason for
the rejection of the state-wide primary idea and for the failure to pass
a comprehensive primary election law.

During the campaign for the constitutional convention in 1901,
the advocates of honest elections and suffrage reform suggested the
inclusion of the primary election system in the new constitution. One
newspaper editor believed that such a move would be "the beginning of a mighty revolution in popular government."[18] Many gave
their support to the convention in hope that the new constitution
would contain provisions for a state-wide primary system. The Birmingham *Age-Herald* recognized the inclusion of a state white primary
in the new constitution as the answer to the problem of disfranchising
the Negro.[19]

The Constitutional Convention of 1901 devoted little attention to the primary system, since the major issue concerned suffrage
and elections. While failing to incorporate the primary as a part of
the fundamental law of the state, the convention required the legislature of 1903 to pass laws governing the primary election system.
The conservatives in the convention not only prevented the inclusion of a state primary provision in the constitution, but they made
the primary optional for political parties in the state.[20]

After the adoption of the Constitution of 1901, demands for a
state-wide primary and for a comprehensive primary election law grew
stronger. Conservative political leaders in Alabama connected the
primary system with the new constitution and declared that it was
now safe for the white men of the state to disagree in the primary
because the Negro had been disfranchised.[21]

[17] Montgomery *Advertiser*, Jan. 21, 1897; Minutes of Democratic State Executive
Committee, Mar. 23, 1900.
[18] Roanoke *Randolph Leader*, Jan. 30, 1901; see also Birmingham *Age-Herald*, May 9, 11,
1901.
[19] *Ibid.*, Apr. 27, 1900, Jan. 20, May 9, 11, 1901.
[20] *Official Proceedings of the Constitutional Convention of the State of Alabama, May 21, 1901, to
September 3, 1901* (Wetumpka, 1940), I, 113–17, 395–96, 1257–66, III, 3328–56, 3846; *Constitution of the State of Alabama, 1901* (Montgomery, 1901), 44–45; see also McMillan, *Constitutional Development in Alabama*, 263–309, 316–17.
[21] Mobile *Register*, Mar. 23, 25, 1902; Minutes of Democratic State Executive Committee, July 10, 1902.

Following hard on the heels of Alabama's disfranchising constitution was the first state-wide Democratic primary election. Early in 1902 the state press and the reform faction of the Democratic party, led by ex-Governor Johnston, launched the battle for a state primary.[22] Such a vigorous campaign ensued that when the state executive committee met in July, 1902 it could not avoid the issue. After two days of argument and debate, the committee ordered a white primary to nominate candidates for state office. County executive committees were directed to conduct the primary election on August 25, 1902, and all candidates entering the race were assessed by the state committee to defray the expenses of printing and distributing the ballots. The plan required each nominee to receive a majority of the votes; in case there was no majority, a runoff or second primary would be held between the two candidates with the largest number of votes. While providing all the rules, regulations, and procedures for holding the primary, the state committee specified that the primary would be held in accordance with the general laws of the state governing primary elections.[23]

Alabama's first state primary in August, 1902 exposed a heated contest between the conservatives, led by Governor William D. Jelks, and the reformers, led by former Governor Joseph F. Johnston, for control of the Democratic Party. This primary provided the first opportunity for these two factions to settle their political differences at the polls without having to worry about the Negro holding the balance of power in the general election. Although the progressives lost in the primary election, they made an everlasting contribution to political reform in Alabama by forcing the first state-wide primary. This primary marked the beginning of the end for Democratic conventions in Alabama.[24]

Shortly after the state primary of 1902, the press began agitation for a state law that would establish and regulate the necessary machinery for conducting primary elections.[25] With strong encouragement from Governor Jelks, the legislature passed Alabama's first complete

[22] Governor Johnston's reform faction of the Democratic party included such men as W. W. Quarles, Jesse F. Stallings, Charles M. Shelley, William H. Denson, A. E. Caffee, Bibb Graves, P. G. Bowman, James Crook, and P. C. Stegall. Birmingham *Daily Ledger,* July 16, 17, 1902.

[23] Minutes of Democratic State Executive Committee, July 10–12, 1902.

[24] Jones, "History of the Direct Primary in Alabama," 281–318.

[25] Eufaula *Times and News,* Aug. 28, 1902; Vernon *Courier,* Sept. 25, 1902.

and comprehensive primary election law in October, 1903.[26] The law allowed party executive committees the power to prescribe qualifications for participants, establish the time and dates for primaries, appoint inspectors, clerks, returning officers and canvassing boards, and try all contests coming out of the primary. All primaries were ordered held at the expense of the political party. Punishment was provided for corruption and fraud in the primaries and the provisions of the general election laws of the state were declared applicable to all primary elections. The new law went into lengthy detail concerning certificates of nomination, canvassing of returns, notice of elections, preparation and counting of ballots, and poll lists. Written solely for the Democratic Party, this law served effectively and without major change until 1915.[27]

Nothing was done during the administration of Governor Braxton B. Comer to alter the primary election laws, but in a message to the 1911 legislature Governor Emmet O'Neal outlined objectionable features of the primary system and recommended a number of reforms.[28] In April, 1911 the legislature responded by providing more government regulation and control of party primaries. The expense of party primaries became a responsibility of the state, with the stipulation that in order to hold a primary a party must have polled more than twenty-five per cent of all votes cast in the last general election. This was designed to prevent the weak Republican Party from holding primaries at public expense. The law standardized the time and date for primaries, listed the offices to be voted for, detailed the process and procedure for contesting the primary, and applied the general election laws of the state to the primary, except that voters were not required to prepare their ballots in the voting place. Employers were directed to permit any qualified elector to leave his employment to cast a vote in the primary without any forfeiture of wage or salary for the time lost in attending the polls. Candidates running in the primary were forbidden to promise anyone an appointment or a reward in return for political support. To protect the candidates from charitable societies seeking donations, the law prohibited any person or

[26] William D. Jelks to Oscar W. Underwood, Sept. 4, 1903, in William D. Jelks Papers, Alabama Department of Archives and History, Montgomery; *Biennial Message of William D. Jelks to the Legislature of Alabama, 1903* (Montgomery, 1903), 4; *Message of William D. Jelks to the Legislature of Alabama, September 1, 1903* (Montgomery, 1903), 6.

[27] *Acts of Alabama, 1903*, 356–65.

[28] *Message of Governor Emmet O'Neal to the Legislature of Alabama, January 10, 1911* (Montgomery, 1911), 60–64.

organization from soliciting money or other contributions from any candidate seeking nomination in a primary. All candidates were forced to file their campaign expenses with the state and no corporation was permitted to pay or contribute any money to aid or promote the nomination of a person in the primary. Other corrupt practice provisions prevented candidates from paying voter's transportation expenses to the polls; made it illegal to serve free drinks or food within one hundred yards of any polling place; required all circulars, posters, and bills affecting any candidate to contain the name and address of the author, printer, publisher, or circulator; and prohibited any candidate from paying any owner, publisher, or agent of a newspaper for aiding or opposing any candidate for nomination.[29]

Democratic Party factionalism produced the next major change in the primary election system. After using the majority system in the state primary of 1902, the state executive committee adopted the plurality plan for the state primaries of 1906 and 1910. This spared the party the time, effort, and expense of a runoff or second primary by declaring the candidate with the most votes the nominee.[30] While only minor opposition appeared to the plurality plan prior to 1914, the state election in this year produced a battle between the progressives and conservatives on the issue of local option or prohibition. The state executive committee, which was opposed to the prohibitionist B. B. Comer, ordered a runoff or second primary for every office in which no candidate received a majority of the votes cast. Although Comer received a plurality in the first primary, Charles Henderson defeated him in the runoff primary by 10,327 votes.[31] When the new legislature convened in 1915, it was controlled by the progressives and prohibitionists, who were determined to further reform politics in Alabama.[32]

The 1915 legislature accepted the recommendations of a special committee of the Democratic state executive committee and passed a new primary election law which was supported by a new registration law and a corrupt practices act. The most significant provision of the

[29] *Acts of Alabama, 1911*, 421–51.
[30] Minutes of Democratic State Executive Committee, July 10–12, 1902, Jan. 9, 1906, and Jan. 24, 1910.
[31] Albert B. Moore, *History of Alabama* (Tuscaloosa, 1951), 753–55; Minutes of Democratic State Executive Committee, Jan. 7, Apr. 21, May 26, 1914.
[32] Maggie Burgin, "The Direct Primary Election System in Alabama" (unpublished Master's thesis, University of Alabama, 1931), 8–9.

new primary law eliminated the "runoff" or "double primary" by establishing a system of first- and second-choice voting. When no candidate received a majority of first-choice votes, the two leading candidates added their second-choice votes and the one with the largest total vote was declared the nominee.[33] In spite of strong opposition in the 1920's, first- and second-choice voting in the primaries was not abandoned until 1931.[34] The secret ballot was extended to the primary elections by the new law, and there were numerous provisions relating to contests, certificates of candidates, and election procedures.[35]

The 1915 corrupt practices act was based on political experience and previous legislation. In 1907 the legislature had made it unlawful for corporations to contribute money or other things of value to any candidate for public office or to any political party.[36] The same legislature passed a corrupt solicitation act that prohibited all county and state officials from accepting fees, money, office, employment, or things of value in return for legislative favors. This law, sometimes called the "Dual Office" act and the "anti-lobby" act, prevented any person from corruptly soliciting or attempting to influence any state legislator in his duties as a public servant.[37] Certain corrupt practices were specified in the general election law of 1903 and the primary election acts of 1903 and 1911.[38]

The corrupt practices act of 1915 attempted to "banish all ills from politics" in Alabama,[39] but the newspapers of the state said the law was a "ridiculous . . . effort to muzzle the press."[40] The Montgomery *Advertiser* charged that the law, written by Comer prohibitionists, was "designed to punish those who had helped defeat their candidates" in 1914 and "to strengthen the political interests of their defeated

[33] *Ibid.*, 9–10; *Acts of Alabama, 1915*, 218–39. The 1915 primary election law was modeled after a law passed by the Florida legislature in 1913. Montgomery *Advertiser*, Dec. 29, 1916.

[34] Burgin, "The Direct Primary Election System in Alabama," 17–50; *Acts of Alabama, 1931*, 73–125.

[35] *Acts of Alabama, 1915*, 218–39.

[36] *Acts of Alabama, 1907*, 406.

[37] *Ibid.*, 693–94. In 1910 a grand jury in Mobile indicated Francis J. Inge, President of the Mobile City Council, and Boykin B. Boone, City Attorney of Mobile, for violation of the "Dual Office Law" of 1907. The same law was used in Mobile in 1910 to remove R. T. Ervin from the Democratic ticket as nominee for the state legislature because he held a federal office of "referee in bankruptcy." Mobile *Register*, Oct. 17, 21, 1910.

[38] *Acts of Alabama, 1903*, 356–65, 438–79, and *1911*, 421–51.

[39] Tuscaloosa *News and Times-Gazette*, Aug. 24, 1915.

[40] *Ibid.*, Feb. 3, 1915. See also Birmingham *News*, Feb. 1, 1915.

heroes."[41] The law limited the use of political cartoons and required that all political advertisements bear the name and address of the person responsible for publication. Because of the excessive expenditures in the 1914 primary, the law limited the expenses of candidates and required all candidates to submit an itemized statement of contributions and disbursements and a list of contributors. By limiting campaign expenditures, it was supposed that a man of limited means could aspire to political office. Other provisions of this "antigraft" law made it unlawful to intimidate an elector, to hire conveyances to transport electors to polls, to campaign or solicit any votes on election day, for corporations and businesses to contribute to any candidate or political party, and for religious and charitable organizations to solicit money and aid from candidates.[42]

Another act passed by the progressive legislature of 1915 prohibited municipal, county, and state commissions and boards from holding executive or secret sessions. Any member who remained in attendance at any such meeting was guilty of a misdemeanor and subject to fine.[43]

While the primary election law and the corrupt practices acts were pointed toward political democracy, the registration law of 1915 reflected the old Bourbon philosophy of a "select electorate" through the limitation of the suffrage. Such a law was in complete harmony with the Constitution of 1901. Under this law the old board of registrars in each county was abolished and registration became the work of one man, who was directed to open the gates for registration every two years between November 15 and January 5.[44] One newspaper editor felt that the purpose of the new registration and election laws was "to take from the election and party authorities those discretionary powers that have given them the opportunity to wield a wide influence in shaping the results in intra-party elections."[45]

In his departing message to the legislature in 1919, Governor Charles Henderson reviewed the progress of primary election laws, observing that "one of the freaks" of the law was its failure to properly protect the ballot.[46] The legislature responded with amend-

[41] Montgomery *Advertiser*, May 9, 1916. See also *ibid.*, June 30, 1918.
[42] *Acts of Alabama, 1915*, 250–57. See also Tuscaloosa *News*, Jan. 7, 29, 1915; Tuscaloosa *News and Times-Gazette*, Feb. 10, 1915; Selma *Times*, May 10, 1916.
[43] *Acts of Alabama, 1915*, 314–15.
[44] *Ibid.*, 239–48. See also Tuscaloosa *News and Times-Gazette*, Nov. 2, 1916.
[45] *Ibid.*, Nov. 29, 1915, quoting Mobile *Register*.
[46] *Message of Governor Charles Henderson to the Legislature of Alabama, January 14, 1919* (Montgomery, 1919), 60–62.

ments to the 1915 law that made the ballot of every voter in the primary secret and inviolate. Another significant change provided for absentee voting in all primary and general elections.[47]

While primary elections were being regulated and reformed by state legislation, the real success or failure of the primary election system rested with the politicians of the state. The Republican Party never adopted the primary for state nominations and only a few north Alabama counties used it infrequently to select nominees for local office.[48] The ruling Democratic Party, however, assured the success of the primary after 1902 by gradually extending its use to the nomination and election of all party offices and positions. In 1904, for example, state supreme court justices and the president of the railroad commission were added to the list of state officers nominated by primary, and in 1906 the state executive committee held a primary election for United States Senators. The domination of party affairs by the state committee was again demonstrated in 1908 when the committee called a primary election to choose candidates for all state offices and to select members of the state executive committee, presidential electors and alternates, and delegates and alternates to the National Democratic Convention.[49] Although the Democratic State Convention of 1912 nominated state supreme court justices (who had been selected by primary since 1904) and chose delegates to the National Democratic Convention, it surrendered its last power and destroyed its political future by adopting a resolution to select in the future "all delegates to the National Democratic Convention . . . by a direct vote of the people in a primary . . ."[50] The 1912 state convention was the last to make party nominations and the state committee, with the help of the primary election system, emerged as the central political agency of the Democratic Party in Alabama. One last Democratic state convention was held in 1922, in which the "Old Guard" from the Black Belt counties attempted to abandon the primary election system and return to convention nominations. The triumph of the primary election advocates over

[47] *Acts of Alabama*, 1919, 70–73, 862–65, 969–79.

[48] George Stiefelmeyer to Oliver D. Street, Mar. 25, 1912, in Oliver D. Street Papers, University of Alabama Library, Tuscaloosa; Tuscaloosa *News and Times-Gazette*, Aug. 7, 1922; Montgomery *Journal*, July 30, 1922.

[49] Minutes of Democratic State Executive Committee, Apr. 20, 1904, Jan. 9, 1906, and Feb. 7, 1908. See also Montgomery *Advertiser*, Apr. 21, 1904.

[50] Minutes of Democratic State Convention, Apr. 17, 1912.

the Black Belt Bourbons in the convention, however, marked the end of the convention system for the Democratic Party of Alabama.[51]

The movement in Alabama to secure the direct election or nomination of United States Senators began during the Populist era. It fell on deaf ears until the late 1890's when the reform faction of the Democratic party picked up the idea as a hope for defeating Senator John T. Morgan.[52] As early as February, 1899 the state legislature expressed approval of a constitutional amendment for the direct election of senators, and by 1900 the state press began agitation for the nomination of senators by primary election.[53] A resolution calling for such a primary was introduced in the state convention of 1900, but was allowed to die quietly in committee.[54] After his defeat by Senator Morgan in 1900, Governor Johnston made another unsuccessful attempt in 1902 to have the primary system used to nominate United States Senators.[55]

The question of choosing senators remained in the background of Alabama politics until December, 1905, when former Governor William C. Oates wrote a letter to the press suggesting that senators be chosen in a state primary election in 1906.[56] Much of the state press gave sanction to the idea. On January 9, 1906, the state executive committee met in Montgomery and adopted a rather unusual primary election plan for nominating United States Senators.[57] Interest-

[51] Minutes of Democratic State Convention, Sept. 7, 1922. See also Montgomery *Journal*, Sept. 8, 13, 1922; Montgomery *Times*, Sept. 8, 1922.

[52] James Crook to Oliver D. Street, Nov. 2, 1899, O. D. Street to James Crook, Nov. 3, 1899, in Oliver D. Street Papers; Montgomery *Advertiser*, June 7, 1899.

[53] Alabama *House Journal, 1898–1899*, 718; Alabama *Senate Journal, 1898–1899*, 795–96; Hamilton *Marion County News*, Sept. 7, 1899; Cullman *Tribune-Gazette*, Sept. 14, 1899; Dothan *Wire-Grass Siftings*, Jan. 4, 1900; Birmingham *Age-Herald*, Apr. 14, 1900; Roanoke *Randolph Leader*, May 23, 1900, quoting the Tuskegee *News*.

[54] Minutes of Democratic State Convention, Apr. 24, 1900.

[55] Joseph F. Johnston to John W. DuBose, Mar. 26, 1902, in John W. DuBose Papers, Alabama Department of Archives and History, Montgomery. The names of Morgan and Johnston appeared on primary election ballots in those counties which held primaries for nominating local officers and state legislators. Candidates for the state legislature were required by county executive committees to abide by the people's vote in the primary for United States Senators. The arrangements for voting directly for United States Senators were made by the county committees and were not ordered by the state committee. Greenville *Advocate*, Apr. 11, 1900.

[56] Birmingham *Age-Herald*, Dec. 22, 1905.

[57] Montgomery *Journal*, Jan. 4, 1906; Minutes of Democratic State Executive Committee, Jan. 9, 1906.

ingly, the complicated plan resembled one suggested by Johnston in a personal letter to a friend in August, 1905.[58]

The state committee's plan gave consideration to the age and health of Alabama's incumbent senators, John Tyler Morgan, age eighty-one, and Edmund Winston Pettus, age eighty-four. The senatorial primary plan allowed Morgan and Pettus to run without opposition, while a "sweepstake primary" was held for alternate senators. Seven candidates—Joseph F. Johnston, John H. Bankhead, Sr., William C. Oates, John B. Knox, William C. Fitts, Jesse F. Stallings, and Richard H. Clarke—appeared on the ballot for alternate senators. The two candidates receiving a plurality of the votes would succeed the two senators in case of their death or resignation. All candidates for the legislature and for governor and lieutenant-governor were required to pledge that they would obey the recommendations of the voters in making appointments to fill any vacancy in the United States Senate.[59]

Democratic politicians as well as the state press were divided over the state committee's alternate-senatorial primary plan. Some opponents referred to the plan as the "Dead-Shoe Primary";[60] others called it the "pallbearers ticket."[61] One editor described the scheme as ". . . ghoulishly blood-chilling—heart-paralyzing—soul-horrifying."[62]

On August 27, after an exciting seven-month campaign, Bankhead won 48,362 votes and became the first alternate-senator; Johnston came in second with 36,107. Knox came in third, followed by Stallings, Clarke, Oates, and Fitts.[63] In 1907 both Pettus and Morgan died and the two alternates, Bankhead and Johnston, replaced them in the United States Senate.[64]

Thus, in 1906 Alabama joined several midwestern states in using

[58] Joseph F. Johnston to John W. DuBose, Aug. 24, 1905, in John W. DuBose Papers.
[59] Minutes of Democratic State Executive Committee, Jan. 9, 1906; Harris, "Racists and Reformers: A Study of Progressivism in Alabama," 320–24; Montgomery *Journal*, Jan. 10, 1906; Montgomery *Advertiser*, Jan. 12, 1906.
[60] Birmingham *News*, Jan. 12, 1906, quoting a letter from Joseph B. Babb; *ibid.*, Jan. 16, 1906, quoting the Athens *Democrat*.
[61] Birmingham *News*, Jan. 10, Aug. 28, 1906.
[62] *Ibid.*, Jan. 16, 1906, quoting Hartselle *Enquirer*.
[63] Minutes of Democratic State Executive Committee, Sept. 7, 1906; Montgomery *Advertiser*, Sept. 8, 1906.
[64] *Acts of Alabama, 1907*, 73–74, 484–85. See also Selma *Journal*, June 16, 1907; Attalla *Mirror*, June 20, 1907; Montgomery *Advertiser*, July 28, 1907.

the primary election system to achieve the direct election of senators. Many politicians in the state actually preferred the use of a state primary to instruct the legislature in choosing senators instead of an amendment to the United States Constitution.[65]

Another new and progressive innovation was introduced into Alabama politics in 1908. The direct democracy provided by the primary election system had been so effective and well-received by the Democrats of Alabama that the state executive committee decided to apply the system to the selection of candidates for President of the United States.[66] Such a suggestion had been made by John W. DuBose in 1891, but it was ignored by both Populists and Democrats.[67]

When the state executive committee met in Montgomery on February 7, 1908, the progressives were in control. In presenting his plan for a preferential presidential primary, Virgil Bouldin of Jackson County argued that "nothing breeds democracy faster than a primary." He stressed the importance of letting each citizen have a direct voice in his government.[68] Under Bouldin's plan the voter would cast his ballot directly for presidential candidates, and those candidates running for delegates and alternates to the national convention had to pledge to support the candidate for President who received the largest vote in the primary. To get on the ticket as a presidential candidate required a petition of at least two hundred qualified Democratic voters of Alabama. All qualified electors who would pledge to support the nominees were invited to participate in the primary.[69]

The "Great Commoner," William Jennings Bryan, was the first to be qualified with the state committee for the presidential primary, but the last minute entry into the race of Minnesota's "dark-

---

[65] Governor B. B. Comer favored an amendment to the United States Constitution allowing direct election of senators and suggested to the state legislature in 1907 that a petition be sent to Congress supporting this idea. *Acts of Alabama, 1907,* 56. Governor Emmet O'Neal expressed his opposition to the direct election of senators in speeches and articles. Inez M. Edwards, "Emmet O'Neal: Alabama Governor 1911–1915" (unpublished Master's thesis, Alabama Polytechnic Institute, 1957), 12–13. See also Emmet O'Neal, "Election of U.S. Senators by the People," *Northern Review,* CLXXXVIII (November, 1908), 702–709.

[66] Minutes of Democratic State Executive Committee, Feb. 7, 1908.

[67] Bessemer *Journal,* June 11, 1891.

[68] Minutes of Democratic State Executive Committee, Feb. 7, 1908.

[69] *Ibid.* See also Montgomery *Journal,* Feb. 7, 1908; Montgomery *Advertiser,* Feb. 8, 1908.

horse" governor, John A. Johnson, created a stir in state politics. A. G. Smith, a former chairman of the Democratic state executive committee and a Birmingham attorney, became the chairman of Johnson's campaign committee in Alabama.[70] Although Johnson had little support from the press of Alabama, the anti-Bryan Mobile *Register* supported him.[71] The surprise of the campaign came when Senator Joseph F. Johnston announced his support for the Minnesota governor.[72]

The results of Alabama's first preferential presidential primary on May 18, 1908 gave Bryan a sweeping victory with 54,931 votes to Johnson's 30,926. Johnson's strength came from south Alabama and the cities and towns, while Bryan polled the vote of the country people in north Alabama. Alabama has held only one other preferential presidential primary in its history, in 1923.[73]

The reform of municipal government in Alabama was somewhat restricted by the conservative Constitution of 1901, but demands for improvement in city government arose from the increasing population of the urban centers in Alabama.[74] The three governors of the state from 1900 to 1910 showed little interest in the increasing problems of the growing cities.[75] Prior to 1910 the business of municipal government in Alabama was directed by mayors and city councils who were charged by the people as being corrupt and inefficient. The wave of reform for municipal government, which began in Galveston, Texas in 1903 with the establishment of a city commission, reached Alabama in 1910. The Mobile *Register* and the Birmingham *Age-Herald* became champions of the new form of city government and pushed for its adoption by Alabama municipalities.[76] Emmet O'Neal, elected governor in 1910, became an ardent supporter of commission government and municipal reforms. Eight pages of his message to the legis-

---

[70] Montgomery *Advertiser*, May 3, 18, 1908.

[71] Mobile *Register*, May 13, 17, 1908; Gadsden *Daily Times News*, May 14, 1908; Montgomery *Journal*, May 13, 1908; Birmingham *News*, May 12, 13, 1908.

[72] Montgomery *Advertiser*, May 13, 1908.

[73] Minutes of Democratic State Executive Committee, May 29, 1908 and Dec. 13, 1923. See also Montgomery *Advertiser*, May 19, 30, 1908.

[74] McMillan, *Constitutional Development in Alabama*, 330–32.

[75] See *Acts of Alabama*, 1900–1901, 1903, 1907, 1909.

[76] Mobile *Register*, Oct. 5, 12, 14, 16, Nov. 1, Dec. 30, 1910; Birmingham *Age-Herald*, Apr. 29, 1911; Birmingham *News*, Oct. 14, 1910.

lature in January, 1911 were devoted to the defects in city government and the need for reform.[77]

Encouraged by the press and the governor, the 1911 legislature
passed four municipality laws in less than a month. They provided
means and procedures for the establishment of commission government in the towns and cities of the state. This legislation became
the basis of urban governmental reform during the next decade, and
the legislatures of 1915 and 1919 made improvements by amending the
1911 statutes.[78]

While the legislature was busy drafting legislation for commission
government, Birmingham, Montgomery, and Mobile made plans to
become the first cities to adopt the new system. The citizens of
Birmingham took the lead in 1910 by voting overwhelmingly for
commission government, and when Governor O'Neal approved the
first law on March 31, 1911 this city became the first in the state to
have a commission government.[79]

In other cities the change from the old mayor-council to the
commission form of government did not come so easily. A mass
meeting of over 5,000 citizens was held in Mobile when local politicians
blocked plans for adopting the commission form of government.
Politicians who favored and opposed the new form of government
bitterly attacked each other. Before adjourning, the citizens approved a petition to the state senators and representatives from
the Mobile district asking them to secure legislation that would
authorize Mobile to change its municipal government to the commission form. The commission form of government became an issue
in Bessemer, Gadsden, Montgomery, Dothan, Decatur, and Huntsville, and by 1915 some of these cities had adopted it.[80]

While campaigning for changes in municipal government, reform
newspapers in the state made an appeal for the initiative, referendum,
and recall. The Mobile *Register* described the initiative and referendum as the "Club and Poker" system; the initiative was a
"poker" for use on lax lawmakers and the referendum was a "club"
for use on crooks.[81] One progressive-minded citizen from Mobile ar-

[77] *Message of Governor Emmet O'Neal to the Legislature of Alabama, January 11, 1911* (Montgomery, 1911), 36–43. See also Florence *Times,* July 22, 1910.

[78] *Acts of Alabama, 1911,* 204–23, 289–315, 330–55, 591–611; *ibid., 1915,* 52–76, 770–73, 789–
807, 869–74; *ibid., 1919,* 97–102, 487–520, 1115–16.

[79] Birmingham *Age-Herald,* Apr. 29, May 2, 5, 1911.

[80] Mobile *Register,* Oct. 5, 9, 12, 14, Dec. 30, 1910; Birmingham *Age-Herald,* May 1, 1911.

[81] Mobile *Register,* Oct. 30, 1910. See also *ibid.,* Oct. 15, 17, 23, Dec. 30, 1910.

gued that the adoption of these three political devices would "emancipate the people from the undue and evil influence of irresponsible and unaccountable representatives."[82]

One of the most outspoken opponents of the initiative, referendum, and recall was Governor O'Neal, who felt that these "unwise" devices would ". . . overthrow the representative principle and inaugurate a radical revolution in . . . American government."[83] In his message to the 1911 legislature O'Neal denounced the recall as a useless and unconstitutional "substitute for the regular and orderly course of judicial procedure by impeachment proceedings."[84] The legislature disregarded his opinions, however, and included a recall provision in the four laws concerning municipal commission government. This was the only level of government for which the recall system was inaugurated. No laws were enacted for the initiative or referendum.[85]

The last political reform achieved in Alabama during the progressive era came with the Nineteenth Amendment to the United States Constitution. The woman suffrage movement in Alabama began in the 1890's and emerged slowly through the first decade of the twentieth century. An era of activity began in 1910 with the formation of local feminist organizations, and by 1915 the suffragists demonstrated their strength by asking the state legislature to amend the state constitution to allow women to vote. When the legislature refused to pass the resolution in 1915, the suffragists reorganized and began making plans for another crusade against the state legislature in 1919.[86]

[82] *Ibid.*, Oct. 17, 1910, quoting a letter from "E. D."

[83] Emmet O'Neal, *Representative Government and the Common Law, A Study of the Initiative and Referendum* (New York, 1911), 6. This was an address which O'Neal delivered at the 143rd Annual Banquet of the Chamber of Commerce of the State of New York at the Waldorf-Astoria on Nov. 16, 1911. See also Emmet O'Neal, *Distrust of State Legislatures, The Cause; The Remedy* (Montgomery, 1913). This is an address delivered at the Governor's Conference, Colorado Springs, Colorado, Aug. 28, 1913. O'Neal debated the question of the initiative, referendum, and recall with Gov. Woodrow Wilson at the Governor's Conference, Spring Lake, N.J., on Sept. 12, 1911. Emmet O'Neal, *Strengthening the Power of the Executive* (Montgomery, 1911).

[84] *Message of Governor Emmet O'Neal to the Legislature of Alabama, January 11, 1911* (Montgomery, 1911), 42.

[85] *Acts of Alabama, 1911,* 204–23, 289–315, 330–55, 591–611. One prominent source states that Alabama made no use whatsoever of the recall. Frederick L. Bud and Frances M. Ryan, *The Recall of Public Officers* (New York, 1930), 5.

[86] Lee N. Allen, "The Woman Suffrage Movement in Alabama" (unpublished Master's thesis, Alabama Polytechnic Institute, 1949), 1–90. See also Lee N. Allen, "The Woman Suffrage Movement in Alabama, 1910–1920," *Alabama Review,* XI (April, 1958), 80–99.

In the meantime strong anti-suffrage sentiment developed in the state, with the Black Belt, especially Selma and Montgomery, providing the leadership. Prior to 1916 most of the opposition to the woman suffrage movement came from the clergy and the state press. The formation of the "Alabama Association Opposed to Woman Suffrage" at Selma in 1916 marked the beginning of organized efforts to check the feminists, and by 1919 a similar and more active organization appeared in Montgomery.[87] These organizations pictured woman suffrage as "the most dangerous blow aimed at the peace and happiness of the people in Alabama and white supremacy since the Civil War."[88] The major argument against woman suffrage and probably the most important reason for its rejection by Alabama voters was the fear that it would reopen the Negro suffrage issue and lead to Negro domination.[89]

With the passage of the constitutional amendment by Congress in 1919, the suffragists launched a losing campaign for state ratification.[90] Alabama's ladies in waiting emerged triumphant in August, 1920, however, when the Nineteenth Amendment was proclaimed to be in effect. A special session of the legislature assembled in September, 1920 and passed laws implementing the Nineteenth Amendment in Alabama. In November, 1920 the women of Alabama participated in their first state and national election.[91]

Political reforms in Alabama during the progressive era appear to be a paradox. While instituting the direct democracy so far described, the state and the Democratic Party in the same era limited the suffrage to the "intelligent and virtuous" white males as "a means of achieving an incorruptible electorate and good progressive government." They denied many people the ballot, but at the same time gave much more participation in the government to those with the right to vote. Perhaps, this paradox explains at least in part why historians have ignored or neglected the progressive era in Alabama and other Southern states.

[87] Allen, "The Woman Suffrage Movement in Alabama," 122–26.

[88] *A Protest Against Woman's Suffrage in Alabama.* This is an updated pamphlet published "By Alabama Democrats On Behalf and in Defense of the Large Unorganized Majority of the Women of Alabama" and is in the possession of the writer.

[89] Allen, "The Woman Suffrage Movement in Alabama," iv–v. Emmet O'Neal opposed the Nineteenth Amendment because "he felt that it was a far-reaching stroke against state sovereignty and was unnecessary." Edwards, "Emmet O'Neal: Alabama Governor 1911–1915," 108.

[90] Allen, "The Woman Suffrage Movement in Alabama," 139–60.

[91] *Acts of Alabama, Special Session, 1920,* 1–6, 124–34, 143–44.

JAMES F. DOSTER

Comer, Smith, and Jones:
Alabama's Railroad War of 1907–1914

The name of Milton Hannibal Smith suggests the Carthaginian general, Hannibal, who took elephants through the Alps.[1] Milton Hannibal was the master of the iron horses that snorted through the hills of Alabama on the steel rails of the Louisville and Nashville Railroad. Smith was the company's chief executive officer from 1882 to 1921, and a doughty character he was. "The whole push jump and skeedaddle when Smith sneezes," wrote one unappreciative employee.[2] Smith ruled his railroad with a firm hand, and even today its management bears his deep impress and is also famous for efficient operation. Unlike most railroad builders and promoters, Smith cared little for accumulating personal wealth. He managed his company faithfully in the interest of its stockholders, and his management inspired confidence. No man did more to promote investment in and development of Alabama's coal and iron industry than Smith.[3] His company invested millions of dollars in Alabama on his recommendations, and he induced

[1] This paper, which was read before a meeting of the Alabama Historical Association on April 20, 1956, is a product of research conducted by the author with the financial aid of the University of Alabama Research Committee. It was published in *The Alabama Review*, X (April, 1957).

[2] George H. Trebaux, Louisville, Kentucky, to Governor Comer, November 8, 1907 (in the Alabama State Department of Archives and History, Montgomery). All other manuscripts cited are in this library.

[3] For full accounts see Ethel Armes, *The Story of Coal and Iron in Alabama* (Birmingham, 1910), and Jean E. Keith, "The Role of the Louisville and Nashville Railroad in Early Development of Alabama Coal and Iron," *Bulletin of the Business Historical Society*, XXVI, 165–174 (September, 1952).

others to follow in the building of the state's industries. He resisted with determination the encroachments on his company's revenues made by shippers, competitors, the Interstate Commerce Commission, and state legislatures and railroad commissions. His home was in Louisville, Kentucky, where the headquarters of the L. & N. were located, but he was a familiar figure in Alabama, where his private car could often be seen on a side-track.

The particular nemesis of Smith was Braxton Bragg Comer, who was determined to secure reductions in rates and to rid Alabama of railroad domination. With this as his platform, Comer in the elections of 1906 won the governorship and secured the election of a legislature and a slate of public officials pledged to carry out his program.

Comer was a wealthy cotton-manufacturer of Birmingham, an aggressive, hard-working, self-made man, who had started out as a cotton planter in Barbour County and who retained large cotton-producing estates in East Alabama. He was sure the railroads were using monopoly powers to charge the farmers too much and that an arbitrary rate-structure was throttling the state's development. For some twenty years he had worked to get the state government to take firm action to protect the people against the railroads.[4]

The building of railroads in Alabama had given the people of the state their first real taste of the problems of an industrial society. The question of how to regulate them in a manner that would best serve the public interest was one on which honest men disagreed. Some thought it best to let them alone; others wanted the state government to fix the rates they might charge and to regulate their practices closely.

When Governor Comer took office in January, 1907, his railroad program was all steamed up and ready to roll. The Governor pulled the throttle, and one measure after another found a clear track in the legislature. Within a few days he could relax with satisfaction, for at last he had secured the adoption of a strict code of laws to regulate the railroad rates and practices in Alabama.

The low Georgia freight rates were made the legal maximum in

---

[4] See James F. Doster, "Alabama's Political Revolution of 1904," *Alabama Review*, VII, 85–98 (April, 1954); "Alabama's Gubernatorial Election of 1906," *ibid.*, VIII, 163–168 (July, 1955); and "The Conflict over Railroad Regulation in Alabama," *Business History Review*, XVIII, 329–342 (December, 1954).

Alabama. The state railroad commission, now filled with Comer's followers, was given greater power, and a drastic anti-free-pass law was enacted. The standard passenger fare was reduced from 3c to 2½c per mile, and a considerable number of other railroad matters were regulated. An "outlaw" act provided that a railroad company should lose its license to do business in Alabama, if it should resort to a Federal court for protection against state laws.

However, the triumph of Comer was short-lived. Waiting like Mephistopheles outside the gate was Milton Hannibal Smith in his private car at the Montgomery station. Under his leadership the main railroad companies operating in the state petitioned Federal Judge Thomas Goode Jones at Montgomery for injunctions prohibiting the enforcement of the Comer laws. The railroads claimed the reduced rates would deny them a fair and just return on the value of their property devoted to intrastate business and were therefore confiscatory. Their argument was based upon a formula used by the United States Supreme Court in the case of Smyth v. Ames (1898),[5] which was sheer buncombe, but the Supreme Court had not seen through it, and the state's attorneys in Alabama did not see through it. Judge Jones, in the absence of effective counter-argument, granted the injunctions. No real light was shed upon the question of whether the rates were confiscatory, but the state's attorneys were baffled.

Judge Jones was an old Confederate soldier. He had been with Lee in those last trying days of the war and was fond of talking about it. This we can easily understand, for little had happened in Alabama since the war that an ex-soldier of the Confederacy could find to grow nostalgic about. His father had been a railroad engineer (of the kind that builds railroads) and a railroad president. Jones himself had been a popular man, and he had served Alabama as governor in the difficult years from 1891 to 1895, a Democrat, of course. He had, however, bolted the Democratic party in the presidential race of 1896 to support Palmer and Buckner, Gold Democrats, against William Jennings Bryan. In 1901 President Theodore Roosevelt, on the suggestion of Grover Cleveland, had made him a Federal judge. The Judge was a good lawyer, but it also happened that he was a corporation lawyer, who had been for many years the L. & N. Railroad's chief attorney in

[5] 169 U.S. 466.

Alabama. He had a deep devotion to what he thought was right and a keen sense of integrity, but he was over-sensitive to criticism and sharp-tongued in reply.

Comer, Smith, and Jones were all men of strong character, not mere figures in a Punch and Judy show. The words they spoke were spontaneous, not those of actors upon a stage. And, oh, what a noise they made!

Comer and his associates, alleging a miscarriage of justice, blamed the Judge and insinuated that his decision had been influenced by his long time and intimate association with railroad interests. There quickly developed then a bitter personal feud between Governor Comer and Judge Jones. The Governor accused the Judge of being "railroad environed" and alleged that he was the protege and puppet of Milton H. Smith, and the Judge said that it was a "wicked thing" for the Governor to "excite the passions of the people against the authority of the courts."[6]

The legal proceedings were prolonged into the summer of 1907. Then, suddenly, the Southern Railway was caught off base on August 1, when it removed a case from a state court to a Federal court in violation of one of the Comer acts against which there was no injunction. Before Judge Jones could act the state cancelled the Southern's license to do business in Alabama, leaving the company in the position of an outlaw. This opened the way for harassing the employees of the company with criminal prosecutions, such as had very recently been pressed in North Carolina, where President W. W. Finley of the Southern had been arrested.

The Southern Railway Company, which was facing simultaneous pressure from the governments of North Carolina, Virginia, Georgia, and Alabama, capitulated to Governor Comer and accepted the reduced rates and the restrictive laws. According to a railroad lawyer in a position to know, the Southern's decision was made by J. P. Morgan, and the company yielded for the sake of peace.[7] Numerous other railroads followed the course of the Southern and yielded to Comer, and all would have done so but for the indomitable lead-

<hr />

[6] Montgomery *Advertiser,* August 10, 1907, July 5, 1908, October 7, 1909.

[7] The lawyer was R. E. Steiner, who gave the information in an interview with the author on December 9, 1941. Steiner had been present at a meeting in Morgan's New York office late in July, 1907, at which representatives of railroad interests in the South had discussed their pressing political problems. Milton H. Smith, not liking what was going on, said Steiner, got his hat and walked out.

ership of Milton H. Smith. Governor Comer threatened and cajoled, but Smith would not yield. The only railroads keeping to the shelter of their injunctions were the L. & N., the Central of Georgia, and their affiliates, the South and North Alabama, the Western of Alabama, and the Nashville, Chattanooga, and St. Louis.

Judge Jones in mid-August issued a new order, restraining sheriffs from arresting and solicitors from indicting railroad employees and sent marshals to serve individual notices of the order on these officials. This action caused widespread resentment in the state. "You need have no fears that Tom Jones is the best hated man in Alabama," wrote one correspondent to the Governor.[8] The Judge charged a Federal grand jury in strong language to watch for violations of the orders of the court, and he sympathized somewhat extravagantly with a delegation of railroad men who called to inquire about the likelihood of their being arrested by the state officials. He cited Henry Steagall, the solicitor of Henry County, for contempt for idle remarks made to a United States marshall. "I could not conceive how far he [Judge Jones], in his excitement and exaggerated egotism, might go," declared Governor Comer, who hurried off to Washington to confer with President Roosevelt. The Governor wrote to Governor Glenn of North Carolina to ask for suggestions on legislation "putting into effect proper railroad legislation that would escape the environments of a judge who has been all his life in the service of the railroads."[9]

The issue was changing. Judge Jones saw the important question as "whether we shall have anarchy or a government of laws." Governor Comer declared, "It is evident that the question at issue is not so much freight rates or passenger rates, but whether the state shall dominate and control its own affairs." Milton H. Smith told the governor that "it was not the rates he objected to but state regulation, and he would fight this to the last ditch."[10]

In framing laws to coerce the recalcitrants, Governor Comer was faced with the problem of securing statutes that would survive the tests of constitutionality and yet strike the L. & N. and its followers

[8] R. W. Phelps to Governor Comer, August 28, 1907 (in Governor's Letterfile No. 140).
[9] Montgomery *Advertiser*, October 7, 1909; Governor Comer to Governor R. B. Glenn of North Carolina, September 17, 1907 (in Governor's Letterbook No. 119).
[10] Montgomery *Advertiser*, August 18, November 7, 1907; Governor Comer to Judge David Shelby, April 20, 1909 (in Governor's Letterfile No. 169).

without injuring seriously the roads which had come to terms. Dozens of letters in the Governor's letterfiles indicate that public sentiment was overwhelmingly behind Comer. R. W. Phelps, a dealer in general merchandise of Salem, Alabama, wrote: "The people would fight anything headed by Tom Jones with that fierceness . . . a bull would fight anything headed by a red flag."[11] A wide variety of gratuitous suggestions as to how to force the railroads to yield poured in.

Governor Comer held a futile conference with Milton H. Smith. Then, finally, he called the legislature to meet in November, 1907, and pushed through an elaborate, drastic, and extravagant code of punitive legislation, designed to make it more attractive for the railroads to settle with him than to fight their cases through the Federal courts. The new laws were carefully framed with the purpose of giving no grounds for injunctions.

Judge Jones promptly enjoined the enforcement of the supposedly injunction-proof laws. The state as its next step, however, took an appeal to the Circuit Court of Appeals at New Orleans, which on April 6, 1909 decided the injunctions had been "improvidently issued" and dissolved them, allowing the statutory rates to go into effect pending the outcome of the litigation.[12]

Meanwhile, some two years having passed since the adoption of the first Comer railroad code in 1907, liquor prohibition had crowded railroad regulation off the front pages of newspapers and had become the state's leading political issue. The harsh railroad code of November, 1907 had turned many against Governor Comer, and his prohibitionist stand lost him the support of others. The legislature, called into special session in the summer of 1909 primarily to deal with the liquor problem, gave the railroad code an overhauling and repealed the most harsh and objectionable of the railroad laws, which no one had any further use for. After a period of actual trial of the statutory rates, the litigation was resumed. Special masters in chancery were appointed to conduct exhaustive hearings, and the cases were prolonged through 1910 and 1911, although they received little publicity.

Comer was not eligible for reelection in 1910, but Governor Emmett O'Neal, his successor, continued to fight the railroad cases through the courts. The contest became obscured by technicalities,

[11] R. W. Phelps to Governor Comer, August 28, 1907.
[12] Railroad Commission of Alabama *v*. Central of Georgia Ry. Co., 170 *Fed. Rep.* 225, 95 *C.C.A.* 117.

and the public largely lost track of what was going on. The state's attorneys were so overwhelmed by the volume of data and opinions poured forth by the railroads that they tended to lose sight of what they were searching for. Their efforts at cross-examination of railroad witnesses were ineffective. The state needed as many and as able legal counsellors and technical advisers as the railroads had but did not get them.

Judge Jones was faced with a very difficult dilemma, which was not of his making. The problem of the railroads was to show that they were not earning a fair and just return on the value of the property devoted to intrastate business. The burden of proof was theirs, and there appeared no way they could overcome it except by the application of some such specious formula as that approved by the Supreme Court in the case of Smyth v. Ames. Without such a formula they could not prove confiscation, if confiscation existed, but with it they could "prove" confiscation when it did not exist. The Fourteenth Amendment, as interpreted by the courts, gave protection against confiscation by rate reductions; could the courts, in the face of this, deny the railroads a remedy by refuting the specious formula? There was no logical way out of this *cul de sac,* and the Judge could only fall back upon his own conceptions and philosophy. Judge Jones, in his final opinions in April and May, 1912, found against the state.[13]

The whole Federal judicial system had been turned into a blind alley. The logical extension of Judge Jones' opinions and those of several other Federal judges about the same time was the conclusion that a state could impose no regulation upon a corporation, if it cost the corporation anything. On Governor O'Neal's instigation, governors of twenty-five states, meeting at Spring Lake, New Jersey, unanimously and vigorously protested. The Federal courts had gone too far, and it was the problem of the Supreme Court of the United States to find a way out of the impasse.

Governor O'Neal, in cooperation with Robert C. Brickell, then attorney-general of Alabama, and the special attorneys for the state, Henry C. Selheimer and Samuel D. Weakley, decided to postpone an appeal of the cases to the United States Supreme Court because of the great expense involved. That court at the time had under

---

[13] Louisville & N. R. Co. v. Railroad Commission of Alabama, 196 *Fed. Rep.* 800; Western Railway of Alabama v. Railroad Commission of Alabama, 197 *Fed. Rep.* 954.

advisement a large number of cases from Minnesota and other states, involving the points at issue in Alabama. In the meantime, the Railroad Commission of Alabama took up and ordered reduced the passenger rates of the railroads which had obtained the injunctions. The commission was able to get around Judge Jones' injunctions, and, when the roads appealed for new ones, the cases were heard before courts made up of three federal judges, under a federal law passed in 1910, and the state won all these cases.

In June, 1913, the United States Supreme Court finally decided the Minnesota rate cases.[14] The court denied it had ever approved the Smyth *v.* Ames formula, which had stymied state control of railroad rates for fifteen years, and to keep this falsehood from being too transparent did not even cite the case. In this and numerous other questions paralleled in the Alabama cases the decision was opposite to that of Judge Jones. The effect was to jettison the protection formerly given railroads by the Federal courts.

The State of Alabama's attorneys began to work on an appeal of their cases, but several influences were working in favor of a settlement out of court. Former Governor Comer aspired to regain the governorship in the election of 1914. Many former Comer supporters disapproved his constant agitation of the railroad issue and his uncompromising extremism, which had come to be known as "Comerism." The prohibition issue divided his former followers and separated him from Governor O'Neal, a local optionist. Charles Henderson of Troy, whom Comer had appointed president of the railroad commission in 1907 and who had subsequently been elected to that office, was ambitious to become governor. S. P. Kennedy, the commission's executive secretary, was stirred with a desire to be appointed president of the commission, if Henderson should vacate the office to become governor. Henderson, a local optionist, secured the support of O'Neal, and Kennedy became Henderson's campaign manager. O'Neal had been stung by Comer's criticisms of his administration.

Suddenly, without consulting the state's attorneys, Governor O'Neal confronted his Attorney General with a draft of a settlement of the railroad cases, which the railroad lawyers were already on hand to sign; with only one important change it was signed, on February

[14] 230 *U.S.* 352.

21, 1914.[15] By its terms the 2½c passenger fare was to be accepted by the railroads without appeal, and the Jones injunctions were to remain in effect but not to prevent the railroad commission from exercising its lawful powers to revise freight and passenger rates. The railroads were not to suffer any liability under bonds posted in the rate cases, and coupons issued to passengers, payable if the railroads lost their cases, were not to be redeemed. There was no acceptance of the statutory freight rates. O'Neal indicated that the agreement had been brought to him through the railroad commission, but Henderson was the only member of the commission who appears to have known anything about it, blanks being left for the signatures of the associate members. That there were railroad brains behind the scheme appears obvious, R. E. Steiner and George W. Jones being suspect. Henderson and Kennedy steadfastly insisted during the gubernatorial race that the invalidated coupons were redeemable.

Comer was publicly beside himself with wrath at the settlement, which he described as a cowardly surrender to the railroads after the state had won. It cut the ground from under him politically and was perhaps a decisive factor in his defeat in the complicated gubernatorial race in 1914, which Charles Henderson won.

It is probable that the settlement was a good thing for the state, despite the circumstances under which it was made. An appeal would have been quite expensive because of the complexity of the cases and the volume of the record. It was high time to heal the open sore of conflict between the state and its corporations and to bring about peace and cooperation. Rising railroad costs were reducing earnings, and the economic effects of the coming World War were soon to weaken the railroads financially. The railroad commission was left in a position to adjust freight rates and did so in the case of the compromising companies.

The warring triumvirate of Comer, Smith, and Jones continued their bitter personal feud. When their utterances had ceased to be news, they each hired at personal expense great amounts of newspaper advertising space to defend themselves and attack each other, in

---

[15] Attorney General Robert C. Brickell to Henry C. Selheimer, March 26, 1914 (in Attorney General's Papers, Drawer 365); "Views of H. C. Selheimer," a typewritten statement; Selheimer to Brickell, March 25, 1914; see also Attorney General of Alabama, *Biennial Report*, 1912–14, p. 31.

language not characterized by restraint. Judge Jones' death in 1914 was probably hastened by his deep hurt at the attacks upon him and at his obvious unpopularity. Comer and Smith kept up the feud. Comer pressed old libel suits against L. & N. officials, and Smith, as late as 1916, violently denounced him in sworn testimony before the Interstate Commerce Commission: "An impossible man. A disordered mind. He will not be placated. [He is] one with a diseased mind."[16]

The mood of the people in 1914 appears to have been accurately gauged by Charles Henderson, who said:

> We have seen enough of rainbow chasing. We have had enough of men riding into office on hobbies . . . We have had enough of strife. We have had enough of dictatorship. . . . We want peace, tranquility and prosperity in Alabama, and unless the signs of the times fail we are going to have it soon.[17]

Corporations continued to be influential in the state's government, but the reform movement had achieved two important things: very substantial steps had been taken to reform corporate abuses, and the public and the legislature had come to understand better the important and difficult problem of regulating corporations so as to require them to serve the public interest without injuring their capacity to do so. Corporate executives, too, were learning through hard experience their obligations to the public. The story here told had its parallel, with local differences of detail and circumstance, in many other states and in the Federal government, and each shared through communication the experiences of the others. The Fourteenth Amendment and the bungling of the Federal courts appear to have been complicating factors that seriously interfered with the working out of practical adjustments of the differences between people and corporations on the basis of mutual interest.

[16]"Hearings before the Interstate Commerce Commission Relative to . . . the Louisville & Nashville Railroad Co.," U.S. 64 Cong., 1 Sess., *Senate Doc.* 461(1916), pp. 362–364.

[17]Montgomery *Advertiser*, February 17, 1914.

HUGH C. BAILEY

Edgar Gardner Murphy
and the Child
Labor Movement

When the 1898–1899 Alabama legislature failed to pass a law to improve working conditions of children employed in cotton mills,[1] Edgar Gardner Murphy, crusading rector of St. John's Episcopal Church, Montgomery, put plans in motion which later resulted in an American social revolution.[2]

Armed with the fact that twenty-five Alabama mills were employing 430 children twelve hours a day, six days a week, for 15c to 30c a day in 1901, Murphy, accompanied by representatives from the Alabama Federation of Women's Clubs, appeared before joint sessions of committees of the Alabama House and Senate to press for the adoption of a twelve-year minimum age limit for factory workers. He was maligned as the tool of New England industrialists who were seeking to destroy the textile industry of the South, and the proposed bill was defeated.[3] It was now apparent that the only hope for success lay in the awakening of public opinion in Alabama, and Murphy undertook this through the formation of the Alabama Child Labor Committee to which he attracted some of the outstanding leaders of the state. Associated with him on the Executive Committee were former Governor Thomas G. Jones, who was soon to become Federal judge through the efforts of Murphy, and Booker T. Washington, Lucien V. La-

[1] This paper was read at the annual meeting of the Alabama Historical Association, Auburn, April 25, 1964. It was published in *The Alabama Review*, XVIII (Jan. 1965).

[2] Maud King Murphy, *Edgar Gardner Murphy, From Records and Memories* (New York, 1943), 42, and Elizabeth H. Davidson, *Child Labor Legislation in the Southern Textile States* (Chapel Hill, 1939), 20–23.

[3] Montgomery (Ala.) *Advertiser*, Feb. 7, 1901, and undated clipping from the Birmingham (Ala.) *Age-Herald* (Murphy Papers, University of North Carolina, Chapel Hill).

taste of Montgomery, John Craft of Mobile, A. J. Reilly of Ensley, and J. H. Phillips, superintendent of the Birmingham City Schools.[4]

The committee's campaign for a law was initiated by the publication in the Boston *Evening Transcript* of "An Appeal to the People and Press of New England." Murphy had married a girl from Concord, Massachusetts and had spent months in New England. He understood the psychology of the area and appealed "to the public conscience of those historic localities from which so much good has come to our common country." Twice as many children under twelve were employed in New England mills as in Southern-owned ones, and he knew that the most effective opposition to a child labor law was likely to come from the "salaried representative of Massachusetts investments."

J. Howard Nichols of Boston, treasurer of the Alabama City Mill, replied to Murphy. Although he conceded that the employment of young children was a mistake, he charged parents forced this on mills by threatening to go elsewhere if they were not employed. He attacked the proposed child labor bill with vehemence, contending that it owed its origin to a "skillful, female labor agitator" and was the entering wedge for an attempted unionization of Alabama factories. He held that all legitimate reform must come from within the state and demanded that Georgia, which had twice as many spindles as Alabama, must act first. He concluded by praising the fine facilities afforded its workers by his company, inviting comparison of them with any others in the state.

Murphy met Nichols' challenges by noting that the Alabama Child Labor committee was composed and directed by Alabamians who had no financial interests in its work; certainly, Nichols could not claim to occupy such a position. He could not see how Nichols could oppose the projected legislation. It would remove from the mills parental pressure to employ children, since no mill would be allowed to do so. Moreover, it was absurd to oppose the measure on the grounds that it might lead to unionization, no matter how much one opposed it. Nichols was demanding that "we must not do a compassionate and reasonable thing, because, somebody might demand an inconsiderate and unreasonable thing." The same lack of logic was displayed in the demand that Georgia act first. Logically, since Georgia had twice as

[4] *Child Labor in Alabama, An Appeal to the People and Press of New England With A Resulting Correspondence* (Montgomery, 1901), 6.

many spindles as Alabama, it would be twice as hard for that state to pass a law. Murphy believed sincerely that for owners and management the "course of humanity is always the course of wisdom." Barbarous conditions "must gradually invite the hatred of the people, must inevitably goad the great masses of our population into the fixed belief that the corporation desires to live, not by production but through destruction; that it is a force to be feared and bound rather than a force to be trusted and liberated." Nichols' presentation of the exceptional nature of his company's mill merely furnished additional proof of the need of a law. If the Alabama City Mill was unique, then its owners should welcome a law that would require other mills to approach its excellent standards.

Nichols did not attempt to reply to Murphy, but the cause was taken up by another Bostonian, Horace S. Sears, treasurer of the West Point Manufacturing Company of Langdale, Alabama, who attacked Murphy as an "ill-advised humanitarian" and contended that before any child labor law was passed a compulsory education law must precede it. However, he hastened to add, this should be contingent upon the passage of education laws by Georgia, South Carolina, and North Carolina; otherwise, the interests of Alabama mills would be jeopardized.

In replying to Sears, Murphy implied that his arguments were ruses. He believed in education as devoutly as anyone but knew that a compulsory education law could not be passed at the time. Moreover, Sears was not ready to accept his own remedy. In making an education law contingent upon action by other states, he was using a strategy "very familiar to the students of economic progress." "Over in Georgia and the Carolinas, some of the mill men are claiming that they are 'only waiting upon Alabama,'" Murphy wrote. Amazingly enough, the compulsory education law Sears supported "owed its origin" to Miss Irene Ashby, a representative of the American Federation of Labor, whom Nichols condemned as an agitator. It seemed incongruous that forces opposing a law to prevent ten- to twelve-year-olds working twelve hours a day could sincerely support a compulsory education act. The child labor system was, if anything, "a system of compulsory ignorance." Murphy knew from experience that children would go to school, if they had a chance. Within twenty miles of his office a factory employed seventy-five children from 6 A.M. to 6:30 P.M. When a night school was established near them, however, fifty of the children promptly enrolled and were so eager to learn, even after their exhausting day's labor, that they expressed disappointment when the evening's sessions were over. This convinced Murphy that the first step in the education of mill children was to get them out of the mills. To Sears's contention that many would promptly get into vice if the discipline of work were removed, Murphy could only ask, "What possible vice can a sub-12-year-old get into in the streets of the rural South or in the model mill villages Sears described so beautifully?"

Murphy believed that Massachusetts' apathy toward Alabama conditions could be explained by the fact that Alabama's mill children were white. "Suppose the conditions were reversed and the mills of Southern men were full of Negro children under twelve—how quickly and how justly New England would ring with denunciation!"[5]

The Alabama Child Labor Committee was conscious of the value of the Murphy-Nichols-Sears correspondence and of the fact that the legislature which would meet in January, 1903 would be the last for four years. Therefore, to bring pressure on the lawmakers, the committee issued the correspondence as a forty-page pamphlet. The success of this publication led Murphy to write at least nine others in the next few months. Frequently he had to pay the costs himself, but they were distributed free and were well received. Murphy's work led the editor of the *Annals of the American Academy of Political and Social Science* to ask him to deal fully with the child labor situation in the South in an extended article for his journal. Extensive research was done in preparation for this work, but illness prevented the meeting of the publication deadline. When this occurred, Murphy incorporated his findings in one of his most influential publications, *The Case Against Child Labor: An Argument.*[6] Here, in unanswerable statistics, he demonstrated that children under sixteen constituted one-fourth of the work force in Southern cotton mills and that in the twenty years from 1880 to 1900 the percentage of such children in Northern mills had been cut in half, thanks to state legislation, while the percentage in the South had remained constant. Basing his figures on North Carolina percentages, the only state with a breakdown below the age of sixteen, he estimated that there were at least 32,000

[5] *Ibid.*, 3–6, 11–38.
[6] (Montgomery, 1902), 3–18, 22–27.

children under fourteen in Southern mills and 10,000 to 12,000 under twelve. Murphy's study had convinced him that "among the most distinctive of the rights of the little child is the divine right to do nothing." Even the horse breeder recognized that the "abnormal straining of muscles and nerves, in the period of immaturity, is an injury to all life." Manufacturers contended that the work required of children was light. They did not see that the nervous tension involved in long hours of monotonous repetition was stupifying. They seemed to regard the factories as "great educational and philanthropical institutions" which offered "children of the poor the progressive advantages of the kindergarten, the grammar school, the high school, the great university—and a trip to Europe—all in one!" And as a "slight addition" to its other advantages, the mill bestowed 10c to 30c on each child for twelve hours of work.

Of course, children were injured in the mills. On one occasion Murphy expressed sympathy when he saw a little girl of eight who had "the two larger fingers of her right hand torn from their sockets at the greater knuckles." Mill men defended this and similar accidents by stating that they were the results of carelessness, adding that the mill families were living better than ever before. Murphy protested against such reasoning. Should not eight-year-olds be careless? He pitied the world when all of its young children became "philosophers of probabilities." He dissented from the belief that the little child must bear the brunt of the new industrial stress. "Let us not be guilty of mental confusion," he wrote. "Let us not credit the good fortune of the family to the misfortune of the child."

Murphy declared that Southerners must realize that they could not "war against the practice of the whole world." He felt the average citizen must demand decent standards in the mills, and industry must comply. He knew from the large profits mill men conceded making that fear for profits could not be the principal factor in using child labor. He suspected that the opposition to a child labor law lay in a dread of unionization and warned manufacturers that the sure way to lose their fight was to oppose reasonable working conditions. In a paragraph pregnant with insight, he advised the mill owners not to underrate the sentiments which would flare up in Southern society if it were aroused to defend its children. "Of all the sections of this world," he wrote, "the South—the land of chivalry, of tenderness, of home—the land where, if we have learned anything, we have learned to suffer for our ideals—the South is the very last place in which to laugh at sentiment, least of all at the sentiment which touches the promise and freedom of our children."[7]

Murphy's concern extended from the individual child to Southern society generally. He felt that as long as child labor continued the entire region would stagnate. Though originally from the poorest of families (his father had deserted his mother when he was six), Murphy had risen to the heights of intellectual and social respectability, but he retained the utmost regard for the potential of the Southern masses from whom he differed in so many ways. He detested child labor because it closed the opportunity for the child's development. Murphy realized that the employment of workers before they could receive an education meant "the condemning of them to the lot of the underprivileged." It relegated the South to the class of producers of coarser goods and its workers to "childlike" labor "even after they became adults."[8]

Murphy's work was attacked by the *Manufacturers' Record* (Baltimore) as "inflammatory," "impractical," "bryanesque," "wandering," and "radical." It classified him as a "demagogue" and an "hysterian of the masculine gender," adding that child labor would be cast off "only by the unimpeded and unantagonized efforts of the representative Southern men" who had already done so much for the South and the owners and managers of the mills.

Murphy replied that in twenty years the mill men had done nothing to improve conditions. He particularly resented the contention that mill men were the only representative Southerners. Certainly, they were no more representative than any other segment of the population, and it was unfortunate that when they wished someone to speak for them they usually turned to a New England figure.[9]

Under Murphy's leadership the Alabama Child Labor Committee organized local committees and letter-writing campaigns. Moreover, it distributed 28,000 copies of Murphy's pamphlets which constituted "the first body of printed material of any considerable extent or value" on child labor produced in the South.[10] One of the most

---

[7] *Ibid.*, 27–34.

[8] *Ibid.*, 19, 34–36, 38, 41–45; DuBose and Gardner Murphy, *Maud King Murphy 1865–1957* (n.p., n.d.), 13.

[9] *The South and Her Children: A Rejoinder in the Child Labor Discussion* (Montgomery, 1902), 3–9, 13, 15, 17–21.

[10] Murphy, "Southern Prosperity Is Not Shackled to Child Labor," *Charities*, X 453 (May 2, 1903); Davidson, 36.

effective of its pieces of propaganda was *Pictures from the Mills,* a pamphlet composed of actual photographs of the young operatives taken by Murphy in the plants.[11] The pressure created by the Alabama Child Labor Committee made the enactment of a law possible, and Murphy's fine hand was, of course, prominent in the victory strategy. Much to the consternation of Miss Ashby, Samuel Gompers, and others, he insisted that the American Federation of Labor stay out of the political campaign in the state. He believed that union association with a fine bill in Georgia had been responsible for its defeat, and he was determined that the same thing should not happen in Alabama.

When the legislature convened, Murphy was instrumental in negotiating a compromise with three mill leaders, among whom was B. B. Comer. It provided far less than he would have liked, allowing ten-year-olds with widowed mothers or dependent fathers to hold jobs, for example, but it was all that was obtainable. The wisdom of Murphy's strategy was evident in the Senate, where the measure passed by only two votes; these would not have been available if the more progressive mill men had not been already converted to support the law.[12]

Murphy's successful campaign in Alabama made him a national figure in the struggle against child labor. Following it, he delivered the most important address at the 1903 meeting of the National Conference of Charities and Corrections in Atlanta. In a message in which he demanded that the humanitarian convert his appeal into practical terms that ordinary people could understand, he called for a nation-wide crusade against child labor. A decade later A. J. McKelway, one of the leading reformers in the field himself, described the address as "the greatest speech against child labor ever delivered in America."[13]

Following the Atlanta meeting, Murphy frequently conferred with Dr. Felix Adler, professor of Political and Social Ethics at Columbia University and head of the Ethical Culture Society. Together, they formed plans for a national organization to fight child labor. Murphy bore the brunt of the effort in contacting key reformers over the nation to ask their support. As a part of the strategy for organiza-

---

[11] (Montgomery, 1902).

[12] Davidson, 37–47, 50; *Advertiser,* Feb. 20, 1903; "Child Labor in Alabama," *Annals of the American Academy of Political and Social Science,* XXI, 331–332 (Jan.–June, 1903).

[13] "Edgar Gardner Murphy Memorial Meeting, New York City, December 7, 1913" (typescript in writer's possession).

tion, he delivered a major address in New York in March, 1904,[14] and in April the National Child Labor Committee was organized with Murphy as temporary secretary. As specific policy, it agreed not to appeal to the Federal government for aid, but to work directly with the people to obtain enactment of proper state laws.

Because of his ill health and the demands of his new position as secretary of the Southern Education Board, Murphy resigned as secretary of the NCLC soon after its organization. For two years, however, he played a leading role in its program. Nothing less could have been expected from "the father and founder" of the committee, as Adler described him.[15] Murphy's own publications had been widely used by state committees, and he served as a member of the committee's publication division. He urged the launching of investigations in the coal mines of Pennsylvania, the glass factories of New Jersey, Pennsylvania, and Ohio, and the cotton mills of Georgia. Above all, he aided in keeping the organization "on the ground"; he insisted facts be obtained before pamphlets were written and that consideration always be given to the totality of the situation. He was not opposed to capitalism in any way, but was concerned with the rights of individuals and the welfare of society generally.[16]

In 1906 a majority of the members of the Board of Trustees of NCLC, discouraged by the slowness of Southern legislatures, voted to rescind their restriction on the endorsement of national action in the field of child labor and to give their support to the Beveridge Bill, a measure that would exclude the goods of all plants employing children under fourteen from interstate commerce. Murphy resigned from the NCLC when this occurred, feeling that the enactment of the bill was "contrary to sound public policy" and would "work the gravest injury to the children." He effectively raised his voice against Federal action by writing leading public men and furnishing articles to the press. An article in the Montgomery *Advertiser* "definitely decided" President Roosevelt to abstain from sending a special message on the subject to Congress.[17] Subsequently, Murphy prepared

[14] Typescript in Murphy Papers.

[15] Minute Book No. 1, April, 1904–April, 1906 (National Child Labor Committee Papers, Library of Congress), Apr. 15, May 4, 1904.

[16] *Ibid.*, May 4, Oct. 3, Nov. 10, 1904; Feb. 6, Nov. 16, 1905.

[17] Murphy to Adler, Dec. 18, 1906 in Minute Book No. 2, October 24, 1906– April 29, 1908 (NCLC Papers); Murphy to Oswald G. Villard, Feb. 24, 1907 (Villard Papers, Harvard University Library); Roosevelt to Murphy, Jan. 17, 1907 (in writer's possession).

a pamphlet containing one of the ablest statements ever made against a Federal child labor law. In it he contended that the educational effects of state campaigns were necessary if any law were to succeed. He challenged the constitutionality of the Beveridge Bill, holding that the central government did not have the power to prohibit the transportation of goods which were not harmful in themselves across state lines. He questioned the effectiveness of the bill since it provided only an age limit as a protection for the children. A truly effective law must establish a *system* of protection, including provisions of inspection and enforcement, compulsory education, and limitation upon the periods and hours of work. As Murphy saw it, the tragedy of the Beveridge Bill lay in its retarding of effective action in the states and in its division of the reform forces.[18]

In the midst of the campaign against the Beveridge Bill, Murphy returned to Alabama to direct the Alabama Child Labor Committee in obtaining passage of the Child Labor Act of 1907. The issue was a tense one since Comer, president of the Avondale Mills, had just become governor. In the campaign the *Advertiser* had quoted Murphy as saying Comer had opposed all legislation in their 1903 conference. Furthermore, Murphy had written, "Mr. Comer has seemed to me the most bitter opponent of child labor legislation I have ever known." As governor, Comer had no choice but to remain at least passive on the child labor issue, especially since the Democratic platform promised additional reform. But many of his lieutenants were bitterly opposed to new legislation. For weeks Murphy conferred with leaders of public opinion and leading members of the legislature in Montgomery, but because of his poor health the strain became so great he had to leave. He advised his associates, however, to wait until the legislature returned from a recess in July to press the question.[19] In the interim he wrote an effective "Plea for Immediate Action" and sent it to each member of the House and Senate. In it he demanded that an absolute age limit of twelve be fixed for all children in the mills. He pleaded for the prohibition of work for all under sixteen from 7 P.M. to 6 A.M. He urged the passage of a compulsory school attendance law and the appointment of competent inspectors to enforce the law. He reminded the lawmakers that in the

---

[18] *The Federal Regulation of Child Labor, A Criticism of the Policy Represented in the Beveridge-Parsons Bill* (New York, 1907), 1–38.

[19] Murphy to Villard, March 10, 1907 (Villard Papers); Davidson, 216.

earlier session they had given ample protection to fish, game and wild life and wondered if they could afford to do less for the state's children. Speaking directly to the Comer forces, he wrote, "We are told that the people do not wish the railroads of this state to write the railroad legislation. Do they then wish the factory legislation of the state to be written by the factories? Have the people of Alabama displaced one set of special interests, only to enthrone another?" He urged immediate action. If the legislature failed to act, it would be four years before another opportunity presented itself. "That will be the day of *other* children," he wrote. "The opportunity to help *these* children is here today; it cannot return; it will pass with them and with you."[20]

Shortly after the legislature reconvened, it passed a measure incorporating all the features of Murphy's demand. He was immensely pleased, feeling that his faith in state action had been vindicated. He realized that much remained to be done, but he felt that in time an aroused state citizenry would respond.[21]

While Murphy was winning his fight in Alabama, his desire to see the Beveridge Bill defeated and NCLC support for it withdrawn was being attained. Undoubtedly, his attack on the bill played an important role in Roosevelt's decision not to give it his support. The President wrote Murphy he had decided not to take immediate action, preferring to see if the states would do their duty.[22] If they did not, he could later call for Federal legislation.

At the same time the NCLC, discouraged because Congress failed to act and the bill's endorsement created division, adopted a statement that it would not take action on a law until the results of a survey of child labor conditions, authorized by the United States Government in February, 1907, became known. After a more searching study, it hoped a policy could be agreed upon which would "unite all forces now devoted to the cause of child labor reform."[23]

In January, 1908 Murphy was urged to return as a member of the

[20] *The Child Labor Question in Alabama—A Plea for Immediate Action*, National Child Labor Committee, Pamphlet 59 (New York, 1907), 1–12.

[21] *Ibid.*, n. 9; New York *Evening Post*, Sept. 19, 1907 (Murphy Papers); Murphy to Villard, Sept. 17, 1907 (Villard Papers).

[22] Nov. 15, 1907 (Murphy Papers).

[23] National Child Labor Committee, Pamphlet 64, *Third Annual Report, for the Fiscal Year Ended Sept. 30, 1907* (New York, 1907), 12–13; Robert deForest to Murphy, May 28, 1907; Jan. 8, 1908 (Murphy Papers).

NCLC. Robert W. deForest, a member of the Board of Trustees, wrote that with the adjournment of the Congress there was no Beveridge Bill and "the attitude of the committee toward any future Beveridge bill is assured. . . . You have won out, and there are no feelings to swallow."

But Murphy was too ill to consider returning. As much as any man he had "pricked the conscience of the country alive to the existence of child labor as a shame and curse to America." To a great extent, due to his efforts and that of organizations he aided in founding and guiding, the public repudiated child labor, and it came to be defended only by a few employers who felt their self-interest depended on a perpetuation of the system.[24] Methods of fighting it would change as the country re-evaluated its theories of government, but Murphy would not lose his status as a pioneer who perceived and attacked a major enemy when few others recognized it or dared raise their voices against it.

[24] "Child Labor in 1913," *Child Labor Bulletin* (Nov., 1913), 9.

MARLENE HUNT RIKARD

George Gordon Crawford:
Man of the New South

In 1907 when United States Steel purchased the Tennessee Coal, Iron and Railroad Company of Birmingham, Alabama, a young Southerner, George Gordon Crawford, returned to the South as TCI's new president. While serving in this capacity from 1907 to 1930, he became one of the most important and influential men of the early twentieth-century New South. He was not a typical flamboyant Southern steelman nor a bombastic New South promoter. Instead, he generally shunned publicity, refused to regard industrialization as a "cure-all," and emphasized a balance between agriculture and industry.[1]

There is a paucity of studies on the economic development of the South after the 1880s.[2] Considering the impact industrialization has had on the region, studies of the New South and its industrial leaders are essential for a balance in Southern historiography. The actions and leadership of George Crawford were a vital aspect of this period.

A son of the Old South—raised on his grandfather's Georgia plantation—Crawford was a member of the first graduating class of Georgia Tech, earning a degree in mechanical engineering.[3] Two years of total

This paper was read at the meeting of the Alabama Historical Association in Birmingham, April 29, 1977. It was published in *The Alabama Review*, XXXI (July 1978).

[1] A more detailed discussion of Crawford is available in Marlene Hunt Rikard, "George Gordon Crawford: Man of the New South" (M.A. thesis, Samford University, 1971). The complete company name was Tennessee Coal, Iron and Railroad Company. It was generally called the Tennessee Company or TCI. A grant from the Birmingham Metropolitan Study Project helped fund the oral histories used in this paper, cited as Oral History Project.

[2] See Gerald D. Nash, "Research Opportunities in the Economic History of the South After 1880," *Journal of Southern History*, XXXII (August 1966), 308–24.

[3] Atlanta *Journal*, November 14, 1907 in Crawford Collection, hereafter cited as CC. This collection is available on microfilm at Samford University, Birmingham, Alabama.

immersion in the study of technical chemistry at Karl-Eberhard University of Tubingen, Germany, were followed by brief employment as a draftsman at Sloss-Sheffield Iron and Steel Company in Birmingham.[4] One of his German professors had told him that the Southern states were at the stage of industrial efficiency of medieval Europe, and his brief stay in Birmingham confirmed this caveat to Crawford. He left the South accepting a position as a chemist at the Edgar-Thomson Works of the Carnegie Steel Company near Pittsburgh. Frequent promotions in the following years allowed him to gain wide-ranging experience in many areas of the steel industry with Carnegie Steel and the National Tube Company of McKeesport, Pennsylvania. When the United States Steel Corporation was organized in 1901, he became manager of the National Department of the National Tube Company, one of the three largest plants of the new corporation.[5]

As a "public service" during the panic of 1907 the United States Steel Corporation decided to purchase the majority of the stock of the Tennessee Coal, Iron and Railroad Company of Birmingham, Alabama, and the giant of the steel industry entered the South. Only at the continued insistence of Judge Elbert Gary, chairman of the board, and President William Corey was Crawford prevailed upon to accept the proffered position as president of the new subsidiary. Crawford knew that the reputation of several men had been ruined by attempts to make steel at Birmingham. Andrew Carnegie had proclaimed to the people of Birmingham, "You have all the elements but you cannot make steel."[6]

No such lack of confidence existed in the Magic City. The U.S. Steel purchase was hailed as a "fulfillment of promise" that would "make the Birmingham district hum as it has never hummed before."[7] To the people of Birmingham the only unknown quantity implicit in the purchase was the young Southerner returning to his native region as president. His advance billing was impressive. The New York papers described him as a "Carnegie protege . . . one of the hustling young heads of the subsidiaries of the Corporation,"

[4] Edwin Mims, *The Advancing South: Stories of Progress and Reaction* (New York, 1926), 92; "Who's Who From Georgia Tech," *Georgia Tech Alumnus,* June 1923, 106–07, CC.

[5] Mims, *Advancing South,* 93; "Who's Who," *Georgia Tech Alumnus,* 107, CC.

[6] Mims, *Advancing South,* 94; McKeesport (Pennsylvania) *News,* November 14, 1907, CC; Ida M. Tarbell, *The Life of Elbert H. Gary* (New York, 1925), 309.

[7] Birmingham *News,* November 13, 1907.

acknowledged by all steel experts to be "one of the most capable men in the employ of the Steel Corporation in the mechanical side of its work."[8]

Crawford arrived in Birmingham in the midst of a business depression that had reduced the number of "stacks blowing" and closed down many furnaces and mines. However, larger concerns dwarfed the immediate crisis. The management of U.S. Steel felt that two major problems confronted Crawford at the Tennessee Company. One was technical—the best employment of Southern low-grade ore. The other was human—the inability to obtain steady, efficient labor.[9] The failure of previous owners to resolve these difficulties had long stifled the potential of this Southern iron and steel complex.

A survey of the living conditions for labor in the Birmingham district helped explain the 400 percent employee turnover rate that confronted Crawford. People were living in a swampy wilderness with primitive sanitary facilities and polluted water supplies. Malaria was a common occurrence. Under the impact of rapid industrialization and an influx of workers from rural areas, the existing public facilities were overburdened, and Jefferson County lacked the resources to provide needed services. The work force in such an environment was plagued by illness and lost work time, and there were few inducements for working men to settle permanently and raise their families in the area.[10]

Firms in the area had done little on their own to improve the living conditions. Industrial negligence created bitter resentment as illustrated in the statement of one employee who said the workers were treated as "mine and furnace fodder," housed worse than mules, and received medical treatment in a dirty shack with no floor. In return, one company official characterized the labor force as "shiftless, thriftless, sloppy and dirty."[11]

If Crawford were to succeed in solving the complicated metallurgical and technical problems and to operate the plants with efficiency comparable to those of the North, an important priority was the establishment of a reliable and healthy work force. Because the Ten-

[8] New York *Herald*, November 14, 1907, CC; New York *Commercial*, November 14, 1907, CC.

[9] Birmingham *Labor Advocate*, November 29, 1907, CC; New York *Herald*, November 14, 1907, CC.

[10] *Tribute to Lloyd Noland: Reunion Volume* (Fairfield, Ala., 1947), 3; Arthur Wiebel, *Biography of a Business* (Birmingham, 1960), 45.

[11] Rose Feld, "Way Down in Alabama," *Success*, VIII (January 1924), 55–56; Sterling D. Spero and Abram L. Harris, *The Black Worker* (New York, 1931), 46.

nessee Company was now a U.S. Steel subsidiary, his solutions had to evolve within the framework of the policies of the parent corporation led by Judge Elbert Gary. Characterized as a man of "tact, smoothness, conciliation, and compromise," Gary decreed that the corporation's policy toward its workers would include fair wages, good working conditions, pensions, compensations, and school and recreation facilities—thus making labor unions unnecessary. This attitude, he claimed, was produced not by the threat of labor unions but a mature social conscience within the industry.[12]

Crawford utilized this philosophy of welfare capitalism in an attempt to create the desired work force in the Birmingham district. The implementation was complex in the South because the cheap labor supply sought by the steel industry included black workers. The programs devised under this paternalistic system varied according to the conditions faced by the management of individual subsidiaries and according to the autonomy allowed the subsidiary president. Possessing to an unusual degree the confidence and friendship of Judge Gary, Crawford's welfare programs were perhaps more his own than those of most subsidiary presidents.[13]

His approach to solving the labor turnover and changing the character of the work force was a rapid clean-up of living conditions in the district. Inadequate shacks and shotgun houses were remodeled in existing villages, and new company towns were built with better constructed, larger houses on sizable lots along curbed, winding streets. Two villages—one for whites and one for blacks—were constructed at most sites. Each included a school building, playground, community house, teachers' cottage, bathhouse, church, and sometimes a swimming pool and a tennis court.[14]

[12] Philip Cabot, "Slavery and Steel—A Day Dream?," *The World's Work*, XLV (December 1922), 223; Rose Feld, "The Public Be Informed," *The World's Work*, LIII (December 1926), 203; C. L. Close, "The Economic Saving of Human Resource," *Scientific Monthly*, IV (May 1917), 428; "The Story of Steel—XIV Welfare Work, or the Human Side of the Steel Industry," *Scientific American*, CXXXII (June 1925), 388. In 1910 a Bureau of Safety, Sanitation, and Welfare was created to oversee the activities of the corporation in sanitation, housing, safety, and education.

[13] Tarbell, *Elbert H. Gary*, 309; Cleveland (Ohio) *Daily Metal Trade*, January 30, 1930, CC.

[14] Hastings H. Hart, *Social Problems of Alabama: A Study of the Social Institutions and Agencies of the State of Alabama as Related to its War Activities* (Montgomery, 1918), 81–83; Mims, *Advancing South*, 100–01; Mollie Beck Jenkins, "The Social Work of the Tennessee Coal, Iron and Railroad Company" (M.A. thesis, University of Alabama, 1929), 4, 33–36; Clyde and Ruby Harper (resided in Muscoda and attended company schools), Oral History Project, January 15, 1976, Birmingham. Tape and transcript in possession of author.

Housing was only a small part of the physical and sociological problem that confronted Crawford. After being advised by a social welfare expert to work from within rather than adopt plans in effect elsewhere, Crawford hired Winifred Collins, an experienced social worker from Chicago, to head a department of social science. She brought in social workers from across the country, primarily young, college-educated women, who went to live and work in the villages. During the succeeding decades this corps of social workers implemented a highly developed, wide-ranging sphere of activities. Domestic science classes taught housekeeping, nutrition, and sewing to wives of the workers; women's clubs, children's groups, drama clubs, and village bands met in the community houses; libraries were established; and a horticultural expert encouraged and aided the villagers in growing gardens and guided school children in planting school plots.[15]

Because the existing county schools were entirely inadequate, housed in shacks and staffed by poorly trained teachers who often had only a grammar school education, Crawford arranged with local authorities for TCI to build, equip, maintain, and administer new schools in the company villages. The company supplemented the county's annual teacher salary appropriation, and well-trained teachers were recruited from major universities across the country. This company school system, operating eight white and fourteen black schools from 1914 to 1933, provided equal facilities and equipment for both races in direct contrast to the practice elsewhere in the state. The teachers lived in the villages, made regular home visits, and supervised scout troops and athletic teams.[16] A Rosenwald Fund survey characterized the system as "excellently managed, equipped and supervised" and concluded that the Tennessee Company schools were probably the best for black children in the entire South.[17]

Another major effort of Crawford to improve living conditions was the creation of a department of health that would cope not only

[15] Mims, *Advancing South,* 102–04; Jenkins, "Social Work," 1–4, 11; Hart, *Social Problems,* 82–84; Feld, "Way Down in Alabama," 110; Mrs. Doris Frost (company teacher and supervisor), Oral History Project, November 15, 1975, Washington, D.C. Tape and transcript in possession of author.

[16] Feld, "Way Down in Alabama," 110; Hart, *Social Problems,* 83; interview with Mrs. Nora Powell (teacher and principal in company school system), Birmingham, September 25, 1970; Jenkins, "Social Work," 7; Horace Mann Bond, *Negro Education in Alabama; A Study in Cotton and Steel* (Washington, D.C., 1939), 242; Frost, Oral History Project.

[17] Cited in Horace Mann Bond, *The Education of the Negro in the American Social Order* (New York, 1966), 349–51.

with work-related accidents but also with the eradication of malaria, typhoid, smallpox, and hookworm. These diseases were so prevalent that the average worker was on the job only twelve days a month. Crawford personally went to Panama to recruit Dr. Lloyd Noland from the staff of Dr. William Crawford Gorgas at the Panama Canal. Noland, equipped with authority equal to operating superintendents and with a generous budget, began an immediate program to close polluted water sources, drain swamps, and create a sanitary division. The voluntary health project he established, costing $1.25 a month, entitled employees and their families to the services of the salaried company physicians—night or day—at the local dispensaries or at home. The program of the department also included dental offices, baby and nutrition clinics in the schools, and eventually a large well-equipped company hospital. Although the expense was great, Crawford justified it by the increased number of work days secured and higher efficiency of the work force.[18]

The TCI president received both praise and severe criticism because of this approach to obtaining a stable work force. White mine owners condemned him for spoiling an illiterate black work force by educating them. Black historian Horace Mann Bond accused him of flattering the black worker to create a bulwark against unionism. In contrast, Tuskegee and Hampton Institutes had a close working relationship with Crawford and the Tennessee Company. The leadership of these black institutions generally supported the welfare programs, deeming them valuable factors in the economic progress of blacks.[19]

Several historians suggest that the welfare programs of the Tennessee Company were the result of the 1908 coal strike, which occurred after Crawford had been in Birmingham only eight months.[20] A 17½

[18] "Tribute to Lloyd Noland," booklet presented to Lloyd Noland at testamentary dinner, May 16, 1947, 7, 9–10, 20, 22–23, 26–27, 32–33; Mims, *Advancing South*, 102; Lloyd Noland, "The Organization and Operation of an Industrial Health Department," *Transactions of the Southern Surgical Association*, XXXVIII (1926), 275–84; Dr. O. E. Wilson (company doctor), Oral History Project, April 11, 1977, Birmingham, and Dr. John R. Orr (company dentist), Oral History Project, April 7, 1977, Fairfield, Ala. Tapes and transcripts in possession of author.

[19] John Fitch, "The Human Side of Large Outputs," *Survey*, XXVII (January 6, 1912), 1540; Bond, *Negro Education*, 144–45, 232, 240–42; Spero and Harris, *Black Worker*, 364; Crawford to Monroe N. Work of Tuskegee Institute, January 31, 1930, and Crawford to G. W. A. Johnston of Tuskegee Institute, January 31, 1930, CC.

[20] See C. Vann Woodward, *Origins of the New South: 1877–1913* (Baton Rouge, 1950), 363–64; F. Ray Marshall, *Labor in the South* (Cambridge, 1967), 73–74; Paul B. Worthman, "Black Workers and Labor Unions in Birmingham, Alabama, 1897–1904," *Labor History*, X (Summer 1969), 404.

percent wage reduction made during the depression of 1907–1908 had triggered the strike. The coal operators felt that the entrance of U.S. Steel into the district greatly strengthened their position since it was well known that the corporation opposed unionism with "especial vigor." With the aid of Governor Braxton Bragg Comer and the National Guard the strike was broken after two months, and the United Mine Workers' organization was almost totally destroyed in the Birmingham district. George Crawford, although he was undoubtedly directing company labor policy during the strike, remained behind the scenes, and no statement directly attributable to him appeared in the newspapers. This low profile was to be the pattern in all subsequent strikes during his administration.[21]

Although one aim of welfare capitalism was the contentment of the worker so that unions would not be desired, it is an oversimplification to charge that the TCI welfare programs were primarily a response to the United Mine Workers and the 1908 strike. The programs were an outgrowth of a complex situation. At the outset labor turnover was more the result of unhealthy, degrading living conditions than of discontent of the workmen with the absence of union recognition. Crawford asserted that a healthy environment must be created so that stable family men would be willing to remain in the district long enough to become skilled and efficient at their jobs.

The last vestiges of unionism in U.S. Steel plants were eliminated by Judge Gary in 1909. The American Federation of Labor, meeting in convention during the steel strike of that year, declared the corporation to be the greatest enemy of organized labor. Gary instructed Crawford and other subsidiary presidents to show the working men "that it is for their interests in every respect to be in your employ." Orders were issued in 1911 to make sure that U.S. Steel employees had conditions as good or better than those obtained by organized labor in the district.[22] Because of the deplorable living

---

[21] Horace R. Cayton and George S. Mitchell, *Black Workers and the New Unions* (Chapel Hill, 1939), 316–17; Herbert George Gutman, "The Negro and the United Mine Workers," in *The Negro and the American Labor Movement*, ed. by Julius Jacobson (Garden City, N.Y., 1968), 112. See Nancy Ruth Elmore, "The Birmingham Coal Strike of 1908" (M.A. thesis, University of Alabama, 1966), and Rikard, "George Crawford," 93–101.

[22] Bernard Mandel, *Samuel Gompers* (Yellow Springs, Ohio, 1963), 302–03; John A. Fitch, *The Steel Workers* (New York, 1911), 136; David Brody, *Labor in Crisis: The Steel Strike of 1919* (Philadelphia, 1965), 38; Tyler Dennett, "United States Steel Corporation, Employer," *Outlook,* CXI (November 24, 1915), 730.

conditions in the Birmingham area, the programs implemented under Crawford's direction were more complex and extensive than those at the other subsidiaries. He did not possess the same freedom of initiative in other areas of labor relations. During times of unrest the actions of TCI reflected the policies of the men at corporation headquarters. Because of his low-key, behind-the-scenes stance during strikes, it is difficult to know Crawford's personal feelings concerning the unions, but there is no evidence that he was in disagreement with Judge Gary's anti-union position.[23]

Crawford's welfare and health programs were successful in reducing the labor turnover in the mines and mills from 400 percent annually to 5.1 percent in 1930, the average work attendance was doubled, and the standards of living and education of the TCI employees and their families were raised above that of other workers in the area.[24] He was not able, however, to maintain industrial peace. Although general working conditions and benefits—safety, pensions, accident compensation—were gradually improved in the corporation subsidiaries, many of the workers' grievances went unheeded until public indignation, strikes, and government intervention during the First World War forced some limited change.[25]

The war years were turbulent ones marked by strikes and violence in the Birmingham district. Although the unions met with defeat in this period, they were destined to eventual success and welfare capitalism to eventual demise. It was characteristic of the time that men like Crawford failed to approach labor relations with the same open-minded, bold innovations with which they approached technological problems. In contrast to his leadership in creating a more healthy, livable environment in the district, Crawford offered no long-range planning and leadership in the encounters between management and unions. His labor relations policies were more reminiscent of the paternalism of the Old South; his technological abilities were of greater benefit to the future of the New South.

[23] Though it could have been that Crawford simply chose to follow corporation policy during strikes, he was probably bound by U.S.S. policy in regard to the union. In this area Gary could not afford to allow any deviation. It is impossible to arrive at a definite conclusion as Crawford made no public statements concerning the union, nor is there any reference to the matter in his private papers. There is, however, no indication that he would have recognized the union if left to pursue his own course.

[24] Lloyd Noland, "Problems of Administration in Industrial Surgery," *The Journal of the American Medical Association,* XCIX (October 1932), 1216–18.

[25] For details see Rikard, "George Crawford," 89–155.

Technological innovation is the area in which Crawford made his most lasting contribution. Though the solutions to the technical problems of TCI required vast amounts of capital, they were more tangible and controllable than the labor dilemma. The promises of Birmingham, a child of the Reconstruction era, had been trumpeted by New South promoters who proudly boasted that all the basic materials for the making of iron and steel lay within an eight-mile radius. But technological problems such as the low iron–high phosphorous content of Red Mountain ore and the lack of capital had stymied the potential of this Southern Pittsburgh. The difficulty of Crawford's task was compounded by the scope of activities of the Tennessee Company—it was the only corporation subsidiary concerned not only with the production of steel and steel products but also with the mining and transportation of coal and ore.[26]

Crawford's dogged determination that the steel corporation would grant the necessary appropriations was as important as the application of his technical knowledge of the steel industry. He had no difficulty in obtaining the cooperation of the "movers and shakers" of Birmingham in extending the hospitality of the city when any of the steel executives from 71 Broadway came to visit the Southern subsidiary. Crawford observed to Judge Gary, "I know of no city where we have interests or where I have been connected that is as friendly and more appreciative of our development as is Birmingham." Crawford eagerly squired the corporation officials to the outlying steel mills and mines in his personal railroad car with its white flags flying. Since Gary was not a technical steelman, Crawford arranged for a variety of social events including the annual spring pageant of the company's school system. Judge Gary joined admiring parents at the company-built stadium to watch thousands of children perform the Highland fling, Slavonic dances, and original dances honoring iron and steel! The Judge was also treated to a ride in a caboose on the newly constructed "High Line" TCI railroad.[27]

[26] For information concerning problems facing the iron and steel industry of Birmingham see Neil M. Clark, "Birmingham—The Next Capital of the Steel Age," *World's Work*, LIII (March 1927), 538; *Steelmaking at Birmingham, Alabama* (Birmingham, 1924), 13; Rupert B. Vance, *Human Geography of the South* (Chapel Hill, 1935), 302–03; Mims, *Advancing South*, 96–97.

[27] Birmingham *Ledger*, December 16, 1909, CC; Birmingham *Age-Herald*, December 17, 1909; Birmingham *News*, December 16, 17, 1909; interview with Margaret Crawford Rives (daughter of George Crawford), Birmingham, March 16, 1970; Birmingham *Age-Herald*, May 3, 1925.

Birmingham showed its gratitude to the corporation through much bowing and scraping as well as concrete evidence of deference to the wishes of Crawford and the corporation. City fathers even drew the municipal boundary to exempt TCI's Ensley furnaces from inclusion in the formation of "Greater Birmingham" in 1910.[28] Many of the city's leading businessmen dug deep in their bank accounts when Crawford emphasized that the city lacked a really fine hotel at which the steel executives might stay during their visits. This effort led to the construction of Birmingham's most opulent hotel, the Tutwiler, built in 1914. It was indicative of Crawford's personal dedication to his adopted home and its future that in ventures such as this his own financial investment backed his suggestions.[29] Crawford's wife, Margaret Richardson Crawford, was a valuable asset in his strategy of impressing the men from headquarters with the hospitable atmosphere of the district. A former New Orleans belle and queen of the Mardi Gras whom Crawford had married after returning to Birmingham, Margaret not only personally charmed the men from north of the Mason-Dixon line but also introduced them to all the charming young women of the city's society.[30]

Crawford often met the U.S. Steel executives on their own ground at corporation headquarters in New York. Although he was considered to be Judge Gary's "fair-haired young man," appropriations were not automatically handed to him. His engineering background and the detailed nature of his plans served him well, but he still agonized over "reducing to words of three syllables my engineering data so financiers can understand without too much effort. They must have predigested pablum."[31]

In twenty-three years at the helm of TCI Crawford matured from a "hustling young protege" to one characterized in the publica-

[28] Concerning "Greater Birmingham" see Martha Mitchell, "Birmingham: Biography of a City of the New South" (Ph.D. dissertation, University of Chicago, 1946), 69; Graham Romeyn Taylor, "Birmingham's Civic Front," *Survey*, XXVII (January 6, 1912), 1468–71.

The question was asked of Birmingham business leader and real estate developer, Robert Jemison, if Crawford had exerted pressure concerning this merger. The reply was that he didn't need to exert pressure—only let his wishes be known. Interview with Robert Jemison, Jr., Birmingham, June 3, 1970.

[29] "Tutwiler File," CC; interview with Jemison; Birmingham *Age-Herald*, April 2, 1912, CC.

[30] Interview with Rives.

[31] Birmingham *News*, October 13, 1909, CC; Crawford to Mrs. Margaret Crawford, June 1911, CC.

tion *Farms and Industries* as the "leading steel master of this day."[32] Remodeling, expansion, and innovations to overcome the problems of the low-grade Southern ore marked each year of his administration. Coal mines were opened at Docena, Edgewater, Bayview, and Hamilton; additional open-hearth furnaces were added at the Ensley plant; a by-product coke plant was installed; production was begun of by-products such as slag and phosphate fertilizer; and an industrial water supply was created with the construction of Bayview Lake.[33]

In spite of Crawford's determined pursuit of expansion at this Southern subsidiary, there were additional problems. Although the Birmingham district had offered "public thanksgiving" for the rescue of TCI by U.S. Steel in the panic of 1907, the specter of monopoly was raised by other voices. According to the *Wall Street Journal,* the steel corporation through its "public service" had swallowed up its strongest competitor in open-hearth rail manufacture. Despite President Theodore Roosevelt's assurances to Morgan and Gary in 1907, the U.S. attorney general filed a suit against U.S. Steel in October 1911 for violation of the Sherman Anti-Trust Act. The acquisition of the Tennessee Company constituted one of the major reasons. To the dismay of the city boosters the corporation took the position that the full extent of planned developments at TCI could not be undertaken until a final decision was reached in the court case.[34] Having laid a sound basis for expansion, Crawford was also frustrated at the delays. Finally, despite the threat of the government suit, demand for war steel gave him the opportunity to obtain Gary's approval of an $11,000,000 appropriation for a group of mills known as the Fairfield Steel Company. This "patriotic construction" began in 1917, and additions continued throughout Crawford's administration.[35]

Beneath the glowing optimism of public utterances, there was a growing awareness by analytical observers such as Crawford that the

[32] "Chosen from Proven Men," *Farms and Industries,* April 9, 1927, n.p., CC.

[33] For details see Rikard, "George Crawford," 50–88.

[34] Birmingham *Age-Herald,* November 25, 1907; *Wall Street Journal,* November 8, 1907, CC; William Glenn Moore, "The Acquisition of the Tennessee Coal and Iron Company by the United States Steel Corporation in 1907" (M.A. thesis, University of Alabama, 1951), 86–105; Yoshimitsu Ide, "The Significance of Richard Hathaway Edmonds and His *Manufacturers' Record* in the New South" (Ph.D. dissertation, University of Florida, 1959), 95–97. It was not until March 1, 1920 that the steel corporation received a favorable Supreme Court verdict. Moore, "Acquisition," 113.

[35] Birmingham *News,* July 16, 1917; Birmingham *Age-Herald,* July 15, 1917.

promises of the "New South creed" were not coming up to expectation. As early as 1910 he was not only publicly questioning the oversimplified approach of some area boosters but also analyzing the situation and suggesting solutions. He cited such problems as the lack of Southern domestic markets, absence of facilities for producing diversified products, inefficient transportation, and inadequacy of Southern ports.[36] Regionalized freight rates, the tariff, and pricing systems such as Pittsburgh Plus and Birmingham Differential also came under attack. U.S. Steel had not created the system of Pittsburgh Plus, but it had certainly utilized it. Although Crawford could not publicly participate in the South's efforts to free itself from the system, he protested within the corporation structure and gave his private support to those Southerners fighting against it.[37]

He was in a unique position to evaluate both the advantages and disadvantages of the corporation's impact on the South. Though a U.S. Steel employee, he had obviously become regional in outlook since taking charge at TCI; but as a practical administrator, he realized that some corporation policies were necessarily designed more for U.S. Steel as a whole than for TCI as an individual entity. Perhaps forced into a sober appraisal because of his connection with a national firm and the need for the capital available through that corporation, Crawford never allowed the "New South creed" to become such a sacred incantation that it obstructed a realistic appraisal of the problems and reforms needed in the South. He believed that a transformation of the area could not be wrought by the development of one segment, and his interests and activities transcended the iron and steel industry to include the entire Southern economic structure, agricultural as well as industrial.

Crawford presented some thoughts concerning industrial-agricultural balance and diversification of industry in a speech before the National Foreign Trade Council meeting in Charleston, South Carolina, in April 1926. Much of his analysis of the South's problems and

---

[36] Article written for the Atlanta *Constitution*, reprinted in Birmingham *Age-Herald*, December 2, 1910, CC. See also Mims, *Advancing South*, 96–97.

[37] See Clarence H. Danhof, "Four Decades of Thought on the South's Economic Problems," in *Essays in Southern Economic Development*, ed. by Melvin L. Greenhut and W. Tate Whitman (Chapel Hill, 1964), 41, for accusations against U.S.S. in such matters as Pittsburgh Plus. George W. Stocking, *Basing Point Pricing and Regional Development* (Chapel Hill, 1954), 7, 64; John Temple Graves (Birmingham newspaper columnist), unidentified clipping, September 10, 1953, CC.

potential was echoed a decade later by regionalists such as Rupert Vance. Crawford saw a lack of capital and credit and the exchange of raw materials for manufactured goods as critical to the South's problems. However, he differed from the colonial economy thesis of the regionalists who emphasized exploitation by outside powers. Crawford blamed historical forces and subsequent shortsightedness by the South's own people. Economic historian Clarence Danhof in the 1960s suggested that the colonial-imperialistic thesis diverted some of the South's ablest men from constructive approaches to the area's problems. Crawford was a notable exception. He was particularly concerned with overcoming the vulnerability of a cotton economy by stimulating agricultural diversity through cooperation between farmers, merchants, bankers, and businessmen. Manufacturing also should be diversified with attention given to producing finished consumer products.[38]

Crawford was not only a student of the economy but also a man of practical action, personally investing time, effort, and money in the South. He was instrumental in obtaining the 1914 annual meeting of the American Iron and Steel Institute for Birmingham, giving the visitors an opportunity to see first-hand the potential of the area; he served as an Alabama delegate to the 1910 Southern Commercial Congress; he worked actively for the development of the Black Warrior River, Birmingport, and the improvement of the state docks at Mobile so Alabama could take advantage of expanded trade opportunities with the opening of the Panama Canal.[39] As the moving force behind the creation of the Alabama State Industrial Board, Crawford enthusiastically promoted everything from peanut-fed hogs to Southern pine newsprint with his borrowed slogan, "What Alabama Makes, Makes Alabama." Crawford volunteered the services of the TCI land engineer to the industrial board to survey the resources of each county. Bearing unexpected fruit, this survey was later used by the WPA to obtain immediate information on needed projects. Crawford worked actively for farm diversification and established a

[38] Speech reprinted in Birmingham *News,* April 30, 1926, CC; Vance, *Human Geography,* 264–66; Danhof, "Four Decades," 50.

[39] Ide, "Richard H. Edmonds," 91; *Manufacturers' Record,* LXVI (November 5, 1914), 51; Birmingham *Age-Herald,* November 1, 1910, CC; John Temple Graves, "This Morning," Birmingham *Age-Herald,* n.d., CC; Birmingham *Ledger,* December 4, 1919, CC; Mims, *Advancing South,* 107. Crawford was appointed the first chairman when the State Docks Commission was authorized in 1923. Marie Bankhead Owen, *Alabama, A Social and Economic History of the State* (Montgomery, 1938), 201.

Farm Products Division at the Tennessee Company to give farmers practical advice and to act as a clearinghouse on the sale of farm products.[40]

In January 1930, after twenty-three years at TCI, Crawford unexpectedly resigned to accept the presidency of Jones and Laughlin Steel Corporation of Pittsburgh. After their most prosperous peace year ever (1929), this independent producer was ready to embark on an expansion program and wanted an "operating" man. Crawford confided to friends in Birmingham that though he was reluctant to leave TCI, he could not resist the generous contract offered by Jones and Laughlin, knowing that it would make his family independent. But instead of the challenge of guiding a program of growth, Crawford spent five years in Pittsburgh desperately trying to weather the depression. Broken in health, he resigned in 1935 at the age of sixty-five and returned to Birmingham, the city to which he had come "with trepidation" in 1907. He died in 1936.[41]

In his presidential address to the Southern Historical Association in 1941, historian B. B. Kendrick proclaimed, "The people of the South, who all their lives had suffered deprivation, want, and humiliation from an outside finance imperialism, followed with hardly a murmur of protest leaders who, if indirectly, were nonetheless in effect agents and attorneys of the imperialists."[42] During the years he was president of TCI, Crawford was a leader of the community. Was he an "agent of the imperialists?" U.S. Steel was an absentee landlord whose prime consideration was not the Tennessee Company, but Crawford's actions indicated not only a desire to promote the interest of TCI but also a regional concern. It was, however, a concern tempered by reason, shrewdness, and sometimes a practical regard for his own position through an awareness of the limits to which he could push disputes with corporation headquarters.

In 1926 Crawford remarked, "The strength of our nation is the

---

[40] Interview with Thad Holt (first director of Alabama Industrial Board), Birmingham, March 2, 1971; Birmingham *Age-Herald*, March 21, 1936; John Temple Graves, *The Fighting South* (New York, 1943), 169–70; Charles Longenecker, *The Tennessee Coal, Iron and Railroad Company* (Pittsburgh, 1939), 834.

[41] Birmingham *Age-Herald*, January 29, 1930, CC; unidentified clipping (Pittsburgh paper), February 6, 1935, CC; interview with Jemison; Birmingham *Post*, February 8, 1930, CC; interview with Rives.

[42] B. B. Kendrick, "The Colonial Status of the South," in *The Pursuit of Southern History*, ed. by George Brown Tindall (Baton Rouge, 1964), 102.

sum of its parts, and if the South has not yet achieved the percentage of economic strength which it had and which it can have and should have, our country is not as strong as it can be and should be."[43] Though he returned to the South reluctantly in 1907, he became an avid promoter of the region within a national context and was one of the more realistic New South spokesmen.

[43] Speech given by Crawford at Roebuck Country Club, Birmingham, Ala., to a delegation of visiting investment bankers, reprinted in Birmingham *News,* November 16, 1926, CC.

WAYNE FLYNT

Religion in the Urban South:
The Divided Religious Mind of Birmingham, 1900–1930

Recent years have seen increasing numbers of academicians struggling with religion as a critical instrument in the comprehension of American culture. Such historians as Kenneth K. Bailey, John Eighmy, and other interpreters of Southern thought have demonstrated an increasing socialization of Southern Protestantism during the twentieth century. Also, historians have treated their audiences to an increasingly refined insight into the urban South and the way in which Progressivism thrived in the metropolitan climate of the early years of this century. Industrialism in the South, as elsewhere, created complex problems that demanded substantial modification of nineteenth-century pietistic Christianity. Southern industrialism also produced a level of religious pluralism that resulted in at least a temporary increase in bigotry and intolerance. But there has been little effort to trace the interaction of church and urban South in order to determine how rural, agrarian religion adjusted to the complexities of industrial cities that sprang up among the wisteria, kudzu, and magnolia trees. Although Birmingham, Alabama, is atypical in both its late nineteenth-century origin and its unique heavy industrial economic base, it does serve as a fascinating case study in the socialization of Southern religion.

It is ironic that two of the most notable symbols of twentieth-century Birmingham have been the giant statue of Vulcan perched atop the ore vein of Red Mountain and the Temple of Vesta domi-

This essay was published in *The Alabama Review,* XXX (April 1977).

nating Shades Mountain. Leaders of the city in the heart of the Bible Belt have boasted that theirs was a "city of churches," while they also have identified it with the Roman god of metal-working and the Roman goddess of the hearth.[1] This curious mixture of paganism and evangelical Christianity is symbolic of the contradictory character of the city. Despite its many churches, it became nationally known as "Bad Birmingham," the city of minerals and murder. Though allegedly dominated by salvationists, other-worldly Baptists and Methodists, it counted a large Catholic population, and for a time the Social Gospel flourished in the city. In theory affirming the brotherhood of man, the religious life of Birmingham was rigidly segregated by race. The Ku Klux Klan thrived on the city's racism and anti-Catholicism.

In religion Birmingham was a city of paradoxes. A number of factors shaped the city's religious attitudes. From Birmingham's earliest beginnings in the 1870s, local land companies provided free plots of land to encourage establishment of Christian congregations. Until the 1890s, most of the people pouring into the town were rural, evangelical Southern Protestants, and despite the later arrival of immigrants who brought religious diversity, Protestants maintained their hegemony over community life. Leading businessmen were proud of their close association with one of the multiplicity of local sects, and the denominations pursued a sometimes unfriendly rivalry trying to enroll the community's "wealthiest and best."[2] Sermons traditionally emphasized individualism, salvation, and civic boosterism, while posing no challenge to the economic and social status quo. Yet the frontier mining nature of the city also gave it a renown for moral looseness and for rip-roaring drunkenness and violence.

Birmingham, as a city of the "New South," could not escape the industrial and urban stresses that were transforming American life

[1] To complete the irony, the Temple to Vesta built by Birmingham Mayor George Ward later was converted into a Baptist church.

[2] See John R. Hornady, *The Book of Birmingham* (New York, 1921), 4–7; George M. Cruikshank, *A History of Birmingham and its Environs* (2 vols., New York, 1920), I, 270–86. A fascinating perspective is offered by Blaine Brownell who suggests not only that pastors were important in instilling a sense of civic responsibility and unity of purpose in their congregations, but also that "success" in the ministry meant promotion from a rural church to an urban one; thus, coming to terms with urban problems as well as not alienating one's own congregation were both measures of a pastor's "success" and hence contributed to his status. See Blaine A. Brownell, "The Urban Mind in the South: The Growth of Urban Consciousness in Southern Cities, 1920–1927" (Ph.D. dissertation, University of North Carolina, 1969), 181, 202–16.

in the late nineteenth century, and her religious institutions strained under new pressures. Industrial urbanization brought social distress to the working classes and alienated them from the church, forcing pietistic Protestantism to begin dealing with the city's critical social problems. By 1900 the religious and ethnic homogeneity of Birmingham had relaxed as southern and eastern European immigrants poured into the region's factories and mines, giving it one of the highest proportions of immigrants of any Southern city. The religious census of 1906 revealed the pattern in unmistakable relief. The largest single denomination of the total church membership was Roman Catholic (7,965 members, 28.9 percent) followed by the National Baptist Convention (black, 4,029 members, 14.6 percent), and the Methodist Episcopal Church, South (3,919 members, 14.2 percent). Southern Baptists were a poor fifth (2,059 members, 7.5 percent). By 1916 the influx of immigrants had slowed, and the religious affiliation of the city's residents reflected a more typical Southern pattern: National Baptists were the most numerous (20,145 members, 26.1 percent of the total church membership), followed by the Methodist Episcopal Church, South (15,477, 20.1 percent), Roman Catholic (12,651, 16.4 percent), and Southern Baptist (8,420, 10.9 percent).[3]

In attempting to deal with the religious life of a community, one must come to terms with both the theological climate of ideas and the social expression of these ideas. Theology presents only minor problems, for evangelical Protestant Fundamentalism characterized the Bible Belt. Excluding Episcopal, Catholic, and Jewish minorities, black and white clergymen alike generally preached a Calvinistic doctrine of man's sinfulness, God's judgment, and the consequent imperative for man to repent and "be saved." The Bible was literally interpreted as the verbatim word of God. Such doctrines as the virgin birth, the atonement, the physical resurrection of Christ,

[3]U.S. Bureau of the Census, *Religious Bodies,* 1916, Part I (Washington, 1919), 123. In 1920 the city population counted over six thousand immigrants and more than ten thousand citizens with at least one foreign-born parent. Most of these came from Italy or Russia. The city was 40 percent black, and the religious diversity intensified. In that same year the following churches were represented: White: Adventist (1), Southern Baptist (33), Christian (5), Christian Science (1), Church of God (1), Congregational (1), Evangelical (1), Greek Orthodox (1), Jewish (3), Lutheran (2), Methodist Episcopal Church, South (37), Methodist Protestant (1), Presbyterian (25), Protestant Episcopal (6), Roman Catholic (13), Unitarian (1). Black: Adventist (1), National Baptist (64), Church of God (4), Congregational (1), Episcopal (1), Methodist (37), Presbyterian (2), Sanctified (2); *Birmingham City Directory,* 1919–1920, XXXIV (Birmingham, 1920), 59–62.

and immortality were equally sacrosanct. Sectarian independence was as fundamental as separation of church and state.

Although the foregoing description would summarize the religious convictions of the overwhelming majority of clergymen and laymen alike in the years from 1900 to 1930, a strain of religious liberalism provided variegation to the otherwise uniform theological landscape. A Unitarian congregation was established with its liberal influence, but more significant is the dissent within mainline Protestant churches. Within the Methodist church there was liberal sentiment, particularly among the faculty of Methodist-related Birmingham-Southern College.[4]

Southern Baptists would appear an unlikely environment for religious iconoclasts, yet Dr. Alfred J. Dickinson, pastor of Birmingham's First Baptist Church, was the city's chief intellectual "mugwump."[5] Upon becoming pastor of the Birmingham congregation in 1901, he accelerated his already active advocacy of the controversial "higher criticism" that sought to subject the Bible to all the canons of literary, historical, and archaeological criticism used to examine any other piece of literature. He saw no conflict between evangelical concern and academic challenges to the literal interpretation of scripture, and, in a series of provocative essays in the state Baptist paper, he defended "higher criticism" against all comers.[6] Frank W. Barnett, a member of Dickinson's church and owner/editor of *The Alabama Baptist,* did not share his pastor's theological liberalism, but the same editorials that challenged liberalism defended the freedom of Baptists to take critical theological positions without fear of retaliation: "Let us shake off a false Baptist demagogy which, boasting of its own self-sufficing orthodoxy, becomes the worst of all tyrannies in striving to force its narrow tests upon all who are willing to receive with open minds truth from any source."[7] Barnett's successor as editor of *The Alabama Baptist* in 1919 was Rev. L. L. Gwaltney, whose defense of theistic evolution and science was in sharp contrast to the anti-

[4] See Charles Marion Prestwood, Jr., "Social Ideas of Methodist Ministers in Alabama Since Unification" (Ph.D. dissertation, Boston University, 1960).

[5] For an excellent thesis exploring Dickinson's theology, see John H. Burrows, "The Great Disturber: The Social Philosophy and Theology of Alfred James Dickinson" (M.A. thesis, Samford University, 1970).

[6] For examples of the liberal/fundamentalist exchange, see *The Alabama Baptist,* August 15, November 21, 1906, February 5, 19, 26, April 2, 23, 1913, September 22, 1915.

[7] *The Alabama Baptist,* August 16, 1916.

evolution sentiment that thrived in the Bible Belt during the 1920s.[8] He spent his editorship arguing that science did not conflict with religion. In his declining years he wrote a manuscript pleading with Baptists to incorporate evolution and modern science in their religion so as not to alienate their young and informed people of all ages.[9]

Perhaps the most dramatic evidence of theological conflict in Birmingham came from the controversy that split South Highlands Presbyterian Church and led to the creation of Independent Presbyterian Church. At the epicenter of the storm was Dr. Henry M. Edmonds. A native of Sumter County, Alabama, Edmonds became pastor of South Highlands in 1913 but was barely settled when "a heresy-hunter was on my trail." The prominent layman, who had attended a "Fundamentalist Bible School," polarized the church against Edmonds, as he had against two previous pastors. Though cautious in his pronouncements, Edmonds's theological views on immortality, the divinity of Christ, the "second coming," human depravity, the virgin birth, and the atonement were in no sense "orthodox."[10] Edmonds's antagonist also assaulted the pastor for his opposition to city "blue laws," which forbade movies and golf on Sundays, and for his social concerns. His antagonist chided: "You are trying to improve relations between husband and wife, between classes, nations, races. We ought to rejoice if those relations grow worse and worse, for when they become intolerable Christ will come again."[11] Finally, Edmonds was brought before the Birmingham Presbytery and censured for his views. He consequently withdrew from South Highlands, together with a large segment of the congregation, and formed the unaffiliated Independent Presbyterian Church. Upon the invitation of Rabbi Morris Newfield, the church met at Temple Emanu-el for ten years, with night services emphasizing social action held at the downtown Lyric Theater.[12]

Ruhama Baptist Church experienced similar friction when Dr. Cecil

---

[8] *Ibid.*, January 3, 1917, November 6, 27, December 11, 1918.

[9] L. L. Gwaltney, "This I Leave With You," unpublished manuscript in Alabama Baptist Historical Society Archives, Samford University. Hereafter cited as ABHS.

[10] Henry M. Edmonds, *A Parson's Notebook* (Birmingham, 1961), 72–86.

[11] *Ibid.*, 73.

[12] For extensive discussion of the theological clash that split South Highlands, see *ibid.*, 72–96; and *The Independent Presbyterian Church of Birmingham, Alabama* (Birmingham, 1950), 8–10.

V. Cook of Kentucky became pastor in 1910. A brilliant pastor orator he nonetheless suffered a brief and stormy tenure, charged by his congregation with tactlessness and liberal theological views.[13] Unlike South Highlands, he had little support, and the church did not fragment when he resigned under pressure.

Sporadic evidence of liberal theology existed in Birmingham, and some clerics also sympathized with ecumenism. Throughout the first two decades of the new century, local congregations had cooperated on issues such as prohibition and evangelization. While there was little demonstrable sentiment for church union among Birmingham clergy and laymen, there was sentiment for a more coordinated social and mission outreach. The focus of this interest was the Interchurch World Movement, an attempt to coordinate church energies in the service of evangelism and social ministries but not to compete with denominational agencies. On March 3, 1920 officials from New York held a conference in Birmingham to explain the Movement. Churchwomen from throughout the state met at First Christian Church, while six hundred ministers discussed the same subject at the First Methodist Church. The ministers, representing every Protestant and evangelical faith in the state, endorsed the organization and returned to their congregations to explain its operations.[14]

The notable exception to this general enthusiasm came from the city's white Baptists. Ever fearful of ecumenism or even close cooperation, the Southern Baptist and Alabama Baptist conventions had rejected association with the Movement. *The Alabama Baptist* conducted a forum on the subject based on correspondence from one hundred state pastors. The response was overwhelmingly negative, reflecting concern that it could lead to Catholic control, church union, or emphasis on social issues to the exclusion of individual salvation.[15] Despite his denomination's opposition, Birmingham's Baptist iconoclast, A. J. Dickinson, enthusiastically endorsed the Movement. It originated out of a basic human desire for progress, he argued, just as had missions, temperance, abolition of slavery, and women's rights. It was a movement for "effecting His Kingdom in the earth"; it was a community organization to serve the needs of

---

[13] Fanna K. Bee and Lee N. Allen, *Sesquicentennial History: Ruhama Baptist Church, 1819–1969* (Birmingham, 1969), 139.

[14] *Birmingham News*, March 4–7, 1920.

[15] *The Alabama Baptist*, February 5, 12, 1920.

the whole city, and this purpose could not be accomplished without cooperative church action.[16]

No matter how intently the climate of thought in Birmingham is studied, theology alone does not provide a complete picture of its religious life. The social manifestation of these ideas is equally significant. The demands of an industrial/urban community posed complex problems for the city's religious structure, and the response ranged across the theological spectrum.

Most representative of the older Fundamentalist attempt to wrestle with urban malaise was the remarkable ministry of Dr. James Alexander Bryan of the Third Presbyterian Church. Fondly known to thousands as "Brother Bryan," he had come to Birmingham in 1888 and spent his entire life loving the city's volatile population. Though minister to a working-class church, friend of blue-collar workers and of blacks, and an honorary member of most local labor unions, his sermons were evangelical with hardly a trace of Social Gospel influence.[17] A loner who believed in welfare organizations, he administered a personal program of vast relief supported by his own church, Jewish businessmen, saloon keepers, and anyone else who offered help. He had no formal organization and kept no records. Yet, he organized a social ministry for Italian immigrants, brought the first district nurse to Birmingham to minister to the city's poor, literally lived at the city's mills, factories, and jails, helping laborers and criminals, and ended each midweek service at his church by inviting all who desired to have lunch with the pastor so that the poor did not have to ask for food. He was so touched by the needs of others that he gave away his horse to a farmer whose beast had died and gave his food to those in greater need. Explaining his legendary ministry, which in time took on an aura of mystical unreality, Bryan wrote:

> Ever since I have been a pastor my work has been partially among needy people. If there are no poor in your congregation, my humble advice is to get another charge or shut your doors. Social service alone will not solve the problem of the poor and hungry, nor can it alone fill the need of the breadless and bedless and jacketless ... Christ taught us to pray, "Give us this day our daily bread." If He gives you your daily bread, you should divide with someone else. A woman came in the other day and said,

[16] *Ibid.*, December 11, 1919, January 1, 1920.
[17] See J. A. Bryan, *A Collection of My Sermons* (Birmingham, n.d.).

"Brother Bryan, one of your friends sent me a sack of flour, some meat and lard, and a half-ton of coal." I saw Christ in that basket of food. People do not read their Bibles, they read you and me.[18]

Despite the individualistic nature of Bryan's ministry, his belief that all men—white and black, native-born and immigrant, poor and rich—were his brothers,[19] propelled him into an urban society festering with many kinds of hurt. His biographer maintains that Bryan had "by all odds relieved more suffering than any man who ever lived in Birmingham."[20] Apparently the people of Birmingham agreed; in 1920, when the *Birmingham News* announced a five-hundred-dollar award to the citizen who had rendered the greatest service to the city during the year, the selection committee was swamped with petitions from labor unions and private citizens nominating Brother Bryan. When he received the first annual award on January 9, 1921, a tremendous throng overflowed the largest theater in Birmingham and by the hundreds spilled over into the streets to honor the man who called them all his Brothers.

The magnitude of social distress in the city caused most religious bodies to follow a more coordinated ministry than Brother Bryan's. The medium of expressing this concern was the Social Gospel, a movement pioneered in the North, but with substantial impact on the urban South as well. Two successive editors of *The Alabama Baptist,* writing from offices in Birmingham, championed social concern as fundamental to making the gospel relevant to modern city dwellers. Though both were theologically conservative, Frank W. Barnett and L. L. Gwaltney turned the pages of their journal into a forum where they advocated control of trusts, political reform, better care for immigrants, and abolition of child labor, the convict lease system, and capital punishment.[21]

The issue that involved so many pastors in social activism was prohibition. To achieve this moral objective the religious commu-

[18] Quoted in Hunter B. Blakely, *Religion in Shoes* (Birmingham, 1967), 43.
[19] For a summary see Dewey Robinson, "The Life of Dr. J. A. Bryan," unpublished manuscript, 1934, in ABHS.
[20] Blakely, *Religion in Shoes,* 43.
[21] For general surveys see Wayne Flynt, "Dissent in Zion: Alabama Baptists and Social Issues, 1900–1914," *Journal of Southern History,* XXXV (November 1969), 523–42, and Robert F. Crider, "The Social Philosophy of L. L. Gwaltney, 1919–1950" (M.A. thesis, Samford University, 1969).

nity had to forsake its passivism and enter politics. In 1907 the Women's Christian Temperance Union and the interdenominational Pastors' Union made common cause against "demon rum," arguing that prohibition would not only reduce the city's legendary violence but also cure many of the community's social ills. Women and children wearing white ribbons surrounded polling places on October 28, 1907 and sang "When the Roll is Called Up Yonder," perhaps as a theological warning to male voters. Five thousand women and children paraded through city streets waving banners proclaiming "Save the Boys" and "Vote for Mothers." When Jefferson County went dry by 1,800 votes (though the city proper voted wet), crowds thronged the polling places singing without regard to the irony involved, "Praise God From Whom All Blessings Flow."[22] Now fully aware of their combined political power, churchmen did not intend to relinquish it.

They turned their new-found muscle to Birmingham's unsavory moral climate. Saloons, dance halls, and brothels thrived along with the city's churches and emotional revivals. Murder, gambling, drunkenness, and prostitution characterized the city's national reputation more than did its fine steel.[23] The editor of *The Alabama Baptist* helped launch the cleanup in 1904 with a blistering editorial noting that Jefferson County had more murders annually than occurred in all of Great Britain with a population of forty million people: "In Jefferson County when a man contemplated killing his fellow man he argues that with a little money and personal influence the probabilities are that he will be given a short prison sentence at most." The pulpits, he thought, should join the secular press to stop lawlessness in Birmingham.[24]

As part of this crusade, religious leaders sought the elimination of prostitution. The "oldest profession" was practiced openly and thrived on local customers as well as the weekend miners who flooded the city to gamble and drink. City officials ignored the problem until 1905 when they sought to confine it to wards six and seven. Churchmen

---

[22] Martha C. Mitchell Bigelow, "Birmingham: Biography of a City of the New South" (Ph.D. dissertation, University of Chicago, 1946), 109–11; *The Alabama Baptist,* November 6, 1907.

[23] Nationally famous evangelist Sam Jones, who held a great revival meeting in the city in the 1890s called Birmingham a "hell-hole."

[24] *The Alabama Baptist,* October 12, 1904.

rejected this policy of segregating prostitution and continued a decade-long battle to rid the city of the practice altogether.[25]

Although partially defeated on the issue of prostitution, the city's religious forces won their struggle against Sunday amusements, to which Birmingham was not so deeply devoted. By 1908 they had pressured the city into passing ordinances forbidding such Sabbath pastimes as golf, baseball, tennis, football, hunting, shooting, gaming, card playing, and even dominoes.[26]

Reviewing church influence, one city historian concludes that prohibition and moral reform in the first decade of the century resulted in clean amusements, increased church attendance on Sunday mornings, a firm insistence on law enforcement, and a moral climate unexcelled in the urban South.[27] Though this conclusion obviously is exaggerated, conditions had improved, and rigorous standards of morality had been enforced.

Concern for the social welfare of the community also helped politicize religion. The problems of labor in a blue-collar city not only were obvious by 1900 but also had alienated many workingmen from the church. Frank Barnett of *The Alabama Baptist* directed much of his attention toward remedying unjust labor conditions in his home city and chided the pulpits: "Churches have frequently shut their eyes to the struggles of labor to get a minimum wage; and have not heard the cry of the children who were being sacrificed in our mills; or cared when a fight was being made for shorter hours and better working conditions."[28] Infuriated by child labor, he exploded in dozens of editorials. After the state legislature postponed meaningful legislation in 1907, he stormed: "Let us call it [child labor] by its right name—murder. But if the death comes quickly enough, it is less cruel than the life to which such boys and girls are condemned."[29] He also propagandized for the end of the convict lease system, whereby many Birmingham area mine owners leased state convicts to work their mines.[30]

Editor L. L. Gwaltney, Barnett's successor, frankly advocated

[25] *Ibid.*, February 27, 1907, June 19, 1912, June 18, 1913.

[26] Bigelow, "Birmingham," 212–13.

[27] Hornady, *Book of Birmingham*, 6–7.

[28] *The Alabama Baptist*, June 18, 1913. For a general survey of Birmingham Baptist attitudes toward social issues, see Flynt, "Dissent in Zion," 523–42.

[29] *The Alabama Baptist*, February 13, 1907.

[30] *Ibid.*, June 25, 1913.

the Social Gospel, contending that he saw no conflict in it and the individualistic gospel of salvation. They were both elements of the complete gospel and neither could endure without the other; the minister who followed Christ "will also preach against the social vices and sins of the day. He will even tell armies what to do, and enter the realm of politics and insist that the levying of taxes must be just."[31]

Many local churches implemented the manifold social interests of Barnett, Gwaltney, and other clerics. Dr. Augustine C. Davidson, pastor of Southside Baptist Church, persuaded his congregation that it should pattern itself after Charles H. Spurgeon's famous "institutional church," to which were attached reading rooms, baths, a gymnasium, and other facilities. The church established a free kindergarten in the southwest part of town, an industrial school to teach workers' children to cook and sew, and a "Goodwill Center" among Birmingham's Italian community (with kindergarten, sewing classes, and Bible teaching).[32]

The Pastors' Union, aided by churchwomen, inaugurated various social ministries in the early years of the new century. The Free Kindergarten Association was formed in 1899 and provided three-day nurseries or kindergartens for small children whose mothers worked. In the summer of 1908, women of the School Improvement Association opened kindergarten and settlement work in the basement of the Paul Hayne School.[33]

Methodists constituted one of the largest religious groups in the city and were active in social ministries. When the Pastors' Union proposed construction of a boarding house for working women, one Methodist layman pledged $25,000. Women from St. John's and First Methodist churches created the City Board of Missions in 1903, and the Board opened a settlement house in June of the same year. The home was situated in a working-class neighborhood and operated an "industrial school" for girls, a day school for children whose parents worked, a night literacy school for working boys, and a free kindergarten. The home ministered primarily to families working in the adjacent rolling

---

[31] L. L. Gwaltney, *Forty of the Twentieth or the First Forty Years of the Twentieth Century* (Birmingham, 1940), 126–27.
[32] James F. Sulzby, Jr., *Annals of the Southside Baptist Church, Birmingham, Alabama* (Birmingham, 1947), 88.
[33] Bigelow, "Birmingham," 153.

mills and foundries. Between 1900 and 1905 some three thousand children attended church-sponsored kindergartens in Birmingham; most of the children came from blue-collar families, and the money for the schools was provided by the Methodist Christmas offering.[34]

The settlement house ministry operated so successfully that in September 1908 a "deaconess" (trained social worker) was employed by the Board of City Missions to open a Wesley House. By the end of the year the facility was in operation with a thirty-eight-pupil kindergarten; the work grew so rapidly by 1909 that a larger house was purchased, an assistant was employed, and plans were begun for construction of an "institutional church." Another Wesley House was built directly behind Avondale Mills, one of the most prominent state textile mills. By 1912 it cared for eleven babies and forty preschoolers, enrolled thirty women in the "Mothers' Club," and conducted a night literacy program three evenings a week.[35]

The City Board of Missions expanded its social ministries in 1912 to five thousand Italian immigrants employed at the Ensley mills of Tennessee Coal and Iron Company. T.C.I. donated a house, playgrounds, heat, light, and $2,000. The Board, assisted by Ensley Methodist Church, employed Miss Dorothy Crim, a trained social worker, in October 1912. By 1913 two assistants had been employed, and the Ensley ministry included all the facilities of the Avondale house plus a boarding home for working girls.[36]

During these same years the Episcopal Church of the Advent became socially active. Its rectors focused their interests on the Boys' Industrial School, the Mercy Home for women, the Northside Community House, and social work among blacks. When Rev. Middleton S. Barnwell became rector in 1913, a smaller rectory was purchased, and the older structure was devoted to social ministries, particularly a free neighborhood kindergarten. In a remarkable example of ecumenical social service, Barnwell joined Rabbi Morris Newfield of Temple Emanu-el and Dr. Henry Edmonds, pastor of Independent Presbyterian, to organize the Jefferson County Children's Aid Society, which subsequently spread statewide and became the Alabama Department of Child Welfare.[37]

---

[34] *The Alabama Christian Advocate,* March 6, 1902, November 26, 1903.

[35] *Ibid.,* January 21, July 22, 1909, June 9, 1910, February 8, 1912.

[36] *Ibid.,* November 7, December 12, 1912, March 6, September 25, 1913.

[37] Mittie Owen McDavid, *Church of the Advent: Its History and Traditions* (Birmingham, 1943), 44–65.

Dr. Henry Edmonds was perhaps the most independent-minded of the city's clergymen. Infuriating many ministers by opposing church movements to ban Sunday movies and golf, he nonetheless retained their respect and was elected president of the Birmingham Pastors' Union. He also led his church in the most active social ministry of any area congregation. When Independent Presbyterian was established in 1915, the "Purpose of the Church" had listed service to humanity as second only to the individual search for God. In order to implement this purpose, Sunday evening services were held in the Lyric Theater, and a downtown office was maintained. A female member of the church staff was assigned the task of assisting the jobless, while a nurse was employed to serve the city's health needs (due to her excellent service to the church, she was subsequently employed by the city as the first Public Health Nurse in Birmingham). The Northside Community House was established, although it was aided by several other congregations as well as Independent. In 1920 the church employed Miss Leila Winn as its city missionary to do case work that was brought to the attention of the church's Social Service Group.

The congregation also sponsored a Children's Fresh Air Farm, a project suggested by Edmonds and funded by the philanthropy of Robert R. Meyer. The thirty-acre farm on Shades Mountain provided summer nourishment and recreation for eight thousand poor children between 1920 and 1950, while doctors from the church performed over one hundred free operations needed by the children. The church also undertook "Winter Work," providing the poor with birthday parties for children, scholarships to school, weddings, baby showers, and other services of a continuing ministry. Independent Presbyterian, noting the disadvantage suffered by poor people of both races in the courts, also employed a lawyer who provided free legal aid.[38]

Much of Independent's social ministry grew from its services at the Lyric Theater. Held for ten years between 1915 and 1925, the services attracted every facet of urban Southern culture—blacks, who sat in a segregated upper balcony, gamblers, prostitutes, and the poor. One prominent "madame" of a "disorderly house" attended for many years, was converted, and became a regular member of Independent Presbyterian. Another convert from the services, formerly

---

[38] For excellent discussions of Independent Presbyterian's far-flung social ministries see *The Independent Presbyterian Church of Birmingham, Alabama*, 14–40, and Edmonds, *A Parson's Notebook*, 96–99.

a prostitute, left a large bequest to the Atlanta Y.M.C.A. when she died. Offerings from the services were used in local social work (for example, one offering purchased a new horse for a vegetable peddler whose animal had died).[39]

Since most of the city's charity and philanthropy was church motivated, virtually all denominations participated in social ministries. In 1895 the Ladies of Charity was organized, composed mainly from the membership of St. Paul's Catholic Church. This group appears to be the earliest Christian welfare agency in the city. Catholic St. Vincent's Hospital was opened in November 1900, and between its opening and 1904 it served over twenty-four hundred indigent patients. A St. Vincent's nursing graduate, Miss Marie Forsman, became the city's first "district nurse" in 1907, with the responsibility of providing medical care to the city's poor whites. Catholics also established an orphanage at East Lake.[40]

Jewish businessmen and rabbis not only contributed individually to city social agencies but also organized collectively. In 1890, the Daughters of Israel began Jewish social work in the city, followed by the Hebrew Relief Society (1897), and the Council of Jewish Charities, which coordinated activities.[41]

Most Birmingham pastors seem to have detected no conflict between social and spiritual ministries, viewing the Social Gospel as a practical necessity. Church membership during this epoch of "Social Gospelism" increased at a phenomenal rate indicating that the church was translating its spiritual interests in the poor and workingmen into social reality. The Methodist Wesley House ministry won the enthusiastic backing of denominational clergymen; the pastor of the nearest Methodist church to the Avondale Mills House praised the tremendous help it provided his parish in attracting mill workers.[42] Southside Baptist Church, founded in the mid-1880s, experienced the greatest spiritual prosperity in its history while operating as an institutional church.[43] For the city as a whole, church membership bounded from 27,578 in 1906 to 77,145 in 1916, nearly a 200 percent increase.[44]

In contrast with the social "liberalism" of Birmingham churches during the "Progressive" era, the growing intolerance and bigotry

[39] Edmonds, *A Parson's Notebook*, 96–97.
[40] Bigelow, "Birmingham," 149.
[41] *Ibid.*
[42] *The Alabama Christian Advocate*, April 25, 1912.
[43] Sulzby, *Annals of the Southside Baptist Church*, 89.
[44] U.S. Bureau of the Census, *Religious Bodies*, 1916, Part I, 123.

that emerged full blown in the 1920s seem shocking. Rabid opposition
to Catholics, Jews, immigrants, or to any deviation from Protestant moral standards threw the churches into a frenzy. Whereas Protestants had organized politically to combat moral deviations earlier,
many members added extralegal violence to political activism during
the 1920s. Despite apparent contradictions, there are strong elements
of continuity in the periods from 1900 to 1915 and 1915 to 1930. Both
eras saw the churches deeply involved in social issues. During each
period the church sought a restrictive, enforced community morality
based on its own standards. In both, churchmen were activists, condemning forces which they felt encouraged religious and social diversity within the city.

Anti-Catholicism was a touchstone of the new period, though the
theme had long been obvious in local Protestant circles. Baptist
editor Frank Barnett, a leader in his denomination's socialization,
believed that Catholics were a menace to American democracy and
defended such organizations as the "Guardians of Liberty," a
fanatical anti-Catholic cult organized in the second decade of the
century.[45] As early as 1916 night riders burned a Catholic church and
school near Pratt City. When two Birmingham public schools were
destroyed weeks after the Pratt City incident, rumors spread that
Catholics had burned them in retaliation. When federal agents warned
of a plot to destroy other Catholic institutions, the local newspapers
maintained a discreet silence. One newsman on the Birmingham *Age-
Herald* staff was dismissed, allegedly for his negative expressions about
the "True Americans," a local anti-Catholic group.[46] The same
year Father James E. Coyle, pastor of St. Paul's Church, Alabama's
largest Catholic congregation, wrote a rebuttal to the anti-Catholicism expressed by Baptist pastor R. L. Durant in the *Age-Herald*.
The dispute broadened when the Birmingham Baptist Ministers' Conference passed a resolution supporting Reverend Durant's views.[47]
Father Coyle's life was threatened in 1917, and federal authorities,
learning of a plot to burn St. Paul's, persuaded the priest to place
an armed guard on the church property at night.[48] By 1919 the editor
of *The Alabama Baptist* not only believed that church union was a

[45] *The Alabama Baptist,* November 6, 1912.
[46] Charles P. Sweeney, "Bigotry in the South," *The Nation,* CXI (November 24, 1920),
586.
[47] For the resolution, see *The Alabama Baptist,* March 29, 1916.
[48] Charles P. Sweeney, "Bigotry Turns to Murder," *The Nation,* CXIII (August 31, 1921),
232.

Catholic conspiracy, but also argued that there was only one struggle in the postwar religious world—Baptist democracy versus "Romanism's" monarchy.[49]

The 1920s deepened the chasm separating faiths. The city was characterized by religious zeal, the growth of civic and social clubs, population expansion, construction of the city's skyscrapers, financial problems, inadequacies in law enforcement and education, and the prevalence of social unrest.[50] Bigotry thrived in such an atmosphere. *The Menace,* a sometimes obscene anti-Catholic publication by Georgia's Tom Watson, was widely available at local newsstands.[51] The "True Americans" dominated city government with a motto of "No Catholics in Public Office." They defeated incumbent officials in the 1920 elections for refusing to fire a Catholic woman stenographer in the county treasurer's office, and they threatened to boycott businesses that employed Catholics.[52]

Even state politics became enmeshed in Birmingham's religious and ethnic strife. Incumbent United States Senator Oscar W. Underwood, a resident of Jefferson County, simultaneously represented conservative political and economic philosophies and opposed the attempt of religious groups to prescribe individual choice through prohibition. Courageously opposing both prohibition and the nativist sentiment of the "True Americans" and Ku Klux Klan, he became the natural target of an unlikely but comprehensible political coalition in Jefferson County. Methodists and Baptists, mobilized by the Alabama Anti-Saloon League, attacked Underwood for his "wet" record. They generally endorsed Jasper businessman L. B. Musgrove, who also had the backing of organized labor.[53] Religious leaders often joined labor spokesmen officiating at Musgrove rallies, and the editor of the state Methodist journal based his opposition to Underwood on the incumbent Senator's "wetness," "anti-

[49] *The Alabama Baptist,* April 24, 1919.

[50] These characteristics are noted as formative patterns in the Ku Klux Klan dominance of Birmingham. For an excellent study William Robert Snell, "The Ku Klux Klan in Jefferson County, Alabama, 1916–1930" (M.A. thesis, Samford University, 1967).

[51] Sweeney, "Bigotry in the South," 586.

[52] Sweeney, "Bigotry Turns to Murder," 232; also see Snell, "Ku Klux Klan in Jefferson County," 25.

[53] *The Alabama Baptist,* December 11, 1919, January 1, 1920; *The Alabama Christian Advocate,* April 22, 29, May 6, 1920. For a fuller discussion of this race see Wayne Flynt, "Organized Labor, Reform, and Alabama Politics, 1920," *Alabama Review,* XXIII (July 1970), 163–80.

progressive" social philosophy, and failure to support the more advanced "liberalism" of the Woodrow Wilson administration.[54] Pamphlets accusing Underwood of pro-Catholic leanings also circulated in the state.[55]

Although Underwood narrowly won the election (69,130 to 61,360), he lost Jefferson County (9,934 for Musgrove to 9,883), the only time in his long career that he lost his home district. Political lieutenants in Birmingham attributed his local defeat to the remarkable coalition forged by organized labor and the Anti-Saloon League.[56]

The Underwood election posed Birmingham's religious dilemma in sharp relief. The social concern of the churches had not changed suddenly to Klan-style bigotry. The nativist sentiment and battles against secularism of the 1920s were continuations of the earlier struggles to impose prohibition and "blue laws"; all of these were attempts to dictate community morality by force. Many churchmen and laymen retained fairly "liberal" social attitudes, but felt that the Klan was working for a common objective—to preserve community moral standards.

There is certainly no question that Birmingham's Protestant churches supported the Ku Klux Klan. The Klan's attempts to end bootlegging and its floggings of "moral undesirables" in the community usually elicited either praise or neutrality from the city's pulpits. The local head of the Klan estimated that 51 percent of the white Protestant ministers in the county where members of the Klan and that at least that proportion of the laity favored the organizaton.[57] Klansmen frequently interrupted church services in Birmingham during the 1920s to make a donation to the pastor for his support; such Klan processionals occurred at Inglenook Methodist, Pike Avenue Baptist, Virginia Mines Baptist, Avondale Baptist, Packer Memorial Baptist, Pentecostal Church of North Birmingham, Alton Methodist, Gate City Baptist, Irondale Baptist, and Antioch Baptist.[58]

[54] See *The Alabama Christian Advocate,* January–April, 1914.
[55] J. B. Long to Oscar W. Underwood, April 20, 1920, Oscar W. Underwood Papers, Alabama State Department of Archives and History, Montgomery. Hereafter cited as Underwood Papers.
[56] Forney Johnston to Oscar W. Underwood, May 13, 1920, Underwood Papers.
[57] Snell, "Ku Klux Klan in Jefferson County," 161.
[58] *Ibid.*

Perhaps the most spectacular incident of religious intolerance during the 1920s occurred on the evening of August 11, 1921. Father James E. Coyle, pastor of St. Paul's Catholic Church and a focus of Catholic-Protestant conflict, was shot to death by Rev. E. R. Stephenson, a Methodist minister and Klansman, who specialized in performing marriages at the local courthouse. Stephenson's daughter had married a Catholic in a ceremony performed by Father Coyle. The enraged father admitted the shooting and was charged with second-degree murder, but the Birmingham community sympathized with Stephenson. His defense council, Hugo Black, a local attorney and active Sunday School teacher at First Baptist Church, won acquittal from a sympathetic jury. National opinion blamed the bigotry on the city's churches and the acquiescence of the press, while denouncing Birmingham as the "American hotbed of anti-Catholic fanaticism," where the "murder of a priest had been added to the achievements of bigotry."[59]

The religious mind of Birmingham was divided, however, even on Klan enforcement of morality. An increasingly vocal minority of ministers denounced the Klan and demanded that police curb its excesses. Although not all the denomination's ministers signed it, Methodist pastors passed a resolution condemning floggings in the city. Ministers such as Dr. Robert N. Simpson of First Christian, Rev. Jack Johnston of Eleventh Street Baptist, Dr. Henry Edmonds of Independent Presbyterian, Dr. J. E. Dillard of Southside Baptist, Rev. Theo Harris of Pike Avenue Baptist, Dr. W. R. Hendrix of Highlands Methodist, and Rev. Hans Reuter of Zion Lutheran all spoke out publicly against Klan violence.[60] When Father Coyle was murdered, Henry Edmonds announced a sermon on the incident. Because Klan control of city government was almost complete, Edmonds's friends tried to dissuade him. Failing this, they attended his service at the Lyric Theater fully armed and scattered through the congregation determined to protect Edmonds should the Klan attempt any violence. Luckily, such an armed confrontation never materialized.[61]

Edmonds went beyond criticism of the Klan. He, Rabbi Newfield,

[59] Sweeney, "Bigotry Turns to Murder," 232. The *New York World* blamed the religious press for its failure to take a stand against the Klan; quoted in Snell, "Ku Klux Klan in Jefferson County," 161.

[60] Snell, "Ku Klux Klan in Jefferson County," 92 ff; also see Birmingham *Age-Herald*, July 11, 18, 19, 24, 1927.

[61] Edmonds, *A Parson's Notebook*, 98.

and Father Eugene Sands, presiding priest at St. Paul's in Birmingham, also organized a Faith Panel, which toured Alabama and neighboring states speaking to civic clubs and colleges. He later aided local Jewish businessmen and Rabbi Newfield in reviving the National Conference of Christians and Jews to stem an ugly rise in anti-Semitism.[62]

Intolerance was not only personalized toward Catholics, Jews, and blacks in Birmingham; it was also aimed at the entire climate of free thought. Anti-evolution sentiment was strong, and in 1928 a women's group sponsored a lecture by noted Fundamentalist Baptist minister Dr. John Roach Straton. Allegedly financed by the Klan, Straton's speech to a packed municipal auditorium verbally roasted Catholic Democratic Presidential nominee Alfred E. Smith.[63] On the opposite side of the issue was *Alabama Baptist* editor L. L. Gwaltney, who quietly waged an energetic campaign for free religious thought. Appalled at the Fundamentalist attack on Baptist professors, he resisted their attempts to force teachers in Baptist institutions to sign statements of faith. The president of Birmingham's Howard College, Baptist affiliated, wanted to announce the willingness of his faculty to sign such a statement, but Gwaltney dissuaded him.[64] When a state Baptist pastor wrote an article attacking President William L. Poteat of Baptist Wake Forest College for his evolutionary ideas, Gwaltney refused to carry the article. The infuriated pastor told a prominent politico in his congregation about the incident, and the layman, who later ran for governor, demanded that Gwaltney carry the article as paid advertisement. Gwaltney again refused, and recalling the atmosphere years later, wrote that the same kind of "dogmatic faith" that had condemned Galileo's science, "happened among Protestants of America, the Baptists included, during the second [third] decade of the twentieth century."[65]

Perhaps the energy diverted into Klan and Fundamentalist movements enervated the city's churches, for membership increased from 77,145 in 1916 to only 125,253 in 1926, a major decline from the nearly 200 percent growth of the 1906–1916 era. Between 1926 and 1936 church membership actually decreased from 125,253 to 109,945 in 1936, a 12.2 percent decline. Only eight of America's fifty largest cities experienced

[62] *Ibid.*, 197, 215.
[63] Snell, "Ku Klux Klan in Jefferson County," 200.
[64] Gwaltney, *Forty of the Twentieth*, 140.
[65] Gwaltney, "This I Leave With You," 40, 65.

a decline during the same period, and Birmingham's was the fourth largest drop in the nation.[66] Though the cause of the decline is more complicated than any single issue, it seems clear that the atmosphere of constant controversy did not enhance the strength of the church in Birmingham.

Analysis of the city's church membership reveals that the largest single religious group in the city after 1910 was the National Baptist denomination representing Birmingham's black population. The African Methodist Episcopal church was close behind, and the preponderance of black churches necessitates further word about the religious expression of the 40 percent of Birmingham's population that was black.

The views of most white Protestants toward blacks were paternalistic. They opposed lynching, favored education for blacks, and even pleaded for better jobs, but beyond these attitudes few were willing to go.[67] Even a man so consistently liberal as Henry Edmonds viewed blacks paternalistically and bemoaned the 1954 desegregation decision which he believed "ended the era of good feeling in the South between the races and halted the progress that was being made . . . under the earlier formula of equal but separate facilities."[68]

Despite such white attitudes, blacks did make undeniable contributions to the religious life of Birmingham during the era. A Juvenile Court Association was organized early in the century composed of one woman from each of thirty black churches. Its task was to take charge of black delinquents. In 1907 the women raised $2,000 and bought twenty-five acres of land near Montgomery. They built a six-room cottage and started an "industrial school" for black males, the beginning of Mt. Meigs Reformatory, which later became a state institution.[69]

The church was more central to the urban black subculture than to white society. Consequently, blacks went to church more frequently, and a larger proportion than whites were church members.[70] Preachers

[66] U.S. Bureau of the Census, *Religious Bodies, 1936*, Part I (Washington, 1941), 71–72.

[67] For fuller treatment of this subject see Wayne Flynt, "The Negro and Alabama Baptists During the Progressive Era," *Journal of the Alabama Academy of Science*, XXXIX (April 1968), 163–67.

[68] Edmonds, *A Parson's Notebook*, 283.

[69] Bigelow, "Birmingham," 155.

[70] *Ibid.*, 218.

had high status, serving as political organizers and providing business leadership.[71] Two of Birmingham's leading black businesses were begun by clergymen: Rev. W. R. Pettiford founded the Alabama Penny Savings Bank, and Rev. T. W. Walker started the People's Home and Insurance Company. Black church societies also were more concerned with the social problems of the black community than were their white equivalents.

Other social interests of both black and white churches were similar. White Baptist pastor B. F. Riley assisted blacks in the organization of the Negro Anti-Saloon League in 1909 with national headquarters in Birmingham.[72] Black pastors also enthusiastically favored the Interchurch World Movement, demonstrating a more cooperative sentiment than their white brethren. One hundred seventy-three black delegates attended the Interchurch conference in Birmingham in 1920, and a special session was held on the last day of the conference at Sixteenth Street Baptist, the leading black church in the city. Black clergymen agreed that the movement would be helpful in promoting better race relations and in combating prejudice, injustice, and lynching.[73]

Whether black or white, the religious mind of Birmingham faced traumatic issues in the first decades of the new century. Responding to the evident challenges of the urban/industrial South, churches charted a new course that led them further and further from the other-worldly salvation gospel of the nineteenth century. Even the conservative individualists such as Brother Bryan demonstrated a social dimension not typical of rural Southern religion. At the opposite pole Henry Edmonds and A. J. Dickinson questioned traditional religious dogma, while black churches and Wesley Houses ministered to estranged laborers. Tragedy came when the attempts of the churches to remake society inadvertently lent support to "True Americans" and the Klan, whose tactics were inimical to Christianity. Reluctantly, chroniclers of Southern thought must come to terms with the fact that the politicizing of Southern religion was not always "good," that the same socialization which resulted in "Social

---

[71] The political function of the black pastor was frequently criticized by white ministers; for example, see *ibid.*, 215–16, and *The Alabama Baptist*, October 22, 1902.

[72] *The Alabama Baptist*, April 21, 1909.

[73] *Birmingham News*, March 7, 1920.

Gospel" reform such as the abolition of child labor and injustice toward laborers also resulted in proscriptive morality and Klan-type intolerance. Perhaps Vulcan is an adequate symbol for the "city of churches," for sin and salvation, churches and violence existed in contradictory union during the first three decades of the twentieth century.

LEE N. ALLEN

The Woman Suffrage Movement in Alabama, 1910–1920

The woman suffrage movement started comparatively late in the South. In New York the first Women's Rights Convention was held in 1848, and in the West women were allowed to vote shortly after the Civil War. But throughout the South agitation for equal suffrage was virtually non-existent before about 1890, and it was not until 1910 that the crusade attracted widespread attention.[1]

The root of the woman suffrage movement in Alabama reaches back to the Reconstruction era. National records reveal that the society had an appointed representative at Huntsville in the 1870's, a Mrs. Priscilla Holmes Drake.[2] No extant facts indicate the scope of her inchoate work, and it is perhaps safe to assume that she accomplished very little in the state. Judging from occasional contemporary edi-

---

This essay was published in *The Alabama Review,* XI (April, 1958).

[1] The standard history of the woman suffrage movement is Elizabeth Cady Stanton, Susan B. Anthony, Matilda J. Gage, and Ida H. Harper, *History of Woman Suffrage* (Rochester and New York, 1889–1922), 6 vols. A briefer survey is Carrie Chapman Catt and Nettie Rogers Shuler, *Woman Suffrage and Politics* (New York, 1926). Biographies of leaders include Ida H. Harper, *The Life and Work of Susan B. Anthony* (Indianapolis, 1908), 3 vols., and Mary Gray Peck, *Carrie Chapman Catt* (New York, 1944). The official publication of the national organization was *Woman's Journal* (Boston, 1870–1917), succeeded by *Woman Citizen* (New York, 1917–27). The annual reports of the National American Woman Suffrage Association, variously titled, but commonly called *Proceedings of the . . . Annual Convention* [1892–1922], contain a wealth of material on national and local suffrage campaigns.

[2] Stanton, *op. cit.,* III, 830.

torial comment, sentiment was almost unanimous in opposition to Mrs. Drake's struggle to win voting rights for women.[3]

Toward the end of the nineteenth century a change in attitude could be observed, however, for in 1892 the first woman suffrage association in Alabama was organized in Decatur. During the next few years similar groups were established in Verbena, Huntsville, Gadsden, Calera, probably Montgomery, and possibly elsewhere.[4] In 1893 a state organization was brought into being with Mrs. Ellen Stephens Hildreth of Decatur as president, and it became affiliated with the National American Woman Suffrage Association.[5]

The work of these early Alabama suffragists was very limited. Newspapers in Columbiana and Decatur regularly granted the organization space during 1893-1894, but no Alabama journalist is known to have come out openly for equal rights.[6] Public lectures in Huntsville and New Decatur in 1895 by two nationally known suffragists, Susan B. Anthony and Carrie Chapman Catt, attracted only local attention.[7] In 1897 two outstanding Alabama leaders, Mrs. Virginia Clay-Clopton and Miss Frances E. Griffin, were among the principal speakers at the Nashville convention held to organize the Tennessee Equal Rights Association.[8]

The climax to this brief era of activity came in 1901, when the Alabama Constitutional Convention met in Montgomery. Delegate Benjamin H. Craig presented a resolution providing for woman suffrage in the new organ. A public hearing was given the women on June 10, 1901, and Miss Frances Griffin, then president of the state associ-

[3] See *Lauderdale Times* (Florence, Ala.), Nov. 14, 1871, Oct. 8, 1872; *Alabama Daily State Journal* (Montgomery), Aug. 31, Oct. 26, 1871; Columbiana (Ala.) *Chronicle*, April 20, 1893.

[4] Stanton, *op. cit.,* IV, 465; *Proceedings of the Thirtieth Annual Convention of the National American Woman Suffrage Association* [Washington, 1898] (Philadelphia, n.d.), p. 81. This title is hereinafter cited as *Proceedings,* with appropriate number and date.

[5] *Chronicle,* April 27, 1893. Mrs. Hildreth's husband, who had moved to Alabama in 1889, was editor of the friendly Decatur *Advertiser.* She died January 6, 1916.

[6] *Chronicle,* Jan. 26, Feb. 2, 1893; *Proceedings . . . 26th* [Washington, 1894] (Warren, Ohio, 1894), p. 89.

[7] Stanton, *op. cit.,* IV, 465; Peck, *op. cit.,* p. 83.

[8] Nashville (Tenn.) *American,* May 13, 1897, cited in A. Elizabeth Taylor, "The Woman Suffrage Movement in Tennessee" (unpublished Ph.D. dissertation, Vanderbilt University, 1943), pp. 25–27 (this thesis was published in New York in 1957). Mrs. Clay-Clopton had married Clement C. Clay in 1843. She was the author of *A Belle of the Fifties,* her reminiscences of Washington society on the eve of the Civil War. Following the death of Senator Clay in 1882, she married David Clopton (1887), chief justice of the Alabama Supreme Court. Her participation in this phase of the suffrage work added greatly to the prestige of the movement in the state. She died June 23, 1915.

ation, ably presented the women's views. When the showdown vote was taken in August, however, the women were denied the ballot by an overwhelming vote of 87 to 22.[9] Following this failure activity in Alabama all but ceased for almost a decade.

The year 1910 marked the beginning of a new era for Alabama women, for it was then that the first of several local chapters of suffrage associations was formed. Organized in Selma on March 29, 1910, its president was Miss Mary Winslow Partridge, a prime mover in its formation, one who believed that only when women could vote would the evil of the saloon be conquered.[10]

Birmingham was the second city to have a woman suffrage association. It came into being on November 11, 1911 as the Equal Suffrage League, the outgrowth of another progressive proposal of the day, the abolition of child labor. Mrs. W. L. Murdoch, a child labor leader of Birmingham, and Mrs. Solon Harold Jacobs, were the organizers.[11] Mrs. Jacobs, who later became a national suffrage leader, was its first president.[12] Subsequently, a number of chapters were organized in other Alabama cities, largely through the missionary efforts of these first two groups. In Huntsville the association that had been so active in the 1890's was revived by Mrs. Oscar R. Hundley, of Birmingham. The women selected the venerable Mrs. Virginia Clay-Clopton, a leader from the early days as president.[13] The Montgomery chapter was formed on January 2, 1913, after Miss Partridge of Selma delivered

[9] Birmingham (Ala.) *Age-Herald*, Aug. 10, 1901; *Official Proceedings of the Constitutional Convention of the State of Alabama . . . 1901* (Wetumpka, Ala., 1940), I, 322–23, 464–71; II, 1388–89; 3814–24; III, 3855–79. Miss Griffin was born in Wetumpka, July 22, 1843, was graduated from Judson College, and taught school first in Verbena and later in Montgomery. Raised in a Baptist family, she joined the Methodist Episcopal Church because, as she explained, it gave a broader field to women in public life. She was active in both prohibition and woman suffrage work. She died June 17, 1917.

[10] Stanton, *op. cit.*, VI, 3; letter, Miss Mary Partridge, Selma, to author, Sept. 24, 1948.

[11] Their inspiration had grown out of a meeting of the National Child Labor Conference held in Birmingham the preceeding March (see Birmingham, Ala., *News*, March 9–13, 1911).

[12] *Age-Herald*, Nov. 12, 19, 26, 1911. Mrs. Pattie Ruffner Jacobs, born October 2, 1875, in Charleston, W. Va., was educated in Nashville at Ward-Belmont Seminary. She was not only a woman suffrage leader, but also crusaded for betterment of conditions for convict labor and for the abolition of child labor. After 1920 she was active in the Democratic party, serving as Alabama's first national committee-woman. During the New Deal days she worked with the NRA and TVA. She died in Birmingham, December 22, 1935.

[13] Huntsville (Ala.) *Mercury-Banner*, Nov. 11, 1912.

an inspiring talk on the subject of equal suffrage. Mrs. Sallie B. Powell was its first president.[14]

The work of these and all other locals formed during the second decade was aimed ultimately at enfranchisement of women. The route to this goal was a long one and necessarily took the workers into many by-paths. Yet, in all their varied activities these honorable ladies of great courage never forgot that they were laboring for the right to vote.

Of necessity, a great amount of their energy was consumed in organizational activity—such routine matters as preparing regular club programs, building and training membership, raising money, keeping contact with national, state, and other local suffrage associations, maintaining adequate offices, and general club administration. So active was the Birmingham group that it maintained a downtown office from 1913 through 1919. A few other towns opened similar headquarters for shorter periods.[15]

To support their multitudinous activities the suffragists raised money by dues and by such activities as dances, bazaars, and contests.[16] Public lectures at which admission was charged were not uncommon. General H. H. Roberts once gave a series of four lectures in Birmingham under the auspices of the Birmingham Equal Suffrage Association.[17] Another device to raise money was publication of suffrage sections in local newspapers. The first of these appeared as a two-page insert in the Huntsville *Mercury-Banner*, November 23, 1913. Later, an eighteen-page supplement to the Birmingham *News* (July 2, 1916) resulted in about $1,000 profit from the sale of advertisements.[18] A third insert appeared in the Selma *Times*, November 25, 1917. These columns were educational, appearing as supplements to the regular club columns in several local newspapers. Miss Amelia Worthington edited the first and finest woman suffrage column for

[14] Montgomery (Ala.) *Advertiser,* Jan. 5, 11, 1913.

[15] For its opening see *Age-Herald,* June 22, 1913. See also *ibid.,* Nov. 26, 1911; Jan. 5, Dec. 7, 1913; Oct. 25, 1914; Jan. 17, 1915; and April 22, 1916 for details concerning routine activities of the organizations.

[16] *Ibid.,* Sept. 24, Oct. 22, 1913; May 6, Dec. 4, 1914; *News,* Nov. 8, 1914; Jan. 10, 1915; Oct. 28, 1917.

[17] *Age-Herald,* Nov. 19, 1915.

[18] Minutes of the Alabama Equal Suffrage Association [1912–1918] (MS in Alabama Equal Suffrage Association File, Alabama State Department of Archives and History, Montgomery), July 26, 1916. This title is hereinafter cited as Minutes.

the Birmingham *News,* beginning in January, 1913. By early 1915, it was reported that there were suffrage columns in at least fourteen Alabama papers.[19]

The local associations devoted much of their energy to educating the public to the need and justice of woman suffrage. In addition to the newspaper columns and special sections, they also prepared publicity releases, sponsored free public lectures, talked personally with leaders and memberships of civic, religious, political, social, and labor groups, distributed literature, and sponsored debates and essay contests. Extension committees, acting as speakers' bureaus, furnished suffragists to address other groups. Their lecturers were preferred by labor and church groups, but the committees provided speakers for many different occasions.[20] The state fairs were favorites of the ladies. They usually maintained well-decorated booths and took advantage of every opportunity to lecture and distribute handbills around the fair grounds.[21] In 1913 at the Alabama State Fair, in Birmingham, some 25,000 sheets of printed matter were given out by the yellow-sashed ladies.[22]

The women also devoted a great deal of this time to social service, humanitarian activities, and war work. This phase of their program was not directly concerned with advancing the suffrage cause, but it did help establish good public relations. It aimed at refuting the careless assertion that women were selfishly seeking the ballot and were not actually interested in public affairs and would not use the vote to improve society if and when they got it.[23] The suffragists were credited with persuading Birmingham merchants to close their stores on Thursday at noon during the summer and earlier than the traditional 10 o'clock on Saturday night. This was for the benefit of the women employees.[24] Gadsden women were responsible for establishing a playground, and they and their counterparts in Tuscaloosa conducted story-telling hours for children. In Huntsville the suffragists presented each prisoner in the local jail with a good Thanksgiving

[19] *News,* Feb. 28, 1915.
[20] *Age-Herald,* June 20, Oct. 26, 1913; March 14, June 4, 1915.
[21] *Ibid.,* Oct. 5, 1912; Oct. 17, 1914; Nov. 2, 1915; *News,* Oct. 8, 18, 1914; Oct. 28, 1917; Montgomery (Ala.) *Journal,* March 7, 1914.
[22] *News,* May 24, 1914.
[23] *Age-Herald,* Jan. 31, July 1, 1913.
[24] *Ibid.,* July 13, 1913; Nov. 6, 1915.

dinner in 1916. Following a bad flood in Selma in 1916, the suffragists made their headquarters a relief center.[25]

Some of the women's most impressive work was done during World War I. After America was drawn into this holocaust, for the most part they relegated suffrage, as such, to a secondary position and promptly took up war work. As a group they assisted in draft registrations, in enlistment of women for volunteer home service, in Liberty Bond Loan drives, and in Red Cross projects.[26] The Birmingham suffragists published a special cookbook of useful wartime recipes, known as *A Hoover Helper*.[27] And they offered a number of free courses in practical subjects, such as stenography, nursing, telephone and telegraph operation, and automobile driving, to help train women for better home service during the war.[28]

Altogether, however, the ladies' most important single activity, and the one that drew to them the most criticism, was legislative lobbying on the state level. In this field they were able to work only twice, in 1915 and 1919, the years the legislature held its quadrennial sessions. This vital element of the suffrage program is best viewed in the light of the struggle to establish a state-wide suffrage organization, co-ordinating the work of the various local societies scattered throughout the State of Alabama.

On October 9, 1912 Selma and Birmingham suffragists, representing local groups in the state, held a meeting to form a state organization, called the Alabama Equal Suffrage Association. Mrs. Solon Jacobs of Birmingham was elected first president. The constitution adopted that day stated that the object of the association was "to secure protection in their right to vote, to women citizens of Alabama by appropriate national and state legislation." The group immediately became affiliated with the National American Woman Suffrage Association and sent delegates to the November convention in Philadelphia. It was further provided by the constitution that missionary work was to be conducted by one of the officers, a

---

[25] *News,* July 16, Aug. 20, Dec. 21, 1916; April 8, 1917.
[26] *Ibid.,* June 3, July 1, 11, 1917; March 3, Dec. 15, 1918; "Fortnightly Suffrage Bulletin" (mimeographed), June 15, Aug. 1, Sept. 1, 1917.
[27] A copy of this book, subtitled *Fifty Tested and Endorsed War-Time Recipes,* is in the Alabama Equal Suffrage Association File.
[28] *News,* Feb. 12, March 24, 1918.

state organizer. Miss Mary Partridge of Selma was elected to the position, and her first job was to form a club in Montgomery.[29]

The first annual convention met January 29, 1913, in Selma; the second in Huntsville in February, 1914; and the third in Tuscaloosa in February, 1915. At the 1916 convention, in Gadsden, the presidency passed from Mrs. Jacobs to Mrs. Julian B. Parke of Selma, and state headquarters were removed from Birmingham.[30] The following year the convention met in Birmingham for two days, followed by three days of a special "suffrage school," staffed by women officials from the national association.[31] In 1918, however, war demands so interfered with normal activities that the meeting in Selma lasted only parts of two days. This was the low-water mark during the decade.[32]

One of the chief operational functions of the Alabama Equal Suffrage Association was assisting locals in their publicity programs. A press committee had been created in the beginning to carry out the work. Its first chairman for two years was Miss Ethel Armes, a Birmingham free-lance writer. Miss Amelia Worthington later assumed the responsibility, and her suffrage column in the Birmingham *News*, mentioned above, became the organization's unofficial voice.[33] The most effective work of the committee was done after the legislative defeat of 1915. Recognizing the tremendous educational task, it sought to use every possible medium of communication. Special news plates were distributed to about one hundred small papers. To some forty larger newspapers, a mimeographed bi-weekly bulletin was dispatched. And for general distribution among members a monthly *Alabama Suffrage Bulletin* was issued about fifteen times during 1915 and 1916.[34]

The function of the Alabama Equal Suffrage Association was not only to co-ordinate the work of Alabama suffragists but also to keep

---

[29] *Ibid.*, Sept. 25, 1912; *Proceedings of the Annual Conventions of the Alabama Equal Suffrage Association* [1912–1915] (Birmingham, 1916), pp. 9–10; *Advertiser*, Jan. 5, 1913. This title is hereinafter cited as Alabama *Proceedings*.

[30] Gadsden (Ala.) *Evening Journal*, Feb. 11, 1916.

[31] *The Handbook of the National American Woman Suffrage Association and Proceedings . . . 49th* [1917] (New York, 1917?), p. 86. This title is hereinafter cited as *Handbook and Proceedings*.

[32] Minutes, May 7, 1918.

[33] Alabama *Proceedings*, pp. 13, 23, 68.

[34] Minutes, Dec. 9, 1916; Oct. 17, June 9, 1917; *Alabama Suffrage Bulletin*, Oct., 1915.

Alabama suffrage activities in line with national objectives. The spirit of co-operation which existed between workers at these two levels was commendable. Alabama suffragists joined nation-wide publicity schemes, such as the May Day demonstrations of 1914 and 1915, the Self-Sacrifice Day of 1914, the Buy-A-Bale Plan for boosting cotton prices in 1915, and the Million Dollar Fund campaign of 1917.[35] At all of the national conventions Alabama was usually well represented, and a few Alabamians rose to national offices. Mrs. Solon Jacobs, the Birmingham leader, was elected second auditor in 1915, and she remained active at the national level for many years.[36] Others served on important committees or appeared on the convention programs.

One dark moment occurred when the loyalty of Alabama suffragists to the national objectives was questioned immediately before 1915 and again just prior to submission of the Federal amendment. Out of deference to the strong state's rights feelings of many local citizens and politicians, the women of Alabama asserted that their primary objective was enfranchisement by state action rather than by Federal authority. Yet, the Alabama Equal Suffrage Association always remained loyally affiliated with the National American Woman Suffrage Association and flatly refused to co-operate with the Louisiana state's rights group known as the Southern Woman Suffrage Conference, which absolutely denied the right of the Federal government to regulate suffrage requirements.[37] Alabama was determined to remain loyal. As it shied away from the conservatives, so it refused to be drawn into the radicals' camp. The Woman's Party, headed by Miss Alice Paul, was a rival organization of the National American Woman Suffrage Association and worked for enfranchisement by Federal amendment only, frequently resorting to the kind of militant tactics often associated with English suffragettes. Miss Paul spent a fruitless week in Birmingham in May, 1917, but she was unable to lure any of the leaders into her own intractable group. The small start she made in the state never achieved any importance.[38] The stout-hearted suffragists of Alabama wanted freedom to work for enfranchisement by

[35] Unidentified clipping in Partridge Scrapbook (owned by Miss Mary Partridge, Selma, Ala.); Minutes, April 9, 1914; Alabama *Proceedings*, p. 73; *Handbook and Proceedings, 49th* [1917], pp. 98, 188; *Age-Herald*, Sept. 28, 1914.

[36] *Ibid., 47th* [1915] (New York, 1915?), p. 42.

[37] Unidentified clippings in Partidge Scrapbook; Minutes, March 11, 1914.

[38] *News*, May 6, 13, June 25, July 1, 1917; Mrs. Ellea C. Thompson to ?, Dec. 31, 1917 (in National Woman's Party Files, Library of Congress, Washington).

any means and refused to be limited in their approach by state or Federal action. The only limitation permitted was a voluntary one— that is, not to work for a Federal amendment until the Alabama State Legislature had been given an opportunity to vote on the issue.[39]

The long-coveted opportunity to present this matter to the legislature of Alabama came in 1915 with the first quadrennial meeting of this body since organization of the Alabama Equal Suffrage Association in 1912. Plans were a long time in the making and strategy was carefully mapped. For example, when the national association sent a Miss Lavinia Engle to assist the Alabamians, they quickly hustled her out into the hinterlands, instead of using her to lobby in the gleaming marble corridors of the imposing Capitol. There was legitimate fear that her presence in Montgomery would be seized upon by hostile legislators as proof that there was so little interest locally among Alabama women that a national worker had to be imported from out of the state to assist in leadership of the campaign.[40]

A number of other preliminary steps were taken by the suffragists. A petition requesting the legislature to submit a woman suffrage amendment to the voters circulated for about a year and, when presented in August, 1915, bore over ten thousand names.[41] Further, the legislative committee chairman, Mrs. Oscar R. Hundley, began to build a file on each legislator, to ascertain his usefulness to the cause.[42] Moreover, men of the state were asked to form separate leagues and apply pressure as voters on the legislators. Only in Cullman and Birmingham, however, did the men so respond.[43]

The legislature convened on January 12, 1915 and on that same day the suffragists opened campaign headquarters in Montgomery. They selected a vacant store in the historic Grand Theater building because, in addition to providing comfortable quarters, it lay on the direct Dexter Avenue route from downtown hotels to the Capitol. The large windows were conspicuously plastered with eye-catching suffrage posters.[44]

---

[39] *News,* May 20, 1917. Mrs. Solon Jacobs to Alice Paul, April 12, 1914 (in *ibid.*).
[40] Minutes, Nov. 23, 1914; Jan. 9, Feb. 2, 1915.
[41] *Age-Herald,* March 8, 1914; May 15, Aug. 10, 1915.
[42] This information is in the Southern Collection of the Birmingham (Ala.) Public Library.
[43] Minutes, Nov. 23, 1914; *News,* Jan. 31, 1915; *Age-Herald,* May 23, 1915.
[44] *Ibid.,* Jan. 17, 1915.

The bill which the women were seeking to have passed provided
that the following constitutional amendment be submitted to the
voters in 1916: "The right of the citizens of this state to vote
shall not be denied or abridged on account of sex." The resolution was
introduced on January 22, 1915 by Representative J. W. Green, of
Dallas county, who had requested the honor almost a year before. It
was referred to the Committee on Privileges and Elections.[45] A joint
session was held February 5, at which time Dr. Anna Howard Shaw, a
national suffrage leader and an ordained minister of the Methodist
Episcopal Church, spoke. She is said to have impressed the legislators,[46] though it was to slight avail, for a few days later the legislature
adjourned for a five month recess without taking further action on
Green's resolution. The intervening months were busy ones for
suffragists.

The legislature reconvened on July 13, 1915, but not until Wednes-
day, August 25, was the final vote taken in the House of Representatives. On the question of submitting the proposed amendment to
the electorate, the House stood 52 *yeas* and 42 *nays,* with two pairs.
This was not a victory, although there was more than a majority in
favor. Actually, the bill failed to carry because it fell short of the
required three-fifths of the entire membership, which would have been
64 votes.[47] With this disheartening action the woman suffrage question, for all practical purposes, was settled for the 1915 legislative
session. However, for the record, the Senate acted a few days later and
administered the *coup de grace*. The vote there was 12 *yeas* and 20 *nays*.[48]

Alabama suffragists were naturally disappointed at the failure of
their measure. These dauntless women had hoped that, even if the
various legislators were personally antagonistic to equal suffrage, they
would at least have been willing to submit the question to the voters
of the state. The indefatigable Mrs. Jacobs commented on the
defeat: "We have received a check. That is all. We will be before the
legislature in its next session, and in all succeeding sessions until our
bill is submitted. We have not by any means given up the fight."[49]

It was clear that the intrepid suffragists had no intention of aban-

[45] *Ibid.,* April 15, 1914; Jan. 22, 1915.
[46] *Advertiser,* Feb. 6, 1915.
[47] Alabama *House Journal,* 1915, II, 2963–64.
[48] Alabama *Senate Journal,* 1915, II, 2846.
[49] *Age-Herald,* Jan. 30, Aug. 26, 1915.

doning their crusade simply because of a single momentary defeat. But the high ideals proclaimed by Mrs. Jacobs were not easily sustained. Activities during the next four years were considerably lessened. There are several identifiable factors accounting for this. First of all, there was what was described by women themselves as "the inevitable letdown" resulting from the unsuccessful conclusion of their prolonged effort.[50] The second factor accounting for slackened interest centered in the formation in 1916 of an anti-suffrage organization known as the Alabama Association Opposed to Woman Suffrage. It was affiliated with a national organization of similar name, but it was active only in the Selma area.[51] A third was the outbreak of war. As has been noted previously, the women devoted their collective and individual energies after 1917 to war work at the expense of the suffrage movement. And the last major factor was the women's uncertainty of their next objective. At the conclusion of the unsuccessful 1915 campaign they had announced that they planned to work next for the adoption of a Federal constitutional amendment. If this proposition were not before the states by 1919, the women later announced, they planned to ask the legislature again for a state constitutional amendment.[52] Yet the fate of the Federal amendment until early 1919 made it impossible for the Alabama leaders to know for what sort of campaign to prepare. Not until the annual national convention was held in March, 1919 were the women of Alabama certain that the Susan B. Anthony amendment would be submitted in time for the Alabama legislators to vote upon it at the 1919 session.[53] On their return from the national convention, the Alabama suffragists, having floundered uncertainly for almost four years, launched plans for their ratification campaign.

On June 4, 1919 the United States Senate concurred with the House of Representatives in submitting the woman suffrage amendment to the states. From the viewpoint of Alabama suffragists, this was an ideal time. The state legislature which had been in session earlier in the year was scheduled to reassemble on July 8. This allowed ample time for the women to put into operation the strategy they had been perfecting for several months. The inauguration of the cam-

[50] *Alabama Suffrage Bulletin,* Oct. 1915.
[51] Unidentified clippings in Partridge Scrapbook; Selma (Ala.) *Times,* Feb. 12, 1916.
[52] Minutes, Oct. 9, 1915; Jan. 19, 1918.
[53] *Proceedings* [1920], (New York, 1920?), p. 132.

paign was officially marked by an impressive "ratification dinner" in Birmingham on June 19.[54] A large committee was formed, members of the legislature, the Governor, and other prominent citizens were interviewed, three experienced organizers were sent into Alabama, and Miss Mary Parke London of Birmingham agreed to serve as an apprentice to these workers.[55] At the national headquarters Alabama was classified as one of the almost hopeless states. However, the eyes of the entire nation were on the vigorous campaign in Alabama, because it might be the first state to act on the amendment; a victory here would materially aid other states.[56]

Some unexpected and unappreciated assistance of questionable value came from the militant Woman's Party. Several of its members, notably Miss Sue White of Tennessee, appeared as the legislature reassembled and remained in Montgomery for about three months. The local suffragists resented their blatant intrusion and refused to work with them but, as Miss White put it later, "they never did repudiate us or show a mean spirit. . . ."[57]

At the other extreme, on June 17 an organization of opponents was formed in Montgomery for the sole purpose of preventing ratification of the Federal amendment, the Women's Anti-Ratification League of Alabama, with Mrs. James S. Pinckard as president, Mrs. Thomas M. Owen, long prominent in women's activities and a daughter of Senator John H. Bankhead (who was known as a bitter foe of woman suffrage), as legislative chairman. Included in its rapidly growing membership were many former suffragists, recusants who were opposed to enfanchisement by the Federal amendment. Such a person was J. Lister Hill, a young Montgomery lawyer from a prominent family, later to become a strong supporter of liberal national policies as Senator from Alabama.[58] In Selma, meanwhile, the Alabama Association Opposed to Woman Suffrage, founded in 1916, actively campaigned at this crucial moment, not only in Alabama but throughout the entire South.[59]

[54] *News,* June 5, 19, 1919. Neither Senator from Alabama favored the proposal. See John H. Bankhead to Miss Margaret Miller, May 23, 1919 (in Bankhead Papers, Alabama State Department of Archives and History).

[55] *Proceedings* [1920], pp. 94, 96, 132–33.

[56] Mobile (Ala.) *Register,* July 17, 1919.

[57] *Journal,* July 11, 28, Sept. 18, 1919; Sue White to Alice Paul, July 14, 1919 (in National Woman's Party Files).

[58] *Advertiser,* June 21, 22, 25, 28, 1919; *Woman Patriot,* Nov. 1, 1919.

[59] *Ibid.,* Aug. 23, 1919; *Advertiser,* July 2, 1919.

When the legislature reassembled on July 8, 1919, both sides were ready for action. The first blow was struck by the opponents of the amendment. Representative J. Lee Long of Butler County introduced a resolution to reject the proposed amendment,[60] thus carrying out the wishes of the national anti-suffragists who desired, not merely to secure defeat of a ratification resolution, but rather to secure adoption of another resolution which specifically rejected the amendment. The anti-suffragists hoped to secure thirteen such rejections, of which Alabama's would be one, and by such clear-cut action, to block any court action in case a future legislature should reverse its predecessor's position.[61]

On July 16 an open hearing before a joint session of the legislature was held. The suffragists divided their time among eight speakers, but their opponents refused to make any vocal presentation, saying that they had no desire to mix in politics, and to argue their points in public debate would contradict their professed feelings. But the opponents were not without a spokesman, for they appealed to Senator James B. Evins to read from the floor their memorial which dramatically pleaded in its touching peroration that the legislators not force them "from the quietitude of our homes into the contaminating atmosphere of political struggle."[62]

On the following day the Senate voted on a resolution, introduced earlier by Senator A. H. Carmichael, to ratify the proposed amendment. It received 13 *ayes* and 19 *nays*.[63] No action was taken on this defeated measure by the other chamber, but in September the House of Representatives voted on the resolution to reject the amendment. This resolution was adopted 95 to 31.[64] Two days later the Senate concurred 19 to 8, and rejection of the proposed Federal amendment on woman suffrage was complete. The anti-suffragists of Alabama had won a complete victory.[65]

One explanation of the defeat of the resolution was the fear that the amendment would have enfranchised the Negro women, or pos-

---

[60] Alabama *House Journal,* 1919, I, 696.
[61] Catt and Shuler, *op. cit.,* p. 463.
[62] Alabama *House Journal,* 1919, I, 846–47.
[63] Alabama *Senate Journal,* 1920, I, 836–39.
[64] Alabama *House Journal,* 1919, II, 2274–77.
[65] Alabama *Senate Journal,* 1919, II, 2064.

sibly re-opened the entire question of Negro voting in the state.[66] Not only is this argument found in much of the printed matter, but it is also suggested by the distribution of votes in the House of Representatives in relation to the Negro population of the state. Of the 90 votes cast, 31 were for the Federal suffrage amendment (34.4 per cent). Within the Black Belt area (with 40 per cent Negro population), there were a total of 43 votes cast, of which only 9 were in favor of the amendment (20.9 per cent). The fact that areas with heavy concentrations of Negro population gave substantially less support to the Federal proposal than did the state as a whole suggests a close relationship between the Negro question and progressive voting practices.

Once again the suffragists of Alabama had gone down in defeat. But in 1919 the prospects did not look so bleak as they had four years earlier. Although the women left Montgomery promising the legislators that they would return again in 1923, few of them believed it would be necessary. Already nearly a score of states had ratified the Federal amendment: certainly within four years the required thirty-six would have acted. Actually, the women had to wait only one year, for in August, 1920 Tennessee dramatically ratified the amendment and women were no longer to be denied the ballot on account of sex.

Months before this, suffragists of Alabama had come to realize that enfranchisement was inevitable. At the Jubilee Convention in April, 1920 the Alabama Equal Suffrage Association was voted out of existence, its records bequeathed to the Alabama State Department of Archives and History, and a League of Women Voters formed, with Mrs. A. J. Bowron, long a leading suffragist of Birmingham, as state chairman.[67]

Their work might have been regarded as a trifle premature, for it was not until August 26, 1920 that the Nineteenth Amendment was proclaimed in effect. Almost simultaneously the Governor of Alabama issued a call for a special session of the state legislature to make provisions for woman suffrage. In September, by a set of three laws,

---

[66] *News*, Jan. 11, March 2, 1918; June 18, 1919. See also assorted anti-suffrage dodgers in the Woman Suffrage File (in Alabama State Department of Archives and History).
    [67] *Journal*, April 8, 9, 10, 1920.

women were officially added to the electorate and Alabama fell into the ranks of the equal suffrage states.[68]

The organized campaign for woman suffrage in Alabama, which had begun haltingly in 1892 and had been in continuous operation since 1910, had at last ended in victory. Women could now vote to carry through the reforms which, they claimed, had precipitated the suffrage movement originally. Even the anti-suffragists who had but lately refused to participate in political meetings were now prepared, as they reluctantly admitted, "to assume the burden of suffrage if put upon them."[69] Together the pros and the cons marched to the voting polls.

---

[68] *Ibid.*, Sept. 14, 1920; *News,* Aug. 26, 27, 1920.
[69] Journal of the Women's Anti-Ratification League, Feb. 21, 1920 (in private possession).

The Twenties

LESLIE S. WRIGHT

Henry Ford and Muscle Shoals

Prospects were bright for development of the Tennessee River Valley, particularly the Muscle Shoals area, following World War I.[1] Writing in 1925, Richard C. Henry described the Tri-Cities region in these words:

> Three Alabama towns—Sheffield, Tuscumbia and Florence—stand near Muscle Shoals. Their combined population is in the neighborhood of 30,000. They are attractive, enterprising and progressive. Paved streets, splendid churches and schools and homelike residences are marked features of all three. Sheffield and Tuscumbia adjoin each other and are on the south bank of the Tennessee River five miles below Wilson Dam. Florence is on the north bank of the river, almost opposite Sheffield. The three are connected by hard surface roads. Three railroads lead into the district—the Southern, Louisville & Nashville and Northern Alabama.
>
> A fourth city has come into being, a city which adjoins immediately the land holdings of the United States government. . . . The city hall is built, ample for the functioning of the first city government and very attractive, indeed, but no visitor to the Muscle Shoals district believes it will long be adequate, so apparent and so vast are the possibilities for the near future.[2]

At the time of the entrance of the United States into the war, the Allies having refused to furnish her with necessary explosives, the government built two nitrate plants and a dam at Muscle Shoals for the purpose of assuring a home supply of munitions. The project was planned and undertaken purely as a war measure, but with the idea in the background that the electric power and the nitrate plants would be useful after the war ended, for the purpose of producing cheap power

---

[1] This paper was read at the annual meeting of the Alabama Historical Association, Selma, April 22, 1960. It was published in *The Alabama Review*, XIV (July, 1961).
[2] *The Truth About Muscle Shoals* (Chicago, 1925), 25.

and nitrates. This led to the use of permanent construction. In the appropriation bill, however, there was no provision for the operation of the project after the war. Congress believed that the manufacture of commercial fertilizers was not a legitimate line of activity for the War Department. Furthermore, public policy demanded that the government not enter into competition with private enterprise, the old established manufacturers of fertilizers, and the importers of Chilean nitrates.

Just as the plants were ready for operation, however, World War I ended. The nitrate plants were closed after their test runs and the building of the dam was abandoned.[3] For some time no action whatever was taken. An amendment to the general civil appropriations bill, which would have provided $10,000,000 for continuing construction of the Wilson Dam, was introduced in February, 1921, but was removed in a House-Senate conference. The general theory seems to have been that it was better to lose a little money altogether and forget it than to expend a greater sum in a salvage effort.[4]

The thought of a deteriorating dam and two costly nitrate plants standing unused was a constant source of irritation to taxpayers; and the thought of the cheap fertilizer which these idle plants could be supplying was a constant source of irritation to the farmers. The tremendously powerful waters of the Tennessee were running to waste. Since it was felt that the Harding administration would not support an expensive government undertaking on the Tennessee, Secretary of War John W. Weeks took action to secure bids from private enterprise willing to do the work.[5] In March, 1921 the Chief of Engineers was therefore requested to ask for bids. Weeks had declared his intention of passing on to Congress any bids that promised "commercial results commensurate with the expenditures that would have to be made."[6]

Henry Ford, at the urging of a number of farm leaders, had begun inquiring into Muscle Shoals in the spring of 1921. Gray Silver, who was the Washington representative of the Farm Bureau Federation, E. A.

[3] Oscar W. Underwood, *Drifting Sands of Party Politics* (New York, 1931), 206.

[4] National League of Women Voters, Committee on Living Costs, *Facts About Muscle Shoals* (Washington, 1927), 17.

[5] Allan Nevins and Frank E. Hill, *Ford: Expansion and Challenge, 1915–1933* (New York, 1957), 306.

[6] *Facts About Muscle Shoals*, 17.

O'Neal, president of the Alabama branch of that organization, and editors of several farm journals joined with the Tennessee Valley Improvement Association in prompting the enlistment of Ford's capital in completing the facilities.[7]

From Thomas A. Edison, Ford had got a "romantic notion of the possibilities of hydro-electric power." He had already built small dams on the River Rouge and attached small factories to them.[8] But Ford's interest in the development of power was not limited to "small streams and grist mills," for he predicted that one day water power would run factories everywhere. Therefore, when a committee of Alabamians proposed that he complete the unfinished project at Muscle Shoals, he turned his attention to it as an idea "worthy of the enthusiasm of the master industrialist."[9]

Henry Ford and Thomas Edison visited Muscle Shoals. They inspected the construction work on Wilson Dam, saw the gigantic power of the swift currents of the Tennessee and went carefully, step by step, through the various processes of the manufacture of nitrates. Ford declared, "The destiny of the American people for centuries to come lies here at Muscle Shoals." When asked his opinion, Edison replied, "I cannot answer because the possibilities are so great."[10]

On July 8, 1921 Ford presented a proposal in writing to Secretary Weeks. After a thorough investigation Weeks was convinced that the Ford offer did not constitute an adequate return to the government and suggested that Ford "modify his offer so that it would be based upon an annual payment equivalent to a rate of interest on the total cost to the Government of completing the projects." On January 13, 1922 Ford presented Weeks a modified proposal in which he agreed to undertake the completion, at actual cost and without profit, of the work referred to in his first offer and, when completed and ready for operation, to pay the United States as annual rental of the property an amount equal to 4 per cent of the total cost of such construction.

In his transmittal letter to the Speaker of the House, February 1, Secretary Weeks wrote,

---

[7] Nevins and Hill, 306.
[8] Garet Garrett, *The Wild Wheel* (New York, 1952), 165.
[9] William A. Simonds, *Henry Ford: His Life, His Work, His Genius* (New York, 1943), 197.
[10] Henry, 27.

The total expenditures on Dam No. 2 [Wilson Dam] have been $16,251,038.14. . . . A large construction camp has been built, a railroad track laid to the site, complete construction plant assembled, and the dam itself approximately 30 per cent completed. . . .

There have been no expenditures on Dam No. 3, which is located 14.7 miles upstream from Dam No. 2. Dam No. 2, when constructed will render 14.7 miles of Muscle Shoals navigable, while Dam No. 3 will overflow the remaining portion of the rapids and will improve conditions of navigation for a distance of 63 additional miles. The present estimates of the Engineer Department for the completion of both Dam No. 2 and Dam No. 3 is $50,000,000. . . .

Situated about 6 miles southwest from Dam No. 2 at Sheffield . . . is United States nitrate plant No. 1 constructed by the United States during the war under an agreement with the General Chemical Company . . . at a total cost of $12,887,941.31. . . .

Four miles northeast of nitrate plant No. 1, and 2 miles distant from Dam No. 2, is located United States nitrate plant No. 2. This plant was constructed at a total expense of $67,555,355.09.

Situated about 20 miles south of plant No. 2 in Franklin County, and five miles southeast of Russellville, Alabama, is located what is known as Waco quarry, acquired by the United States in connection with the operation of nitrate plant No. 2, embracing an area of 460 acres, acquired at a total cost of $52,962.88. This quarry has a crushing plant sufficient to produce 2,000 tons of crushed and sized limestone per day. The total cost of said quarry, including buildings and plant, was $1,179,076.80.

Situated about 88 miles southeast of nitrate plant No. 2, in Walker County, Alabama, is located what is known as the Government-owned Warrior steam plant at Gorgas, Alabama. This plant was constructed under contract with the Alabama Power Company, dated December 1, 1917, on land owned or acquired by said company. It was built in the vicinity of a coal mine with a view of using coal direct from the mines. It has a capacity of 30,000 kilowatts, and the electric power produced at said plant is carried over a transmission line extending a distance of about 88 miles to nitrate plant No. 2, to furnish power for the operation of said plant. The total cost of the plant was $4,979,782.33.[11]

Ford's offer for all of these properties may be roughly outlined as follows:

1. Ford would organize a corporation backed by a cash capital of at least $10,000,000, the stock and securities of which would be owned and controlled solely by the citizens.

[11] U.S. 67 Cong., 2 Sess., *House Report* 1084 (Washington, 1922), 3–5.

2. The Ford Corporation would lease Dams Nos. 2 and 3 and property incidental to them for a period of 100 years.

3. Annual rental for the lease was to be computed on the basis of 4 per cent of the government expenditures for construction.

4. The Ford Corporation would purchase for $5,000,000 Nitrate Plants Nos. 1 and 2, the Waco Quarry, and the Gorgas-Warrior Steam Plant with all appurtenances.[12] For his $5,000,000 Ford was also to receive filtration stations, fully lighted and heated houses, railway tracks, tool cars, and locomotives, and, according to one commentator, platinum worth $500,000 with total assets equal to $84,000,000.[13]

5. Ford was to manufacture each year commercial fertilizer with a minimum fixed-nitrogen content of 40,000 tons.

6. In order that farmers might obtain fertilizer at a fair price, profit was not to exceed 8 per cent of the cost of manufacture.

7. Representatives to be nominated by the President of the United States, national farm organizations, and the Ford Motor Company were to act as a governing board, advised by non-voting representatives of the Department of Agriculture.

8. Research was to be carried on to discover ways to manufacture cheaper and better fertilizers.[14]

At the same time he was developing hydroelectric power and supplying cheap fertilizer, Ford would also maintain the larger nitrate plant in constant readiness should it be needed for defense.[15]

Naturally, Ford expected to derive some benefit from the project other than that of being looked upon as a public benefactor. His main business, apparently, was to be that of producing potash. Alunite, which is 12 per cent potash, 37 per cent aluminum, and 38 per cent sulphuric acid, had been discovered in Utah and could be shipped to Muscle Shoals at a low rate. Once the potash was removed, the aluminum could be obtained for use in automobile manufacture.[16]

Another of Ford's plans deserves special mention—much-debated "Seventy-Five Mile City." This fabulous proposal was made in an

[12] Martin Clary, *The Facts About Muscle Shoals* (New York, 1924), 139–140.
[13] Charles Merz, "Muscle Shoals," *Century*, CVIII, 617 (Sept., 1924).
[14] Clary, 139–140.
[15] Nevins and Hill, 306.
[16] "Why Henry Ford Wants the Muscle Shoals Property," *Current Opinion*, LXXII, 262–263 (Feb., 1922).

effort to retain the factory system and to cleanse it of its evil features. Ford had seen and perhaps felt some measure of responsibility for the poverty and hardship of the industrial class. His solution was to make a factory worker a part-time rural or semi-rural worker. Between the electric furnaces and fertilizer factories strung out along the seventy-mile lake formed between Wilson Dam and the upper dam, he envisioned small farms of from five to eighty acres. Employees of the factories would buy these farms at the rate of $50.00 an acre, on reasonable time, and would be released from factory work at certain periods during the year so that they could plant or harvest. Demonstration agents would show them the proper use of farm tools they rented from the factory. Their absence from work would not greatly hinder factory output because each man would know several jobs, and substitution could be carried out efficiently. Because their homes would thus be self-supporting their salaries from factory work would be supplementary income.[17]

Although Ford had not really promised to bring about the millennium, somehow the people of the United States seemed to feel that he had. The idea was propagated by real-estate boosters who had laid plans for a city that would make New York look like a prairie village and Southern senators who had "a 'mash' on Henry Ford as persistent and as heady as the shopgirl's dreams of Douglas Fairbanks."[18] Among those Southern senators who favored signing a contract were Joseph T. Robinson of Arkansas, William J. Harris of Georgia, and Oscar Underwood and Tom Heflin of Alabama. The American Federation of Labor voted approval of the offer at its 1922 convention.[19]

Although it was generally agreed that the development of Muscle Shoals was important, Edison set forth three major reasons for leasing the area to Ford: (1) developing the project would be a safeguard against emergency munitions needs, and Ford's proposal would include preserving this safeguard; (2) Ford was the man who would be most likely to operate it successfully—he had proved himself to be a "great manufacturer, with great conceptions, who moves rapidly to their realization"; and (3) Ford would operate the business, not

[17] Littell McClung, "The Seventy-Five Mile City," *Scientific American*, CXXVII, 156–157, 213–214 (Sept., Oct., 1922).

[18] Merz, 616–617.

[19] Nevins and Hill, 307.

for personal gain, but for the benefit of the majority of the American people.[20]

Newspaper opinion was one with farm leaders and Southern senators and businessmen. The Kansas City (Mo.) *Star* reported that 600,000 horsepower would be developed by the project. (This figure takes on greater importance when it is realized that the total horsepower developed in the entire United States at that time was only 8,000,000.) An industrial and manufacturing area second to none in the United States would be established, for there would be a surplus of 500,000 horsepower which could be used by cities within 300 miles of the plant. In addition, cheap fertilizer would reduce the cost of production of an average cotton crop by $75,000,000. The New York *American* joyously announced that at last the government would get some real money for a war investment. A Birmingham (Ala.) *Age-Herald* story read in part: "Mr. Ford offers to convert into an asset what is at present a tremendous liability to the Government, and should his bid be refused, the Administration will have a hard time making an explanation to the agricultural interests of the country." And the Birmingham *News* said that "Congress will not dare in this emergency to reject the Ford offer unless a better one is made."[21] Other newspapers supporting Ford in his offer included the Charleston (W. Va.) *Gazette;* St. Louis (Mo.) *Dispatch;* Raleigh (N.C.) *News and Observer* and the Boston (Mass.) *Post.*[22]

What inspired this tremendous faith in one man? William C. Richards, Ford's biographer, gave the answer in these words:

> Ford was a victim . . . of the reasoning that because a man piles up a vast fortune making a girdle or baking soda or a tonic or a flivver, the value of what he thinks improves with his net cash worth. Preeminence in one field, that is, guarantees capacity in all.[23]

On February 1, 1922 Secretary Weeks referred Ford's formal bid to Congress. The House Committee on Military Affairs and the Senate Committee on Agriculture and Forestry began hearings on February 8 and 16, respectively. Five days later a rival bid from the Alabama

---

[20] "Henry Ford's Bid for Muscle Shoals," *Literary Digest,* LXXVII, 11 (Jan. 28, 1922).

[21] *Ibid.,* LXXVII, 10 (Jan. 28, 1922).

[22] "Ford Winning Muscle Shoals," *Literary Digest,* LXXX, 11 (March 29, 1924).

[23] *The Last Billionaire* (New York, 1948), 2.

Power Company was transmitted to Congress.[24] Dan E. McGugin, general counsel for the Tennessee Manufacturers' Association, claimed that before Ford's offer was made the Alabama Power Company had proposed to the government that it would complete, lease and operate the Wilson Dam for fifty years under the Federal Water Power Act.[25] Whether this new bid was superior to that of Ford was a topic of long and heated debate. The Providence (R.I.) *Journal* stated that at the end of fifty years the government would net $90,998,300 from the Ford proposal and $136,400,000 from that of the Alabama Power Company. On the other hand, Gray Silver, the Farm Bureau's representative in Washington, examined the two offers and disclosed that the Ford proposal would, at the end of fifty years, net $130,526,800 in contrast with a return of $87,800,000 for the Alabama firm.[26]

On April 10, 1922 Senator George W. Norris of Nebraska, a lifelong conservationist and opponent of transferring resources of the public domain to private individuals, submitted his bill (S.3420), outlining a plan for a government operation. On June 9 a majority report, recommending acceptance of the Ford proposal with the elimination of the Gorgas-Warrior Steam Plant, was brought in from the House Committee on Military Affairs. However, the Congress adjourned without taking action.

When Congress reconvened, Ford declared that his offer still stood. During the next few weeks additional offers were received from the Alabama Power Company, which had meanwhile joined forces with the Tennessee Electric Power Company, the Memphis Light and Power Company, and the Union Carbide Company.[27] The final bid of the series was made by W. W. Atterbury, Elon H. Hooker, and J. G. White.[28]

On March 10, 1924 a bill (H.R.518) for the acceptance of Ford's bid passed the House and was sent to the Senate.[29] Sponsored by John C. McKenzie, a member of the House Committee on Military Affairs, this measure received a vote in the House of 227 for and 142 against.[30]

[24] *Facts About Muscle Shoals,* 17.
[25] Dan E. McGugin, *Shall Henry Ford Get Muscle Shoals?* (Nashville, 1924), 7; Merz, 619.
[26] "The Rival Bids For Muscle Shoals," *Literary Digest,* LXXXI, 10 (May 10, 1924).
[27] *Facts About Muscle Shoals,* 17–18.
[28] "The Rival Bids For Muscle Shoals," *Literary Digest,* LXXXI, 10 (May 10, 1924).
[29] *Facts About Muscle Shoals,* 18.
[30] "Ford Winning Muscle Shoals," *Literary Digest,* LXXX, 10 (March 29, 1924).

By that time, however, public opinion had begun to change mark-edly. Some of the worse features of Ford's proposal had become more obvious, and "despised, neglected, forgotten Muscle Shoals, appar-ently destined for the scrap heap, became a great national asset. . . ."[31] The Lincoln (Neb.) *State Journal* declared: "The Ford Lease has had popular support on the theory that Ford is primarily a philanthropist, but this view has weakened in the last few months." Former Secretary of War Newton D. Baker stated that surrendering Muscle Shoals would be like "giving away all the coal that will be discovered in the next century."[32]

Objections were found in the Norfolk (Va.) *Virginian-Pilot,* the Cleveland (Ohio) *Plain Dealer,* the Sacramento (Cal.) *Bee,* the Phil-adelphia (Pa.) *Public Ledger,* and the Chicago (Ill.) *Tribune.* Papers called the offer "something approaching an act of treason to the public," "a questionable bargain . . . ," and "the purchase of an empire for some chicken feed." An editorial cartoon in the Chicago *Tribune* showed "King Henry the Ford" seated upon a throne of money bags, holding as a scepter the Ford Agency, and being offered Muscle Shoals by a kneeling page.[33] Senator Norris called the offer the "most wonderful real-estate speculation since Adam and Eve lost title to the Garden of Eden,"[34] and charged that the terms by which Ford would secure the property made it "the greatest gift ever bestowed upon any mortal man since salvation was made free to the human race."[35] Edwin Dakin pointed out that the ruler of that day, in contrast to despots of earlier ages, was not the man who owned human labor but the man who controlled natural forces, such as coal and oil and water. His feeling was that "within the next few weeks another Napoleon is planning to be born."[36] The Teapot Dome scandal was frequently mentioned in connection with the question of Ford's receiving the Shoals property. The New Haven (Conn.) *Reg-ister,* for example, asked, "If it is criminal to lease away the gov-ernment oil's [*sic*] privileges at Teapot Dome, is it entirely com-mendable to give a century's lease to private interests of the

[31] Simonds, 198.
[32] "The Rival Bids For Muscle Shoals," *Literary Digest,* LXXXI, 10 (May 10, 1924).
[33] "Ford Winning Muscle Shoals," *ibid.,* LXXX, 11 (March 29, 1924).
[34] Merz, 620.
[35] William Hard, "Mr. Ford Is So Good," *Nation,* CXVIII, 340 (March 26, 1924).
[36] Dakin, 36.

government's possibilities of power and other treasures at Muscle Shoals?"[37]

Why did the change in opinion take place? What transformed Henry Ford from a good fairy to a swindler in the eyes of the public? Opposition might be placed under the following headings: the length of the lease and the legality of certain clauses; the lack of restrictions; the actual monetary return to the government; the feasibility of Ford's plans; and the political implications of his action.

Early opposition on the basis of financial return was brought forth by Rowland Thomas in a series of articles for the New York *World*. Thomas had figured out that Ford's offer amounted to only $3.39 per horsepower per year, whereas the lowest market rate was $18.00.[38] Charles Merz added up the assets which Ford would obtain for $5,000,000 and arrived at a sum of $84,000,000. He claimed that the scrap value of property worth that much would be about $11,000,000. In addition, he argued that Ford would actually pay only 2.85 per cent interest instead of the apparent 4 per cent expected.[39]

In rebuttal, Ford pointed out that his offer was made at a time when many wartime facilities were being sold for low salvage prices. The Old Hickory Powder Plant had gone for 5 per cent of its cost and wooden ships had sold for less than ½ of 1 per cent of cost.[40]

Opposition based upon the theory that Ford's plans were not practicable sprang from two points. The Gadsden (Ala.) *Star* summed up one argument by saying that Ford "would have to build a network of transmission wires at great cost before [the plant] could get started." The Alabama Power Company, on the other hand, already had the distribution system and, being a local concern, "would naturally favor Alabama in the distribution of power."[41]

As the controversy over Muscle Shoals became increasingly political, the name of Henry Ford was frequently heard in discussions of potential candidates for President of the United States. When Ford did not remove his name from the primary ballot in Nebraska, both sides became nervous. A headline in one Democratic paper read,

[37] *The Muscle Shoals Situation As Viewed By the Press of America*, Series 2 (Nashville, 1924), 5.
[38] "Henry Ford's Bid For Muscle Shoals," *Literary Digest*, LXXVII, (Jan. 28, 1922).
[39] Merz, 617–618.
[40] Nevins and Hill, 306.
[41] *Views and Opinions of Alabama Editors on Muscle Shoals and the Alabama Power Company* (Birmingham, 1926), 6.

"G.O.P. Delighted at Pushing Ford Into Democracy" and a Republican daily bannered, "Democrats Pin Hopes to Ford's Party Dividing Vote."[42] Whether on the Republican, Democratic, or the third party ticket, Ford was Coolidge's only formidable rival. When, one day, Coolidge invited Ford to the White House, many predicted a trade was in the making—Ford's candidacy for Muscle Shoals.[43] A company employee, who saw Ford often in those days, believed that he was totally indifferent to politics and much more deeply interested in developing something like Muscle Shoals.[44] Ford did declare his allegiance to Coolidge, and the newspapers went wild. The Danville (Ind.) *Gazette,* March 29, 1924, recalled that in 1921 Republicans heartily opposed Ford's offer and went on to state that, since Ford had thrown his support behind Coolidge,

> . . . a good many Republicans who were opposed to his Muscle Shoals proposition have seen the light, and with great enthusiasm, have rushed through the House a bill accepting his offer. This may be a mere coincidence, but it is an interesting one.[45]

The fact that the House vote accepting the Ford offer was composed of 170 Democrats and only 57 Republicans might belie this contention that Ford was getting the Shoals as a reward for his support of the Republican candidate.[46]

Nonetheless, in October, 1924 Ford notified President Coolidge that his offer was officially withdrawn,[47] possibly more as a result of the political struggle than of any other one factor. In Ford's own words:

> A simple affair of business which should have been decided by any one within a week has become a complicated political affair. We are not in politics and we are in business. We do not intend to be drawn into politics.
> We are moving so fast and the settlement of Muscle Shoals' future seemed so far away that we had to find other means to do the things we could have accomplished at Muscle Shoals. In fact, we have passed Muscle Shoals. Productive business cannot wait on politics. Therefore, we are withdrawing our bid.

---

[42] "Ford Politics in Muscle Shoals," *Literary Digest,* LXXIX, 14 (Oct. 27, 1923).
[43] Garrett, 164, 166.
[44] Nevins and Hill, 305.
[45] *The Muscle Shoals Situation As Viewed By the Press of America,* 20.
[46] "Ford Winning Muscle Shoals," *Literary Digest,* LXXX, 12 (March 29, 1924).
[47] *Facts About Muscle Shoals,* 19.

Besides, when we were first approached we did not have the coal and
engines and turbines which we have. That is, when we bid for Muscle Shoals
we could have used it. Now we can achieve the same results in another way.

Ford also stated that he still wanted to help the South, and that
he still believed that nitrate production at Muscle Shoals was the
country's "greatest guarantee for peace on the one hand and for
the farmers on the other."[48]

With the withdrawal of Henry Ford's offer, Muscle Shoals stood idle,
a sore spot for politicians and farmers, until the creation of the
Tennessee Valley Authority, May 18, 1933, during the administration
of President Franklin D. Roosevelt.

[48] Samuel Crowther, "Henry Ford Tackles a New Job," *Collier's*, LXXIV, 5 (Oct. 18, 1924).

WILLIAM R. SNELL

Fiery Crosses in the Roaring Twenties:

Activities of the Revised Klan in Alabama,
1915–1930

In 1965 a few interested persons gathered in Pulaski, Tennessee, at
the building where the Ku Klux Klan was organized by former Confederate soldiers, to commemorate the hundredth year of its long, but
not continuous, existence. The original organization was an attempt
to combat the abuses, real and imaginary, heaped upon the South by
the Radical Republicans and their local agents, the carpetbaggers and
scalawags. After the Klan had drifted into lawlessness, Imperial Wizard
Nathan Bedford Forrest disbanded it in 1869 and it disappeared from
public view by 1871, not to be revived again until the second decade
of the twentieth century.

William J. Simmons, the founder of the revised Klan, was born in
Harpersville, Alabama in 1880.[1] Unsuccessful in the Methodist ministry,
Simmons turned his interests to the numerous fraternal organizations he had joined. While hospitalized for three months as a result
of a car accident, he projected a fraternal organization patterned
after the romantic image of the Reconstruction Ku Klux Klan. He
interested others in his plans, and on Thanksgiving Eve, 1915, while
the pro-Klan movie, *The Birth of a Nation,* was being shown in nearby
Atlanta, he and others formally inaugurated the movement by climb-
ing the granite heights of Stone Mountain and lighting a fiery cross.
It was not until the 1920's, however, that the movement grew sig-

This essay was published in *The Alabama Review,* XXIII (October 1970).
[1] There is disagreement about the birthdate of Simmons; others indicate 1882.

nificantly. Adopting the habit and ritual of the first Klan, the reha-
bilitated Klan affected an exaggerated nationalism growing out of
World War I and increased concern over the moral laxity of the times.
Conceived at a time when clubs of all types thrived and flourished, its
secrecy and elaborate ritual appealed to many who felt lost in the
masses; its colorful pageantry attracted numerous members and sym-
pathizers. It was similar in many ways to other fraternal orders of the
day. It was dedicated to what its members believed was one hundred
percent Americanism, the supremacy of the Caucasian race, and Protestant religious tenets and morals. The members pictured themselves
as protectors of morals threatened by immigration, urbanization,
industrialization and the increased use of automobiles. Though this
latter invention, in Klan opinion, threatened morals, it also provided greater mobility to the group and a larger area from which to
draw members. The Ford car, which was frequently used in parades and
later in floggings, came to be almost as symbolic of the Klan as the
fiery cross.[2]

The newly self-appointed judges of public morals checked into affairs
throughout the South. Klansmen intervened in a shipyard strike in
Mobile, hunted draft dodgers, and on occasion marched in patriotic
parades. Considerable public sentiment seemed favorable to their
efforts. By 1920 the Klan had enrolled about five thousand members,
most of whom were in Georgia.[3]

From Georgia the organization spread to Alabama, Florida, and
other Southern states. The Robert E. Lee Klan, No. 1 (Birmingham),
evidently the first klavern in Alabama, was organized in 1916, less
than a year after the Invisible Empire was revived. Bessemer Klan,
No. 2 and Montgomery Klan, No. 3 were soon organized. These groups
grew very slowly during their early years, as was true nationally. The
Klan's rapid growth in membership came in 1921.[4]

[2] David M. Chalmers, Hooded Americanism, The First Century of the Ku Klux Klan, 1865–
1965 (Garden City, 1965), 28–38, hereinafter cited as Chalmers. See also S. Rice, The Ku
Klux Klan in American Politics (Washington, 1962), 14–16, hereinafter cited as Rice. In
addition to Simmons, the group included two members of the original Klan and the
speaker of the Georgia Legislature.
[3] Chalmers, loc. cit. See also Francis B. Simkins, "Ku-Klux Klan," The American Encyclopedia (New York, 1964), XVI, 549–51.
[4] Chalmers, 78–84. "In September of 1923, Birmingham's Robert E. Lee Klan No.
1 staged a monster rally to celebrate its seventh anniversary. A city park was leased and
invitations were sent out across the South," 79. See also Rice, loc. cit. The only known
title by an Alabama author about the revised Klan was written by the Exhalted Cyclops
of the Goodwater klavern, John Stephen Fleming, What Is Ku Kluxism? Let Americans
Answer—Aliens Only Muddy the Waters [Birmingham, 1923].

When Simmons' recruitment efforts were not so successful as he had hoped, he employed Edward Young Clarke and Mrs. Bessie Tyler, professional publicity agents formerly of the Southern Publicity Association, to inaugurate a nation-wide canvass for members. To the Klan's announced beliefs were added antiSemitism and anti-Catholicism, the latter becoming the strongest selling point of the revived order. Other selling points were added later.[5]

Two efforts to frustrate the Klan had quite the opposite effect: a hearing by the House Rules Committee in October, 1921 and, in the same year, a series of articles in the New York *World* attempting to expose the secret order. Rather than thwarting the Klan, these gave it nation-wide publicity and resulted in increased membership, which was largely middle class and remarkably cross sectional. Contrary to general belief, the Klan was not primarily a small-town and rural phenomenon; cities, large and small, both North and South, were prominent in Klan organization and activity. Whites who thought their jobs would be threatened by equal opportunity for Negroes or aliens were quick to join the hooded order.[6]

Enjoying national publicity, Imperial Wizard Simmons chose the year 1921 to launch a recruitment drive in the Birmingham area. In an open letter he charged that the Klan's enemies "have attempted to lynch the Ku Klux Klan by discrediting it in the eyes of the public before it had a chance to defend itself, to state its case, or to obtain a fair and impartial hearing." Enumerating the efforts of its antagonists, the Klan claimed the "right to live and be let alone, because it stands unfalteringly for true Americanism, for the preservation of our ideals and institutions and for the glorious principals enumerated by our fathers, and because it stands first, last and all the time for maintenance of law. . . ." He appealed for a fair chance for his fledgling organization to prove itself, and presented it as an underdog struggling for life.[7]

---

[5] Among the other elements added later were strong feelings against the foreign born, see Rice, 19.

[6] Chalmers, *loc. cit.*; John Moffatt Mecklin, *The Ku Klux Klan: A Study in the American Mind* (New York, 1963), 96–109. "The Klan was in the main a village and small town phenomenon," Rice, 13. Contrawise see Charles C. Alexander, *The Ku Klux Klan in the Southwest* (Lexington, 1965), 27–29. See also Carl N. Degler, "A Century of the Klans: A Review Article," *Journal of Southern History,* XXXI (November, 1965), 439.

[7] Birmingham *News,* October 26, 1921, hereinafter cited as *News.* The Robert E. Lee Klan unanimously adopted a resolution urging better salaries for the Birmingham police force and additional policemen to protect personal and property rights, *News,* October 5, 1925.

The Klan received a sympathetic hearing in the Magic City. A huge rally was planned in September, 1923 for Edgewood Park, when a number of "aliens" were to be "naturalized" as the Klan's initiation was called. A public invitation was extended more than a week in advance in a front-page story in the Birmingham *Age-Herald.* In addition to the ceremony there was to be swimming, dancing, a barbecue, stunt flying, a fireworks display, and a concert by the Chattanooga Klan Band. About 5,000 Klansmen were present to initiate from 1,250 to 1,750 new members. Crowds estimated at from 20,000 to 25,000 were present to witness the ceremony, while an estimated 40,000 to 50,000 people came sometime during the day. The ceremony, said to be the largest in the South, attracted more people than a similar ceremony in Chattanooga a few weeks earlier. Hugo L. Black was among the initiates who took part in the stately ritual conducted by the Robert E. Lee Klan.

At a strategic point,

> ... the entire procession began to move and the circles moved clockwise and stopped before each of the three stations situated at intervals of 450 feet, where a portion of the obligation was received. At the close of the march the entire assembly was marched in front of the imperial wizard where the final touches of the ceremony were given. At this point the famous band of the Chattanooga Klan struck up "America" and was followed by the drum and bugle corps of the same organization.[8]

A host of national Klan officials from Atlanta were present, including Imperial Wizard Dr. Hiram Wesley Evans. Born in Ashland, Alabama, Evans was a Vanderbilt graduate and a reasonably successful dentist in Dallas, Texas. He dressed well, was a good public speaker, and recognized and appealed to the "groups in America with interests parallel to those of the Klan, especially large corporations."[9] He was favorably impressed with Birmingham and the growth of the Klan there. He

---

[8] Birmingham *Age-Herald,* September 12, 1923, hereinafter cited as *Age-Herald; News,* September 12, 1923; Chalmers, 78–84, 314–16. The *News* indicated that about 400 candidates were unable to reach the park due to the congestion. At this time the *News* was not as sympathetic with the Klan as was the *Age-Herald.* An editorial comment on the meeting could not be found in either paper. An editorial on immigration in the *Age-Herald,* September 18, 1923, reflected the general Klan attitude, although it may be a reflection of the general state or Southern thinking on the issue as well.

[9] William Peirce Randel, *The Ku Klux Klan, A Century of Infamy* (Philadelphia, 1965), 195.

called Birmingham Klansmen "Americans one, and all." Visiting delegations estimated at 7,500 were present from Georgia, Mississippi, Florida, Tennessee, Louisiana and Texas.

The Chattanooga Klan Band and Drum and Bugle Corps, composed of 55 members, led a parade of Klan officials through downtown Birmingham in the afternoon. Police officers were on hand at Edgewood Park to direct the traffic, which was unusually heavy. The local Klan evidently enjoyed the approval of the City's commissioners.

The following week a Klan convention (Klorero) was held in Montgomery. Among the main items adopted was a resolution pledging support of prohibition in the state. The Grand Dragon reported a 50 percent increase in the number of state Klans organized during the past year and a 500 percent increase in membership.[10]

Soon after the Edgewood initiation the Nathan Bedford Forrest Klan, No. 60 held a public service at East Lake Park. In addition to an initiation ceremony, there was a barbecue, a fireworks display, and a giveaway of a car. An estimated 50,000 curious and interested persons crowded the park during the afternoon and evening. Electric lights were strung across the field, and extra streetcars were added on the East Lake Park and Tidewater lines. Dr. Lloyd P. Bloodworth, Imperial Lecturer, addressed the evening crowd, saying that the Ku Klux Klan was the "embodiment of the old-fashioned and now almost forgotten principles on which the American government was founded. . . ." and the "principles of the Klan and the doctrines of Americanism and Christianity were one and the same." He pledged the strength of the Klan to make "America a better place for Americans to live in." In a plea for law enforcement, he praised Jefferson County Sheriff T. J. Shirley, a longtime national Klan official, Police Commissioner W. H. Cloe, Rev. George R. Stuart, pastor of the First Methodist Church, and the editors of the Birmingham *Age-Herald* whose newspaper was lauded as an "exponent of a high standard of Americanism." Within three years thereafter, however, the *Age-Herald* had become a bitter opponent of the Klan.[11]

The naturalization ceremony at East Lake Park inducted approximately 2,000 new members in an impressive ritual.

---

[10] *News,* September 16, 1923.

[11] *Age-Herald,* September 2, 12, 1923, November 1, 6, 21, 1923; *News,* September 12, 1923.

There was a parade of thousands of white-robed figures moving in a steady line with their robes standing out in bold outline against the landscape forming the background for the ceremony. From out of the woods they came, thousands of them, and almost as far as the eye could see they could be observed marching to the commands of their officers.

A part of the parade preceding the address was lighted by red torches, which the members carried in their hands lending a sombre light to the whole scene.[12]

This naturalization was reputed to be the "biggest ever held in the South. . . ."

On June 10, 1924 following the East Lake ceremonies an extended parade opened a concerted recruitment drive for new members. Exploding fireworks during the afternoon signaled the parade for the evening. Policemen on motorcycles, a band and drum corps and local and state Klan officials led 5,000 Klansmen in full regalia through the streets of Fairfield, Ensley, and Birmingham. Literature listing the qualifications for membership was scattered by one of the advance cars, and announcement was made of another large ceremony to be held two weeks later in East Lake Park. This event originated at Oakwood Cemetery near Fairfield, and over a thousand cars were in the parade, which terminated in East Lake about 9 P.M. Many members carried electric torches, slogans, and patriotic buntings, but all tags had been carefully covered by cloth, "so secret was the parade." Traffic lights along the route were stopped, and regular traffic was held up for 35 minutes at some points.[13]

One of the largest crowds to gather in Alabama—40,000 people— witnessed the initiation of over 4,000 candidates at this second East Lake Park meeting. 50,000 persons visited the park during the day. Throughout the day the Birmingham Electric Company again added extra cars to handle the crowds, and automobiles were parked in all directions from the festivities.

Five local Klans participated in the joint "naturalization" at East Lake Park. Tallied by the turnstiles the numbers were: Robert E. Lee Klan, 2,000 candidates; Woodlawn [Nathan B. Forrest Klan,

---

[12] *Age-Herald*, November 21, 1923. The *News* evidently did not carry an account of this event.

[13] *News*, June 11, 1924. The account called this "the first Klan parade of the year," and was "one of the most successful and most orderly to be carried out here in some time. . . ."

No. 60], 1,100; Ensley, 500; Bessemer, 367; and Avondale, 140; a total of 4,107. Registration headquarters indicated that these had been enrolled since May 1. "Klansmen asserted that it was not only the biggest fraternal day in Birmingham's history, but the largest Ku Klux function ever held in the Southeast." By 1924 Robert E. Lee Klan was estimated to have from 7,500 to 10,000 members.

Special trains brought visiting Klansmen from Chattanooga, Anniston, Sylacauga, Goodwater, Alexander City, Mobile and Tuscaloosa. There were even ten visitors from as far away as Evansville, Indiana, a center of mid-Western Klan activity.

It took two leaders 20 minutes to administer the Klan oath, in which the initiates pledged their allegiance to the United States, its Constitution and flag, the Klan and its members, and the tenets of the Christian religion. One reporter concluded that "the most stolid anti would have admitted that the ceremony was impressive."[14]

The initiations in the Birmingham area were the largest and most impressive in the state, but were not the only ones in 1924 by any means. A Clanton initiation attracted between 8,000 and 10,000 spectators to see 250 inducted. Malone Park was the scene where 630 Decatur Klansmen conducted a public initiation. More than 7,000 watched the Gadsden Klan parade up and down Broad Street and initiate a number of candidates. A Klan demonstration marked the dedication of the state highway through Goodwater. The Greenville ballpark was chosen by the local Klan to initiate 75 new members. More than 10,000 were attracted to the fairgrounds at Huntsville to witness 1,000 members march through town in the third public ceremony there. A large Klan parade of several hundred at Jacksonville attracted a great deal of local interest. After a speech the Klan members drove to Weaver and participated in a barbecue given to aid in the rebuilding of the Methodist Church. The first public ceremony in Jasper attracted 2,000 to watch several hundred enrolled in the hooded order. In historic Mobile, 6,000 spectators looked on as 250 "aliens" were "naturalized" at Old Government and Mohawk

---

[14]*News*, June 27, 28, 1924; *Age-Herald*, June 28, 1924. A front page notice in the Sylacauga *Advance* announced a special train from Sylacauga to the Birmingham ceremony. A story in the next issue indicated that approximately 500 members from Alexander City, Goodwater, and Sylacauga had made the trip. They were met at the train and carried to the park for the evening's activities. Leaving Birmingham at midnight they arrived in Sylacauga at 2 A.M. Sylacauga *Advance*, June 25, 1924, July 2, 1924.

streets. "The klansmen formed a living cross at the end of the march, outlined by red fire and with a fiery cross burning at each arm. A brief ceremony of initiation was conducted as the aliens were marched from the woods and knelt before the flag and the open-air altar. . . ." In Montgomery the Klan enjoyed a large membership, estimated at 1,800 in 1924, and made plans to erect a klavern building at a cost of $40,000 or $50,000. More than 4,000 automobiles, bearing 2,000 Klansmen and 10,000 spectators, were parked around the site at Snowdown where some 500 candidates swore allegiance to the Invisible Empire; this was the largest Klan ceremony held in central Alabama.

Klansmen were angry because the Alabama delegation to the recent Democratic national convention had continued to support favorite son Oscar W. Underwood for many ballots. The Alabama Senator was an outspoken critic of the Klan and proposed to include an anti-Klan plank in the Democratic platform.[15] The robed men pledged a "political death warrant to the 49 people" who supported the anti-Klan plank. A parade was announced for Graham Field by the Reform Klan. The Five Oaks Klan (Russellville) attracted 8,000 to 12,000 visitors to East Side Park to watch 162 candidates enlisted. Brunswick stew was enjoyed by 150 Jackson County Klansmen and a large crowd at Scottsboro. Entertainment was furnished by the Vaughn Quartet, and special trains from Sheffield and Huntsville brought approximately 300 Klansmen to aid in the ritual. A ceremony at Slocumb High School attracted almost 1,000 to view 50 robed and hooded members and to hear the Rev. Caleb T. Martin deliver an address. In Tuscaloosa a caravan of 250 cars of parading Klansmen "attracted to the streets . . . the largest crowd of persons and the biggest number of automobiles ever seen here." Starting at Stallworth's Lake, they had to circle Northport because of some road work being done. "At one time the city was completely surrounded by the

---

[15] An extra edition of the New York *World* quoted Senator Oscar W. Underwood as saying that the Birmingham parade was an effort of "a secret, political organization to intimidate me, the Alabama delegation and the democratic party [then in national nominating convention]. . . . It will not succeed. I am not afraid either in a political or a personal sense of the Ku Klux Klan. I maintain that the organization is a national menace. . . . It is either the Ku Klux Klan or the United States of America. Both cannot survive. Between the two, I choose my country." *Age-Herald*, June 29, 1914.

cars of the Ku Klux Klan and . . . the leading car returning passed the last car going at the river bridge."[16]

Initiation ceremonies and parades were held in the following cities in 1925 and 1926: Evergreen, Haleyville, Greensboro, Russellville, Tuscumbia and Birmingham. In the latter city 6,000 robed and hooded figures including a number of women and "junior Klansmen" paraded through the downtown area to the municipal auditorium. A rough spot in the pavement at Twentieth Street and Second Avenue, North, caused a number of the marchers to stumble and some had face masks blown over their heads, but they were quickly pulled back in place. "Crowds on the corner laughed, and the klansmen seemed to enjoy it, too." At the auditorium a more serious matter awaited them, a "Lodge of Sorrow" to memorialize the more than 120 Klansmen who had died in Alabama since the Klan was revived. Attracting dignitaries from all parts of North Alabama, known as Province No. 1, Realm of Alabama, the program included the Klan dirge, special music, a memorial address, and impressive rites for the dead. This service was in addition to separate rites provided for individual Klansmen who died. For example, when Bailey G. McClendon, Civil War veteran and former surveyor of Calhoun County died, Odd Fellow and Masonic rites and "K.K.K. mysteries featured the funeral ceremony." In nearby Talladega, C. L. Stockdale, postmaster and state Woodman of the World officer, was buried with a short Klan service.[17]

The Klans in the Birmingham area enjoyed financial as well as numerical success. A building for the Robert E. Lee Klan was announced in February 1924. To be located on the northeast corner of Twenty-First Street and Sixth Avenue, North, the proposed $250,000 build-

---

[16] *News,* March 3, 1924; Albany-Decatur *Daily,* October 3, 1924; Gadsden *Evening Journal,* June 30, 1924, July 2, 1924; *Age-Herald,* June 17, 1924. Interview of November 25, 1966 with W. B. Prater, who was Sheriff of Coosa County and a Klan member present on this occasion. Members from Goodwater, Sylacauga, and Alexander City participated in the Goodwater demonstration. Huntsville *Daily Times,* May 27, 28, 1924; Anniston *Star,* June 20, 1924; (Jasper) *The Mountain Eagle,* June 18, 1924, July 23, 1924, August 6, 1924; Mobile *News-Item,* June 20, 21, 1924; Montgomery *Journal,* June 27, 1924, July 3, 1924; Montgomery *Advertiser,* July 4, 1924; *Age-Herald,* June 29, 1924, July 4, 6, 1924, June 17, 1924; *News,* May 2, 1924; Slocumb *Observer,* March 20, 27, 1924, April 24, 1924, May 8, 15, 22, 1924; Tuscaloosa *News and Times-Gazette,* June 16, 17, 1924.

[17] *Age-Herald,* December 14, 1925, May 7, 1925, June 21, 1925, March 26, 1925, June 11, 1925; The Birmingham *Post,* June 11, 1925, hereinafter cited as *Post.*

ing would be "one of the most beautiful buildings in Birmingham." But in May 1925 this site was sold for $70,000 and the Athletic Club property at 510 North Twentieth Street purchased for $190,000. Thorough plans were made for extensive redecorations and early occupancy. By February 1926, however, the Klan sold this structure to the Y.M.C.A. for $200,000 and decided, temporarily at least, to rent quarters.[18]

By May 1924 it was rumored that the Ensley Klan had purchased for $10,000 a lot on the northeast corner of Twenty-Third Street and Avenue E (Ensley). A two-story brick klavern was to be erected on the site.[19]

Contracts for the Nathan B. Forrest Klavern Building were let in December 1924 at a cost of $120,000. The two-story brick structure located in Wahouma at Edmonds Street and First Avenue, contained Klan offices upstairs and rental space on the ground floor and was described as the "last word in architectural beauty."[20] Other klaverns had ample if less commodious lodges. In Sylacauga the meetings were held in the Masonic Hall, while in Jasper they met in the Tweedy Building over the telephone exchange.[21]

Klan success was attributable not only to its secrecy, which appealed to an adventure-seeking group of men, but also to the protection promised members and their families who might be in need. Aid was often promised individuals in unfortunate circumstances. The Anniston Klan proposed to help furnish school books to students unable to buy them. While parading down Noble Street, four Klansmen carried a large sheet into which the sympathetic crowd "contributed freely to the book fund" as the parade progressed.

An unusual financial shortage caused the Birmingham Board of Education to close the schools April 24, 1925, five weeks short of the regular nine-month term. Some teachers continued to work even though they were not promised a salary. Civic and community groups responded to the crisis, among them the Klan, which sponsored a minstrel at the municipal auditorium. Featured were the Original Four Quartet and Little Willie, a fiddler from Blount County. The

---

[18] *News,* February 13, 1924. A Klan supported Protestant hospital was projected for a later date. *Age-Herald,* February 13, 1924, May 15, 1925, February 28, 1926.

[19] *News,* May 23, 1924.

[20] *Age-Herald,* December 21, 1924.

[21] Interview with J. A. Prater, February 6, 1966; *Age-Herald,* March 24, 1925, April 9, 1925.

show made $3,445.50 which was turned over to county treasurer C. E. Harrison to pay the teachers who remained at their posts. Names of recipients and the amounts received, ranging from $10 to $100, were listed in the *Age-Herald*.[22]

In other ways the Klan stressed the importance of education. The "little red schoolhouse" was often portrayed in Klan parades and demonstrations. The Klan of York sponsored a spelling match and awarded a $5 prize to the winner of each grade. Fifty white robed men presented Etowah High School with a flag pole and an American flag. N. O. Patterson and A. H. Nabers, the local Baptist and Methodist ministers, helped in the presentation. Ministers and churches also received consideration from the Klan. At the conclusion of three weeks' revival services 24 members of the Andalusia Klan presented evangelist Bob Jones a check for $1,568. Rev. J. O. Hanes in Tuscaloosa preached on "The State, The Klan and The Church" before a Thursday evening crowd of 3,000 and endorsed the Klan's stand for law enforcement. At the Sunday morning service, members of the local Klan presented him with a check for $50. Fifty Gadsden Klansmen gave Rev. Caleb A. Ridley an envelope which contained money and a letter of appreciation for his work there. In accepting, Ridley said that he had been an officer in the national Klan for eight years. In nearby Attalla the following month, 400 Negro delegates of the Baptist district conference were "popeyed" when robed Klansmen marched into the church and presented the pastor with $25 and a letter of commendation. "The act was appreciated, it is said, because of the widespread impression that the negro is the klansmen's pet object of hatred. It is said, too, that it was something entirely new in the tactics of the hooded order."[23]

All ministers and churches did not fare as well with the Klan. Crosses were burned before St. Matthew's Catholic Church in Oakdale (Mobile) while services were being conducted inside. George R. Seiple and his brother E. R. Seiple were arrested for this offense, but denied that

[22] Interviews with J. A. Prater, February 6, 1966; W. B. Prater, January 16, 1966; Anniston *Star,* September 21, 22, 23, 24, 1925; *Post,* April 24, 1925; *Age-Herald,* June 23, 24, 1925; Talladega *Daily Home,* June 5, 1924. The Original Four Quartet was composed of: Al Fennell, Sebe Kernodle, Fred Wellborne, and Vance Busby. The original minstrel proved so successful that they were booked for East Lake Park in June. *Age-Herald,* June 21, 23, 1925.

[23] *Age-Herald,* April 21, 1925, May 21, 1925, September 1, 1925, August 9, 1924; Gadsden *Evening Journal,* June 12, 1924, July 12, 1924; *Age-Herald,* July 14, 1924.

they represented the Klan. Numerous crosses were burned that same night in Mobile, which made the spontaneousness of their action doubtful.[24]

The zeal of some Klansmen was aflame for enforcement of laws and strict morals. Cars parked along the roads leading from Gadsden were called to the attention of the Sheriff of Etowah County in a personal letter, a copy of which was sent to the local papers. The problem had reached such proportions that "people living a few miles distant from town are loathe to start to town after dark with their families for fear of running into a scene. . . ." Promising their aid both day and night, the Klan planned to furnish the sheriff with car tag numbers and the occupants' names. Klansmen in the Troy area created a similar situation. They proposed to have delegations watch the roads and report names to parents and the police. An open letter said,"We do not resort to violence and in this instance we do not propose to harm anyone. We simply mean to stop this practice. . . ." On Red Mountain near Birmingham, robed Klansmen burned crosses, "flashed lights on occupants of parked cars and ordered them to move on." Parking was not the only vice attacked. At Dothan the local Klan distributed handbills warning "no loafing—the fields are white with cotton. Don't let Monday morning see you idle—white and black." "The days of the blind tiger [bootlegger] and rum runner in Houston county are numbered. We stand for the right—we will back up our stand."[25]

The stand of the Birmingham area Klans was unmistakably known. Early in 1924 they sought to bring moral reform to Jefferson County. White robed men lighted fiery crosses along the Montgomery highway and the valley regions south of Birmingham "to break up road houses." These raids were conducted with the approval of the county authorities who wanted to "clean up the places, anyhow." In January 1925, similar raids were conducted against houses of ill repute. City detectives M. W. Alexander and Frank Watson received a letter demanding that several locations be cleaned up because "they were immoral and were selling liquor." It was signed "K.K.K." One house was visited on a Thursday and five on Friday, January 16, 1925. Witnesses reported that "several automobile loads of white-robed

---

[24] *Age-Herald,* April 2, 1925.

[25] Gadsden *Evening Journal,* April 25, 1925; *Greenville Advocate,* June 18, 1924; *Post,* August 28, 1926; *Age-Herald,* August 31, 1925.

figures drove up, planted the cross, set it on fire and then silently drove away." Birmingham's Commissioner of Public Safety W. B. Cloe announced a "dramatic campaign against disorderly houses, following the sensational burning of fiery crosses. . . . Police believe that the Ku Klux Klan was responsible for burning the crosses, as a warning to inmates of the houses." Later Commissioner Cloe said, "I welcome outside aid of whatever nature, as long as it is an orderly effort to help rid Birmingham of immorality."[26] Several days later the Birmingham *Post* reported that the "disorderly houses, which have operated openly in Birmingham for years, were quiet and deserted today." Early in February six additional men were added to the police force to help curb lawlessness. In addition to the houses of prostitution, there had been a rash of robberies and considerable evidence of a crime wave in the city.[27]

The fourth in a series of similar incidents occurred February 6, when crosses were burned at three houses of ill fame. The clean-up committee was composed of 75 Klansmen in automobiles whose tags were covered. Staff representatives of the city's newspapers were invited to be waiting at 8 P.M. at the corner of Sixth Avenue and Twenty-Sixth Street. A reporter from the Birmingham *Age-Herald* accompanied the raiding party, but no representatives came from the other papers. The roving reporter wrote that all occupants protested their innocence, although one of them, Miss Ida Cartwright, said she would return to Evansville, Indiana.[28]

Meanwhile, a public controversy had developed about the extralegal actions of the robed raiders. Then, on January 2, 1926, the "crusade" took a new turn. A group of robed Klansmen armed with search warrants for liquor (and a gun or two) staged sensational raids on three Chinese restaurants in Birmingham. In addition to searching the premises, some took the liberty of searching some of the patrons. The Klan had violated propriety as well as law. An editorial outcry was raised against such an outrage by the Klan, and a call went out for law enforcement by legally constituted authorities. Within two weeks, four Klansmen had been arrested and convicted. W. J. Worthington, Exhalted Cyclops of Avondale Klan, No. 59, and W. W. Israel were fined $100 and given 90 days in jail. T. C. Harwell was fined $100 and given

---

[26] *News,* January 17, 1925; *Post,* January 17, 1925; *Age-Herald,* January 18, 1925.
[27] *Post,* January 23, 1925; *Age-Herald,* February 4, 1925.
[28] *News,* February 7, 1925.

30 days, while W. D. Haynie, the youngest member of the party, was fined $50 and given a suspended jail sentence of 30 days. When their decision was appealed, Worthington was tried separately and acquitted. Hugh Locke, lawyer for the defense, argued that the search warrants were properly drawn and that the deputy sheriff with the group made their actions within the law. The case against the others was dropped, because officials felt that their strongest case was against Worthington.[29]

In some areas of the state, the Klan exercised a great deal of political influence. Although the Klan failed to prevent the reelection of R. E. Chadwick to the Birmingham Board of Education in April 1925, the results of the city commissioner's election in October were considered a "tremendous victory" for the Klan. Two of the three Klan-supported candidates won election, although only John H. Taylor, Commissioner of Public Safety, was a member of the secret order. In Sylacauga, Mayor H. H. Howard was Exhalted Cyclops of the local Klan. In adjoining Coosa County a slate of important county officials were members of the hooded order: Probate Judge George B. McDonald, Circuit Court Clerk G. W. Miller, and Sheriff W. B. Prater.

In the 1926 elections the Klan enjoyed important political victories. Governor-elect Bibb Graves and Attorney General-elect Charles C. McCall were both members of the Montgomery Klan, the former being Exhalted Cyclops. Although the two were members of the same klavern and enjoyed the taste of political victory, before long the breach of feelings between the two widened into a full-fledged feud. Hugo L. Black, newly elected United States Senator, was a member of the Robert E. Lee Klan in Birmingham. Birmingham lawyer George Frey and a number of other state representatives were members of the Invisible Empire. Frey shared an office in the First National Bank Building with fellow lawyer, James Esdale, Grand Dragon of the Realm of Alabama. When election results were conclusive, Esdale checked the list of new legislators and "found that some of the members of that body" did not belong to the Klan. He advised various Klans throughout the state that legislators who were not members should be encouraged to join, and that his office be informed of the success of the campaign.[30]

[29] *Age-Herald,* January 3, 14, 1926; *Post,* April 29, 1926, May 1, 1926.
[30] *Post,* April 4, 21, 1925, October 20, 1925; *News,* October 20, 1925. Interview with J. A. Prater, February 6, 1966; Interview with W. B. Prater, January 16, 1966. *Age-Herald,* December 12, 29, 1926.

One of the flagrant outrages perpetrated by the revised Klan was flogging. The total number of those to suffer this outrage will never be known. The Birmingham *News* estimated in 1927 that hundreds had felt the Klan's lash in the previous five years. A typical incident occurred in 1921, when a band of masked men in two Ford cars carried C. S. Cooley and Mrs. Kate Alexander to a spot on Birmingham's Vanderbilt Road. They were formally charged with miscegenation because they had had "friendly relations with Negroes," and were flogged. Mrs. Alexander was first and received five lashes, while Cooley received several more. Abandoned near East Lake Park, the couple returned to town in a taxi. Expressing a desire that there be no investigation, Cooley related that the men appeared to be "educated and refined," and he would soon be leaving town. But there were many protests. The directors of the Junior Chamber of Commerce scorned the "apathetic attitude" of the police, while Judge H. P. Heflin admonished the county grand jury to make a thorough investigation of the incident. Numerous whippings were carried out in 1922 and 1923, but there were no arrests, hence no convictions.[31]

Attention was focused on Gadsden in 1924, when J. Nadler, a prominent Jewish merchant, was taken from his house, driven into the country and forced to surrender a house lease and a small check. Although he was not harmed, the incident created a commotion in the Gadsden area. Three men were indicted. Civic clubs adopted resolutions; public indignation prompted a proposed antimask law. At the November trial, a hat bearing the name of one of the accused was presented as the major piece of evidence. During the course of the trial, the hat band bearing the name disappeared from the sheriff's office. Although a majority of the jury favored conviction, the case resulted in a mistrial.[32]

In 1925 a series of floggings occurred in Birmingham and Jasper during a brief period of time. In Birmingham, where four of the floggings took place, an outpouring of public, civic, and judicial indignation occurred, which resulted in the indictment of three men. The first case resulted in an acquittal, and the others were not brought to trial. The results in Walker County were different. A band of masked men, while searching automobiles for one Robert Christian, discovered

[31]*Age-Herald*, July 24, 25, 27, 1921, August 2, 1921, March 1, 1924; *Post*, March 1, 1924; *News*, July 24, 25, 1921, April 13, 14, 1924; *Post*, April 14, 1924, June 14, 1924.
[32]Gadsden *Evening Journal*, July 7, 8, 1924; *News*, July 7, 1924; *Age-Herald*, July 8, 1924; *Post*, July 8, 1924; *Age-Herald*, November 20, 25, 26, 1924.

George Tallant, an outspoken critic of the Klan because of its operating under cover of night. The masked men tied him to a tree, and a group of eight men took turns flogging him with a rawhide whip. Within a few days indictments were handed down against five men accused of the crime, among them Will Dupree, the group's alleged leader. All five were convicted, but the Alabama Supreme Court set aside the conviction on technical grounds, assuring a new trial, in which, after deliberating 36 hours, the jury was unable to reach a verdict—a mistrial.[33]

Klansmen from Oneonta and Tarrant City participated in an evening service June 26, 1927 at Antioch Baptist Church near Oneonta, in which three white-robed men spoke from the pulpit. While they were leaving, they seized Jeff Calloway, a 19-year-old orphan who had a bottle and had been drinking. They drove to Jefferson County, where he was severely kicked and beaten with a hickory stick. Attorney General Charles C. McCall, himself a Klansman, demanded the names of the men responsible for the crime from state Grand Dragon, James Esdale. Seven men were tried for kidnapping and flogging Calloway; two defendants were found guilty, and subsequently the others entered guilty pleas. This conviction was so important that the *Age-Herald* compared it to the fall of the Bastille.

These convictions marked the beginning of a rapid descent of the power, respect, and influence of the Invisible Empire in the state. By 1925 over 115,000 members had been inducted into the secret order in Alabama; in 1926 actual membership had declined to 94,301. As 1927 drew to a close, membership stood at 10,431, then dropped to about half this figure in 1928. In 1929 there were only 3,213 members, and the membership fell to 1,349 during 1930. That year marked, for all practical purposes, the demise of the Klan as an organization, although local units continued into the 1930's.[34]

The decline of the Klan nationally and locally was precipitous;

[33] *Post*, March 16, 1925; *Age-Herald*, March 3, 1925, September 3, 1926; *News*, September 4, 1926.

[34] *Post*, July 5, 6, 9, 11, 12, 1927; William Edward Gilbert, "The First Administration of Governor Bibb Graves, 1927–30," unpublished M.A. thesis, University of Alabama, 1953; Charles N. Feidelson, "Alabama's Super Government," *The Nation*, CXXV (September 28, 1927), 311–12; The Washington *Post*, quoted in the Birmingham *News*, November 23, 1930. These figures when presented to former Klan officials in Pennsylvania were judged accurate, Emerson H. Loucks, *The Ku Klux Klan in Pennsylvania, A Study in Nativism* (New York, 1936), 208.

"even its rapid rise to prominence seems leisurely by comparison." In 1924 the Klan was riding high; by 1926 it had lost its influence in every Southern state except Alabama. The decision to enter politics and the propensity toward violence started the order on its road to oblivion; and continuous feuds in the state and national orders aided in wrecking the organization. Many people who were otherwise in sympathy with the beliefs of the Klan condemned its use of the mask, intimidation, and violence. Its own excesses virtually destroyed it, especially in the South; in fact, opposition to the hooded order was more serious and outspoken in the South than anywhere else.

LEE N. ALLEN

The 1924 Underwood
Campaign in Alabama

After a long and distinguished political career Senator Oscar Wilder
Underwood in 1924 offered himself as a nominee for the presidency on
the Democratic ticket.[1] Twelve years before he had unsuccessfully
sought the same high office.[2] The political climate now seemed more
conducive to victory, however, for encouraging 1922 congressional
elections predicted national Democratic political superiority and in
January, 1923 the legislature of Alabama, Underwood's home state,
had adopted a resolution officially requesting him to toss his hat into
the ring.[3] At first Underwood remained cautious,[4] delaying his answer,
and, before deciding definitely, he considered the matter carefully on
a long tour with his wife throughout Africa and Europe.[5]

While he was abroad his supporters in Washington and in Alabama

[1] This article is based upon a larger, unpublished study, "The Underwood Presidential Movement of 1924," prepared as a doctoral dissertation in history at the University
of Pennsylvania (1955). The Underwood Papers, freely used in the preparation of both,
are in the Alabama State Department of Archives and History (Montgomery). "The
1924 Underwood Campaign in Alabama" was published in *The Alabama Review*, IX (July,
1956).

[2] See Arthur S. Link, "The Underwood Presidential Movement of 1912," *Journal
of Southern History*, XI, 230–245 (May, 1945). Other data about Underwood (1862–1929)
may be found in *Biographical Directory of the American Congress, 1774–1949* (Washington, 1950),
p. 1943; *Dictionary of American Biography* (New York, 1936), XIX, 117–119; Evans C. Johnson,
"Oscar W. Underwood," unpublished doctoral dissertation, University of North Carolina (1952); and Underwood's own *Drifting Sands of Party Politics* (New York, 1931). Underwood's former private secretary, Oakley W. Melton, of Wetumpka, Alabama, was personally
helpful in an interview on August 27, 1953.

[3] Alabama *House Journal*, 1923, I, 407.

[4] Underwood to R. Cuyler Gordon, January 22, 1923; Oscar W. Underwood, Jr. to
author, November 12, 1954.

[5] See Underwood to E. D. Kenna, February 2, 1923; New York *Times*, February 24, April
30, 1923; and Montgomery *Advertiser*, February 25, 1923.

looked forward to his favorable decision, generally behaving as if his candidacy were a foregone conclusion.[6] Forney Johnston, Washington lawyer and son of the late Alabama Senator Joseph F. Johnston, was in charge of Underwood's political affairs during these months (February–July, 1923). He answered the Senator's correspondence and arranged for a certain amount of financial support. A Southern news service supplied the rural press with favorable editorial comment and clipping bureaus throughout the nation were employed to check Underwood's popularity with the newspapers.[7] Meanwhile, in Underwood's home, Birmingham, Walter Moore, Democratic national committeeman busied himself circularizing party leaders throughout the country, seeking their consideration and support for the Senator. Alabama's enthusiasm for Underwood resulted in two significant endorsements, one in April by the potent Alabama Bar Association and the other in June by the all-important state Democratic Executive Committee.[8]

Upon his return from Europe in early July Underwood refrained from comments, but agreed to answer the Alabama legislature's official invitation with an address before a joint session in Montgomery on July 31, 1923. In the interim he had concluded that there was enough sentiment to justify a campaign. Therefore, in his talk to the legislators he stated that, if they still thought that there was ample cause for his candidacy, he would make the hard race. They warmly encouraged him, and the following day Underwood made his formal announcement, thus becoming the first avowed candidate for the 1924 Democratic nomination for the presidency. The nominating convention was yet eleven months in the future.[9]

At the time several other possible candidates were being mentioned across the nation. Henry Ford, the automobile industrialist, had widespread support among certain Democratic liberals and farmers, who had been aided by his low-cost tractor. But before the end of the year he had removed himself from the political scene by pledging his support to President Coolidge.[10] More popular than Ford was William

[6] Birmingham *News*, February 28, 1923.

[7] Mrs. Marian E. Martin, Underwood's office secretary, to H. J. Rowe, March 13, 1923; *ibid.* to E. D. Kenna, March 31, 1923; *ibid.* to Frank Gilreath, February 27, 1923. Clippings accumulated during this campaign, and now a part of the Underwood Papers, fill about eight filing-cabinet drawers.

[8] Montgomery *Advertiser*, April 29, June 16, 1923.

[9] *Ibid.*, July 3, 6, 10, 21, 29, August 1, 2, 1923.

[10] Keith Sward, *The Legend of Henry Ford* (New York, 1948), pp. 105–130.

Gibbs McAdoo, former Secretary of the Treasury, now a California attorney. Although he was actively denying an open candidacy, among his closest friends it was common knowledge that at the appropriate time he would make his announcement.[11] Certainly, Underwood felt that McAdoo was to be his principal opponent, although McAdoo did not make formal announcement until December, 1923.[12]

Following Underwood's address before the Alabama legislature, endorsements poured in from every sort of group, including the Alabama Press Association and the Alabama Manufacturers' Association, as well as from many personal friends and admirers. Most of the local Democratic leaders supported him. Only an occasional voice of opposition was heard (for instance, a Birmingham labor group expressed "hearty disapproval and opposition" to his candidacy),[13] but the person around whom much unfavorable sentiment seemed to crystallize was the Jasper, Alabama millionaire coal operator, Lycurgus Breckenridge Musgrove, a perennial Underwood opponent.[14]

While Musgrove was not regarded as a serious threat by the state legislators, they nevertheless made legal provision for Senator Underwood's absolute control of the Alabama delegation in the event of his expected primary victory. Back of this lay the memory of the 1912 fiasco, when Underwood's home delegation had forced him to withdraw his name prematurely. Subsequently, friends convinced Underwood that the disloyalty of the Alabama delegates had cost him the Democratic nomination.[15] It was to prevent a repetition at the 1924 convention that Underwood's friends introduced and pushed through the legislature what came to be known as the Verner law, taking its name from C. B. Verner, the Tuscaloosa representative who introduced it. According to its provisions, any citizen of Alabama who was campaigning for the presidency might name the entire delegation, if he received a plurality of the votes in the party primary. This aroused a certain amount of opposition, but, as such, it seems to have cost the Senator few votes, if any.[16]

[11] Daniel C. Roper to Thomas B. Love, May 18, 1923 (in Love Papers, Dallas Historical Society, Dallas, Texas).

[12] New York *Times,* December 18, 1923.

[13] Montgomery *Advertiser,* August 1, 2, 6, 7, 1923; *Weekly Bulletin of the Alabama Manufacturers Association,* September 8, 1923.

[14] Montgomery *Advertiser,* May 4, 10, 20, August 3, 1923, May 18, 1924. Musgrove eventually turned his support to McAdoo.

[15] Johnson, *op. cit.,* pp. 315–316.

[16] Montgomery *Advertiser,* August 29, September 7, 1923.

Meanwhile, Underwood was preparing his own campaign. The first phase consisted of a series of speaking trips through the South. Beginning in Alabama, he spoke in several towns there, as well as in Mississippi, Tennessee, North Carolina, Texas, Kentucky, South Carolina, and Georgia before Congress reconvened in December, 1923.[17] Probably, the most significant speech he made was in Texas, when he openly censured the Ku Klux Klan at Houston, in the heart of its stronghold.[18] Thereafter, although a Southerner, he became the leading anti-Klan candidate and was consequently unable to win any appreciable following in Klan-ridden areas of the South, outside of Alabama.

Underwood's campaign made little progress until a formal organization had been shaped. Outside the very informal group of close friends in Washington, there was no national organization until November, when former Congressman Charles Creighton Carlin of Alexandria, Virginia, was installed as manager. Thereafter, an extensive organization worked on a nationwide basis for Underwood's nomination.[19] Meanwhile, local organizations had been formed in half a dozen Southern states. Alabama's was formally announced on November 17, 1923. This committee grew out of a temporary organization which had been directed by Governor William W. Brandon. The definitive committee was headed by sixty-year-old Alfred M. Tunstall of Greensboro; Robert B. Evins, a younger Birmingham lawyer and chairman of the Alabama Democratic Executive Committee, was chosen vice-chairman.[20] The committee was charged with the responsibility of the campaign in several neighboring states as well as in Alabama.[21] Its work in Alabama was supplemented by campaign committees in every congressional district and in most of the state's sixty-seven counties. Moreover, in this new day of woman suffrage, the recently enfranchised women had their own organizations. A Montgomery leader was Mrs. Marie Bankhead Owen, whose late father, the elder Senator John H. Bankhead, had been Underwood's campaign manager in 1912.[22]

As political campaigns go, the spring primary in Alabama was very unexciting. Underwood was virtually the only contestant. There was

---

[17] *Ibid.*, August–October, 1923, *passim.*
[18] New York *Times,* October 28, 1923.
[19] Underwood to Francis S. Russell, November 17, 1923.
[20] Montgomery *Advertiser,* November 18, 1923.
[21] Forney Johnston to Charles M. Lewis, October 11, 1923.
[22] Montgomery *Advertiser,* December 5, 1923, January 26, 1924.

no real campaign issue, and the result was a foregone conclusion. As a matter of fact, following the official launching of the Alabama campaign, Senator Underwood did not even bother to come into the state, entrusting conduct of his entire race to local friends. However, he was not destined to win control of the Alabama delegation by default, for two other contestants filed papers and entered the field against him—the aforementioned L. B. Musgrove and Marvin A. Dinsmore, a Birmingham attorney, who was generally considered the Klan's candidate in the race.[23] Both men were expected to throw their support to McAdoo at the national convention.[24]

The campaign which followed was one strictly of personalities. On the one hand there was Underwood, a man of well-known views, widely respected by Alabamians, and enjoying substantial press support in the state. Nationally his associations were largely among the middle-of-the-road and conservative Democrats, and he was very far removed from the radical left wing of the party personified in the unpredictable senator from Montana, Burton K. Wheeler. Underwood had personally opposed the woman suffrage and prohibition amendments, both on the grounds of state's rights. He was now opposed to the so-called soldiers' bonus. He favored leasing Muscle Shoals to Henry Ford, a restriction on immigration, and the tax plan formulated by Secretary of the Treasury Andrew W. Mellon. His antipathy to the Ku Klux Klan was well known. Opposing Underwood, the candidate with a clear and open record, was Musgrove, a political dry, who could only boost himself by crying out that the veteran solon was "reactionary and wet," while he himself professed to be "progressive and dry."[25] Dinsmore, the third man, remained an unknown figure in the campaign. While both he and Musgrove were presumed to be campaigning in behalf of a delegation pledged to McAdoo, neither was an official candidate for the popular Californian. And McAdoo denied any responsibility for either man, saying that he would make no campaign effort in Alabama, in keeping with his policy of refraining from contesting with any favorite sons.[26]

The Musgrove and Dinsmore politicians, while ignoring each other, freely threw mud at Underwood. False rumors were widely circulated to

[23] *Ibid.*, December 29, 30, 1923, January 1, 1924; New York *Times*, January 13, 1924.
[24] Montgomery *Advertiser*, December 30, 1923; Birmingham *News*, January 27, 1924.
[25] Montgomery *Advertiser*, January 18, 1924.
[26] *Ibid.*, January 31, 1924.

the effect that he had been born in the North, that his ancestors had fought with Union forces, that he had renounced his Masonic affiliations, and that he had become a Roman Catholic. The purpose of these baseless charges was to rouse the Klansmen of the state against Underwood; but they did no harm, for the campaign committee effectively answered each in turn.[27]

Nationally, probably the most influential event of the campaign was the revelation, during the famous Teapot Dome investigation, that McAdoo was an attorney for the untouchable Edward L. Doheny.[28] The immediate reaction of many people was that McAdoo, while personally guilty of no crime, was at least now unavailable for the nomination and for the sake of political expediency should drop out of the race.[29] Underwood's national campaign manager was greatly encouraged by this turn of events.[30] Even a few of McAdoo's closest advisers were certain that his chances for nomination in 1924 had been ruined.[31] It was therefore only natural that Underwood's enemies should attempt to use the oil investigation to destroy the Senator also, and the Musgrove forces lost no time in fabricating unsubstantiated charges against Underwood. However, they were speedily denied, hardly heard from again, and probably did not prove damaging.[32]

The only accusations made against Underwood which bore any resemblance to a real national issue involved his attitude toward prohibition. Not only was Underwood's record of opposition to the Eighteenth Amendment well known, but it was generally recognized that his personal proclivities were toward sympathy for the wets. The fear of the prohibitionists was that Underwood would throw his strength to the very wet Alfred E. Smith, if he saw that he could not be nominated. Musgrove assumed his usual role of champion of the drys, but Underwood won many of their leaders in Alabama by a frank acknowledgement of his previous record, which he justified by a state's rights argument. He pledged that, if elected, he would uphold the existing law without change, enforcing the Volstead Act with the same enthusiasm that Governor Brandon was enforcing the compan-

---

[27] Birmingham *News*, January 13, 1924; W. H. May to A. M. Tunstall, February 15, 1924.
[28] Montgomery *Advertiser*, February 2, 1924.
[29] *American Review of Reviews*, XLIX, 465 (May, 1924).
[30] C. C. Carlin to W. R. Pattangall, February 6, 1924.
[31] Thomas B. Love to D. L. Rockwell, February 8, 1924 (in Love Papers); Daniel C. Roper, *Fifty Years of Public Life* (Durham, 1941), p. 218.
[32] Montgomery *Advertiser*, February 29, 1924.

ion state law in Alabama. He convinced the Reverend Dr. W. B. Crumpton, a retired Baptist minister serving as the state president of the Anti-Saloon League, and Braxton Bragg Comer, generally regarded as the political leader of the drys of the state. They and other longtime prohibitionists joined in endorsing Senator Underwood.[33]

The most serious threat to an Underwood victory in the entire Alabama campaign came not from the mud-slinging opposition, but from the internal breach which developed within the Underwood ranks during the early part of the campaign. Former Governor Comer, serving on the state's campaign committee, grew alarmed at the number of the anti-prohibitionists working for Underwood. He had been one of the earliest of the Underwood supporters, having joined with all the living former governors of Alabama in endorsing Underwood's candidacy early in the fall of 1923.[34] Largely because of the prestige of his name, he was soon placed in a position of campaign leadership from which he viewed with alarm the changing complexion of the committee. Now he announced to Underwood that he wanted assurance that the Alabama delegation to the Democratic convention would never join forces with wet delegations to demand a plank in the party platform, calling for repeal of prohibition. Comer's menacing threat to withdraw from the Underwood campaign resulted in an arrangement which allowed him to choose half the delegation and to name one of his own men to the convention's platform committee. Harmony was again restored to the Underwood committee, and the complete story was given to the press.[35]

The only further diversion during the campaign was a visit of William Jennings Bryan, now of Miami, to the northern part of the state. During late February he was brought under the auspices of Musgrove and made several addresses for which he was said to have been handsomely paid. However, his service for Musgrove was more in the spirit of a "labor of love"; his antipathy for Underwood knew no bounds and he was more than willing to go to any lengths to prevent his winning the Democratic nomination.[36]

[33] Birmingham *News,* December 18, 1923, March 9, 1924; Montgomery *Advertiser,* August 1, 6, 1923.

[34] *Ibid.,* September 3, 1923.

[35] *Ibid.,* February 8, 10, 1924; B. B. Comer to Underwood, December 8, 1923; Underwood to B. B. Comer, December 10, 1923; Donald Comer to author, August 31, 1953.

[36] Montgomery *Advertiser,* February 23, 25, 26, 27, 1924; Bryan to Ira Champion, December 31, 1923 (in William Jennings Bryan Papers, Library of Congress, Washington, D.C.).

The Alabama election was held March 11, 1924 as the first primary of the season. The friendly executive committee had doubtless set this early date in order to give Underwood a certain psychological advantage to be gained by winning the first election of the year. As expected, he won an overwhelming majority. The official vote was Underwood 65,798, Musgrove 37,837, and Dinsmore 2,001.[37] The results cheered the Underwood campaign in other states. Because of the victory, Underwood was widely publicized as the first candidate to win official control of delegates to the national convention. For a week he led the entire field of candidates with his twenty-four votes, which were later to become so famous.

The subsequent story of the national Underwood campaign does not present so rosy a picture. Simultaneously, he was waging active campaigns in Georgia, Texas, Tennessee, Mississippi, and Florida, but in none did he secure instructed delegations. In most of them he was defeated by a McAdoo majority. During the spring the ambitious Californian built up a tremendous following, despite the Teapot Dome disclosures, and Underwood did not go to the national nominating convention with that core of Southern strength on which his campaign plans had been initially built. Defeat begets discouragement, and as one failure followed another, Underwood dwindled from one of the leading national contenders to the status of a favorite son, sharing this honor with a full stable of dark horses.

A note of disharmony was sounded in Alabama on the eve of the convention, when Underwood undertook to name the delegates as provided for by the controversial Verner law. In accord with the so-called Tunstall-Comer pact, publicized in February, each of these men was to name half of the delegation, and Underwood was to ratify the choices. The only stipulation made at the meeting was that every delegate should give an unqualified, iron-clad pledge of loyalty to Underwood's candidacy. However, in the intervening months Underwood's national campaign was being built around an anti-Klan plank. Late in May, 1924, when Comer and Tunstall were making their appointments, Underwood insisted on an unqualified pledge of support on this additional issue also. Comer, however, was not in full sympathy with the Senator's new crusade and refused to extract any such pledge from his twenty-four appointees. In a last-minute concession, to maintain state unity Underwood agreed to accept these men

[37] Montgomery *Advertiser*, March 22, 1924.

without a promise to support his anti-Klan plank. The Alabama delegation, with "Plain Bill" Brandon as chairman, went to New York, agreeing only on their complete loyalty to Underwood. When the platform was under consideration, the Alabama delegation, voting under the strictures of the unit rule, supported the Senator's preference, but the vote within the group was very close.[38]

At the Democratic National Convention, held in Madison Square Garden, Underwood was but one of sixteen men placed in formal nomination. His name was the first presented, and the honors for naming the Senator went to Forney Johnston, who attracted much attention by means of a dramatic speech. During the balloting which followed, a deadlock between McAdoo and Governor Al Smith prolonged the convention into a record-breaking third week. Not until after the 99th roll call did the two men withdraw, and for the next four ballots the convention searched for an acceptable candidate. During the 101st and 102nd ballots a considerable number of delegates considered Underwood, and he made a fair showing on the latter tabulation. However, the ultimate victor on the 103rd ballot was the "Wall Street" lawyer, John W. Davis, a former West Virginia congressman, who had served one term in the House while Underwood was still there.[39]

Thus did Oscar W. Underwood make his second unsuccessful attempt to win the Democratic presidential nomination. There is little doubt why he again failed. To begin with, the Democratic party in 1924 was not likely to draw its standard bearer from so safely Democratic a state as Alabama.[40] Secondly, Underwood was generally classed as a wet, and the convention was predominantly dry.[41] Thirdly, Underwood was an anathema to the Ku Klux Klan. It is improbable that a majority of the delegates were Klansmen or even sympathetic with its position. However, most of the delegates were unwilling to offend so potent a group as the Klan by nominating a man as uncompromising in his attacks on that hooded order as was Underwood.[42] He demanded a

[38] B. B. Comer to Underwood, May 6, 1924; Underwood to A. M. Tunstall, May 31, 1924; A. M. Tunstall to Underwood, June 4, 1924; B. B. Comer to each of his 24 delegates, June 6, 1924.
[39] Charles A. Greathouse, compiler, *Official Report of the Proceedings of the Democratic National Convention . . . 1924* (Indianapolis, n.d.), *passim.*
[40] Josephus Daniels to S. A. Ashe, July 31, 1924 (in Josephus Daniels Papers, Library of Congress, Washington, D.C.).
[41] Montgomery *Advertiser*, July 5, 1924; New York *Times*, February 28, 1923.
[42] *Ibid.*, July 10, 1924.

platform plank that would have censured the Ku Klux Klan by name.[43] And finally, it should not be overlooked that Underwood was not the preference of two important men at the convention. James M. Cox, the 1920 standard bearer, had come to the convention during the closing hours and attempted to manipulate a successful choice. Underwood did not receive his benediction.[44] Nor was he at all acceptable to the ubiquitous William Jennings Bryan, who was thought still to wield a significant, if unmeasurable, degree of influence.[45]

Underwood's 1924 attempt to capture the Democratic nomination for the presidency did, however, produce a bit of political publicity, which is even now remembered nationally. When diminutive Governor "Bill" Brandon stood up in his chair at each roll call and repeatedly shouted in stentorian tones, "Alabama casts twenty-four votes for Oscar W. Underwood," he uttered words which still ring down the halls of the Democratic party.

[43] *Ibid.*, January 23, 1924.

[44] James M. Cox, *Journey Through My Years* (New York, 1946), p. 328; Carter Glass to Harry F. Byrd, July 22, 1924 (in Glass MSS, Alderman Library, University of Virginia, Charlottesville).

[45] Montgomery *Advertiser,* August 3, 1923.

WILLIAM E. GILBERT

Bibb Graves as a
Progressive, 1927–1930

During the years immediately following World War I, the South, like
the Mid-West, was in a period of transition, which had begun prior to
the turn of the century during the prominence of the Populist
movement. These changes continued during the first quarter of the
twentieth century, when Alabama was shifting from a predominately
agricultural state to one with a better balance between industry and
agriculture. Agriculture itself was expanding and improving even while
this industrialization was in progress. The phenomenal growth of
Alabama's cities—particularly Birmingham—created problems of urbanization that had to be solved. The advent of the automobile
brought increasing demand from all parts of the state for more and
better roads and bridges. Federal aid for road building projects, which
had been first begun during the Wilson administration, was continued
during the 1920's. These demands for more public services made it
necessary for the state government gradually to desert the old Jeffersonian ideal of simple government and to expand its functions.

Bibb Graves was recognized throughout his political career as a
leader of the progressive forces of Alabama. He believed that the
state should provide more services for its citizens. The conservatives, however, were still strong in the state, and they wanted to
maintain a simple government, such as that of the Bourbons in the
last quarter of the nineteenth century. They vigorously opposed

This paper was read at the annual meeting of the Alabama Historical Association,
Montgomery, April 21, 1956. It was published in *The Alabama Review*, X (January 1957).

Graves and his program throughout his entire tenure of office, from 1927 to 1931.

Bibb Graves' political career began early. He was first elected to the Alabama House of Representatives from Montgomery County in 1898, and he served in that body for two terms.[1] He was very active in the Democratic party. In 1916 he was elected chairman of the state Democratic executive committee.[2] He first sought the Democratic nomination for governor in 1922, but he was defeated in the primary election by W. W. Brandon.[3] Following this unsuccessful campaign, Graves spent the next four years getting ready for the next. He entered the 1926 contest very early, and the ensuing campaign was one of the bitterest in Alabama history.[4] The Brandon administration's choice was Lieutenant-Governor Charles S. McDowell, Jr., of Eufaula.[5] Archie H. Carmichael, a Tuscumbia attorney, and Andrew G. Patterson, the president of the Alabama Public Service Commission, ran on progressive platforms that were similar in many respects to that of Graves.[6] Graves was not believed to have a chance for election, and, therefore, he was virtually ignored by the other candidates.[7]

While his opponents fought each other, Graves quietly won the governorship. He ran strongest in the rural sections of North Alabama, but he received a substantial vote from every section of the state, except the Black Belt.[8] He drew considerable support from the Ku Klux Klan, organized labor, and the World War veterans, and he received some support from the educational and professional groups.[9] The major portion of his strength, however, came from the "plain people" of the state. His campaign appealed to them, and they followed him, because he was free from the so-called "taint" of corporate influence.[10]

The Graves administration distinguished itself for its expansion

[1] "Biographical Sketch of Bibb Graves" (MS in Alabama State Department of Archives and History, Montgomery).
[2] Birmingham *Age-Herald*, August 15, 1926.
[3] *Alabama Official and Statistical Register*, 1923 (Montgomery, 1923), pp. 364–365.
[4] Montgomery *Advertiser*, January 31, 1926.
[5] Albert B. Moore, *History of Alabama* (University, 1934), p. 769.
[6] Montgomery *Advertiser*, August 2, 1927.
[7] New York *Times*, August 9, 1926.
[8] *Alabama Official and Statistical Register*, 1927 (Montgomery, 1927), pp. 362–363.
[9] New York *Times*, August 9, 1926.
[10] Moore, *op. cit.*, p. 770.

of the state's educational system. The present school system is largely the outgrowth of the unified program worked out during this administration.[11] Prior to 1927, most of the school money which the counties received from the state was apportioned on a per capita basis— so much for each child of school age. This school fund proved to be entirely inadequate to maintain a reasonable school term. While the richer counties could supplement it from local taxation, the poorer counties, which had low values of taxable property, found themselves unable to do so.[12] During Graves' term every effort was made to increase the educational standards in Alabama. Especially in the rural areas was progress immediately apparent in lengthened school terms.[13]

On November 3, 1926 Governor-elect Graves received a delegation of the state's educational leaders, consisting of Mr. Robert E. Tidwell, state superintendent of education-elect; Dr. George H. Denny, president of the University of Alabama; Dr. Spright Dowell, president of the Alabama Polytechnic Institute; Dr. Henry J. Willingham, president of the Florence State Normal School; and Dr. E. M. Shackelford, president of the Troy State Normal School. They outlined the needs of the state's institutions of higher learning during the next four years.[14]

The Graves legislature began its work in a special session which met on December 28, 1926. One of the purposes of this short session was to organize the legislative machinery so that the legislators could get down to actual work at the beginning of the regular session on January 11, 1927. The 1927 session consisted of fifty legislative days. After appointing a number of interim committees, the legislature recessed from February 18 until June 7, and did not finally adjourn until September 2, 1927.[15]

Governor Graves urged the legislature to approve a $600,000.00 emergency appropriation for the public schools.[16] A bill carrying out this recommendation passed the legislature on January 28, 1927.[17] An unexpected obstacle arose, however, on February 3 when Attorney General Charles C. McCall held that the law was unconstitutional. He

[11] *Ibid.*, p. 748.
[12] Interview with Robert E. Tidwell, University of Alabama, March 11, 1953.
[13] Birmingham *News,* January 15, 1931.
[14] Montgomery *Advertiser,* November 4, 1926.
[15] Alabama *House Journal,*1927 (Montgomery, 1927), pp. 3017–3018.
[16] *Ibid.*, p. 159.
[17] Alabama *Acts,* 1927 (Montgomery, 1927), p. 80.

ruled that it violated sections 110 and 256 of the constitution because the appropriation was not made on a per capita basis, but was made on an arbitrary basis according to the amount needed by each county in order to provide a school term of seven months.[18] Immediately following the announcement of McCall's opinion, Graves submitted a request to the Alabama Supreme Court for an advisory opinion.[19] Four days later the court reversed McCall's ruling and held that the emergency appropriation for education was constitutional.[20]

Administration leaders had agreed that approximately $20 million would be needed for educational purposes during the quadrennium. They realized that there would be considerable opposition to such a large sum. These needs were embodied in the Ward education bill, which made the most liberal appropriations in the state's history up to that time for the support and maintenance of the public schools and higher institutions.[21] Over $25 million was provided for educational purposes during the quadrennium—$22 million for public schools and the remainder for normal schools and higher institutions.[22] The Ward education bill became law on August 25, 1927.[23] Public opinion seemed to be very much in favor of the expansion of the state's educational program. Even the Montgomery *Journal,* which was generally very critical of the Graves administration, complimented it highly on its farsighted educational plans.[24]

The necessity for better teacher training was basic in any program for improving the public schools of the state. Bibb Graves said repeatedly that the state received more immediate returns from the money spent upon its normal schools than upon any other educational expenditure.[25] The unified program act of 1927 appropriated $35,000.00 annually to each of the normal schools at Florence, Jacksonville, Livingston, and Troy.[26]

Since the funds available were not adequate for the maintenance of a school of education offering all needed services at each of the state's three higher institutions, the State Department of Educa-

[18] Mobile *Register,* February 4, 1927.
[19] Montgomery *Advertiser,* February 4, 1927.
[20] 215 *Ala.,* 524; Montgomery *Journal,* February 8, 1927.
[21] Mobile *Register,* June 3, 1927.
[22] *Alabama State Department of Education Report,* 1927 (Montgomery, 1928), p. 57.
[23] Alabama *Acts,* 1927 (Montgomery, 1928), pp. 442–455.
[24] Montgomery *Journal,* July 14, 1927.
[25] Montgomery *Advertiser,* January 19, 1927.
[26] Alabama *Acts,* 1927, p. 443.

tion deemed it advisable to eliminate duplication of courses as far as possible. Toward this goal the heads of these institutions reached a tri-presidential agreement on June 26, 1927. In this agreement, Dr. Denny of the University, Dr. Dowell of Alabama Polytechnic Institute, and Dr. Carmichael of Alabama College planned to work together in the expansion of their courses of study and in the establishment of new schools and colleges.[27]

A committee of the State Department of Education devoted considerable study to the normal schools in an effort to provide more adequate facilities for the training of teachers. Upon its recommendation the normal schools at Florence, Troy, Jacksonville, and Livingston were made state teachers colleges in 1929 and empowered to grant the B.S. degree.[28] The physical plants of all four were found to be inadequate for the expansion, and a building program was instituted with funds appropriated by the legislature.[29]

An effort was made to improve also Negro educational opportunities in the state during the Graves administration. The General Education Board of the Rockefeller Foundation and the Julius Rosenwald Fund were active in the promotion of Negro education and school building programs.[30] Increased appropriations and building programs were provided by the state for Negro as well as white schools.[31] Appropriations were also provided for the Negro colleges. Tuskegee Institute received $5,000.00 per year, the state teachers college at Montgomery received $20,000.00 per year, and the Agricultural and Mechanical Institute at Normal $15,000.00 per year.[32]

The eleemosynary institutions of the state shared with the public schools and higher institutions in the increased public interest in social legislation of the time. The legislature appropriated $159,040.00 per year for the Deaf, Dumb, and Blind Institute at Talladega, and in addition appropriated $300,000.00 for the construction and repair of buildings and equipment there.[33] The state greatly enlarged its provisions for the insane and feeble-minded. During the quadrennium there was completed a dormitory at the Negro

[27] *Alabama State Department of Education Report,* 1928 (Montgomery, 1929), pp. 42–57.

[28] Interview with Tidwell, March 11, 1953.

[29] *Alabama State Department of Education Report,* 1929 (Montgomery, 1930), pp. 23–24.

[30] Horace M. Bond, *Negro Education in Alabama* . . . (Washington, 1939), p. 274.

[31] Interview with Tidwell, March 11, 1953.

[32] *Alabama State Department of Education Report,* 1930 (Montgomery, 1931), pp. 82–88.

[33] *Annual Report of the Alabama Institute for the Deaf and Blind,* 1929–1930 (Montgomery, 1930), p.11.

hospital at Mt. Vernon designed for 225 beds, and a dormitory at Bryce Hospital at Tuscaloosa for 200 beds. In addition, some 3,000 acres of farm lands were acquired at Tuscaloosa for a farm colony.[34] The Boys Industrial School at East Lake and the Girls Industrial School at Birmingham received generous appropriations from the Graves legislature,[35] $112,433.00 and $50,550.00, respectively.[36]

Such then is Bibb Graves' record in the educational and charitable fields. It speaks for itself in proving him to be one of Alabama's most liberal governors. But these services cost money, and the increased revenue was not sufficient to take care of the increased appropriations. This resulted in an annual deficit in the treasury, which left the state in debt at the conclusion of Graves' term of office. Moreover, a depression began during the last year of the term. State revenue declined, terms of the public schools had to be cut short, many teachers were paid in warrants, and the colleges received only a small portion of their building funds. The Graves administration was severely criticized by many as an "orgie of extravagance and waste."[37]

One of the most important reforms of the Graves' administration was the abolition of the convict leasing system. For many years the leasing of convicts had been a leading social question, and much had been written concerning the abuses suffered under it. As early as 1882, Warden John H. Bankhead had reported the convict camps to be "totally unfit for use, filthy beyond description, and infested with vermin."[38] In 1893 Miss Julia S. Tutwiler said that the lease system had been "well described as one that combines all of the evils of slavery without one of its ameliorating features."[39] Other humanitarians insisted upon good treatment of the prisoners, even if it involved public expense, and they wanted to institute a program of regeneration so that the convicts might return to society as useful citizens.[40] However, the general public had apparently been apathetic

---

[34] Alabama *Acts,* 1931, p. 9.
[35] *Annual Report of the Auditor of the State of Alabama,* 1927 (Montgomery, 1928), pp. 718–719.
[36] *Ibid.,* pp. 173–174.
[37] Quoted in Moore, *op. cit.,* p. 781.
[38] Malcolm C. Moos, *State Penal Administration in Alabama* (University, Ala., 1942), p. 12.
[39] Moore, *op. cit.,* pp. 814–815.
[40] Elizabeth B. Clark, "The Abolition of the Convict Lease System in Alabama, 1913–1928" (unpublished Master's thesis, University of Alabama, 1949).

to this agitation. The main reason for this was the large income that
the convicts brought into the state treasury. Governors who had
leased convicts shrewdly and realized a handsome profit for the state
were congratulated on their business ability. The series of "business" governors pointed with particular pride to what they had made
for the state from convict leasing.[41] For example, in the four year
period ending September 30, 1926, Alabama's net profit from her
convict labor was $3,269,098.00.[42] Therefore, it can be readily seen
why there would be opposition to the abandonment of such a lucrative
source of revenue.

One of the first measures to be introduced in the Senate when the
legislature convened on January 11, 1927, was a bill banning the leasing
of convicts. It prohibited the further leasing of them after March
31, 1927 and provided that after December 31, 1927 it would be unlawful
to work convicts in the coal mines.[43] Governor Graves was very
much concerned about alleviating the conditions of the convicts.
In devising plans for employing them after the abolition of the
leasing system, he investigated the successful use made of convicts
on the roads in other states.[44] From the time of his inauguration he
had been laying the groundwork for the removal of the convicts. He
found that under existing conditions the state leased the mine property from the owners, mined the coal with the convicts under state
control, and sold the coal back to the mine owners.[45]

Following a conference on February 12, 1927, between Governor
Graves, Chairman Moffett of the State Board of Administration,
and Chairman Finnell of the State Highway Department, it was announced that all the county convicts would be removed from the
mines by June 1, 1927.[46] The first consignment of 125 convicts was
removed on February 13, 1927, and taken to prison camps at Speigner
and Kilby, where they were worked in the state cotton mills and shirt
factory.[47] To care for the increased number of prisoners, additional
buildings had to be provided at all the prisons then in existence.

[41] Moore, *op. cit.,* p. 814.
[42] Fred E. Haynes, *The American Prison System* (New York, 1939), p. 175.
[43] Birmingham *News,* January 11, 1927.
[44] Interview with Mrs. Bibb Graves, March 20, 1953.
[45] "Alabama's Convict System Under Fire," *Literary Digest,* LXXXIX, 10–13 (April
10, 1936).
[46] Montgomery *Advertiser,* February 13, 1927.
[47] Mobile *Register,* February 14, 1927.

Finding that this was not sufficient to supply the need, the State Board of Administration purchased a farm in Escambia County, near Atmore.[48] A crew of prisoners was sent to Atmore in the spring of 1928, and they erected the prison camp themselves, so the cost to the state was not excessive. It is interesting to note that a policy of self-discipline was established among the convicts, who were engaged in the construction of the Atmore buildings. More than a hundred of them went about their work with many of the privileges of free men.[49] By 1931 the farm had become a source of profit to the state. An automobile tag mill was built at Kilby Prison at a cost of $95,000.00, and new machinery was installed at the Speigner cotton mill at a cost of $100,000.00. By the close of the Graves' administration these enterprises were a source of revenue to the state.[50]

After almost a quarter of a century of agitation, the practice of convict leasing in Alabama had finally come to an end. Governor Graves had advocated in his gubernatorial platform the end of the lease system and the legislature co-operated by enacting a law forbidding it. This legislation stands out as one of the lasting achievements of the Graves' administration, because these prison reforms mark the beginning of a whole new chapter in the history of penology in Alabama.

Governor Graves and his administration are remembered for the accomplishments made during this time in providing a system of highways and bridges throughout the state. Graves considered his election to be a popular mandate in favor of the $25 million bond issue, which he had advocated during the campaign.[51] Governor Brandon co-operated with Graves by calling a special session of the newly-elected legislature to meet on December 28, 1926. Brandon limited his call to the submission of the bond issue amendment and the levying of a two-cent gasoline tax to retire the bonds.[52] The special session passed the necessary legislation in the form Graves requested, and then it adjourned on January 4, 1927.[53] The amendment was ratified by the people of Alabama in a special election on April 12,

---

[48] *Quadrennial Report of the State Board of Administration,* 1926–1930 (Montgomery, 1930), p. 26.
[49] New York *Times,* July 1, 1928; Montgomery *Journal,* October 9, 1928.
[50] Alabama *Acts,* 1931 (Montgomery, 1931), p. 11.
[51] Birmingham *Age-Herald,* December 30, 1926.
[52] Alabama *Acts,* Special Session, 1926–1927 (Montgomery, 1927), pp. 787, 788.
[53] Birmingham *News,* January 4, 1927.

1927.[54] Immediately, the State Highway Commission completed plans for the expenditure of the money. In addition to the $25 million proceeds from the bond sales, the commission also received approximately $1½ million annually from Federal appropriations. Therefore, the total amount available for road purposes in Alabama during the quadrennium was over $30 million.[55]

On August 31, 1927, the Legislature passed a law, authorizing the creation of the State Bridge Corporation, delegating to it authority to issue bonds for the construction of fifteen toll bridges to span the principal rivers of the state.[56] The personnel of the commission consisted of the director of the State Highway Department, the president of the State Board of Administration, and the chairman of the State Tax Commission.[57] The corporation issued $5 million worth of toll bridge bonds in the spring of 1929 and used the proceeds to build the bridges. Provision was made for the eventual freeing of the bridges when the income from the toll had paid the bonds and the interest.[58]

Bibb Graves and his administration are usually best remembered for their major reforms in the fields of education, highways, and convict leasing. Often overlooked is the progress made in other fields that, while not so spectacular, was nevertheless very important. Public health specialists came from all over the nation to study the organization of the Alabama Health Department.[59] Alabama achieved a position of national leadership in the percentage of its rural population provided with full-time health service. By the end of the quadrennium, fifty-four counties, embracing 88 per cent of the state's population, were participating in the state health program. That is, each had a county health officer and one or more nurses at work to improve the health and lower the death rate among their citizens.[60]

Closely related to health and education was the Child Welfare Department, which was under the supervision of a director, Mrs. A. M. Tunstall, who became nationally recognized for her work in the field.[61]

[54] Mobile *Register*, April 14, 1927.
[55] *Ibid.*, April 13, 1927.
[56] New York *Times*, September 11, 1927.
[57] Alabama *Acts*, 1927 (Montgomery, 1927), pp. 278–284.
[58] Montgomery *Journal*, July 20, 1927.
[59] Moore, *op. cit.*, p. 819.
[60] *Annual Report of the State Board of Health of Alabama*, 1930, pp. 10–11.
[61] Marie B. Owen, *The Story of Alabama* . . . (New York, 1949), II, 402.

The department was charged with the enforcement of the child labor act and was given authority to receive children through the juvenile courts and to place them in family homes under supervision. On August 18, 1927, the legislature made an appropriation of $100,000.00 each year for the first two years of the quadrennium and after that time, October 1, 1929, $125,000.00 each year.[62]

In his gubernatorial campaign Bibb Graves had pledged himself to provide more generously for the necessities of Confederate veterans and their wives in their declining years.[63] A bill was passed by the legislature, which provided for a gradual increase in pensions from $25.00 to $40.00 per month.[64] Moreover, during this period the state still maintained the Confederate soldiers home at Mountain Creek, located between Birmingham and Montgomery on the Louisville & Nashville Railroad. Through the years this institution had provided a home for numbers of indigent veterans.[65] After the increase in veterans' benefits had been made, the pension commissioner reported that there was an immediate and marked drop in the rate of mortality among the Confederate veterans. This would seem to indicate that the pension increase was sorely needed by many in order to provide the actual necessities of life.[66]

Prohibition had ceased to be a major political issue in the state with the passage of the Eighteenth Amendment. During the period from 1927 to 1931, however, this issue was re-emerging as demand for repeal began to be heard all over the nation. The electorate of Alabama had never ceased to require of candidates for public office their stand with regard to the liquor question. The Anti-Saloon League and the Woman's Christian Temperance Union were still powerful organizations which wielded tremendous influence in the state— political as well as social.[67] The enforcement of the prohibition law became more and more of a problem as the people became more and more disgusted with the farce that it had proved to be. The automobile complicated matters by making it easier for the "bootleg-

---

[62] *Annual Report of the Department of Public Welfare of Alabama*, 1930 (Montgomery, 1930), p. 1.

[63] Birmingham *Age-Herald*, July 4, 1926.

[64] Alabama *Acts*, 1927, pp. 71–73.

[65] *Annual Report of the Auditor of the State of Alabama*, 1926, p. 211; *ibid.*, 1927, p. 183.

[66] Birmingham *News*, January 15, 1931.

[67] James B. Sellers, *The Prohibition Movement in Alabama, 1702 to 1943* (Chapel Hill, 1943), p. 192.

ger" to transport his product without being apprehended. The legislature of 1927 attempted to remedy this situation by enacting a law making it illegal to transport liquor or similar beverages, the sale or possession of which was prohibited in Alabama. The penalty for the violation of this law was unusually severe—imprisonment of from one to five years.[68]

The Graves' administration made notable progress in its attempt to conserve and develop the natural resources of Alabama. This work was directed by three departments of the state government—the Department of Agriculture and Industries, the Commission of Forestry, and the Department of Game and Fisheries.

The main objective of the Commission of Forestry was to encourage the development of forests by educating the people to the fact that there were profits to be derived from the growing of timber. It endeavored also to protect the existing forests and to provide for reforestation of lands that were no longer profitable for farming.[69] The state parks were placed under the jurisdiction of the commission by an act of the legislature on September 26, 1927. Another important duty that it performed was to aid in the prevention of forest fires.[70]

Bibb Graves was vitally interested in the development of Alabama's only seaport at Mobile and the system of waterways which served it. The state docks were constructed, beginning in 1928, and by the end of the Graves quadrennium the port of Mobile had harbor facilities comparable with those of the other Gulf ports. No longer were vessels compelled to load and unload their cargoes in the harbor because of the lack of proper port facilities.[71]

Governor Graves did not accomplish the passage of two of the reforms he advocated. These were reapportionment of representation in the legislature and biennial sessions of the legislature. In his first message to the legislature on January 18, 1927, he said, "I believe it is your duty to carry out the provisions of the Constitution upon reapportionment of representation in the legislature."[72] The legislature failed to take any action on reapportionment and did not provide for biennial sessions of the legislature. One would certainly be

[68] Alabama *Acts,* 1927, pp. 704–705.
[69] *Alabama Commission of Forestry,* 1930 (Montgomery, 1930), pp. 5–12.
[70] *Ibid.,* p. 15.
[71] Owen, *op. cit.,* II, 46–47.
[72] Alabama *Acts,* 1927, p. 75.

justified in saying, however, that Governor Graves was unusually
successful in getting his program enacted into law.

In conclusion, the four years of Bibb Graves' first administration
as governor were eventful years in Alabama history. His term began in
1927 when money seemed plentiful and prosperity here to stay; it
ended in 1931 when the despair of the worst economic depression in
the nation's history gripped the land. Meeting the problems that
arose as a result of these changing conditions required ability and
leadership. Many decisions had to be made and many new programs
put into operation. The dynamic manner with which Graves pursued
his policies captured the imagination of the people. His admirers
claimed that he was the forerunner in this state of Franklin D. Roosevelt in the nation and that he was one of the first leaders to
recognize the responsibility of the government to provide certain
social services for its citizens. His opponents, on the other hand,
referred to him as a radical who really accomplished little of permanent
value, but only managed to waste the people's money in extravagant
schemes and to keep the state in a constant turmoil about something. As usual, perhaps, the truth lies somewhere between these two
extremes.

Bibb Graves was one of the best stump speakers and campaigners
in the state's history. His impressive voice often convinced his audience that he was an earnest and true friend of the people. Because of
their faith in him the voters of Alabama elected him again to serve
as their governor in 1934. It was generally thought that he would
have been elected to a third term, in 1942, had not his death occurred
on March 14 of that year.[73]

Bibb Graves was one of the best educated men ever to occupy the
governor's chair in Alabama. He was so clever and diplomatic in his
dealings with the legislature that an open break never occurred between him and any member. He always waited until the most opportune
time to make his views known, and then he usually expressed himself
through his subordinates. Because of his political astuteness, Graves
never suffered a major defeat at the hands of his opponents. All of
the important pieces of legislation that he advocated were enacted
into law.

It is apparent that Graves possessed a great deal of vanity and

---

[73] Montgomery *Advertiser,* March 15, 1942.

personal egotism. He liked to be called "The Little Colonel" and "Bibb the Builder." As testimony to the fact that he liked to see his name perpetuated in stone, there is a building named Bibb Graves Hall on the campus of every major state-supported institution of higher learning in Alabama.

Bibb Graves was sincerely interested in the people's welfare, and he gave the state a progressive administration. Under his leadership some important reforms were achieved, the most notable of which was the ending of the convict lease system. Needed tax reforms which broadened and improved the state's base of taxation were instituted. His administration greatly improved the state's system of highways and bridges and instituted a health program which became a model for the entire nation. Probably the most important of all, however, was the contribution to educational advancement in Alabama. Perhaps the best brief summation of Bibb Graves as a chief executive was that of Grover C. Hall, the editor of the Montgomery *Advertiser*, who generally opposed Graves and his policies. Hall said, "Bibb Graves makes a good governor, but an expensive one."[74] Certainly, the Bibb Graves administration made a profound and lasting impression upon the social progress of the State of Alabama.

[74] Quoted in Birmingham *News*, March 15, 1942.

J. MILLS THORNTON III

Alabama Politics, J. Thomas Heflin, and the Expulsion Movement of 1929

The fall of the Bourbons from power in Alabama after the turn of the century was more a voluntary than a forced abdication. Ever pragmatic in their approach to politics, the majority of the Bourbon elite took the lesson of the populist period to heart. Without the Negro vote, they could not maintain themselves in power. But as long as Negroes remained legal voters, there was always the danger that a dissident white group might capture the Negroes' confidence, and with these allies go on to effect a complete revolution in state government. Clearly, the way to prevent such an eventuality was to admit to some degree of power the excluded white groups from whose ranks dissident movements had time and again arisen, while concurrently eliminating the Negro from politics. Of course, such a program meant a considerable diminution of power for the Bourbons, but, "half a loaf was better than none." The result was the Constitution of 1901. The Bourbons contented themselves with disproportionate power in the malapportioned legislature, while largely—through the institution of the direct primary—abandoning executive offices to the formerly excluded white groups. The Negro was removed as a possible bone of contention between the two segments of the white electorate by his disfranchisement.

By the time of the Henderson Administration (1915–1919), it was clear that the Bourbon ploy had been successful. North Alabama,

This essay was published in *The Alabama Review*, XXI (Apr., 1968).

home of the dissident whites, had accepted the degree of power that the Constitutional Convention had granted it, and made no further attempts to dislodge the Bourbons from their remaining strong-holds. Bourbons continued to control Black Belt county govern-ments. The Black Belt bloc was unrivalled within the legislature for its coherence, consistency, and continuity. But very few of the in-tellectual heirs of the old Bourbon elite ever again achieved statewide eminence.[1]

By the end of the twenties the number of important officials who might fairly be called descendants of the old ruling class was small indeed. Henry De Lamar Clayton II, after a distinguished career in Congress culminating in the passage of the Clayton Antitrust Act, was now one of Alabama's federal judges. Chief Justice John C. Anderson of Demopolis dominated a Supreme Court made up largely of North Alabamians by his sheer legal brilliance. William A. Gunter, Jr., mayor of Montgomery, controlled with genial paternalism Ala-bama's most famous city machine, and his influence spread far beyond his city's boundaries. J. Lister Hill, scion of a distinguished Black Belt family, represented Alabama's second district in Congress. Edmund W. Pettus II of Selma, grandson of Alabama's longtime United States Senator and son of a former Speaker of the Alabama House and Pres-ident of the Alabama Senate, served as chairman of the state Dem-ocratic Executive Committee. These men and others like them had just lived through a decade that had left them apprehensive for their positions—and with good reason.

The twenties were hard times in Alabama. Like their forebears of the nineties, North Alabamians were growing restless under a Bourbon-

---

[1] For a fuller account of the events surrounding the Constitutional Convention of 1901, see the author's "The Changing of the Guard in Alabama" (unpublished senior thesis, Princeton University, 1966). See also Malcolm C. McMillan, *Constitutional Development in Alabama: A Study in Politics, the Negro, and Sectionalism* (Chapel Hill, 1955), 233–359.

A word about the geography of Alabama is in order. The Black Belt is a band of fourteen counties across the south-central portion of the state. It is so named because its soil characteristically is rich in humus. Historically it has been a center of political and social conservatism. It is generally allied with four or five counties in the southwestern corner of the state whose social structures resemble those of the Black Belt. North Alabama is a mountainous region of small farms and has historically harbored liberalism and indeed radicalism within its confines. It is allied politically with the Wiregrass region, a group of eleven counties in the southeastern part of the state. The term "North Alabamian" as used in this paper is intended to include residents of the Wiregrass. In the antebellum period the Tennessee Valley constituted a distinct political region, but by the time with which we deal here it differed from the rest of North Alabama in little except geography.

engineered order. Though they might control the governorship, they seldom saw the legislature pass any laws regarded by the Black Belt bloc as radical. If North Alabamians were ever aroused and organized, there was danger that they might force the adoption of a program that would be anathema to the remnants of the Bourbons. The levees of power, however, had been carefully and lovingly constructed at the turn of the century. Only by breaking clear of, or taking over entirely, the Democratic Party and striking out as a self-consciously revolutionary force could North Alabamians hope to disturb the political *status quo*. The remaining Bourbons, aware of this fact, sought constantly to emphasize the necessity for white solidarity and party unity. It was particularly important to prevent the Republican Party from becoming a socially acceptable alternative to Democracy. But any organization that tended to give structure and purpose to North Alabama frustrations was characterized by the Bourbons as dangerous.

At the dawn of the twenties, the Republicans were still regarded as too radical to appeal to any but the most disenchanted voters.[2] Two other groups, however, were tending to weld North Alabamians into an effective political bloc—the Anti-Saloon League and the Ku Klux Klan. The former had been a power in Alabama politics for some time, but the twenties saw it reach such a position that no candidate dared incur its active opposition. The sectional character of the League, and of its ally the Women's Christian Temperance Union, was marked. Wet sentiment had always been strongest in the Black Belt. At the outset of the prohibition crusade, however, there had been considerable sympathy for the effort in some urban centers. The progressive movement had been particularly enamoured of the cause. But once prohibition had become a fact and the progressive movement had been laid to rest, the experiment rapidly lost its urban support. By the twenties, the backbone of the League's strength was in the rural hill counties.[3] Curiously, this narrowing of the League's base seems only to have strengthened it as a political instrument. As its membership took on a homogeneous character, it came to be regarded by its membership as a spokesman for their class. They were thus far more likely than before to support the candidates which it endorsed. Therefore, despite growing repeal sentiment, no admitted wet ventured

[2] There were 30,000 to 40,000 Alabama Republicans in this period, out of a total registration (1930) of 356,627.
[3] See the map contained in A. B. Moore, *History of Alabama* (Tuscaloosa, 1934), 796.

to offer himself for statewide office during the decade. It should be emphasized that this enforced conformity on the prohibition question was largely abstracted from the nominal issue involved. The hill county residents would have regarded a candidate advocating repeal as engaging in a calculated insult to their entire socio-economic group, and would have repudiated him on this basis, quite apart from their sentiments on temperance. And it was to emphasize that they did not hold small farmers in contempt that candidates no longer questioned the wisdom of prohibition. Indeed, the Anti-Saloon League might well have become the political voice of the hill counties had not its scope been so clearly limited to one issue. This fact forced those North Alabamians who were seeking a vehicle for general protest to look elsewhere.

The vehicle to which they turned was the Ku Klux Klan. The rise of the Klan during the twenties was phenomenal. Starting from almost nothing at the beginning of the decade, but building on the political awareness created among North Alabamians by the Anti-Saloon League, the Klan grew rapidly. It offered elaborate ceremonial to take the member's mind off his poverty. It offered specific villains who could be blamed for causing that poverty. And it promised vigorous, positive action to punish those villains and to undo their work. The hardpressed farmers were eager to support any organization that purported to identify their enemies and to take action to foil the anti-farmer conspiracy. Klaverns sprouted all over North Alabama.

The height of the Klan's political success came in the elections of 1926. In the gubernatorial campaign, the incumbent administration of W. W. Brandon gave its support to Lieutenant Governor Charles S. McDowell, Jr., who also received the support of the Bourbon press, led by the Montgomery *Advertiser*. Also in the campaign was A. H. Carmichael, who was regarded as a candidate of the small business, education, and prohibition forces. A. G. Patterson, president of the state public service commission, canvassed as a "pay-as-you-go" highway construction advocate. The final candidate in the race, Colonel Bibb Graves, was distinct in the field for having no support among any important segment of the state press or party leadership. He proclaimed his support of heavy taxation of corporations, improved educational facilities, the end of the convict lease system, and extensive highway construction.[4] Graves' attitude toward corporations,

---

[4]*Ibid.*, 769–770.

the open hostility to him shown in Bourbon circles, and his self-proclaimed friendship for the "common man" attracted to his cause one major voting bloc—the Klan.

In the senatorial race, the Klan endorsed a young Birmingham attorney, Hugo L. Black. Black had served a term as solicitor of Jefferson County before World War I, but since then had done nothing to draw attention to himself, and was practically unknown politically. Some three weeks after Black announced his candidacy, however, the aged incumbent Oscar W. Underwood, a bitter enemy of the Klan, decided to retire without a fight.[5] This decision left John H. Bankhead, Jr., a major corporation lawyer, as Black's principal opponent. Black took his campaign to every hill and hollow in North Alabama, lambasting the "Big Mules" and attacking Al Smith, a likely candidate for the Democratic presidential nomination in 1928.[6] The Klan's Imperial Wizard, Hiram Evans of Georgia, endorsed L. Breckinridge Musgrove, a millionaire industrialist who had given generously to the Klan cause.[7] But there was never any doubt as to whom the state Klan was supporting for the Senate. Klansmen simply could not resist Black's oft-repeated cry, "I am the candidate of the masses!"[8]

It should be noted also that in no race in 1926 was the Klan an open issue.[9] Here, as in the case of prohibition, a direct attack upon the Klan would have been considered by a substantial part of the electorate to be an expression of upper class contempt for "plain people." No candidate dared risk alienating this vote.

When the votes were counted, the extent of the Klan's victory became apparent. It had taken Graves, who had virtually no other organized support, and had made him governor over McDowell, who had a superior organization and great financial resources. It had made the almost completely unknown Black a Senator over three of the most famous names in the state. It had elected the state's attorney general, "a large number of minor officials, a majority of county officials, a number of " congressmen, and about half of the membership of each house of the legislature.[10] The mechanics of this achieve-

[5] John P. Frank, *Mr. Justice Black* (New York, 1949), 39. A rather naive account of the campaign is contained on 39–43.
[6] New York *Times*, Aug. 9, 1926.
[7] *Ibid.*; Frank, *Mr. Justice Black*, 42. This endorsement was made despite the fact that both Black and Evans had been born, five years apart, in the small Alabama town of Ashland, Clay County.
[8] Frank, 42.
[9] Montgomery *Advertiser*, Aug. 21, 1929.
[10] *Ibid.*, May 29, 1929.

ment are extremely important for the understanding of later developments.

In 1915, the Anti-Saloon League had engineered the passage of the so-called double-choice primary law.[11] Prior to the passage of this act, Alabama primaries had been conducted under resolutions adopted by the party executive committee. These resolutions specified that when no candidate for an office received a majority of the votes cast, a runoff primary was to be held.[12] The new law, however, altered this procedure. It provided that the voter be permitted to indicate on the ballot a first and a second choice for each office. In the event that no candidate received a majority of all first-choice votes, the second-choice votes of the two leading candidates were to be added directly to the first-choice, and the candidate with the larger total was to be declared nominated. The Anti-Saloon League hoped that this complicated procedure would aid well-organized minority blocs, and indeed it did.

In the late twenties, the Montgomery *Advertiser* commented: "In Alabama it is hard to tell where the League ends and the Klan begins."[13] Certainly the two organizations spoke for very similar socio-economic groups. As the best-organized pressure groups in the state, they had made the double-choice primary their road to political power. The complicated procedures for casting a double vote deterred many voters from attempting to indicate a second choice. But the Klan and the League carefully instructed their members in the intricacies of the primary ballot. Moreover, when a voter through personal loyalty or family commitment was constrained to cast his first choice for a candidate other than the Klan favorite, he could nevertheless designate the Klan favorite as a second choice. In 1926 a model ballot, with the X's already marked in, was distributed "by the tens of thousands" from Klan headquarters in Birmingham, and many voters followed its recommendations absolutely.[14]

The operation of the double-choice law may be clearly seen in the

---

[11] *Ibid.*, Nov. 12, 1929. For an extremely interesting account of how prohibition forces had snatched control of the 1915 legislature from the Henderson Administration, see *ibid.*, Jan. 28, 1915; "General Law 78," *General Laws of the Legislature of Alabama Passed at the Session of 1915* (Montgomery, 1915), 218–239.

[12] "Resolution of the Alabama Democratic Executive Committee Adopted January 7, 1914," *Alabama Official and Statistical Register, 1915*, 396–398.

[13] Montgomery *Advertiser*, Nov. 13, 1929.

[14] Selma *Times-Journal*, Dec. 29, 1929.

1926 gubernatorial results. In first choice votes, Graves, McDowell, Carmichael, and Patterson received approximately 61,000, 60,000, 54,000, and 47,000 votes respectively. In second-choice votes, however, Graves, with his Klan endorsement, polled 21,978. McDowell received only 7,943. Graves was declared the winner by almost 16,000 votes. About two-thirds of those who participated in the primary, 141,770 voters, did not bother, or were unable, to indicate a second choice, while 40,954 second-choice ballots were voided because they were cast either for Carmichael or for Patterson.[15] It seems likely that a runoff would have resulted in a very different outcome. Graves may perhaps have fallen heir to some portion of Patterson's support, but the greater part of Carmichael's vote would have gone to McDowell. Thus, under a runoff system, Charles S. McDowell would probably have been nominated by the Democrats and elected governor of Alabama in 1926. As it was, Graves was chosen on the basis of the Klan bloc—the one-third or more of the vote that the Klan and the League controlled "in all weathers and under all circumstances."[16] An almost equally convincing case may be made for the nomination of Hugo Black for Senator and Charlie McCall for Attorney General, though each received a somewhat larger percentage of the first-choice vote than did Graves.

The Bourbons were startled and disturbed by the Klan showing in 1926, and they determined to make a strong effort at the 1927 session of the legislature to break the back of the Klan movement by enacting anti-masking legislation and a runoff primary bill.[17] At the same time, the Klan was determined to use its newly acquired legislative strength to enact Governor Graves' legislative program and to pass a so-called "press muzzling bill," designed to amend the libel statute in such a way as to suppress editorial criticism of the Klan. Klan supporters (whom the Bourbon press dubbed the "bedsheet bloc") held a slight majority in each house, but the Bourbons possessed an advantage in their many years of legislative experience and their thorough knowledge of parliamentary rules and procedures.

[15] Figures from *Alabama Official and Statistical Register, 1927*, 362–363.

[16] Montgomery *Advertiser*, Nov. 12, 1929.

[17] The Bourbons, out of touch with movements among the hill county farmers, seem almost universally to have felt that McDowell and Carmichael were the front-runners, and that Graves was lagging badly. (New York *Times*, Aug. 9, 1926; Montgomery *Advertiser*, Aug. 21, 1929).

The Goodwyn-Rogers runoff primary bill slipped through the House in the early days of the session, before the opposition to it had solidified. In the Senate, the bill was referred to the Privileges and Elections Committee, which was controlled by forces inimical to it. Late in the session, John M. Bonner of Wilcox, the leader of the Black Belt forces in the Senate, moved to recall the bill from Privileges and Elections and recommit it to the Judiciary Committee, which was prepared to report it favorably. The Klan and League forces, led by Administration floor leader L. H. Ellis of Shelby, vigorously contested this move. When the vote came, it resulted in a 15 to 15 tie, which was broken by Lieutenant Governor W. C. Davis of Jasper in favor of the Administration.[18] The defeat of the runoff primary bill, as we shall see, played a crucial role in the development of the expulsion movement.

Meanwhile, clever tactics on the part of the Bourbons killed the "press muzzling bill." While Bourbon leader R. Tyler Goodwyn fought a valiant delaying effort in the House, where he was clearly outvoted, his allies in the Senate arranged for that body to adjourn early at its forty-eighth sitting. Administration forces were dismayed to learn later that, under the rules, the Senate was thus precluded from acting on the bill before the end of the session. The anti-masking fight resulted in a compromise. The bill was defeated, but another was passed raising flogging from a misdemeanor to a felony. The rest of Graves' program was enacted. The convict lease system was abolished. A two and one-half per cent gross business tax was placed on all public utilities and the corporation franchise tax was doubled.

The Montgomery *Advertiser,* a Bourbon organ, decried the anti-corporation spirit of the Legislature.[19] When the revenue bill was passed, it commented that "the most radical legislature since 1907 has fallen upon the industries and business of Alabama," and concluded bitterly that a good portion of the new money would go "to make the mothers of countless office-hungry politicians exclaim: 'I'm glad I raised my boy to be a Klansman!' "[20] Actually the funds were put to good use. Expenditures for highways and for public education were vastly increased.[21]

---

[18]*Journal of the Senate of the State of Alabama, Session of 1927,* 1708; Montgomery *Advertiser,* Aug. 22, 1929.

[19]Montgomery *Advertiser,* July 13, 1927.

[20]*Ibid.,* July 15, 1927.

[21]Summaries of the session are in the Montgomery *Advertiser,* Sept. 5, 1927, the New York *Times,* Sept. 11, 1927, and in Moore, *History of Alabama* (1934 edition), 771–776.

We cannot leave the legislature of 1927 without pointing out how archetypical its session was of all those held under the 1901 Compromise System. Even in their hour of greatest triumph, holding virtually every executive office and a majority in the legislature, the forces of North Alabama were compelled at every turn to negotiate with and often to yield to the Bourbons, still secure in the legislative fastnesses that remained of their once total power. Always the legislature placed a check on the reformist impulses of the "liberal" governors. Always the governors goaded the legislature into more action than it would otherwise have taken. Inexorably, but almost imperceptibly, Alabama government moved toward a more liberal position. If North Alabama wished to effect any substantial reforms in a brief period of time, it would have to break out of and destroy this compromise system. It could not be content with primary victories, for control of the executive was not enough. And it seemed that in order to control the legislative branch, North Alabama would have to leave the Democratic Party.

While the "progressive" Klan bloc spent its strength during the long summer months of 1927 battering against immovable Black Belt boulders, Alabama slipped closer to anarchy. In the 1926 election the Klan captured a majority of county offices. And, as Alabama Grand Dragon James Esdale revealed, Governor Graves "made all of his appointments by and through the Klan."[22] As a result, something like a reign of terror gripped some rural sections of the state. For instance, in the Wiregrass county of Crenshaw law enforcement largely ceased to function.[23] Floggings and lawlessness over the state caused the Bourbon press to attack the Klan's power. As usual, the Montgomery *Advertiser* was in the vanguard of this movement.

In late June, Jeff Calloway, a young orphan, was severely flogged in the hill country of Blount County. On July 3, editor Grover C. Hall of the Montgomery *Advertiser* wrote the first of a series of editorials with which he won the Pulitzer Prize. Entitled "The Glove of the Beast—Will the State Pick It Up?", it was typical of Hall's poetic style of writing and of the power of his imagery. Throughout the summer and fall the editor of the *Advertiser* kept up his attacks on the Klan. He was joined by editors of other newspapers, notably those of the Selma *Times-Journal*, the Dothan *Eagle* (whose editor was

[22] Montgomery *Advertiser*, May 28, 1929.
[23] Moore, *History of Alabama* (1934 edition), 776.

Grover Hall's nephew), the Birmingham *News,* and the Columbus *Enquirer-Sun.* Although published in Georgia, the latter had a substantial circulation in east Alabama. So much pressure was placed on the Klan that by the end of 1927, it had almost ceased to use flogging as a method of intimidation.

The chief result of the vigorous attacks launched by the Bourbon press was to convince many North Alabamians that the Klan was indeed a dangerous organization. The recruiting power of the Klan had so little to do with its ideology and so much to do with politics in this period that it was difficult for many hill county residents to believe that the organization was as evil as the Bourbons declared. The power of the Klan was concentrated in a limited area, and one does not usually suspect one's friends and neighbors of being vicious thugs. The farmers had been told that Catholics, Jews, and other groups were responsible for the economic and social distress of North Alabama. Violence represented primarily a protest against that distress. The floggings were abandoned chiefly because they did not appear to be ameliorating conditions in the section and because, thanks to the press campaign, they were alienating non-Klansmen who had formerly sympathized with the organization's political efforts. The *Wiregrass Farmer* of Headland, a journal sympathetic to the group named in its title, warned, "If the Klan is to survive as a political organization in Alabama, it will have to . . . repudiate floggings and intimidations as a Klan principle."[24]

The abandonment of violent means of protest did not mean, however, that North Alabamians abandoned their hopes of using the Klan in order to effect political and social reforms. Indeed, 1928 saw the Klan and its ally the Anti-Saloon League mount a major political effort, led by the state's senior United States Senator, J. Thomas Heflin, a dedicated Klansman. J. Thomas Heflin came from a notable hill county family. Robert S. Heflin, his uncle, had been a Scalawag and had served a term in Congress from 1869 to 1871.[25] His father, Dr. Wilson L. Heflin, was a country doctor in Randolph County. He was the only doctor in that section of the state "equipped for performing surgical operations."[26] Doctor Heflin had eight sons. One of these, John Heflin, a farmer, represented Randolph County in the Constitutional

[24] *Wiregrass Farmer,* quoted in Montgomery *Advertiser,* Sept. 4, 1927.
[25] Thomas McA. Owen, *Dictionary of Alabama Biography,* III, 783–784.
[26] Moore, *History of Alabama and Her People* (Chicago, 1927), III, 443.

Convention of 1901. Another son, Harrington Heflin, was for many years Jefferson County solicitor, but in 1914 was defeated in a bid for re-election by Hugo Black. After 1915 Harrington served as a circuit judge.[27] J. Thomas Heflin, affectionately known as "Tom," was elected mayor of Lafayette, Alabama in 1893. He was state representative from his adopted county of Chambers from 1896 to 1900, and in 1901 he represented Chambers in the Constitutional Convention. From 1902 to 1904 he was secretary of state, and for the next sixteen years was a congressman.[28] In 1920 he was elected to replace the deceased Senator John H. Bankhead, Sr.

Tom Heflin was an extremely large man who insisted upon wearing wide-brimmed black hats, cream-colored frock-tailed coats, ornate vests, and string ties. His theatrical qualities were greatly appreciated by his constituents. A New York *Times* correspondent thus described him in debate with another senator: "Mr. Heflin raved. His face was a bright red and he swung his great body to and fro, coughing as he clinched his hands and swung one fist into the other. At times the two Senators shouted at the same time, waving their hands at each other." When Heflin said that the press gallery was filled with "squirrel headed" people, his opponent invited him to "compare their heads with his own."[29]

Heflin gained a reputation at the 1901 Constitutional Convention as a leader of the racist forces, and indeed his racism was of the most virulent sort. During the 1930 campaign, he published a circular detailing his congressional record, in which he wrote that "the failure to have separate street cars for whites and Negroes in Washington caused him to have to inflict severe punishment upon a drunken Negro who had insulted a white woman on the car." National publicity had followed the incident in which he shot a Negro on the street car in Washington and announced to the public that he carried a pistol to protect himself from his enemies.[30]

Other than on racial policy, however, Heflin's record was far from consistent. His opponents impugned his sincerity. The *Advertiser* commented:

[27] *Ibid.*
[28] Owen, *Dictionary,* III, 783.
[29] New York *Times,* Feb. 21, 1929.
[30] "By Their Fruits Ye Shall Know Them," 1930 campaign circular in private possession; see also John S. Ezell, *The South Since 1865* (New York, 1963), 377.

If 51 per cent of the voters of Alabama were Catholic, the Pope couldn't
have alarmed Tom in a thousand years—on the contrary, Tom would have
been the leader of the anti-Klan forces of the State and probably would
have advocated the nomination of Smith. It is only in very recent years,
when Tom found himself in need of an issue, that he discovered the Pope,
in regard to whom he had been silent for 20 years before. When Bryan was
powerful in Alabama, Tom was a noisy Bryanite; in the days of Underwood's
ascendancy, Tom was hot for him. He never turned on W. P. G. Harding
until the chairman of the Federal Reserve Board became unpopular and
seemed to have in himself the makings of a very good devil, in 1920 when
economic distress in the South created the need for a devil. Tom never
took any serious risks with prohibition. In 1909, when he, like a number of
other politicians thought it would be ratified, Tom voted for the State
prohibition amendment. It was beaten. Nine years later, when few thought
it would be ratified, Tom voted and spoke against submission and ratification of the Eighteenth Amendment. It was ratified, and soon after Tom
became so hot for National prohibition that many supposed he had been
for it ever since Bishop Cannon was a boy. A few years ago Tom was in
demand as a Fourth of July speaker under the auspices of the Knights of
Columbus. Today Tom is teaching young Americans that the Knights of
Columbus can have no possible interest in the Fourth of July.[31]

This summary of Heflin's intellectual evolution is factually accurate,
but we cannot assume that his frequent conversions were altogether
self-serving. Heflin may merely have been a son of North Alabama,
whose opinions followed, and were formed under the same pressures
as, those of his constituents. His fervent embrace of prohibition, for
instance, coincides with the rise of the Anti-Saloon League as a political
spokesman of the hill county farmer. At any rate, by the end of the
twenties Heflin was firmly identified in the public mind with prohibition, anti-Catholicism and, at least in some intellectual circles, with
political buffoonery.

During his early career in Congress Heflin was ignored or granted
minimal toleration by the Bourbon group. He talked a great deal but,
not having the respect of his fellow legislators, he was rendered very
nearly impotent in terms of actual accomplishment. Hence his enemies
considered him harmless. Grover C. Hall, who strongly supported the
Goodwyn-Rogers runoff bill, was merely amused when Heflin issued a
statement opposing the legislation.[32] On another occasion, the paper

---

[31] Montgomery *Advertiser*, Apr. 27, 1929.
[32] *Ibid.*, July 7, 1927.

spoke of "the slender talents and negligible influence of this utterly commonplace man," and concluded patronizingly, "We do not know whether Tom is out of his head, or whether he is merely a simpleton. He is one or the other."[33]

A crisis in Heflin's senatorial career was reached on January 19, 1928. After one of Heflin's attacks on Catholicism, Senator Joseph T. Robinson of Arkansas, the minority leader, rose to reply. Robinson was a prohibitionist and an opponent of Smith. Evidently he hoped that his reaffirmation of the virtues of religious toleration would free his forces from the taint of Heflinism. Rather than accepting Robinson's rather mild rebuke, however, Heflin shouted that if the Arkansan ever came to Alabama, he would be tarred and feathered. He demanded that Robinson resign as minority leader. Robinson accepted the challenge and called a caucus for the following day to consider the matter.[34] The meeting of the caucus found Heflin utterly deserted by his brethren. The vote went against him by 33 to 1. Hugo Black, the junior senator from Alabama, abstained from voting.[35]

The encounter with Robinson marked something of a turning-point in the Bourbon attitude toward Heflin. He no longer was a harmless nuisance. He was now a menace to the Democracy. Shocked at Heflin's attack on a fellow Democrat, a fellow Southerner, and a man greatly admired throughout the section, the Alabama press was nearly unanimous in its condemnation of the Alabamian. Unlimbering the prose style for which it was famous, the *Advertiser* commented:

> What a callous and wretched demagogue Heflin is! What a disgrace to a proud State that its senior Senator should invite the Democratic leader of the Senate to come to Alabama to be 'tarred and feathered'! How humiliating and depressing a thing it is that such a man should be the keeper of Alabama's good name abroad! O, that the heart and soul of this people had a voice in the United States Senate![36]

Meanwhile, Montgomery's Mayor Gunter invited Robinson to speak there as the city's guest and the Mobile City Council adopted a resolution censuring Heflin.[37]

[33] *Ibid.*, Aug. 19, 1927.
[34] New York *Times*, Jan. 19, 1928.
[35] *Ibid.*, Jan. 20, 1928. The lone dissenter was Park Trammell of Florida.
[36] Montgomery *Advertiser*, Jan. 19, 1928. For other derogatory comment, see Mobile *Register*, Decatur *Daily*, Selma *Times-Journal*, and Dothan *Eagle* of same date.
[37] New York *Times*, Jan. 21, 1928.

Alabamians were united in their opposition to Al Smith. The New Yorker received but one of Alabama's votes at the Houston convention.[38] But for the Bourbons the maintenance of party regularity was of prime importance, regardless of the identity of the nominee. As we have seen, as long as North Alabama's protest was confined within the bounds of the political *status quo,* the Bourbon position was secure. Only when protest spilled over the party levees and challenged the foundations of the system were the remnants of Bourbon power in danger. Senator Heflin's attack on the leader of Senate Democrats bespoke a dangerous tendency on his part to put principle above party. It was deeply disturbing that a Democratic caucus had chastened an Alabamian for lack of deference to party authority. And Heflin's course in succeeding months fulfilled the Bourbons' worst fears. If Heflin were able to take his North Alabama constituency out of the party, the compromise of 1901 was in real danger.

Immediately after Smith's nomination, Heflin announced himself "shocked and dismayed," and predicted that Smith would lose.[39] This was not the sort of statement that a man contemplating acquiescence in the party's decision would be likely to make. On July 4 State Chairman Edmund Pettus, attempting to forestall a bolt, warned that the Democratic Executive Committee had the power to bar the heterodox from the party's primaries.[40] In the weeks immediately following, Heflin remained silent—so silent, in fact, that by September 9 the New York *Times* predicted that Heflin might yet "slide into the Smith camp, or at least the Alabama end of it." On September 21, in an effort to force the issue, former Governor William W. Brandon invited Heflin to speak in behalf of the Democratic ticket. He refused.[41]

On September 22, the State Democratic Executive Committee convened in Birmingham to organize for the coming campaign. Chairman Pettus read a telegram from the Lee County Committee stating that Heflin had met with Republican strategists in Opelika on the twentieth and had announced that he would make an anti-Smith speech on the twenty-fifth. The wire concluded, "He must not

[38] The one vote for Smith was that of W. S. Childers, chairman of the Walker County Democratic Committee. The bulk of the state's vote was divided about equally between Walter F. George and Cordell Hull.
[39] New York *Times,* June 29 and 30, 1928.
[40] *Ibid.,* July 5, 1928.
[41] *Ibid.,* Sept. 22, 1928.

longer be tolerated."[42] Great excitement was generated by this revelation. A motion was carried to dismiss from the Committee two
members, Hugh Locke of Birmingham and Hamp Draper of Wetumpka, who were actively campaigning for Hoover.

The Democratic leadership was greatly disturbed by the fact that
"white men and women" were "preaching the Republican doctrine," thus making the Republican Party a respectable opposition
force in Alabama. With a United States Senator supporting a Republican, and any number of his followers thus having their habit of
obedience to party decisions shattered, the *status quo* was in grave
jeopardy. Chairman Pettus made it clear that opposition to Al
Smith was not the sin involved. The sin was failing to recognize the
outcome of an intraparty struggle as binding on all concerned.[43]
Appealing beyond the established institutional limits of the party
directly to the voters was a threat to the entire system.

The Committee invited the state's congressional delegation, including Heflin, to serve upon the state campaign committee. This
action finally induced Heflin to break his silence. On September 24, in
an open letter to Chairman Pettus, he declined the offer and attacked Smith and John J. Raskob, Democratic national campaign
manager.[44] The campaign grew increasingly heated as frightened Bourbons fought back. Montgomery's Mayor Gunter, whose powerful machine was an old and bitter enemy of Heflin, denied the Senator the
use of the city auditorium. When Heflin came to the capital anyway,
Governor Graves had to dispatch a contingent of the state police
to protect him.[45] On October 26, the state campaign committee
adopted a resolution denouncing him.[46] Finally, on October 30, Heflin
took the step for which everyone had been waiting. Addressing a
Dothan crowd, he declared, "I will vote against Al Smith, so help me
God!"[47] The next week an Anniston audience pelted him with
eggs.[48]

When the votes were counted, Smith won over Hoover by a vote

---

[42] Quoted in "Minutes of the Meeting of the Alabama Democratic Executive
Committee, September 22, 1928," manuscript in Alabama Department of Archives and
History, Montgomery.

[43] *Ibid.*

[44] New York *Times,* Sept. 25, 1928.

[45] *Ibid.,* Sept. 20, 1928.

[46] *Ibid.,* Oct. 26, 1928.

[47] *Ibid.,* Oct. 31, 1928.

[48] *Ibid.,* Nov. 6, 1928.

of 127,796 to 120,725.[49] Many observers felt that only manipulation of the returns accounted for the Democratic victory. The sectional character of the vote was marked; the hill counties provided the backbone of Hoover's support and the Black Belt went solidly for Smith.[50] The bolt was no longer an abstract fear, but a reality. It now seemed that only canny leadership and vigorous action could keep the Bourbons in control of the Democratic party. Bourbon Democracy's one last hope was the expulsion movement. On November 25, it was launched.

The first public suggestion of the expulsion movement came from Geneva County businessman Edward C. Boswell, who had recently headed the losing effort to keep his county in the Democratic column. In a telegram to each member of the State Executive Committee, he lashed out at the bolters and urged that they be barred from the 1930 primary.[51] The Bourbon leadership, however, did not so quickly endorse this course of action.

If the Goodwyn-Rogers runoff bill could yet be passed, there would be little need to take such radical action as expulsion. Heflin and the Klan-backed gubernatorial candidate Hugh Locke would be defeated in a primary in which the Klan's bloc vote would not be sufficient to ensure nomination. Without a public office, these officials would no longer be in a strong position to lead a political revolt. Hope for the runoff was stimulated by the likelihood that Governor Graves would soon be forced to call a special session of the legislature in order to obtain additional appropriations for the highway program. Graves was aware of the Bourbon plans, however, and was determined to confine any special session to the highway question. In order to control a rebellious House he depended on its Speaker, J. Lee Long. Long had in the past been lukewarm at best in his support of the Administration. But Graves hoped to effect a *rapprochement* with him. In late January the governor summoned Long to Montgomery to discuss the situation. There, on February 2, Long suffered a heart attack and died. Without Long's gavel in the House, a special session was too risky. The new speaker was likely to be Alf Tunstall of Hale, an old legislative warhorse who in 1927 had been unable to control the

[49] *Alabama Official and Statistical Register, 1931*, 511–512.
[50] See V. O. Key, *Southern Politics in State and Nation* (New York, 1949), 324–325.
[51] New York *Times*, Nov. 26, 1928.

House.[52] In addition, the number of vacancies that had occurred in the legislature, five in the Senate alone, would most likely be filled by nomination by the State Democratic Committee. Were five senators hostile to the Administration to be chosen, it would break Graves' hold over that body. By February 14, Graves had decided against a special session.[53]

At this point a split developed within the Bourbon group as to the proper course to follow. One group, typified by Hugh S. D. Mallory, Jr., of Selma, felt that the enactment of runoff legislation would be the only effective way to deal with bolters. They desired to continue agitation for a special session. Mallory and other members of this group were closely identified with the industrial forces in the state.[54] Their position was best expressed by Birmingham Congressman George Huddleston in his reaction to the Boswell telegram. "If we bar the anti-Smith Democrats from the next primary, it may easily transpire that we will raise up a respectable white opposition party that will plague the Democrats permanently," he said.[55] The other Bourbon group, led by Black Belters and typified by S. H. Dent of Eufaula, wanted to expel the bolters, feeling that expulsion, as an example of swift retribution for rebellion, would prevent future attempts to leave the party.

In mid-April, Mallory dispatched a telegram to Mrs. Mabel Jones West, president of the Alabama Women's Democratic Club and of the Alabama Woman's League for White Supremacy, vigorously attacking the double-choice primary and demanding the institution of runoffs.[56] Some days later Dent replied in a letter to the *Advertiser*. He joined in deploring the double-choice primary, but maintained that Graves would never allow a special session to consider its repeal, as he "was largely responsible for the present primary law, if indeed he was not its author." With the legislature thus precluded from acting, the task of preserving the party devolved upon the Committee. Expulsion was the only answer.[57]

Dent's letter also revealed that a movement was afoot to have

[52] Montgomery *Advertiser*, Feb. 9, 1929; *ibid.*, Sept. 5, 1927.
[53] *Ibid.*, Feb. 17, 1929; Demopolis *Times*, Feb. 14, 1929.
[54] Moore, *History of Alabama* (1927 edition), II, 8.
[55] New York *Times*, Nov. 26, 1928.
[56] Montgomery *Advertiser*, Apr. 15, 1929.
[57] *Ibid.*, Apr. 19, 1929.

all anti-Klan forces unite on a single candidate in the senatorial and gubernatorial contests. If such an alliance were achieved, of course, the disadvantages of the double-choice primary would be eliminated. But Dent disparaged the movement's chances for success, calling it "impractical." "There is no authority to enforce it and no machinery to execute it," he concluded.[58] The following week the Woman's White Supremacy League went on record as repudiating "Heflin as our representative in any sense" and deploring "his foolish and fanatical assaults upon those of our fellow citizens who are members of the Roman Catholic Church."[59]

While the discussions as to the best course to pursue continued, the Bourbon press set out to discredit Heflin in the eyes of his farmer constituency. While Congress was in extraordinary session considering farm relief legislation in 1929, Senator Heflin occupied fully half of its time attempting to induce the Senate to adopt a resolution deploring a mob attack on him at Brockton, Massachusetts. Commented the *Advertiser*, "What does he care about the progress of the farm bill? His thoughts are occupied with something infinitely more important than the welfare of the farmers. He is thinking about himself . . . For the simple fact is that Senator Heflin, Democrat, Alabama, considers himself far more important than any farmer, or all the farmers put together."[60]

On May 10, the *Advertiser* announced the decision of the first two Committee members to commit themselves publicly. They were for expulsion. But the Mallory faction was far from convinced. On July 7, Mallory, evidently still hoping to force a special session, released a statement flatly opposing expulsion. On July 10, Dent replied with a letter deploring minority rule by organized blocs, and demanding expulsion of all bolters. On July 12, the *Advertiser* broke its long silence on the issue with an editorial seeking to effect a compromise among its warring children. It suggested that all bolters be barred from becoming candidates in the party primary, but that anyone who pledged to support its choices be permitted to vote in it.[61]

The summer was also an active one for the anti-expulsion forces. Congressmen and county officeholders put substantial pressure on the

[58] *Ibid.*
[59] *Ibid.*, Apr. 27, 1929.
[60] *Ibid.*, May 4, 1929.
[61] *Ibid.*, July 7, 10, and 12, 1929.

Committee members. Their position was a difficult one. Whereas over the state as a whole anti-Klan forces had a majority, in several congressional districts and many counties supporters of the bolters held dominance. If the Democrats expelled the bolters, their supporters might well wreak vengeance on the local party representatives at the general election.[62] Frightened by the prospect of alienating a group that was a majority in many counties and the largest single voting bloc in many more, county officeholders succeeded in convincing a number of committeemen of the rationality of their fears. By August 30 the *Advertiser*'s political columnist, Atticus Mullin, was forced to acknowledge the effectiveness of these efforts. Whereas in May thirty-one committeemen had been for expulsion, he wrote, at this time only twelve to fourteen could be counted on.[63]

This admission marked the low ebb of the expulsionists' fortunes. The *Advertiser* feared that the state, after all, was in for another Heflin campaign. "The serious public questions of the hour must be forgotten in the storm and fury that the Heflin jehad will raise . . . The drill sergeants of organized hatred and fear are to march again in Alabama. Whispering couriers are to skulk from post to post by night and scatter their poison."[64] Mullin's revelation served to rally Bourbon leaders to action and by September 10, Mullin reported hopefully that "supporters of the move [expulsion] say that there has been a noticeable stiffening of Democratic backs, so far as the state committee is concerned, in the last ten days." At the same time he suggested the compromise that was eventually to turn the tide. Admitting that "ninety-five percent" of the state's county officials were opposed to expulsion, he suggested that the State Committee's bar apply only to statewide races, and that the setting of qualifications for local races be left to the party's county committees.[65] During the coming days Mullin conducted a vigorous campaign in an attempt to alter public sentiment on the issue. Supporting him editorially, the *Advertiser* called the readmission of the bolters as candidates "unthinkable."[66]

[62] Cf. speech of J. C. Inzer, "Minutes of the Meeting of the Alabama Democratic Executive Committee, December 16, 1929," manuscript in Alabama Department of Archives and History, Montgomery.
[63] Montgomery *Advertiser*, Aug. 30, 1929.
[64] *Ibid.*, Aug. 31, 1929.
[65] *Ibid.*, Sept. 10, 1929.
[66] *Ibid.*, Sept. 13, 1929.

Meanwhile, the effort received support on September 4, when Governor Graves announced that there definitely would be no special session of the legislature. With the last hope of removing the mechanics of Klan control through legislation thus eliminated, almost all of the Bourbons began to accept the expulsion movement as the only avenue left open for dealing effectively with the bolters' challenge. In addition, Mullin's compromise severely undercut the argument of the county officials, for it would have the effect of placing the contest strictly on a pro-Heflin or anti-Heflin basis. Local personalities would not be drawn into the controversy, and local sentiment was consequently not so likely to be stirred up.

As a result of these factors, Mullin was able to report, on September 15, that the crisis had passed. There had been, he said, "a big change of heart" within the Committee in "the last week."[67] The tide was now running in favor of the expulsionists. Even so, as a Heflin ally reported to him, the situation still remained fluid.[68]

On October 29 the Selma *Times-Journal* made one final effort to rally all of the anti-Klan forces behind the gubernatorial candidacy of W. C. Davis. But Davis' strong support from labor[69] made him unacceptable in some Bourbon circles. With the failure of this movement, the *Times-Journal* joined the expulsionist bandwagon and was soon saying that the existence of the double-choice primary in Alabama had compelled the crusade.[70]

By November the battle lines were clearly drawn. The Bourbons had decided to risk everything on their belief that expulsion would crush the North Alabama revolt. Once this commitment by the Bourbon forces had been made, Governor Graves could no longer hold aloof from the fray. He delegated his chief political lieutenant, Gaston Scott, to organize the anti-expulsionist forces and he himself went to Washington to consult with Senators Black and Heflin.[71] While Scott traveled the state rounding up support for the Administration position, Klan leaders from all of northeast Alabama gathered in Birmingham to plot strategy with Hugh Locke.[72] On November 12 Senator Black issued a statement pleading for party harmony and

[67] *Ibid.*, Sept. 15, 1929.
[68] Ben F. Ray to Heflin, Sept. 16, 1929, J. Thomas Heflin Papers, University of Alabama Library, Tuscaloosa.
[69] Montgomery *Advertiser*, Aug. 21, 1929.
[70] Selma *Times-Journal*, Nov. 17, 1929.
[71] Montgomery *Advertiser*, Nov. 2, 1929.
[72] *Ibid.*, Nov. 7, 1929.

opposing expulsion. The *Advertiser* replied that the "harmony boys" "know that with their minority-rule primary law, with numerous candidates for each office, they stand a good chance of electing their ticket in the next Democratic primary—provided the bars are kept down . . . Klan politicians and Anti-Saloon League politicians . . . are now exerting themselves to 'keep the bars down' not because they love real party harmony, but because they love . . . the Klan and the Anti-Saloon League." The paper called the situation in Alabama an example "of what can be done by well-organized, shrewdly led minorities that know what they want . . . Unless [the] majority finds some way to center on its own ticket in 1930, it is doubtful whether they can free themselves from this . . . minority gag rule."[73]

The leaders of the expulsionist forces within the Committee were Chairman Pettus; Cyrus Brown of Montgomery, the political arm of the powerful Gunter organization; and Thomas J. Judge III, a Birmingham lawyer, former state legislator, and grandson of a prominent antebellum jurist.[74] One of the problems they faced was that many politicians who faced election in 1930, fearing to anger any substantial voting bloc, remained neutral in the fight.[75] Indeed, John Bankhead, Jr., Heflin's only announced opponent, actively opposed expulsion, believing that Heflin would be easier to beat in a primary.[76] However, toward the end of November Bankhead was induced to release those committeemen pledged to him, to vote as they chose on expulsion.[77]

Having achieved this major breakthrough, the expulsionists arranged a caucus in Birmingham for Thanksgiving Day, just before the football game between the University of Alabama and the University of Georgia. A count revealed that twenty-six of the fifty committee members were likely to vote for expulsion. Although a decision as to when to call the State Committee together for a vote on expulsion could not be made at the Birmingham meeting, it was later decided that the Committee would meet in Montgomery on December 16, 1929.[78]

[73] *Ibid.,* Nov. 12 and 13, 1929.

[74] Ray to Heflin, Nov. 12, 1929, Heflin Papers.

[75] Montgomery *Advertiser,* Nov. 17, 1929.

[76] V. J. Dooley, "United States Senator James Thomas Heflin and the Democratic Party Revolt in Alabama, 1930" (unpublished M.A. thesis, Auburn University, 1965), 34.

[77] Montgomery *Advertiser,* Nov. 27, 1929.

[78] *Ibid.,* Dec. 4, 1929; Ray to Heflin, Nov. 30, 1929, Heflin Papers. Alabama lost the game, 12–0.

It being now obvious that Pettus had the votes, the opposition began frantic last-minute maneuvers. On November 22 Heflin had written an admirer that the "situation is fine in Alabama. The masses are for me."[79] After Pettus' announcement, however, Heflin's forces tried to cut loose from their erstwhile ally Hugh Locke. A movement was launched to have the Committee bar Locke but not Heflin, since Locke had actually voted for Hoover, whereas Heflin had merely refrained from voting.[80] On December 11, the Montgomery *Advertiser* carried an editorial condemning this plan. On that same day, Judge Harrington Heflin wrote to his brother that the Committee's action now seemed certain. It would endorse expulsion.[81]

The day before the Committee was to meet, the anti-expulsionists played their last cards. Gaston Scott released a letter from W. L. Lee of Dothan, a bolter, promising to run for governor if the bars were not put up. Thus, Scott argued, the Klan vote would be split between Locke and Lee, and its power as a bloc would be destroyed. The argument was so clearly one of desperation that it was received with a laugh by the expulsionists.[82] A different reaction greeted a telegram from Democratic National Chairman Jouett Shouse opposing expulsion.[83] His interference in local politics merely provoked resentment.

The Committee meeting went as expected. Committeeman Seybourn A. Lynne introduced the resolution, which included both sections of the *Advertiser*'s compromise. It excluded from candidacy in statewide races all persons who had either voted for Hoover or campaigned actively against Smith. But it welcomed back as voters bolters of all stripes, provided that they pledged to support in November the nominees of the August primary. And it left to the discretion of the county committees the qualifications for local office.[84] Lynne told the Committee, "Gentlemen, if we are to have a Democratic party, we must play the game . . . If we are to have an organization, we must be willing to bow our heads when the majority is against our cause." John D. McQueen thundered, "Democrats

---

[79] Heflin to L. Fitzpatrick, Nov. 22, 1929, Heflin Papers.
[80] Emmett P. Smith to Heflin, J. Johnston Moore to Heflin, Dec. 4, 1929, Heflin Papers.
[81] Harrington P. Heflin to Heflin, Dec. 11, 1929, Heflin Papers.
[82] Montgomery *Advertiser*, Dec. 16, 1929.
[83] *Ibid.*
[84] "Minutes, December 16, 1929." Dooley reports (page 47) that thirty-three counties barred bolters, twenty-eight did not, and that the action of six is unknown.

must know that the rules of the Party mean something. They must know that when a primary election is legally called and legally held, that those men [nominated] of right are entitled to the support of Democrats." McQueen placed emphasis upon observing the results of primaries, when in theory what was at issue was the outcome of a presidential nominating convention. In this statement he revealed the true source of Bourbon fears.

Arthur F. Fite, speaking against expulsion, said that the bolt of 1928 "was not a revolt against the Democratic Party; it was a revolt against one man."[85] He pled with the Committee not to turn its back on the bolters of 1928, some of whom were good and loyal Democrats in 1896, when other Alabamians bolted against William Jennings Bryan in order to follow the gold standard banner of Palmer and Buckner.

The expulsion resolution was adopted 27 to 21. A correspondent for the New York *Times* analyzed the vote as follows: "When the roll-call came on the resolution . . ., it became apparent that the central section of Alabama was opposing the bolters almost to a man. All the five committee members from the Sixth District voted to bar the men who supported Hoover. It was this district which was principally responsible for the 7000 majority given Smith in 1928. In the Eighth District, which was carried by the Hoover supporters, four of the five committee members voted not to read Heflin and Locke out of the party."[86] Indeed, only one Black Belter—Henry McDaniel of Marengo —voted against expulsion.

The campaign of 1930 is beyond the scope of the present inquiry. The post-expulsion situation was well summarized by the Thomasville *Times:* "If Alabama had not had its crazy election law, the bolters would never have been barred from becoming candidates . . . The bolters are united. They have concentrated on one man for each office, knowing that the bolter vote would elect them in a field of three or four. But their hopes have been shattered and now they must fight it out against one man, picked from the ranks of the loyal Democrats."[87] Heflin and Locke were barred from running in the Democratic primary. They ran as independents in the general election and

---

[85] *Ibid.*
[86] New York *Times,* Dec. 17, 1929.
[87] Quoted in Selma *Times-Journal,* Dec. 21, 1929.

received enough votes to indicate that they would have been nominated against a field of candidates under the double-vote primary
law. In the general election, their opposition concentrated on the
Democratic nominees and both Klansmen went down to defeat.

It is too much to maintain that the expulsion of their leaders from
the primary crushed the Klan movement. The Klan had already been
dead for some years in surrounding states.[88] Only the unique function
that the Klan was serving in Alabama had kept it vital there. It had
been losing members ever since its defeat in the presidential election
of 1928 and to some extent even before that date.[89] In addition, the
advent of the Depression of 1929 played a role in dissipating political
protest. There seems to be a point beyond which discontent, such as
characterized Alabama in the twenties, is converted into despair.
And the plight of Alabama in the early thirties was nothing if not
desperate. Alabamians turned in greater numbers toward Washington
and national politics for deliverance. The "New Deal" came with
Franklin D. Roosevelt in 1932, opening new avenues of approach to
some old problems.

Nevertheless, at least as important as these factors in suppressing
the Democratic revolt was the nature of the political structure in
Alabama, and the determination of the Bourbons, as proven by the
expulsion movement, to enforce the limits of that structure. Alabama had experienced hill county political revolts before—the Greenbackers in the seventies and the Populists in the nineties. The
Populist Revolt was crushed by fraud and manipulation of the then
existing political structure. The Klan movement, which was in Alabama essentially a recrudescence of Populism, was dealt with far more
effectively, thanks to the political structure that had grown out of
the Constitution of 1901. Only by outright repudiation of the system
could North Alabama have achieved its political goals. The demonstration that the Bourbons could still effectively discipline protest-
ers who transgressed the borders of the *status quo* ended, for the
present, all North Alabama ambitions in that direction. It seemed
to North Alabamians that revolt was unnecessary and inexpedient if
the opposition to Bourbonism could win in the primary anyway. This
was exactly the misconception that the Bourbons wanted to perpet-

[88] Cf. Charles C. Alexander, *The Ku Klux Klan in the Southwest* (Lexington, Ky., 1965),
passim, especially p. 209.
[89] Montgomery *Advertiser*, May 28 and July 22, 1929.

uate. And it was to make sure that this myth was accepted in the future that Tom Heflin was expelled from the Democratic primary in 1930.

Thus, in 1935, Bibb Graves, a Klansman and progressive, who stayed within the party in 1928, became Alabama's first governor since the Constitution of 1901 to be elected to a second term. And Hugo Black, who got overwhelming Klan support in 1926 but remained a loyal Democrat in the crisis of 1928, was re-elected to the United States Senate in 1932.

The pattern remained fixed. A progressive under the system that had evolved out of the 1901 structure could win the governorship, but the Bourbons prevented the reapportionment of the legislature. With their power in that body and in the party councils, they stood ready to discipline bolters who threatened their control.

The Great Depression

WAYNE FLYNT

Spindle, Mine, and Mule:
The Poor White Experience in Post-Civil War Alabama

The April 1980 meeting of the Alabama Historical Association began the same day as the abortive raid to rescue American hostages in Iran. That afternoon, television station WSFA in Montgomery frequently interrupted its regular programming, not so much to give the latest news from the Middle East, as to assure its viewing audience that the special program on country music star Hank Williams, originally scheduled for that evening, would be shown at a different time because of the international crisis.

The almost cultic interest in Hank Williams is one of the few examples of an Alabama poor white reaching the status of celebrity. It is entirely appropriate that one of the folk heroes of poor and lower middle-class Alabamians is barely known beyond his own kind. Among people who never heard of William Rufus King, John Tyler Morgan, or B. B. Comer, Hank Williams's memory is revered.

The semi-literate Williams grew to manhood amid the grinding poverty of central Alabama. Later, he forged his fame, not with pen or from podium, but with a guitar. In Nashville they called him the "Hillbilly Shakespeare." To anyone familiar with the terrain around Georgiana, it would be difficult to determine whether the geographical or literary allusion is more exaggerated. I prefer a different designation of him—"father of the white man's blues"—because he wrote his music for the people I want to describe.

This Presidential Address was read at the meeting of the Alabama Historical Association in Tuscaloosa, April 25, 1981. It was published in *The Alabama Review*, XXXIV (October 1981).

Among the potential Alabama audience for that April television program, one of every four individuals and one of five families ranked at or below the official poverty line.[1] Although 47 percent of all black Alabama families were poor compared to only 13.6 of white, there were actually more poor whites in the state than blacks (93,614 whites, 86,821 blacks). Of the poor whites who headed families, 59 percent had only elementary schooling; the median education was 8.2 years, which was 3.8 years below the median for all Alabama whites.[2]

The Source

The origin of such widespread poverty traces to complex sources. Descent down the economic ladder was a common experience in the troubled years after Appomattox. Livestock was decimated by marauding armies wearing both blue and gray. Thievery by desperately hungry whites and blacks during Reconstruction also took its toll on herds. Perhaps a change in diet from high-protein range pork to fat, pen-fed hogs, from unrefined corn to milled corn, increased the incidence of pellagra, a crippling disease caused by vitamin deficiency.[3]

Lack of education also played a role. In 1860 the census reported 868,000 persons who had attended school in the eleven future Confederate states. Unreliable though it may be, the 1870 census cannot be entirely dismissed, and it could locate only 519,000 white Southerners who had received some schooling. The rate of illiteracy climbed in every Southern state, and in some it doubled. Alabama, which had boasted seventeen colleges with 2,120 students in 1860, had only eight enrolling 1,026 ten years later.[4] A new generation of farmers, reaching maturity without even functional literacy, could not read farm journals, or understand the causes and perils of erosion, or insist on written contracts from landowners or country merchants that would have protected their legal and economic rights.

[1] The Federal Interagency Council defined poverty in 1969 in terms of family size, sex, age, whether a person was a head of family, the total amount of family income, and the amount of food necessary for a nutritious diet. The statistics are for the year 1970.

[2] Mary Lee Rice Shannon, *Poverty in Alabama: A Barrier to Postsecondary Education* (University, Ala., 1976), 8, 14, 15, 17–18.

[3] Grady McWhiney, "The Revolution in Nineteenth-Century Alabama Agriculture," *Alabama Review*, XXXI (January 1978), 21–31.

[4] *Ninth Census. The Statistics of the Population of the United States . . .* , Vol. I (Washington, D.C., 1872), 394, 456, 474–76.

Nor can the tumultuous upheaval of the war itself be eliminated as a cause for white poverty. To the political and economic confusion of the 1870s, one can add family instability and changing values that tended to glorify acquisitive and material instincts. The same chaotic forces that produced Alabama outlaws Steve Renfroe and Rube Burrow caused others to despair of putting the world right again. One Clarke Countian expressed it as an "apparent hopelessness for working up again in life."[5]

Clarke County, located in southwest Alabama below the prosperous cotton belt, escaped marauding armies and the physical destruction of the Civil War. But the worthlessness of Confederate currency, the loss of life by so many young men in their prime, the upheaval of Reconstruction, all contributed to the growing poverty of the county. During the 1860s 150 of Clarke's 901 farms failed, and 174,000 acres of farmland went untilled. The number of improved acres declined from 99,000 in 1860 to 61,000 in 1870. The county produced only one-third as much cotton in 1870 as it had ten years earlier. Production of peas, beans, potatoes, and corn dropped below 1850 levels.

Between 1860 and 1880 Clarke was transformed from a plantation economy to a system of farm tenancy. By the latter year, only half of the county's farms were cultivated by owners; 22 percent were rented for a fixed sum, and 28 percent were rented for a share of the crop. Landowners preferred sharecropping to cash rent because a crop failure almost certainly meant a default in payment among renters. Also, sharecroppers had less control over what they grew, meaning that the landowner could insist that virtually every acre produce cotton. This policy, in turn, made the tenant increasingly dependent on the owner or local merchant who furnished him with seed, coffee, sugar, and other necessities, with the cropper's share serving as collateral.[6]

Clarke County was not exceptional. Across Alabama people of both races descended into tenancy from quite different directions, blacks coming from slavery, while many whites entered from the more prosperous life of yeoman farmer, planter, or merchant. No typical pattern emerges, but three case studies offer insights.

[5]T. H. Ball, *A Glance into the Great South-East, or Clarke County, Alabama, and its Surroundings, from 1540 to 1877* (1879, reprint ed., Tuscaloosa, 1962), 295.

[6]Jonathan Kaledin, "The Economic Consequences of the Civil War in Clarke County, Alabama," *Alabama Historian,* II (Fall 1980), 9–16.

Mary Wigley Harper rose from the poverty of a Sand Mountain tenant farm by obtaining an education, becoming a rural school-teacher, home demonstration agent, and then marrying a distin-guished Tuscaloosa geographer, Dr. Roland Harper. In 1900 her father owned a combination country store/post office and farm and was a respected community leader. He bought on credit from a railroad furnishing agent, and the post office in his store attracted customers. But when Rural Free Delivery came to Sand Mountain, fewer people patronized his store. His supply merchant shipped inferior quality goods, and Mr. Wigley became over-extended. When the Mynard Post Office closed in October 1904, trouble followed. So desperate was her father that he secretly sold Mary's pet cow, which he could no longer afford to feed. In time the Wigleys sold their store and farm to pay debts. Mary Wigley sought deliverance through prayer:

> How I felt when I finally decided to pray the all-important prayer for money to pay the debts is one of the most distinct memories of my life. It was almost dark when I slipped out alone in the side yard at the chimney-end of the house. There on my knees, with my eyes tightly closed, I poured out my heart to God. I pleaded that he save me from being like a little orphan girl with no home. I told Him I did not want one penny for myself—just enough to pay the debts—and would he please put the money for the debts in the empty trash can nearby.
>
> With my eyes still tightly closed and with my face buried in my hands, I waited and kept waiting. I was afraid to look in the can. When I finally did and found it empty, I remember thinking to myself and probably said out loud, "Just about as I expected."[7]

From their prosperous farm on the main road the Wigleys moved to a tenant farm at the end of a rutted dirt trail. On the Tinney place her father rented land for one-third of his corn and one-fourth of his cotton. The rest of the crop was mortgaged to a Lebanon, Alabama, supply merchant who provided the necessary implements, food, and clothes, at 25 percent interest for six month's credit. For fertilizer they used cow manure mixed with pine straw and distributed from a twenty-five-pound lard can.

After an ornery mule kicked Wigley and broke his arm, he taught his daughter how to plow. She grasped the right handle of the turning

---

[7] Mary Harper, "The Wind Is from the East" (typed manuscript), 88, in possession of Dr. Dennis Rouse, Auburn University, Auburn.

plow while he held the left. When the self-confident youngster begged her father to release his side so she could demonstrate her new proficiency, he decided to see if she really could manage by herself.

> Before I knew it, the plow was almost out of the ground and I did what seemed right—I pressed down on both handles. Contrary to reason, that made the plow come out of the ground completely, and with the load suddenly lighter, Old Beck struck up a fast walk.
>
> Things were going wrong. I wanted to get the plow back in the ground and in my excitement yelled in a loud voice, "Wait!" That made the mule go faster. . . . As I yelled louder and louder, she trotted across the field faster and faster until she reached the pasture fence.
>
> Father had followed his new plow girl part of the way, but when I finally had a chance to look back, he was all bent over, slapping his knee with his good hand, laughing and hallooing. It sounded like he did in the evenings gone by when Mother read funny stories to us from the Atlanta *Constitution.*[8]

Although the Wigleys maintained both their sense of humor and the closeness of family, there was little to laugh about. When a new owner purchased the land and told them that they could no longer grow vegetables and cut flowers, the proud tenant family decided to move. Conditions became even worse, as months passed when they received no money at all. Old clothes were mended and worn. Cornmeal mush extended the scarce supply of bread. Meat was limited to wild game or fish, and wild greens and fruits supplemented a drab diet. Drink substitutes were made from roasted grain, okra seed, and dry crusts. Medicines were concocted from herbs, wild leaves, bark, and roots.

The family adopted the migratory habits common to tenancy. They moved frequently, always seeking better soil and a kinder landlord. The Johnston place followed the Tinney farm, then the Everett place, each epoch identified in memory by the name of the person who owned the land, or whose farm it once had been. Because they were proud and had once been prosperous, the Wigleys doubly resented their fate. Mary Harper remembered those years "both mentally and physically" as the "most difficult period of my life."[9]

James Homer Flynt followed a different route into poverty. He was

---

[8] *Ibid.,* 99.
[9] *Ibid.,* 113.

born in 1868 to a family who had owned a small Georgia plantation before the Civil War. Times were hard, schools were closed, his mother died, and at the age of sixteen, he ran away from home. He obtained work in a foundry in northeast Alabama and married. Unable to read or write and tiring of foundry work, he began to sharecrop and remained a tenant all his life.[10]

Mrs. L. A. House entered poverty from yet another direction. She came from sturdy Shelby County yeoman stock. Her father owned a farm and rural saloon, and her mother was a skilled seamstress. Mrs. House married when she was fourteen, in 1899: "Married real young. Been married all my life." Her husband bought a farm, and they lived comfortably for fourteen years. Tragedy befell them in the form of throat cancer. When medical bills piled up, they mortgaged their farm. By the time her husband died, they had lost everything. She was left alone with five young children to tenant farm a twenty-acre plot. Several years of hard, back-breaking labor brought too meager a return, so she left the rural Methodist church she loved and her five children in the care of a relative and moved into Sylacauga's mill town.[11]

There are almost as many stories of downward mobility as there are people to tell them, but the pattern is obvious. In the eight decades between 1860 and 1940 tenancy covered the land like a winter frost. In 1900 38.8 percent of Alabama's white farmers were tenants. By 1920 only four states (Georgia, Oklahoma, South Carolina, and Texas) exceeded Alabama's total rate of tenancy, which had risen to 57.9 percent. Ten years later, 64.7 percent of all farms were operated by tenants.[12]

Tenancy involved many different financial arrangements. Some

---

[10] Personal interview with Lillie Mae Beason in Steele, August 17, 1975, tape and transcript in Samford University Archives, Birmingham.

[11] Personal interview with Mrs. L. A. House in Sylacauga, July 10, 1974, tape and transcript in Samford University Archives, Birmingham.

[12] Statistics differ somewhat depending upon how tenancy is defined and whether the comparison is to all farms or only to cotton farms. For examples see Benjamin H. Hibbard, "Tenancy in the Southern States," *Quarterly Journal of Economics*, XXVII (May 1913), 482–96; W. G. Poindexter, Jr., "Sharecroppers in the South," *The Southern Workman*, LXVI (April 1937), 118–26; Richard A. Harvill, "The Economy of the South," *Journal of Political Economy*, XLVIII (February 1940), 33–61. Two sources were used for statistics: *Fifteenth Census of the United States, Agriculture*, Vol. II, Pt. 2, *The Southern States* (Washington, D.C., 1932), 30–31, 35, and Vol. III, *Type of Farm*, Pt.2, *The Southern States* (Washington, D.C., 1932), 705.

farmers paid "standing rent," or a set amount of money per year, perhaps seventy-five dollars for a forty-acre tract. But the largest category of tenants consisted of sharecroppers, who surrendered a predetermined percentage of their corn and cotton.

In retrospect, many Alabamians remember sharecropping to be a mainly black institution. Although that perception was correct in the predominantly black counties, it was not true for the state as a whole. In 1930 there were approximately 37,500 white sharecroppers to only 27,500 blacks. Alabama's rate of tenancy remained virtually unchanged into the mid-1930s at 64.5 percent of all farmers, with white sharecroppers still outnumbering blacks (though the margin had narrowed considerably: 34,717 to 33,257).

Because tenants were often proud people drifting inexorably lower in economic status, they found various ways to protest what they viewed as the injustice and inhumanity of their plight. One historian of Alabama protest movements wrote in the mid-1940s that "Alabama has had perhaps the longest and most consistent history of militant agrarian unionism of any State in the southern Cotton Belt."[13] Such conflict may be attributed to many causes: the sharp divisions in types of farming due to geographical differences; regional political conflicts between north Alabama poor white counties and white-dominated central Alabama counties where most tenants were black; and the fact that Alabama was the most highly industrialized of the Southern cotton states with a strong labor union movement located in the Birmingham District.

Although the Populist party of the 1890s cannot be considered entirely a poor white party, that class was certainly an element in the protest movement. Populists usually chose their leaders from the middle class because rural ministers, physicians, teachers, and small landowners typically had better educations and more leadership skills. But Alabama's agrarian revolt of the 1890s was born in the turbulent agricultural policies of Reconstruction and after, which produced a steadily growing number of angry, dispossessed tenant farmers, coal miners, and cotton mill workers.[14]

[13] *Labor Unionism in American Agriculture,* U.S. Department of Labor Bulletin No. 836, 1945, p. 289.
[14] The best study of the agrarian revolt in Alabama is William Warren Rogers, *The One-Gallused Rebellion; Agrarianism in Alabama, 1865–1896* (Baton Rouge, 1970); see especially 29–30.

Progressivism produced little political reform for Alabama farmers, but the 1930s brought stirrings of change. During the Depression the Farmers' Union organized both white and black laborers, sharecroppers, and small farm owners. The union was strongest in counties adjacent to Birmingham and aimed its reforms at improving conditions among black and white tenants and farm laborers. However, the union clashed with the Communist-backed Sharecroppers' Union, which siphoned off its black support, and in 1937 many of its locals near Birmingham voted to affiliate with the newly organized CIO.[15]

New Deal programs affected far more poor white farmers than the radical organizing efforts of the Farmers' Union, the Sharecroppers' Union, or the Southern Tenant Farmers' Union. Despite bitter opposition from Edward O'Neal and the Farm Bureau Federation, Alabama's Senator John H. Bankhead co-sponsored a Farm Tenancy Act in 1937, which created the Farm Security Administration. Southern reformers dominated the new agency, which provided loans to 20,000 tenant farmers to allow them to purchase land. Conservative opposition and inadequate funding severely crippled the agency, but Alabamians whose lives were touched by the FSA remember it fondly.

Carl Forrester, now a prosperous peanut farmer in Houston County, was a typical recipient of an FSA loan. Born in 1906, Forrester began sharecropping in 1927 and continued to work someone else's land until 1941. In that year the FSA lent him money to purchase 100 acres and furnished him with farm equipment and technical advice. Three years later government officials gave him permission to sell his mules, plow stocks, two wagons, and a cultivator, and buy a used Farmall tractor. Forrester used a relative's service pay during World War II to purchase forty more acres. With his credit established he borrowed money from a bank to finance the purchase of 120 additional acres. A smart, diligent farmer, he abandoned cotton for wheat, then turned to hog-raising, and finally converted to peanuts, corn, and soybeans. By 1970 he was a well-to-do, respected member of his community and established his son in farming. Forrester represented only a small percentage of Alabama farmers who received direct federal assistance, but it wrought a miracle in his life.[16]

For white tenants who were not so lucky as Forrester, life followed

[15] *Labor Unionism in American Agriculture*, 291–92.
[16] Personal interview with Carl Forrester in Dothan, January 18, 1975, tape and transcript in Samford University Archives, Birmingham.

a more confused course. During the summer of 1936 two unlikely visitors journeyed to Hale County, Alabama, to prepare an article about share-croppers. Novelist James Agee and photographer Walker Evans spent most of that miserably hot summer living with three poor white families: the Fields, the Burroughs, and the Tingles (who appear in the book under the pseudonyms of Woods, Gudger, and Ricketts). Their essay never appeared in *Fortune* magazine, which had commissioned the work, but was published in expanded form in 1941 under the provocative title, *Let Us Now Praise Famous Men*. Virtually ignored in its time (it sold less than 600 copies), it was republished in the 1960s and became a classic in the literature of Southern poverty. Agonized, impressionistic, cosmic in scope, it captured in word and photograph the squalor, despondency, and degradation of its sub-jects, without ignoring their perseverance, their strength, and even the aesthetic quality of their folk architecture and crafts. To Agee's mind, these people were the legion of the damned, without hope, despite their courage. He saw for most of them the fate he predicted for Mary Fields: "years on years of cold, hopeless nights."

Life wasn't quite that bad. Recently, New York *Times* reporter Howell Raines, himself a product of a small Alabama farm, returned to Hale County to track down the three sharecropper families, or what was left of them. Ruby Fields Darby, who was eight years old in that fateful summer when Agee lived with her family, resented the photo-graphs that made her family better known than any sharecroppers in America: "I know it's all of us and that's the way we looked back then. But just to take our lives now and compare it to that life back then, it seems a dream. It seems like it just didn't happen to me."[17]

But it did happen, and the intervening years have carried the lives of Agee's famous men and women across uneven terrain. William Fields, who appeared in the book as a half-naked three-year-old, earns thirty-five dollars a day as a farm laborer on another man's land. One of the Burroughs boys works at a meat-packing plant in Tuscaloosa. Bud Fields, in some ways the tenant hero of Agee's book, died in 1957 at the age of seventy-seven, never realizing his dream of owning land. Appropriately enough, he died in late August, in cotton-picking time, on another man's land. Floyd Burroughs, who headed a second

[17] Howell Raines, "Let Us Now Revisit Famous Folk," New York *Times Magazine*, May 25, 1980, 32.

of Agee's three cropper families, was among only a handful of white tenants left in Alabama when he died of stomach cancer in 1959. He left his widow landless and without money. One of Frank Tingle's boys helped his father sharecrop until the boy died of tuberculosis. Frank Tingle, patriarch of the family, if such people can be said to have patriarchs, died in 1962 at the age of ninety. Only Tingle of the three croppers attained their lifelong dream—his own land. In 1959 the Farm Security Administration made him one of the lucky few who received a loan. With it, he purchased 129 acres.

Mary McCray, daughter of one of the sharecroppers, married an older man to escape the rigors of agricultural poverty. Instead, she bore him five children and because of his dereliction, became a sharecropper herself, forced by her husband's failure of will to contract the crop, work the fields, and pick the cotton. While she labored in the cotton patch, her shiftless husband tinkered with a water wheel:

> He'd go down there and work on that water wheel and I'd go hoe cotton from sun to sun for four pounds of lard, and tote it back to the house. If I didn't get the lard, I'd get 50 cents. But now he wouldn't work for 50 cents. Now he just wouldn't do it. But he was going to build that water wheel and make electricity. That was his plan. He always had big ideas, what he could do, but he never did accomplish it.

In 1953 Mary McCray had her best year as a cropper: "That was the year I cleared more money than I had ever cleared. I cleared right close near about a thousand dollars. And do you know, he stuck right in there till he spent every penny of it."[18] Finally, Mary left her husband, supported her five children until she was incapacitated with asthma, then obtained a job at a nursing home through the Alabama state rehabilitation service.

Howell Raines notes sardonically that one of Walker Evans's 1936 photographs of the sharecroppers, which are now considered classics in the genre of photographic journalism, fetches four thousand dollars among collectors: "So it happens that . . . this man who spent his 56 years looking at a mule's rump from between two plow handles and never owned so much as a postage stamp of his own land came to be worth more dead than he was alive."[19]

[18] *Ibid.*, 38, 40.
[19] *Ibid.*, 36.

For many poor whites stranded on the land, almost any fate was better than what befell Bud Fields and Floyd Burroughs. Beginning in the late nineteenth century, tens of thousands of them began to drift into villages where they went to work at cotton mills. If a farm laborer earned the southwide average of thirty-five dollars a month in 1928, and that was unusual for Alabama, he made 420 dollars annually. The same man could find employment in Alabama's cotton mills, which paid the lowest average full-time salaries in the country (thirteen dollars, forty-two cents per week), and earn 698 dollars.[20] That may explain why Alabama's mill workers were so docile and generally kept their distance from labor unions. They compared their lives, not to what textile workers elsewhere might be paid or how they were treated, but to Alabama's rural poverty from which most of them came.

From 1885 until 1895 the number of male textile mill operatives in Alabama increased by 31 percent, the number of women by 75 percent, the total of girls under the age of eighteen by 158 percent, the boys under eighteen by 81 percent.[21] By 1925 Alabama was the fourth leading Southern state in the number of manufacturing jobs with 66,806; of these 23,443 (more than one in three) were employed in textile mills.[22] By 1929 the South contained 280,000 textile mill workers, 60 percent of the nation's total. Of these, 27,724 worked in eighty-three Alabama mills. The sex of Alabama's cotton mill force was almost equally divided.[23]

The presence of females and children in the work force was one distinguishing characteristic of the industry. Although my conclusions are still tentative due to the tedious process of gathering information about why poor white women left the land for the mill village, I

[20] G. T. Schwenning, "Prospects of Southern Textile Unionism," *Journal of Political Economy,* XXXIX (December 1931), 783–810.
[21] Harry Boyte, "The Textile Industry: Keel of Southern Industrialization," *Radical America,* VI (March–April 1972), 4–49.
[22] "Workers in Southern Manufactures," *American Federationist,* XXXVI, Pt. 1 (May 1929), 588.
[23] Broadus Mitchell, "Why Cheap Labor Down South?" *Virginia Quarterly Review,* V (October 1929), 481–91; *Fifteenth Census of the United States, Manufactures: 1929,* Vol. III, *Reports by States* (Washington, D.C., 1933), 48, and *Population,* Vol. IV, *Occupations, By States* (Washington, D.C., 1933), 110. The 1930 figures reflect a sharp decline in employment throughout the industry. The first year of the Depression had been disastrous for the industry, and Alabama's textile work force had declined from 27,724 in 1929 to only a little over 21,000 in 1930.

have uncovered enough information to establish some patterns. Farming involved grueling physical toil amid considerable social isolation. Some women could perform the toil as well or better than their husbands (as the life of Mary McCray well demonstrates), but if a woman had no man, the labor required just for survival was oftentimes beyond her limits. It is not surprising then, in a region with no social welfare programs and few industrial jobs open to females, that so many single, deserted, divorced, and widowed women viewed the mill as a passage from impossible agrarian poverty to a more prosperous and sociable environment.

Sybil Chandler was born into an Alabama tenant family but dreamed of becoming a nurse. Her rural county provided school only through the seventh grade. Unwilling to sacrifice her future, she moved to Birmingham and began working at Avondale Mills in 1924, intending to continue her education. As the eldest of seven children, she assumed responsibility for the entire family after her father died. Her dream of becoming a nurse perished where it began, in front of a spindle.[24]

For women more interested in survival than dreams, mill life was not always so grim. Mrs. L. A. House, a widow with five children, left a tenant farm for Comer's mill in Sylacauga. She had adjustment problems, disliked the twelve-hour shifts, and didn't care much for the mill village Methodist church, but the pay was good compared to the poverty of the countryside, and the work was steady and predictable.

Mrs. Nancy Nolan tried to survive on a Dale County tenant farm after her husband died, leaving her with three sons, the oldest nine. She put her nine-year-old behind a plow but gave up after five years of sharecropping and moved to Cowikee Mill in Eufaula. Two of her sons, the oldest fourteen, also obtained jobs in the mill. The youngest son entered school and at night taught the two older boys to read.

Mrs. Jim Lauderdale's decision to move to a mill town had a different source. When she converted to Pentecostalism, she tried to get her husband to stop selling whiskey, get a steady job, and provide for the family. When her irresponsible spouse ignored her, she deserted him, taking her daughter and moving to Sylacauga, where they obtained jobs in Comer's mill earning a combined salary of twenty-two dollars a week.

[24] Edward N. Akin, "Mr. Donald's Help: The Birmingham Village of Avondale Mills During the Great Depression" (unpublished paper read at the Southern Historical Association meeting, Atlanta, November 1980).

Not all women came to mill towns of their own free will. Julia Rhodes was born on a farm in Tallapoosa County. Her father moved to Alexander City when she was a young girl in order to put his two older daughters to work in the mill. Julia, too young to work, attended school briefly. But she was terrified of her teacher and soon dropped out. When she reached the age of fifteen, she married an older textile worker and spaced eight children around her work schedule at the mill.

Mrs. Lee Snipes also began her career in Eufaula's Cowikee Mill as a small child. Mrs. Tom Alsobrook began work at Cowikee as a "spooler hand" for fifty cents a day when she was nine years old. Her mother-in-law had also been a female head of family who brought her family to Eufaula and obtained a job at Cowikee.[25]

Life remained difficult for most of them, a fact many accepted with fatalistic resolve. But there were occasional "Norma Raes" among them who joined unions and walked picket lines as well as any man. In the summer of 1934 5,000 textile workers walked off their jobs in Huntsville. The strike, organized by the United Textile Workers of America, spread quickly to twenty-eight mills—two in Birmingham, six in Huntsville, three in Florence, and others in Anniston, Gadsden, Jasper, Piedmont, Guntersville, Albertville, Gordo, and Winfield. Although the UTWA had been defeated in the mills of central Alabama, the strike still involved 23,000 operatives and was one of the largest in the state's history. The strike to protest miserable wages and working conditions was opposed both by the national leadership of the UTWA and by officials of the State Federation of Labor, who warned textile workers in Anniston to stay on their jobs "unless conditions are extremely bad." Apparently they were, because the very next day Anniston workers shut down the mills.

Conditions threatened to turn violent when the organizer of the Huntsville strike was kidnapped, allegedly by a former state commander of the American Legion, and driven to Fayetteville, Tennessee. Fearing that the kidnapping might precipitate violence, mill owners had armed guards patrol the streets of Huntsville. At Haleyville a

[25] Personal interview with Mrs. L. A. House; Federal Writers Project interviews with Julia Rhodes, Mr. and Mrs. Tom Alsobrook, Mrs. Lee Snipes, Nancy Nolan, and Jim Lauderdale, Federal Writers Project, "Life Histories," Folders 110–84, Microfilm Reel 1 (Originals in Southern Historical Collection, University of North Carolina, Chapel Hill). These biographies constitute a major source on Alabama poor whites. James S. Brown of Samford University is currently editing the project under the tentative title, "Depression Alabama: 'Life Histories' from the Alabama Writers Project, 1938–39."

truckload of union members and organizers sought to gain support of workers at the Alabama Mills Company but were turned away by armed guards who would not let them enter the town. A similar incident occurred in Opelika. Deprived of both incomes and their mill village houses, Birmingham strikers poured into the city's parks to take up residence.[26]

Not all workers were so militant, however. Mrs. L. A. House never liked the union, despite economic hard times. She accepted her fate stoically and probably spoke for many "lint-heads" when she slumped during our interview and muttered: "It's been a hard life." After a long pause she brightened and with a twinkle in her eye looked firmly at me and added: "But it hasn't been all bad either."

If cotton mill work was the most thoroughly mixed for poor whites of both sexes, coal mining was the most thoroughly segregated. The cool blackness of the mine shaft was a man's world. In 1930 all but nine of Alabama's 23,965 coal miners were men.[27]

By 1929 Alabama had 202 active coal mines producing nearly 18 million tons of coal, valued at more than 37 million dollars. The industry employed 25,208 miners who worked an average of 231 days a year. Despite a modest decline 22,000 miners were still employed in the industry in 1944.[28]

The story of what brought them to the mines is as diverse as the one told by textile workers. Sam Cash was a farmer who lived on Lookout Mountain and mined a small seam four miles east of Mentone. Except for one desperately bleak year when he left Alabama to mine coal in Harlan County, Kentucky, and in West Virginia, he spent all of his seventy years in northeast Alabama: "I have been farming and mining ever since I can remember and I still don't know which one is the worse to make a living at."

Joseph Davis was a miner at Brookwood, north of Birmingham. His father had been a Methodist minister and blacksmith in Tennessee. Davis and six of his seven brothers became coal miners. He began picking slate out of the coal when he was twelve years old for seventy-five cents a day. Mining and schooling didn't mix, so Davis had only nine months of education before he met his schoolteacher wife, who

---

[26] Alexander Kendrick, "Alabama Goes on Strike," *The Nation*, CXXXIX (August 29, 1934), 233–34.

[27] *Fifteenth Census of the United States, Population*, Vol. IV, 109.

[28] O. E. Kiessling, "Coal Mining in the South," *Annals of the American Academy of Political and Social Science*, CLIII (January 1931), 84–93; *Labor in the South*, U.S. Department of Labor Bulletin No. 898, 1947, p. 92.

taught him to read and write. Davis made a good living mining until he was laid off in the early 1930s. He bought a farm but failed at that, losing his mortgage. Despite poor health he was forced to return to mining, earning so little on short shifts at the Sayreton Mines that his wife saved the family financially by obtaining a Federal Emergency Relief Act job teaching illiterate miners to read.

Sam Brakefield mined coal in the same area of north Alabama as Davis. Like Sam Cash and Davis, he also farmed on the side. He left his father's farm at the age of fourteen to escape the poverty and drudgery of the land. As he explains it: "When I was a boy growing up, I talked my dad out of letting me leave our hillside farm that was so poor we couldn't even raise enough for the cows and pigs to eat." He began his mining career at Gamble Mines in 1887 making eighty cents a day working from "sunup to sunset." By a combination of hard work, frugality, and good fortune, he saved enough money to buy forty-six acres and build a house. But all his life was a cycle of feast or famine, prosperity during good times, suffering and deprivation during bad.

A bit farther south, John Gates mined coal in the Cahaba Valley. He rose long before dawn and at 5:00 A.M. began the three-mile walk to Paramount Mines near Helena. After years of effort, he managed to build a new house for his family. But like so many of his dreams, this one was smashed, by a tornado in the early 1930s. Fortunately, a New Deal relief agency came to his assistance and helped him rebuild his cherished house.

Charley Ryland was not so lucky. When the Federal Writers Project interviewer located him, he was living as a derelict in a remote cabin on the Coosa River. For a living, he fished trotlines and made whiskey. An illiterate, he had once been an industrious Birmingham district coal miner with a wife and seven children. When times turned hard in Alabama, he left for a mining job in West Virginia. Far from home, fate dealt him a double blow: he lost an eye in a mining accident, and his wife died. His children married coal miners or entered the West Virginia mines themselves, and the lonely old man returned to the Alabama river where he was born, lest he be a burden to them. Reflecting on his life, he remembered: "We never had no money much; ain't no ignerunt miner wuth much. . . ."[29]

[29] The preceding biographies are taken from interviews conducted in the 1930s by the Federal Writers Project with Sam Cash, Mr. and Mrs. Joseph Davis, Sam Brakefield, John Gates, and Charley Ryland.

Despite the legendary fatalism usually attributed to Appalachian poor whites, many of these independent people banded together to alter their lives. As early as 1894 the United Mine Workers organized miners in Jefferson, Walker, Tuscaloosa, Bibb, and Shelby counties. Some 8,000 coal miners conducted a bitter and protracted strike in that earlier depression year against wages and wretched conditions. They made common cause with angry farmers in the Populist party and gave that party in Alabama an industrial constituency which it lacked elsewhere in the South. Despite the opposition of operators, the state government, and public opinion, the miners won some concessions during their violent four months' strike.[30]

Subsequent labor unrest reached crisis state periodically in Alabama: in 1908, just after World War I ended, and again in 1922. Such strikes involved considerable suffering because strike benefits consisted of little more than navy beans, salt pork, potatoes, flour, and sugar.

Yet, Alabama miners demonstrated a loyalty to their union, and especially to John L. Lewis and Franklin D. Roosevelt, that was nearly idolatrous. John Gates of Helena generally voted the straight Republican ticket. But not during the 1930s, when he regularly voted for Roosevelt: "If he hadn't stood behind us working men, I don't know where we'd be now. Too bad we didn't have him in '20 and '22." Sam Cash was also a strong UMW man and a great admirer of John L. Lewis, who would save the poor man: "Everybody else lives offen us farmers and miners and all we gits for our labor is grubstake, and a po' one." A deeply religious man, he was convinced in the 1930s that God, Lewis, and Franklin Roosevelt would improve conditions: "things can't go on much longer like they is going, cause they is too unjust in the sight of God."[31]

If coal miners were the best organized group of poor whites in Alabama, timber workers may well have been the worst. Although lumbermen have received little attention, their numbers match or exceed the totals for the textile and mining industries. In 1929 Alabama contained 1,141 lumber and timber mills, which employed 25,954 wage earners.[32] The industry was like mining in two respects: the work force was virtually all male, and there was a generous sprinkling of black

---

[30] For details of this affair see Robert David Ward and William Warren Rogers, *Labor Revolt in Alabama: The Great Strike of 1894* (University, Ala., 1965).

[31] Federal Writers Project interviews with Sam Cash and John Gates.

[32] *Fifteenth Census, Manufactures: 1929*, 48.

workers among the poor whites. Like miners also, they came from various backgrounds.

Isaac Johnson was a second-generation logger and turpentine worker in Washington County on the Tombigbee River. His father had made a good living felling the huge pine trees of southwest Alabama and had managed to buy a forty-acre farm with his savings. The scrub pine of Isaac Johnson's time was less profitable to cut, and by the 1930s many of the county's sawmills had closed down. Johnson tried to earn a living collecting turpentine, but the liquid brought only fourteen cents a gallon during the great Depression. His schoolteacher wife had taught him to read and write, although he did both poorly. Describing his life, Johnson told an interviewer in 1938:

> I tell you, when things was so bad back in 1932, I'd a-get up in the mornings, and I swear I didn't know where I was a-going to get something to eat for the day. But I got it, just the same. I guess life's like that; you got to scratch for everything.[33]

George Carter was a contemporary of Johnson's, who lived at Talladega Springs. He was a classic example of the degenerate envisioned in the term "poor white trash." He never knew his mother or father who gave him and his sister to a Talladega County farmer when they were infants. He hated the man who worked him unmercifully. He ran away when he was fifteen, but the farmer caught him and beat him until his shirt stuck to his bloody back. The second time he ran away he reached Selma, where he begged food until he could get work with a traveling circus. He ran away from the circus after hitting his boss in the head with a sledgehammer because the man kicked him. He returned to Coosa County, where he took up with a Negro, Tom Green. They made whiskey, gambled, and generally raised hell until Green was killed in a drunken incident in a sawmill village. Carter, a strapping six-foot three-inch 220 pounder, then began his forty-two year career as a logger. He worked all day for fifty cents a day.

Although these four occupations—tenant farming, textiles, mining, and timbering—accounted for the overwhelming majority of Alabama's poor whites, others were employed in various low-paying industries where one could labor long without escaping poverty. The state's iron and steel industry, centered in Birmingham, employed

---

[33] Federal Writers Project interview with Isaac Johnson.

11,651 wage earners in 1929, and railroad shops provided wages to another 7,183. Cast-iron pipe shops employed an additional 9,335.[34] During normal times these skilled workers were relatively well paid. Also, TCI in Birmingham, the largest employer in this group, had pioneered a successful program of company welfare for its employees. During the Depression, however, many workers in these industries suffered as badly or worse than their rural counterparts. Without land and often knowing little about farming, they had few alternatives. Alabama had the largest drop in employment of any Southern state during the decade of the 1930s. In Mobile 51.7 percent of all wage-earning families received less than one thousand dollars a year in 1935–1936, and 21 percent of the native white families earned less than five thousand dollars annually; 10.3 percent of all native white families in the city were on relief.[35]

To assist such people, Alabama's Senator John H. Bankhead introduced a bill in 1933 to create subsistence farms for unemployed industrial workers. Passed as an amendment to Title II of NIRA in June 1933, the provision appropriated twenty-five million dollars. The largest recipient of funds was Alabama, where five projects were begun in Jefferson and Walker counties.

Jefferson County, with some 100,000 people on relief, had been hard hit by the Depression. In fact, Birmingham's economy was so bad that locals coined the expression, "When Birmingham is not black it is blue." With the city's furnaces down, its coal and iron ore mines closed or on reduced shifts, its economic life paralyzed, it was definitely blue in the 1930s.

Four subsistence farm communities were built at Cahaba, Greenwood, Mt. Olive, and Palmerdale. Unemployed laborers applied, were interviewed by social workers, and a lucky 697 families were allowed to buy the farms on generous, deferred terms. Curiously, those who were most successful on the new homesteads formerly had been machinists or skilled artisans; those who did worst had been professionals or in service occupations. Although most families came to their new home-

[34] *Fifteenth Census, Manufactures: 1929,* 48.

[35] Joseph B. Gittler and Roscoe R. Giffin, "Changing Patterns of Employment in Five Southeastern States, 1930–1940," *Southern Economic Journal,* XI (October 1944), 169–82; A. D. H. Kaplan, et al., *Family Income and Expenditure in the Southeastern Region, 1935–36,* U.S. Department of Labor Bulletin No. 647, 1939.

steads broke, in debt, and with shattered spirits, they quickly recovered both economically and psychologically.[36]

The resilience of Alabama's poor whites depended on many factors: whether their poverty was caused by temporary conditions such as the Depression, or dated back through generations; whether they were rural or urban folk; whether they retained a sense of family stability and personal pride; and whether or not they had at least minimal education and job skills.

Sunup to Sundown: Poor Whites and Their Work

Although a purely external view of their poverty provides useful data on the numbers of poor whites engaged in various occupations and even suggests how they arrived at their low economic status, it results in a largely sterile, lifeless panorama. To probe beyond an essentially statistical profile requires an internal perspective. What was life at the bottom like? How did poor whites feel about their jobs, houses, bosses, food, and health? What was their self-image and did it correspond with the ways that others viewed them? What hope persisted for the future?

Most of Alabama's poor whites worked hard without escaping poverty. For them, long hours, low wages, and poor working conditions were common. The occupations that employed them were traditionally labor intensive, low-wage industries.

The average Alabama cotton mill operative in 1924 earned about half what his counterpart did in Massachusetts. Whereas Massachusetts limited the work week of mill workers to forty-eight hours, the legal limit in North Carolina and Georgia in 1926 was sixty hours, and Alabama had no legal maximum at all.[37]

Although textile wages went up with the passing years, they never kept pace with comparable wages in other regions or with the cost of what the mill hand had to purchase. In 1885 women spinners in Alabama earned two dollars and seventy-six cents a week; by 1895, a depression

---

[36] See Paul W. Wager, *One Foot on the Soil, A Study of Subsistence Homesteads in Alabama* (University, Ala., 1945).

[37] Mitchell, "Why Cheap Labor Down South?" 481–91; Dexter M. Keezer, "Low Wages in the South," *The Survey*, LVII (November 15, 1926), 226–28.

year, their wages had declined to two dollars and thirty-eight cents. By 1920 the average mill worker in Alabama earned slightly more than eight and a half dollars a week, but this varied according to sex, age, and skill. Unskilled sweepers earned three dollars a week in 1930, while skilled weavers earned the top scale of twenty-three dollars weekly. The average for all Alabama mill workers was thirteen dollars per week. The average work week in 1928 was fifty-five hours, but that declined quickly when the market collapsed in 1929.[38]

The testimony of individual mill hands confirms the general pattern. Nancy Nolan began working the twelve-hour night shift at Cowikee Mill in Eufaula shortly after the turn of the century for twenty-five cents a night. Tom Alsobrook obtained employment at the same mill as a sweeper for fifty cents a day. Mrs. Lee Snipes and Mrs. Sam Anderson began at the same mill working a shift that began at 6:00 A.M. and ended at 6:00 P.M. Mrs. Anderson also complained about working conditions. The mill had neither electricity nor indoor toilets: "We had to draw the warps in by hand, and threading them looms by mouth was something terrible. I'm shamed to tell it, but that's why I started dipping snuff; to keep the lint out of my mouth."[39]

Such conditions were typical. When Mrs. L. A. House began working in Comer's Sylacauga mill at the end of World War I, she worked the same 6:00 to 6:00 shift five days a week and half a day Saturday, for nine dollars a week (which averaged seven and a third cents per hour).[40]

Wages for miners differed somewhat because of the use of company script. Alabama coal miners averaged four dollars twenty-five cents per day in 1930 and worked an average of three days a week. By 1936 the national hourly wage for coal miners was seventy-three cents, compared to fifty-four cents for Alabama miners.[41]

Sam Brakefield began mining at Gamble Mines in 1887 for eighty cents a day. In 1903 he became a foreman and supported his wife and five children on a straight salary of seventy-five dollars a month.

[38] Boyte, "The Textile Industry," 9; Elizabeth L. Otey, "Women and Children in Southern Industry," *Annals of the American Academy of Political and Social Science,* CLIII (January 1931), 164; Louis Stark, "The Meaning of the Textile Strike," *New Republic,* LVIII (May 8, 1929), 324; William Green, "At the Crossroads," *American Federationist,* XXXVII, Pt. 1 (January 1930), 28.
[39] Federal Writers Project interviews with Nancy Nolan, Tom Alsobrook, Mrs. Lee Snipes, and Mrs. Sam Anderson.
[40] Personal interview with Mrs. L. A. House.
[41] Green, "At the Crossroads," 28; *Labor in the South,* 92.

Because he was paid once a month, he usually had to obtain an advance on his salary in the form of company script. The script, or "clacker," could be redeemed in the company commissary at a rate of eighty cents to the dollar. When he first began working at Gamble, company spies reported any miner who bought goods anywhere except the commissary, and the miner was fired.[42]

John Gates of Helena found a way to outsmart the commissary system at Paramount Mine. The commissary usually charged prices considerably higher than Helena merchants. One exception, however, was snuff, which was sold at the regular price. So Gates spent all his script for snuff, which he bought by the case; then he carried it to the merchants in Helena and swapped it for groceries at the regular noncommissary prices.[43]

Tenant farmers stood at the bottom of the economic ladder in terms of disposable income. A 1935 study of some 700 sharecroppers in ten Alabama counties revealed that they "broke even" for almost one-half the total years of their lives spent in sharecropping. In 30 percent of the years they lost, and only about one year in four ended with a profit. More than 31 percent of the tenants in the sample had been indebted to the landlord for more than a year. Frequently, the illiterate tenant did not even know how much he owed. Even when they received government checks to reduce their cotton acreage, landlords generally took the money, reasoning that it was their lands being removed from production.[44]

Returning prosperity had little effect on agricultural poverty. Tenants drifted into the status of farm laborers, the major difference being that they worked for a stipulated salary. In July 1942 Alabama farm laborers earned an average of one dollar thirty-five cents per day without board, while even unskilled industrial laborers were making three dollars forty-three cents for an eight-hour day.[45]

Although some historians of America's lower class have perceived a Marxist kind of class conflict emerging from such conditions, few Alabama poor whites expressed their grievances in such terms. They might complain vaguely about the injustice of life, or join a union,

[42] Federal Writers Project interview with Sam Brakefield.
[43] Federal Writers Project interview with John Gates.
[44] Harold Hoffsommer, "The AAA and the Cropper," *Social Forces,* XIII (May 1935), 494–502.
[45] Herman Jay Braunhut, "Farm Labor Wage Rates in the South, 1909–1948," *Southern Economic Journal,* XVI (October 1949), 189–99.

or vote for a party or candidate as a method of protest, but they seemed to have believed that the economic system could be corrected, that life would improve, if not for them, then certainly for their children. This general acceptance of their fate has been attributed to many factors: the fatalistic religious tradition of poor whites; the paternalism of their bosses, mill and factory owners; the widespread American belief in economic mobility; the contrast between their previous condition and their prevailing situation.

There were exceptions, however. George Carter, a logger who lived in a shanty seven miles from Talladega Springs in the 1930s, harbored resentment. He began working for fifty cents a day but in time earned two dollars as "boss logger" to a black crew. His official workday was eight hours, "but I could count on my ten fingers how many times I got out of the woods before good dark." Disgusted with his pay, he complained to his boss:

> and he put on a mouth that was as poor as a widow woman. He says "George, you know I'm your friend; I'd pay you more if I could. But my sales is way down. If I'm going to keep eating myself, I can't pay my help no more. It'd bust me, and then we'd all be out in the cold." Well, I ain't been to him since that day. He thinks I'm a damned fool, but I ain't blind. A man that's been lumbering as long as me knows a few things. I can look at the stock in his sheds and know that he was lying with a face as bare as a baby's rump. I know what I cut in the woods, and I know how much lumber it will make. Blalock [his boss] is so stingy he wears buttons on his pants made out of his own wood. He's that tight all right.[46]

For other poor whites, perceptions of their bosses varied with the years. Textile operative Tom Alsobrook began working for a Captain Tullis, who was president of the Eufaula Cotton Mill. He remembered the mill as a haphazardly run business. Mrs. Lee Snipes entered the same mill and complained of wages too low and hours too long. That ended when Donald Comer bought the mill in 1908, installed new machinery, and modernized the facility. Nancy Nolan, Tom Alsobrook, Mrs. Champion, and Mrs. Lee Snipes all praised Comer as a wonderful man. He installed running ice water, "five commodes, all cleaned every day," marble floors in the bathrooms, purchased different-color uniforms for each department, and provided loans so workers' children could attend college. They praised their foremen and

---

[46] Federal Writers Project interview with George Carter.

vowed to stand by Comer if union representatives ever tried to organize their mill.[47]

Tenant farmers often felt the same way, damning unjust landlords but providing generous praise for good ones. James H. Flynt admired Anniston banker Charlie Bell, who owned his land and always treated him fairly. Sharecropper Orrie Robinson praised Shep Cooper: "I don't know what we'd do if it wasn't for Shep, so I don't grudge him nothing. He's let us have something to eat when they wasn't a penny he could hope to get." M. B. Truitt, a tenant farmer living near Opelika, also esteemed his landlord: "a fine man, the best boss I ever worked for."[48]

Obviously, not every coal miner, tenant farmer, logger, or textile worker was bound to his boss by ties of trust and affection. That is the reason they joined unions, moved so often, and complained so vociferously about injustice. But paternalism was a common sentiment among affluent Alabamians. One mid-1930s survey recorded that 89 percent of Alabama's landowners interviewed believed it was their duty to maintain their sharecroppers during times of distress.[49]

Unfortunately, that was little protection to the tenant buffeted by declining prices and economic uncertainty. Indeed, the same survey found that 22 percent of the white tenants interviewed claimed that their landlords forced them against their wills to turn over their government crop reduction checks.

Home Sweet Home

Although wages and working conditions emerge as the central issues in the lives of most poor whites, housing was also important. Until the 1940s many mills and mines provided housing for their employees. Company housing originated from mixed motives of paternalism and desire to control the work force. The threat of eviction was one of the most effective anti-union tools.

The Ellawhite mill village one mile east of Uniontown was a typical company town. Founded in 1909 it was named for Mrs. Ella Sims White,

[47] Federal Writers Project interviews with Mrs. Lee Snipes, Tom Alsobrook, Mrs. Champion, and Nancy Nolan.
[48] Personal interview with Lillie Mae Beason; Federal Writers Project interviews with Orrie Robinson and M. B. Truitt.
[49] Hoffsommer, "The AAA and the Cropper."

wife of one of the largest stockholders of the California Cotton Mill, whose facility dominated the community. The village contained a general store, a filling station, a main street that led into Uniontown, and two streets parallel to it, with a hundred or so mill houses spaced along the roads. Housing for the foreman, the mill church, and school were located across from the mill. Farther away were trim but less pretentious dwellings. At the edge of town unskilled workers lived in dilapidated houses fronted by bare yards.[50]

Tenant farmers did not fare so well as poor whites in mine and mill towns. Their typical housing was a dogtrot, so-called because a breezeway connected two rooms. The open center provided relief from the oppressive heat of an Alabama summer, and the house was easily constructed and additions readily made. James Agee described tenant folk architecture in a brilliant, poetic, and moving passage:

> It is put together out of the cheapest available pine lumber, and the least of this is used which shall stretch a skin of one thickness alone against the earth and air; . . . and the work is done by half-skilled, half-paid men under no need to do well, who therefore take such vengeance on the world as they may in a cynical and part willful apathy; . . . A look of being most earnestly hand-made, as a child's drawing, a thing created out of need, love, patience, and strained skill. . . . Nowhere one ounce or inch spent with ornament, not one trace of relief or of disguise. . . .[51]

Ranging downward from this, the poorest of the poor lived in simple one-room cabins. A Federal Writers Project employee described such a structure near the Coosa River in 1938:

> The cabin that sat before us on crumbling pillars was only a squat heap of rough pine lumber, thrown together carelessly. It was a dirty gray from the buffetings of many winds, and it seemed . . . that one more good wind would tear it asunder. On the narrow front porch, a zinc water bucket sat on a shelf, with the washpan and a bar of cheap soap. Fish hooks and lines were strung from a dozen nails that had been driven into the walls.
>
> Inside the cabin was freshly scrubbed, but its cleanliness served only to emphasize its bareness. There was one bed made of two-by-four lumber, and covered with a straw mattress. Nearby was a dilapidated cot, covered only by a patchwork quilt of great age. In a corner stood a wood stove that seemed to be yearning to crumble off its weary legs.

[50] Federal Writers Project interview with Susie R. O'Brien.
[51] James Agee and Walker Evans, *Let Us Now Praise Famous Men* (1941, reprint ed., New York, 1978), 129–30.

In the other room—smaller than the first and added without much planning to the original structure—a long table and a bench had been nailed to the wall.[52]

Inadequate housing was one of many reasons for the legendary mobility of poor whites. When too many babies appeared for the house to hold them all, or when debts piled up, or when landlords changed or became too demanding, tenants simply left. Generally, white tenants moved more often than blacks, perhaps an indication of their superior expectations. Moving posed no problems for people who had so few material possessions. Herman C. Nixon, who had observed tenants closely in his early days near Piedmont, remembered that "All they have to do is to call the dog and spit in the fire."[53]

My own grandfather moved so often that my aunt pegs her childhood chronology to the names of farmers who built the houses in which they lived or who owned the land. There was the Francis place, the Johnson place, and the Bell place: "We just moved every time there was a baby. . . ." I inquired why they moved so often:

> Well, he was looking for something better. You know, he had a lot of pride. I think my dad had more pride than was really good for him. And he was always bettering himself. I can just see him now coming in and telling my mother that one time when we moved to Wellington . . . how . . . everything was just going to be rosy. He was gonna have this and this and this. . . . He always bettered himself, he said, as he moved. I'm not so sure about it, but he said he did. . . .[54]

Mrs. Kathleen Knight's family sharecropped in the Mississippi Delta and near Guin, Alabama. She remembered moving frequently because of grievances against landlords: "I reckon they was just trying to find something better all [the] time—better house and better way of being treated."[55]

Mrs. E. J. Alexander grew up in Texas, the daughter of a carpenter who moved frequently trying to find work. They lived nowhere more than a year. When her father moved to Birmingham, she met and

[52] Federal Writers Project interview with Charley Ryland.
[53] H. Clarence Nixon, "The Changing Background of Southern Politics," *Social Forces*, XI (October 1932), 17.
[54] Personal interview with Lillie Mae Beason.
[55] Personal interview with Mrs. Kathleen Knight in Guin, January 23, 1975, tape and transcript in Samford University Archives, Birmingham.

married E. J. Alexander. They rented a farm in Perry County and
began their own rural odyssey, moving many times, "hoping by
each move to better their conditions."[56]

Meat, Meal, and Molasses: The Poor White Diet

One of the byproducts of poverty was poor diet and health. For
the poorest, hunger was a reality. One Federal Writers Project investigator discovered a family on the banks of the Coosa River who
subsisted on fish and cornmeal. Orrie Robinson complained in answer
to a question: "Hungry?—Hell, I'm allus hungry." The same interviewer investigated the section of another one-room cabin that was
devoted to cooking and found a sack of cornmeal and a bag of coffee
on an otherwise empty grocery shelf. Catfish was the staple source of
protein.[57]

Usually there was sufficient food, but it was of inadequate variety
to provide the vitamins necessary for good health. Frequently mentioned dietary items included turnip greens, peas, collards, cornbread,
biscuits, hoecakes, fried pork, gravy, sorghum and ribbon-cane syrup.

Poor diet complicated other health problems. Cabins were poorly
insulated against insects in summer and cold in winter, and spare money
to buy shoes was uncommon. Outhouses were too near wells and im-
properly maintained. Hence, poor whites suffered from endemic diseases: hookworm, malaria, typhoid, and pellagra.

Family Life

Closely related to health was the size of poor white families. Lack
of education and money limited access to birth control devices, to
which many poor whites objected anyway on religious grounds. As a
consequence, Appalachian poor whites had the highest fertility rates
in America during the first half of the twentieth century. Coal miner
Sam Brakefield and his wife had thirteen children. Textile worker Julia
Rhodes married when she was fifteen. Her first child was born a year later.

---

[56] Federal Writers Project interview with E. J. Alexander.
[57] Federal Writers Project interviews with Charley Ryland and Orrie Robinson.

By her thirty-fifth birthday she had eight children ranging in age from an infant to a nineteen-year-old son.

Although most poor whites married, established normal families, and lived temperate lives, some lapsed into various kinds of excesses. They often drowned their frustrations and failures in a sea of alcohol. Drinking problems appear in poor white family histories as a source of more family friction than any other single factor. Mrs. Champion, a widow and operative at the Cowikee Cotton Mill, complained: "My ole man died 'bout three years ago. He was good, but he kilt hisself drinking liquor. 'Fore God, he drinked enough to float a creek."[58]

From such people came many of the classic stereotypes of poor white degeneracy. Orrie Robinson insisted that his family was not "poor white trash." But he did recall an evening when he got roaring drunk, took a prostitute to a hotel room, and woke up the next morning to discover the girl and the meager contents of his wallet both gone.

George Carter took up with a poor white woman whom he met in the logging camp where he worked. Although he could not remember her last name, he considered her a good woman. That did not prevent him from physically abusing her or from infidelity. When she died, he began living with a second poor white from a different sawmill town. After she died, he vowed to abstain from even the nominal responsibilities of his irregular living arrangements: "I been 'round lots in my day, and I done buried two ol' women. You couldn't give me another'n. They's too many runnin' bout that you don't have to feed." He was as good as his word, at least on this subject. After moving to a sawmill in Shelby County, he found the female population un- usually promising: "That was one place where they was enough women to suit me, and I runned after 'em 'til my tongue was rolling out like a damned dog's."[59] When Carter's hordes of illegitimate children were old enough, he wasted no time pushing them from his crowded nest.

Neeley Williams proved that degeneracy was not limited to men.

---

[58] Federal Writers Project interview with Mrs. Champion. Similar episodes involving women who left their husbands because of drinking problems, bootlegging, and alcohol abuse abound in the F.W.P. interviews.

[59] Federal Writers Project interviews with Orrie Robinson and George Carter.

She lived in a two-room pine-board shanty twelve miles south of Sylacauga on the Coosa River. She made a living begging for food and snuff from the fishermen along the river, various ones of which claimed to have fathered her six children. Her oldest boy, twenty in 1938, refused to work. Welfare workers had removed the oldest girls from the family, and the younger children greeted a government investigator in unorthodox style. Most were naked, and the primary vocabulary of the speech-impaired four-year-old seemed to be: "Dod-dammit—dod-dammit—dod-dammit."[60]

Central to the story of Alabama's poor whites is the contrast between internal and external perceptions of life. Most knowledge about them has been based on the perceptions of others. Better class whites often pitied and sometimes despised them. Every crime and vice within the community was placed on their humble doorsteps. They committed the lynchings, elected the demagogues, made the illegal whiskey, lived the debauched lives, practiced bizarre religions, and hardly ever exerted themselves to improve their lives.

Even blacks looked down on them. In 1915 a professor at Auburn University, who gained renown later as a pioneer folklorist, collected a song from one of his students. The student had recorded the lyric from a black guitar picker in Choctaw County:

> I went to the crap game the other night,
>   Which was against my will.
> I bet the last hundred that I had
>   On the whip-o-will,
> Ever since then I've been wearing good clothes,
>   Living on chicken and wine,
> I'd rather be a nigger than a poor white man—
>   Since I got mine.[61]

The self-perceptions of poor whites diverged sharply from such prevailing stereotypes. Although white tenant farmers did not attend church as regularly as landowners (59.5 percent of the South's farm owners were members of churches in the mid-1930s compared to only 33.5 percent of the tenants), they considered themselves just as religious. Often they did not attend church because they had to work

---

[60] Federal Writers Project interview with Neeley Williams.
[61] Newman I. White, *American Negro Folk-Songs* (1928, reprint ed., Hatboro, Pa., 1965), 197.

on Sundays, their clothes were not good enough, they lived too far away, or their mobility cut them off from familiar home congregations. Often, however, miners and mill workers were active in churches that consisted mainly of miners or mill hands. Even the pastor might be a bivocational laborer. In such congregations poor whites often became stewards or deacons. Although Baptist and Methodist denominations attracted most poor whites, Pentecostal sects became increasingly popular in the twentieth century.[62]

Poor whites did not share in many of the routine experiences of life. Neeley Williams, who lived at Fayetteville, near Sylacauga, had never seen a movie and had heard a radio only once when interviewed in 1938. Orrie Robinson, an illiterate who had never been to a movie, heard a radio, or read a newspaper, remembered the first time he heard an airplane: "I honest-to-God thought it was Old Man Stamps' sawmill boiler a-blowing up. The airplanes scared me at first, but I like to watch 'em pass over . . . now."[63]

Such cultural isolation resulted in discontent and low self-esteem. Sharecropper Orrie Robinson complained in two different 1938 interviews: "Ever since I's knee-high to a grasshopper I ain't knowed nothing but hard times"; "we don't have no good times. In the summertime we'uns enjoy being good and warm, but hit gets pretty bad in winter." Sharecropper Mrs. E. J. Alexander did not like farm life: "I ain't old, just forty-two, but I feel pretty old. If I could have looked ahead I guess maybe I would have picked a different road." Another sharecropper's wife, Mrs. "Bull" Elliott of Lowndesboro, avoided her neighbors and didn't go shopping more often than necessary because of her embarrassment at being poor.[64]

Although low self-esteem is more common among white tenant farmers, one encounters it also among mill workers and miners. Cotton mill worker Mrs. L. A. House of Sylacauga remembers the fights at ball games between children of mill workers and "uptown" children. She recalled a parade where she heard children complaining about all the "lint heads" who had left mill town to crowd city streets. She

[62] Charles M. McConnell, "Farm Tenants and Sharecroppers," *Missionary Review of the World*, LX (June 1937), 288. This paper's conclusions concerning the religious views of poor whites are based on the interviews cited earlier.

[63] Federal Writers Project interviews with Neeley Williams and Orrie Robinson.

[64] *Ibid.*, and Federal Writers Project interviews with Mrs. E. J. Alexander and Mrs. "Bull" Elliott.

angrily snapped: "if it wasn't for the cottonheads you wouldn't have nothing to eat in Sylacauga."[65]

When Dera Bledsoe decided to marry Birmingham coal miner Joseph Davis, her father was furious. He had been a justice of the peace for twenty years, was a member of the Birmingham Chamber of Commerce, and was influential in local politics. He had provided all his children with a college education and judged all miners by the ones who appeared in his courtroom. His daughter remembered that he "looked down on the laboring class." He exploded when he discovered that she was dating an older miner who was widowed and the father of three children:

> Dera Bledsoe you haven't got one bit of marrying sense in your head. To think of Al Bledsoe's daughter even speaking to a coal miner! You know very well that miners are all a bunch of ignorant, profane crapshooters with no ambition. I won't stand idly by and let my daughter marry one of 'em. I forbid you even to see him again, and if he keeps on seeing you after what I've just said—well, I guess there's nothing left but to shoot him, and damned if I won't do it.

Naturally, they married, and Joseph Davis proved to be a gentle, loving husband and a loyal family man. Even Dera's father came to admire him as a tireless worker and good provider.

But even good providers encountered hard times. After losing his mining job in the mid-1930s, Davis tried farming but failed. Moving back into the Sayreton mining camp he reentered the mines. Until his first payday the family could not afford to have the electricity turned on in their company house. They used kerosene lamps to the considerable chagrin of their socially conscious children, who preferred a dark house to advertising that the family didn't have sufficient money to turn on the electricity.[66]

Such adolescent embarrassment was not uncommon among the children of poor whites. James L. Townsend later established a successful career in journalism; but he grew up poor in Lanett, Alabama. He remembered not having a car, how his family had a woodstove and icebox long after neighbors bought electric ranges and refrigerators. Their outdoor toilet was a source of embarrassment only slightly greater than having to bathe in a number 10 washtub, sometimes in

---

[65] Personal interview with Mrs. L. A. House.
[66] Federal Writers Project interview with Mr. and Mrs. Joseph Davis.

water already used by his brother. When his family finally moved to a house with an indoor bathtub, Townsend invented ways to introduce the subject of bathing in conversations with friends:

> "I like to jump into the bathtub at night. It makes me sleep better." Or this: "Does the phone ring every time you get in the bathtub?" That was a way of showing that we had both a bathtub and a telephone, and remembering it makes me feel silly yet.

Even worse, the family slept under homemade quilts instead of the more fashionable store-bought blankets:

> any time I brought a friend home, there was always the chance that there would be a quilt frame hanging from the ceiling. It was bad enough that we didn't own a car nor have a telephone, but to have my West Point [Georgia] friends learn that we even made our own bed coverings was more than I could bear.[67]

To cope with such realities, poor whites developed many protective devices. They carefully distinguished between themselves and people whom they acknowledged to be "poor white trash." Orrie Robinson explained: "We ain't got nothing but a shirt tail and a prayer, but we ain't low-down. We ain't like them Ellisons. . . . They ain't never tried to do nothing but beat people outa everything they could, and they'd steal the handles off'n a coffin."[68]

Or they contrasted their earlier status as sharecroppers or cotton mill workers to their present condition. Mrs. Lee Snipes, a spinner at Cowikee Cotton Mill, contrasted old ways and new: "It used to be we were just factory folks or 'lint heads.' Now we are 'mill operatives' and we hold our heads high. All work is honorable, you know, and we are proud of ours."[69]

Although few sharecroppers expressed pride in the work they did, such sentiments were common among mill workers and miners. Contrasting her unhappy early years in a poorly run, exploitive mill with her work in Donald Comer's establishment, Mrs. Snipes concluded: "My work is such happiness." Julia Rhodes, who worked at Avondale Mills in Alexander City, also was happy with her occupation.[70]

---

[67] James L. Townsend, "Fatback Mystique," *Brown's Guide to Georgia,* clipping in possession of author.

[68] Federal Writers Project interview with Orrie Robinson.

[69] Federal Writers Project interview with Mrs. Lee Snipes.

[70] *Ibid.,* and Federal Writers Project interviews with Julia Rhodes and Tom Alsobrook.

Coal miners often expressed similar pride in their jobs. Bennie Amerson had lived through nine disasters and prolonged strikes, but he would consider no other occupation: "It sort of gets a fellow when he follows it awhile." Sam Brakefield briefly gave up mining for a safer occupation, but he eventually returned to the mines. It had become so much a part of his life that he couldn't quit.[71]

To such prideful people, education was the key to a better life. Deprived of all but minimal schooling, they blamed their fate primarily on illiteracy. In 1900 13.5 percent of Alabama's adult whites could neither read nor write. Ten years later the rate for the state had dropped to 10.1 percent, but wide geographical variations still existed. For instance, the rate of white adult illiteracy was only 3 percent in the Black Belt; but it rose to 12 percent in the Tennessee Valley, 11 percent in the Warrior Coal Basin, 13 percent in the Appalachian counties, and 14 percent in the eastern clay hills.[72]

Specific examples abound. No one in the family of sharecropper Orrie Robinson could read or write. Mrs. Champion, a textile worker in Eufaula, could not read, her oldest son left school after the seventh grade to join the navy, and her other children quit after only three years of school. The wives of coal miner Joseph Davis and sawmill worker Isaac Johnson taught them to read.[73]

Their children's future depended heavily if not entirely on education. Coal miner Sam Brakefield was satisfied with his life; he was even proud to be a miner. But he was glad none of his children had chosen to follow his trade. He insisted that his children complete school, and he took inordinate pride in a son who had finished at the University of Southern California and was teaching at Howard College. Helena coal miner John Gates missed a supervisory job in the mines because of his limited education; he therefore sacrificed his own welfare so that his oldest son could attend Howard College.[74]

Education was one way out of poverty; a guitar could be another. Such an unlikely route led Hank Williams away from the W. T. Smith Lumber Company to Nashville. His career provided a concrete example of how at least one of Alabama's poor whites escaped poverty.

[71] Federal Writers Project interviews with Bennie Amerson and Sam Brakefield.
[72] Roland M. Harper, "Rural Standards of Living in the South," *Social Forces,* II (January 1924), 261.
[73] Federal Writers Project interviews with Orrie Robinson, Mrs. Champion, Mr. and Mrs. Joseph Davis, and Isaac Johnson.
[74] Federal Writers Project interviews with Sam Brakefield and John Gates.

Born in the Mt. Olive community near Georgiana in 1923, Williams experienced most of the traumas common to poor whites. His father had dropped out of school in the sixth grade and became a water boy in lumber camps. Alonzo Williams enjoyed upward mobility; in succession he graduated to sawing logs, driving oxen, and running a locomotive. He even ran a small store and bought a three-acre strawberry patch.

But in 1930 good times ended for the Williams family. Alonzo entered a VA hospital for treatment of physical and psychological damages sustained in World War I. He was confined for ten years. Deprived of the family's breadwinner, seven-year-old Hank sold peanuts at the logging camp, shined shoes, delivered groceries, and did other odd jobs. His mother finally got a WPA job at a cannery making a dollar a day. A Georgiana woman remembered those hard times: "People were so poor then you can't imagine." Irene Williams, Hank's sister, recalled the era in contradictory terms: "We were poor people but we weren't in poverty. No matter what anyone says, we never begged." She did not approve of the rags to riches characterization of her brother's career. In a typical defensive response she denied her own poverty by redefining it. Only if one had to beg was she poor.[75]

What Lilly Williams could not give her son in material advantages, she supplied from her culture. She taught him the gospel songs that she played on the organ each Sunday at the Baptist church. He began singing with his mother when he was six; for his eighth birthday she dipped into her precious earnings to buy him a guitar. By fourteen, he had organized his own band, playing hoedowns and square dances.

The half-literate school dropout knew only a few technical rudiments of music, some of which he learned from a black street musician in Georgiana. But with this apprenticeship the teenager moved to Montgomery, where he won an amateur night prize of fifteen dollars for a composition that must have embarrassed his sister. Entitled "The WPA Blues," it contained lyrics drawn from his life:

> I got a home in Montgomery,
> A place I like to stay,
> But I have to work for the WPA,
> And I'm dissatisfied—I'm dissatisfied.

[75] Roger M. Williams, *Sing a Sad Song: The Life of Hank Williams* (New York, 1970), 8–13.

Encouraged by this early recognition, he got a job with radio station WSFA and sang in honky-tonks and for club meetings. Unable to make a decent living, he briefly departed for a shipyard job in Mobile until his mother arranged enough appearances for him to return to the capital.

He finally decided to move to Nashville, the capital of country music. Arriving by bus, he began to introduce himself to the stars. When the Willis Brothers, then called the Oklahoma Wranglers, first met him, they were unimpressed by his Baptist hymns and country blues. His singing was unprofessional and his lyrics amateurish: "We hadn't been used to hearing a country singer who was as country as he was." A Nashville friend and songwriter, Vic McAlpin, well remembered Williams's entry to "Music City":

> He was just a country hick like me. The kind of hick that comes from so far back in the country that you're like a damn whipped dog people kick around in this business. You don't make friends too easy because you got your own thing, and you don't trust nobody very much and to hell with 'em. A backwoods cat, that's what I call 'em. That's kinda the way he was.[76]

His popularity exploded among poor whites who were moving to cities after 1945 to take industrial jobs. In 1947 he got a job as a songwriter with Roy Acuff in Nashville's first country music publishing firm. He left briefly for a successful stint on the Louisiana Hayride before returning to Nashville in 1949 with the Grand Ole Opry. Four of the top ten country hits in 1949 were written by Hank Williams: "Love Sick Blues," "Mind Your Own Business," "You're Gonna Change," and "My Bucket's Got a Hole in It." Four of his 1950 songs earned him gold records ("I Just Don't Like This Kind of Livin'," "Lone Gone Lonesome Blues," "Moaning the Blues," "Why Don't You Love Me"). In 1951 he made the charts with seven hits including "Cold, Cold Heart," "Dear John," and "Hey, Good Lookin'." In 1952 he followed with "Jambalaya," "Honky Tonk Blues," and "Setting the Woods on Fire." Even after his death on New Year's Day 1953, at age twenty-nine, his records continued to dominate the charts for years.[77]

[76] Jack Hurst, *Grand Ole Opry* (New York, 1975), 175–77.
[77] Irwin Stambler and Grelun Landon, *Encyclopedia of Folk, Country and Western Music* (New York, 1969), 333.

His early poverty, divorce, the alcohol and drug abuse that finally took his life, were common experiences for millions of poor whites who were pouring into the cities. This semi-literate "Hillbilly Shakespeare" understood their frustrations and their dreams, and his white man's blues allowed country music to penetrate urban American subculture. Music critic D. K. Wilgus best captured the ambience of his songs:

> Hank Williams was as country-based as they come, or rather he was a typical product of the forces of urbanization on the southeastern poor white. He reeked of the parched fields of Alabama, the dirty streets and dives of Montgomery. He embodied drunken Saturday nights in the tavern and soul-saving Sundays in the country church. It was all there in him, and it was all there in his music. He had the gospel, blues, and sentimental tradition from folk and professional sources. He had inhaled the postwar honky-tonk style with every breath. . . . He presented–in fact he was–the dichotomy, the polarization of the urban hillbilly: he went "honky-tonkin'," but knew he was "Headed Down the Wrong Highway"; he cheated, was cheated on, cursed her "Cheatin' Heart," "Dreamed About Mama Last Night," and looked forward to the land "Beyond the Sunset."[78]

Alabama poor white culture had given a whole class its most articulate spokesman and its most popular hero.

To call Hank Williams's people "famous men," as James Agee did, even with license for excluding all those memorable women, is to idealize history and romanticize the class. The reality of their lives, the foibles, phobias, and grinding poverty, or the occasional failures of spirit, sexual promiscuity, drunkenness, and violence, are too apparent to honor them with so grand a title. But they deserve better than they have gotten, which is comic stereotype and historical obscurity. They were people with a fierce will to survive, whose folk culture and family cohesion often contrast favorably to the standardized forms of "Dallas" and "Dynasty," to the familial disintegration and narcissism of the "me generation." If not "famous men," then at least people determined to endure, whose past, I trust, will not be forgotten.

---

[78] D. K. Wilgus, "Country-Western Music and the Urban Hillbilly," *Journal of American Folklore*, LXXXIII (April–June 1970), 172–73.

World War II
and Beyond

WILLIAM D. BARNARD

The Old Order Changes:
Graves, Sparks, Folsom, and the
Gubernatorial Election of 1942

The State Democratic executive committee met in Montgomery in
early January of 1942 to issue the call for a gubernatorial primary the
following May.* Everyone expected the forthcoming campaign to be
dull and dispirited. Atticus Mullin, the astute but partisan political
columnist for the Montgomery *Advertiser,* predicted that this would
be "the least interesting State campaign in history."[1]

The South is known for its colorful political contests, and Alabama
has seldom had a placid campaign. The Democratic party in Alabama
was split in the 1940s, as it had been in rough fashion since Reconstruction, into two factions. One, favoring an expansion of state services
and identifying with Franklin Roosevelt's New Deal in the 1930s, drew
its strength from the mining and farming regions of north Alabama,
from organized labor, city and county officeholders, the elderly, and
educators. The other, favoring low taxes and economical government
at all costs and vehemently anti-New Deal, drew its strength from
the business and industrial community and from conservative agricultural interests, particularly in the Black Belt. With each faction
sure to contest the gubernatorial race, why was 1942 expected to differ
from the bitter and colorful campaigns of the past? Because no one
seriously expected it to be a contest at all. Former Governor Bibb

This essay was published in *The Alabama Review,* XXVIII (July 1975).
*Brief segments of this article have previously appeared in William D. Barnard,
Dixiecrats and Democrats: Alabama Politics 1942–1950, University, Ala.: The University of
Alabama Press, 1974.
[1] Montgomery *Advertiser,* January 8, 1942.

Graves was running for a third term, and Graves was seemingly invincible in Alabama politics.

Atticus Mullin was convinced that a majority of the Democratic executive committee would officially endorse Graves if they could. Graves was "the friend of Roosevelt and a progressive," Mullin wrote, and was so highly respected by the Alabama electorate that against any conceivable opponent he would win better than three to one.[2]

Bibb Graves had twice served as governor of Alabama. First elected in 1926, he succeeded the amiable conservative, "Plain Bill" Brandon, whose administration had been one of economy and retrenchment. During Brandon's administration, there had built up among the progressive forces within the state a demand for increased expenditures for schools, roads, social services and for increased taxes on corporate wealth to pay for these expansive programs. With economic issues most prominent, the 1926 contest had resolved, as A. B. Moore put it, into a classic struggle "between the conservative and progressive wings of the Democracy."[3]

Despite opposition by the major newspapers, by the outgoing Brandon administration, and by the business and industrial interests of the state, Graves forged a winning coalition of veterans, organized labor, supporters of education, and expanded welfare services—and the Ku Klux Klan.[4]

With the addition of county and municipal officials and aided by the popularity of Franklin Roosevelt, this was the same coalition that returned Graves to office in 1934, after the required intervening term. Despite the unyielding opposition of "one of the most powerful and persistent lobbies in the history of the State," appropriations for education, for roads, and for other social services increased substantially in Graves' two administrations. Though the tax burden on the "Big Mules," the great corporate interests and the

[2] *Ibid.*

[3] Albert Burton Moore, *History of Alabama* (Tuscaloosa, 1951), 767–70.

[4] *Ibid.*, 770. This is not the place for an extended discussion of the connection, or lack of it, between the Klan and Southern progressives in the 1920s. Suffice it to say that many progressive Southern politicians did join the organization initially. In the middle of Graves' first administration violence perpetrated by the Klan led many prominent politicians to break with the organization and call for measures to curb its activities. Graves did not take as strong a stand against the Klan as many would have liked, but he did act to end the "reign of terror" that existed in some counties, and, according to the Montgomery *Advertiser,* resigned from the organization in 1928 for the good of the state. Moore, *History of Alabama,* 774–77.

wealthy, had been increased, these expanded state programs had also been financed by one of the most regressive of taxes, the sales tax.[5]

The bust of Graves that stands on the capitol grounds carries a simple epitaph: "Bibb Graves—The Builder." And so he was. Almost every public institution of higher learning then in existence has its Bibb Graves Hall. Highways and county roads were paved and improved. While he lived, particularly during the 1930s when his brand of bread-and-butter liberalism combined with his genial manner to endear him to the Alabama electorate, he was unbeatable. Atticus Mullin had judged the political climate correctly. But 1942 was to prove a year of surprises in Alabama politics.

Graves' only opponent of consequence at the start of the campaign was Chauncey Sparks, long-time legislator and runner-up to Frank Dixon in the gubernatorial contest of 1938. Sparks was from Barbour County and had been dubbed "the Bourbon from Barbour." His legislative record was largely nonideological, though he had been identified with the conservative "economy bloc" in the state senate during Graves' second administration.[6]

Despite Sparks' strong showing against Dixon in 1938, Graves seemed unbeatable. He had consolidated his support among progressive forces in the state and had the support of the schoolteachers, the oldsters, city and county officials, and labor. His identification with Roosevelt further aided his cause.[7]

Sparks could not repudiate Roosevelt and the New Deal. He could not openly run an anti-New Deal campaign. That was politically impossible. He could, however, expect considerable aid from the business and industrial community, which was anti-Roosevelt. The size and character of that support depended in large measure on incumbent-Governor Frank Dixon, acknowledged leader of the anti-New Deal forces in the state.

Dixon and other conservative leaders were reluctant to support Sparks, however. He lacked color, many said, and could not be elected.[8]

---

[5] Moore, *History of Alabama*, 771–76; Malcolm C. McMillan, *The Land Called Alabama* (Austin, Texas, 1968), 312–14, 361.

[6] W. D. Malone to Chauncey Sparks, June 23, 1936, in Sparks Papers, Alabama Department of Archives and History, Montgomery, Alabama. (Unless stated otherwise, all Sparks communications cited are in this collection.) See also Sparks to Jeff Beeland, June 20, 1936; Sparks to A. B. Aldrige, June 25, 1936.

[7] Birmingham *News*, September 20, 27, 28, October 3, 1941.

[8] Robin Swift to Sparks, October 24, 1940.

Sparks was aware of his lackluster image and of the hesitancy of Dixon to support him. As early as April, 1939, he set out what his strategy would be. Dixon, he argued, would do anything to prevent Graves from serving a third term. Therefore, "we should try to build up such strength that Dixon will throw in with us or keep hands off. . . . We ought first to encourage talk of Graves and second strengthen our own fences and make them so high as to keep D[ixon] from putting a man on our track."[9]

Sparks wanted to define the issue clearly as a contest between the liberal, free-spending Graves and those opposed to him and his policies. He hoped to compel the support of all anti-Graves factions by making himself the only possible candidate with a chance of defeating Graves. "If there is to be a Graves and anti-Graves fight," he wrote a friend and advisor, "then we should have high hopes that the anti-Graves forces would have to look to us. This would well define the issue and remove the necessity of having to approve or disapprove present [Dixon] administration."[10]

Well into 1941, with the primary less than a year away, Sparks had failed to secure support from the conservative wing of the party. James A. Simpson, respected Birmingham businessman and a leader of the conservative faction, feared that Sparks could not be elected. Governor Dixon continued to express his reservations about Sparks' candidacy. He agreed that the anti-Graves forces should unite on one candidate, but, he confided rather pointedly to Sparks, one who can win. Dixon's reservations were echoed by others to whom Sparks looked for support. According to Sparks' closest personal and political friend, some business leaders in the state were resigned to the inevitability of a Graves victory and would not make a serious effort to oppose the two-term governor. "Let Graves have it," they said, "he never hurt business and his sales tax is our salvation."[11]

On into 1941 conservative leaders continued to search for a more colorful candidate to lead the anti-Graves forces. Robin Swift, Sparks' friend of long standing, warned Sparks that "they are going to exhaust every possibility before they come to you."[12] But Sparks was

[9] Sparks to Robin Swift, April 1, 1939.
[10] Ibid.
[11] Robin Swift to Sparks, October 24, 1940; Emmett Hildreth to Sparks, February 6, 1941; Sparks to Swift, February 28, 1941.
[12] Robin Swift to Sparks, February 17, 1941.

increasingly confident that in the end the conservatives would be forced to turn to him as the only candidate of statewide reputation capable of running a plausible campaign against Graves.

In mid February of 1941, Sparks was told by Sydney Smyer, another conservative business leader from Birmingham, that influential businessmen, centered in Birmingham, had concluded that they did not wish to see a third Graves administration and that Sparks was the most logical candidate to oppose him. "Many of my friends," Smyer reported, "say that you cannot win." But, he added, "this state has been combed for a candidate other than you. . . . So far, none has been found."[13]

Smyer urged Sparks to declare his candidacy early to forestall the spread of a defeatist attitude among the conservatives. But by this time Sparks was relishing the predicament of the anti-Graves forces. "Let them stew in their own pepper sauce," he wrote his friend Swift. "An early announcement might stop [their] search [for another candidate] but might cause resentment and consequent half handed support."[14]

Sparks was cheered by these indications of increasingly firm support from the conservative faction of the state party. Yet rumors continued to spread in early 1941 that even the "good citizens," in Swift's phase, recognized the inevitable and would support Graves. Governor Dixon was still unwilling to endorse Sparks. The Governor met with Sparks in late February and assured him that he, Dixon, was not behind the efforts to boom candidacies of other anti-Graves possibilities. Nonetheless, Dixon wondered aloud if perhaps someone with fewer political scars than Sparks should carry the anti-Graves banner in 1942. He urged Sparks not to withdraw, though—at least not yet.[15]

In the months before the campaign officially opened, Sparks continued to seek the support of the business and industrial community. Robin Swift had urged him to "give a lot of thought" to his stand on labor. It was a year of labor unrest, "and the rank and file of the people are mighty sore about these strikes. It is my guess," Swift added, "that they are going to get sorer, for organized

---

[13] Sidney Smyer to Sparks, February 19, 1941.
[14] *Ibid.;* Sparks to Robin Swift, February 21, 1941; see also Sparks to Sidney Smyer, February 24, 1941.
[15] Robin Swift to Sparks, April 24, 1941; Sparks to Swift, February 28, 1941.

labor has no patriotism, no sense of responsibility, and in its greed would wreck this Country." Besides, Swift argued, Graves already had the union vote and Sparks could not damage himself by criticizing the overweening power of organized labor.[16]

Sparks must have been impressed with Swift's argument. In a Labor Day speech in a laboring district in industrial Birmingham, he jolted his audience with a call for the regulation of organized labor and the cessation of the right to strike during a wartime emergency.[17] Swift was elated. "Here is the issue between you and Graves," he wrote. "I mean the new issue. The real issue of good government is now *old* and *stale*," he argued, "but the question of whether or not Union Labor is going to rule or ruin means the very existence of this State and Nation."[18]

Sparks' strategy had apparently worked. In July he had received what he took to be a firm offer of support from Dixon. And in the same week that he delivered his Labor Day speech he met with a group of influential businessmen in Birmingham to discuss his campaign and to establish a committee to raise the necessary funds.[19]

Sparks was increasingly optimistic. To Robin Swift, he exulted, "Before long it will be asked, 'Has Graves a chance' instead of have I a chance." And as 1942 dawned and the May primary neared, he was further encouraged by Graves' inability to run an aggressive campaign. Graves was already past seventy and on a "bed of apparent permanent affliction."[20]

Graves' health and age had been of concern to his friends for some time. In 1939, at the end of his second term, he was one of the South's oldest governors to serve in the decade from 1938 to 1948, and he had suffered two painful and serious attacks of kidney stones.[21] Nonetheless, with the progressive faction of the party entrenched in all

---

[16] Robin Swift to Sparks, June 7, 1941. See the Birmingham *News,* September 14, 19, 27, 30, and October 21, 1941, for the impact of a number of strikes on the Birmingham economy. By late October, twenty of Birmingham's key industries were idled by strikes.

[17] Birmingham *News,* September 2 and 7, 1941.

[18] Robin Swift to Sparks, August [September ?] 2, 1941.

[19] Personal memorandum of conference with Governor Dixon written by Sparks, July 22, 1941; Memorandum on Organization Plans, September 2, 1941; Memorandum by Sparks, September 12, 1941.

[20] Sparks to Robin Swift, September 4, 1941.

[21] Graves was the third oldest of the forty-six governors to serve in the eleven Confederate states plus Oklahoma in the decade 1938–1948. See Cortez A. M. Ewing, "Southern Governors," *Journal of Politics,* Vol. X, No. 2 (May, 1948), 390; Birmingham *News,* November 6, 1941.

but the governor's chair, he still remained, as John Temple Graves put it, "Governor-in-Waiting."[22]

By late 1941, despite his age and fragile health, Graves looked like the winner to the established politicians in the state. He was overwhelmed with endorsements from county commissioners, and by November, he had secured the endorsement of "practically every [politically] potent group in Alabama."[23]

That same month, however, the fears of his partisans materialized. Graves was taken to a Montgomery hospital with an apparent attack of kidney stones.[24]

The outbreak of war in December, 1941, overshadowed the news of Graves' illness. Interest in state politics dimmed. Both Graves and Sparks tried to turn their campaigns in the direction of the people's major concern, issuing repeated statements of support for Roosevelt and the nation in the war effort.[25]

Other issues were not forgotten, however. Sparks continued to criticize Graves' past administrations as lavish and wasteful. In the speech officially opening his campaign, he charged that the main issue was clear, "the merit system against the spoils system." This election, he contended, would decide whether Alabamians "will return to the yoke of governmental dishonesty and abuse of power or whether they will continue the progress already made [by the Dixon administration] and advance along new lines." Alabamians will choose their governor in 1942, Sparks said, "despite all sinister schemes to disallow any choice of the people by limiting the number of candidates to only that one whose two terms of unsurpassed extravagance some refer to as experience, whose tried and true record—long since damned by all who love Alabama—guarantees again the opportunity for feasting on the public treasury by unscrupulous swarms of political locusts."[26] This same "wanton, willful and wasteful group" was trying to force its way back to the political trough in the hope that the people had forgotten "the political stench which accompanied them out of office" the last time.[27]

Such heated charges had little impact, however. Sparks' campaign

[22] Quoted in Birmingham *News,* November 9, 1941.
[23] *Ibid.,* October 19, 23, and November 16, 1941.
[24] *Ibid.,* November 6, 1941.
[25] See, for example, *ibid.,* November 21, 1941.
[26] *Ibid.,* January 9, 30, 1942.
[27] *Alabama: News Magazine of the Deep South,* Vol. VIII, No. 5 (January 30, 1942), 7.

was in trouble. Less than 150 people turned out in Huntsville to hear his opening speech. Interest in state politics had waned after the Japanese attack upon Pearl Harbor and, as Dixon and others had feared, Sparks lacked the dash and flamboyance to fire the voters' interest. Sparks was in a box. He was up against a powerful but absent foe.[28]

Graves was now in Baltimore, at Johns Hopkins. His followers issued optimistic statements about his condition, and he himself told his campaign leaders to "tell the boys to keep on keeping on." It was reported that he might see F. D. R. about the war effort, that he was more interested in the defense of the nation than in politics.[29]

Sparks might decry those "sinister schemes" to smother debate through calls for unity before the foreign foe, but the appeals of Richard Rives and other leaders in Graves' campaign had an undeniable impact. Rives, an ardent New Dealer, was Graves' campaign manager. In February, he issued a statement arguing that "this is not the time to undermine faith and confidence in our democratic processes, to divide and embitter our people for the purpose of serving the political ambitions of any man."[30]

Sparks found it difficult to respond to such statements. Not to do so or to do so meekly meant that his campaign would remain stalled. Yet to do so with vehemence took on the appearance of an unsporting attack upon a sick man. Perhaps for that reason the harvest responses were left to his brother Leon. "Alabamians will not be misled," Leon Sparks charged, "by the red herring of 'peace and unity' which Mr. Rives seeks to drag across the spoil-strewn trail of Col. Graves' two past administrations. Nor will they follow blindly the banner he has raised with its meaningless motto: 'Keep on keeping on.' " Graves "has twice paid his political debts with the people's money. Let him now renounce his own personal ambitions in the interests of 'peace and unity.' "[31]

With Sparks' campaign floundering and with Graves' health increasingly uncertain, there was a flurry of interest in other candidates in early 1942. Three major candidates had already entered the race. Henry J. Carwile hailed from the same county that spawned the Populist

[28] Birmingham *News,* January 30, February 1 and 15, 1942.
[29] *Ibid.,* January 24 and 26, 1942.
[30] *Ibid.,* February 15, 1942.
[31] *Ibid.*

orator, Joseph C. Manning, and the liberal senator and jurist, Hugo Black. Carwile ran as the "poor man's" candidate. Traversing the state in a red, white, and blue Model T, "the man from the mountains" proclaimed his campaign slogan: "Save the perishing and care for the dying." W. O. Broyles, an elderly furniture dealer from Birmingham, campaigned chiefly with a promise of $60 per month for the aged, and an Ozark dentist pledged to improve the quality of education in the state. None was a serious contender.[32] In late February, James E. Folsom of Cullman announced his candidacy, but it was little noticed by the press.[33]

The press paid considerably more attention, however, to the entry of another candidate, Chris Sherlock. Sherlock had held the politically sensitive post of highway director in the Dixon administration. Unlike the other candidates, he spoke bluntly about Graves' health and predicted that even if the Little Colonel lived to be elected he would not serve out his term. Graves was "a very weak, sick old man," Sherlock charged, and "would be controlled by a bunch of sycophants."[34]

Sherlock immediately attracted support from conservatives who had never been enthusiastic about Sparks. He might be able to defeat Graves if Sparks could not. At the very least he might split the Graves vote. From Wilcox County, in the heart of the Black Belt, former Governor B. M. Miller announced his support. And Sherlock later told Chauncey Sparks that he had been urged to declare his candidacy by Governor Dixon.[35] "Ain't it hell!!!" Robin Swift had written Sparks a few months earlier, "all this crossing and double crossing."[36]

Sherlock later claimed that he had had secret information on the seriousness of Graves' condition. Perhaps Sherlock hoped to gain the support of the Graves faction should Graves withdraw or die before the upcoming primary. This support, combined with that of Miller and Dixon, might very well elevate Sherlock to the state house rather than Sparks.[37] If that was Sherlock's hope, it proved a misplaced one

[32] *Ibid.*, October 29, 1941; February 22, 1942.

[33] *Ibid.*, March 1, 1942.

[34] Montgomery *Advertiser,* April 9, 1942.

[35] Birmingham *News,* March 8, 1942; Memorandum by Sparks on a conversation with Sherlock, June 5, 1942.

[36] Robin Swift to Sparks, November 9, 1941.

[37] Memorandum by Sparks on a conversation with Sherlock, June 5, 1942.

when news of Graves' death reached Alabama in the second week of March.

Graves' passing was genuinely mourned by a majority of Alabama's citizens. He had graduated Phi Beta Kappa from Yale, but he was known as "a man of the people." He had an aura of personal magnetism that attracted the same fierce loyalty that Jim Folsom and George Wallace later had. The people regarded him somehow as a personal friend, the Birmingham *News* commented. His interest in the people's welfare, the *News* contended, was not merely campaign rhetoric. He had ended the "wretched convict-lease system," lessened the inequities in the state tax structure, and improved the quality of education.[38]

Cooper Green, the capable and progressive mayor of Birmingham, said that Alabama had lost "its greatest liberal statesman," and many recalled the oft-quoted remark of Grover Hall, Sr., late editor of the Montgomery *Advertiser*. Bibb Graves, Hall had said, "makes a good governor but an expensive one." The Birmingham *News* thought Hall was right and that whether you were for or against Graves depended largely on whether you placed governmental economy first or progressive government "even if it was somewhat expensive." The majority of the people of Alabama had placed progressive government first and had revered Bibb Graves.[39]

Graves' death removed the strongest liberal contender in the race for governor. But it could not have been less propitious for Chris Sherlock. Overnight, in the eyes of most Graves supporters, Sherlock became not simply a political insurgent rebelling against an aging master, but a rebel against a revered and departed leader. To the Graves forces he was now political anathema. To the anti-Graves forces he was no longer a viable candidate. Governor Dixon had long since lost interest. Sherlock's campaign was destroyed, though he did not know it yet.

But what were the Graves men to do? They could not support Sherlock. They did not want to support Sparks. Carwile and Broyles were impossible, and no one took Folsom's rustic liberalism seriously. The qualifying deadline had passed. No last-minute candidacy could

[38] Birmingham *News*, March 14, 15, 1942.
[39] *Ibid.*

be launched. In the end, the majority of Graves' backers supported Sparks. It was reluctant support, however.[40]

A small group of Graves' lieutenants broke ranks and supported Folsom. A few weeks later the Birmingham *News* reported that "one of the mild surprises of the campaign" was the overnight strength of Folsom, who had "looked down in bucolic bewilderment when he found a group of Graves' men had decided to have a fling with him." Folsom's candidacy reportedly was being pushed by "a comparatively small but potent group" of Graves' followers who felt that they could not support Sparks or Sherlock but who hoped to force the two into a run-off in order to enhance their own bargaining position.[41]

Folsom's campaign was essentially a one-man effort. Without the support of the courthouse rings he was forced to go directly to the people. And he was suited by temperament and by philosophy for just such a campaign. His campaigns were unlike any other Alabama had known. Familiar with the techniques of other mass leaders of the South, Folsom drew upon their innovations and adapted them to his own use. He recalled Jackson's ploy of brandishing a hickory broom and promising to sweep the rascals out of Washington, and he acquired a cornshuck mop of his own. Up-country bands, the passing of the bucket, the outlandish rhetoric damning the corrupt politicians who represented "the interests"—all became his stock in trade.

These were the techniques of men both of good intent and ill. Folsom mastered them for his own purposes. But his greatest asset was himself. Folsom was not a grand orator of the old school. He did not stir the masses with fevered phrases. He was not grandiloquent.[42]

---

[40] *Alabama: The News Magazine of the Deep South,* Vol. VII, No. 12 (March 20, 1942), 6. It was suggested that Richard Rives, Graves' campaign manager, enter the race if the Democratic Executive Committee would reopen the eligibility list. That was impossible, however, for the State Chairman, Gessner McCorvey of Mobile, was anti-Graves and refused to call the committee into session.

[41] Birmingham *News,* March 22, 1942.

[42] Young Grover Hall, Jr., the observant political commentator from Montgomery, first heard a Folsom speech in 1946. He was disappointed. "It was not the show we had expected. It was, in fact, flat, nasal and devoid of pageantry. . . . The Folsom show had no pace and the lines were neither bright nor sharp." Still, judging from his columns and editorials of later years, Hall himself was ineluctably drawn to Folsom. A political critic he remained, but he was a bemused and sympathetic observer. "Hallmarks," [Montgomery] Alabama *Journal,* March 4, 1946. Clipping in Scrapbook of Chauncey Sparks, Alabama Department of Archives and History, Montgomery, Alabama. (Hereinafter referred to as Sparks Scrapbook.)

No, it was not Folsom's oratory that captured the allegiance of the plain folk who heard him. Indeed, he was the antithesis of the great orator. When introduced he would walk to the podium with a rather ambling gait, almost a shuffle. Usually dressed in a conservative suit or in shirtsleeves, he would speak to his listeners in long, loping sentences that resembled more the across-the-fence talk of neighbors than the heightened periods of a politician's speech.

It was low-key, despite the inflated rhetoric and pungent phrases. Replete with stories drawn from rural folklore, his performance was captivating. In this, his first statewide campaign, he was every town's overgrown boy, faintly bashful but full of mischief. He exuded a sincerity of purpose and an integrity of intent that found ready adherents among those who heard him.[43]

Folsom's campaign opened in Ft. Payne, a DeKalb County town of 4000 in the northeastern corner of the state. This was the hill-country where Folsom's brand of politics found ready and historic acceptance. It was a county whose yeoman farmers had looked askance at the swollen wealth and power of the Black Belt before the Civil War. It was an area that had been less than wholly enthusiastic about secession and the Civil War. Its hills had harbored many who fought for the Confederacy but who had doubts about a war to defend slavery when they had no slaves, about a war that took the sons of an insular people far from their families and crops. To some the Civil War had been "a rich man's war and a poor man's fight." The Lost Cause was not revered here in quite the same manner as in the Black Belt counties of Dallas and Wilcox and Lowndes. DeKalb, like Folsom's adopted county of Cullman, had remained a center of discontent both within and without the Democratic party. These hill-country counties nurtured a sizable Republican minority and provided the progressive wing of the Democratic party with their primary allegiance. Third parties and unorthodox economic nostrums found fer-

---

[43] For comments on the character of Folsom's appeal in a later campaign, see Atlanta *Journal,* June 9, 1946; Birmingham *Post,* August 27, 1946. Clippings in the vertical files of the Birmingham Public Library's Southern Collection (hereinafter referred to as BPL Files). One of Folsom's political rivals once tried to account for the public response to Folsom. "Jim appeals to the popular imagination," he said. "He's like a big awkward puppy. People love him on sight and, for no apparent reason, feel kindly toward him. It doesn't seem to matter what he says or does, or even if he says or does anything. They just vote for him regardless. To them, he's not a politician...." Birmingham *Post,* August 20, 1945. Clipping in BPL File.

tile breeding ground in the poor lands of the hill counties.[44] Here Folsom opened his first campaign for governor.

When Folsom and the two or three men traveling with him reached Ft. Payne, they hired a local band to play for the rally and to attract a crowd.[45] The evening went well, but when the band was paid the campaign treasury was exhausted. Somehow his entourage made it to Walker County, another mountain county to the west of Birmingham, in the heart of the mining district. Here labor violence and liberal economics had mixed freely throughout the state's history.

Funds were low or nonexistent, and activity in Walker was limited to handshaking down the mainstreets of little mining communities and delivering impromptu street-corner speeches wherever a group of voters could be corralled. After Graves' death, however, funds were more readily available.

One source of campaign funds proved to be the opposition, the Sherlock campaign itself. Sherlock's campaign leaders realized that Sparks was the frontrunner. Sherlock's only hope was to deny Sparks a majority, to force him into a run-off. To do so required that Folsom draw a sizable number of votes. Thus when Folsom's campaign leaders approached members of Sherlock's organization and told them that Folsom's campaign might founder from lack of funds, Sherlock's leaders quickly diverted some of their own money to Folsom's campaign.[46]

Sherlock's willingness to subsidize Folsom's campaign in the hope of forcing a run-off was indicative of Sparks' growing strength. City and county officials, who had been solidly behind Graves, had turned to Sparks as the most likely winner. Many of the state's newspapers had joined the mounting bandwagon. And the nucleus of Graves' personal machine, centered in Montgomery, lent their support.[47]

With Graves no longer living, each of the remaining candidates sought to wrap himself in the dead leader's mantle. Richard Rives, Graves' former campaign manager, spoke for much of the state's liberal faction in supporting Sparks. Folsom and Sherlock, Rives contended, were "two self-styled liberals" and it would be "a sad

[44] See, for example, Moore, *History of Alabama,* 353, 416–17, 581–82, 639; V. O. Key, *Southern Politics in State and Nation* (New York, 1949), 42, 45–46.

[45] Interview with James E. Folsom, Cullman, Alabama, July 29, 1968. Unless otherwise noted, the description of Folsom's campaign which follows is based on this interview.

[46] Interview with Folsom, Cullman, Alabama, July 29, 1968; Grover Hall, Jr., "Hallmarks," [Montgomery] Alabama *Journal,* November 27, 1945, Sparks Scrapbooks.

[47] Birmingham *News,* March 29, April 5, 12, 19, 1942.

day for the true liberals in Alabama if . . . either . . . should be elected."[48]

Rives' effort to portray Chauncey Sparks as the "true liberal" in the race was not wholly convincing. Sherlock's campaign advertising highlighted Sparks' conservative legislative record and pointed to himself as the genuine "New Deal" candidate. Organized labor also refused to accept Sparks' recent conversion to liberalism. The A. F. of L. refused to endorse anyone, indicating that Folsom would be their choice if he had a chance. The C. I. O., however, switched support from Sherlock to Folsom in mid-campaign.[49]

Folsom also sought to identify himself with Graves, to cast himself as the genuine liberal in the race. He was pleased, he said, that Alabama had turned to "a real Democrat who believes in the principles of our leadership in Washington and in the political philosophy practiced by that great humanitarian, the Hon. Bibb Graves. . . . I will carry on from where he left off."[50]

Despite last-minute charges by Sherlock, a Catholic, that Sparks was guilty of religious prejudice and had avoided military service in World War I, Sparks won by a small majority. Predictions that he would garner 60 to 75 percent of the vote were wide of the mark, however. To the surprise of most observers and especially to the Sherlock camp, Folsom ran second with 26 percent of the vote. Whether or not there would be a run-off was in doubt for several days. But when the official count was released, Sparks had a margin of 6,071 votes out of some 279,000 cast. A run-off was unnecessary.[51]

The confusion and disarray inherent in the 1942 primary is apparent in the returns. The clarity of factional lines had been blurred after the death of Bibb Graves. What had begun as a clear-cut clash between the progressive and conservative wings of the Democratic party had been muted.

Chauncey Sparks received a plurality in fifty-one of the state's sixty-seven counties. His support was quite general throughout the state and fits no established pattern. Generally his support was strong-

[48] *Ibid.*, May 3, 1942.

[49] *Ibid.*, May 4, April 12, 1942; *Alabama: The News Magazine of the Deep South,* Vol. VII, No. 13 (March 27, 1942), 6; No. 16 (April 17, 1942), 6; No. 18 (May 1, 1942), 4.

[50] Birmingham *News,* May 3, 1942.

[51] *Ibid.*, April 19, 26, May 9, 11, 1942. The vote stood: Sparks 145,798; Folsom 73,306; Sherlock 53,448; Carwile 4,745; and Broyles 2,157. The Ozark dentist had withdrawn earlier.

est in the Black Belt counties and in a cluster of counties in the east-central section of the state. He ran relatively poorly in the Wiregrass, where both Folsom and Sherlock were strong contenders. He also ran relatively poorly in counties in the southwestern corner of the state, counties included in the old First Congressional District.

The old First was generally a conservative stronghold in state politics. Conservative political circles centered in Mobile exercised great influence within the district. Though Sparks carried all the counties in the district except populous Mobile, the old First was the center of Sherlock's greatest strength and counties in the area generally gave Sparks a relatively small plurality. Aided perhaps by the relatively high percentage of his fellow Catholics in Mobile and perhaps by the lingering reluctance of some conservatives to support Sparks, Sherlock ran relatively well throughout the southwestern third of the state, with scattered strength in the western Black Belt and in portions of the Wiregrass, which was the home of his wife.

Despite the lack of clear-cut pattern in the vote for Sparks and Sherlock, the returns nonetheless reflect not only the passing political alignments of the moment but deep and persisting divisions in the Alabama body politic as well. This is most apparent in the pattern of support for "Big Jim" Folsom.

The sectional basis of Folsom's strength approximates most closely the historic political divisions within the state. Folsom ran strongest in a band of ten contiguous counties stretching from the northeastern corner of the state, down the lower bank of the Tennessee, dipping into the mountainous mineral district and thence westward to the Mississippi line. A second pocket of strength lay in a cluster of five counties in the southeastern corner of the state, the Wiregrass.[52]

Folsom had been born in the Wiregrass county of Coffee and resided in the north Alabama county of Cullman. His strength in these areas is evidence of the tendency of Alabama voters to support candidates from their section of the state.[53] But it also reflects the enduring sectional alignments in state politics.

The hill country of north Alabama and the Wiregrass—both regions

---

[52] The only county in which a minor candidate polled a significant percentage of the vote was Clay. Henry J. Carwile carried his home county with 47.7% of the vote. In only one other county did his vote exceed 5% of the total and generally it was much lower than that. His percentage of the statewide total was 1.70%.

[53] Key, *Southern Politics*, 37–41.

of low Negro population and peopled by subsistence farmers or urban laborers rather than great planters and their dependents—had often been united in political outlook. These were areas that had been strongest in support for Jackson, weakest in enthusiasm for secession and the Confederacy. They had provided strong support for the repeated attempts of white farmers to overthrow or alter conservative Redeemer control in the late nineteenth century.[54] And, in the case of north Alabama, these counties harbored a significant Republican minority. Here had been the breeding ground for political dissidence and a kind of truculent democratic revolt against the "better elements" for over a hundred years.

Conversely, Folsom ran poorly in counties of high black population. He received least support in that area of the state, the Black Belt, that had been the seat of planter power, that had been Whig rather than Democratic before the Civil War, and that had been the mainstay of political, economic, and racial conservatism since Reconstruction. Eleven of the seventeen counties in the lowest quartile of support for Folsom are in or border the Black Belt. Here, with a great concentration of Negro population, the pressure for social and political unity among whites historically had been greater than in the hill country. These were the counties most ardent in their support of the conservative Redeemers after Reconstruction. And it was in these counties that the Populists and Greenbackers had received least support.[55]

Folsom's ability to mount a strong campaign with a minimum of support from the courthouse politicians, the press, or the great business and financial interests of the state was one of the many surprises of the 1942 electoral year. The outcome of the contest, however, was scarcely surprising. It had not been in doubt since the death of Bibb Graves.

The meaning of the election, what it portended for the future, was less clear. Sparks won in 1942 under conservative aegis. But the most powerful leader of the state's liberal faction had been removed from

[54] Moore, *History of Alabama*, 416–17, 582, 639; McMillan, *Land Called Alabama*, 115–17, 119–21, 188–90, 193, 265–68, 275–77; C. Vann Woodward, *Origins of the New South* ([Baton Rouge], 1951), 78–79, 84, 247; Key, *Southern Politics*, 42, 45–46.

[55] These counties also were strongest in support of the 1946 Boswell Amendment that sought to restrict Negro suffrage, and it was from these counties that much of the leadership of the States' Rights revolt of 1948 came. William D. Barnard, *Dixiecrats and Democrats: Alabama Politics 1942–1950* (University, Ala.: The University of Alabama Press, 1974), 63, 97–101; Key, *Southern Politics*, 332–33, 634–35.

the contest by death, and factional lines had been blurred when most of Graves' supporters swung to Sparks.

Intent upon reasserting conservative influence in state politics, the conservative faction sought in 1942 to retain control of the governorship they had won in 1938 with Frank Dixon. The governor's chair was one of the few major offices held by conservatives. Though they succeeded in 1942 almost by default, leaders of the conservative faction could take encouragement from Sparks' election. Prevailing political winds seemed decidedly favorable to those of conservative bent, and the conservative faction could look forward with enthusiasm to the Senate race against Lister Hill in 1944 and to the gubernatorial contest in 1946. The groundwork for the long sought post-New Deal resurgence by conservatives had apparently been firmly laid.

However, the surprisingly strong showing by Folsom should have served as a cautionary warning to conservatives. Here was an engaging candidate who had polled a sizable vote with a frankly liberal appeal and a great deal of personal magnetism. Here was a candidate who might prove an obstacle to conservative expectations of a postwar resurgence.

But few commentators grasped the full impact of the emergence of Folsom as a force in Alabama politics. Folsom's showing was regarded by many as a fluke, a one-time chance happening rooted in the peculiar circumstances of 1942.[56] Few could take seriously the ballyhoo artist from Cullman with his rube band and unorthodox campaign theatrics. The gubernatorial election of 1946 was to prove how mistaken the skeptical judgments of 1942 were.

The primary campaign of 1942 had not been the quiet affair Atticus Mullin had expected in January. The few short months from January to May had witnessed the passing from the political scene of the man who had come closest to dominating Alabama politics in the 1920s and 1930s, Bibb Graves. Though ambiguous in its import for the future, the election represented another episode in the continuing struggle between factional alliances for dominance in state politics. And in the course of that primary year, there had emerged the man who would dominate Alabama politics throughout much of the 1940s and 1950s, James E. "Big Jim" Folsom. It had not been an uneventful year.

[56] See, for example, Birmingham *News,* March 31, 1946.

LEONARD DINNERSTEIN

The Senate's Rejection of Aubrey Williams as Rural Electrification Administrator

Two days after his fourth inaugural in 1945, President Franklin D. Roosevelt nominated Henry Wallace for Secretary of Commerce and Aubrey Williams for Rural Electrification Administrator. The selections, perhaps a harbinger of more liberal domestic policies, were not well received on Capitol Hill. Informed sources indicated that neither candidate would have an easy time winning Senate approval. To Southern Democrats Wallace and Williams symbolized "the left wing element of the party," and conservatives of both parties feared that once in office they might engage in foolhardy and lavish expenditures.[1] The Senate eventually confirmed Wallace. It rejected Williams and in so doing let the White House know that the solons would not look with favor upon an expanded New Deal in the postwar years. A probing of Williams' background may help to explain why he became the target of the Senate's irascibility.

Aubrey Williams was born in Springville, Alabama, in 1890. Although descended from prominent Southern planters, the young Williams was forced to begin working at the age of seven, as a bundle-boy in a Springville laundry for $1.00 a week, because his family needed the money. By the age of ten he had tripled this weekly wage, as a cash-boy in a Birmingham department store. Thereafter he worked as a hat salesman, window-dresser, sign-painter, and coal miner before be-

This essay was published in *The Alabama Review*, XXI (Apr., 1968).
[1] *The Times-Picayune* (New Orleans), Feb. 4, 1945.

coming a student for the Presbyterian ministry at Maryville College in the mountains of eastern Tennessee. After five years of study, however, he changed his vocational choice and left school. During World War I he served overseas with the Young Men's Christian Association and then decided to join the French Foreign Legion. When the United States entered the war he switched to an American artillery unit. While in France, he attended the University of Bordeau and received a degree in 1919. He then returned to the United States, studied economics and sociology at the University of Cincinnati, and received his baccalaureate in 1920. From 1922 to 1932 he served as Executive Director of the Wisconsin Conference of Social Work and also taught at the University of Wisconsin. After the depression began in 1929, he worked with the American Public Welfare Association and helped organize relief services in Mississippi and Texas. Harry Hopkins, President Roosevelt's relief administrator, brought Williams to Washington in 1933.[2]

Williams worked with Hopkins on the Civil Works Administration, the Federal Emergency Relief Administration, and the Works Progress Administration. As assistant director of the WPA, he also served as head of the National Youth Administration, which Congress had established in 1935. The latter organization helped unemployed youths between 16 and 24 to find jobs and assisted full-time students who desired part-time employment. In 1939–1940, at its peak, the National Youth Administration aided some 750,000 people. Under Williams' direction, the agency won plaudits from impartial observers. For example, one commentator wrote that in its short existence the NYA had "done more to create a feeling of self-reliance in young America than anything since the Alger books."[3]

Few doubted that Williams was a talented administrator. But many opposed his liberalism, and conservatives wanted to deny him a place of power that he might use against them. To his credit he vigorously espoused equality of opportunity for all people to rise from the depths of acute poverty. His public expressions on the subject aroused consid-

[2] *Hearings Before the Committee on Agriculture and Forestry on the Nomination of Aubrey Williams to be Administrator, Rural Electrification Administration,* 79th Congress, First Session, 1945 (U.S. Congress, Senate, Committee on Agriculture and Forestry), 3–4. Cited hereafter as *Hearings;* New York *Times,* Mar. 5, 1965; *Current Biography,* 1940, 872–873; George Creel, "Dollars For Youth," *Collier's,* XCVI (Sept. 28, 1935), 10; *Literary Digest,* CXX (June 6, 1935), 6; Washington *Post,* Mar. 5, 1965.
[3] *Hearings,* 5; *Current Biography* (1940), 873; Creel, *Collier's* 10.

erable controversy, however. "The government has always been charged with the responsibility of extending the frontiers of opportunity,"[4] he said on one occasion. Another time he insisted that our economy could "yield abundance to all instead of poverty to many, happiness to all instead of misery to many."[5] In 1935 he told a West Virginia audience that an "overwhelming majority of the children born in the last 25 years will never rise above a hand-to-mouth existence, that all their steps from the cradle to the grave will be dogged by poverty, sickness, and insecurity." Ten years later, when challenged to defend these words by South Dakota's conservative Republican senator, Harlan Bushfield, Williams stood his ground. "I do not take back one word of that statement," he said.[6]

Williams' strong convictions frequently resulted in other tactless remarks and the enunciation of somewhat radical ideas. "I am not sure," he reputedly stated in a North Carolina speech in November, 1938, that "class warfare is not all right." To an American Youth Congress group, later found to have some Communist associations, he advised: "You must organize to get power in the hands of the workers. The law be damned. Unemployment . . . is here to stay. Millions now out of jobs will never find jobs again."[7] Such utterances won him few friends among American conservatives. In 1940 Representative Hamilton Fish of New York rose in the House of Representatives and denounced the Alabamian as "the most dangerous man in America."[8]

Prosperity returned when America entered World War II, and Congress abolished the National Youth Administration, thereby severing Williams' connection with the government. Economic recovery, however, not only precipitated prosperity but hardened the conservative opposition to the New Deal. Southern Democrats joined hands with reactionary Republicans in carefully scrutinizing domestic expenditures and stifling liberal sentiment in Washington. In September, 1944, the outspoken Williams, then an organizer for the National

[4] Aubrey Williams, "Standards of Living and Government Responsibility," *The Annals of the American Academy of Political and Social Science,* XLXXVI (November, 1937), 127.
[5] Williams, "Youth and Our Economic Problem," *Vital Speeches of the Day,* V (Aug. 15, 1939), 662.
[6] *Hearings,* 47.
[7] Quoted in *Newsweek,* XXV (Feb. 19, 1945), 47–48.
[8] Quoted in the New York *Times,* Mar. 5, 1965.

Farmers Union, wrote a column denouncing this "Republican-Southern Tory coalition [which] had succeeded in running almost every decent man out of the government. Those that are left alive are in constant fear of having their heads cut off."[9]

In January, 1945, President Roosevelt nominated Williams to head the Rural Electrification Administration. Liberals applauded the selection. The National Association for the Advancement of Colored People found the nominee "absolutely straight on our question."[10] Williams also received enthusiastic support from hundreds of students, farmers, civic minded citizens, and organizations like the Farmers Union Grain Terminal, the National Popular Government League, and the American Federation of Labor.[11] A more skeptical Senate, however, decided upon open hearings to determine the nominee's qualifications. *Business Week* warned that Williams faced "the toughest fight of his long career."[12] The conservative coalition welcomed the opportunity for a public confrontation with one of its most vitriolic critics.

The Senate Agriculture Committee opened hearings on February 2, 1945. Williams' enemies could find so little in his record to excoriate that most of the questions verged on irrelevancies. Senators Harlan Bushfield of South Dakota and Kenneth McKellar of Tennessee[13] had copies of the Dies Committee Report, which accused Williams of Communist associations, and they interrogated him about these charges.[14] Despite the Alabamian's denial and evidence submitted by the Fed-

---

[9] Quoted in *ibid.*, Feb. 24, 1945.

[10] Telegrams from NAACP headquarters to branches in Baltimore, Boston, and Detroit. Copies are located among Aubrey Williams Papers (Franklin D. Roosevelt Library, Hyde Park), Box 37. All references to the Williams Papers are from Box 37. Cited hereafter as Williams Papers.

[11] *Ibid.*

[12] "Fighting For Power," *Business Week*, Feb. 10, 1945.

[13] Senator Kenneth McKellar, senior senator from Tennessee, was not a member of the Senate Agriculture Committee. He requested permission, however, to question the witness, and his colleagues permitted him to do so.

[14] On July 21, 1937, Congressman Martin Dies of Texas introduced a resolution in the House of Representatives providing for a special committee to investigate un-American propaganda activities. Ten months later the House approved the resolution and the committee was thereafter popularly referred to as the Dies Committee. In one of its reports Williams was accused of being a member of three Communist organizations: the American Youth Congress, the Washington Committee for Democratic Action, and the Workers Alliance. The Committee was never able to substantiate its charges, nor could anyone else prove that Williams had any Communist affiliations. William Gellermann, *Martin Dies* (New York: The John Day Co., 1944), 6; *Hearings*, 46.

eral Bureau of Investigation specifically exonerating him of any sub-
versive activities, the two senators persisted in belaboring the
point.[15] McKellar objected also to Williams' liberal fiscal policies as
National Youth Administrator and even cast aspersions upon his
religious beliefs. The Senator inserted into the record a telegram he
had received from an Ohio minister alleging that Williams had "denied the divinity of Christ . . . [and was therefore] utterly unworthy
of any official position in our government."[16] Some other committee
members protested that Williams' religious views were inviolate and
in no way indicative of his capacity for government service. McKellar's
bomb had been planted, however.

At the final session of the hearings, on February 19, Senator Bushfield intensified his attack. He read from one of Williams' earlier writ-
ings, which denied the "enormous blessings that this Nation conferred
upon all its citizens. That has been a lot of bunk. I think the poor
have been getting poorer and the rich have been getting richer all
the years of my life," Williams said.[17] Sharp words immediately ensued
between the two concerning the truth of this statement. Finally
Bushfield exploded: "There isn't anybody in the United States
of America in the last fifteen years that has died from starvation,
and you know it." Williams shot back: "I certainly do not know it.
I know they have died and they have been crippled, many of them
for life, because they did not have proper nourishment when
children."[18]

The last round of cross-examination came from Mississippi's Theodore Bilbo. The Senator wanted to know if Williams had been influential in getting the President to abolish discriminatory employment
practices in government defense plants. "I did as much as I could to
persuade him to issue the order," Williams acknowledged. "Would
you subscribe," Bilbo continued, "to the provisions of that order,
which has resulted in the breaking down of the barriers in all the public
offices in the District of Columbia where cafeteria partitions have
been eliminated and the two races have been forced to eat together
and all the toilets torn out for the colored and the whites are forced

---

[15] *Hearings,* 46, 57, 76, 79, 148, 178.
[16] *Ibid.,* 168.
[17] *Ibid.,* 293.
[18] *Ibid.,* 294.

to use toilets with the blacks? Do you subscribe to that?" "Completely," Williams replied.[19]

After the hearings, William S. White noted in the New York *Times* that despite Williams' liberal views and Congress' belief that he and Henry Wallace were cut out of the same cloth, the "greatest threat" to confirmation came from the Senate's reaction to Williams' much-too-explicit remarks about the "Republican-Southern Tory coalition." One does not needlessly antagonize Southern Senators in a Democratic administration, White added, and quoted a reliable informant as saying that if confirmation were denied, the "real reasons" would be Williams' outspoken opinions.[20]

During the Senate's debate on confirmation, characterized by *Time* as "a debate notable for irrelevant oratory and the bored absence of most Senators,"[21] McKellar, Bilbo, and Bushfield echoed sentiments similar to those that they had expressed at the hearings. Some other Senate conservatives, however, had different reservations about the nominee. Robert Taft of Ohio considered the former director of the National Youth Administration a "wasteful administrator."[22] The Indiana Republican, Raymond Willis, feared that Williams' "record of . . . extravagance in government administration . . . would recklessly . . . saddle farmers with ruinous debts."[23] Scott Lucas of Illinois, on the other hand, accused the opposition of "intolerance and bigotry." Never in his memory, he said, "had a nominee for an important post been treated with such disrespect or subjected to such irresponsible attacks."[24] Also in defense of the nominee, Senator Allen Ellender of Louisiana proclaimed: "It may be [that] the crime which has been committed by Mr. Williams is that he has devoted his entire life to helping the underprivileged."[25]

Alabama's Lister Hill may have come closer to the truth when he

---

[19] *Ibid.*, 318. In a letter, dated February 16, 1945, Bilbo wrote to the Honorable Ralph H. Herrin of Collins, Mississippi, that "we do not want this negro lover on this job." Williams Papers.

[20] New York *Times*, Feb. 24, 1945.

[21] *Time*, XLV (Apr. 2, 1945), 17.

[22] *Congressional Record*, 79th Congress, First Session, 1945, 2647. All future citations are from the same Congress and Session.

[23] *Ibid.*, 2481.

[24] *Ibid.*, 2409; *New Republic*, CXII (Mar. 5, 1945), 317.

[25] *Congressional Record*, 2481.

summarized: "We see politics, prejudice, animosity and the might of powerful vested interests combined to defeat Aubrey Williams' nomination."[26] Senator George Aiken of Vermont outlined more clearly what Hill had only hinted at. The Copperweld Company had previously been getting "the lion's share of the orders for R.E.A. construction materials," Aiken explained. Since the copper interests "have the inside track in obtaining R.E.A. orders, and . . . intended to run the R.E.A. so far as it was possible for them to do so," they had sent a Mr. Craig to reach an understanding with the nominee. Outraged, Williams had refused to participate in any unholy alliance. "When the representatives of the Copperweld Co. found that they could not handle him," Aiken concluded, "it would appear they then turned on all the heat they could everywhere in the United States to prevent his becoming administrator of the R.E.A."[27] Aiken's explanation did not alter the convictions of his colleagues. By a vote of 52 to 36 they refused to "advise and consent" to the appointment of Aubrey Williams as head of the Rural Electrification Administration.[28]

The Philadelphia *Record* immediately attributed the defeat to "reasons born of hatred, malice, bigotry and greed." The editor doubted "that in its whole history the United States Senate has ever stooped lower in the muck of vindictiveness, race prejudice and reaction."[29] Negro newspapers such as the San Francisco *Reporter* believed Williams had "doomed" his chances "when he dared to defend the FEPC and the rights of Negro workers . . ."[30] *Time* ascribed the rejection to Williams' "leftish views."[31] The nominee himself concluded that the Senate had refused confirmation because of his belief that "the wage-earners, the farmers, and the little people should be an articulate part of our economic life."[32] But two decades later, in Williams' obituary, the New York *Times* indicated that one

---

[26] *Ibid.*, 2610.

[27] *Ibid.*, 2649–2650.

[28] *Ibid.*, 2652.

[29] Philadelphia *Record*, Mar. 24, 1945, clipping, Williams Papers.

[30] San Francisco *Reporter*, Mar. 10, 1945. See also Chicago *Defender*, Mar. 10, 1945; Chicago *Bee*, Mar. 11, 1945; Atlanta *Daily World*, Mar. 9, 1945; *The Journal and Guide* (Norfolk, Virginia), Mar. 10, 1945; Washington *Tribune*, Mar. 10, 1945; *People's Voice*, Mar. 8, 1945; *The Afro-American*, Mar. 10, 1945. All of the above are clippings in the Williams Papers.

[31] *Time*, LIV (Nov. 21, 1949), 51.

[32] Quoted in *The Nation*, CLX (Mar. 31, 1945), 349.

of the main reasons for Williams' failure to become Rural Electrification Administration director was that the private power companies feared that he might be too energetic in setting up electrical cooperatives.[33]

No one would deny, of course, the validity of these postmortems, but it is equally unreasonable to accept any one of them as the sole explanation. Williams' positions on the racial question, fiscal expenditures, and aid to the underprivileged probably lost him votes, but a similar philosophy had also handicapped Henry Wallace, who had been confirmed for the post of Secretary of Commerce.[34] For an understanding, therefore, of why Williams lost, it behooves us to look not at the similarities in the opposition to the two, but at the differences.

An analysis of the Senate votes on the two nominees reveals that only five Democrats,[35] four of whom were from the South, voted against Wallace, whereas nineteen Democrats,[36] including fifteen Southerners, refused to sanction Williams. Ten Republicans supported Wallace,[37] while only four backed Williams.[38] Perhaps Carleton Kent of the Chicago Times had the answer for this division: "a number of confederate gentlemen, who, choking with distaste, voted to confirm Henry Wallace . . . now intend to vote against Williams to absolve themselves of any taint of liberalism."[39] Or perhaps the editors of The

[33] New York Times, Mar. 5, 1965, 33.

[34] The Senate confirmed Henry Wallace as Secretary of Commerce on March 1, 1945 by a vote of 56 to 32. Congressional Record, 1616.

[35] Harry Byrd of Virginia, Kenneth McKellar of Tennessee, Lee O'Daniel of Texas, Tom Stewart of Tennessee, and Pat McCarran of Nevada.

[36] The following Democrats voted against Williams: Bailey, Bankhead, Bilbo, Byrd, Chandler, Connally, Eastland, Fulbright, George, Gerry, McCarran, McClellan, McKellar, O'Daniel, Overton, Radcliffe, Russell, Stewart, and Tydings. The non-Southerners were Peter Gerry of Rhode Island, Pat McCarran of Nevada, and George Radcliffe and Millard Tydings, both of Maryland.

[37] George D. Aiken of Vermont, Joseph S. Ball of Minnesota, Owen Brewster of Maine, Thomas C. Hart of Connecticut, William Langer of North Dakota, Leverett Saltonstall of Massachusetts, Wayne Morse of Oregon, Henrik Shipstead of Minnesota, Charles W. Tobey of New Hampshire, and George A. Wilson of Iowa. Congressional Record, 1616.

[38] Aiken, Langer, Morse, and Milton R. Young of North Dakota.

[39] Chicago Times, Mar. 5, 1945. See also "Power and Politics," Time, XLV (Apr. 2, 1945), 17: The Senate "coalition of Republicans and Southern Democrats, only half successful in its fight against Henry Wallace, has been pointing up for a fuller victory. If they could not keep Wallace out of the Commerce Department, there was one thing they could do: keep leftish, New Dealer Aubrey Willis Williams from becoming Rural Electrification Administrator," Time said.

Nation discovered the key: "There is little doubt," they wrote, "that Williams might have been confirmed despite his New Deal record if he had been willing to 'play ball' with certain copper interests."[40] Finally, one cannot ignore the fact that while Southerners might have reluctantly endorsed a liberal from the North or the West, a *Southern* liberal might have been just too much for them to stomach.

The forces working against Williams were numerous and complex, and even in retrospect it is difficult to say which single factor, if any, proved decisive. His indiscreet radical utterances in the 1930's, the column denouncing the Republican-Southern Tory coalition, the feeling among conservatives that one liberal at a time was all that they could tolerate, perhaps even the unconscious resistance to a Southern liberal, and the opposition of the copper interests became too much for Alabama's humanitarian son to overcome. But one cannot overlook the possibility that Aubrey Williams symbolized the goals and aspirations of the common man—and his failure to win approval might have been a warning to the President that the temper of the Congress was such that it would not accept a new barrel of liberal proposals from the White House when the war ended. The St. Louis *Post-Dispatch* intimated as much when it wrote that "every poisoned dart," verbally thrust by the "Dixie demagogues" and their cohorts in the Senate, "was expected to go through Williams and then lodge in the President, whom these geographical Democrats hate."[41]

Aubrey Williams continued to espouse the causes that he believed in during the final two decades of his life. In the 1950's, he published a liberal newspaper, *The Southern Farmer,* which advocated racial equality, and he also served as president of the Southern Conference Educational Fund, which promoted the same cause. When he died in 1965 the New York *Times* noted that he had "devoted his life to fighting poverty, ignorance, and intolerance."[42]

[40] "The Lesson of the Defeat," *The Nation,* CLX (Mar. 31, 1945), 349.
[41] St. Louis *Post-Dispatch,* Mar. 24, 1945.
[42] New York *Times,* Mar. 5, 1965, 33.

CARL GRAFTON

James E. Folsom's 1946 Campaign

James E. Folsom served two extraordinarily important terms as governor of the state of Alabama in the years 1947–1950 and 1955–1958. Folsom, a Jacksonian populist who was often drastically out of phase with public and elite opinion in Alabama, actively opposed the 1948 Dixiecrat split in the Democratic party, appointed officials who registered blacks to vote, worked for legislative reapportionment, vetoed or refused to sign nearly all of the many segregation laws that gushed out of the legislature after *Brown* v. *Board of Education,* encouraged the Montgomery bus boycott, took no part in the race baiting that was so popular when he was governor, and worked for women's rights. In addition to his amazingly open and blunt advocacy of civil liberties in election campaigns, Folsom presided over an enormous growth in Alabama state government, which, though not as dramatic as his civil liberties battles, was no less important.

Folsom's terms of office were also important in the sense that he and the civil rights movement that coincided with his career represented serious threats to interests who had dominated state government since the late 1800s. Folsom's efforts to reduce these interests' influence, combined with increasingly intense federal civil rights pressure, forced them to retaliate openly, revealing much about ways political elites function in a democracy.

Folsom's first successful gubernatorial campaign, waged in 1946, was critical both because it placed such an unusual figure in the governor's

This essay was published in *The Alabama Review*, XXV (July 1982).

The author wishes to thank Dr. Anne Permaloff for her important contributions to this study.

441

chair and because Folsom used campaign techniques never before seen in Alabama. These techniques were adopted by his protégé George Wallace and emulated by many other candidates for state office up to the most recent election. But no one matched the skill and imagination that Folsom put into his 1946 effort. Wallace came closest, but he felt obliged to add racism while reducing or distorting Folsom's mixture of gentle, often self-deprecating humor, country music, critiques of the state's political elite, and appeals to the humane and constructive elements of human nature. Wallace kept Folsom's staging and discarded the best of his message.

In January 1946 there seemed little doubt of the outcome of the forthcoming Alabama gubernatorial election. Almost everyone agreed that the only question was whether Commissioner of Agriculture Joe Poole or Lieutenant Governor Handy Ellis would win. It was also agreed that both men were lucky not to be facing stiff competition. Poole was a colorless campaigner and a man of narrow vision, and Handy Ellis, known in some circles as "Mule Skinner Ellis," was a cigar-chomping, square-jawed veteran officeholder who was almost a caricature of a career politician. Still, both men had important strengths. Poole, as a major Black Belt plantation owner, enjoyed the support of many of the most conservative and wealthy Bosses (Sheldon Hackney's terminology), especially those in the Black Belt. The powerful Alabama Farm Bureau Federation was the largest single group behind his candidacy. He was also supported by large segments of the Agricultural Extension Service (which was supposed to be nonpolitical, but which rarely sat out any election of consequence), Alabama Power Company, and U.S. Steel Corporation.[1] Many had won

---

[1] Montgomery *Advertiser*, March 9, May 1, 1946; Huntsville *Times*, April 16, 1946; Birmingham *News*, November 11, 18, December 2, 1945; confidential personal interviews in Decatur, July 1974. Unless otherwise noted, the cities in which personal interviews were conducted are in Alabama. In his classic account of Alabama's 1901 constitutional convention Sheldon Hackney categorizes delegates into four groups: Bosses, Planters, Agrarians, and Progressives. These categories are just as useful in portraying politics in the Folsom era. The Boss category represents an alliance among the wealthiest Black Belt, Birmingham, and Mobile farmers and industrialists. The Bosses are roughly equivalent to C. Wright Mills's power elite or what Folsom and before him Bibb Graves called the Big Mules. Planters are those plantation owners not quite large enough to make it into the ranks of the Bosses. The Agrarians have a north Alabama and populist orientation. The Progressives are small businessmen who, like the Planters, are not sufficiently affluent to be included in the Boss elite. See Sheldon Hackney, *Populism to Progressivism in Alabama* (Princeton, 1969), 210–14.

the governor's office with less support than Poole had. Ellis, a highly experienced lawyer and a clever parliamentarian, was the candidate of both Progressives and the considerable number of Bosses who believed that Poole's inadequacies as a campaigner would keep him from winning. Two other candidates, Elbert Boozer and Gordon Persons, were able campaigners, but they lacked the resources necessary to win. They were never serious contenders. Nor was James E. Folsom, a part owner in his family's small insurance company and its north Alabama representative, given much of a chance. He had lost elections in 1933, 1936, 1938, and 1942, and he had never held public office. He finished second in the 1942 gubernatorial election, traditionally an indication of future success, but that was only because the certain winner Bibb Graves had suddenly died, leaving the field open to hopelessly weak campaigners.[2] He had been elected as a delegate to the 1944 Democratic party convention, but he had cancelled this success by appearing to commit the blunder of supporting the hated left-leaning Henry A. Wallace for vice-president over the popular Alabama Senator John H. Bankhead.[3] On January 2, 1946 the Montgomery *Advertiser*'s leading political columnist Atticus Mullin commented: "No well posted political observer believes that Jim Folsom will run for governor. It is true that Jim has personal strength but he has no statewide organization, and such an organization takes time and money."[4] But Mullin did not know that Folsom had been quietly establishing political contacts throughout north Alabama as he traveled about selling insurance.[5] Folsom was moving quietly, not wanting his plans revealed prematurely. There was little danger that a reporter isolated in Montgomery would discover Folsom's strategy as early as January. Folsom had eight years before moved from Elba, his boyhood home in south Alabama, to Cullman in north Alabama. His two homes amid Alabama's northern and southern "white counties" with their white popula-

---

[2] William D. Barnard, "The Old Order Changes: Graves, Sparks, Folsom, and the Gubernatorial Election of 1942," *Alabama Review*, XXVIII (July 1975), 173; Carl Grafton, "James E. Folsom and Civil Liberties in Alabama," *Alabama Review*, XXXII (January 1979), 11, and "James E. Folsom's First Four Election Campaigns: Learning to Win By Losing," *Alabama Review*, XXXIV (July 1981), 163–83.

[3] William Dewey Murray, "The Folsom Gubernatorial Campaign of 1946" (M.A. thesis, University of Alabama, 1949), 29–30.

[4] Montgomery *Advertiser*, January 2, 1946.

[5] Birmingham *News*, April 8, 1945.

tion majorities and small farms bracketed the Black Belt with its black majorities and large plantations. This carefully planned move was designed to take advantage of a strong pattern of "friends and neighbors" electoral politics so common in one party multi-factional states; Folsom would receive the support of two sets of friends and neighbors instead of only one.[6] In addition, Folsom's two homes were located in the state's two areas of populist strength, a circumstance that coincided with his strongly held ideological beliefs.[7] But perhaps Folsom's greatest advantage was his comprehension, born out of history reading and four election losses, that a campaign style new to Alabama (although used for at least two decades in Texas and Louisiana among other states) could allow a statewide candidate unconnected to county rings (organizations very similar to Northern urban machines) to win.

Prior to Folsom, the standard campaign approach was for a candidate, when he arrived in a town, to go directly to the courthouse where he would confer with the "courthouse crowd" and try to win their support with promises of appointments and other patronage. Then he might stroll out on the courthouse steps, make a perfunctory speech, shake a few hands, and then move on to the next county seat. As election day approached, large newspaper advertisements would appear, and the candidate might make a few boring radio speeches. Although they were far more active than past candidates, this method was essentially the way Ellis and Poole campaigned. Folsom short-circuited the entire process.

Not long before Mullin wrote Folsom's premature political obituary (at least as far as the governor's race was concerned), musicians in north Alabama were answering nondescript newspaper advertisements asking for people who could play "string" music, what today would be called "country and western." The call was for accordion, fiddle, banjo, and guitar players. A string band called the Strawberry Pickers formed to play as part of Folsom's campaign. At first, members of the new band were not even told what office he was pursuing.[8] The "Strawberry Pickers" was a good name; it carried the country imagery that Folsom wanted, and it contained a little play on words that neatly described a string band.

[6] V. O. Key, Jr., *Southern Politics in State and Nation* (New York, 1949), 37–41.
[7] *Ibid.*, 42–46.
[8] Confidential personal interviews with two members of the Strawberry Pickers in Cullman, April 1974.

The 1946 Campaign

The basic strategy, an extension of what Folsom did in 1942, called for mailings of circulars announcing his rallies.[9] Campaigning began in January, months earlier than normal, in the smallest towns. The conventional wisdom was that to start a campaign so early was a waste of time because by voting day in May people who had heard a speech four months before would have long forgotten it. Folsom's logic was that people in rural areas had few sources of entertainment and little to do in January and February, so they would welcome a good string band (and the Strawberry Pickers were first rate) even if it was accompanied by a politician. And, as it turned out, Folsom was as entertaining as his string band. As the months clicked by, the group slowly spiraled in from the small towns to larger ones where entertainment was more plentiful, life quicker, and memories shorter, and where fewer people were busy with spring planting.[10]

Folsom, the Strawberry Pickers, John Steifelmeyer, a Cullman friend who had assisted in the 1942 effort, and a few others started on a cold, cloudy morning in friendly territory—north Alabama. They began with less than $200 in expense money. Folsom had ample personal resources, but he did not seem inclined to use them, preferring to run the campaign on a shoestring. By the end of their first day of campaigning, food and hotel expenses had drained most of their cash. The next day they were obliged to pass the hat, which actually was a bucket. One of the band members recalls: "When Jim came out with that bucket on the second day I was shakin' in my shoes—I didn't know whether it was goin' over or not. But the first haul was 27 dollars and some odd cents."[11] That was in Elkmont. The second rally on the same day netted more than $40. Another Strawberry Picker remembers: "When Jim counted the money on our first day of passing the bucket it came to more than $100 and Jim said, 'Boys, I'm gonna be the next governor of the state.' We figured that $100 a day would keep us on the road."[12]

---

[9] Personal interview with James E. Folsom in Montgomery, May 1978.

[10] *Ibid.,* in Cullman, June 1973. See the listings of the candidates' speaking schedules in the Huntsville *Times,* March 17, 1946. For that week Folsom averaged four or five rallies per day, Ellis one or two, and Poole one or two plus a statewide radio speech. See also Huntsville *Times,* April 7, 1946.

[11] Confidential personal interview in Cullman, April 1974.

[12] Confidential personal interview in Cullman, April 1974.

This campaign was the high point of Folsom's life. When he talks about it today, he relives it. He repeats the speeches as if he were back on a makeshift platform, on a tree stump, on the back of a pickup truck, in a high school auditorium, or on the courthouse steps. He sits in his living room in an old arm chair, suddenly erect, his pale gray eyes staring into the past:

> "You see this corn shuck mop? You know what I'm goin' to do? I'm going to take that mop and scour out the kitchen and open up the windows and let a green breeze out of the north," called it a green breeze, "a green breeze out of the north and you'll have the freshest, sweetest smell that you've seen in that old Alabama capitol since it was built." Or somethin' like that. "Now while the boys strike up a tune of Down Yonder in the Governor's Chair"—We also used the Yellow Rose of Texas—the copyright had run out on them—the theme song was really Banjo on my Knee—of course, that was old and the old folks remembered it. That was a good banjo song. We had a good banjo picker and that went over big—"we'll pass the bucket."[13]

When he was asked who thought of the bucket strategy, he replied:

> Well, Huey Long. I had read his book, and Huey Long had passed the bucket. Pappy O'Daniel in Texas, he got elected governor of Texas—he was a flour salesman—and he carried his band around and he was the one who really passed the bucket and on his bucket it said, "Flour and not pork."[14]

Those pale eyes see crowds of tough, taciturn farmers in baggy bib overalls, jackets, muddy workshoes, and weather-beaten, felt snap-brim hats.

> And another story in that campaign was—it was just before I passed the bucket. That was my come on, passin' the bucket. I had an old corn shuck mop . . . You used to scour out your kitchen every Saturday night and the rooms that didn't have no carpet—the front room had a carpet—we scoured out the boys' room and the kitchen every Saturday—that cleanin' out the capitol—that was it with the old corn shuck mop and I'd get off onto a side issue and I was tellin' the story. And I'd say, "Turnip greens. I remember my mama she would be cookin' turnip greens and I'd see her hittin' those turnip greens on her hand, put 'em in water. And I truly didn't know what she was hittin' them on her hand until I was in Atlanta

[13] Personal interview with James E. Folsom in Cullman, June 1973.
[14] *Ibid.*

and I went to the Alabama football game—I was a freshman in college—Georgia Tech beat 'em—I hoboed over there—I went with the team—I had to stay hid. Turnip greens! Black eyed peas! I remember my mama cookin' those turnip greens. Folks, I didn't know what she was hittin' those turnip greens on her hands for till I was 19 years old and I was in Atlanta, Georgia right across from the Langley Hotel where the Alabama football team was staying and we was eatin' turnip greens—the first storebought turnip greens I ever ate in my life, and I got into the turnip greens and tastin' sand, and right then I knew what ma was a hittin' those turnip greens on her hand for. Cornbread! Ham! Put that all in together. You see this corn shuck mop? You know what I'm going to do? . . .[15]

These accounts illustrate several important Folsom campaign tactics. In interviews with the author he emphasized his use of the word "green" in the phrase "green breeze out of the north." He said that he used it not because of any literal meaning the word held but because it added something to the phrase "breeze out of the north," and because it reinforced the next part of the sentence that concerned the fresh, sweet-smelling capitol. Many have observed that he seldom read a formal speech word for word but instead used a script as a foundation for extemporaneous remarks, often straying far from the written word. Those who conclude from this observation that everything he said publicly was extemporaneous are mistaken. Folsom developed campaign set pieces (not entire speeches) the same way many stand-up comedians build routines. He often started with a memory or an observation (his mother hitting turnip greens on her hand) that he would then gradually build into an organized piece in speech after speech, changing a word here, adding a sentence there until it elicited the kind of response he intended. It would then be used repeatedly in that perfect form. These routines served as building blocks for speeches, and they could be moved around, used or not used, as each audience and the time available required.[16]

Folsom used symbols masterfully. Turnip greens have nothing to do with politics, but his dissertation on that subject established him as one of the crowd, a candidate for the highest office in state government who actually knew what their lives were like because he had lived the same life.[17] He would tell his audiences:

[15] *Ibid.*
[16] *Ibid.*, in Montgomery, May 1978.
[17] Murray, "The Folsom Gubernatorial Campaign of 1946," 49.

> Black eyed peas, cornbread, turnip greens, throw them in that black iron
> pot. They talkin' about these fancy cookin' pots advertisin' as the greatest
> in the world—they'll keep the vitamins and they'll do this—but mama's old
> black iron pot didn't do so bad.[18]

Folsom's reference to the sand in restaurant greens contained quiet suggestions that he and his back country listeners were together against an alien and somewhat grimy outside world. This theme is typically populist, but rarely is it conveyed with such subtlety and warmth.

But effective as they were, none of his many symbolic devices compared with the corn-shuck mop and the suds bucket. The corn-shuck mop again established him as part of the society of common men, and the analogy between cleaning a house (notice how he used rich detail to carry his listeners with him into his home) and cleaning the capitol was very powerful. It is also completely meaningless when applied to the complexities of governing a state, but symbols need have little relationship with reality to be effective. The suds bucket was his premier technique. It carried the suds (money) that would enable Big Jim to clear out the capitol (with the mop).

Collections from the suds bucket represented a major source of funding for the campaign prior to the runoff when money was in critically short supply. If the suds bucket had failed to produce the needed funds, Folsom would have abandoned the campaign or lost. The bucket saved them on several occasions. His group was sometimes so low on funds that impromptu rallies had to be held just so that the bucket could be passed. Sometimes they reached this point because they stayed in the best hotels and ate the finest food their budget could tolerate; shades of things to come. But the suds bucket was also a psychological ploy; when a person made his contribution, even if it was only a nickel or a dime he had made a commitment to the Folsom movement, and commitments were as important as the money collected.

> That little boy you was talking to [John Steifelmeyer] was one that
> passed [the bucket] and there was a black man. John just passed him up,
> and the black man called him back—he was 65, 70 years old. "Come here
> boss," he said and he reached down into his dogeared pocketbook, got a

---

[18] Personal interview with James E. Folsom in Cullman, June 1973.

dime out, put it in there and said, "Boss, I wants to jin up with y'all."
Couldn't even vote y'know. That was during the disenfranchisement
[*sic*].[19]

This story is one of Folsom's favorites. As he tells it he pantomimes
the opening of the clasp on the old pocketbook, the removal of the
dime with infinite care, and when he says, "I wants to jin up with
y'all," it sounds like poetry. Experience brought increasing sophisti-
cation in the bucket's use. When it passed through the audience, he
would emphasize that no one was allowed to contribute more than $2
apiece. His purpose was to "get them to put in $5 just to show that
they could do it."[20]

Folsom refused to play on racial fears in this or any other election
campaign. In 1946 segregation and black voting rights issues were not
as important in Alabama as they were in other Southern states, but,
nevertheless, they frequently bubbled to the surface. Folsom
comments:

> Gene Talmadge, Herman Talmadge's daddy. . . . got elected in 1946. I got
> elected cookin' turnip greens and he got elected on the race issue. That
> was his personal reservation, and I never did use it. The same time right
> in adjoining states—the same background—ethnic background—Alabama
> was part of Georgia at one time. He got elected just raisin' hell about the
> race question. Negro, Negro, Negro, Negro, and I never mentioned the
> thing. And I shook hands with the Negro. . . .[21]

By shaking hands with "the Negro" he was committing an as-
tounding breach of Southern mores; he was treating blacks as *men*,
not boys. Sometimes during campaigns and later as governor he would
get out of a car, march past white dignitaries, and shake hands first
with black laborers watching on the fringes of the crowd.[22] With all his
tricks and artifices, amid a cool and rational drive for power that he
truly wanted, he insisted on using the campaign to "agitate for
liberty," as he had been taught to do by his populist uncle John
Dunnavant and populist father-in-law Judge J. A. Carnley of Elba.[23]

[19] *Ibid.*, June 1974.
[20] *Ibid.*, in Montgomery, May 1978.
[21] *Ibid.*, in Cullman, June 1974.
[22] Marshall Frady, *Wallace* (New York, 1968), 106; confidential personal interview in
Montgomery, July 1974.
[23] Grafton, "James E. Folsom and Civil Liberties," 5–9.

Meanwhile, Joe Poole was making prohibition the centerpiece of his campaign. He started with a flourish, attacking Handy Ellis, a former dry, as the "pride and joy of the honky-tonk and gambling fraternity."[24] Many of Poole's conservative supporters sympathized with his desire to end the bane of liquor, but the state depended heavily on revenues from alcoholic beverage sales and their termination would mean that new sources would have to be found, a prospect few wanted. As Poole recognized the consequences of his stand, he softened it over the protests of his campaign manager J. Bruce Henderson, a fanatical prohibitionist. Poole was quoted as saying: "I am neither extremely dry, nor am I really wet."[25] His campaign continued at this level and never recovered. Ellis, employing classic Progressive rhetoric, portrayed Poole as a Big Mule puppet. By keeping a low profile, Folsom encouraged the two front-runners to attack each other. "They're both right," he would quip cheerfully.[26]

Ellis, Poole, and the press ignored Folsom and his platform until far into the campaign. There seemed no reason to take him seriously. In its early months his campaign appeared to be a shambles. Grover Hall, Jr., attended one rally when by accident the mailings announcing the rally had not been delivered. The audience was small and unresponsive, and Folsom's performance was weak.[27] Even as late as March Hall found that little had changed in the rallies, but he had, for reasons he did not make clear, begun to doubt his perceptions. William Barnard suggests that Hall was unaccustomed to judging reactions of laconic country people, and that local newspaper editors were alerting him to the fact that Folsom was stronger than he appeared.[28] Reporters seeking evidence of Folsom's progress in the magnitude and tightness of his organization also underestimated his progress. In his speeches Folsom flayed his opponents for maintaining headquarters in Montgomery, "where they gather in little cliques

[24] William D. Barnard, *Dixiecrats and Democrats: Alabama Politics, 1942–1950* (University, Ala., 1974), 25.

[25] *Ibid.*, 26. Ellis took full advantage of Poole's awkward retreat saying, "Joe began to crawfish out—a crawfish, you know, always moves backwards." Montgomery *Advertiser*, March 31, 1946. Also see Grover Hall, Jr.'s account of the Alabama Temperance Alliance's campaign on Poole's behalf, Montgomery *Advertiser*, April 14, 1946.

[26] Personal interview with James E. Folsom in Cullman, June 1973. See Ellis ad in Birmingham *Post*, April 29, 1946, and Poole ad in Birmingham *Post*, May 4, 1946. Huntsville *Times*, April 2, 1946.

[27] *Ibid.*; Montgomery *Advertiser*, February 26, 1946.

[28] Barnard, *Dixiecrats and Democrats*, 36.

and clans to huddle up in rooms, plot and plan more double talk. My headquarters are on the political stump and I have no managers, being responsible to the people and the people alone."[29] There was considerable truth in his description of his organization. Gould Beech, editor of the populist *Southern Farmer,* was attracted to Folsom early in 1946, so he called the Folsom office in Cullman, where he spoke to O. H. Finney, one of Folsom's key aides. Beech asked to speak to the campaign manager, and Finney responded that there was no such person but that he was the office manager and he would be happy to help. Beech volunteered to run Folsom's ads at no charge in his newspaper, and he asked Finney to send campaign materials that he could reproduce and print. Finney replied that he had none, but anything that Beech cared to print would be fine. Similarly, it often happened that after a rally someone would pull Folsom aside and tell him that he had a sum of money—on one occasion it was $150—to invest in a newspaper ad, and he would ask what Folsom wanted printed. Folsom would drape his arm over the person's shoulders and say, "You know the local situation better than I do. Whatever you put in is all right with me."[30] On another occasion Beech attempted to contact Folsom headquarters in the state's second largest city, Mobile. The long distance operator had no listing, but her supervisor happened to know that Folsom supporters often congregated in a particular barber shop, which in fact turned out to be the official headquarters![31]

The organizational looseness suggested by these examples was partly the result of rational calculation. Folsom reasoned that people worked hardest for a campaign when they held the hope that their efforts would be rewarded by a high position in government. It followed that one's future governmental position could be estimated by one's present position in the campaign machine, and if this machine was hierarchical (campaign manager, district managers, etc.), only those few near the top would work diligently. No hierarchy meant that more people could be motivated to put more effort into the cam-

[29] Unlabeled newspaper clipping in Folsom scrapbook, James E. Folsom Papers, Alabama State Department of Archives and History; Montgomery *Advertiser,* May 26, 1946; Alabama *Magazine,* April 5, 1946; *Time,* May 20, 1946.

[30] Confidential personal interview, September 1973. When a city and the interview criteria combine to reveal a confidential interview subject's name it is omitted.

[31] *Ibid.*

paign.[32] The loose structure also fit Folsom's personality. There has probably never been a major political figure in this country less inclined toward neat organization charts and careful supervision of subordinates than Folsom.

Still, we must not push this point too far. It would probably be fair to say that William (Bill) Drinkard, a Cullman mortician and businessman, was the campaign manager and central fund raiser. Drinkard handled mailouts, dealt with printers, coordinated rally schedules, and performed many other critical functions. He was one of the first financially comfortable (but not wealthy) individuals to support Folsom.[33]

The Folsom "organization" was assembled over a period of years in a seemingly casual and haphazard manner. Ward McFarland, one of his leading central and southwestern supporters, met Folsom at the University of Alabama when they were both students. It would be difficult to exaggerate the political importance of "The University," as it is often called. Informal groupings among both undergraduates and law students often last for decades of governmental service. McFarland was a Tuscaloosa Bibb Graves supporter who turned to Folsom after Graves's death in 1942. By then he was an attorney, and few others of his stature were willing to work for Folsom in that part of the state.[34] In both 1942 and 1946 McFarland's major responsibility was the creation of campaign committees in counties from Tuscaloosa to Mobile. These committees consisted largely of people he had met at the University of Alabama and through his law practice. McFarland was the kind of person Folsom had in mind when he opted for a looseknit campaign organization. McFarland had little or no interest in Folsom's desire to break Big Mule power. His sole concern was the development of personal contacts from which he could profit in later business ventures.

Folsom met his driver Bill Lyerly at an American Legion conference in January 1946, where Lyerly, who had just bought a new car (which in the period immediately after the war, when automobiles were in short supply, was quite important), volunteered to work in the campaign. Folsom paid no attention to the brash young man, but a

<hr />

[32] Personal interview with James E. Folsom in Cullman, June 1973.
[33] Confidential personal interviews in Albertville, June 1974, and in Cullman, April 1974.
[34] Confidential personal interviews in Tuscaloosa, July 1973.

few weeks later Lyerly appeared at a rally in Prattville, and Folsom immediately accepted his assistance. Like McFarland, Lyerly was essentially nonideological, but Lyerly was not nearly as ambitious; he developed a personal loyalty to Folsom that was honest, straightforward, and very strong.[35]

The ultra-conservative Representative Ira Thompson was another early Folsom supporter. When asked about him Folsom responded:

> He was a captain of the National Guard unit when I was in high school in the adjoining county to mine . . . The *Advertiser* had wrote scorchin' editorials accusing him of being in the Ku Klux . . . and Thompson was a good friend of Horace Wilkinson [a notorious racist who also supported Folsom for a short time]. . . . I inherited the old Bibb Graves followin' and Ira Thompson was part of it. I remembered the trouble he got in when the *Advertiser* exposed him as a Kluxer, but the Kluxer business was dead and I wanted Thompson on my side in the legislature and he always was on my side. . . . His politics and mine—now, I'm anti-Klux, but the Klux business was used for political purposes. My folks were agin' it *from the word go. Always have been.*[36]

As the campaign developed it was joined by Gould Beech, editor of the *Southern Farmer,* a brilliant young journalist who had held editorial positions with the Birmingham *News* and Montgomery *Advertiser.* He had also done free-lance speech writing for several legislative candidates and for Handy Ellis early in 1946. Beech's multifarious past belied his strongly held populist-liberal beliefs. Before enlisting in the Folsom cause (they were brought together by a mutual acquaintance, a politically active plumber), Beech quizzed Folsom as to the sincerity of his populist ideas. Folsom satisfied the writer with a recitation, delivered while lying on a hotel bed wearing combat boots with no socks, of how his grandfather and uncles had opposed Alabama's entry into the Civil War. In Beech, Folsom had a writer who could fit his simple, straightforward style of speaking. The *Southern Farmer,* published by liberal activists Aubrey Williams and Marshall Field, with a circulation of one million nationwide and eighty thousand in Alabama, was aimed at small farmers. Its advertising leaned to Charles Atlas bodybuilding courses and chinchilla breeding ventures. Beech

---

[35] Confidential personal interviews in Montgomery, June 1974; personal interview with James E. Folsom in Cullman, June 1973.

[36] Emphasis is Folsom's. Personal interview with James E. Folsom in Cullman, June 1973.

wrote almost everything in the paper, often using pen names, including a column of advice to the lovelorn. He shared Folsom's ability to communicate clearly and dramatically with people who were barely literate.[37]

O. H. Finney was a bulwark of order in the 1946 campaign as he had been when serving as Folsom's administrative assistant in his Marshall County WPA days. Anyone who is as unstructured as Folsom and who attempts anything that involves administrative complexity needs someone who is intelligent and (above all) systematic, and Finney fit both requirements. In addition, like Beech, he was a populist, and he had a strong personal loyalty to Folsom.[38]

McFarland, Lyerly, Thompson, Beech, and Finney were typical of the untypical nature of the Folsom camp. Surely few political candidates have ever had as fluid and heterogeneous a campaign "organization" as the one that came together around Folsom in 1946.

In the midst of the campaign on April 18 Folsom's mother suddenly died. She was a strong, loving disciplinarian described in the warmest terms by the people in Elba who knew her. Folsom had not fully recovered from the deaths of his wife and brother in 1944 and 1945, and he was jolted by this third loss, but, after a few days of mourning, he plunged back into the campaign.

The campaign with its eight to ten rallies a day quickly developed into a routine. According to one Strawberry Picker:

> We would start playing 15 minutes before the scheduled beginning of the speech. You could hear the music all over town. Folsom would hit the edge of town with Bill Lyerly about five minutes before his time and wait until he heard his cue and then they would drive in on cue.
>
> At first we couldn't get a local person to introduce him, so a member of the band would. Then we kept it up to avoid irritating local factions. Also, the propaganda was that we didn't have a chance because none of the local people wanted to get involved, and this helped our image.[39]

When Folsom arrived at a rally he did not always begin speaking immediately:

---

[37] Personal interview with Gould Beech in Houston, Texas, September 1973.
[38] Personal interview with O. H. Finney in Albertville, June 1974, and Cecil Noel (Folsom's WPA chief highway engineer) in Boaz, April 1974.
[39] Confidential personal interview in Cullman, April 1974.

It has been his common practice upon arriving at a speaking location to announce that he is tired and will have to rest. Whereupon he removes his brogans and, taking care to show that he wears no socks, extends himself on the bare ground. In due time the giant stirs, sits upright, studiously brushes the dirt from his toes, puts on his shoes and gets up for business. With a hearty handshake for every man, woman and child in sight he is ready for his speech which consists largely of praise for pretty women, thoughts of the old mule who was dear to him, and reminiscences of how his mother used to fix turnip greens.[40]

Asked about his practice of removing his shoes in public Folsom responded tersely: "Got big feet. Shoes hurt. Can't think when my feet hurt, so I took off the shoes. Helps my thinkin' to be able to wiggle my toes."[41]

Folsom's rallies developed into an art form. Bob Kyle, a reporter for the Tuscaloosa *News,* described one:

Snappy fiddling tunes that would make grandma take on hepcat ways, mixed with lonesome numbers that moaned of trouble between a gal and her man attracted a crowd of some 400 Tuscaloosa Countains Saturday morning to hear J. E. (Big Jim) Folsom. . . .

It looked like an ancient Fourth of July celebration observing the termination of a community logrolling, lacking only a plate of turnip greens, side meat and a snort of apple cider to complete the picture. . . .

One man parked a truck full of cows in front of the courthouse steps where Big Jim spoke and stayed through the speaking. The cows didn't even switch their tails.[42]

As the campaign developed, new set pieces were added: "Roland," Folsom would command a band member, "hold up that foot." Roland Johnson would then exhibit a muck-encrusted shoe from a rain-soaked, mud road. "There ain't gonna be no more mud on that boy's foot when we come back," Folsom would say.[43] Road construction was a major issue in 1946. Few rural roads were paved, and many roads connecting county seats were either unpaved or a complete ruin, but while Poole and Ellis were dully proclaiming that they would construct

[40] Montgomery *Advertiser,* June 2, 1946.
[41] Personal interview with James E. Folsom in Montgomery, May 1978.
[42] Undated Tuscaloosa *News* clipping in Folsom scrapbook, Folsom Papers.
[43] Confidential personal interview in Cullman, April 1974.

new roads in an efficient, businesslike manner, Folsom was making the
point with Roland Johnson's foot.

The platform that he outlined in his speeches was ambitious. He
advocated free textbooks through high school, more schools, a nine-
month school term, increased salaries for teachers, increased Workmen's Compensation, increased unemployment insurance, occupa-
tional diseases (e.g., black lung) compensation, paved farm-to-market
roads, a $50 monthly minimum pension to every person over sixty-
five years of age (which was more than double the average at that
time), repeal of the poll tax, and reapportionment of the state
legislature on a one-man-one-vote basis via a constitutional convention. He opposed the Boswell Amendment, a proposed addition to
the state constitution designed to circumvent U.S. Supreme Court
voting rights decisions. To some contemporary eyes Folsom's platform may appear modest, even conservative, but in Alabama in 1946
it was radical, i.e., it would, if enacted, have fundamentally changed
the status quo. Alabama's political elite regarded a malapportioned
legislature and disfranchisement of blacks and poor whites as crucial to
their defense of power and privilege, and as it slowly became clear to
them many months later that Folsom was serious, he began to loom
in their eyes as a major threat.

As the weeks passed, his speeches became ever more fluid, mixing folk
history, blunt position statements, and self-destructive ad libs. He
chose conservative Montgomery as a good place to proclaim his
opposition to the Boswell Amendment. At the same rally he spoke
against the Marshall Plan in general and aid to England in particular;
at that time the Marshall Plan, which brought assistance to war-torn
Europe, was enjoying extraordinarily widespread bipartisan support
throughout the country.[44] Here he was following his father-in-law's example of using an election speech to educate the populace.

Some of his ad libs would have ruined a normal candidate:

> We had a rally scheduled for Talladega. I'd spoke at Sylacauga and I got
> up to Talladega 15, 20 minutes late and I was mad as hell about bein' late.
> It was the first hot day of the year, and I commented in my speech that if
> I had a cold bottle of beer I could make a lot better speech. Afterward
> . . . one of the local people told me that they was havin' a wet-dry election.

[44] Montgomery *Advertiser*, April 26, 1946.

I hadn't known it, but it was too late then. I led the ticket and the county went dry. That told me it didn't matter what you say so long as you tell the truth and you are sincere.[45]

He seemed to enjoy taunting conservative whites in the Black Belt during his infrequent rallies there, knowing that he would receive few of their votes no matter what he said. He would sometimes look around the audience and observe that he saw a lot of people they called "black" who were nearly as white as he was, and "I want you to know that the sun didn't bleach 'em."[46]

After he had finished a speech Folsom would work his way through the crowd engaging people in quick, friendly conversations. An especially tall individual would be greeted with, "Hi, big 'un!" To others he would say, "What's your name, boy?" One of his campaign workers overheard people say in awe, "He was interested in what my name was." As he moved slowly along, people would reach out and gently touch the edge of his jacket or his shoulder. By the time he had finished, strangers believed that they knew him personally. Folsom generated an affection and a loyalty unlike anything seen in this state before or since.

It was often difficult for schedule-conscious aides to pull him away from crowds. Folsom loves people, or more precisely, he loves being loved. On one occasion Bill Lyerly managed to get him to the car where he briefly left Folsom to the business of accepting large contributions (averaging between $20 and $50) that people did not want to place anonymously in the suds bucket. Upon his return Lyerly discovered that Folsom had disappeared. After several inquiries Lyerly tracked him to a grocery store while grumbling to himself about having managed to lose a six-foot-eight-inch candidate and found him juggling oranges in a back room to the delight of surrounding admirers.[47]

Adherence to a tight schedule was made even more difficult by Folsom's habit of stopping for catnaps and meals on the road. Between rallies he would abruptly command Lyerly to stop, whereupon he would fall asleep in the back seat and awake a few minutes later

---

[45] Personal interview with James E. Folsom in Cullman, June 1976.
[46] *Ibid.*, and confidential personal interview in Cullman, June 1973.
[47] Personal interview with Bill Lyerly in Montgomery, July 1973.

completely alert. This pattern helps to explain how he maintained the grueling schedule of eight to ten rallies per day week after week; Lyerly put almost 30,000 miles on his car and wore out two sets of tires. His trips were often frequently interrupted by more or less random snack stops at the homes of complete strangers—a habit he had developed in earlier campaigns. All over Alabama the author was told how Big Jim had arrived unannounced at the Smiths' or Joneses' asking for something to eat, preferably cornbread and buttermilk, which he would wolf down on the front porch. These visits were often accompanied by promises of road paving, which by all accounts he remembered and acted on as governor.[48] During one such stop he noticed a housewife struggling with wet laundry on a line while a car sped past on a dry dirt road, enveloping the laundry with clouds of red dust. Folsom turned to Bill Lyerly and said sadly and quietly, "No one ought to have to live like that."[49]

Folsom won the May 7 primary with 104,152 votes, 28.5 percent of the total, far short of a majority but nevertheless an amazing victory. In its post-election analysis the press determined that he had won largely because of his personal charm combined with voter ignorance of his ties to labor unions, especially the hated CIO. Newspaper editors agreed that once voters had cleared their heads, Ellis, who ran a close second with 24.2 percent, would win the runoff.[50] Ellis quickly adopted this theme, saying that the people had had their "small fun in the first primary," but that the time had passed "for clowning and hippodroming and putting on a medicine show. It is time now, and high time to get down to business—serious business . . . to turn back the most serious threat that has faced us since reconstruction days."[51]

At first glance, Ellis's position after May 7 appeared fairly sound. He was only 4.3 percentage points behind Folsom, and a logical argument could have been made that Folsom would receive few votes from the relatively conservative Poole, Boozer, and Persons camps. A few days after the primary Poole and Boozer had thrown their support to Folsom, but Persons favored Ellis together with most other

---

[48] Innumerable personal interviews with reporters, Folsom campaign workers, and state legislators in all parts of the state except the Black Belt.

[49] Personal interview with Bill Lyerly in Montgomery, July 1973.

[50] Montgomery *Advertiser*, May 10, 1946.

[51] *Ibid.*, May 26, 1946.

political influentials in the state, and there was no guarantee that Poole and Boozer supporters would follow the suggestions of their leaders and vote for Folsom rather than Ellis with whom they were in much greater ideological sympathy.[52] Still, Ellis, whose career had by and large been one of progressive moderation, must have felt some desperation as he turned to a nasty mixture of red baiting and racism. At one rally he said: "The principle involved is whether a political agitator and rabble rouser . . . a man who was born and reared in Russia, can fasten his greedy clutches on the free Americans in the State of Alabama, slap a ring in their noses and tell them what they must do in a local Democratic primary." He then added coyly that he was referring to Sidney Hillman, head of the CIO's Political Action Committee (CIO-PAC). Ellis spoke of a "dark and ugly plot against our institutions, our cherished traditions, our free Democratic institutions." CIO-PAC, to whom Folsom was beholden, would, Ellis charged, "disrupt our fine and wholesome race relations by breaking down our segregation laws."[53]

Folsom responded with his deadliest weapon, wit. He told a Montgomery crowd:

> Before May 7 all you heard was that Folsom was a nice country boy—with no organization, no machines, no corporations, no state politicians—just a country boy out in a sea of humanity trying to get himself a few votes.
> But since May 7, Big Jim is a *bi-ig, ba-ad booger!*[54]

Folsom remembers this critical period today:

> Right up to that time they had ignored me. But in the runoff I was a Henry Wallace communist. Oh, I was just everything—really *bad*. They really pictured me sinister. I remember this rally in Montgomery and it was just slam runnin' over, and, of course, they had to lock the doors and there were just as many outside . . . And I sighted way back in the history of the family. 'Course I didn't go way back in 1630 when they landed. . . . "There's one thing between me and pa. He run all his life and never was beat, and I've run all my life and never was elected, and I'm tellin' you I

[52] *Ibid.*, May 21, June 1, 1946.

[53] Montgomery *Advertiser*, May 26, 1946; Birmingham *News*, May 13, 21, 1946. Ellis was not the first to use racial slurs in the campaign. This "honor" rests with the Alabama Temperance Alliance, which was working on Joe Poole's behalf. Montgomery *Advertiser*, April 14, 1946.

[54] Montgomery *Advertiser*, May 22, 1946, and personal interview with James E. Folsom in Cullman, June 1973.

wants on the payroll!" That just tore the house *down*. And I tole them up to that first primary I was a good ole country boy, and now I'm a big bad bugger. That got a wonderful response. And I told them another joke. I had old Army shoes. They didn't have these king size then and I had to order my shoes and I didn't have anything except the Army shoes. They was comfortable. They was *wide*. And it just so happened that some of those Army shoes had the size stamped on the side. I had two pair. One pair had the number stamped on the side: fifteen and a half. . . . And I told this story: "They tellin' a big ole political lie on me. They tellin' it on salt water down on the Gulf. They tellin' it in the Piney Woods. They tellin' it around the state capitol. They tellin' it through the mountains. What they tellin' on me? I want y'all to help me beat it down. Its a big ole political lie." And they'd say, "What in the world are they tellin' on Big Jim now?" "They tellin' that I wear a size 16 shoe, and it ain't so folks I just wear a 15½."[55]

At this point he would elevate his monstrous hoof into the air and point with delight at the 15½ stenciled on the instep. The laughter was deafening. As the days went by, Folsom's performance became ever sharper, new set pieces were developed, now with Gould Beech's expert assistance, and audiences became more responsive. People at Folsom rallies laughed, applauded, and danced. Even Ellis loyalists and hardened newspaper men found themselves reacting in spite of themselves.

Once again, Folsom had more than comedy in mind when he used the combat boot routine. He was able to say things clearly and directly, but he preferred symbols and parables. While people laughed at the "15½" an important message was being imprinted on their minds: his footwear was no ordinary boot, it was a U.S. Army combat boot that meant that *Folsom was a veteran*, "the only war veteran in the governor's race," as the idea was less subtly expressed in an infrequently run newspaper advertisement. Folsom possesses his own sense of taste and propriety. He did not care for the flag waving so popular among World War II veteran political candidates in 1946. It was crude and obvious and unseemly. The size 15½ boot was in a peculiar way graceful and smooth. He dealt with religion in the same manner. He was sensitive about overusing religious symbolism in his campaign.

Handy Ellis tried in vain to project a "man of the people" image by having himself photographed behind a plow mule. But the rigging was wrong. Folsom spotted the mistake, had the picture blown up,

---

[55] Personal interview with James E. Folsom in Cullman, June 1973.

and exhibited it at rural rallies while lecturing audiences on the proper way to hitch a mule: ". . . if you don't do this right he's going to fill up his stomach with air. . . ." His audiences knew how to hitch a mule, and they knew that he knew and that Ellis was nothing but another city slicker trying to fool them.[56]

Folsom defeated Ellis by 195,000 to 140,000 votes. Predictably, Folsom's strength lay in the Northern and Southern populist-oriented "white counties." Folsom's victory, together with the election of more than one hundred new legislators out of a total of one hundred thirty-five in both houses, was widely interpreted as a "revolt of the 'outs' against the 'ins.'" Most analysts agreed that the election result could not be explained by CIO-PAC power because Folsom's victory margin had been far too large and because many CIO-PAC candidates had been defeated even in industrial counties.[57] One clue to the outcome could be found in the makeup of Folsom's most active supporters. Bill Lyerly was typical. He was a young veteran returning home after defeating two of the greatest war machines ever created with vastly expanded feelings of what he could accomplish. In Folsom's words:

> In 1946 World War II was just over. War experiences encouraged dissatisfaction with the status quo. Vets saw what things were like elsewhere and what could be accomplished with determination. Before we went we didn't realize where taxpayers' money was going. When we got back we didn't have anything to come back to—no money, no jobs, nothin'.[58]

This statement was far from being an accurate description of Folsom's own circumstances, but he understood the deepest feelings of his fellow veterans just as he understood the plight of the woman with her clean, wet wash being ruined by the dust from passing cars on an unpaved road. The returning veterans faced a choice between, on one side, four Big Mule candidates who seemed more closely tied to 1901 than 1946, men who seemed completely removed from their daily world who clearly represented only monied interests and who often spoke in gloomy tones about the future and, on the other, Big Jim for whom all men were equal and everything was possible.

[56] Confidential interview of political reporters in Decatur, July 1973.

[57] Birmingham *Post,* June 6, 1946; Huntsville *Times,* June 5, 1946.

[58] Personal interview with James E. Folsom in Cullman, June 1973. See also Montgomery *Advertiser,* March 5, 1946.

And there was his charm. He possessed, at least as seen from a distance, a little boy's charm. His awesome frame was not used to intimidate—there were no loud, mean-spirited harangues—he was low-keyed and funny. He seldom preached political sermons, and those few he delivered carried a positive, constructive tone—not hell fire but salvation. And he was charismatic. Even in later years, with his capacities diminished by ill health, he radiates an indefinable *something*. It partly derives from his size—breadth as well as height. When that bearlike figure lurches into view, the effect is startling and disquieting. And his charisma remains even when his dimensions are tamed by a chair. Part of the magnetism derives from his single-minded devotion to politics—ideological politics—politics with goals. He is far more interested in where people stand on the *issues* (one of his favorite words) than who is likely to win or lose. Politics, in his view, is not a game; it is, despite the jokes and humor, a deadly serious centuries-old struggle of working people versus kings, slaveholders, or corporate elites.[59] Nothing else really matters. This single-minded passion compels one to pay attention to him.

Folsom's 1946 victory was a vivid demonstration that the county rings could be circumvented by direct appeals to voters combined with the efforts of ad hoc county and city organizations. No more would candidates be able to win just by collecting the endorsements of wealthy men in courthouse meetings. With one exception all other gubernatorial candidates emulated Folsom's approach in whole or in part through the 1978 primary. The lone exception was the 1978 winner Forrest (Fob) James. Like Folsom twenty years before, James, who had never before run for any election, realized that by using new techniques—this time techniques based on scientific public opinion polling and television—he could defeat even highly experienced opponents still relying on old ones.

[59] Grafton, "James E. Folsom and Civil Liberties," 3–27.

J. MILLS THORNTON III

Challenge and Response in the Montgomery Bus Boycott of 1955–1956

Shortly after five o'clock on the evening of December 1, 1955 Mrs. Raymond A. Parks boarded the Cleveland Avenue bus of the Montgomery City Lines at Court Square in Montgomery, Alabama. She sat next to the window on the side opposite the driver, in the first row of seats in the black section of the bus. The bus driver, James F. Blake, wrenched the yellow bus into gear and headed it up Montgomery Street towards its stop in front of the Empire Theater—towards that moment when Mrs. Raymond A. Parks and James F. Blake would change the course of American history.[1] In order to understand how their disagreement could have had such an effect, one must understand the context of past experiences and relationships that shaped the reactions of Montgomerians to it.

At the end of 1955 municipal politics in Montgomery was in the

This essay was published in *The Alabama Review*, XXXIII (July 1980).

[1] Montgomery *Advertiser*, December 2, 1955; Montgomery *Alabama Journal*, December 5, 1955; Trial Transcript, *Rosa Parks* v. *City of Montgomery* (Records of the Alabama Court of Criminal Appeals, Office of the Clerk, Supreme Court Building, Montgomery), 9. This article has greatly benefited from interviews conducted with the following people on the dates noted: Ralph D. Abernathy, February 28, 1979; Joe F. Bear, March 9, 1979; Eugene W. Carter, October 16, 1978; Jack Crenshaw, July 15, 1977; Virginia F. Durr, May 2, 1979; C. T. Fitzpatrick, January 11, 1979; Fred D. Gray, October 17, 1978; Mark W. Johnston, July 19, 1977; Walter J. Knabe, August 5, 1977; Rufus A. Lewis, July 27, 1977; William V. Lyerly, September 2, 1976; William R. Lynn, December 29, 1976; Edgar D. Nixon, August 2, 1977; Rosa L. Parks, May 22, 1978; James G. Pruett, Sr., January 2, 1977; Jo Ann Robinson, January 27, 1978; William F. Thetford, September 4, 1976. At the request of Mr. Pruett, I have regarded his interview as confidential.

midst of a fundamental transformation. For essentially the preceding half century Montgomery had been ruled by the Gunter Machine, headed for most of that time by William A. Gunter, Jr., the city's mayor from 1910 to 1915 and from 1919 to his death in 1940. Mayor Gunter had come to power after more than a dozen years of bitter factional warfare between two groups of the city's wealthy older families. Thereafter, he turned back all challenges to his rule. He could always rely upon the unwavering support of the city's morning newspaper, the Montgomery *Advertiser,* whose editor, Grover C. Hall, Sr., was one of his closest advisers, and upon the allegiance of the majority of Montgomery's older families. In the final two decades of his life he also had the unanimous support of city employees, whom—as a result of an act which he pushed through the state legislature—he could in effect hire and fire at will.[2]

If there were no successful challenges to the Machine after 1919, however, the unsuccessful challenges were many. During the 1920s Gunter's uncompromising opposition to the Ku Klux Klan made him a special object of Klan hatred. His repeated expressions of disapproval for the prohibition experiment placed the Anti-Saloon League in the ranks of his enemies, and fundamentalists condemned him for his generally lax enforcement of public morality. During the 1930s he turned the city government into a relief operation, putting hundreds on the public payroll and earning the bitter hostility of fiscal conservatives for unbalancing the city budgets. At the time of his death in 1940 he was admired by much of Montgomery's upper class and by large numbers of the city's unemployed. But he was also detested by many owners of small businesses and conservative citizens, strict Baptists and Methodists, and others to whom his values— rooted in the easygoing tolerance and aristocratic paternalism of his planter and Episcopalian background—were anathema.

After Gunter's death the Machine spent the next decade searching for a leader. The mayor was immediately succeeded by Cyrus B. Brown, who had long been one of Gunter's most powerful lieutenants and was at the time president of the Montgomery County governing body, the Board of Revenue. But Brown, an elderly man, died in 1944. David

---

[2] Thomas M. Owen, *History of Alabama and Dictionary of Alabama Biography* (4 vols., Chicago, 1921), III, 716; Montgomery *Advertiser,* April 1, 2, 1911, May 18, 20, 1919; *Acts of Alabama,* 1911, pp. 289–315, 1915, pp. 52–76, 1919, pp. 97–102; *House Journal,* 1915, pp. 1461–66; *Senate Journal,* 1915, pp. 1144–49, 1170–71, 1173–75.

Dunn, who had earlier been a political protégé of former Governor Bibb Graves, obtained Machine endorsement to succeed Brown but resigned in 1946 to go into private business.

The mayoralty then passed to City Attorney John L. Goodwyn, a cousin of Gunter's wife, whom Gunter had appointed city attorney in 1930. Goodwyn resigned in 1951 to accept a position in the state government; this position led eventually to his being appointed to the state Supreme Court. Goodwyn was succeeded by William A. "Tacky" Gayle, a Machine stalwart who had been a member of the City Commission since 1935.[3]

During this decade of rapid changes in leadership the Machine grew steadily weaker. The rapidity of these changes itself contributed to the process. Another factor in the Machine's decline was Gunter's penchant for surrounding himself with colorless, if often quite competent, administrators. Early in the century the Gunter forces had secured the abolition of the mayor-council form of government for the more easily controlled three-man commission.

In addition to the mayor there was a commissioner of public affairs, who administered the police and fire departments, and a commissioner of public works, who had charge of parks, libraries, street maintenance, and garbage collection. During the 1930s Gunter turned to two retired military men to fill these posts. Gayle, a veteran of World War I, had subsequently served as Alabama's adjutant general and had returned to active duty in World War II. In 1943 while serving in Britain as an air force colonel, Gayle was elected to his third term on the City Commission in absentia. The other commissioner, General William P. Screws, had been the commander of the Alabama contingent in the famed Rainbow Division during World War I. This tradition continued when George L. Cleere, another former state adjutant general, was selected to succeed Gayle as commissioner of public works when Gayle became mayor in 1951. These men, for all their efficiency, were by no means Gunter's equals as politicians, and without him they had trouble in holding the voters' affection.

By far the most important reason for the Machine's decline, how-

[3] Montgomery *Advertiser,* March 15, 16, 1943, August 9, 12, September 5, 6, 1944, March 8, May 5, 9, 1946, March 18, 1947, March 19, 20, 1951; Montgomery *Alabama Journal,* May 9, 1946, March 18, 1947. Dunn had resigned in order to permit returning soldiers to participate in the choice of their mayor—one of his campaign pledges in 1944—but had declined himself to become a candidate in the special election "as I am entering private business here in Montgomery."

ever, was the changing character of the city's population and residence patterns. During the first half of the twentieth century Montgomery grew rapidly, at an average of 30 percent a decade. This steady growth concealed after 1940 an important change in the city's racial composition. In 1910, as Gunter was first taking office as mayor, Montgomery's white population for the first time achieved parity in numbers with blacks. During the remainder of the Gunter years the relative proportion of the two races remained stable at 55 percent white and 45 percent black. But after Mayor Gunter's death the proportions began to change, under the impact both of increased black emigration to the North and of increased rural white movement into the city. In 1950 Montgomery was 60 percent white and 40 percent black; the white population grew by 47 percent during the 1940s and the black by only 23 percent. This trend continued during the 1950s. By 1955 Montgomery contained about 120,000 people, of whom some 63 percent were white and 37 percent were black.

The increasing white population meant that the number of residents in the city who could vote was growing even faster than was the population at large. The Machine had no hold upon either the gratitude or the affection of many of these new voters. Moreover, changing residence patterns reinforced this development. Resentments of Gunter's policies on the part of the lower middle class had existed in the 1920s and 1930s, but the resentment had found little institutional support. The town was small and could sustain few institutions alternative to the ones controlled by the well-to-do. During the 1940s and early 1950s the development of housing subdivisions on the edges of the city with small homes intended for the white lower middle class, effectively separated that group from the institutional control of the upper class and the upper middle class. In the eastern section of Montgomery—Capitol Heights, Dalraida, and Chisholm—there developed churches whose congregations did not contain a mix of classes and within which leadership could therefore fall to the lower middle class. In 1931, for instance, there were only seven white Baptist churches in the city, and in 1940 there were still only eleven, but by 1952 there were twenty. The number of white churches belonging to the Pentecostal sects, always a refuge for poorer elements of the population, also advanced rapidly. In 1931 white Pentecostal congregations constituted less than a fourth of the city's white churches, but by 1940 they were a third of the total, and by 1952 almost 40 percent of it.[4]

Similarly, East Montgomery developed alternative men's clubs; the Lions Club and the Exchange Club, for instance, both established separate East Montgomery units, leaving the downtown clubs in the hands of the businessmen who had dominated them. The growth to the east also demanded new schools, and with them came PTAs to be run by men and women unlikely to be leaders in a PTA in which the various classes were commingled—as had been the case with the PTAs of the few schools in the earlier, smaller city. Power in these earlier organizations had gravitated toward social leaders. East Montgomery also developed separate shopping and entertainment areas. In these and countless other ways the simple growth of the city gave the white lower middle class a separate community life and allowed it some measure of self-consciousness as a unit.

Meanwhile, this institutional "de-intermixture" of white classes was proceeding from the other side as well when subdivisions for wealthier residents were developed in South Montgomery, particularly in the Cloverdale section. Between 1951 and 1954 no less than sixty new subdivisions were completed in East and in South Montgomery, and in 1955 another thirty-three were reported to be in the planning stages.[5]

The first hint of what these developments portended for the Machine came in the city elections of 1947, when General William P. Screws, a member of the City Commission since 1931, was challenged by a young East Montgomery schoolteacher and football coach, Earl D. James. James's connection with physical education at Capitol Heights Junior High School placed him in an excellent position to capitalize upon the emerging sense of community in that section of the city. Screws beat James in Cloverdale, while James swamped all of his opponents in Capitol Heights and also ran well in an older, lower middle class ward, Oak Park. James thus erected a majority upon a basis not previously seen in Montgomery politics. The division between South Montgomery and East Montgomery that was demon-

---

[4] The figures as to churches were developed from Montgomery city directories. After 1952 city directories ceased to designate their entries by race. Dalraida and Chisholm were not within the city limits at this period.

[5] Montgomery *Advertiser*, February 20, March 15, 1955.

strated in these returns was to become characteristic of municipal elections for the next thirty years.[6]

Nevertheless, the Machine did not yet foresee its doom. It still controlled two of the Commission's three seats. James proved an able and relatively tractable official. He was elected to a second term in 1951 but resigned in 1953 to enter business. In the special election to choose James's successor the newly emerging shape of city politics first became completely clear. State Representative Joe M. Dawkins gathered endorsements for his candidacy from Montgomery's most prominent citizens. In the first primary Dawkins carried every precinct in the city and missed winning without a run-off by only 523 votes. In the second primary Dawkins faced Dave Birmingham, a man whose candidacy was regarded by the city's upper class as a bad joke. Birmingham had been an early and zealous supporter of former Governor James E. Folsom, and he shared much of Folsom's aggressive hostility to the wealthy. Birmingham was a classic demagogue. During his campaign he suggested that the chlorination of the city's drinking water had caused the preceding summer's devastating polio epidemic. He charged—contrary to well-documented fact—that the red color that sometimes appeared in the water was not iron but mud. The burden of Birmingham's appeal was an attack on the Machine. Dawkins was, Birmingham said, "hogtied to the old ring masters. . . . It is never good for a city to let one 'click' [*sic*] completely dominate it. Progress would stagnate." He opposed appointive municipal boards: "The ring masters through the board masters are strangling you to death with taxes without any responsibility to you as to how they will spend this tax money." He unremittingly attacked "that cesspool of gangsters at City Hall" and particularly decried the taxes that had been levied in order to finance the extension of services to new areas of the rapidly growing city.

Birmingham beat Dawkins in the run-off by a margin of 53 percent to 47 percent. Dawkins carried the wealthier precincts; his best ward was Cloverdale. Birmingham swept the lower middle class and lower class white precincts; he ran best in Capitol Heights and did well in precincts in which a substantial minority of the voters was black. The meaning of this election for the fortunes of the disintegrating Ma-

<hr>

[6]Montgomery *Alabama Journal,* March 18, 1947; Montgomery *Advertiser,* August 28, 1953, October 28, 1955.

chine was unmistakable. *Advertiser* editor Grover C. Hall, Jr., commented that, with Birmingham a member of the Commission, "The City Hall is going to be notably different for the foreseeable future." Doubtless, Hall had no real conception of just how right he was.[7]

The principal reason for the Machine's demise was the growing independence of the white lower middle class. Politicians called this phenomenon "the silent vote." In a 1955 article the *Advertiser's* city editor, Joe Azbell, explained the meaning of the term. In the 1920s and 1930s, in a city dominated by personal acquaintance, family alliances and personal favors rather than issues really decided the outcome of elections. But the growth of the city had added many voters to the rolls who were not members of the family alliances. The abolition of the city spoils system in favor of appointment by civil service examination had deprived the Machine of much of its power to bind voters to it by favors. By 1955, Azbell noted, voters lacked personal knowledge of the candidates and had thus begun to make voting decisions on the basis of issues, as filtered through the mass media. Politicians therefore lacked any real sense of where the voters were moving until the election returns were counted. In 1953, 1954, and 1955 knowledgeable observers had repeatedly guessed wrong about the election outcome because the voters no longer were members of cousinries or other blocs whose behavior could be predicted. Of the 1955 municipal elections Azbell commented, "No one seemed to care how the Hills were moving. No one seemed concerned about the political blocs. But twenty years ago a political observer would not dare comment on an election without first determining how the blocs were going. For the first time in city political history, ring politics played no important part in the local election, because the old ring politics has been overshadowed by a growing city where there is no control or method of determining how the voters will cast their ballot." As a result, city administrators feared their new constituents.[8]

If the growing independence of the white lower middle class was the principal factor that had altered the structure of municipal politics, another factor of almost equal significance was the newly important

---

[7] Montgomery *Advertiser*, September 15, October 3, 4, 18, 24, 27, November 1, 3, 4, 1953.
[8] *Ibid.*, March 27, 1955; cf. May 12, 1954.

black vote. The white lower middle class might be unfamiliar to the politicians, but the black community was virtual *terra incognita*. The state Democratic primary of 1946 represented the first primary in which blacks could legally vote; earlier such elections had been conducted under the white primary rule, which the Supreme Court had forbidden in 1944. Because they could now participate in the only elections that mattered in Alabama, blacks sought to register in increasing numbers during the late 1940s and early 1950s, particularly in the cities. The number of blacks registered in Montgomery grew slowly but steadily, and by 1955, 7.55 percent of the city's 22,210 registered voters were black. This percentage was well above the 5 percent ratio statewide. Moreover, in some wards black voters represented a substantial proportion of the total: 31 percent in Beat 7W, almost 25 percent in Beat 2, and 20 percent in Beat 6. Seven and a half percent is quite a small figure, but given the near equiponderance in the rivalry between South Montgomery and East Montgomery during these years, blacks could easily represent a balance of power.[9]

The returns in the special election of November 1953 appeared to black leaders to demonstrate that Birmingham owed his margin of victory over Dawkins to blacks, and they prepared to press the new commissioner for interest on this debt. Moreover, Birmingham stood ready to respond, both because he needed to hold the political allegiance of the blacks and because his racial views appear to have been genuinely, remarkably liberal.[10] The inauguration of Dave Birmingham as a city commissioner, therefore, marked the beginning of a heady period for the black leadership in which it found itself with genuine access to the city government for the first time.

The most important black spokesman in making demands upon the newly constituted City Commission was Edgar D. Nixon, a sleeping-car porter who was also president of the Montgomery local of the International Brotherhood of Sleeping Car Porters. Moving beyond his union power base, Nixon in the late 1940s and early 1950s had become more and more publicly active in demanding amelioration of conditions for members of his race. Throughout these years he was the dominant figure in the Montgomery chapter of the NAACP and was

---

[9] *Ibid.*, May 8, 1946, November 9, 1953, March 25, 1955; *Smith* v. *Allwright*, 321 U.S. 649.
[10] E.g., Dave Birmingham to James E. Folsom, October 28, 1955, James E. Folsom Papers, Manuscripts Division, Alabama State Department of Archives and History, Montgomery.

state president of that organization in 1948–49. He was also president of the Montgomery chapter of the Alabama Progressive Democratic Association, which had been organized during the 1940s as a black alternative to the regular party apparatus. In 1954 he created a great stir in Montgomery as a candidate for the County Democratic Executive Committee, the first black in living memory to seek public office. Though he lost to a white candidate, Joseph W. Carroll, he won more than 42 percent of the vote in the precinct, only a fourth of whose voters were black. In 1955 Nixon sought unsuccessfully to purchase a ticket to a Jefferson-Jackson Day dinner in Birmingham; the evening's principal speaker, Governor G. Mennen Williams of Michigan, abruptly cancelled his appearance in protest against Nixon's exclusion. Such highly visible efforts made Nixon the best known "activist" in Montgomery and gave him a considerable following in the black community.[11]

Equally as prominent in the dealings with the City Commission were two other blacks, Rufus A. Lewis and Mrs. Jo Ann Robinson. A former football coach at Alabama State College, Lewis was at the time a successful businessman and the chairman of the Citizens' Steering Committee, a group that had been formed in the fall of 1952 to press for better treatment for blacks. Mrs. Robinson, an English teacher at Alabama State College, was the moving spirit behind the black Women's Political Council, a group organized in 1949 to urge black women to register to vote; thereafter, the Council became the most militant and uncompromising organ of the black community. Led by Mrs. Robinson, Mrs. Mary Fair Burks, and Mrs. Thelma Glass, all of the Alabama State College faculty, and Mrs. A. Wayman West, Jr., the wife of a dentist, and sometimes aided by the more moderate Federation of Negro Women's Clubs, the Council repeatedly protested to the City Commission against discrimination and injustice in Montgomery. Indeed, with exceptions such as Nixon and

---

[11] Montgomery *Advertiser,* February 6, March 21, April 20, May 6, 1954, September 23, 30, 1955; Montgomery *Alabama Tribune,* September 30, October 14, 1955; Montgomery *Alabama Journal,* February 2, 1956; Clifford J. Durr to Hubert T. Delany, September 4, 1955, Durr to Herbert H. Lehman, March 25, 1957, both in Clifford J. Durr Papers, Alabama State Department of Archives and History, Montgomery; Thomas J. Gilliam, "The Montgomery Bus Boycott of 1955–1956" (M.A. thesis, Auburn University, 1968), 12–13. Nixon today believes that he may have been counted out in the executive committee race (interview, August 2, 1977).

Lewis, the blacks who addressed complaints to the City Commission in this period usually were women.[12]

The election of Dave Birmingham encouraged these groups for the first time to seek redress from the city government for long-standing grievances: the lack of black policemen, the inadequacy of parks and playgrounds in black sections of the city, and the conditions on the city buses. Immediately after Birmingham's election the Montgomery County Grand Jury and the Montgomery *Advertiser* had both urged the city to join Dothan, Anniston, and Talladega in hiring black policemen. Possibly supporters of the Machine saw this action as a way to cope with Birmingham's popularity in the black community. But the two Machine commissioners apparently remained dubious. After Birmingham's inauguration a delegation of black leaders met with the Commission; at this meeting Birmingham extracted from his colleagues a promise to hire black officers if funds could be found to pay their salaries. Birmingham continued to press the proposal and finally, in early May 1954, succeeded in obtaining the addition of four blacks to the force. Their hiring caused consternation among the city's extreme segregationists, whose resentment expressed itself two years later, during the boycott, when the home of one of the four, Patrolman Arthur G. Worthy, became a target for bombers. In the summer of 1955 Police Chief Goodwyn J. Ruppenthal sought to placate still hostile citizens by reassuring them that the new policemen were "just niggers doing a nigger's job."[13] But the doubts of many Montgomerians were not so easily assuaged, and the controversy rendered Birmingham's two colleagues increasingly unwilling to join him in taking other similar actions. The Machine could not afford to alienate either black or white segregationist voters. This difficulty

---

[12] Trial Transcript, *M. L. King, Jr.* v. *State of Alabama* (Records of the Alabama Court of Criminal Appeals, Office of the Clerk, Supreme Court Building, Montgomery), 256–57, 349–59; Martin Luther King, Jr., *Stride Toward Freedom: The Montgomery Story* (New York, 1958), 34, 73; Montgomery *Alabama Tribune,* December 23, 1955. Mrs. Burks and Mrs. Robinson organized the Council when they were refused membership in the League of Women Voters. Mrs. Robinson suggests that black women were able to be more aggressive in dealing with whites than were black men because in the environment created by segregation, women were under somewhat fewer strictures (interview, January 27, 1978). Lewis had been employed by the Montgomery Board of Education at the end of World War II to organize classes under the GI Bill for returning black veterans, and the veterans whom he taught became the backbone of his organization (interview, July 27, 1977).

[13] Montgomery *Advertiser,* November 7, December 17, 1953, April 15, 17, 23, June 20, 1954; Juliette Morgan to William A. Gayle, July 13, 1955, Juliette Morgan Scrapbook, Alabama State Department of Archives and History, Montgomery.

virtually immobilized the two Machine commissioners on every racial issue from late 1953 through early 1955, as the city prepared for the crucial municipal elections of late March 1955. In addition, their position was rendered even more awkward by the considerable heightening of white fears and black hopes that followed the Supreme Court's school integration decision in mid-May 1954.

Meanwhile, no such hesitation bound Birmingham or the black leadership. The question of parks in black areas escalated to a new level of public controversy in January 1955, when a delegation from the Women's Political Council appeared at a City Commission meeting to urge the appointment of a black to the city Parks and Recreation Board and to suggest Council member Mrs. A. Wayman West, Jr., for the position. Commissioner Birmingham immediately moved that the next vacancy go to a black, but Mayor Gayle persuaded him to withdraw the motion until a vacancy actually occurred. The mayor, who had actively supported a city program under which three new playgrounds for blacks had been recently built, assured the delegation that its request would be given every consideration when there was a vacancy. He continued his effort to define a medial position later in the same week when he appeared before a large group of blacks gathered to celebrate the inauguration of Governor James E. Folsom and there praised the work of the city's black policemen. But the question of black representation on the Parks and Recreation Board could not be dismissed so easily. It was to become a principal issue in the city elections in March. In August, Commissioner Birmingham, now a lame duck, offered a motion to expand the Parks and Recreation Board from five to seven members and to designate the two new places for blacks, but Gayle and Cleere voted the resolution down. However, the mayor in July and the Parks and Recreation Board in September assured angry black delegations that if the city's voters would approve the proposed issuance of a million dollars in parks bonds, significant improvements in Negro parks would immediately be forthcoming.[14]

---

[14] Montgomery *Advertiser,* December 20, 1953, January 19, July 20, August 10, September 14, 1955; Montgomery *Alabama Tribune,* January 28, August 19, 1955. The *Advertiser* alleged editorially that Birmingham's August resolution was merely the opening gun in his rumored race for a seat on the County Board of Revenue. At the July meeting with the blacks Cleere and Birmingham almost came to blows and had to be separated by the mayor. The land that was promised as the site of a large new Negro park at the September meeting ultimately became a parking lot for a white football stadium.

While the public was concerned with the issues of black policemen and black membership on the Parks and Recreation Board, tension over racial relations on the city's buses had quietly been mounting. At the end of 1953, encouraged by Birmingham's recent election, the Women's Political Council met with the City Commission to lodge three complaints: that blacks sometimes had to stand beside empty seats, in cases where the black section was filled but the white section was not; that black passengers were compelled to get on at the front door to pay their fare and then to get off and to reboard at the back door to take a seat, rather than being permitted simply to walk down the aisle of the bus; and that buses stopped at every corner in white neighborhoods but only at every other corner in black neighborhoods. Allegations of discourtesy by drivers and of buses' passing by waiting black passengers were also made. The meeting was inconclusive, but representatives of the bus lines, who were present, evidently offered to investigate specific charges of discourtesy. Several months later, in the spring of 1954, the Women's Political Council again met with the Commission and representatives of the bus company to reiterate its three complaints and to offer a list of specific instances of abuse by bus drivers. At this meeting the delegation from the Political Council was accompanied by Rufus Lewis representing the Citizens' Steering Committee, by a delegation from the Federation of Negro Women's Clubs, and by a large group representing black trade union locals. At this meeting as at the earlier one the principal spokesman for the blacks was Jo Ann Robinson of the Political Council.

As a result of this meeting the problem of buses' stopping only at every other corner in black areas was remedied. Addressing the issue of seating, the Commission, on the advice of City Attorney Walter Knabe and bus company attorney Jack Crenshaw, informed the blacks that it was legally powerless to do anything about the problem of black passengers' being compelled to stand beside empty seats. The city ordinance and the state statute on the subject were both read aloud to the petitioners. The meeting was evidently a stormy one. Subsequently, Mayor Gayle testified that several days later Mrs. Robinson called him angrily "and said they would just show me, they were going in the front door and sitting wherever they pleased." In April 1954 the Reverend Uriah J. Fields, a militant young black minister who was later to break spectacularly with Martin King, brought the seating complaints before the public with a letter to the Montgomery *Advertiser* demanding that the policy be altered. There the matter rested until the following spring.[15]

Meantime, the elections that could kill the already moribund Machine were approaching. Gayle and Cleere both sought re-election. Gayle's only opponent was Harold McGlynn, a candy wholesaler who was a political associate of Commissioner Birmingham. Cleere's principal opposition came from Frank Parks, an East Montgomery interior decorator who was a former Grand Master of Alabama's Masons. Parks set out to create an electoral coalition like that which had enabled Birmingham to upset Dawkins a year and a half earlier. Though Gayle and Cleere supported each other, and Birmingham supported McGlynn and Parks, it is unclear whether or not Gayle and Cleere supported one of the candidates opposing Birmingham; at any rate, they did not do so publicly. Birmingham drew two principal opponents. Sam B. Stearns, the owner of a downtown parking garage and a nephew of a former Montgomery County sheriff, ran a vigorous and well-financed campaign, but the returns showed him much less popular than observers had thought. The real threat to the incumbent was former State Representative Clyde C. Sellers, a resident of South Montgomery and the owner of an exterminating business. Sellers effectively emphasized his extensive experience in law enforcement; he had joined the state Highway Patrol shortly after its formation, had worked his way up through its ranks, and in 1945 had been appointed director of the department by Governor Chauncey Sparks. His four years in the state legislature also strengthened his credentials. That he had been a star football player for Auburn University in the 1920s gave him additional popularity. But the issue that was to carry him to victory was provided by the events of the canvass.

Birmingham launched a typically demagogic campaign. His two colleagues on the Commission had voted to increase the city sewerage fee in order to finance the extension of sewer mains into the Allendale-Wildwood section, a South Montgomery area. Birmingham denounced this decision as class legislation and demanded that the wealthy homeowners in the section pay for the sewers themselves. Frank Parks loudly echoed this argument. Birmingham revived his accusation that chlorination of the water supply was dangerous; he alleged as

---

[15] Trial Transcript, *King* v. *State*, 141, 256–57, 349–59; Montgomery *Advertiser*, April 6, 1954.

proof that city water would kill camellia bushes. He also charged that Gayle and Cleere might have favored the construction of a city sewage treatment plant only in order to make a private profit by selling the plant's effluent for fertilizer. With such allegations Birmingham hoped to hold, and Parks to build, constituencies of whites of the lower class and the lower middle class. McGlynn refused to stoop to this level, and perhaps for that reason his campaign against Gayle never really gained momentum. McGlynn did join Birmingham and Parks in a strong effort to gain the allegiance of the black vote.[16]

As the campaign of 1955 began, black leaders hoped to use the black balance of power between South Montgomery and East Montgomery to extract real concessions from the candidates. They had just passed through a year in which the city government had shown unprecedented willingness to listen to their proposals. Birmingham, Parks, and McGlynn were eager for black support. One of Birmingham's opponents, Stearns, was equally as willing to seek black votes. Nor, indeed, were Gayle and Cleere hostile. Though more reticent than were their opponents about openly campaigning for black ballots, still both men were racial moderates. The remnants of the Machine that they represented could command a certain residue of good will in the black community. Mayor Gunter's actions in the 1920s and 1930s had endeared him to many blacks, and after World War II the Machine-dominated city government had constructed a number of low-rent public housing projects for poor blacks. By 1955 the Montgomery Housing Authority, which was headed by the late Mayor Gunter's son-in-law Charles P. Rogers, administered four such developments and had a fifth in the planning stages. Its public housing record was not an unmixed asset for the Machine, however, because many blacks resented the demolition of their homes and their removal into crowded apartments, however modern.[17]

All of these circumstances so emboldened the black leaders that they decided in February to hold a public meeting in order to question the various Commission candidates about their stands on racial issues. The candidates subsequently also appeared before organized labor and

[16] Montgomery *Advertiser,* February 1, 6, 9, 13, 16, 20, 27, 28, March 10, 13, 16, 20, 23, 24, 27, 1955.
[17] 1956 Montgomery City Directory; Montgomery *Advertiser,* May 9, 1954, February 1, 9, 1955. An additional highly visible alteration in race relations, though one unconnected with politics, was the hiring in the winter of 1953–54 of black players for the city's professional baseball team.

the Junior Chamber of Commerce.[18] But the spectacle of office seekers appearing before blacks to submit to interrogation was a sight for which the electorate was unprepared.

The meeting, held under the auspices of Nixon's Progressive Democratic Association, convened in the Ben Moore Hotel, the city's only black hotel, on the evening of February 23. All of the candidates were present. The session commenced with Nixon's distributing to them a questionnaire asking their position on a number of specific black grievances. The first area of complaint on the list was "the present bus situation. Negroes have to stand over empty seats of city buses, because the first ten seats are reserved for whites who sometime never ride. We wish to fill the bus from the back toward the front until all seats are taken. This is done in Atlanta, Georgia, Mobile, Alabama and in most of our larger southern cities." Next came requests that a black be appointed to the Parks and Recreation Board and that blacks be considered for all municipal boards. The third subject mentioned was the lack of middle-class housing subdivisions for relatively well-to-do blacks. The authors of the questionnaire had been upset by the city's decision a week earlier to forbid the development of such an area because of the protests of neighboring whites. The fourth plea was that qualified black applicants be considered for civil service jobs with the city. "Everybody cannot teach," the questionnaire noted, in reference to the limited professional opportunities available to Montgomery's middle-class blacks. The document concluded with three complaints about the inadequacy of city services in black neighborhoods. It asked for the installation of more fireplugs in these sections, the extension of sewer mains to eliminate outdoor privies, and the widening and paving of streets and the addition of curbing.

In their responses Birmingham, McGlynn, and Parks all agreed to appoint a black member of the Parks and Recreation Board. Stearns, who had adopted the strategy of attempting to defeat Birmingham by outbidding him for the allegiance of the city's various groups, also agreed, and added a proposal for a sixteen-member all-black advisory board as an adjunct of the Parks Board. The press reported that black leaders were as a result closely divided as to whether they should endorse Birmingham or Stearns. Gayle and Cleere remained noncommittal on the Parks Board issue. Sellers gave a general talk that did

---

[18] Montgomery *Advertiser,* February 9, 16, March 16, 1955, January 13, 1956.

not speak to any of the points in the questionnaire; he said later that he did not see the document until the end of the meeting. Accounts of the session do not indicate any reply by any of the candidates to the questionnaire's proposal on bus seating.[19]

After the candidates had completed their presentations, the meeting adjourned, but its repercussions were still being felt years later. Clyde Sellers quickly saw that the black proposals and their deferential handling by his two opponents presented him with the issue that would allow him to win a majority. It appeared that Stearns and Birmingham were going to divide the black vote. Sellers, as a South Montgomerian, could count on a large vote from that section in response to Birmingham's vociferous attacks on its residents. Previously, though, there had seemed to be no way to cut into Birmingham's solid following in East Montgomery. Now, demagogic exploitation of racial tensions promised to counter Birmingham's exploitation of class tensions and thus to capture support in the eastern wards. During March, before the election on the 21st, Sellers made the most blatantly and insistently racist addresses heard in Montgomery since the days of J. Johnston Moore, the Ku Klux Klan's candidate against Mayor Gunter in the 1920s. Sellers converted the Ben Moore Hotel meeting into the principal issue of the canvass. He answered the questionnaire point by point in his speeches and advertisements. He asserted flatly that the blacks' bus seating proposal would violate state law—not bothering to explain how, in that case, the system could be used in Mobile. He pledged himself to oppose the appointment of blacks to city boards. To the request that qualified blacks be allowed to apply for civil service jobs, he said, "If the commission were to comply with this request, it would be only a short time before negroes would be working along side of whites and whites along side of negroes . . . I have always felt that if a man wanted a job bad enough, he could go where the job, for which he is qualified, is available. There are places in this nation where civil service jobs for negroes in cities are available but not in Montgomery. I will expend every effort to keep it that way."[20] Sellers's campaign was aided by

[19] *Ibid.*, February 18, 24, 25, March 1, 16, 20, 1955. Abernathy gives the membership of the committee that drafted the questionnaire as including himself, Nixon, Lewis, Robinson, Mrs. A. Wayman West, and James E. Pierce, a professor of political science at Alabama State (interview, February 28, 1979). Nixon, who presided at the meeting, says that all of the candidates chose to duck the bus-seating question (interview, August 2, 1977).
[20] *Ibid.*, March 16, 20, 1955.

the first of the bus incidents, the arrest on March 2 and the trial on March 18 of Claudette Colvin for violation of the segregation ordinance.

Sellers had been correct about the effect of his racial appeal upon the electorate. In the returns he took 43 percent of the poll, to 37 percent for Birmingham, 16 percent for Stearns, and 4 percent for a minor candidate, John T. Weaver. Birmingham carried the wards with substantial black registration and also took the poorest white wards. But the white lower middle class areas of East Montgomery that he had swept in 1953 now went to Sellers. Capitol Heights, which had given Birmingham 62 percent of its vote in 1953, making it his banner precinct, now gave him only 31 percent, to 44 percent for Sellers. At the same time South Montgomery voted heavily against Birmingham; Sellers took 60 percent of the poll in Cloverdale. Despite Sellers's solid lead over Birmingham, a run-off between the two men would have been necessary. However, two days after the election Birmingham collapsed while preparing to give a television speech; his doctor diagnosed his condition as "overexertion and exhaustion" and advised him to withdraw from the race. Birmingham did so, and Sellers was declared elected. We can never know whether Birmingham could have defeated Sellers. Birmingham had come back from an even more substantial deficit to defeat Dawkins in 1953, but Birmingham's chances of repeating this accomplishment in 1955 were poor. Sam B. Stearns, the third important candidate in the race, had made shrill personal attacks on Birmingham. It is unlikely that a white voter who had cast his ballot for Stearns in the first round would thereafter have moved to the support of Birmingham.

In the mayoral election McGlynn had seldom indulged in the demagogic appeals of Birmingham and Parks. He may have been hurt by the fact that he was a Roman Catholic, but on that point evidence is lacking. Although McGlynn received 40 percent of the vote and carried the wards with substantial black registration and also the city's poorest white ward, West End, nevertheless Mayor Gayle won easily.

In the election for commissioner of public works the incumbent, George Cleere, had refused to follow Sellers in exploiting the racial issue. Instead, he had attempted to answer with reason the strident class-oriented accusations of Parks, particularly with reference to the sewerage fee. The result was that Parks was elected on returns whose geographical distribution was virtually identical to the distribution of the support for Birmingham in his race against Dawkins in 1953.

Cleere swept the South Montgomery wards, taking more than 75 percent of the vote in Cloverdale, but Parks carried the substantially black precincts and those of the white lower class and lower middle class.[21]

The election's outcome puzzled Grover C. Hall, Jr.; why should the voters have elected Parks, Birmingham's ally, over Cleere, Gayle's ally, but then have repudiated Birmingham himself and returned Gayle?[22] The meaning of the election was probably much clearer to Gayle, now the sole Machine survivor in municipal politics, seated between an uncompromising segregationist on his right and an adversary of Montgomery's wealthy on his left. The Machine's traditional policies of moderate, paternalistic racial attitudes, and a firm alliance with the city's upper class had failed to sustain it, and they held little likelihood of endearing Gayle to the constituencies that had elevated either of his two colleagues. Clearly, Gayle needed a new strategy immediately. The lesson of Parks's victory appeared to be that, given the new social realities produced by the city's rapid postwar growth, an East Montgomerian would always defeat a South Montgomerian when the issues remained class oriented. The lesson of Sellers's victory appeared to be that the vigorous exploitation of racial antipathies could give a South Montgomerian at least a fighting chance of defeating an East Montgomerian. Gayle was, of course, a South Montgomerian. But Gayle's dilemma was much more complicated than this analysis would imply. First, he was unlikely to abandon a set of beliefs that he had held sincerely for many decades merely because political strategy seemed to dictate this course. Second, developments within the business community rendered it less than certain that a sound strategy actually dictated this course. To understand this factor, we must briefly explore the attitude of Montgomery's businessmen towards their city government.

The business community believed that the source of all genuine social ills was the lack of industrialization. Montgomery's economy rested primarily on the presence of the state government and of two air force bases, Maxwell and Gunter. One in every seven families in the

---

[21] *Ibid.*, February 9, 13, March 16, 20, 22, 24, 25, 29, 1955. Because of the presence on the ballot of a minor candidate, George J. Rivers, the race between Parks and Cleere was forced into a run-off, but the geographical distribution of the vote was identical in both elections.

[22] *Ibid.*, March 30, 1955.

city was an air force family in 1955. Aside from income generated by federal and state governmental expenditures, Montgomery relied almost exclusively on its role as a marketing center for the surrounding agricultural area.[23] By 1955 businessmen were armed with legislation passed during the preceding decade providing Alabama municipalities with powerful tools for attracting industry to the state, particularly in the form of tax advantages and of public financing of plant construction. Business leaders therefore had high hopes of broadening Montgomery's economic base.

This zealous commitment to industrialization was the source of the tension between businessmen and the city government. Business leaders believed that the city's politicians had been inept in attracting industry. Near the end of October 1953 the *Advertiser* had broken the story that DuPont had purchased 850 acres near Montgomery "as a prospective site for an industrial plant." The article had concluded excitedly, "Announcement is expected soon on the type of plant to be constructed." Months passed, and no such announcement was forthcoming. Reportedly, four other "very large companies" that had considered building factories in Montgomery had been lost to other cities during 1954 and 1955. Worried businessmen sought to discover what they were doing wrong. The Chamber of Commerce desperately debated ways to attract favorable national publicity for the city. Chamber of Commerce President James G. Pruett ominously warned the Rotary Club that "industry will come to Montgomery and Alabama only when there is a healthy climate for it and when government on all levels is not hostile to it." In this atmosphere of frustration at the repeated recent failures in the drive for industrialization, forty of the city's most important businessmen met in mid-October 1955 to organize the Men of Montgomery. Adopting the frank motto "We Mean Business," they chose as their first project a campaign to compel the City Commission to act on a proposal that had languished in the City Hall bureaucracy for years: to construct a new terminal for the municipal airport to give visitors to the city a more favorable first impression.[24]

[23] Montgomery *Alabama Journal,* January 13, 1956.
[24] Montgomery *Advertiser,* October 28, 1953, January 15, 1954, February 20, 24, March 7, 10, October 19, December 11, 1955, March 4, 1956; Montgomery *Alabama Journal,* November 3, December 9, 1955, January 10, 1956.

Mayor Gayle had always counted on business support. The Gunter Machine had been closely allied with business interests. Gayle himself was a brother-in-law of one of the most influential businessmen in Alabama, Birmingham industrialist Donald Comer of Avondale Mills.[25] Now the mayor faced a business community organized with a new efficiency and motivated by a new hostility. By the fall of 1955 his dilemma was acute. His colleagues on the Commission each represented constituencies only recently defined, and Gayle had no real access to either. The black leadership was making militant demands upon the city for the first time and was asking for public responses. The business community was suddenly dubious of his competence and disposed to press him for positive action. If he moved towards one of the newly emerging constituencies, he risked permanently alienating the elements in the city upon which he had relied ever since he had first entered politics. Against this background the city moved towards the events of early December.

At the Ben Moore Hotel meeting on February 23 bus seating had headed the list of grievances. On the afternoon of March 2 came the arrest of Claudette Colvin, a fifteen-year-old black girl who refused to vacate her seat when ordered to do so by a bus driver, Robert W. Cleere. Miss Colvin, who was returning from school, was seated far back in the bus, just forward of the rear door, on a seat with an older black woman, a Mrs. Hamilton. The bus was entirely filled, and Cleere ordered the two blacks to stand in order to give their seats to boarding whites. Mrs. Hamilton refused, and Cleere summoned police. When the police arrived, a black man got up, gave his seat to Mrs. Hamilton, and left the bus. Miss Colvin, who apparently was led into her resistance by the actions of Mrs. Hamilton, now found herself deserted to face the music alone. She became hysterical, kicked and scratched the arresting officers, and had to be carried bodily from the bus.[26]

Because of her age Miss Colvin was brought to trial before Juvenile

---

[25] Montgomery *Advertiser,* December 11, 1955.

[26] *Ibid.,* March 6, 1955; Trial Transcript, *Aurelia S. Browder* v. *William A. Gayle,* Civil Action 1147-N, U.S. District Court, Middle District of Alabama (Federal Records Center, Atlanta, Georgia, FRC Box Number 426114), 17–20, and Colvin arrest warrant and complaint contained in case file.

Court Judge Wiley C. Hill, Jr., a first cousin of U.S. Senator J. Lister Hill. She was not the first person to be arrested for violation of the bus seating ordinance, but according to Commissioner Birmingham she was the first person ever to enter a plea of not guilty to such a charge. Her twenty-four-year-old attorney, Fred D. Gray, one of two black lawyers in Montgomery, interposed two defenses. The first, that segregated seating violated the U.S. Constitution, was overruled in short order by Judge Hill. The second defense was more troublesome. When the city ordinance requiring segregation on public conveyances had first been adopted in 1900, it had provoked a black boycott of the city trolley lines. This boycott had lasted throughout the summer of 1900 and had ended only when the City Council agreed to amend the new ordinance to forbid compelling anyone to vacate his seat unless there was another seat to which he could move. This proviso remained a part of the city code. Because both sides in the Colvin case agreed that the bus had been entirely filled, the bus driver, rather than Miss Colvin, had violated the segregation ordinance.

State laws supersede city ordinances, however. In 1945 the state legislature had enacted a statute requiring the Alabama Public Service Commission to see that all bus companies under its jurisdiction enforced racially segregated seating. This statute, unlike the city ordinance, gave bus drivers absolute power to seat passengers. It was unclear whether or not the Public Service Commission had jurisdiction over municipal bus lines. A year later the state was to contend in federal court that the state law was inapplicable in such situations in order to avoid having it at issue in the suit seeking to declare the segregation of Montgomery buses unconstitutional. Now Circuit Solicitor William F. Thetford moved to meet Gray's defense by amending the complaint so as to allege a violation of the state law rather than of the city ordinance. Judge Hill overruled Gray's objection that the state law did not apply, found Miss Colvin guilty both of violating the state bus segregation statute and of assault and battery on the arresting officer, declared her a juvenile delinquent, and ordered her placed on probation. Gray filed an appeal to Circuit Court, but on the appeal the state pressed only the charge of assault and battery, and on that ground Miss Colvin's sentence of probation was affirmed. As a result Gray was deprived of any way to use this case as a means to contest the various questions that had been raised with regard to the segregation laws.[27]

Meanwhile, Miss Colvin's arrest had moved the city's black leaders to make one more effort to deal with the bus problem through the political mechanism. In mid-March, as the municipal election campaign climaxed, blacks arranged two meetings with white officials. At the first one Commissioner Birmingham and the bus company's manager James H. Bagley met in Bagley's office with a delegation that included the Reverend Martin L. King, Jr., a twenty-six-year-old Baptist minister who had moved to Montgomery the preceding September to take up his first pastorate, and who in the intervening six months had become quite active in the city's NAACP chapter. It appears that, at this meeting as at earlier ones, the principal spokesman for the blacks was a conspicuous member of King's new congregation, Jo Ann Robinson.

This encounter was relatively amicable. Birmingham was eager to conciliate the blacks, and Bagley did not wish to offend his customers gratuitously. The black delegation pointed out that forcing a passenger to stand in order to seat another passenger violated both company policy and the provisions of the city code. Bagley acknowledged that the policy did forbid such action; he promised to investigate and to reprimand the bus driver in the Colvin case if it was warranted. The blacks evidently brought up the seating plan proposed in the questionnaire presented at the Ben Moore Hotel meeting; Birmingham promised to secure a formal opinion from City Attorney Walter Knabe on what seating arrangements were legally permissible. Unfortunately, nothing came of either of these promises.[28]

Birmingham's failure to act is understandable; within two weeks he was a lame duck, his influence greatly diminished and his health precarious. Bagley's inattention to the matter was simply shortsighted. A principal source of friction on the buses was the company's loosely

---

[27] Montgomery *Alabama Journal,* March 18, 19, 1955; Montgomery City Code of 1952, Chapter 6, Sections 10–11; Code of Alabama, 1940, Recompiled, Title 48, Section 301 (31a); Gilliam, "Bus Boycott," 17. Gray had only returned to Montgomery six months earlier, after attending law school in Cleveland, Ohio. The Colvin case was his first joust with the segregation laws (interview, October 17, 1978). But he quickly became a leader of the black community; that summer found him serving as a spokesman for the black delegation in the meetings with the city concerning the parks.

[28] King, *Stride,* 41–42; Trial Transcript, *King* v. *State,* 240, 344–46; Gilliam, "Bus Boycott," 18–19; Montgomery *Alabama Tribune,* March 16, 1956.

defined seating policy. In practice the policy varied enormously from route to route and from driver to driver. Even under the company's official policy, the middle sixteen seats of the bus had no fixed racial designation; it was the responsibility of the driver to shift the racial line forward or back in order to provide a number of seats roughly proportionate to the racial composition of the group of riders at any given moment. Under these circumstances the drivers had to reseat passengers rather frequently. The embarrassment and humiliation to blacks of being thus publicly forced to acknowledge and accept legal discrimination was exacerbated by the fact that the harried drivers usually adjusted the seating simply by shouting peremptory commands over their shoulders. If Bagley had attempted to specify the seating policy more fully and had sought more vigorously to enforce company rules requiring courtesy from drivers, he could have eliminated much of the ill will between the bus line and the black community. If he had emphasized to the drivers the company policy against unseating passengers when other seats were unavailable, he would have forestalled both the Claudette Colvin and the Rosa Parks incidents.[29]

The second meeting in response to Miss Colvin's arrest appears to have been much stormier than that with Bagley and Birmingham. Bagley arranged this meeting for the blacks. The black delegation included, as usual, members of the black Women's Political Council and the Federation of Negro Women's Clubs. It also included Rufus A. Lewis of the Citizens' Steering Committee and attorney Fred Gray. Mayor Gayle and City Attorney Knabe represented the city. The bus company was represented by its attorney, Jack Crenshaw. The blacks apparently pressed the seating proposal contained in the questionnaire distributed at the Ben Moore Hotel meeting. Gray believed that the proposal violated no existing law. Crenshaw adamantly maintained that the proposal flouted both the city ordinance and the state statute, an opinion in which Knabe concurred.

The importance of Crenshaw's intransigence both in producing and in sustaining the bus boycott can hardly be overstated. He was an excellent lawyer, educated at Harvard. He was a political ally of the racially moderate Governor Folsom. Despite this background, however, he proved incapable of understanding the strategic advantage

[29]Trial Transcript, *King* v. *State*, 360–486, 510–47; Trial Transcript, *Browder* v. *Gayle*, 58–69.

of accepting a modest compromise in order to forestall a full-scale assault on segregation. He dismissed Gray's arguments out of hand and informed his client Bagley that the law left the bus company absolutely no room for compromise. The meeting adjourned with the complaints of the blacks still unanswered.[30]

Through the summer and fall of 1955 a series of events kept the bus question before the public. Early in the year a black woman, Sarah Mae Flemming, had sued the city bus line of Columbia, South Carolina, for damages for its having enforced the segregation laws against her. In mid-July the U.S. Court of Appeals for the Fourth Circuit ruled in this case that segregated seating on buses was unconstitutional—a decision that received headline treatment in the Montgomery *Advertiser*. Later in July a young black, James M. Ritter, had defied the order of a bus driver in Richmond, Virginia, to move to the rear and had been fined ten dollars for his action. In Montgomery itself another black teenager, Mary Louise Smith, was arrested on October 21 for refusing to yield her seat to a white woman. This case did not create the furor which the Colvin incident had, however, because Miss Smith chose to plead guilty; she was fined five dollars.[31]

Equally important in focusing attention on the bus company was the fact that its franchise was about to expire. National City Lines, Inc., of Chicago, owned the Montgomery bus company. That firm had been granted a twenty-year city franchise in 1936; the franchise would come up for renewal in March of 1956. In late October an official of the company came to Montgomery to open negotiations. He and the city commissioners surveyed the city from the air in order to plan revisions in the bus routes, and delegations from a number of the new subdivisions on the city's outskirts appeared before the Commission to seek the extension of bus service to their areas. At the same time the bus company was bargaining with the bus drivers' union for a new two-year contract. Montgomerians who recalled that

---

[30] Trial Transcript, *King* v. *State*, 256–57, 344–46, 357–59, 539–40. On Crenshaw's and Knabe's opinions of the legality of the Negro proposal, see below, notes 43, 47. Crenshaw and his brother had handled Governor Folsom's suit to compel the Dixiecrat presidential electors to vote for Harry Truman: *Folsom* v. *Albritton*, 335 U.S. 882; *State* v. *Albritton*, 251 Ala. 422.

[31] *Flemming* v. *South Carolina Electric and Gas Co.*, 128 F. Supp. 469, 224 F. 2d 752; Montgomery *Advertiser*, July 15, 1955; Montgomery *Alabama Tribune*, July 22, 29, 1955; Trial Transcript, *Browder* v. *Gayle*, 10–12.

all bus service had been suspended during a brief strike in December 1953 watched the progress of the negotiations apprehensively.[32]

In the fall of 1955 the press was filled with accounts of events in Selma. There a group of twenty-nine blacks in September petitioned the city board of education urging the integration of the schools. In mid-September the head of the recently organized Dallas County White Citizens Council, attorney M. Alston Keith, reported that the efforts of the Council had resulted in the firing of sixteen of the twenty-nine petitioners from their jobs. Blacks retaliated by refusing to buy the milk of a dairy that had agreed to discharge a petitioner. Next came incidents of arson and kidnapping, both directed against a black grocer who had been a participant in the boycott of the dairy. Finally, in late October six young white men, two of them members of the Selma police force, were arrested and indicted for the actions directed at the grocer, and one of the accused policemen thereupon committed suicide.[33]

In early November black Congressman Adam Clayton Powell visited Montgomery to speak to the Progressive Democratic Association. Congressman Powell spent the night at the home of Edgar D. Nixon. In his speech Powell warned the Citizens Councils that their economic pressure "can be counter met with our own [black] economic pressure." The example of the events in Selma and the force of Powell's remark doubtless made an impact upon Nixon, who because of his background in the labor movement and because of his long association with and intense admiration for his union's president, A. Philip Randolph, was predisposed in any case to believe in the efficacy of economic action.[34]

The arrest of Rosa Parks struck a spark to this tinder. When Mrs. Parks boarded the bus, it was divided into twenty-six seats for blacks

---

[32] Montgomery *Advertiser*, December 12–16, 1953, October 25, 27, December 7, 20, 1955, January 25, February 16, 1956.

[33] *Ibid.*, September 8, October 22, 23, 26, 1955; Montgomery *Alabama Tribune*, September 16, October 28, 1955. A petition seeking the integration of Montgomery's schools was also presented to the local board of education in August, and similar petitions were submitted throughout Alabama, evidently at the instance of the national NAACP. These petitions appear to have been the trigger for the establishment of a great many of the Alabama chapters of the White Citizens Council.

[34] Montgomery *Advertiser*, November 6, 1955; interview with Nixon, August 27, 1977. In the 1930s both Powell and Randolph had organized black boycotts of Northern merchants who refused to hire blacks.

and ten for whites. Two blocks farther on, when the bus stopped in front of the Empire Theater, it was completely filled, and both whites and blacks were standing; all white standing room was taken. Driver James F. Blake undertook to readjust the seating to a more equitable ratio by clearing one row of seats, altering the racial division to fourteen white and twenty-two black. Since the four unseated blacks would have to stand, Blake's action violated both company policy and the city code. At the same time, inasmuch as company policy forbade allowing whites to stand in the black section, if Blake had not taken his action, none of the whites waiting to board could have been accommodated, although standing room was available in the rear of the bus.

Rosa Parks had been for most of the preceding decade the secretary of the Montgomery chapter of the NAACP. She had grown up on a farm in southern Montgomery County. Against great odds she obtained a high school diploma in 1933. Montgomery then provided no public high school for blacks. But Mrs. Parks's family, ambitious for her advancement, had arranged to send her to the laboratory school of Alabama State College. Although she thus became one of a very small number of black high school graduates in the city, she found herself unable to obtain employment commensurate with her educational level. She worked at a number of relatively menial jobs; in 1955 she was a seamstress altering ready-to-wear clothes in the city's principal department store, the Montgomery Fair. This situation very probably produced a certain bitterness in her and contributed to her decision during World War II to become an active member of the NAACP. She was elected the chapter secretary in 1943 and later also became the adviser to the chapter's youth auxiliary. She had therefore been particularly concerned with the arrest of Claudette Colvin. In the summer of 1955 she had attended an integrated seminar on race relations at the Highlander Folk School, an invitation she had received at the suggestion of Mrs. Clifford J. Durr, the wife of a liberal white attorney. Mrs. Parks worked for Mrs. Durr on a part-time basis as a seamstress. All of these circumstances had made Mrs. Parks peculiarly sensitive to the importance of the series of meetings, petitions, and remonstrances in relation to the bus situation during the years before 1955. We may well suppose that, had she not been so intimately connected with the controversy, she might have been inclined to join the other three blacks on the row of seats in obeying Blake's instruction. But she, alone of the four, did not move. Blake summoned the police, who took her to the city jail. From the jail she contacted her colleague in the NAACP chapter, Edgar D. Nixon. Nixon made bond for her.[35]

If Mrs. Parks had not been a close friend of Nixon's and a prominent figure in the black community, Nixon might not have been moved to such decisive action, and the people whom he contacted might not have responded so readily. But Mrs. Parks and her husband, a barber at Maxwell Air Force Base who had resided in the city for more than a quarter of a century, were distinctly civic leaders and, at least socially, members of the middle class. Nixon returned from the jail and began calling the city's most prominent blacks to suggest that blacks stage a strike of the buses. Those called phoned others. One of these calls took the matter out of Nixon's hands. Attorney Fred Gray called Jo Ann Robinson.

Mrs. Robinson and her associates in the Women's Political Council saw Rosa Parks as one of their own, a woman of similar social status and community standing. The Council did not await the outcome of Nixon's consultations; it acted. Early the next morning, December 2, Mrs. Robinson mimeographed at her office at Alabama State College a call for a boycott of city buses on December 5, the day of Mrs. Parks's trial: "Another Negro woman has been arrested and thrown into jail because she refused to get up out of her seat on the bus and give it to a white person. It is the second time since the Claudette Colbert [*sic*] case that a Negro has been arrested for the same thing. This must be stopped. . . . Until we do something to stop these arrests, they will continue. The next time it may be you or you or you." Council members busied themselves throughout the afternoon and evening of December 2 distributing these handbills in the black sections of the city.[36]

[35] Interview with Rosa L. Parks, May 22, 1978; interview with Virginia F. Durr, May 2, 1979; Trial Transcript, *Parks* v. *City of Montgomery*, 7–9; Montgomery *Advertiser*, December 2, 6, 1955; Montgomery *Alabama Journal*, December 5, 1955. From the jail Mrs. Parks telephoned her mother, who located Nixon. Nixon called his close friend Durr, a former member of the Federal Communications Commission during World War II, and together they arranged the bond.

[36] Gilliam, "Bus Boycott," 22–23; B.S. Thompson, Sr., ed., *A Century of Negro Progress in Montgomery City and County, 1863–1963* (Montgomery, 1963), 2; interview with Jo Ann Robinson, January 27, 1978. Furious, Alabama State's president H. Councill Trenholm threatened to dismiss Mrs. Robinson for having placed the college in danger of white retaliation by her actions. She retained her job only by swearing to keep her role secret. In this she was eminently successful; Solicitor Thetford stated that despite his most diligent efforts, he was never able to discover the origin of the handbills (interview, September 4, 1976). Rufus Lewis believes today that the real source of the boycott was the prominence and popularity of Mrs. Parks, which moved the city's black women to take action (interview, July 27, 1977).

Meanwhile, Nixon's calls to black civic leaders during the night of December 1 and the morning of December 2 had produced sufficient support for a boycott to set up a meeting for the night of December 2 at the Dexter Avenue Baptist Church. But when the forty or so leaders convened, they found themselves faced with a *fait accompli* because of the action of the Women's Political Council during the afternoon. The meeting was reduced to attempting to assure that the boycott that had been called by the handbills would be successful. Committees were appointed to attend to various organizational details, and a mass meeting was scheduled for the night of December 5 to consider future action in the light of how successful the boycott that day might prove.[37]

When sixteen black leaders met on the afternoon of December 5 to plan the evening's mass meeting, they considered two new pieces of information. The boycott had been brilliantly successful, far more so than leaders had permitted themselves to hope. And Rosa Parks had been convicted and fined ten dollars. At the trial City Prosecutor D. Eugene Loe had faced the problem of the city code's prohibition of unseating a passenger unless another seat was available and had met it as had Solicitor Thetford in the Colvin case, by moving to amend the complaint so as to allege a violation of the state law rather than of the city ordinance. Mrs. Parks's attorney, Fred Gray, had again contended that the state law did not apply to municipal bus lines,

[37] King, *Stride,* 43–49; Trial Transcript, *King* v. *State,* 446–48; Montgomery *Alabama Tribune,* December 9, 16, 1955. Additional copies of Mrs. Robinson's handbill were run off by King and Abernathy in the church office after the meeting that night and were distributed on December 3 and 4. The text of the handbill also was reprinted on the front page of the Montgomery *Advertiser* on December 4 and was read from the pulpits of many black churches that day, a Sunday. The persons whom Nixon called after the arrest were largely people who had been active in the NAACP and thus had known Mrs. Parks. But Nixon evidently recognized that this group of activists—many of whom were Alabama State faculty members—was unlikely to be successful in involving the black masses without the support of the clergy. Nixon had very little contact with the black clergy, but he did know Abernathy well. Abernathy was one of the few ministers who was also a leader of the NAACP. He was therefore the ideal bridge between the two groups. Nixon requested Abernathy to arrange for the attendance of the leading black ministers, and Abernathy did so. Abernathy states that King offered his church as the site of the meeting in the hope that he would not be asked to do anything further for the cause. But because the church was King's, he necessarily was appointed along with Abernathy to prepare the additional copies of the handbills that night, thus involving him reluctantly in organizing the boycott (interview, February 28, 1979).

but his argument had been overruled by Recorder's Court Judge John B. Scott, a nephew and appointee of the late Mayor Gunter.[38]

The success of the boycott's first day and the conviction of Mrs. Parks made it clear that the boycott would continue, at least until the blacks received conciliatory overtures from the city. The sixteen persons present at the afternoon meeting decided to create a formal organization to run the boycott. At the suggestion of the Reverend Ralph D. Abernathy, twenty-nine-year-old pastor of the First Baptist Church (black), they adopted the name Montgomery Improvement Association. They constituted themselves the Association's Executive Board and proceeded to choose officers. Presiding at this meeting, as at the meeting on December 2, was the Reverend L. Roy Bennett, a Methodist who was the president of the black Interdenominational Ministerial Alliance. Bennett's gavel had been wielded in an extremely high-handed fashion at the December 2 session, thus provoking much resentment. When Bennett opened the floor for nominations for president of the new organization, Rufus A. Lewis of the Citizens' Steering Committee saw an opportunity to depose Bennett gracefully. He suggested Martin L. King. Lewis, as a member of King's church, had some knowledge of King's talents; King had recently submitted a dissertation to Boston University for the S.T.D. degree, which marked him as considerably better educated than most of Montgomery's black ministers. The selection of King did not proceed, however, from any clear recognition of his potential for leadership but rather from general hostility to Bennett. Lewis chose King largely because King was Lewis's pastor. King was quickly and unanimously elected, and Bennett was then made vice-president. King's election determined the element within the MIA that would become dominant in shaping its policy. Bennett was an older man and a Methodist. King's advisers were almost uniformly Baptists and were usually young, often not out of their twenties. It is also interesting to note that, in February, Bennett was to become the sole member

---

[38] Montgomery *Alabama Journal,* December 5, 1955; Montgomery *Advertiser,* December 6, 1955. On Judge Scott, see Montgomery *Advertiser,* September 25, 1955. Gray states today that whether the prosecution was carried out under the state law or the city ordinance seemed a matter of no real importance to him (interview, October 17, 1978). Abernathy states that none of the boycott's leaders had ever dreamed that the boycott could last longer than four days (interview, February 28, 1979).

of the black leadership to urge the acceptance of the business community's proffered compromise.[39]

The Board next named a committee to draft a resolution for the consideration of the mass meeting that evening. The resolution explicitly attributed the boycott to the failure of the bus company to clarify its seating policy following the two March meetings and to the resultant misunderstandings that had produced the Smith and Parks arrests. It called on "every citizen in Montgomery, regardless of race, color or creed" to participate in the boycott, and urged employers voluntarily to afford transportation to their employees.[40]

The Montgomery chapter of the Alabama Council on Human Relations, the Alabama branch of the Southern Regional Council, arranged a meeting with the MIA, the City Commission, and the bus company on December 8—a success due primarily to the ironic circumstance that the ACHR's most prominent white member in the city, the Reverend Thomas Thrasher, an Episcopalian, was the rector of Mayor Gayle's church. The task before the meeting was large. Both the bus company's manager James H. Bagley and its attorney Jack

[39] King, *Stride,* 30, 46–58, 72–74; Montgomery *Advertiser,* January 19, 1956; Trial Transcript, *King* v. *State,* 106–28, 334. Abernathy reports that at the outset of the December 2 meeting there were perhaps 125 people present, but that Bennett's conduct of the meeting had reduced the attendance to 40 by the time that the vote was taken on the resolution endorsing the boycott. Lewis states that in suggesting King, he was merely searching for another name as an alternative to Bennett; he calls the nomination the luckiest accident of his life. Nixon claims that he had early recognized King's talents and was planning to nominate King if Lewis had not done so. But Abernathy says that Nixon barely knew King at the outbreak of the boycott; he says that when Nixon telephoned him on December 2, he himself suggested King's name to Nixon as a minister who might be cooperative. I am inclined to believe that Nixon's memory of his early appreciation of King's talents is influenced by the bitter struggle for King's mantle of leadership in which Nixon and Lewis engaged between 1961 and 1968—a struggle that culminated in Lewis's victory and that has left Nixon rather embittered. Indeed, Abernathy believes that Lewis suggested King's name as a way of preventing Nixon's own election as president, but I think that Abernathy is reading the later fierce rivalry back into an earlier time (interviews with Abernathy, February 28, 1979, Lewis, July 27, 1977, Nixon, August 2, 1977).

Nixon says that when he called the president of the Montgomery NAACP chapter, Robert L. Matthews, to report Mrs. Parks's arrest, Matthews refused to allow the chapter to become involved in a boycott without the approval of the NAACP national headquarters. Nixon states that it was this attitude of Matthews which forced the creation of a separate organization to run the boycott. But Abernathy reports that he and King had been discussing for months the need for an umbrella organization to bind Montgomery's blacks together, and that he seized the opportunity afforded by the boycott to suggest the creation of one.

[40] Trial Transcript, *King* v. *State,* 59–61, 344–46; Montgomery *Alabama Tribune,* December 16, 1955.

Crenshaw had emphasized in their public statements their belief that the company could not legally alter bus seating arrangements. Crenshaw had maintained that blacks "have no quarrel with our company. If they don't like the law we have to operate under, then they should try to get the law changed, not engage in an attack on our company." To this position King had replied, "We are not asking an end to segregation. That's a matter for the Legislature and the courts. We feel that we have a plan within the law." Thus a principal question before the December 8 meeting, as before all the earlier ones, was whether the law allowed its enforcers any discretion.[41]

The meeting began with Martin King's reading a list of three demands, satisfaction of which was a prerequisite to the end of the boycott: more courtesy from bus drivers; the hiring of black drivers on the four predominantly black routes; and the seating of blacks from the back towards the front and of whites from the front towards the back without insisting that a section always be kept clear for each race. The demands appear to reflect the thinking of Edgar D. Nixon; the seating proposal was lifted from the questionnaire of the Ben Moore Hotel meeting, and the request for black drivers was consistent with Nixon's long-standing commitment as a labor leader to opening additional occupations to blacks.

Crenshaw replied by denying that drivers were discourteous, except in the rarest instances; by flatly rejecting the idea of black drivers, at least for the coming decade; and by declaring the seating proposal illegal. On this last point he joined battle with Gray. Gray offered a full-scale legal brief attempting to demonstrate that the 1945 state statute did not apply to Montgomery City Lines and urged the City Commission to seek a formal opinion from the state attorney general on the question. In any case, he noted, both city code and state statute simply required separate but equal accommodations; they made no attempt to specify the precise arrangements by which this goal was to be accomplished. As King put it in a statement issued two days later, presumably written in consultation with Gray, "The Legislature, it seems clear, wisely left it up to the transportation companies to work out the seating problem in a reasonable and practical way . . . We feel that there is no issue between the Negro

[41] Montgomery *Advertiser,* February 1, December 7, 1955; Montgomery *Alabama Journal,* December 7, 1955.

citizens and the Montgomery City Lines that cannot be solved by negotiations between people of good will. And we submit that there is no legal barrier to such negotiations." At the meeting King emphasized that the suggested seating plan was in use in Mobile and other Southern cities. Crenshaw did offer to have every other bus on the heavily black Washington Park route designated exclusively for blacks, but beyond this concession he simply reiterated that the company could not "change the law."

After some hours of these exchanges, Mayor Gayle suggested that it might be useful if a smaller group conferred in private. He then withdrew, taking the press, television cameramen, spectators, and peripheral participants with him. King, Gray, and perhaps other blacks remained to talk with Bagley and Crenshaw and the two new commissioners, Sellers and Parks. According to King's account of this session, as soon as the reporters had gone, Parks—who had defeated Cleere with black votes—ventured, "I don't see why we can't arrange to accept this seating proposal. We can work it within our segregation laws." At once Crenshaw replied, "But Frank, I don't see how we can do it within the law. If it were legal I would be the first to go along with it, but it just isn't legal. The only way that it can be done is to change your segregation laws." Then he added, "If we granted the Negroes these demands, they would go about boasting of a victory that they had won over the white people, and this we will not stand for." Facing this determined opposition from Crenshaw and knowing that Sellers could not be brought to compromise, Parks crumbled, and the next day resignedly informed the press that he regretted that the conference had produced no settlement but that "We cannot break the law."[42]

[42] King, Stride, 108–13; Trial Transcript, King v. State, 239, 248–50, 336, 346–47; Montgomery Advertiser, December 9–11, 1955; Montgomery Alabama Journal, December 8, 9, 1955; Browder v. Gayle case file, Exhibit A: "Legal Requirements Concerning the Segregation of Races on City Buses." Abernathy states that the three demands were composed at a meeting at noon on December 5 consisting of Abernathy himself, Nixon, and Edgar N. French, director of the pensions office of the A.M.E. Zion churches in Montgomery, and were subsequently accepted by the MIA Executive Board (interview, February 28, 1979). He may, however, be confusing the demands with the resolution of the December 5 mass meeting. King's statement that the demands were adopted by the mass meeting (Stride, 63–64, 108–09) is erroneous. Gray cannot today recall whether he helped King prepare the statement issued on December 10 (interview, October 17, 1978), but its argument clearly is derived from Gray's brief. Crenshaw does not recall the interchange with Parks which King reports, but he does confirm that Parks was more amenable to accepting the MIA's demands than were the other two commissioners—

This sequence of events had been most peculiar. Although all the blacks were integrationists, the thrust of their efforts was so to reform the actual practice of segregation as to make it acceptable and thus to remove the impetus for its elimination. Crenshaw, a firm segregationist, was by implication urging the blacks to seek the complete abolition of segregation in the courts.

Since March the blacks had repeatedly pointed out that their plan was in effect in many Southern cities, including Mobile. King had reiterated this point at the meeting on December 8. Yet, Bagley subsequently testified that he had been unaware of this fact on December 8 and found it out only later. When the *Advertiser* printed on December 31 an article confirming the accuracy of the blacks' statements, the article was thought worthy of prominent treatment and seems to have caused surprise among whites. Nevertheless, the illogic of maintaining that the state law permitted in Mobile what it forbade in Montgomery escaped the white citizenry; when Bagley was asked about the inconsistency, he replied merely, "I cannot testify what they would do in Mobile, or what they can do, but I know what we can do in Montgomery." True, the Mobile City Code specifically required the seating plan in use in that city. But it is also true that the Montgomery City Code prescribed no specific seating plan.[43]

Similarly, Gray had argued at length at both the Colvin and the Parks hearings that the state statute did not apply to municipal bus lines and had submitted a brief to the Commission and the bus company expounding this position. No one in authority, except possibly Frank Parks, appears to have paid any attention. Gray had

---

particularly Sellers. As Gayle and the reporters left the meeting, Gayle told those remaining that he wanted them to find a settlement as quickly as possible. Crenshaw even today rather resents that remark, feeling that it was an effort on the mayor's part to pass the buck to the bus company, which Crenshaw still regards as an innocent third party in the dispute (interview, July 15, 1977).

[43] Trial Transcript, *King* v. *State*, 539–41; Montgomery *Advertiser*, March 20, December 31, 1955; King, *Stride*, 110; Mobile City Code of 1947, Chapter 20, Article 1. Crenshaw continues to believe today that the Montgomery Code required in detail the bus company's specific seating arrangement; when I told him that the Code merely required that the seating be separate and equal, he replied that he was positive that I was wrong. He is also under the impression that Mobile had adopted its seating plan only a few months before the outbreak of the boycott. He states that the Montgomery company had always been willing to accept the Mobile plan if the City Commission would amend the ordinance to permit the arrangement, but that the Commission adamantly refused to do so (interview, July 15, 1977).

suggested that the Commission seek a ruling from the attorney general; the Commission toyed with the idea of doing so but in the end took no action. The following spring, however, when Gray joined the Public Service Commission as a defendant in his federal court suit to void bus segregation, in order to have the state law as well as the city ordinance declared unconstitutional, the state suddenly took up Gray's earlier argument in its entirety. At the trial the president of the Public Service Commission, C. C. "Jack" Owen, flatly denied that his agency had any jurisdiction over municipal bus systems. The Court read the state statute of 1945 to Owen and asked him if his construction of the act was that it "does not include common carriers such as busses in the City of Montgomery?" Owen, evidently nonplussed by the question, stammered in reply, "I had never thought of it in that particular line of thinking. This is the first time that point has ever been brought up. It seems to me like that means segregation as far as segregation is concerned."[44]

Whites simply did not reflect carefully on the legal points which the blacks raised. Indeed, President Owen—a Montgomerian whose position ought to have made him more than ordinarily concerned with this aspect of the controversy—did not even know that the question of the applicability of the 1945 act had been at issue throughout the preceding year. These attitudes appear particularly puzzling because what Gray and his associates were actually trying to do was to rationalize the segregation system. Why did segregationists find it so difficult to accept the modest reforms which the blacks suggested—reforms whose acceptance would clearly have strengthened segregation itself, by diminishing opposition to it? Consideration of three efforts to reach a compromise will help provide an answer to this question.

Mayor Gayle's copy of the resolution adopted by the black mass meeting on December 5, which Fred Gray had handed to the mayor at the December 8 meeting, was offered in evidence at King's trial for violation of the anti-boycott law. On its back someone, presumably the mayor, had jotted in pencil, "How about *again* appointing [a] com[mittee of] Retailer[s] *etc.* to meet with [K. E.] Totten [vice-

---

[44] Trial Transcript, *Browder* v. *Gayle,* 46–48; Motion of Public Service Commission for Dismissal of Complaint, in *Browder* v. *Gayle* case file. This reversal of positions was so complete that it has left Crenshaw confused about what his position had been on the issue earlier in the boycott. He believes that he had argued to the City Commission that the state statute was not applicable and that Gray had maintained that it was (interview, July 15, 1977).

president of National City Lines of Chicago] to bring some recommendations to [the] City Com[mission]?" The reference was to
the course which the commissioners had successfully followed in the bus
drivers' strike of December 1953. At that time the Commission had
named a committee of six—the presidents of the Chamber of Commerce, the Retail Merchants Association, the white Ministerial Association, and the PTA, an attorney, and a prominent black—to me-
diate the conflict. When the December 8 meeting produced no
settlement, the Commission evidently decided to make use of this
precedent.

Totten returned to Montgomery on December 15 to continue
negotiations for the renewal of the company's expiring franchise. After
conferring with him the Commission called a meeting of all parties
to the controversy on the morning of December 17, and there the
mayor suggested the appointment of a ten-member committee—
eight whites and two blacks—to act as mediators between the MIA
and the bus company. Jo Ann Robinson at once insisted that the
number of whites and blacks on the committee be equal. Apparently,
the commissioners conceived of the dispute as being between the bus
company and the MIA, and of the committee as a neutral mediator,
while the MIA thought of the dispute as being between Montgomery's
whites and blacks, and of the committee as a sort of collective
bargaining arrangement. After some discussion the mayor agreed to
add six MIA members to his original ten. These sixteen people met
on the afternoon of December 17 and again on December 19 but
reached no agreement.[45]

The blacks included King, Abernathy, Robinson, attorneys Fred
Gray and Charles D. Langford, the Reverend Hillman H. Hubbard,
pastor of one of the city's largest black congregations and one of the
few older black preachers prominent in the MIA's leadership, and the
two well-to-do black businessmen who were Gayle's choices, Pluie M.
Blair, who owned a dry-cleaners and who was called the "Negro Mayor
of Montgomery," and Dungee Caffey, a realtor with diverse interests.
The white delegation, balancing the black one, included also three

---

[45] Trial Transcript, *King* v. *State*, 346; Montgomery *Advertiser*, December 13, 1953;
Montgomery *Alabama Journal*, December 16, 1955; King, *Stride*, 117–18. Just as the Commission apparently thought of the MIA and the bus company as the principal disputants,
so the bus company thought of the MIA and the Commission as the principal disputants.
This odd situation tended to inhibit both the company and the city in the negotiations with the blacks.

ministers: Dr. Henry Allen Parker of the First Baptist Church (white), the Reverend G. Stanley Frazer of St. James Methodist Church, and the Reverend Henry Edward Russell of Trinity Presbyterian Church, brother of U.S. Senator Richard Russell of Georgia. There were two businessmen: James J. Bailey, the manager of a furniture store and president of the Furniture Dealers Association, and William H. Fields, the manager of a local J. C. Penney store and president of the Retail Merchants Association. Mrs. Earnest R. Moore was the wife of a dental technician and the president of the city-county PTA. Mrs. Logan A. Hipp, Jr., the wife of an insurance adjuster, worked as a secretary in the office of the city Chamber of Commerce. The final white member was William G. Welch, a bus driver for the Montgomery City Lines and president of the bus drivers' local union.[46]

King charged that the mayor had "not appointed a representative committee of whites." At first glance the allegation would appear unfounded. But an investigation of the committee's deliberations casts the notion into a different light. The blacks advanced their seating proposal, and Gray argued that it could be effected within existing law. At the initial session the white delegation, unlike the black, contained no lawyers. The whites relied for legal advice upon City Attorney Walter Knabe, who attended the meetings. Knabe had been involved in the negotiations stretching back to the preceding spring and was committed to the position that the seating proposal was illegal. He informed the whites that Gray was simply wrong, and the whites adopted this position in their final report, issued on January 18. King states that K. E. Totten acknowledged to him privately that the black proposal was used by National City Lines' Mobile affiliate; Totten, King reports, said that he could not see why what worked in Mobile could not work in Montgomery. If Totten made this admission privately, he refused to do so publicly. Instead, he declined to become involved in the local negotiations, saying only that National City Lines would abide by any arrangement accepted by Montgomerians. Understandably, a national firm that dealt with cities across the country would wish to avoid becoming entangled in heated municipal controversies. This motive must have

---

[46] At the second meeting Luther Ingalls, an attorney prominent in the Montgomery White Citizens Council, was added to the white delegation, and Mrs. Hipp became a non-voting secretary of the committee—an alteration that provoked an outraged protest by King.

been particularly strong in the Montgomery situation because Totten was at this very time attempting to secure a new franchise from the city government. However, Totten's refusal to intervene, coupled with the whites' reliance upon Knabe's advice, left the committee within the limits of the controversy that had previously been defined, unable to approach the problem from a new perspective.

Of course, the whites on the committee were segregationists; had they not been, they would not have reflected accurately the sentiment of the community which they represented. Yet segregationist attitudes in themselves were no real barrier to a settlement, because the black delegation emphasized that it had no desire to disestablish segregation. Ill will between the two sides on the committee was exacerbated by the inability of Frazer and Russell to resist the urge to lecture the blacks on the morality of segregation and the immorality of ministerial involvement in politics. The black clergymen responded with lectures of their own. Still, the white committee members were not opposed to compromise. Frazer presented what he took to be a compromise: that fixed lines of racial division be marked on every bus, determined by the proportion of the races on each route, but that riders be permitted to sit forward or back of the line until the seats were needed by the other race. The proposal, as Charles Langford noted, ignored the principal black complaint, the unseating of passengers already seated. At least Frazer's proposal demonstrated a willingness to try to find a solution. Bailey even stated to the committee, "I came here prepared to vote for liberalization of interpretation of the city's laws with certain conditions."[47]

The failure of the committee to discover a compromise was not entirely attributable to the racial attitudes of the committee members, though such attitudes doubtless contributed to the impasse. None of the whites on the committee was a member of Montgomery's upper class; Bailey, the member of the white delegation who seems to

[47] King, *Stride*, 114–21; Montgomery *Advertiser*, December 18, 20, 1955; Montgomery *Alabama Journal*, December 17, 19, 20, 1955, January 18, 1956; Trial Transcript, *King* v. *State*, 233–36, 248–50, 336, 539–41. Knabe states today that he never doubted the legality of the MIA's seating proposal. He says that he opposed granting the concession only because he was convinced that doing so would not really produce an end to the boycott (interview, August 5, 1977). But if he held such an opinion at the time, he certainly never gave any public hint of it. Crenshaw believes that Knabe supported his position (interview, July 15, 1977).

have been most favorable to compromise, was the one member who was at all prominent in the city's business community. This fact is significant. When King called the whites unrepresentative, what he evidently meant was that they were all too representative. The situation demanded men and women who were sufficiently confident of their social position to allow them to be original in their approach to the problem. The committee contained no such members, and it is primarily for that reason that its deliberations proved sterile.

The mayor had not appointed any of the city's social and economic leaders to the committee because of his weak political position. The March elections had emphasized that Gayle could no longer permit himself to seem a front man for Montgomery's upper class. Rather, he needed to seek the support of other social elements among the whites. He certainly could not permit himself the luxury of an action that flew in the face of white community sentiment. A compromise suggested by the committee he did appoint would give some promise of generating community consensus. Precisely because the committee was representative, its deliberations were doomed without the intervention of some outside figure like Totten. Gayle may initially have hoped that Totten would help, but when Totten refused, the committee became an exercise in futility.[48]

The encounter between the city and its black citizens entered a new stage in late January, when attitudes in both camps had hardened considerably. After the December 19 meeting the biracial committee held no further sessions. On January 6 Clyde Sellers appeared at a meeting of the White Citizens Council and dramatically announced that he was joining the organization. On January 9 the City Commission met with an MIA delegation for two hours at King's request, but neither side would modify its position. On January 18 the white members of the biracial committee issued a final report publicly acknowledging the failure of their efforts and urging all parties to accept Frazer's compromise proposal. At least by the same time in mid-January some MIA leaders were concluding that further negotiations would be fruitless and were beginning to discuss the possibility

[48] Crenshaw states that National City Lines hoped that by refusing to get involved, it could avoid making anyone mad (interview, July 15, 1977). The national company's determinedly noncommittal position is well illustrated by B. W. Franklin [executive vice-president] to Wilhelmina D. Long, March 20, 1956, enclosed in Wilhelmina D. Long to James E. Folsom, May 9, 1956, in Governors' Correspondence: Folsom II, Civil Archives Division, Alabama State Department of Archives and History, Montgomery.

of a federal court suit to have bus segregation declared unconstitutional.[49]

During this period discontent had been growing among those black ministers who were not a part of the MIA's leadership. The boycott had so captured the imagination and the loyalties of the city's blacks that the failure of a black minister to be included occasionally as a speaker at the frequent mass meetings which were the movement's backbone demeaned him in the eyes of his congregation. Probably, jealousies thus generated lay behind the decision of three black ministers to contact white officials with the offer to negotiate a settlement. The Reverend Benjamin F. Mosely, pastor of the First Presbyterian Church (black), Bishop Doc C. Rice, pastor of the Oak Street Holiness Church, and the Reverend William K. Kind, pastor of the Jackson Street Baptist Church, one of the few prominent black preachers in the city who had not been chosen a member of the MIA's executive board, perhaps expected that, if they were able to engineer the creation of a compromise acceptable to the black community, they might gain for themselves a portion of the public attention being focused upon King, Abernathy, Gray, and their associates.

On January 21 the City Commission met with the three ministers, together with Paul B. Fuller, the executive secretary of the Chamber of Commerce, and the Reverend Thomas Thrasher of the Alabama Council on Human Relations. The meeting produced a compromise under which ten seats in the front would always be reserved for whites, ten seats in the rear for blacks, and the remaining sixteen seats would

---

[49] Montgomery *Advertiser*, January 7, 10, 1956; Montgomery *Alabama Journal*, January 18, 1956; Montgomery *Alabama Tribune*, January 20, 1956; Gilliam, "Bus Boycott," 114–16. The origins of the idea for a federal suit are disputed. Gray states that he had favored filing a federal suit from the outset but had been unable to convince the MIA Executive Board to authorize the action, both because the strategy was new and untried for Montgomery blacks and because many MIA leaders had high hopes for negotiations in the early weeks (interview, October 17, 1978). Abernathy states that the idea of a federal court suit was first suggested to him near the end of December, he believes by Gray (interview, February 28, 1979). Nixon states that the idea of a federal court suit was suggested to him by his friend Clifford J. Durr. Nixon says that he passed the suggestion along to King and Abernathy; he dates this exchange to mid-February, however, which is impossible (interview, August 2, 1977). Mrs. Durr says that her husband originally suggested the idea to Gray after Ball's letter of January 9. She also states that Durr helped Gray with all the briefs and submissions in the boycott suit and that she personally typed them (interview, May 2, 1979). Lewis states that no one proposed a suit until shortly before it was actually filed, after the negotiations had proved unsuccessful (interview, July 27, 1977). Despite these differing accounts, it would appear certain that MIA leaders were discussing filing suit at least by mid-January, and it seems highly unlikely that the idea was much considered before late December.

be filled as the MIA proposed, blacks sitting from the rear and whites from the front; in addition, all-black buses would be provided during rush hours on three predominantly black routes. The proposal did not specify whether passengers seated in the middle sixteen seats could be unseated. It stated that the City Commission had no authority to alter the bus company's hiring policies; the company had repeatedly refused to hire blacks, so this statement implied the rejection of the request for black drivers.

The MIA promptly denounced this agreement and stated that the three ministers did not speak for the city's blacks. It soon became apparent, moreover, that virtually the entire black community supported the MIA's position in this regard. The three ministers thereupon repudiated the compromise; they told King that they had not understood the proposal and had attended the meeting under the impression that it was to discuss the city's insurance. The commissioners were livid with rage at this turn of events. Mayor Gayle subsequently swore that both Fuller and Thrasher had read the agreement carefully to the ministers who had fully understood and approved of it. On this basis the commissioners had publicly committed themselves to the compromise. All three commissioners were increasingly in awe of Montgomery's rapidly growing White Citizens Council, whose membership local newspapers reported to be 6,000 at the beginning of February and 12,000 by the end of that month. By that time it had become the largest single organization in Montgomery County. Sellers, in a speech to the council on January 6, had pledged to continue fighting the blacks' demands and had repeated the promise in even stronger terms on January 17. Gayle and Parks had been somewhat less vocal but naturally wished to avoid offending council members unnecessarily. Now all three commissioners found themselves revealed to the voters as willing to compromise but deprived at the same time of any compromise to show for their pains. They felt betrayed.[50]

[50]Trial Transcript, *King v. State*, 252–53; Montgomery *Alabama Tribune*, January 27, 1956; Montgomery *Advertiser*, January 7, 18, 19, 22, 24, February 5, 28, 1956; Montgomery *Alabama Journal*, January 23, 24, 1956. My account of this episode differs considerably from that in King, *Stride*, 124–26. King accepted the three ministers' explanation at face value. I am led to reject it and to credit Gayle's testimony at King's trial on the point for two reasons. Most important, King's version does not adequately account for the nature and content of Gayle's statement of January 23. Secondly, an attempt by the city to perpetrate a hoax is inconsistent with the presence of Thrasher at the meeting. The Montgomery chapter of the White Citizens Council had been organized at a meeting on October 3, 1955 with about 300 persons in attendance. It was the tenth chapter to be organized in Alabama (Montgomery *Advertiser*, October 3, 4, 1955).

On January 23 Mayor Gayle announced, "The Negro leaders have proved they will say one thing to a white man and another thing to a Negro." He said, "The City Commission has attempted with sincerity and honesty to end the bus boycott in a businesslike fashion. We have held meetings with the Negroes at which proposals were made that would have been accepted by any fair-minded group of people. But there seems to be a belief on the part of the Negroes that they have the white people hemmed up in a corner and they are not going to give an inch until they can force the white people of our community to submit to their demands—in fact, swallow all of them. . . . We attempted to resolve their reasonable complaints but they proved by their refusal to resolve the reasonable ones that they were not interested in whether the bus service was good or not. What they are after is the destruction of our social fabric." He called the black leadership "a group of Negro radicals" whose only real goal was to "stir up racial strife." He stated, "The white people are firm in their convictions that they do not care whether the Negroes ever ride a city bus again . . ." He concluded, "When and if the Negro people desire to end the boycott, my door is open to them. But until they are ready to end it, there will be no more discussions."

This statement appears to have been the product of a moment of anger, but the astonishing approbation with which whites greeted it transformed it into fixed policy. Appreciative calls swamped the City Hall switchboard; hundreds of congratulatory telegrams flooded in, and voters eager for the opportunity to shake Gayle's hand crowded the mayor's office. Commissioner Parks reported himself "amazed with the avalanche" of approval. He concluded, "There is no need for us to straddle the fence any longer. I am taking a stand and so are the other commissioners." Both Gayle and Sellers moved at once to identify themselves even more firmly with the "get tough" stand. Gayle called for whites to refuse to drive their domestics to and from work or to pay their taxi fare; "the Negroes are laughing at white people behind their backs" because of the whites' willingness to do so, he warned. Sellers instructed the police to arrest blacks waiting to catch a ride and to charge them with loitering. "A person has a perfect right to wait for a ride," he noted, "but the practice of six or eight Negroes huddling together for an hour or more, trampling lawns and making loud noises in white residential districts must cease." On January 24 Mayor Gayle and Commissioner Parks announced that they, too, had joined the

White Citizens Council. Within weeks all members of the County Board of Revenue also had joined. The council's attorney proclaimed that the group was now so large that blacks would never again be able to influence candidates for local office by "dangling their bloc votes" before aspirants.[51]

Stronger and stronger statements followed, as politicians rushed to associate themselves with the City Commission's popular stand. The pronouncements soon bore fruit. On the night of January 30 a stick of dynamite was thrown onto the porch of Martin L. King's home; his wife and a visitor narrowly escaped injury. The MIA leadership had been discussing the advisability of a federal court suit for at least two weeks, as a political settlement seemed increasingly illusory. However, the bombing of King's home convinced the MIA that simply to continue pressure on the city through the boycott to force agreement to the blacks' demands was no longer a reasonable strategy. If negotiations ever could produce an agreement, it would be in the far future. Meantime, the boycott would be fraught with excessive risk. On February 1 Fred Gray filed suit challenging the constitutionality of bus segregation.[52] Mayor Gayle denounced the suit as "proof beyond any doubt that Negroes never wanted better bus service as they were claiming, but complete integration." The blacks, he said, stood convicted of double-dealing.[53]

These events strikingly illuminate the commission's ignorance of sentiment among both blacks and extremist whites. First, the events emphasize how tenaciously the commissioners and their advisers believed that the MIA did not actually speak for the city's

[51] Montgomery *Advertiser*, January 24–26, February 14, 1956; Montgomery *Alabama Journal*, January 24, 1956.

[52] Montgomery *Advertiser*, January 31, February 2, 1956; Montgomery *Alabama Journal*, January 31, 1956. Between January 26 and January 29, with the situation obviously deteriorating rapidly, Governor James E. Folsom attempted a secret mediation. Abernathy states that Folsom intervened after a delegation of blacks requested him to do so. But the governor's efforts proved fruitless (interview with Abernathy, February 28, 1979; interview with William V. Lyerly, September 2, 1976; Trial Transcript, *King* v. *State*, 254–55, 496–97). Gray confirms that the bombing was the trigger for the filing of the federal suit. He states that many in the MIA leadership remained hopeful even through January that the boycott would produce concessions and so, though he had begun preparing the suit, the MIA Executive Board had continued to hesitate about filing it. But the bombing, he says, clearly made it necessary for the MIA to appear to be taking firm retaliatory action, and therefore the Executive Board, at a meeting the morning after the bombing, instructed him to file, which he did later the same day (interview, October 17, 1978).

[53] Montgomery *Advertiser*, February 3, 1956.

blacks. The commissioners had repeatedly urged the masses of blacks to repudiate King and other spurious leaders who owed their apparent positions as spokesmen for the black community only to the apathy of many blacks and to the intimidation of the remainder by MIA goon squads. Commissioner Sellers estimated that 85 to 90 percent of the city's blacks would immediately resume riding the buses if there were no danger of physical reprisal. "The innocent Negroes should wake up," Commissioner Parks warned. "They don't know what they are doing, but I'm afraid they're going to find out. The white people have been their friends, and still want to be, but we can't sit here and watch them destroy our transportation system." Mayor Gayle accepted both Parks's emphasis on ignorance and Sellers's emphasis on fear, although there is relatively little evidence of intimidation and none linking the intimidation to the MIA. Unfortunately, one of the few instances in which intimidation was alleged involved Mayor Gayle's father-in-law's cook. The mayor's closeness to this particular incident perhaps increased his sense of the violence surrounding the boycott. Whether because of Sellers's dark, conspiratorial explanation or because of Parks's more benign one, the city's political leaders were convinced that the MIA's claims to represent Montgomery's blacks were false.

This attitude accounts for the commissioners' otherwise inexplicable notion that the three non-MIA black ministers constituted, as the statement of January 21 claimed, a "group representing the Negroes of Montgomery." At the time of the appointment of the biracial committee on December 17 Gayle had insisted on appointing two prominent blacks, Blair and Caffey, who had not been nominated by the MIA, perhaps partly in the hope that he would tap the reservoir of anti-MIA feeling which he thought to exist. This expectation failed; Blair and Caffey proved to be completely committed to the MIA's demands. When the three ministers approached white leaders in late January, the commissioners evidently felt that they had at last forced from hiding a leadership alternative to King. Of course, the commissioners knew that no organized group had appointed the three ministers. On the other hand, the commissioners regarded the views of the three ministers as more fully consonant with those of the black masses. If the commissioners had been correct in their analysis, it would have been reasonable to have supposed that the conclusion of a settlement with the ministers would give most blacks sufficient encouragement to return to the buses. The compromise produced no such result simply because the Commission was wrong; Montgomery's blacks were dedicated to the achievement of the MIA's program. Unfortunately, the repudiation of the settlement by the three ministers obscured this fact for city political leaders.[54]

The Commission betrayed similar ignorance in failing to gauge the effect upon the city's racist extremists of the intemperate statements issued in late January. The extremist element evidently took the "get tough" policy and the resulting public ovation as a license for violence. In addition to the bombing of King's home on January 30 the home of Edgar D. Nixon was bombed on February 1, though the latter explosion caused no damage. In later months, incidentally, the belief became general in Citizens Council circles that blacks themselves had staged both of these bombings to gain sympathy and contributions from Northerners.[55] The absence of any sense of the state of sentiment among blacks and among white racial extremists is a complementary phenomenon with a single culprit: these segments of the population were essentially excluded from political life, and the Commission had such limited contact with them that it lacked any mechanism for understanding their motives and assumptions.

Contemporary with the events of January, the third and last effort to formulate a compromise acceptable to the MIA emerged from the business community. The Men of Montgomery, already du-

---

[54] *Ibid.*, December 5, 1955, January 18, 26, 1956; Montgomery *Alabama Journal*, January 24, 27, 1956; Trial Transcript, *King* v. *State*, 213–27; Trial Transcript, *Browder* v. *Gayle*, 32–36; King, *Stride*, 115, 118, 120. White Montgomery leaders repeatedly told me that they knew there had been intimidation of many blacks to keep them off the buses because they had been told so by their servants or other employees. I am inclined to believe that these stories were usually told employers in an effort to offer acceptable explanations for cooperation with the boycott. But the tales, while protecting the individual black from reprisal, had the harmful effect of preventing whites from recognizing the extent of black support for the MIA. Abernathy reports that the commissioners made repeated efforts to divide King from the remainder of the MIA leadership as well (interview, February 28, 1979).

[55] Montgomery *Advertiser*, February 2, August 26, 1956; Gilliam, "Bus Boycott," 114, 137; Clifford J. Durr to Corliss Lamont, February 7, 1957, Durr Papers. Jack Crenshaw believes even today that rivalries among various factions within the MIA leadership produced the bombings (interview, July 15, 1977). At the other extreme, Fred Gray still suspects the City Commission of having ordered the bombings (interview, October 17, 1978). Many of the whites whom I interviewed believe that the boycott was prolonged unnecessarily as a sort of confidence game through which sympathetic Northerners were being rooked for contributions.

bious of city politicians, were persuaded by January that the Commission's mismanagement of the crisis had prevented a settlement and that businessmen might well succeed where politicians had failed. Moreover, the organization had three good reasons to try. The boycott had intensified racial hatred in the city, damaged trade, and directed such unfavorable publicity to the city as to complicate any effort to attract industry to the area. Mayor Gayle's announcement on January 23 that the Commission would not negotiate further made the politicians' inability to secure an agreement explicit. The bombing of Dr. King's home clearly announced that the entire affair had gotten out of hand and that unless a compromise could be found quickly, seriously unfavorable reports in the national press would be inevitable.[56] These two events moved the Men of Montgomery to intervene in the boycott. Thus, rather ironically, the same set of circumstances convincing the black leadership that additional negotiation would be fruitless, finally moved the city's economic powers to undertake the mediation of the controversy.

During the first three weeks of February a committee of the Men of Montgomery held two full-scale negotiating sessions with MIA leaders and at least one with the City Commission. It was also in almost constant informal contact with the two groups in an effort to locate tenable middle ground. The Men of Montgomery members advanced no proposals of their own; they apparently saw themselves as brokers rather than as parties to the conflict. King later wrote of them that they had proved themselves "open-minded enough to listen to another point of view and discuss the problem of race intelligently," and in reference to their arbitration he concluded, "I have no doubt that we would have come to a solution had it not been for the recalcitrance of the city commission." However, the obstacles to any such happy outcome appear genuinely insuperable. The commissioners' statements during the last week of January had made it virtually impossible for them to agree to any substantial concessions; and their receptiveness to compromise was not increased by the fact that on February 10, at a White Citizens Council rally which filled the state

---

[56] It is worth noting in this regard that stories about the boycott had not yet reached the front page of the New York *Times* and did not do so until the indictment of MIA leaders for violation of the anti-boycott law, except for one article on the White Citizens Council rally at the state coliseum on February 10.

coliseum, a crowd of some 12,000 gave both Mayor Gayle and Commissioner Sellers sustained, emotional standing ovations.[57]

For its part the MIA was no longer in a position to negotiate. At no time would it have been easy for the MIA to have made concessions; as King had noted in mid-January, "We began with a compromise when we didn't ask for complete integration. Now we're asked to compromise on the compromise."

The filing of the federal court suit on February 1, however, had eliminated even the small basis for an accord that had been present. The MIA's initial requests had sought only a reform of specific practice within the general framework of segregation; the MIA had repeatedly and strenuously affirmed its view that its proposals were in keeping with city and state law. But the suit sought the elimination of segregation. It so changed the MIA's position that King had evidently given serious consideration to recommending that the boycott be called off. The boycott had been intended to move the City Commission and the bus company to action. If the MIA were going to rely on a court order to produce the action, there was no longer a reason for a boycott. Indeed, the only difficulty with this logic was that the MIA could not be certain that the federal courts would declare bus segregation unconstitutional. Despite the decision of the MIA to continue with the boycott, the organization could hardly be expected to agree to a compromise perpetuating segregation while it was at the same time asking the courts to compel full integration. The Men of Montgomery's efforts would appear therefore to have been doomed from the outset.[58]

[57] King, *Stride*, 121–22; Montgomery *Advertiser*, February 11, 1956. A considerable number of businessmen participated in the negotiations at one stage or another, but the principal business negotiators appear to have been Joe F. Bear, owner of a lumber and construction firm, C. T. Fitzpatrick, owner of a laundry and dry-cleaning business, James G. Pruett, president of the local division of the Trailways bus system, and Mark W. Johnston, vice-president of a bank. Bear was the Men of Montgomery chairman for February; the organization's chairmanship rotated monthly, on an alphabetical basis. Fitzpatrick, Pruett, and Johnston were the presidents of the Chamber of Commerce for, respectively, 1954, 1955, and 1956.

[58] Montgomery *Advertiser*, January 19, February 8, 9, 1956. Despite King's statement most of the surviving black leaders agree with my assessment (interviews with Abernathy, February 28, 1979, Gray, October 17, 1978, Robinson, January 27, 1978). Rufus Lewis adds the interesting point that because white leaders, after years of ignoring blacks, were at last taking them seriously, the MIA was rendered quite reluctant to end the boycott that had finally given them access to power (interview, July 27, 1977). The business negotiators are unanimous in stating that, though they approached the negotiations with high hopes, convinced that a settlement could be found, they quickly came to see that the blacks were unwilling to make any concessions. I should also note

Nevertheless, the Men of Montgomery pressed mediation because the city's good reputation could be restored only if Montgomerians solved the boycott themselves. Their task was made especially urgent when some prominent Montgomery lawyers began to advocate a course that would almost certainly destroy whatever respect for the city remained among national opinion leaders: the mass indictment of virtually all the city's most prominent blacks for violation of the Alabama anti-boycott law.

The anti-boycott law had been passed in 1921 as a part of a series of statutes provoked by a bloody strike of Birmingham coal miners in that year. From the beginning of the bus boycott the applicability of this act to the situation had been discussed, but the question was not taken very seriously because, as the *Advertiser* noted editorially on December 8, "As a practical matter, we doubt that either the bus company or the solicitor will attempt to jail 5,000 Negroes." As the hatreds generated by the dispute deepened, some Montgomerians considered prosecution as a realistic weapon. On January 9 Frederick S. Ball, an important figure in both legal and social circles in the city, dispatched a letter to the *Advertiser* demanding the boycotters' indictment. "An individual has the right to ride a bus or not as he or she sees fit and that right should not be interfered with and should be protected by the police," he wrote, "but when certain so-called leaders call a group together and organize a boycott, they are taking the law into their own hands and should be prosecuted. Whether the bus company or its drivers have or have not always themselves obeyed the law and given colored passengers their rights is not the question at all, because two wrongs do not make a right and there is always legal redress against the bus company for anything it does wrong. The question is whether the officials whose duty it is to enforce the law are going to sit idly by and permit the illegal destruction of a transportation system which is most certainly needed by both races." He added pointedly, "A copy of this letter goes to the county solicitor with the suggestion that he give consideration to presenting this matter to the grand jury . . ."

Gray's statement that after February 1, all elements of the white community expressed to him privately a willingness to accept the MIA's original proposals if he would withdraw the federal suit and even offered him bribes to secure his agreement (interview, October 17, 1978). The sequence of events during February and early March makes this assertion seem implausible to me.

Grover C. Hall, Jr., clearly shared the view of the business leaders that this course would be sheer folly. Hall attempted to dispose of Ball's argument with gentle ridicule. "Atty. Ball ... is against lawlessness. So he has asked Solicitor Thetford to prosecute. What leaves us confused is the question whether Atty. Ball is also opposed to the lawlessness of defying the U.S. Supreme Court, the supreme law. . . . We ask then, is Atty. Ball for law-abiding at the local level and lawlessness at the Supreme Court level? And, as we asked Dec. 8, what if Atty. Ball got some bus boycotters convicted in a Montgomery court? Would not the Supreme Court automatically reverse the convictions? Another perplexity left by Atty. Ball's brief letter is whether he is against all persons who have entered an 'arrangement' to boycott? For example, Police Commissioner Clyde Sellers is a card-carrying member of the White Citizens Council, an organization dedicated to boycott and economic sanctions against Negroes. Does Atty. Ball want White Councilman Sellers indicted also?"

But Ball was not so easily dissuaded. On January 12 he replied, "The question is not, as put in your [editorial], how far to 'cast the net' of law enforcement, or whether we should abide by our own state laws or the most recent ruling of the federal Supreme Court on segregation in public schools. The question is not what the White Citizens Council stands for. . . . The law against boycotting is not a segregation law. It applies to all instances where people organize to prevent the operation of a lawful business. The single question here is whether certain religious and other misguided leaders who are openly and publicly violating the law against boycotting should be permitted to do so at the expense of the risk of our city losing a much-needed bus system, or whether the law against boycotting should be enforced. I think it should be enforced, and soon, before it is too late."

Hall continued to believe that sensible officials would not pursue Ball's suggestion. On January 15 Hall referred to "the contradictions and impracticality of Lawyer Ball's vexed demand that the solicitor jug the bus boycott leaders for violation of the anti-boycott law," and noted, "The polite silence of the solicitor substantiates our reservations about the Ball formula." On January 17 an *Advertiser* reader, George C. Poulos, wrote the paper, "If an organized boycott is against the law, as Mr. Fred Ball states . . . , then why should anyone have to present his letter to the Circuit Solicitor?

Doesn't the Solicitor know his job? Why does he have to be reminded of his duty? Maybe he is worried about the Negro vote. He had better start worrying about the white vote."[59]

Hall's confidence and Poulos's fear were both misplaced. On January 10, the day after Ball's initial letter appeared, Circuit Solicitor Thetford contacted Commissioner Sellers and asked that two detectives be assigned to the solicitor's office to investigate the boycott. Sellers agreed at once, and the investigation was launched on January 11. That it was being conducted did not become public knowledge during January, but by February 13 it had become clear that officials had determined to seek indictments; on that day Circuit Judge Eugene W. Carter charged the new county grand jury to determine whether the bus boycott violated the anti-boycott law.[60]

The negotiating efforts of the Men of Montgomery now became a race against time to find a settlement before the forces seeking prosecution could obtain the adoption of their strategy. On February 8 the Men of Montgomery published in the newspapers the name and telephone number of their executive secretary, William R. Lynn, and urged anyone having a suggestion for a compromise formula to contact him. In the end the City Commission was not in a position politically to offer much more than it had previously conceded to the three non-MIA black ministers: the reservation of ten seats at

[59] Montgomery *Advertiser*, December 8, 1955, January 11, 12, 15, 17, 19, February 15, 1956; Code of Alabama, 1940, Recompiled, Title 14, Section 54.

[60] Trial Transcript, *King* v. *State*, 161–62, 186–87, 190; Montgomery *Alabama Journal*, February 13, 1956; Montgomery *Advertiser*, February 14, 1956. Thetford states that he was deeply dubious of indictments under the anti-boycott law as a tactic; he felt that, after a series of lengthy and emotional trials, the prosecution would result only in small fines for the boycotters or at most brief jail terms, without doing any real damage to the boycott itself. His own preference was for the bus company to seek a broad injunction against the MIA on the ground that its carpool operation was violating the company's exclusive franchise. If the MIA then disobeyed the injunction, its leaders could be jailed indefinitely for contempt. This strategy, he believes, would have broken the boycott. But he was unable to convince Crenshaw to adopt it. Crenshaw states that he was equally dubious of prosecuting under the anti-boycott law, but that he was unwilling to sue for an injunction because doing so would have involved abandoning the company's position as an innocent, neutral third party and was not, he thought, likely to end the boycott in any case. Thetford says that his hand was finally forced on the anti-boycott law when, as a result of the Ball letter, Judge Carter became convinced of the necessity to enforce the statute and came to him with the information that he intended to charge the next grand jury on the subject. Judge Carter does not recall the Ball letter, but he confirms that he decided to charge the grand jury about the act and thereupon informed Thetford of his intention (interviews with Thetford, September 4, 1976, Crenshaw, July 15, 1977, Carter, October 16, 1978).

front and rear, with blacks seating from the rear and whites from the front in an unreserved middle section of sixteen seats. The Men of Montgomery sought to make this proposal more palatable to blacks by adding other reforms, such as mechanisms for more effectively institutionalizing the right of blacks to enter complaints against drivers. After a two-hour meeting on the morning of February 20 the Men of Montgomery succeeded in extracting from the commissioners a public promise "that there will be no retaliation whatsoever resulting from the bus boycott"—almost certainly a reference to the grand jury investigation then entering its final stages. The concessions, which might well have satisfied the black leadership a year earlier, came far too late. At an MIA mass meeting on the evening of February 20 the audience shouted the proposals down; only the Reverend L. Roy Bennett and his assistant pastor openly supported the compromise. On February 21 the grand jury returned indictments of eighty-nine blacks, twenty-four of whom were ministers, for the misdemeanor of conspiring to boycott.[61]

The collision between the business community and the bar over the correct tactics to pursue in the crisis is worth some comment. The Men of Montgomery contained but a single lawyer among its forty founding members; it was composed of merchants, realtors, land developers, contractors, insurance men, bankers, brokers, and other men of similar occupations.[62] From the outset the most inflexible of the whites were lawyers. The differences in attitude which the differing vocations produced is one of the most puzzling aspects of the

---

[61] Montgomery *Advertiser,* February 6, 21, 22, 28, 1956; Montgomery *Alabama Journal,* February 8, 20, 21, 1956. The MIA Executive Board's only white member, the Reverend Robert Graetz, also favored the compromise but did not support it publicly (Trial Transcript, *King* v. *State,* 486–92). There may have been unpublished elements in the compromise; in his letter to the Men of Montgomery reporting the compromise's rejection, Abernathy refers to the "proposals submitted by your organization approved by the City Commission and City Bus Line and with the fare conveyed to me by telephone . . ." Abernathy no longer recalls what he meant by the latter phrase (Abernathy to Men of Montgomery, February 20, 1956, in File 2279, Records of the Solicitor's Office, Fifteenth Circuit, Montgomery County Courthouse, Montgomery; interview, February 28, 1979). Lynn reports that the Men of Montgomery did not receive a single suggestion as a result of its appeal (interview, December 29, 1976). Thetford says that he was convinced that the Men of Montgomery mediation would fail, but that if the blacks had accepted the compromise, he would have entered a *nolle prosequi* as to the indictments (interview, September 4, 1976).

[62] Montgomery *Advertiser,* October 19, 1955; Montgomery City Directories for 1955 and 1956.

episode. We may in part explain the attitudes of Judge Carter and Circuit Solicitor Thetford by pointing to the pressures of an elective position; though Judge Carter was quite strong politically, Solicitor Thetford was a young man just beginning his second term in office. That explanation does not account for the stance of such men as Crenshaw, Knabe, and Ball. One might think that they would have seized upon the black proposals as a way to preserve segregation. In fact, however, they repeatedly displayed an absolutist predisposition that precluded compromise.

Nor is their temperament to be explained as a narrow devotion to the letter of the law. Gray's reading of the text of the acts was at least as reasonable as Crenshaw's and Knabe's—a fact proved when the contending parties actually later switched sides, as a result of the federal court suit, on the question of the applicability of the state statute. Ball's construction of the anti-boycott law involved considerable legal difficulties as well. The constitutionality of the law had been specifically considered and affirmed by the Alabama Supreme Court in 1943. However, in that opinion Justice William H. Thomas, writing for the court, had saved the act by interpreting it very strictly. The statute prohibited conspiring to boycott "without a just cause or legal excuse." Such a law could be upheld, Justice Thomas said, when regarded as an effort by the legislature to prohibit the use of force, violence, or other unlawful activities to prevent someone from engaging in his business. If the statute were so construed as to permit the state to interfere with protest carried out by lawful means, it would be unconstitutional. But when limited in its scope and application simply to conspiracies to hinder a lawful occupation by actions otherwise illegal, the statute was within the state's police power. The U.S. Supreme Court had indicated its satisfaction with this decision by denying certiorari in the case. When Martin King was brought to trial in March—the first and only one of the boycotters to be tried—the prosecution was clearly aware of Justice Thomas's opinion and sought to prove that the boycott had indeed been accompanied and maintained by violence: shots had been fired at buses and a number of blacks had been forcibly restrained from riding, the testimony alleged. There was, however, no evidence connecting the MIA to these actions. In fact, at the conclusion of the trial Judge Carter, though convicting King, refused to sentence him to prison on the grounds, explicitly stated, that King had worked to prevent violence. At the very least the applicability of the anti-boycott law to the Montgomery situation was debatable.[63]

One might, of course, attribute the lawyers' maladroit handling of the boycott situation to ignorance or to poor legal training. But Crenshaw and Knabe had both received their legal education at Harvard. Knabe had been an undergraduate at Yale. Ball had been graduated from Princeton and had attended law school at Columbia and Emory. If these men desired to preserve segregation, as they certainly did, it was surely not a lack of mental acuity that prevented their seeing that acceding to the blacks' modest demands would strengthen, rather than weaken, the system.

Racism is no adequate explanation for the phenomenon; Montgomery's attorneys were no more nor less racist than were her business leaders, who were eager to compromise. Neither a literalist reading of the law nor a defective legal education provides an explanation; indeed, the facts contradict both contentions. Perhaps the answer lies in the role demanded of a lawyer as a representative of his client. Lawyers are poorly prepared to participate in the give-and-take of negotiations because they are trained to think of themselves as defending their clients' interests from the assaults of hostile adversaries. Such an attitude does not lend itself easily to the search for common ground. Rather, it almost inevitably conceives of the parties to a negotiation as enemies and tends to emphasize the elements in each position that are irreconcilable. In the boycott this tendency was exacerbated by racial prejudice and by the threat which the black effort seemed to pose to the white attorneys' own social position. But prejudice and social position could as readily have become motives to seek some settlement that would have preserved segregation in an ameliorated form, as the example of the business community shows. The key to the puzzle must be the legal turn of mind upon which the prejudice and the fear of social disintegration were acting, not merely the racial and class positions themselves.

However that may be, by the end of February 1956 both black and white leaders had abandoned the search for compromise and with it the political process and had determined to trust their respective causes to the rigid and unconditional judgment of the courts. The

---

[63] Montgomery *Advertiser,* March 23, 1956; Trial Transcript, *King* v. *State,* 193–227; *Lash* v. *State,* 244 Ala. 48; *Lash* v. *Alabama,* 320 U.S. 784, 814.

pressures leading to this decision among the whites have already been explained. Equally perplexing is why the blacks had not reached this decision much earlier. As logic would indicate that the whites should have been willing to compromise to preserve segregation, so logic would appear to dictate that blacks should have turned to the courts at once to attack the system which they despised. Indeed, as the *Advertiser* noted editorially at the conclusion of the boycott, the boycott itself accomplished absolutely nothing; only a decision of the courts ended the encounter, and that decision could have been obtained at any time, without the necessity for a boycott, simply by entering suit.

This riddle is solved in part by the observation that Montgomery's blacks had not yet developed the faith in the federal court which future years would generate. The city's federal judge, Frank M. Johnson, Jr., was still an unknown quantity, not a legend. He had held his position for just three months and had received Senate confirmation only the day before Gray filed the suit seeking to enjoin bus segregation. Southern federal judges certainly had not proved particular enemies of segregation in previous years. In fact, in the Montgomery bus suit itself, one of the three federal judges who heard it, Seybourn H. Lynne of Birmingham, dissented strongly from his colleagues' holding that the school integration decision of 1954 was applicable to bus seating.[64]

Yet lack of faith in the courts is not the most important explanation for the initial willingness of the black leadership to settle for a compromise within the framework of segregation. The real reason is that the bus boycott in its origins was much less a social than a political movement. During the year and a half that Dave Birmingham served on the City Commission black leaders developed a strengthened sense of the malleability of the system. The size of the black vote grew every year, and the city government paid new attention to black complaints. The decision to hold a public session to interview candidates for commissioner in 1955 and to release a list of endorsements reflected this growing confidence that politics could be made to subserve the needs of blacks. However, the outcome of the

[64] *Browder* v. *Gayle*, 142 F. Supp. 707; Montgomery *Advertiser*, October 23, 25, November 6, 1955, February 4, December 9, 1956, June 6, 1959; Montgomery *Alabama Journal*, October 24, 1955, January 31, 1956.

election dealt a considerable blow to this optimism. Black leaders had been permitted a brief experience of a happier relationship with their rulers, only to have it snatched away.

Bus seating had been one of the areas in which blacks had genuinely expected that they would be able to make progress. In the conferences that had followed the arrest of Claudette Colvin they had been promised public clarifications, which would have represented a clear acknowledgment of their ability to compel the city to respond to their concerns. No clarifications were forthcoming; the Commission formally rejected Birmingham's motion to add black members to the Parks and Recreation Board; the segregationist Sellers was inaugurated; and Mrs. Parks was arrested under the same circumstances as Miss Colvin. The MIA's statements at the beginning of the boycott emphasize unmistakably the connection between the city's failure to define the precise requirements of the segregation ordinance following the Colvin incident and the decision to boycott. The city elections, which had seemed in the spring so likely to produce an amelioration of the blacks' lot, had produced instead a situation that if anything was the worse for having earlier seemed so hopeful.

If government was ever really to benefit blacks, it now seemed, black leaders would have to discover some mechanism other than the electoral process by which to influence politicians. The boycott was intended to be such a mechanism. In the minds of its organizers, at least, it appears to have been analogous to a strike—a way for persons individually weak to bring collective pressure to bear upon the powerful once negotiations have failed. The boycott was not a revolution; it was merely an extension of the negotiations. The black leaders persisted in offering in December their seating proposal advanced in March precisely because they initially conceived their movement not so much as a direct action against bus segregation itself as rather a search for a means to manipulate the political process. They genuinely believed that, faced with this proof of how seriously blacks took the grievance, the City Commission would be compelled to seek a remedy.[65] For this device to work successfully, the blacks could only ask

---

[65] Montgomery *Alabama Tribune,* December 30, 1955. The purpose of the boycott is a matter of some dispute among surviving MIA leaders. Mrs. Robinson states that, because of the progress which the Women's Political Council had already been able to secure, she was initially quite optimistic about the prospects for negotiations. Gray says that he never had any hopes for the negotiations and favored a federal suit from the beginning, but he also says that most of the members of the MIA Executive Board

for something which the commissioners could legally grant—an amelioration of segregation.

Both the Ben Moore Hotel meeting and the boycott were politically naïve. Under other circumstances the black leaders surely would have known that public endorsement of a candidate by blacks was likely to be counterproductive. They would similarly have known that for the commissioners to respond to pressure applied openly through a boycott—to knuckle under to blackmail, as it would have seemed to segregationists—would have infuriated a large part of the electorate. One cannot condemn the black leadership for its naïveté in these matters; inasmuch as blacks had been almost entirely excluded from political life in Alabama for two generations, it could hardly have been otherwise. Yet, the political process was clearly not analogous to an industrial dispute precisely because the interests involved were so many and varied and the conflicting pressures upon the Commission were so manifold. Surely, there was never any real likelihood of achieving a negotiated settlement of the boycott.

At the outset of the boycott the *Advertiser* had stated editorially, "The boycott makes an innocent sufferer of the bus company. Had the company defied city and state laws, its franchise would have been canceled. The quarrel of the Negroes is with the *law*. It is wrong to hold the company a hostage."[66] The blacks replied over and over again—though the whites never seemed to listen—that their quarrel was not at all with the law, that they had no intention of asking the

---

believed that the negotiations would produce a settlement. Abernathy says that because the city and bus company officials had seemed willing to listen at earlier meetings and because the black proposals seemed to him so modest, he expected the whites to accept the MIA's position. Lewis states that at the outset no one really thought about whether or not the boycott was likely to produce concessions; he says that the boycott was born in the anger over Mrs. Parks's arrest and that its initial purpose was not to gain alterations in the bus seating policy but to demonstrate forcefully the extent of black resentment. Nixon says that the exchanges at the time of the Colvin arrest had convinced him of the futility of negotiating, and that he supported the boycott not because he thought it likely to produce concessions but because he thought that by making Mrs. Parks's case a *cause célèbre*, blacks would be able to prevent the white courts from shunting her case aside. He feared, he says, that white judges would never consider a test of the segregation laws seriously unless the test was so surrounded with publicity that they were compelled to do so (interviews, January 27, October 17, 1978, February 28, 1979, July 27, August 2, 1977). Each of these positions is entirely plausible, and very probably each reflects some aspect of the historical reality. At the same time the memory of each participant has necessarily been shaped to some extent by his knowledge of and reaction to subsequent events. In the final analysis the historian must ground his judgment in the sense which he has derived from the contemporary documents.

[66] Montgomery *Advertiser*, December 8, 1955.

company to abandon segregation, that they merely wished to have the company apply the law in Montgomery as it did in Mobile. In a peculiar sense, however, the *Advertiser* was right, and the blacks were wrong. What the boycott taught the city's black leaders as it dragged on was that their quarrel was—had to be—with the law. Compromise with segregation was impossible because segregation so forged and underlay social relationships that even the most modest reform of its requirements threatened—just as the white politicians claimed— the entire social fabric. In such a situation reform was impossible; only "revolution" would do. The white response to the boycott revealed this truth forcefully to the blacks; that revelation is the boycott's supreme achievement, and it is something which no court suit could ever have accomplished.

Perhaps the most interesting single aspect of the boycott is that the inflexibility of segregation was something which black leaders had to learn. It was so much the fundamental presumption of the civil rights movement in later years that we find it difficult to believe that there could have been a time when a black—when anyone—was unaware of this characteristic of the system. Indeed, it is this difficulty that makes the MIA's position in the initial stages of the boycott seem so peculiar. But segregation revealed the true extent of its inflexibility only under the pressure of the civil rights movement itself. For those who had lived inside the segregation system, black and white, the pervasiveness of its impact was not so readily apparent. It is not the author's intention to maintain that blacks were not acutely aware of the constant humiliation that segregation entailed. Yet, the enormous variety of interracial associations even under segregation made the institution seem less fundamental to the shaping of attitudes than in fact it was. Particularly in a city like Montgomery, in which the Gunter Machine had defeated the Ku Klux Klan and ruled with relative benevolence, it was easy not to know how exceedingly far, into how many unrelated organs, the infection had spread. Black leaders had been too ready to believe that the brief thaw that Dave Birmingham's tenure had represented for them marked the beginning of spring. The writer believes that they made this mistake because they, in common with most white Southerners, had conceived of their world, though suffused with segregation, as fictile. Only after segregation came under assault and its supporters roused themselves to fight back were blacks, and later whites, able to discover the omnipresence and the rigidity of the system.

In a sense Martin King, having learned these lessons during the bus boycott, spent the rest of his career arranging demonstrations of them for others. Blacks, especially older blacks, in other Southern cities had to be shown that they were more fully imprisoned than they had believed. Moderate whites had to be shown that, whatever the extent of their good will, segregation had the power to render their best efforts vain. In these demonstrations the medium was the message; the immediate goals in a given city were less important than the process of placing segregation under stress in order to reveal the nature of its hold upon society. Iconoclasts sometimes note that King did not create the boycott, as a way of questioning his greatness. But King's greatness actually lies in the fact that during the boycott, by observing what was happening, he grew. He, far more than any of his contemporaries, white or black, learned the truths which the events of the boycott contained about the nature of the Southern dilemma.

In the end, the bus boycott teaches that segregation could have been disestablished only in the way in which it was disestablished: by internal pressure sufficient to compel intervention from outside the South. For all its diversity and complexity—in large part because of its diversity and complexity, since any fundamental reform would affect an infinite variety of interests—the South did not possess within itself the capacity to save itself. The strength of segregation was bound up with the pluralism of Southern society. As no man could untie the Gordian knot, so segregation would not—could not—yield to negotiation. Thus the boycott, because it failed to achieve its initial goals, succeeded for that reason in changing the course of American history.

Contributors

Lee N. Allen is dean of the Howard College of Arts and Sciences, Samford University.

William D. Barnard is chairman of the Department of History, The University of Alabama.

Hugh C. Bailey is president of Valdosta State College, Valdosta, Georgia.

Peter A. Brannon was director of the Alabama Department of Archives and History until his death.

James F. Cook is a member of the faculty of the Department of History, Floyd Junior College, Rome, Georgia.

Leonard Dinnerstein is a member of the faculty of the Department of History, University of Arizona.

James F. Doster is retired from the faculty of the Department of History, The University of Alabama.

Ralph B. Draughon, Jr., is curator of manuscripts, The Historic New Orleans Collection.

Wayne Flynt is a member of the faculty of the Department of History, Auburn University.

Joseph A. Fry is chairman of the Department of History, University of Nevada, Las Vegas.

William E. Gilbert was a member of the faculty of the Department of History, Livingston University, until his death.

Carl Grafton is a member of the faculty of the Department of Government, Auburn University in Montgomery.

Allen W. Jones is a member of the faculty of the Department of History, Auburn University.

Grady McWhiney is a member of the faculty of the Department of History, Texas Christian University.

Marlene Hunt Rikard is a member of the faculty of the Department of History, Samford University.

Frances Roberts is retired from the faculty of the Department of History, The University of Alabama at Huntsville.

William Warren Rogers is a member of the faculty of the Department of History, Florida State University.

William R. Snell is a member of the faculty of the Department of History, Lee College, Cleveland, Tennessee.

William N. Still is a member of the faculty of the Department of History, East Carolina University.

J. Mills Thornton III is a member of the faculty of the Department of History, University of Michigan.

Frank E. Vandiver is president of Texas A. & M. University.

Jonathan M. Wiener is a member of the faculty of the Department of History, University of California at Irvine.

Sarah Woolfolk Wiggins is a member of the faculty of the Department of History, The University of Alabama.

Leslie S. Wright is chancellor, Samford University.

Index

Abernathy, Ralph D., 491, 497, 501
Abolitionism, 9, 14–17
Acuff, Roy, 410
Adams, Samuel M., 163–64
Adler, Felix, 237–38
African Methodist Episcopal Church, 276
Agee, James, 385–86, 400, 411
Agricultural Wheel, 144, 166
Agriculture: changes in, 109–32; diversification, 137, 254; Farmers' Alliance, 162–72; the Grange, 133–44; legislation, 136, 142–43, 171; poor white, 380–87
Aiken, George, 438
Alabama, U.S.S., 198
Alabama Agricultural and Mechanical Institute at Normal, 340
Alabama Association Opposed to Woman Suffrage, 289, 290
Alabama Baptist, 260–75 *passim*
Alabama Child Labor Committee, 231, 232, 236, 237, 239
Alabama City Mill, 232–33
Alabama Council on Human Relations, 492, 501
Alabama Department of Child Welfare, 268
Alabama Equal Suffrage Association, 284–87, 292
Alabama Extension Service, 442
Alabama Farm Bureau Federation, 442
Alabama Farm Journal, 138–39
Alabama Federation of Women's Clubs, 231
Alabama Manufacturing Company, 19
Alabama Mills Company, 390
Alabama Polytechnic Institute (Auburn University), 138, 166, 167
Alabama Power Company, 300, 303–304, 306, 442
Alabama Progressive Democratic Association, 471, 477, 487
Alabama Public Service Commission, 483
Alabama State Bank, 174
Alabama State Docks (Mobile), 254, 346
Alabama State Exchange, 169–71

Alabama State Fair, 139, 283
Alabama State Grange. *See* Grange, the
Alabama State Industrial Board, 254
Alabama Suffrage Bulletin, 285
Alabama Supreme Court, 513
Alabama Women's Democratic Club, 365
Alabama Women's League for White Supremacy, 365, 366
Alexander, E. J., 402
Alexander, Mrs. E. J., 401–402, 405
Alexander, Kate, 323
Alexander, M. W., 320
Alliance Cooperative School, 167
Alliance Journal, 138–39
Alliance News, 164
Alsobrook, Tom, 396, 398
Alsobrook, Mrs. Tom, 389
Alvis, Thomas S., 93
American Coal and Coke Company, 185–87
American Federation of Labor, 237, 248, 302, 428
Amerson, Bennie, 408
Amnesty, 80, 85–86
Anderson, John C., 350
Anderson, Mrs. Sam, 396
Andersonville Prison (Camp Sumter), Georgia, 34–35, 37
Andrews, Rufus F., 69
Anthony, Susan B., 280, 289
Anti-Boycott Law, 509–14
Anti-Catholicism, 271–75, 360, 361, 428
"Anti-Lobby" Act. *See* "Dual Office" Act
Anti-Saloon League, 272–73, 332, 345, 351–52, 354–69 *passim*, 464; black, 277
Anti-Semitism, 275
Applegate, Andrew J., 68–69
Arkansas, CSS, 32
Armes, Ethel, 285
Ashby, 81, 91
Ashby, Irene, 233, 237
Atmore, 343
Atterbury, W. W., 304
Auburn University. *See* Alabama Polytechnic Institute